# Thailand

routard

**Series director:** Philippe Gloaguen
**Series creators:** Philippe Gloaguen and Michel Duval
**Chief editor:** Pierre Josse
**Assistant chief editor:** Benoît Lucchini
**Coordination director:** Florence Charmetant

**Editorial team:** Yves Couprie, Olivier Page, Véronique de Chardon, Amanda Keravel, Isabelle Al Subaihi, Anne-Caroline Dimas, Carole Foucault, Bénédicte Solle, André Poncelet, Jérôme de Gubernatis, Marie Lung and Thierry Brouard.

**English translation:** Florence Brutton
**Managing editor:** Liz Coghill
**Editorial:** Eileen Townsend Jones and Hilary Hughes
**Proofreader:** Maria Morgan

**Additional research and assistance:** Sofi Mogensen, Michael Hutchinson, Maria Trewin, Ben Davies and Christine Bell.
**Index:** Dorothy Frame

We have done our best to ensure the accuracy of the information contained in this guide. However, addresses, phone numbers, opening times etc. do invariably change from time to time, so if you find a discrepancy please do let us know and help us update the guides. You can contact us at: hachetteuk@orionbooks.co.uk or write to us at Hachette UK, address below. Hachette UK guides provide independent advice. The authors and compilers do not accept any remuneration for the inclusion of addresses in this guide. Please note that we cannot accept any responsibility for any loss, injury or inconvenience sustained by anyone as a result of any information or advice contained in this guide.

**Hotels, restaurants, B&Bs – price guide**
Because of rapid inflation in many countries, it is impossible to give an accurate indication of prices in hotels and restaurants. Prices can change enormously from one year to the next. As a result we have adopted a system of categories for the prices in the guides: 'Budget', 'Cheap', 'Moderate', 'Chic' and 'Très Chic' (in the guides to French-speaking countries), otherwise 'Expensive' and 'Splash out' in the others. These categories do vary from guide to guide, however. If the 'Budget' or 'Cheap' hotels start at £2/$3 per night, then those costing £5/$7.50 per night will belong to the 'moderate' category and those costing £10/$15 and upwards will belong to the 'chic' or 'expensive' category. It therefore follows that in a guide where the 'Budget' option costs £10/$15 per night, the price ranges in the other categories will increase accordingly.

As prices may change so may other circumstances – a restaurant may change hands, the standard of service at a hotel may deteriorate since our researchers made their visit. Again, we do our best to ensure information is accurate, but if you notice any discrepancy, do let us know at the address already given above. The only thing we can't predict is when a hotel or a restaurant changes its standing (gets better or worse) and moves into a different category. If this happens, then we look forward to hearing from you, either by e-mail (see above) or by post (see below for address).

First published in the United Kingdom in 2001 by Hachette UK.

© English Translation Hachette UK 2001
© Hachette Livre (Hachette Tourisme) 2000
© Cartography Hachette Tourisme

Distributed in the United States of America by Sterling Publishing Co., Inc. 387 Park Avenue South, New York, NY 10016-8810.

A CIP catalogue for this book is available from the British Library.

ISBN 1 84202 029 3

Typeset at The Spartan Press Ltd, Lymington, Hants.
Printed and bound in France by Aubin Imprimeur, Poitiers.

Hachette UK, Cassell & Co, Wellington House, 125 Strand, London WC2R 0BB.

Cover design by Emmanuel Le Vallois (Hachette Livre) and Paul Cooper.
Cover photo © Tony Stone. Back cover photo © Tony Stone.

# Thailand

**The guides for travellers**

HACHETTE

# CONTENTS

## GETTING THERE 13

## GENERAL INFORMATION 20

## BACKGROUND 52

## BANGKOK AND THE SURROUNDING AREA 87

## THE NORTHWEST 161

# LIST OF MAPS

# JUST EXACTLY WHO OR WHAT IS A ROUTARD?

You are. Yes, you! The fact that you are reading this book means that you are a Routard. You are probably still none the wiser, so to explain we will take you back to the origin of the guides. Routard was the brain-child of a Frenchman named Philippe Gloaguen, who compiled the first guide some 25 years ago with his friend Michel Duval. They simply could not find the kind of guide book they wanted and so the solution was clear – they would just have to write it themselves. When it came to naming the guide, Philippe came up with the term Routard, which at the time did not exist as a bona fide word – at least, not in conventional dictionary terms. Today, if you look the word up in a French-English dictionary you will find that it means 'traveller' or 'globetrotter' – so there you have it, that's what you are!

From this humble beginning has grown a vast collection of some 100 titles to destinations all over the world. Routard is now the bestselling guide book series in France. The guides have been translated into five different languages, so keep an eye out for fellow Routard readers on your travels.

## What exactly do the guides do?

The short answer is that they provide all the information you need to enable you to have a successful holiday or trip. Routards' great strength however, lies in their listings. The guides provide comprehensive listings for accommodation, eating and drinking – ranging from campsites and youth hostels through to four star hotels – and from bars, clubs and greasy spoons to tearooms, cafés and restaurants. Each entry is accompanied by a detailed and frank appraisal of the address, rather like a friend coming back from holiday who is recommending all the good places to go (or even the places to avoid!). The guides aim to help you find the best addresses and the best value for money within your price range, whilst giving you invaluable insider advice at the same time.

## Anything else?

Routard also provides oceans of practical advice on how to get along in the country or city you are visiting plus an insight into the character and customs of the people. How do you negotiate your way around the transport system? Will you offend if you bare your knees in the temple? And so on. In addition, you will find plenty of sightseeing information, backed up by historical and cultural detail, interesting facts and figures, addresses and opening times. The humanitarian aspect is also of great importance, with the guides commenting freely and often pithily, and most titles contain a section on human rights.

Routard are truly useful guides that are convivial, irreverent, down-to-earth and honest. We very much hope you enjoy them and that they will serve you well during your stay.

Happy travelling.

The Hachette UK team

# SYMBOLS USED IN THE GUIDE

*Please note that not all the symbols below appear in every guide.*

- ■ Useful addresses
- **ℹ** Tourist office
- ✉ Post office
- ☎ Telephone
- 🚂 Railway station
- 🚌 Bus station
- 🚗 Shared taxi
- **T** Tram
- 🚢 River transport
- ⛴ Sea transport
- ✈ Airport
- ⌂ Where to stay

- ✕ Where to eat
- ❢ Where to go for a drink
- ♪ Where to listen to music
- ⸙ Where to go for an ice-cream
- ★ To see
- 🔒 Shopping
- ● 'Other'
- **P** Parking
- ✕ Castle
- ⁂ Ruins

- 🤿 Diving site
- ⛺ Shelter
- ⚱ Camp site
- ▲ Peak
- ● Site
- ○ Town
- ✕ Hill
- ⚲ Abbey, chapel
- ⮜ Lookout
- ⚓ Beach
- ⚑ Lighthouse
- ⚶ Wat (temple)

# INTRODUCTION

*For a general map of Thailand, see the colour pages*

They call it the 'land of smiles', where life is gentle; a kingdom whose people exhibit religious tolerance and open-mindedness, exquisite delicacy, infinite courtesy and natural kindness. All this is true, of course, although it perhaps needs some qualification as Thailand is such a multi-faceted country.

On the one hand there is Bangkok, a suffocating and over-active megalopolis of 10 million inhabitants, lacking any real seductive powers although attractive to some as an urban monster and cauldron of humanity (and cars – it is impossible to speak of Bangkok without mentioning pollution). Then there is the south, with its islands, beaches and rocks soaring from the sea, its spicy cuisine, and generally a different view of life, more marked by Islam. And there is the north, the profound, original Thailand, with its ancient royal founders, its relaxed way of life, its thousands of Buddhist temples and fertile earth. The result is three Thailands, each with its own distinctive physical and cultural traits.

Despite this, there are national qualities which are to be found the length (2,000 km/1,250 miles from north to south) and breadth of the country. Firstly, a strong sense of identity: Siam was never colonized, and developed its own art, culture and even alphabet. Secondly, a developed sense of social conventions and courtesy, a certain susceptibility and high levels of propriety, calm and dignity, combine with a strong religious nature that goes hand in hand with veneration for the royal family. All this is rounded off by a humorous and yet philosophical nature, and a hearty appetite for everything: the Thais are epicureans, with a mischievous side to their characters, and are always ready to enjoy a celebration or a good meal.

Unfortunately, commercial considerations and the tourist influx have in places tainted the amiable Thai nature. Though given that the one intention of many of these tourists is to live it up at all costs, it is difficult to see why the Thais should force themselves to be pleasant all the time.

In this land known as Muang Thai (which means 'land of the free') it's as easy to discover vast emerald rice fields or hillsides carpeted in jungle as it is to avoid the big tourist ghettoes where prices continually rise as the standard of service falls.

Catch a train from hectic Bangkok and within hours you could be relaxing in a raft house on the River Kwai; or take a 60-minute flight and find yourself in the magnificent hills above Mae Hong Son within easy reach of the colourful hill tribes. In islands too, Thailand has something for everyone, from pristine beach hideaways to fine diving, five-star hotels and swinging nightclubs.

While Thailand is no longer an undiscovered paradise, it still has almost everything that you could dream of for a holiday, from balmy coastlines and exotic temples, to some of the finest food on earth. Add one or two more personal ingredients such as a touch of tolerance, zest and open-mindedness, a drop of curiosity and a pinch of self-denial; it's hard to see how your holiday could be anything but a success.

# GETTING THERE

## BY AIR

### FROM THE UK

The major airlines that fly direct to Bangkok from London include the following: **Qantas**, direct flights, twice a day (flight time 11 hours). **Eva Airways**, direct flights, three times a week (11 hours). **Thai Airways**, direct flights three times a week (11 hours). **British Airways**, direct flights, twice a day, (11 hours). **Garuda Airlines**, direct flights twice a week (12 hours).

Several other major airlines offer indirect flights to Bangkok from London. They include the following: **Aeroflot** flies via Moscow once a day during the peak season from Heathrow and twice a week during the off-peak season (9 hours 30 minutes). **Cathay Pacific** flies via Hong Kong once a day although this crosses the International Date Line and the flight takes two days because of this. **Air France** flies via Paris to Bangkok once a day. **Lauda Air** flies via Vienna three times a week (12 hours 30 minutes). **Kuwait Airlines** flies via Kuwait five times a week (12 hours). **Swissair** flies via Zurich to Bangkok daily and twice a day on Wednesday and Saturday (16 hours). **Finnair** flies to Bangkok via Helsinki three times a week (14 hours 30 minutes). **Virgin Atlantic** flies to Bangkok via Kuala Lumpur once a day (12 hours 45 minutes) and via Hong Kong once a day (14 hours 40 minutes). **Malaysia Airlines** flies twice a day from London to Bangkok via Kuala Lumpur (14 hours 30 minutes). **Air Canada** and **Canadian Airlines** also fly to Thailand via London (*see* more details in 'Canada' section).

The price for a standard London to Bangkok return fare varies considerably, from as low as £365 with Kuwait Airlines, £405 with Garuda and £438 with Aeroflot during the off-peak season, which runs approximately from the beginning of July to the end of August and during the month of December. It is worth checking with travel agents for special promotions and offers throughout the year, as they can often undercut the airlines' published prices.

● **Aeroflot**: Terminal 2, Heathrow Airport, Hounslow, Middlesex. ☎ (020) 8562 7175. Website: www.aeroflot.co.uk

● **Air Canada**: 7–8 Conduit Street, London W1R 9TG. ☎ (0870) 524 7226. Website: www.aircanada.ca

● **Air France**: 100 Hammersmith Road, London W6 7JP. ☎ (0845) 084 5111. Website: www.airfrance.com

● **Air New Zealand**: Elsinore House, 77 Fulham Palace Road, London W6 8JA. ☎ (020) 8741 2299; and The Travel Centre, New Zealand House, 80 Haymarket, London SW1 Y4T. Website: www.airnz.co.nz

● **British Airways**: PO Box 365, Harmondsworth, West Drayton, Middlesex UB7 0GB. ☎ (0345) 222 111. Website: www.britishairways.com

GETTING THERE

- **Canadian Airlines**: 45–46 Piccadilly, London W1V 9AJ. ☎ (020) 8577 7722. Website: www.cdnair.ca

- **Cathay Pacific**: 7 Apple Tree Yard, Duke of York St, London SW1Y 6LD. ☎ (020) 7747 8888. Website: www.cathaypacific.com

- **Eva Airways**: Evergreen House, 160 Euston Road, London NW1 2DT. ☎ (020) 7380 8300. Website: www.evaair.com.tw

- **Finnair**: 14 Clifford Street, London W1S 4BX. ☎ (020) 7408 1222. Website: www.finnair.com

- **Garuda Airlines**: 35 Dukes Street, London W1M 5DF. ☎ (020) 7486 3011. Website: www.garuda-indonesia.com

- **KLM UK Ltd**: Endeavour House, Stansted CM24 1RS. ☎ (0990) 074 074. Website: www.klmuk.com

- **Kuwait Airways**: 16-20 Baker Street, London W1M 2AD. ☎ (020) 7412 0007. Website: www.kuwait-airways.com

- **Lauda Air**: 10 Wardour St, London W1D 6BQ. ☎ (020) 7630 5924/ (0845) 601 0934. Website: www.laudaair.co.uk

- **Malaysia Airlines**: 247–249 Cromwell Road, London SW5 9GA. ☎ (0870) 607 9090. Website: www.malaysia-airlines.com

- **Qantas**: 395 King Street, Hammersmith, London W6 9NJ. ☎ (0345) 747767. Website: www.qantas.com.au

- **Singapore Airlines**: 143 Regent Street, London W1R 7LB. ☎ (0870) 608 8886. Website: www.singaporeair.com

- **South African Airways**: St George's House, 61 Conduit Street, London W1S 2NE. ☎ (020) 7312 5001. Website: www.saa.co.za

- **Swissair**: Second Floor, Gemini House, 10–18 Putney Hill, Putney, London SW15 6AA. ☎ (020) 7434 7300. Website: www.swissair.co.uk

- **Thai Airways**: 41 Albemarle Street, London W1S 4BF. ☎ (0870) 606 0911. Website: www.thaiair.com

- **United Airlines**: 7–8 Conduit St, London W1S 2XF. ☎ (0845) 844 4777. Website: www.ual.com

- **Virgin Atlantic**: The Office, Crawley Business Quarter, Manor Royal, Crawley, West Sussex RH10 2NU. ☎ (01293) 747747. Website: www.fly.virgin.com

## FROM THE REPUBLIC OF IRELAND

There are no direct flights from Ireland to Thailand. The cheapest option is to fly via London or take the ferry to England and book your flight from London.

## FROM THE UNITED STATES

There are no direct flights from New York and the East Coast to Bangkok, although **KLM Airlines**' partner **Northwest Airlines** has a direct flight from Los Angeles once a day (10 hours). This can be booked via KLM. Many major airlines run indirect flights to Bangkok including the following: **Aeroflot** flies from Washington via Moscow twice a week. **Cathay Pacific** flies from New York via Hong Kong once a day, although this crosses the International Date Line and the flight takes two days because of this. **Air France** flies from New York via Paris once a day (25 hours 40 minutes) and also from Los Angeles to Bangkok via Paris once a day (26 hours 35 minutes). **KLM** flies via Amsterdam once a day (17 hours 30 minutes). **Singapore Airlines** flies from New York (JFK) daily to Bangkok via Singapore and from New York (Newark) four times a week via Singapore. **United Airlines** flies from New York via Tokyo, (21 hours), four times a day and from Los Angeles via Hong Kong twice a day (23 hours).

• **Aeroflot**: 1620 First Street NW, Suite 500, Washington DC 20006. ☎ (202) 466-4080/(888) 340-6400. Website: www.aeroflot.com

• **Air France**: 125 West 55th Street, New York NY 10019. ☎ (800) 237-2747. Website: www.airfrance.com

• **Cathay Pacific**: 590 Fifth Avenue, Fifth Floor, New York NY 10036. ☎ (800) 233–2742. Website: www.cathaypacific.com

• **Northwest/KLM**: Northwest Airlines, Central Airline Terminal, 100 East 42nd Street, Second Floor, New York NY 10017. ☎ (800) 225-2525. Website: www.nwa.com (has link to KLM site: www.klm.com)

• **Singapore Airlines**: 55 East 59th Street, Suite 20B, New York NY 10022. ☎ (800) 742-3333. Website: www.singaporeair.com

• **United Airlines**: 1 World Trade Center, New York. ☎ (800) 538-2929. Website: www.unitedairlines.com

## FROM CANADA

There are no direct flights from any Canadian cities to Thailand. It is necessary to fly to London and then transfer to a different carrier. **Canadian Airlines** flies from Toronto to London Heathrow once a day (7 hours), from Vancouver once a day (9 hours 15 minutes), from Ottawa to London on Tuesday, Saturday and Sunday (6 hours), and from Montreal to London once a day (6 hours 45 minutes). **Air Canada** flies once a day from the same locations as Canadian Airlines, with flights from Toronto during the peak season. **British Airways** flies from Toronto to London twice a day and once a day from Ottawa, Montreal, Quebec and Vancouver. Flight times are approximately the same for all three airlines. *See* 'By Air from the UK' for information on flights from London to Bangkok.

• **Air Canada**: 333 Fifth Avenue SW, Suite 100, Calgary AB. ☎ (800) 776-3000. Website: www.aircanada.com

• **British Airways**: 4120 Yonge Street, Suite 100, Toronto, Ontario M2P 2B8. ☎ (416) 250-0880/(800) 247-9297. Website: www.britishairways .com

• **Canadian Airlines**: 615 18th Street SE, Calgary AB T2E 6J5. ☎ (800) 665-1177. Website: www.cdnair.com

## FROM AUSTRALIA AND NEW ZEALAND

The major airlines that fly direct from Australia and New Zealand to Bangkok are as follows: **Thai Airways** flies from Sydney to Bangkok twice a day (8 hours 30 minutes). There are connecting flights from

Auckland to Sydney (3 hours 15 minutes). **Qantas** flies direct from Sydney to Bangkok twice a day, (9 hours), and there are connecting flights from Auckland to Sydney (3 hours 15 minutes). **Malaysia Airlines** flies from Sydney to Bangkok once a day (8 hours), and from Auckland to Bangkok once a day (10 hours 45 minutes).

Several other major airlines offer indirect flights from Sydney and Auckland to Bangkok. These include the following: **Garuda** flies from Sydney to Bangkok via Bali three times a week (15 hours), and Auckland to Bangkok via Bali four times a week (18 hours). **Air New Zealand** flies from Auckland to Bangkok via Singapore (12 hours 15 minutes) twice a day. **Singapore Airlines** flies from Auckland to Bangkok daily and twice a day on Wednesday and Saturday.

- **Air New Zealand**: 5 Elizabeth Street, Sydney NSW 2000. ☎ (02) 9223 4666/(13) 2476. *New Zealand*: Air New Zealand House, 72 Oxford Terrace, Christchurch. ☎ (03) 379 7000/(0800) 737 000. Website: www.airnewzealand.com

- **Garuda**: 55 Hunter Street, Sydney, NSW 2000. ☎ (02) 9334 9900/(800) 800-873. *New Zealand*: Garuda Westpac Tower Building, 10th Floor, 120 Albert Street, Auckland 1. ☎ (09) 366 1855. Fax: (09) 366 1866. Website: www.indodirect.comgaruda/defaultc.htm

- **Malaysia Airlines**: MAS, 16th Spring Street, Sydney, NSW 2000, Australia. ☎ (02) 913 2627/(13) 2476. *New Zealand*: MAS, 12th Floor, The Swanson Centre, 12–26 Swanson Street, Auckland, PO Box 3729, Auckland. ☎ (09) 373 2741/(09) 357 3000. Website: www.mas.com.my

- **Qantas**: Qantas Centre, 203 Coward Street, Mascot, Sydney, NSW 2020. ☎ (02) 9691 3636/(13) 1211. *New Zealand*: 191 Queen Street, Auckland. ☎ (09) 357 8900/(0800) 808 767. Website: www.qantas.com

- **Singapore Airlines**: Singapore Airlines House, 17–19 Bridge Street, Sydney, NSW 2000. ☎ (02) 9350 0100/(13) 1011. *New Zealand*: 10th Floor, West Plaza Building, Corner Albert and Fanshawe Streets, Auckland 1. ☎ (09) 379 3209/(0800) 808 909. Website: www.singaporeair.com

- **Thai Airways**: Fourth Floor, 145 Eagle Street, Brisbane, Queensland 4000. ☎ (07) 3215 4700/(13) 1960. *New Zealand*: First Floor, Kensington Swan Building, 22 Fanshawe Street, PO Box 4559, Auckland 1. ☎ (09) 377 0268/(09) 377 3886. Website: www.thaiairways.com

## FROM SOUTH AFRICA

**South African Airways** flies direct from Johannesburg to Bangkok three times a week (10 hours 55 minutes). The other major airlines that fly from South Africa to Bangkok include the following: **Air France** flies from Johannesburg to Bangkok via Paris in conjunction with **Thai Airways**, once a day. **Malaysia Airlines** flies from Johannesburg to Bangkok via Kuala Lumpur (10 hours 10 minutes), four times a week. It is also possible to fly direct to London with several major airlines and then fly to Bangkok from London. These airlines include the following: **Virgin Atlantic** flies once a day from Johannesburg to London and direct from Cape Town to London on Saturdays. **South African Airways** flies from Cape Town to London daily (11 hours 25 minutes), and from Johannesburg twice daily and once on Wednesday (10 hours 50 minutes). **British Airways**

flies from Cape Town to London daily except Tuesday (11 hours 55 minutes) and from Johannesburg to London twice a day (11 hours 10 minutes).

- **Air France**: 196 Oxford Road, Oxford Manor, Illovo, Johannesburg 2196. ☎ (11) 0860 340 340. Website: www.airfrance.com

- **British Airways**: Second Floor, 195 Grosvenor Corner, Rosebank, Johannesburg 2196. ☎ (11) 441 8600/(0860) 011 747. Website: www. britishairways.com

- **Malaysia Airlines**: First Floor, Barclay House, 261 Oxford Rd, Illovo, Johannesburg 2196. ☎ (11) 880 9614. Website: www.mas.com.my

- **South African Airways**: Airways Park, Jones Road, Johannesburg International Airport 1627. ☎ (11) 978 1000. Website: www.saa.co.za

- **Thai Airways**: Eighth Floor, Norwich Life Towers, 13 Fredman Drive, Sandown, Sandton, Johannesburg 2146. ☎ (11) 883 9068/-9. Website: www.thaiairways.com

- **Virgin Atlantic**: Olivetti House, 17 Lower Long Street, Cape Town 8001. ☎ (11) 340 3400. Website: www.virginatlantic.com

# PRICES AND DISCOUNTS ON FLIGHTS

Prices vary considerably during the season and often individual travel agents are able to undercut the airlines' official published fares. Airlines frequently run special promotions, particularly if their main competitors are doing so, and if their sales are down in off-peak months. Virgin Atlantic runs a discount policy for senior citizens. Youth (under 26) and student travel agencies will be able to give you up-to-the-minute discounted fares for young people and full-time students in possession of an NUS (National Union of Students) card or ISIC (International Student Identity Card). Before purchasing a ticket it is important to shop around, contacting several travel agents and comparing prices.

For air travel from the UK to any destination contact the Air Travel Advisory Bureau, which will give free impartial advice on cheap, world-wide flights:

- **Air Travel Advisory Bureau Ltd**: Columbus House, 28 Charles Square, London N1 6HT. ☎ (020) 7636 5000. Website: www.atab.co.uk

## UK TRAVEL AGENTS AND DISCOUNT TRAVEL COMPANIES SELLING FLIGHTS TO THAILAND

There are many companies selling discounted flights worldwide. You could try looking in the back of the Sunday newspapers for special deals. Always check that they have ABTA or ATOL registration and check for any surcharges for credit card bookings. A selection of recommended companies follows:

- **Airline Network**: The Trident Centre, Port Way, Ribble Docklands, Preston PR2 2QA. ☎ (0870) 241 0033. Website: www.netflights.com

- **Bridge the World**: 47 Chalk Farm Road, Camden Town, London NW1 8AJ. ☎ (020) 7911 0900. Website: www.bridgetheworld.com

- **USIT Campus** (mainly serves students and under-26-year-olds): 52 Grosvenor Gardens, London SW1W OAG. ☎ (0870) 240 1010. Website: www.usitcampus.co.uk

- **USIT Now**: 13B Fountain Centre, College Street, Belfast, BT1 6ET. ☎ (01232) 324073.

- **Quest Worldwide**: Quebec House, 10 Richmond Road, Kingston upon Thames, Surrey KT2 5HL. ☎ (020) 8547 3322.

- **STA Travel** (mainly serves students and under-26-year-olds): Priory House, 6 Wrights Lane, London W8 6TA. ☎. (020) 7361 6262 (long-haul). Website: www.statravel.co.uk

- **Thomas Cook**: 11 Donegal Place, Belfast, BT1 5AJ. ☎ (028) 9088 3900.

- **Trailfinders** (for long-haul travel): 42–50 Earl's Court Road, London W8 6FT. ☎ (020) 7938 3366. Website: www.trailfinders.com

- **Travel Bag**: 52 Regent Street, London W1R 6DX. ☎ (020) 7287 5558. Website: www.travelbag.co.uk

- **Wasteels** (specializes in independent travellers): 2 Victoria Station, London SW1V 1JT. ☎ (020) 7834 7066. Website: www.wasteels.dk/uk

## TRAVELLING FROM OUTSIDE THE UK

For discount travel obtained outside the UK, the two main companies to start with are USIT (Council Travel and Travel Cuts) and STA travel. They both have offices worldwide and will provide information on discounts, insurance, tours, car hire and accommodation. Although these companies are aimed at the youth and student market, they also handle the needs of independent travellers. Addresses for their head offices, and branches of other discount travel agents in Australia, Canada, Ireland, New Zealand, South Africa and the United States are as follows:

### From the Republic of Ireland:

- **USIT Now**: 19–21 Aston Quay, O'Connell Bridge, Dublin 2. ☎ (01) 677 8117/(01) 602 1600.

- **Thomas Cook**: 118 Grafton Street, Dublin 2. ☎ (01) 1677 1721.

- **Trailfinders**: 4/5 Dawson Street, Dublin 2, ☎ (01) 677 7888. Open 7 days a week.

### From the United States of America:

- **STA Travel USA**: 920 Westwood Boulevard, Los Angeles, CA 90024. ☎ (310) 824-1574/(800) 777-0112. Website: www.sta-travel.com

- **USIT (Council Travel) USA**: 931 Westwood Boulevard, Los Angeles, CA 90024. ☎ (310) 208-3551. Website: www.counciltravel.com

- **USIT Now USA**: 895 Amsterdam Avenue, West 103rd Street, New York, NY 10025. ☎ (212) 666-4177.

**From Canada:**

• **Travel Cuts (USIT World)**: 187 College Street, Toronto, ON M5T 1P7
☎ (416) 979 2406/(800) 667-2887.

**From Australia:**

• **STA Travel Australia**: 222 Faraday Street, Carlton, Melbourne, Victoria
3053. ☎ (03) 9349 2411/(1 300) 360 960 (fares hotline).

• **Student Uni Travel (USIT)**: Level 8, 92 Pitt Street, Sydney, NSW 2001.
☎ (02) 9232 8444.

**From New Zealand:**

• **STA Travel New Zealand**: 10 High Street, Auckland. ☎ (09) 309 0458/
(0800) 100 677 (fares hotline).

• **USIT Beyond**: Corner of Shortland Street and Jean Batten Place (18
Shortland Street), Auckland. ☎ (09) 379 4224/(0800) 788 336 (freephone).

**From South Africa:**

• **STA Travel South Africa**: Level 3, Leslie Social Sciences Building,
University of Cape Town, Rondebosch 7700, Cape Town. ☎ (21) 685
1808.

• **USIT Adventures**: Rondebosch Shopping Centre, Rondebosch Main
Road (next to McDonalds), Rondebosch, Cape Town. ☎ (21) 685 2226
(telesales).

GETTING THERE

# GENERAL INFORMATION

## ACCOMMODATION

You shouldn't have any problem finding somewhere to stay. Thailand is full of places to suit every taste and every purse: guesthouses galore in Bangkok, teak houses surrounded by gardens in Chiang Mai and bamboo bungalows on the beach in the islands. Some are more comfortable than others, of course, and come with or without ventilation (these days most come with) or air-conditioning, and with or without shower and WC. Cleanliness isn't a problem either – even if much of the accommodation is cheap and cheerful, you can be pretty certain it will be clean and tidy. For more information *see* 'Prices'.

### YOUTH HOSTELS

– People of any age can stay in a youth hostel, you simply need to be a member.

– The Youth Hostel Association (YHA) for England and Wales publishes useful directories: the *YHA Accommodation Guide* (free to members), which details hostels in England and Wales, and the *Hostelling International Guide Books* (£8.50 each), which give information on Europe and the Mediterranean (volume one), and Africa, the Americas, Asia and the Pacific (volume two). These can be bought using credit/debit cards from: YHA (England and Wales) Ltd, Trevelyan House, 8 St Stephen's Hill, St Albans, Hertfordshire, AL1 2DY. ☎ (0870) 870 8808. Fax: (01727) 844126.

– YHA members can book their bed abroad through the International Booking Network (IBN). A small booking fee of £3 guarantees you a bed in over 300 key hostels overseas. You can reserve beds in shared dormitories for up to nine people, for a maximum of six nights, up to six months in advance. You pay for everything in pounds sterling before leaving Britain and in exchange you get a receipt, which you present on arrival at the hostel. Three days' notice is needed for cancelling bookings, and the cost will be refunded in full minus a small administration fee (about £3.50–£5). For details of how to join the YHA, *see* above or check its website (address below).

– **International Booking Network**: PO Box 67, Matlock, Derbyshire DE4 3YX. ☎ (01629) 581418.

● Website: www.yha.org.uk

● Email: customerservices@yha.org.uk

– YHA Membership Desk, YHA Adventure Shop: 14 Southampton Street, Covent Garden, London WC2E 7HY. ☎ (020) 7836 8541 (for booking accommodation in person).

An international youth hostel card is valid in 62 countries and entitles you to stay in any of the 6,000 youth hostels all over the world. Opening times vary according to the country and the hostel. You will find the card particularly useful in Europe, the United States, Canada, the Middle East and the Far East (Japan).

# BRINGING THINGS INTO THE COUNTRY

## DUTY-FREE ALLOWANCES

The duty-free limits for entering Thailand are as follows: 200 cigarettes or 250g (9oz) of cigarettes, cigars or tobacco plus one litre of wine or spirits.

## PROHIBITED ITEMS

You are prohibited from taking into Thailand the following items: narcotics, pornographic material and some species of wildlife.

## PERMITTED ITEMS

You can take firearms, ammunition and explosives providing you have a police permit detailing what you are carrying. You can take living plants and planting materials such as seeds, providing you have a permit from the Department of Agriculture detailing what you are carrying.

## FOREIGN CURRENCY

You are allowed to carry any amount of foreign currency or Thai currency into Thailand. You are also allowed to take up to 50,000 baht out of the country. If you are travelling to Cambodia, Laos, Malaysia or Vietnam you can take up to 500,000 baht out of the country.

# BUDGET

Prices in Thailand have always seemed pretty low to Westerners – even lower since the 1997 stock market crash and the recession that followed. The baht fell by a quarter of its value in just one month, forcing the country to change direction in a number of areas (*see* 'The Economy').

## ACCOMMODATION

Generally speaking, accommodation in the seaside resorts of the south (Phuket for example) is around three times more expensive than in the north. Bangkok is also more expensive than the north, although there are still a few good-value guesthouses to be found.

There are seasonal as well as geographical variations: it is not unusual for an establishment to charge almost double in high season. And, of course, on some islands it seems to be high season all year round: high season prices in Phuket can go through the roof. By contrast, the difference between low and high seasons is far less evident in the north. Despite all these variables, we have attempted to provide a price guide throughout

GENERAL INFORMATION

the book based on the cost of one bedroom for two people. Where possible, specific price ranges are indicated next to the category headings (Budget, Moderate etc.) in the text; where there is no indication of price, please use the general guide below:

– **Budget**: 50–200 Bts.
– **Moderate**: 200–400 Bts.
– **More Expensive**: 400–1,000 Bts.
– **Splash Out**: (for an exceptional hotel with loads of charm) 1,000+ Bts.

## RESTAURANTS

As for eating out, price differences between north and south are less marked. This is particularly true in Bangkok, for example, where it is always easy to find something decent to eat in the small street canteens, at very good prices. Restaurants, on the other hand, are a little more expensive than in the north and this difference is accentuated still further in the south.

As a result we have simplified the categories for eating out, bearing in mind the fewer differences. In the north, it is practically impossible to eat out for more than 300 Bts, unless you are intent on rupturing your stomach, and you can easily get by on 50 Bts a day. Consequently, there is little point in trying to find entries for the 'Splash Out' category!

Likewise in the south, prices are more or less low across the board so we have not listed them, especially since in a single restaurant you can spend next to nothing if you order the fried noodles, or spend five times more if you go for a seafood option. We have basically stuck to three categories:

– **Budget**: popular eateries where a full meal will set you back less than 100 Bts.

– **Moderate**: likewise good value but where you can spend a little more if you feel like it.

– **Expensive**: where you can spend 300 Bts or more – generally establishments aimed specifically at tourists or offering genuinely gourmet food.

All things considered, even if prices do go up, the exchange rates tend to favour our well-heeled economies so you'll never lose out.

# CLIMATE

Whatever time of year you choose to visit Thailand, you will almost inevitably find it hot or humid, and sometimes both. The country does, however, have three distinct seasons. The best time to visit Thailand is during the 'cooler' months from November to February, when the weather is balmy, the skies are blue and temperatures generally around 30°C (mid-80s°F). From March to May is the hot season, with temperatures reaching a scorching high of 39°C (103°F). This is the least pleasant time of year, when you will find the countryside brown and arid and the once mighty waterfalls and rivers reduced to a trickle. The rainy season begins in July and generally lasts until October. During this period,

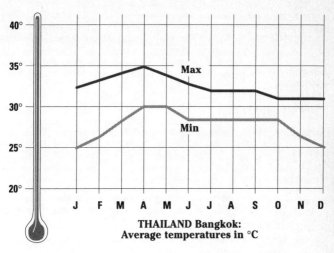

**THAILAND Bangkok:**
**Average temperatures in °C**

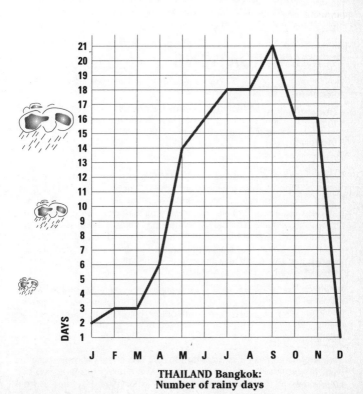

**THAILAND Bangkok:**
**Number of rainy days**

torrential downpours can occur every day – but typically only for a few hours, so there is plenty of time to enjoy life in the open. In the south you will find considerably less variation in climate throughout the year. The southeast monsoon will generally bring rain to Phuket between May and October, while in Koh Samui, on the east coast some of the heaviest downpours occur between November and February.

# CLOTHING

Opt for light clothing, especially cotton, in Thailand's generally warm and humid climate. Even if you are arriving in the hottest months, be sure to bring some long-sleeved shirts and long trousers. These will protect you from mosquitoes and may also be useful if you are going to, say, a temple festival or out for dinner in a smart restaurant.

Up in the north and northeast, during the winter months, you would be strongly advised to bring a light sweater as temperatures can drop sharply at night and in the early morning.

For the most part, Thais dress smartly and don't approve of sloppy dressing. While it is normal to wear shorts and T-shirts on beaches, topless sunbathing, although common among foreigners, embarrasses the locals and is best avoided.

# COMMUNICATIONS

## EMAIL / INTERNET

These days you'll find Internet centres everywhere in Thailand, even on the smallest islands. Surfing the net, sending an email or looking in your mail box costs about 100–150 Bts per hour.

## POST

Post offices are usually open from 8am to 5.30pm Monday to Friday in big towns, 4.30pm in small towns; from 8am to 12 noon on Saturday and are closed all day Sunday except in Bangkok. Staff are usually efficient and service is excellent. Parcels can be sent by surface or air mail from any post office; sending a parcel by surface mail takes 3 months. Boxes can be bought at any post office in the major towns and you can weigh your parcel on the scales. It's all very reliable. For once the English are at a disadvantage (linguistically speaking), since all the dispatch notes in Thailand are written in Thai and French.

Private postal services have also multiplied recently, particularly in the major towns, offering postal, telephone and email services. Opening hours are often slightly different with offices generally staying open later.

## TELEPHONE

The telephone service is growing rapidly. The cheapest way to call is from a telephone exchange (there is one in every town) and you can choose between a station-to-station call, where you are charged from the moment the call is answered, or a person-to-person call (you specify the person you want to speak to and if they are not there, you only pay a nominal fee).

In some places, you can make collect or reverse-charge calls to certain countries. In this case the person you are calling pays a standard price based on the first 2 to 3 minutes of the call. More and more reverse-charge calls are now charged by the minute.

You can also make overseas calls from the many telephone kiosks you find in all the main towns. Some guesthouses let you do this too. It costs a bit more but at least you can call from where you are.

Another good idea, assuming you are not in any hurry, is to call from the post office. This may be your only choice in many of the villages.

Card-operated telephones have now been installed in most large towns, which is great for anyone planning a mainly urban trip. There are two types: international and national. The international ones are green and take overseas phonecards (costing 500 Bts), available from small shops or the post office). A national phonecard costs 100 Bts. Be sure to buy the right card for the right phone, since there are two different operating companies. Find out which company operates in your area before investing in a card.

Lastly, don't forget email, which is by far the cheapest option (*see* above).

## TELEPHONE DIALLING CODES

To call Thailand from the following countries, use these international dialling codes:

From the UK: ☎ 00 66
From the Republic of Ireland: ☎ 00 66
From the USA: ☎ 011 66
From Canada: ☎ 011 66
From Australia: ☎ 0011 66
From New Zealand: ☎ 00 66
From South Africa: ☎ 09 66

To make calls from Thailand, use the following codes:

To the UK: ☎ 001 + 44
To the Republic of Ireland: ☎ 001 + 353
To the USA: ☎ 001 + 1
To Canada: ☎ 001 + 1
To Australia: ☎ 001 + 61
To New Zealand: ☎ 001 + 64
To South Africa: ☎ 001 + 27

To call Bangkok from the rest of Thailand: ☎ 02 + the rest of the telephone number.

# CUISINE

Sharpen your tastebuds and prepare to be overwhelmed by the sights and smells that make Thai cuisine such a richly intoxicating experience. You'll find the same high standards of culinary art wherever you eat – in luxury restaurants in Bangkok or on the pavements of Chiang Mai.

Whatever you eat – elaborate dishes or plain fried rice – you're unlikely to be disappointed.

Restaurants stay open all day but don't turn up later than 10pm.

The Tourist Authority of Thailand (TAT) provides a useful brochure called *Eating in Thailand* which gives the Thai and English names of a variety of delicious dishes as well as a guide to pronouncing their names.

Rice is the basis of Thai cuisine, served fried and prepared in a thousand different ways with fish, beef, pork, crab and shrimps. Most of the dishes are spicy, which means they can be mild or very hot. So a word of warning: learn the word *mai phêt* – ไม่เผ็ด, which means 'mild'. Some restaurants serve a spicy sauce separately in a little saucer and more and more restaurants in tourist areas ease off on the heat, to make sure their customers come back.

Apart from fried rice, the fried noodles *(kway tiao phat* – ผัดไทย), are absolutely delicious and so are the fried local vegetables or vegetables cooked in gravy that they serve in Chinese restaurants.

Thai cuisine owes its unique, mysterious taste to the freshness of the ingredients and the range of herbs and spices used in the cooking: coriander, chillies, white saffron, mint, lemon grass and ginger. Fish sauces, and sauces made from mussels and oysters, plus soy sauce, of course, are all commonly used to season the dishes. All quite spicy for Western palates, but very tasty when tempered a little, something that the majority of eateries do as standard for tourist customers.

Fried rice and noodles may be the basis of culinary art in Thailand, but restaurants in Bangkok and Chiang Mai are now using modern-day skills to revive a more ancient, refined cuisine. The results speak for themselves (check out *Bussaracum* – บุษราคัม, in Bangkok, or *Heun Soontaree* – หวนสุนทรีย์, in Chiang Mai). Thai cuisine today has managed to retain its personality despite the Chinese and Indonesian influences. So you can be sure that there are not many bad restaurants in Thailand and it doesn't cost a lot to eat well.

When it comes to puddings, these are few and far between – and those you do find are very sweet. All the same, look out for the gelatinous-looking squares in fluorescent colours (they're hard to miss). The coconut flans are worth trying too.

Fruits occur in mouth-watering abundance: pineapple, papaya, mango, coconut, rambutan, pomelo (like a pink grapefruit), mangosteen, water-melon, jack fruit and, of course, the famous durian – smells awful and tastes great! This is a fruit that looks like a rugby ball decorated with triangular spines and is much prized by the Thais. The price, however, is prohibitive for the average Thai income and buying one represents a large financial outlay. You probably won't like it, but you really must try it once!

These classic dishes will help you find your way around the menu.

## FRIED DISHES

*Khao phat* – ข้าวผัด: fried rice

*Phak bung phat* – ผัดผักบุ้ง: fried beef in oyster sauce with onions

*Nua phat nam man hoi* – เนื้อผัดน้ำมันหอย: crispy noodles prepared with meat or shrimps

*Thod man pla* – ทอดมันปลา: fried fish fritters

*Mi krob* – หมี่กรอบ: crispy noodles with meat or shrimps

## SOUPS

*Kaeng chut* – แกงจืด: vegetable soup with shrimps or pork

*Tom yam* – ต้มยำ: sweet-and-sour pork, chicken or fish

*Tom yam kung* – ต้มยำกุ้ง: shrimp soup flavoured with lemon grass

*Khao tom pla* – ข้าวต้มปลา: soup with fish sauce

## NOODLES

*Kuai tiao haeng* – ก๋วยเตี๋ยวแห้ง: noodles served with spicy strips of meat and vegetables

*Kuai tiao phat siiu* – ก๋วยเตี๋ยวผัดซีอิ้ว: fried noodles with Chinese sauce, meat, vegetables and eggs

*Ba mi krob rat na kung* – บะหมี่กรอบราดหน้ากุ้ง: crispy yellow noodles with shrimps

## OTHER DISHES

*Kam pu tot* – ก้ามปูทอด: fried crab

*Kai yang* – ไก่ย่าง: grilled chicken

*Hu cha lam sai pu* – หูฉลามใส่ปู: shark's fin with crab

*Keng pla nam khao* – แกงปลาน้ำขาว: pomfret (a kind of fish) cooked in a *court-bouillon* and served with a white sauce

*Khai phat phrik* – ไก่ผัดพริก: spicy grilled chicken

*Pla prieo wan* – ปลาเปรี้ยวหวาน: sweet-and-sour fish

*Ho mok pla tchon* – ห่อหมกปลาช่อน: curried fish steamed in a banana leaf

# DRINKS

It is advisable not to drink the local tap-water as you're likely to suffer from an upset stomach. However, if you'd rather drink water than soft imported fizzy drinks then ask for *Nam kwat* – น้ำขวด: boiled, filtered water in sealed litre bottles which is widely available.

– If you're short of cash, bring your own water purifying pills, otherwise hydroclonazone pills are available just about anywhere. Tea is also easy to find although it's likely to be Lipton's or a pale imitation.

– You must taste the local whisky. It's called *Mekong* – แม่โขง and you mix it with lemonade or cola. Hardly the same as a single malt back home, but it costs much the same whether you buy your own bottle to drink in the restaurant or pay restaurant prices.

– Drink the fresh fruit juice by all means (available everywhere) but don't overdo it. If you're wise, you'll give the ice-cubes a miss. Do taste the *Vitamilk* – ไวตามิ้ลค์ – sweetened soya milk and absolutely delicious.

– The coffee is American – let's just call it weak – but it's increasingly popular with the Thais themselves.

– *Singha Beer* – เบียร์สิงห์ – is fine but rather expensive. Try the cheaper *Leo* or *Chang* beer or better still opt for the more upmarket imports.

– Stay away from crushed ice – it's lethal. Stick to cylindrical-shaped ice-cubes, which are produced under more hygienic conditions.

# DRUGS

No one is trying to preach here, but you should be aware of the high price you will pay in Thailand for trying any kind of drug – including soft drugs. The sanctions are terrible and a number of Europeans are currently in prison for breaking the law, often for long stretches (20 to 30 years). A prison specially for Westerners has recently been built, and is basically full of drugs offenders. The drug dealers are the most likely to shop you to the police, in exchange for a gratuity and the return of their dope. So don't say you didn't know!

## A BRIEF HISTORY OF OPIUM

Picture an old bamboo hut on stilts. At the back of the hut, an emaciated old man lies in the shadows surrounded by a halo of smoke. He pulls on a strange-looking pipe and doesn't appear to have noticed you. This kind of scene isn't uncommon in the mountains of northern Thailand. The ritual attached to opium smoking, along with the trade itself, started long ago in this part of the world and long before hard drugs spread their mayhem to the West several decades ago.

What is opium? Opium is a resin that comes from the poppy flower (*Papaver somniferum*). When a small incision is made in the pistil of the poppy flower, it releases a white paste that is left to turn brown in the sun before being collected the following day. It takes the pressed contents of 20,000 poppies to make one joy (about 1.6 kilograms/3.5lbs). This is the unit of measure of pure opium and has a trading value of about £700 ($1,050). Twenty kilograms of refined opium produce enough morphine to make (through further refinement) one kilogram of pure heroin. By the time heroin reaches the streets and the hands of the 'dealers', it has been 'stepped on' by dozens of middlemen – which gives you some idea of what a £100 ($150) gram is actually worth . . .

The Greeks were the first to cultivate the *Papaver somniferum* in the Mediterranean basin, before Arab traders took it to the Far East. By the 13th century, opium was already being grown for its narcotic properties in southern China, Burma and Thailand. The peasants smoked some of it, but in remote areas the harvest was also a valuable form of barter. Back then, it was strictly between you and your neighbours. The boom dates back to the post-World War II period, when ethnic minorities in China and Burma fled persecution at home. The peasants who settled in northern Thailand emigrated with their pockets full of poppy seeds and it wasn't long before the fields blossomed with pretty red flowers. Not in a big way to begin with, since until the 1950s any trafficking was limited to Southeast Asia. But the war with Vietnam and the not altogether proper contacts made by some Americans round here helped to develop the European and American markets, despite Thailand's ban on the cultivation of poppies in 1958.

The people in charge of the trafficking were KMT (Kuomintang) rebels – soldiers who fled Chang Kai-Chek's army in 1949 and who sought refuge in Burma (before they were thrown out), then settling in northern Thailand where they built villages deep in the jungle. This was the new base from which they carried out anti-Communist guerrilla raids with the blessing of the American secret service. But opium trafficking offered them another, less dangerous and more lucrative way to make a living. To judge from the speed with which their commercial activities developed into an international business, political struggles can't have taken up too much of their time.

The boom in world demand for heroin in the 1970s proved particularly lucrative, despite the ongoing battle between the different political minorities and armed bands of the Golden Triangle. If the reason for the fighting was ostensibly political, the real objective was to gain control of the drug trade.

Since the beginning of the 1980s, the Thai authorities have been at war with the ringleaders, but without success. Today the Thai and Burmese armies are determined to come down hard on trafficking, and measures are underway to return the land to tea or coffee cultivation; they use force where necessary.

It is interesting to note the government's awareness of the cultural and even pathological aspect of opium in relation to the hill tribes: it authorizes the cultivation of around 1 hectare (2.5 acres) of poppies per village, for locals' own consumption. Needless to say, however, the Lisu, Yao or Meo peasants continue to cultivate and sell these attractive red flowers on a clandestine basis given the tidy income that they can represent.

# ELECTRICITY

The standard electric current throughout Thailand is 220V. Although most hotel rooms have a point for shavers, you should bring an adaptor kit as several different types of plugs and sockets are in use.

# EMBASSIES

## ABROAD

**UK**: The Royal Thai Embassy, 29–30 Queen's Gate, London SW7 5JB. ☎ (020) 7589 2944. Fax: (020) 7823 9695.

**Ireland**: The Royal Thai Embassy, 19 Harcourt Street, Dublin 2. ☎ (01) 475 3928. Fax: (01) 475 3943.

**USA**: The Royal Thai Embassy, 351 East 52nd Street, New York, NY 10022. ☎ (212) 754-1770. Fax: (212) 754-1907.

**Canada**: The Royal Thai Embassy, 180 Island Park Drive, Ottawa, Ontario K1Y 0A2. ☎ (613) 722-4444. Fax: (613) 722-6624.

**Australia**: The Royal Thai Consulate General, Second Floor, 75–77 Pitt Street, Sydney, NSW 2000. ☎ (02) 9241 2542/3. Fax: (02) 9247 8312.

**New Zealand**: The Royal Thai Embassy, 2 Cook Street, Karori, Wellington (PO Box 17226). ☎ (04) 476 8618. Fax: (04) 476 3677.

**South Africa**: The Royal Thai Embassy, 428 Hill Street, Pretoria, 0083. ☎ (12) 342 5470. Fax: (12) 342 4805.

## IN THAILAND

**British Embassy**: 1031 Wireless Road, Bangkok 10330. ☎ (02) 253-01-91. Fax: (02) 254-95-78. Open weekdays only, 7.45am–noon (for visa applications).

**American Embassy**: 120–22 Wireless Road, Bangkok 10330. ☎ (02) 205-40-00. Fax: (02) 254-29-90/(02) 205-41-31. Open weekdays only, 7am–noon (for visa applications).

**Canadian Embassy**: 990 Abdulrahim Place, 15th floor, Rama IV Road, Bangrak, Bangkok 10500. ☎ (02) 636-05-40. Fax: (02) 636-05-66. Open weekdays only, 7.30am–12.15pm (1pm Fri) and 1–4.15pm (except Fri).

**Australian Embassy**: 37 South Sathorn Road, Bangkok 10120. ☎ (02) 287-26-80. Fax: (02) 287-20-29. Open weekdays only, 8am–12.30pm.

**New Zealand Embassy**: 93 Wireless Road, Bangkok 10330. ☎ (02) 254-25-30. Fax: (02) 253-90-45. Open weekdays only, 7.30am–noon and 1–4pm.

**South Africa Embassy**: 6th Floor, The Park Place, 231 Soi Sarasin, Lumphini, Bangkok 10330. ☎ (02) 253-84-73. Fax: (02) 253-84-77. Open weekdays only, 8am–noon.

## NEIGHBOURING COUNTRIES

**Embassy of Cambodia**: สถานทูตกัมพูชา: 185 Ratchadamri Road – ถนนราชดำริ, Lumphini, Pathumwan, Bangkok. ☎ (02) 254-66-30. Fax: (02) 253-98-59. Open weekdays only, 9am–noon. Visas are easily obtainable.

**Embassy of the Lao People's Democratic Republic**: สถานทูตลาว: 520, 520/1–3 Soi Ramkamhaeng 39 – ซอยรามคำแหง, Bangkapi, Bangkok 10310. ☎ (02) 539-66-67/(02) 539-66-79. Fax: (02) 539-66-78/(02) 539-3827. Open weekdays only, 8am–noon and 1–4pm. In principle you can only obtain a visa through a travel agency. The rules are unclear, to say the least (*see also* 'Khon Kaen and Nong Khai').

**Indian Embassy**: สถานทูตอินเดีย: 46 Soi Prasarnmit 23 – ซอยประสานมิตร, Sukhumvit Road, Bangkok 10110. ☎ (02) 258-03-00. Fax: (02) 258-46-27. Open weekdays 8.30am–1pm and 1.30–5pm.

**Indonesian Embassy**: สถานทูตอินโดนีเซีย: 600–602 Petchburi Road, Bangkok 10400 – ถนนเพชรบุรี. ☎ (02) 252-31-35(-39). Fax: (02) 255-12-67. Open weekdays 8am–noon and 1–4pm.

**Embassy of Malaysia**: สถานทูตมาเลเซีย: 33–35 South Sathorn Road, Tungmahamek, Sathorn, Bangkok 10120. ☎ (02) 679-21-90. Fax: (02) 679-22-08. Open 8.30–noon and 1–4pm.

**Embassy of the Union of Myanmar** (formerly Burma): สถานทูตพม่า: 132 Sathorn Nua Road, Bangkok 10500 – ถนนสาธรเหนือ. ☎ (02) 233-22-37/ (02) 234-47-89. Fax: (02) 236-68-98. Open weekdays 8.30am–noon and 2–4.30pm. No. 17 bus. The relevant laws may have changed by the time you get there, so double-check when you arrive.

**Office of Immigration Bureau**: สำนักงานตรวจคนเข้าเมือง: The Royal Thai Police Department, Ramal Road, Bangkok 10500. ☎ (02) 287-31-01/10. Fax: (02) 287-13-10. Open 9am–4pm. Best to go in the morning. If you need to extend your visa, it's simpler to go to the immigration office at the airport but be prepared for at least an hour's paperwork.

# ENTRY FORMALITIES

For members of the European Community, visas are not necessary for visits of less than 30 days. For visits of under 30 days (and consequently without visas) it is essential to have a passport valid for three months as of the date of entry into Thailand. For visits of more than 30 days (with visa), passports must be valid for six months after the date of entry into Thailand. Remember to check the time limit entered in your passport as you are sometimes given slightly less than the full 30 days.

American, Australian, New Zealand and South African citizens can obtain a tourist visa for entry into Thailand from the Thai Embassy in their respective countries. You should submit two passport photographs along with your passport, which must be valid for at least six months. The process takes two working days, and a same-day service is also possible, for an extra charge. The visa is valid for three months from the date of application and once a visitor has entered Thailand the visa is valid for 60 days. Tourist visas cannot be extended beyond 60 days without leaving and re-entering the country.

Work is permitted in Thailand for non-Thai people providing the company they will be working for in Thailand contacts the embassy in writing and shows that the job could not be done by a Thai person – teaching English as a foreign language, for example.

If you plan to visit Thailand and its neighbouring countries and your stay in Thailand doesn't exceed 30 days, you'll have no problem obtaining a 'transit without visa' stamp at the frontier.

## A FEW HINTS

– **Extending your visa**: The Thai police take a dim view of anyone who attempts to outstay their welcome. Stay within the limits of your visa or you become liable for a fine of 200 Bts per day for every day of 'overstay', payable as you leave the country. It's worth knowing that, if you happen to be close to the border with Malaysia when your visa is about to expire, one trip there and back will get you a 30-day visa (complimentary, of course). *See* 'Where to Extend your Visa' under the entry on Hat Yai.

– An **airport tax** is payable on leaving the country (500 Bts) and each time you take an internal flight it costs 30 Bts. Bear in mind that these taxes could rise substantially with fluctuations in the baht.

– **Dress properly for customs**: Wear something that covers your shoulders and legs, rather than faded Bermuda shorts and a sleeveless T-shirt.

# FESTIVALS AND PUBLIC HOLIDAYS

Since most of the public festivals are determined by the lunar calendar, the dates tend to vary from one year to the next. As a rule, there are no paid holidays in Thailand, so public holidays are awaited with much anticipation.

– **Thai New Year** or **Songkran** (31 December–1 January): both days are public holidays. Huge crowds and lots of pushing and shoving in the immense Sanam Luong square in Bangkok. All the hotels in Chiang Mai are packed. Trains at this time of year contain twice as many passengers as seats so reserve your sleeper berths at least two weeks in advance.

– **Magha Puja** (end of February): Buddhist festival. People go to the temple and attend candle-lit processions.

– **Pra Buddhabaht** (February and March): the grand festival of Saraburi, 136 kilometres (84 miles) from Bangkok. People gather at the Altar of the Footprint believed to have be made by the Buddha.

– **Chinese New Year** (early February): a family festival. Nothing much happens except that many shops are closed for four days and the buses, trains and hotels tend to be packed.

– **Kite fighting** (March–April): contestants have to knock down each other's kites. Takes place from around 3.30pm onwards every afternoon in Bangkok on Sanam Luong.

– **Chakri Day** (6 April): festival of the reigning dynasty. Ceremonies are held in the Temple of the Emerald Buddha in Bangkok.

– **Songkran** (13 or 15 April): Buddhist New Year. People spray each other with water. Very popular in Chiang Mai and in Phra Praokong, a suburb of Bangkok.

– **Coronation Day** (5 May): official celebration of the coronation day of King Bhumibol.

– **Labour Ceremony** (mid-May): festival marking the start of the rice planting season. The King and Queen make an appearance on Sanam Luong in Bangkok.

– **Visahka Puja** (May): anniversary of the Buddha's birth. One of the loveliest of the Thai festivals, with candle-lit processions in all the temples.

– **Asalaha Puja** (July): also called Khao Pansa, start of the Buddhist 'Lent'. The monks shut themselves away in the temples, lots of boys become novices, and many monks are ordained.

– **Queen Sirikit's birthday** (12 August): public holiday.

– **Ok Pansa** (October): end of 'Lent' and start of the Season of Kathin, when people give new robes to the Buddhist monks. Lots of musical processions. Something you won't get to see, sadly, because it doesn't happen any more, is the spectacular parade of golden barges on the river in Bangkok.

– **Day of Chulalongkorn** (23 October): anniversary of the death of King Rama V. People place flowers around his statue, near the Dusit Zoo in Bangkok.

– **Loy Krathong** (November): the loveliest of all the Thai festivals. At night, thousands of tiny boats (*krathongs*) made of banana leaves and containing a single illuminated candle and some incense are set adrift down the rivers and *khlongs* in honour of the spirits of the waters. Particularly beautiful in Bangkok on the Chao Phraya river beside the Memorial Bridge, in Chiang Mai on the River Ping. In Sukhothai there's a festival of light and sound with dancing as well.

– **Festival of the Golden Mount** (9–11 November): the festival of the temple of Wat Sakhet in Bangkok. Illuminations, street theatre and thousands of street traders.

– **Deejavali** (November): Thai Hindu festival. Particularly worth seeing in the temple on Silom road in Bangkok. Lots of flagellation.

– **Elephant Round-up** (November): hundreds of specially trained elephants on show in Surin (northeastern Thailand). First held in 1955 and organized by the Thai Tourist Authority. Probably the only chance you'll get to see so many elephants in one place.

– **King's birthday** (5 December): national holiday. In Bangkok, the majority of events happen in the area around the the Chittlâdâ Palace, the National Assembly and the Grand Palace: open-air cinema, dancing, concerts.

– **Christmas**: even if Christmas means nothing to the Thais, many of the supermarkets put up as many decorations as those in Western countries. You can now celebrate New Year in style in many parts of Thailand.

# HEALTH

## HEALTH CARE

Hospitals in Thailand are generally of a good standard and many of the doctors, especially in Bangkok, have been trained in Europe or the USA and speak English.

Few people know that Thailand has a reputation for the good quality of its dentistry. You could take this opportunity to get dental work done that you wouldn't be able to afford back home, for unless you've got dental insurance in the UK, you will save money. Do make sure, however, that you seek out a reputable dentist (all of whom should undertake basic hygiene precautions to avoid the transmission of the AIDS virus or hepatitis) as there are plenty of cowboys in the trade.

Standards of medical care are adequate and certainly higher than anywhere else on the peninsula. Nevertheless, you are strongly advised to take out medical insurance before you leave. Useful advice can be obtained from:

GENERAL INFORMATION

● **The Expedition Advisory Centre**, **RGS-IBG**: 1 Kensington Gore, London SW7 2AR. ☎ (020) 7591 3030.

## AIDS AND STDS

Official figures taken from the national press in 2000 stated that there were one million people infected with the HIV virus in Thailand. A frightening prospect. The causes of this explosion are above all negligence and ignorance, the belief that this is an illness that only affects homosexuals and heroin addicts. It is not as if the homosexual community in Thailand is particularly large, certainly no bigger than elsewhere and much smaller than in the United States. As far as intravenous drug users are concerned, there are far fewer than in the Western world. In addition, as the epidemic took some time to strike in this part of the world, people were slow to realize the severity of the consequences of these conceptual errors. This proved to be literally fatal as, needless to say, AIDS can be transmitted by heterosexuals much like any other virus; and the more liberal and active sexual life for which Thailand is famous has favoured the large-scale onslaught of the disease.

Before the gravity of the situation was realized and suitable defensive measures put into place, a million people were contaminated. As for prostitutes, any statistical estimate would be pointless, as the situation is evolving so quickly, but it cannot be too far off the mark to say that one in every two or three is contaminated. The systematic use of condoms is consequently vital.

The government has now started to take action, better late than never, and condoms are available free of charge from pharmacies all over the country (the idea was mooted by one of the royal family's princesses). The Americans adopted a scandalous position in January 2000, when the Thai government decided to produce its own version of the treatments imported from the United States (at a tenth of the cost) which contaminated Thais would be able to afford (currently this is not the case for 90 per cent of them). However, the Americans complained and threatened economic sanctions. It is high time that G7 or another official body stepped in to prevent the desire for financial gain putting human lives at risk in such a scandalous manner, particularly where health matters are concerned.

## VACCINATIONS

Check with your doctor about vaccinations well in advance of departure (preferably at least two months) as some immunizations take time to be effective.

Although there are no special vaccination requirements for Thailand, inoculation is generally recommended against diphtheria, tetanus and poliomyelitis, as well as typhoid, for a protracted stay and against rabies for anyone staying in rural areas. You are also advised to have a combined jab (Twinrex) against hepatitis A and B if you plan to stay several months. Additionally, the World Health Organization (WHO) recommends vaccination against Japanese encephalitis for those planning to spend more than a month in rural areas.

Hepatitis A is prevalent in this area and usually caught from consuming contaminated food or water. So it's worth having a single hepatitis A jab (Havrix 1440, 'Monodose', Avaxim or Vaqta) before you leave. Remember to have a booster six months or a year later to ensure long-term protection (at least 10 years) during trips to other destinations.

If you are travelling from an African country or if you are planning to travel to Africa prior to visiting Thailand, you are required to have a yellow fever vaccination, which is an international health requirement.

## MALARIA

All the books and brochures on Thailand will tell you about a 'multi-resistant' form of malaria. While this does exist, it's worth knowing the following:

– This kind of malaria is only present in a few forested and border regions and is completely absent from the plains and paddies that make up the rest of the country.

– In malaria-infested regions, you are only at risk of infection at night.

– All the major towns and cities are completely malaria-free.

You are not at risk, for example, of catching malaria in the course of a typical tourist trip that takes in Bangkok, Pattaya, Phuket (by plane), Chiang Mai, Chiang Rai and a daytime visit to the northern border territory. Yet tourists continue to be misinformed and regularly arrive stuffed full of strong anti-malarial preparations with side-effects that occasionally spoil the entire trip.

Anti-malarial prophylaxis is only necessary if you plan to spend the night in villages in the border regions. What you need then is a daily dose of 100 mg of doxycycline (Vibramycine). Starting the day before you arrive in the malaria-infested region, take it throughout your stay there and for four weeks after you leave. This is the only anti-malaria preparation to offer protection against the multi-resistant form of malaria.

## DENGUE

During the monsoon season, outbreaks of dengue can occur anywhere in Southeast Asia and that includes Thailand. Dengue is viral in origin and is transmitted by mosquitoes. It presents as a strong fever rather like a dose of flu; and, like the flu, there is no known cure. So prevention is definitely the best option, and that means protecting yourself from mosquito bites day and night.

## MOSQUITO REPELLENTS

Mosquitoes are everywhere in Thailand so mosquito repellents are a must. Despite the wide variety of sprays, creams and lotions available from supermarkets and pharmacies, some are highly effective while others are completely useless. Specialists say the most effective products are those containing deet (diethyltomide). For children, and those who prefer a more natural remedy, 'Musiguard Natural' (containing lemon eucalyptus) has been clinically tested and shown to be effective. Since frequency of application differs with the product, always read the manufacturers' instructions carefully.

### A few tips

– Keep your arms and legs covered after sunset. Sleep in properly screened rooms and use a 'knockdown' spray to kill any mosquitoes in the room.

– Screen your bed with a mosquito net (preferably impregnated with insecticide) at night – make sure that there are no holes in it and that it is well tucked in.

## WHAT TO TAKE WITH YOU

A mosquito net impregnated with insecticide (to spend the night in places where there is no air-conditioning), mosquito repellents, insecticides, sun creams and other articles and items of equipment you are likely to need en route. You can buy many of these by mail order from:

● Nomad Travellers' Store and Medical Centre: 3–4 Wellington Terrace, Turnpike Lane, London N8 OPX. ☎ (020) 8889 7014 for a catalogue.

● Medical Advisory Service for Travellers Abroad (MASTA): these products are also sold in the British Airways Travel Clinics. Credit card order phone line: ☎ (0113) 238 7575 (UK number).

# INSURANCE

Prior to departure make sure that you purchase comprehensive travel and health insurance from a reputable company to cover you in the case of any unwelcome occurrences. Always check the small print to be sure that your insurance policy will cover adventure activities like diving or trekking as well as other vital items such as loss or theft of cash.

# INTERNATIONAL STUDENT CARDS

An international student card entitles you to all the advantages of being a student wherever you are, including all sorts of student reductions (transport, museums, accommodation etc.).

To find out more, check out details of the international student card on the international website: www.istc.org

# LANGUAGE

English is the only tourist language used in Thailand and it is spoken to a greater or lesser degree in Bangkok and by staff in the hotels of Phuket, Pattaya and Chiang Mai. Elsewhere, brace yourself for a complete lack of communication and get ready to mime and make lots of little drawings . . .

The Thai national language that is taught in school is in fact a synthesis of the four different dialects spoken in the centre of the country. Each of the four principal regions has its own dialect and they have about as much in common as Portuguese, Spanish, Italian and French – you see the problem.

On top of this, there is *rachasap*, the special vocabulary used in the presence of monarchs, which is rather like the language still spoken in Cambodia. The Thai language was originally similar to Chinese, since the people themselves came from southern China. Subsequently, it was enriched with Khmer words and phrases, and Sanskrit and Pali, which both originated in India.

The alphabet is composed of 44 consonants and 11 vowels plus four intonation signs. Words are written from left to right and look rather like orderly spaghetti. Popular Thai grammar is rudimentary at best. There is no gender, no article, no plural and no conjugation. The same word can be a noun, a verb, an adjective or an adverb depending on how it is intoned. There are five intonations and they are the basis of 'spoken' Thai. The same word written five times can therefore mean five different things, the difficulty being demonstrated in the famous phrase: 'Mai mai mai mai mai?' Roughly translated, this means 'new wood burns, doesn't it?' So all in all you can forget about learning even basic Thai in a month. Start taking lessons well in advance of departure if you hope to have conversations when you arrive. Meanwhile, learning to count in Thai might come in handy, particularly when it comes to bargaining.

You will probably find most guidebooks vary in the way they spell Thai words written in Roman letters. The truth is that once you leave the phonetic alphabet behind, there's no longer a right or wrong way of writing Thai words and they become impossible to transcribe correctly. Even the Thais themselves are known to chop and change all the time. To be fair, the Roman alphabet doesn't offer a phonetic equivalent of every Thai sound. Names like Bhumibol for instance (the present king) can be written 'Phumiphon', and Thavee (a place name) can be written as Tavi, or Thawee . . . But don't panic. Get the old grey matter working when you're there and you'll find the legendary kindness of the Thais will do the rest.

## A FEW RULES OF PRONUNCIATION

There are five intonations in Thai: neutral (a – unaccented); low (à – with a grave accent); falling (â – with a circumflex); high (á – with an acute accent); and rising (ǎ – with an upside-down circumflex/háček). Note that these accents look like, but are not used the same way as, accents used in European languages The letters *p, t, k* followed by an *h* are aspirated and *ph* is pronounced like the 'p' in 'prime'. The stress falls on the last syllable of every word. The letter *u* is pronounced like the 'oo' in 'goo', the *ai* like the 'uy' in 'guy', the *j* like 'dj', and every *r* is rolled.

## COMMON WORDS AND PHRASES

The vocabulary given below is transcribed phonetically. This may not be ideal but it's the best you're going to get. To make life easier, you will find the Thai renderings of a selection of words and phrases likely to prove essential on some occasions. So instead of jabbering on in the vernacular, just wave your favourite guidebook under their noses. Good luck!

## GREETINGS AND POLITE EXPRESSIONS

| | |
|---|---|
| Hello, goodnight, goodbye | *sawat di* – สวัสดี |
| Please | *karuna* – กรุณา |
| Thank you | *kop khun krap* – ขอบคุณครับ (said by a man) |
| | *kop khun kha* – ขอบคุณค่ะ (said by a woman) |
| Sorry | *ko tot* – ขอโทษ |
| Yes | *tchaï* – ใช่ |
| No | *may tchaï* – ไม่ใช่ |
| Sir, Madam | *khun* – คุณ (also the pronouns 'you') |
| How are you? | *(khun) sabai di ru?* (คุณ) สบายดีหรือ |
| Very well | *sabaïdi, krhap (ou kha)* – สบายดีครับ |
| I don't understand | *may kao ja* – ไม่เข้าใจ |
| Speak slowly please | *phut cha cha* – กรุณาพูดช้าๆ |
| I don't speak Thai | *phûut thai mai pen* – พูดไทยไม่เป็น |

## QUESTIONS, VERBS AND COMMON WORDS

| | |
|---|---|
| How much? (price) | *raka tao-rai?* – ราคาเท่าไหร่ |
| What? | *arai?* – อะไร |
| How? | *yang rai?* – อย่างไร |
| Why? | *thammai?* – ทำใม |
| When? | *mua rai?* – เมื่อไหร่ |
| Where? | *tii naï?* – ที่ไหน |
| What time? | *wèla tao rai?* – เวลาเท่าไหร่ |
| To change | *plien* – เปลี่ยน |
| To buy | *su* – ซื้อ |
| To sell | *khai* – ขาย |
| To go | *pai* – ไป |
| To come | *ma* – มา |
| Give me | *khor* – ขอ |
| To sleep | *non lap* – นอนหลับ |
| To eat | *kin* – กิน |
| Open | *pe* – เปิด |
| Closed | *pid* – ปิด |
| Rather | *pho lêo* – พอแล้ว |

| | |
|---|---|
| More | *mak kwa* – มากกว่า |
| Less | *noi kwa* – น้อยกว่า |
| It's expensive | *paeng mak* – แพงมาก |
| It's pretty | *suay dee (di)* – สวยดี |
| Much/many | *maak* – มาก |
| Not good/bad | *mai dee (di)* – ไม่ดี |
| Amusing, funny | *sanouk* – สนุก |
| Buddha | *pra* – พระ |
| Bonze (monk) | *phrasong* – พระสงฆ์ |
| Tailor | *ráan tát sûa* – ร้านตัดเสื้อ |
| Doctor | *phêêt* – แพทย์ |
| White foreigner | *farang* – ฝรั่ง |

## EXPRESSIONS OF TIME

| | |
|---|---|
| Today | *wan nii* – วันนี้ |
| Tomorrow | *phrûng nii* – พรุ่งนี้ |
| Yesterday | *mûea wan nii* – เมื่อวานนี้ |
| Morning | *tonn tchao* – ตอนเช้า |
| Afternoon | *tonn bai* – ตอนบ่าย |
| Night | *tonn kam* – ตอนค่ำ |
| At noon | *thiang* – เที่ยง |
| Before | *konn nii* – ก่อนนี้ |
| After | *lang* – หลัง |

## IN THE TOWN

| | |
|---|---|
| Where are you going? | *khun kamlang jà pai nai?* – คุณกำลังจะไปไหน |
| Right | *kwa* – ขวา |
| Left | *saï* – ซ้าย |
| Turn right | *leo kwa* – เลี้ยวขวา |
| Turn left | *leo saï* – เลี้ยวซ้าย |
| Drive straight on | *khap rôt trong pai* – ขับรถตรงไป |
| Take a *tuk-tuk* | *nâng tùk tùk pai* – นั่งตุ๊กตุ๊กไป |
| What do I have to pay? | *khâa rot thâu rai?* – ค่ารถเท่าไร |
| More slowly | *cháa cháa noi* – ช้าๆหน่อย |
| Where is the bus-stop? | *pâi rôt mey yùu thêe nai?* – ป้ายรถเมล์อยู่ที่ไหน |
| Street | *thanon* – ถนน |

GENERAL
INFORMATION

| Station | *sathani rot faï* – สถานีรถไฟ |
| Bus station | *sathani rot meh* – สถานีรถเมล์ |
| Cycle-rickshaw | *samlor* – สามล้อ |
| Beach | *talay* – ชายทะเล |
| Police station | *sathani tamrouat* – สถานีตำรวจ |
| Hospital | *roeng phayaabaan* – โรงพยาบาล |
| Post office | *praisanii* – ไปรษณีย์ |

## AT THE HOTEL

| Hotel | *rong raem* – โรงแรม |
| Bedroom | *hong* – ห้อง |
| Shower | *hbong abnam* – ห้องอาบน้ำ |
| Telephone | *thorasap* – โทรศัพท์ |
| Hot water | *náam rorn* – น้ำร้อน |
| Blankets | *phâa hom* – ผ้าห่ม |
| Towels | *phâa chétr tua* – ผ้าเช็ดตัว |
| What is the cost of a room for the night? | *khuen là thâu rai?* – คืนละเท่าไร |

## AT THE RESTAURANT

| Restaurant | *ran a han* – ร้านอาหาร |
| Water (jug) | *nam plao* – น้ำเปล่า |
| Water (bottle) | *nam kwat* – น้ำขวด |
| Bread | *khanom pang* – ขนมปัง |
| To drink | *dum* – ดื่ม |
| Rice | *khao* – ข้าว (with the suggestion of an 'r' between the 'k' and the 'h') |
| Fried rice | *khao phat* – ข้าวผัด |
| Noodles | *kway tiao* – ก๋วยเตี๋ยว |
| Fried noodles | *kway tiao phat* – ก๋วยเตี๋ยวผัด |
| Egg | *khai* – ไข่ |
| Fish | *pla* – ปลา |
| Meat | *neua* – เนื้อ |
| Chinese soup | *feu* (usually just called 'soup') – ซุ้ป |
| Is there a menu in English? | *meynuu phaasaa angkrit mee mai?* – มีเมนูเป็นภาษาอังกฤษไหม |
| What do you recommend? | *mee arai aroiybâang?* – มีอะไรอร่อยบ้าง |
| Not too spicy | *ao mai phêt* – เอาไม่เผ็ด |

| | |
|---|---|
| I'd like mine very spicy | *ao phêt phêt* – เอาเผ็ดๆ |
| Tea | *nam tcha* – น้ำชา |
| Coffee | *kaafae* – กาแฟ |
| Chinese tea | *chaa jeen* – ชาจีน |
| Thai whisky | *Mekong* – แม่โขง |

## NUMBERS

| | |
|---|---|
| One | *neung* – หนึ่ง |
| Two | *song* – สอง |
| Three | *sam* – สาม |
| Four | *si* – สี่ |
| Five | *háa* – ห้า |
| Six | *hok* – หก |
| Seven | *jet* – เจ็ด |
| Eight | *paet* – แปด |
| Nine | *kao* – เก้า |
| Ten | *sip* – สิบ |
| Twenty | *yi sip* – ยี่สิบ |
| Thirty | *sam sip* – สามสิบ |
| Forty | *si sip* – สี่สิบ |
| One hundred | *roï* – ร้อย |
| Two hundred | *song roï* – สองร้อย |
| One thousand | *neung pan* – หนึ่งพัน |
| 1 Bt | *rian báat* – เหรียญบาท |
| 5 Bts | *rian háa báat* – เหรียญห้าบาท |
| 10 Bts | *bai la sip* – ใบละสิบ |
| 20 Bts | *bai la yi sip* – ใบละยี่สิบ |
| 50 Bts | *bai la háa sip* – ใบละห้าสิบ |
| 100 Bts | *bai la roï* – ใบละร้อย |
| 500 Bts | *bai la háa roï* – ใบละห้าร้อย |

## PLACES

| | |
|---|---|
| Bay | *ao* – อ่าว |
| Village | *ban* – บ้าน |
| Town | *chiang* – เชียง |
| Hill | *khao* – เขา |
| Canal | *khlong* – คลอง |

| Island | *koh ou ko* – เกาะ |
| Mountain | *phu* – ภู |
| Khmer-style religious building | *prasat* – ปราสาท |
| Lane | *soi* – ซอย |
| Port, landing-stage | *tha* – ท่า |
| Street | *thanon* – ถนน |

## FINDING YOUR WAY AROUND A TEMPLE

– *Wat*: name given to a Buddhist monastery complex made up of different religious buildings.

– *Bot* or *ubosot*: assembly hall reserved for the monks in a monastery (*wat*) and where they are ordained.

– *Vihara* or *vihan*: according to Indian tradition, the room housing the images of the Buddha and where the faithful meet.

– *Phra chedi* or *chedi*: name given to a funeral monument or any building containing relics and most especially the *stupa*.

– *Stupa*: dome (usually with a layered, parasol-like roof) containing Buddhist relics or serving as a cult building or Buddhist memorial.

– *Mondop*: Thai pronunciation of the Sanskrit word *mandapa*, meaning 'assembly hall for the faithful'.

– *Prang*: name describing a tall, square sanctuary building raised up on high foundations with a very impressive roof. The *prang* resembles the Khmer *prasat* (Angkor Wat-style) but is even higher, and is characteristic of the architecture of the Ayutthaya and Bangkok periods.

– *Prasat*: sanctuary tower.

– *Dvârapâla*: guardian of the door. The guardian on the right of the door wears a pleasant expression, whereas the one on the left looks terrifying. By the end of the Ayutthaya period they had all acquired the same terrifying expression as the *yakshas*.

– *Chofas*: ornaments hanging from the ends of the roof-gables and generally representing snakes (*nâgas*) or birds such as *hamsas*.

*See* 'The Thai Temple' for more information.

# MONEY

## CURRENCY

The unit of currency is the baht (Bt).

### Currency exchange

There is no black market in Thailand, and you can exchange currency just about anywhere including sterling and sterling traveller's cheques – so there's no point in bringing dollars. But it is worth bringing traveller's cheques in large denominations, since a small commission is charged on each cheque. Holders of a post office cheque account will be pleased to hear that no commission at all is charged on post office traveller's cheques, which can be exchanged at any post office in Thailand.

Every town, irrespective of size, also has its 'money-changers', who stay open until 8pm or even later, including weekends. So all in all, you shouldn't have any problems changing money.

## BRINGING MONEY IN AND TAKING IT OUT
*See* 'Bringing Things into the Country', *above*.

## BANKS
Banks are open Monday–Friday, 8.30am–3.30pm.

### Bank debit and credit cards
Nearly all the banks take Visa, MasterCard and American Express and other major cards. The bank with the best exchange rates by far is the Thai Farmers Bank – ธนาคารกสิกรไทย.

Most banks are also equipped with cash machines, which operate from 6am–10pm. Some operate 24 hours a day.

Before leaving home, contact your bank for a complete list of names and addresses of banks in Thailand with cash machines.

– Various UK bank cards entitle the bearer and his or her family (provided they are travelling together) to immediate repatriation in the event of a medical emergency. Contact your bank for details.

– If your Visa card is stolen, contact the number given to you by your bank.

– If you have problems with your American Express card, the number to contact is: ☎ +44 (0) 1273 693555.

# PHOTOGRAPHY
Rolls of film are much cheaper than in Britain, and it is definitely worth stocking up. On the other hand, film developing is generally fairly mediocre, so take your exposed films home with you and get them developed there.

# SAFETY
It is not worth getting unduly worried about safety in Thailand, although like any other country, you should take basic precautions. Avoid sensitive border areas, which may be subject to bandit activity. On Phuket and some of the other major islands, the authorities advise tourists to avoid isolated beaches where they could be subjected to unwanted approaches or targeted by thieves. At night, beware of visiting establishments that are too far off the beaten track. Don't tempt criminals by flaunting valuable items or ostentatious clothes. Finally, watch out for small criminal elements which are especially active in the main bar and entertainment

areas in Bangkok, Pattaya and Phuket. Crimes should be reported immediately to the Tourist Police: ☎ 16-99, most of whom speak English. Alternatively, in case of emergency, contact your embassy.

# SHOPPING

Thai craftsmanship isn't always in the best of taste, except in certain areas, where it excels. Watch out for cheap imitations: poor-quality products masquerading as famous brands. It's illegal to import these into Europe in any quantity, and smuggling them back is an offence for which Customs may prosecute you.

If paying for your purchases with a credit card, don't let it out of your sight for a moment and don't forget to get a copy of the sales voucher.

– **Cotton fabrics** are well priced and come in a wide variety of woven and printed, contemporary and traditional designs. This is the chance to get clothes made for next to nothing, in any one of the little workshops that you find here. In fact, clothes here are so cheap that unless there's something you want copied at a very reasonable price, don't bother bringing much out with you.

– **Precious stones**: Bangkok has become the world centre for the cutting of precious stones, particularly sapphires and rubies. However, it's best to avoid jewellery shops that sell precious stones, ornaments, souvenirs and assorted curios. Generally speaking, you'll find reputable jewellers in major hotels (who have their reputation to maintain). Also, you get a 25 per cent reduction on 5 December (the King's birthday).

Never go into a shop with a guide from a tourist agency, as they automatically get commission.

Fake stones, as you would expect, are all over the place. In fact, Bangkok is one of the principal markets for the world's leading producer of synthetic rubies, which is located in France.

For more information and advice, *see* the section on 'Precious Stones'.

– **Silver** is embossed with traditional symbolic or mythological designs using the *repoussé* technique. The *niello* itself is obtained from silver, which is usually golden in colour and inlaid with another alloy. This type of craftsmanship dates from the days of King Narai of Ayutthaya (1656–88) and you can see some very fine examples of it in the National Museum. Any silver that looks like aluminium contains only 20 per cent silver and is practically worthless. Always ask for 'sterling' silver.

– **Gold jewellery** is cheaper than in Britain but you won't necessarily like it. What's more, unless you really are a connoisseur, you stand a good chance of being ripped off (even if it is hallmarked, it might be copper or 14-carat gold). Jade and onyx bracelets are often reasonably priced.

– You can also get some good **lacquerware** in Thailand (it's a northern speciality).

– **Bronze** has been a feature of Thai craftsmanship for centuries. You can buy copper and bronze temple bells in every shape, size and colour, including in the shape of a leaf from the Bodhi tree *(Ficus religiosa)*.

– **Pottery**, particularly in Chiang Mai, where there's a growing revival in an ancient artform called 'celadon' pottery. This is made by a process involving high temperatures and is distinguished by its delicate finish and exquisite jade green colour.

– **Brass-rubbings**: Impressions are taken of bas-reliefs in Bangkok's main temples, using tracing paper, charcoal, gold dust or oil paint.

– **Thai dolls** made of brightly coloured silks represent characters in classical Thai dance as well as members of mountain tribes.

– **Kohn masks**, used in the masked dramas of Thai popular theatre, are also on sale. They represent the demons, monkeys and other characters from the *Râmakien*, the Thai version of the *Râmâyana*. Great to take back as ornaments.

– **Teak** from the dense jungles of the north is used to produce all kinds of objects, from trays and eating utensils to statues and elegant furniture.

– The **rattan basketwork** and **bamboo furniture** is sensational as well as inexpensive but rather cumbersome, which tends to put people off. Most tourists settle instead for the pointed Chinese (straw) hats and the umbrellas made of stretched paper (particularly in Chiang Mai).

– Allow three months for any packages to be shipped back to Europe and elsewhere, and always post them yourself (recorded delivery). *See* 'Post'.

## BARGAINING

Yes, it's traditional, but you don't always know just how far you can go. In some cases, the price can be reduced by as much as 50 per cent but usually the most you can expect is a 5 to 10 per cent reduction. Have a go all the same, but bear in mind that some of the smaller craftsmen have hardly any profit margin at all and that, since the economic and financial crisis, standards of living have fallen through the floor. So act accordingly, though never be afraid to bargain, even in chic boutiques where everything is labelled. It's a far cry from how things are back home!

You will generally get a reduction, particularly if you make the most of the fierce competition between traders in Bangkok and Chiang Mai. Always go to several shops to see who can come up with the best deal. And never forget that the sales policy here is to sell as much as possible even if it means squeezing the profit margins. Enjoy it while it lasts – this pleasing ceremony is gradually falling apart thanks to the hordes of tourists in the southern islands.

Even if the merchant won't budge, he'll keep smiling or even laughing. Try laughing even louder yourself – nothing throws them like a laughing tourist.

## VAT

When you leave the country you can claim VAT back on any purchases you have made for a minimum of 5,000 Bts in any of the big stores or well-established shops. You will need to fill out the relevant reimbursement form on the day you make your purchase: each form must refer to purchases of at least 2,000 Bts. On your way home, before you check in at the airport hand over your forms and the articles in question at the special customs window and they will happily return your money.

# THEFT AND OTHER CRIME

Pickpockets are pretty common, either on their own or in groups, so take a few elementary precautions and don't trust to luck. A little common sense can save you endless hassles. Try to take at least half your money in traveller's cheques and always keep your money and passport with you.

There are tourist advice centres in all the main towns and tourist resorts, and addresses are given for each of the towns in question. Staff at these centres are employed by the police and the Ministry of Tourism. Their official purpose is to give all possible help to foreign visitors who find themselves in an awkward situation (personal security, safety, dishonest practices, fraud etc.). That's the theory anyway.

In the event of a problem, call the Tourist Police: ☎ 16-99.

When paying by banker's card, make sure you keep the carbon copy and avoid using your card for small bills in dubious-looking places.

Never let your credit card out of your sight. Certainly don't leave it in the hotel safe when you go trekking. Too many people have returned home to find their accounts hugely overdrawn. Read more on this subject in the 'Bangkok – Chiang Mai – Chiang Rai' section.

# TIME

Thailand is six hours ahead of British Summer Time and seven hours ahead of Greenwich Mean Time (GMT + 7). When it's midday in London, it's 6pm (in the summer) or 7pm (in the winter) in Bangkok.

# TIPPING

Tipping is not generally common in Thailand, even if Thai nationals working in large hotels and major tourist centres have readily become accustomed to it, so don't feel you have to.

# TOILETS

Toilets range from the good old basic squat variety in some of the older guesthouses and bungalows to Western-style toilets in the vast majority of restaurants and hotels. Toilet paper is not always provided – so if you are heading off to one of the more remote areas, bring your own. To find the nearest toilet, simply ask for '*hong nam*'.

# TOURIST OFFICES

## ABROAD

**United Kingdom, Ireland and South Africa**: Tourism Authority of Thailand, 49 Albemarle Street, London WIS 4JR. ☎ (020) 7499 7679. Fax: (020) 7629 5519.

**United States of America and Canada**: Tourism Authority of Thailand, First Floor, 611 North Larchmont Boulevard, Los Angeles, CA 90004.

☎ (323) 461-9814. Fax: (323) 461-9834 (covers west Canada). Tourism Authority of Thailand, 1 World Trade Center, Suite No. 3729, New York, NY 10048. ☎ (212) 432-0433/(212) 432-0435. Fax: (212) 912-0920 (covers east Canada).

**Australia and New Zealand**: Tourism Authority of Thailand, Second Floor, 75 Pitt Street, Sydney, NSW 2000. ☎ (02) 9247 7549. Fax: (02) 9251 2465.

**Useful websites to consult before you go:**

www.tat.or.th
www.franco-thai.com

# TRANSPORTATION

Travelling around Thailand is easy and inexpensive. Countless agencies offer you all sorts of deals and even the meanest local café can sometimes sell you an airline or train ticket. When it comes to transport, great competition means great service.

## TRAINS

Trains in Thailand are surprisingly punctual but very slow (express trains go at an average speed of about 40kph (25mph) and cost a bit more than the bus. They all have a buffet car and there is also a non-stop stream of soft-drink vendors. You can also buy pineapples, peanuts, fried chicken, biscuits etc. in every station.

There are three types of ticket: first-, second- and third-class. Third-class has ventilation (or, very occasionally, air-conditioning) and is very cheap (about half the price of second class). Second-class has ventilation or air-conditioning and offers a high standard of comfort. First-class always has air-conditioning and is very classy indeed. If you are planning to travel in an air-conditioned carriage, remember to pack some woollens: the temperature is positively arctic both night and day. Also watch out for the extras on fast, express and special express trains and in air-conditioned carriages and couchettes. The first- and second-class couchettes are impeccable, with immaculate sheets and occasional blankets and you really have to try them out at least once. Note that top couchettes are cheaper and narrower than bottom couchettes. Ask at the main station in Bangkok (Rama IV road) สถานีรถไฟหัวลำโพง (ถนนพระรามี) for the useful little region-by-region brochures that give times and ticket prices in English.

For long journeys (like Bangkok to Chiang Mai) the train is more comfortable and safer than the bus.

NB: The given durations of journeys by train or plane are approximate as the number of stops or stop-overs will vary.

## BUSES

Buses go everywhere and particularly where the trains do not. They also go slightly faster but cost less. It is worth pointing out that the very fierce level of competition pushes some private companies to employ inexperienced drivers and give them crazy timetables. Bus accidents are rare but they do happen. For long journeys, it's best to use the train, which is safer and more comfortable even if it is slower.

There are three types of bus:

– **Government-run buses with or without air-conditioning**. Usually caught from a bus terminal, non-air-conditioned buses stop in all the towns and villages around the main towns and are rather like local buses. They are very frequent and a useful way of getting to places close by but drivers do have an unfortunate tendency to put their foot down. They are also often overcrowded and don't run all day. For long journeys take an air-conditioned bus, which is cheaper than a private bus but not so comfortable (no drinks either).

– **Private air-conditioned buses**. You will find these in every town where there are tourists. They are comfortable, fast, punctual and more expensive than the others. Drinks are served on board and even meals on some journeys, though they are not always edible. Generally they are long-haul buses and run mainly at night, often with an on-board TV showing very noisy films. Theft is occasionally a problem, and you are sure to have heard the stories involving people being drugged and having their belongings stolen. Such incidents are less common now than they were a few years ago, due to a clampdown by police. Be vigilant whenever you travel, keep an eye on your bags or belongings at all times and never leave them unattended or in a stranger's care.

– **Private minibuses** are the most comfortable as they rarely hold more than 10 passengers, but they offer a fairly dull experience with little opportunity to meet people.

– **VIP buses**. These are deluxe air-conditioned buses fitted with just a few, fully reclining seats. These buses are fast and more expensive but you arrive fresh and well rested. Once again, take something warm to wear at night.

## AIR TRAVEL

– **Thai Airways** has increased its routes in recent years and now flies, sometimes several times a day, to medium-sized provincial towns like Mae Hong Son, Chiang Rai etc. The company has an office in London where you can obtain information about flight times and frequency of departures. In high season it's a good idea to make your reservations in London before leaving. Flights are reasonably inexpensive and a combination of plane and overland travel can save quite a bit of time. It seems there is no longer any need to confirm an internal flight but since it doesn't cost anything, do it anyway for your own peace of mind. Bangkok: Thai Larn Lauang Office, 6 Larn Luang Road, Pom Prab Satrupai District, Bangkok 10100. ☎ (02) 280-0060/(02) 628-2000 (reservations). Website: www.thaiair.com

– **Bangkok Airways** flies to Koh Samui (15 flights a day) and Ranong from Bangkok. It also provides a service between Koh Samui and Phuket (two to three flights per day). There is also one flight per day from Bangkok to Sukhothai and one flight from Chiang Mai to Sukhothai (it is the only company to provide a connection with Sukhothai). Bangkok: 60 Queen Sirikit National Convention Centre, New Ratchadapisek Road, Klongtoey, Bangkok 10110. ☎ (02) 229-3456. Fax: (02) 229-3454. Email: restkt@bangkokair.co.uk. Website: www.bkkair.co.th

| MAIN DISTANCES FROM BANGKOK (KM/MILES) | | | |
|---|---|---|---|
| TOWNS | DISTANCE | TRAIN TIME | FLIGHT TIME |
| Ayutthaya | 105 (65) | 1 hr 20 min | |
| Bangsaen | 106 (66) | | |
| Chanthaburi | 245 (152) | | |
| Chiang Mai | 696 (432) | 14 hrs | 1 hr |
| Chiang Rai | 785 (488) | | |
| Chumphon | 463 (288) | 9 hrs | |
| Hat Yai | 933 (580) | 19 hrs | 1 hr 15 min |
| Hua Hin | 230 (143) | 4 hrs | |
| Kanchanaburi | 128 (80) | 2 hrs 30 min | |
| Khon Kaen | 449 (280) | 8 hrs 30 min | 1 hr |
| Lampang | 599 (372) | 11 hrs 30 min | |
| Lamphun | 670 (416) | 13 hrs 30 min | |
| Nakhon Pathom | 56 (35) | 1 hr 40 min | |
| Nakhon Phanom | 647 (402) | | |
| Nakhon Ratchasima | 259 (161) | 5 hrs | |
| Nakhon Si Thammarat | 780 (485) | 16 hrs 45 min | |
| Nan | 668 (415) | | |
| Pattaya | 140 (87) | | |
| Petchburi | 123 (76) | 4 hrs | |
| Phitsanulok | 377 (234) | 7 hrs | 40 min |
| Phuket | 862 (536) | | 1 hr 10 min |
| Rayong | 179 (111) | | |
| Songkhla | 1024 (636) | | |
| Sukhothai | 427 (265) | | |
| Trat | 315 (196) | | |
| Ubon Ratchathani | 629 (391) | 10 hrs 30 min | 1 hr 35 min |
| Udon Thani | 564 (350) | 10 hrs 30 min | 1 hr 35 min |
| Yala | 1084 (674) | 20 hrs | |

Source: All distances in kilometres are provided by the Tourism Authority of Thailand except for Bangsaen, Hua Hin, Pattaya and Songkhla (estimated).

**NB** Mile conversions are estimated to the nearest mile. Also, train and flight times are indications only and liable to vary depending on the number of stops.

GENERAL INFORMATION

– **Angel Airlines** flies to Chiang Mai, Phuket and Udon Thani from Bangkok. It is the only airline to provide direct flights between Udon Thani and Chiang Mai, from November to the end of March. Bookings can be made on the spot: 499/7 Vibhavadee–Rangsit road, or by fax: (02) 953-2261.

## HITCHHIKING

Hiking is not done much in Thailand, either by tourists or by the locals. As you know, it can prove an enriching experience but not always, as some find to their cost. Do it if it really grabs you but going by bus or train is much faster and more acceptable.

## CAR HIRE

Renting a car has become an increasingly popular means of touring the country – giving you the opportunity to get off the beaten track and the ability to return to civilization at will. Major tourist destinations like Bangkok, Chiang Mai, Chiang Rai, Phuket and Koh Samui all have international car-rental agencies. Many of the major hotels can also arrange car rental, although at inflated prices. Before renting a car, always check carefully to see what condition it is in and note down any scratches or dents as otherwise you could be held responsible for the damage on your return. You will be required to show an international driving licence as well as your passport. Make sure that you arrange comprehensive vehicle insurance since it is not always included in the cost of rental.

Before you hit the accelerator, here are a few words of warning. Thais normally drive on the left. Out in the countryside though, you will often find them driving in the middle of the road and sometimes even over-taking in the face of oncoming traffic. Priority almost inevitably goes to the biggest vehicle, so you should always be ready to pull off to the side of the road to make way for oncoming trucks or buses. Driving in Bangkok is mayhem and under no circumstances should you attempt it unless you know the ropes.

Most Thai road signs are easy to understand and make use of standard international symbols. Generally the official speed limit is 40kph (25mph) in towns and 80kph (50mph) on highways. If these limits are exceeded, the police will often impose on-the-spot fines.

Fuel and oil are readily available and prices are considerably lower than those in Europe.

## MOTORBIKES

Motorbikes are great for getting around some towns, particularly for touring the outskirts. In places like Chiang Mai, Chiang Rai and the island of Phuket, for example, the motorbike is ideal. It also leaves you free as a bird if you're touring the mountains in the north and it's a treat motoring around the islands of the south.

If the motorbike seems to offer a good compromise between independence and cost, remember that there's no system of social security in Thailand and that insurance is still in its infancy. Only time will tell how efficient it's going to be. So if you are offered a hire contract, read it carefully and be very precise about what will and will not be your responsibility. When it doesn't come with insurance (most of the time) that means that in the event of an accident that's your fault, you have to pay your own hospital costs as well as those of any passengers in the other vehicle. In any case, you always have to pay for any damage to the bike. So, yes, motorbikes can be fun but you should approach with extreme caution. Although it might cost a few extra bahts, you should plump for a new bike where possible to avoid the risk of mechanical problems. Before paying, try it out, test the brakes and check for any external evidence of previous accidents or scrapes. Make sure you carry your international driving licence with you, as checks are often carried out and there are fines if you fail to produce it.

Beware of any vehicle-hire places that insist on keeping your passport until you bring the bike back. When you do, they're just as likely to point out every last scratch and charge you for the repair costs even if it's nothing to do with you – either that, or you don't get your passport back. It's best to be firm about this at the outset – or look elsewhere.

## FOUR-WHEEL-DRIVES

A four-wheel-drive is very useful in the islands, where most of the roads aren't surfaced (Koh Samet, Koh Chang, Koh Tao for example). Sometimes you can hire one from bungalow owners. Prices tend to be high compared to motorbikes, because competition is less fierce.

# WORKING IN THAILAND

Like many countries in Southeast Asia, Thailand employs a significant number of foreigners, especially in the fields of banking and finance, industry, teaching, the diplomatic corps and non-governmental organizations. Since mid-1997, their numbers have dwindled, however, as a result of the sharp economic downturn. There are opportunities for teaching English privately or at one of the international schools (if you have the relevant experience and qualifications). Various charitable organizations welcome volunteers. The United Nations may also occasionally recruit new staff locally. You are strongly advised to contact official organizations in advance to find out about job opportunities.

## WORK PERMITS

To get a work permit, you will need a letter from your employer together with a photocopy of your passport, a set of passport photos, a copy of any recent tax returns and a non-immigrant visa. All documents should be presented at the One-stop Service Centre for Visas and Work Permits: Krisda Plaza, Third–Fifth Floors, 207 Ratchadapisek Road, Dindaeng, Bangkok 10310. ☎ (02) 693-9333(-9). Fax: (02) 693-9340. This is a one-stop organization set up to coordinate with the labour and immigration ministries. Allow one week for the permit to be processed, although with regulations constantly changing, it can often take considerably longer and involve an excruciatingly long-drawn out and bureaucratic process. The cost ranges from 500–2,000 Bts depending on visa requirements, etc. Prices for the various services are clearly displayed inside the office.

# BACKGROUND

## VITAL STATISTICS

**Population**: just over 61 million

**Surface area**: 513,115 square kilometres (198,000 square miles)

**Capital**: Bangkok, with around 10 million inhabitants

**Languages spoken**: Thai (the official language), Chinese and English

**Currency**: the baht (Bt)

**Political regime**: constitutional monarchy

**Head of State**: King Bhumibol Adulyadej (since 1946)

## GEOGRAPHY

Thailand, with a land area of 513,115 square kilometres (198,000 square miles), is more than twice the size of Britain. The country is identified by a large, rather shapeless mass in the north and a long, narrow strip reaching southwards. What you see today is a country shaped by its history of war – though in this respect Thailand is the same as anywhere else. Today, it borders four other countries – Cambodia, Laos, Myanmar (formerly Burma) and Malaysia – and has two separate coastlines, one on the China Sea and the other on the Andaman Sea. Broadly speaking, Thailand can be divided into four regions:

– **The North**: mountainous, thick with jungle and the last rare teak woods, and scored through with deep valleys planted with paddy fields. The north is home to some incredible tribes which attract many tourists. There are mountains, of course, but this is not the Andes – the highest peak is 2,590 metres (8,500 feet).

– **The Northeast**: the least touristy part of Thailand. No more fertile mountain slopes, but a succession of arid plateaux. Tough but fascinating.

– **The Centre**: a large basin, lush and fertile, with ideal rainfall. Lots of rivers, rich soil, a climate made for planting. The cradle of Thai civilization.

– **The South**: a region that tapers to the south, planted with hevea trees. The main attraction for tourists is its beaches. It's popular as a place to hang out, and you can see why. The beautiful islands of the Andaman Sea and the Gulf of Thailand have become a meeting place for holidaymakers as well as a playground for development companies. A significant proportion of the financial manna derived from tourism is generated in the south. The extreme south, populated by Muslims, lags behind in economic terms, having neither the lushness of the centre nor the tourist appeal of the rest of the south.

# THE ENVIRONMENT

Throughout the last century, the last great rain forests of Southeast Asia have been systematically exploited and destroyed (and this is now happening in Myanmar and Laos too) just as the mangrove swamps have been flattened all along the coast. Consequently, Thailand has lost practically all its teak. The reason for this has been financial, and no matter what they do now, including reforestation with eucalyptus trees and the creation of national parks with all the interest that this arouses, nothing can ever restore the original balance of nature. In addition, there are now many seaside resorts choking under a tide of debris that threatens to destroy their marine life and their coral. Despite recent town planning works carried out by the municipal authorities, Bangkok is still one of the most polluted cities in the world. All in all, the ecologists have got their work cut out.

# HISTORY

## FROM PREHISTORY

The remains of an early man dating back more than 100,000 years have been found in the north of the country. Early modern human populations of this area spread prolifically across the whole of Southeast Asia and even into southern China. Linguistic research combined with recent archaeological finds suggest that these Thais were among the first real farmers and some of the first to work in metal.

There is little evidence of the culture that blossomed in Thai territory before the advent of Christianity, but it is known that Buddhist monks started to leave India for a country called *Suvanabhumi* ('land of gold') in the second and third centuries BC. It seems that this was an area extending from Burma across the centre of what is now Thailand to the east of Cambodia.

## FIERCE TIMES: THE DVÂRAVATÎ PERIOD

Dvâravatî (from the Sanskrit meaning 'places with doors') was the name given to a breeding ground of city-states that existed from the 6th to the 11th centuries and again from the 12th century to the present day. These city-states were probably built by the Mons – descended from Indian immigrants who had bred with native Thais – but everything else about them remains a mystery. The Chinese got to hear about the region (which they called *T'o-Lo-Po-Ti*) through the travels of a monk called Xuan Zang. All that's left today are some outstanding works of art, particularly representations of the Buddha (clearly influenced by Indian art of the Gupta period), earthenware busts and a few stucco bas-reliefs in the temples and grottoes. Few traces of the architectural elements have survived intact. The Dvâravatî culture declined rapidly from the 11th century under the advance of the conquering Khmers.

## THE MIDDLE AGES: THE APOGEE OF KHMER INFLUENCE

The Khmer influence dominated in art, religion and language from the 11th to the 13th centuries. Many of the monuments of the period, located in Kanchanaburi, Lopburi and other sites in the northeast, can be compared with Angkor architecture. But it was at this time too that the first Thai people, who had migrated towards China in the prehistoric period, retraced their footsteps, leaving the province of Yunnan for Thailand. The Khmers called these Thais 'Syams', meaning 'dark skinned', because of the way they looked, and this is probably how the name Siam came about. One of their descendants would later found the kingdom of Lan Xang (Laos – 'land of a million elephants') in 1353.

## THE RENAISSANCE AND THE FIRST KINGDOM OF SUKHOTHAI

During the 13th and 14th centuries, several Thai principalities in the Mekong valley joined forces to fight the Mons, seizing Haripunchai where they founded Lan Na. Next they attacked the Khmers and recovered the region of Sukhothai, and by this time Khmer power and the Angkor government were in decline. So it was that in 1238 the Thais laid claim to the first kingdom and state entirely under their own rule.

The period also led to the emergence and flourishing of an authentically Thai culture, political system and religion. The name *Sukhothai* (from the word *Sukha-udaya*) means 'dawning of happiness' and the Thais today regard this period as a golden age. Everyone was so rich that no one had to pay any taxes. One of the kings, Ram Khamheng, authorized a system of writing that forms the basis of modern Thai. When he died, the kingdom split into several states. Meanwhile, a new capital was waiting in the wings.

## AYUTTHAYA – A CAPITAL WITH A MILLION INHABITANTS

Compared to the wealth and power of Ayutthaya, Europe's capital cities were still like villages. The new capital was founded in 1350 by King Ramadhipati I and, even though the Khmer remained hereditary enemies and the fighting was as fierce as ever, the court of Ayutthaya adopted their language and customs. As a result, the Thai kings became absolute monarchs with the title 'divine king'. The Khmer capital of Angkor fell in 1431 and for four centuries the Thais, smiling though they were, were feared and dreaded throughout Southeast Asia.

In 1498 Vasco da Gama and his Portuguese fleet, having successfully navigated the Cape of Good Hope, opened a new shipping route and launched an era of European expansion in Asia. The first Portuguese embassy was established in Ayutthaya in 1511. The Dutch followed in 1605, the English in 1612, the Danes in 1621 and the French in 1662.

## THE FALL OF AYUTTHAYA

Throughout the 18th century the principalities of Siam were constantly at war with each other. This was to the advantage of the Burmese, who invaded the country and flattened the splendid capital of Ayutthaya after a two-year siege that began in 1769. Some of the ruins can still be seen today. But while the Burmese laid waste to the ancient city, they never managed to gain a foothold in Siam. A new capital, Thonburi, was built opposite what would later become Bangkok, on the banks of the River

Mae Jam Chao Phraya. In charge of this was Phya Taksin, a Thai general who had himself proclaimed king and reigned for a short time. Phya Taksin was a megalomaniac and a religious fanatic who claimed to be almost on an equal footing with the Buddha. He was assassinated by his ministers. In 1782 another general, Phya Chakri, ascended to the throne under the name of Rama I and founded the present capital of Bangkok. The sovereigns of the Chakri dynasty who remain in power today all bear the name of Rama.

## THE BEGINNINGS OF MODERN TIMES

The seeds of modern-day Thailand were sown in 1851 when King Mongkut ascended to the throne to reign as Rama IV. Mongkut was an educated, refined and courteous man who had spent 26 years of his life as a Buddhist monk before becoming king (almost every Thai aspires to be a monk at least once in his lifetime). While he was at the monastery, Mongkut studied modern Western science and became an expert in languages, including Pali and Sanskrit, as well as English and Latin that he learned at the Christian missionary school. King Mongkut even spearheaded a thorough programme of religious reform (which remains unfinished), demythologizing Buddhism and adapting it to the demands of the modern world. A great admirer of the West, he corresponded regularly with the then President of the United States, James Buchanan – even offering him some elephants to help improve the American transport system. Mongkut also signed a number of treaties, with Great Britain among others.

Once in power, Mongkut surrounded himself with Western counsellors. He put a Dane in charge of the police and installed an Italian major at the head of the Military Academy. His closest counsellor was a Belgian and he appointed several Europeans – most of them British – to run his various ministries (imagine the same scenario in reverse in Britain). But despite this tide of Western influence, Mongkut, like his successors, never lost his taste for Thai tradition. He was an avowed polygamist with no less than 82 legitimate children and 35 wives. He retained the services of a British governess, Anna Leonowens, whose reminiscences inspired a stage musical and several movies, the most famous of which is Rodgers and Hammerstein's *The King and I*.

## A REVOLUTIONARY KING

Thailand at the time was like a buffer state between British Burma and French Indochina, and it only escaped colonization thanks to some skilful diplomacy. King Chulalongkorn Rama V (1868–1910) was the heir to the throne and a gifted politician. He made the best of a bad job, conceding 100,000 square kilometres (38,600 square miles) of land, including the whole of Laos, to the thieving French and English – a stroke of genius that kept Siam independent until the present day. The name Thailand was officially adopted in 1939.

So passionate was King Chulalongkorn about the need for new institutions and modern policies that even his own son called him revolutionary. In 1873, the year of his coronation, he decreed that his subjects were no longer to bow down before him. Mind you, even the famously excessive ceremonies of the Spanish court of the time looked relaxed, even casual, compared to the etiquette that applied at the Thai court, where heads tended to roll like marbles in a playground. An event that no doubt contributed to the King's concern about etiquette was the death of one of his wives: she drowned while her servants stood by, as they had been expressly forbidden ever to touch her. Ironically, such extreme rules had evolved from a wish to protect the royal family from assassination attempts.

## THE FOUNDATIONS OF PRESENT-DAY THAILAND

During his reign, the revolutionary King Chulalongkorn Rama abolished slavery, founded a ministry of finance and set up a system of provincial government. He built the first railways and laid the first roads. He also obliged the Thai aristocracy to send its children to Western-type schools, to ensure that intellectual standards kept up with his own ambitions for the kingdom. So it was that the Thai people were able to enter the 20th century with relative serenity after centuries of independence and progress, adapting and even supporting various Western ideas. Having escaped suffering from the 'colonial complex', they have always been able to face the rest of the world as equals.

## THE MONARCHY TODAY

Thailand has been a constitutional monarchy since 1932: the King is head of state but all the power is in the hands of the government. For years that meant the generals, but this changed in 1978 when democracy returned to Thailand. The ruling monarch today is King Bhumibol (born 1927) who reigns under the name of Rama IX.

Prime Minister Chatichai was deposed by the army after the coup in February 1991 and steps were taken to hold immediate elections. In the meantime a temporary prime minister was elected following angry protests from some political parties who suspected yet another military takeover. The United States didn't like the situation either and immediately blocked all military aid. The new constitution, passed in December, increased the power of the military – but there was continued instability. In March 1992, no more than a month after he was elected, Narong Wongwan was replaced by General Suchinda and the country was rocked by violent demonstrations. Suchinda decided to throw in the towel and resigned.

In September 1992, the new Prime Minister Chuan Leekpai formed a coalition government. This was not a resounding success either, and fresh elections were held in 1995. A new coalition government was voted in, led by Banharn Silpa Archa, but corruption and other scandals soon forced him to resign him as well. The country went to the polls once again in November 1996 and elected General Chavalit Yongchaiyudh, leader of the New Aspiration party.

## LIGHT AT THE END OF THE TUNNEL?

The country was hit by an unprecedented economic crisis in July 1997 (*see also* 'The Economy'). In November, the Democratic party, led by Chuan Leekpai, returned once again to lead the government. However this change had no effect whatsoever: the gravity of economic factors such as unemployment and devaluation was such that the International Monetary Fund (IMF) was forced to come to the rescue. Meanwhile, the country suffered massive redundancies, decreases in salaries (from 20 to 30 per cent in most companies), the expulsion of immigrant workers and a mass exodus from Bangkok to rural areas, where at least there was food available.

However, the crisis seemed to bring about a certain social change: the privileged classes put their hands in their pockets and a genuine system of mutual aid developed. The most critical period now seems to have passed (an unfailing barometer is the price of rice, which now appears to have stabilized). Recovery looks to be durable and healthy even if the pre-crisis stock market euphoria is very much a thing of the past.

## PRINCIPAL DATES

– **7th century**: the Mon kingdom of Dvâravatî.

– **8th century**: Thai kingdom of Nanzhao in the Yunnan.

– **11th century**: the Thais descend towards the Menam basin.

– **1181–1218**: reign of the Khmer sovereign, Jayavarman VII.

– **1220**: foundation of the kingdom of Sukhothai.

– **1253**: the Mongols conquer the kingdom of Nanzhao.

– **1292**: the kingdom of Sukhothai grows increasingly important and spreads into Vientiane in Laos.

– **1350**: Rama Tdhipati I proclaims himself king of Siam in Ayutthaya.

– **1376**: the kingdom of Ayutthaya annexes Phitsanulok then Kampheng-pet.

– **1438**: end of the Sukhothai dynasty.

– **16th century**: Siam and Burma are constantly at war and Siam becomes Burmese.

– **1593**: Siam regains its independence together with its 1549 borders and imposes its sovereignty on Cambodia.

– **1656**: beginning of the reign of Phra Narai.

– **1688**: end of the reign of Phra Narai.

– **1767**: the Burmese invade Ayutthaya.

– **1782**: beginning of the reign of Phya Chakri, first of the present-day dynasty.

– **1855**: Siam opens up to the West.

– **1868–1910**: reign of Chulalongkorn.

– **1910–25**: reign of Vajirawdh (Rama VI).

– **1925–35**: reign of Prajadhipok.

– **1932**: a coup puts an end to the absolute monarchy. Siam gets its first constitution and its first military government.

BACKGROUND

– **1939**: Siam becomes officially known as Thailand.

– **1935–46**: reign of King Ananda Mahidol, later to be assassinated.

– **1946**: beginning of the reign of King Bhumibol Adulyadej (Rama IX).

– **1947–57**: the Pibul Songgram government.

– **1963**: the Thanom Kittikachorn government (second time around).

– **1980**: General Prem is appointed prime minister.

– **1985**: the Vietnamese army occupies the headquarters of the Khmer Rouge in Phnom Malai. Attempted coup in Thailand.

– **1991**: military takeover in February. The prime minister is arrested, the country put under martial law and the constitution is suspended.

– **1992**: following March elections a prime minister is appointed but immediately rejected by the Americans, who suspect him of being involved with drugs. A member of the military is appointed in his place, and this time it's the people who protest. There are violent demonstrations and riots in the spring and the army fires on the crowd. The king plays for time, the prime minister resigns, there is a general amnesty and the democrats win the autumn elections.

– **1995**: Prime Minister Banharn Silpa Archa is elected in July.

– **1996**: the government is overthrown in September and legislative elections are planned for November. General Chavalit Yongchaiyudh, leader of the New Aspiration party, becomes prime minister.

– **1997**: serious financial and monetary crisis in the spring. The International Monetary Fund (IMF) intervenes but insists on banking reform and an increase in taxes. A new democratic government led by Chuan Leekpai is elected in November.

– **1999**: drastic measures facilitated an upturn in the economic situation, and at least succeeded in plugging the wound (*see* above).

– **2000**: armed and diplomatic troubles with Burma and the Karen liberation army at the beginning of the year. A Karen commando, sent by two charismatic leaders aged 10 and 12 respectively, held to be invincible by their men (allegedly untouchable by bullets), attacked a Thai hospital, demanding care and money. The army mounted a charge and the commando surrendered. However, things appear to be hotting up. Watch this space.

# THE ECONOMY

The Thai economy is based on agriculture (it ranks fourth in the world as an exporter of rice, and there is significant market-gardening and fruit production in the centre and the north), mining and mechanics (no big national names, but some important international factories: Toyota, General Motors, etc.). However, despite a number of natural gas deposits, the country turns elsewhere to meet its energy requirements.

It was on this fairly healthy base that Thailand launched itself into pure, hard capitalism and to its credit, managed to achieve some significant figures in terms of economic statistics. Some even saw Thailand as an up-and-coming front runner, soon to join the ranks of the 'Young Tigers', along with Hong Kong, Singapore, Taiwan and South Korea.

But 1997 was a black year for Thailand, and things went rapidly from bad to worse. On 3 March the impending economic crash forced the Bangkok stock exchange to close, for the first time in its existence. The crunch came in the summer, when Bangkok took the decision to float the baht (which had previously been linked to the dollar), hurling the country into immediate devaluation. Faced with a slump and very heavy debts, Thailand teetered on the brink of disaster.

As the financial screws were tightened, Thailand looked for a way to correct the economic imbalance. It appealed to the International Monetary Fund (IMF) for help, receiving a rescue package worth more than £7 billion – but there were strings attached. In exchange, the Thai government had to take a firm line, forcing no less than 56 finance companies to fold in the face of impossible debts. The belt had to be tightened if confidence and stability were to be restored.

Conditions in Thailand may have gone into remission for the time being, but the bad times are by no means over yet and the Thais continue to feel the pinch. Salaries have dropped by an average of 20–30 per cent in the bigger companies and two million people have found themselves out of work. In addition to job losses, buying power has fallen and VAT has risen from 7 per cent to 10 per cent. In accordance with IMF demands, the government has reduced its budgets and made serious cutbacks in private borrowing. That is to say nothing of the 300,000 foreign workers (Burmese, Malaysians etc.) who have been unceremoniously repatriated.

Thailand has shown itself capable of responding to this serious crisis, but with considerably less urgency than Malaysia or South Korea. By all accounts, Thailand has the natural and human resources as well as the infrastructure (good road and rail networks, irrigation, good energy distribution) to achieve recovery. And while things look set to improve with Gross Domestic Product (GDP) forecast to grow by 6 per cent in the year 2000, the economic problems are likely to continue for many years to come. In short, although the country is not out of the tunnel yet, the light can certainly be seen at the end.

What you can glean from all this is that while Thailand isn't out of the woods, you'll find the cost of living in Thailand pretty low in comparison with the West.

# THE CHINESE INFLUENCE

The Chinese have been coming to Thailand in droves during the past 200 years, mainly to escape food shortages and the political regime. Many of them started as labourers and rickshaw drivers, but the Chinese are an enterprising, determined people with a strong sense of community, so it doesn't take them long to enter and master the fields of commerce and finance. Pretty soon, all that was left for the Thais themselves was agriculture and administration. Today, practically the whole of the banking sector is in Chinese hands and they also manage 90 per cent of the private sector in industry and services.

The absence of religious barriers meant that the Chinese were able to become an integrated part of Thai society – something that was never possible in Malaysia and Indonesia. Young Chinese now communicate in Thai and mix freely with the local population, which results in mixed marriages, so you can barely tell who is Chinese and who is Thai.

# HUMAN RIGHTS

Astonishing as it may seem, Thailand, like a number of ASEAN tigers, is recovering little by little from the cold shower of the 1997 Asian financial crisis. However, although macroeconomic indicators promise 6 per cent growth in Thailand in the year 2000, the negative effect on the population's economic and social rights brought on by increased unemployment and inequality is worrying some NGOs (non-governmental organizations) concerned with civil liberties. Per capita income has dropped by a third in three years (to reach US$2,000 per year), in a country where any social assistance system is almost non-existent.

The situation is particularly worrying where the numerous workers of foreign origin are concerned (Laotians, Cambodians, Vietnamese). Many of them have not been able to renew or extend their work permits and have, as a result, become illegal aliens. Throughout 1999, the government returned some 108,000 migrant workers and their families to the country's borders.

In addition, the political tensions in the region have led to refugee flows into Thailand from Myanmar, Cambodia, Laos and Vietnam. To its credit, the Thai government has begun to cooperate with the United Nations High Commission for Refugees (UNHCR) in dealing with this problem, both in terms of negotiating voluntary repatriation and setting up civilian refugee camps, particularly near the Myanmar border where the situation is currently at its most fraught. However, this recent moderation in approach follows several years where refugees were prevented from entering Thailand by the Thai army, and often left in considerable danger in Myanmar. NGOs report that the change in attitude has been only partial and that this type of action still occurs. There have also been concerns over the security of the refugee camps which have been subject to attack in cross-border raids by forces loyal to the Burmese army.

From a domestic perspective, the most pressing human rights issue is the inferior position of women and girls in Thai society. The Government has attempted to address the problem through the establishment of the National Commission for Women's affairs, and through gender equality legislation, including the Constitution of 1998. However, the situation on the ground is not much improved, and the legislation is not extensively enforced. In particular, Thailand still has a problem with high levels of prostitution, and the trafficking and sale of women and girls for this purpose. The country remains a prime destination for 'sex tourism'. New laws, which came into force in 1996 and 1997, aimed at strengthening the State's efforts in matters of prevention, enlarged the field of responsibility but also made the penalties, particularly in relation to child prostitution, much harsher. However, although some progress has been made in this area (and the figures provided must certainly be treated with caution), NGOs claim that the child prostitution networks have simply been displaced to neighbouring countries (Laos, Cambodia). Many countries, including Australia, the USA, New Zealand and many EU states, have now made child prostitution an extra-territorial offence, so that offenders may be prosecuted in their country of residence even if the offence took place overseas.

Thailand is a nation in which a culture of corruption is ingrained at all levels: government authorities, police and armed forces. Although this behaviour is not necessarily evident to tourists, it certainly exists. Nevertheless, this corruption appears not to have tarnished the elections of 5 March 2000. It is thought that some votes were 'bought' but the turn-out for the elections attained a record high (more than 60 per cent), implying that the people are willing to give the current constitution a genuine chance.

Thailand must also be given credit for the behaviour of its authorities during the negotiations regarding the statute for the future international criminal court; behaviour which placed the country in the most liberal camp alongside Germany and Great Britain (against France and the United States). A National Commission on Human Rights was finally set up by a law passed in November 1999. This is a government institution and its function will lie in the preparation of an annual observatory report on the human rights situation for the National Assembly. It may also offer a certain number of recommendations to the assembly, as well as amendments to existing laws. However, human rights NGOs are already decrying the lack of independence of the 11 members of this commission.

To find out more, contact:

• **Liberty** (London office of the **International Federation of Human Rights**): 21 Tabard Street, London SE1 4LA. ☎ (020) 7403 3888. Email: liberty@gn.apc.org

• **Amnesty International**: 99–119 Rosebery Ave, London EC1R 4RE. ☎ (020) 7814 6200. Fax: (020) 7833 1510. Email: info@amnesty.org.uk Website: www.amnesty.org.uk

# THAI BUDDHISM

## LIFE OF THE BUDDHA

In 563 BC, a prince called Siddhartha Gautama was born at the foot of the Hindu Himalayas. This prince had everything: a kingdom, a loving wife, a child, but he knew nothing of the world. When he was 20, the prince decided to venture beyond his palace and he had three separate encounters. The first was with an old man, the second with a sick man and the third with a dead man being carried to the funeral pyre. Thus the prince came to understand that there is no escape from time, sickness and death. His fourth encounter was with a wise beggar who persuaded the prince to renounce his easy life. Gautama turned his back on family and fortune, and devoted himself to asceticism. His teachers were among the most famous gurus of the time but he was not convinced by the approach they offered, which was based on suffering. So he set out to discover an explanation of his own. After 49 days spent in motionless meditation, resisting the temptations of Mara, the Lord of Death, and all his friends, Gautama reached Nirvana, the state of the Buddha, of perfect enlightenment and perfect knowledge.

If you want to know more, read *Siddhartha* by Hermann Hesse (Picador, 1998, £6.99).

## THE BUDDHA'S TEACHINGS

'Life is subject to suffering.' *(duhkha)*

'Suffering is caused by desire.' *(tanha)*

'Renouncing desire therefore brings an end to suffering.'

'This state is attainable by renouncing the world, becoming detached from the self and following the Eightfold Path.' The Eightfold Path is a way of living based on eight interdependent principles:

– right understanding

– right intention

– right speech

– right action

– right way of life

– right effort

– right consciousness

– right concentration

By accepting the four truths, following the principles of the Eightfold Path, and leading a life based on sincerity of feeling, you can free yourself from the endless circle of death and rebirth *(samsâra)* and attain Nirvana through meditation.

## THE SPREAD OF BUDDHISM

Buddha's disciples left India three centuries before Christ, to spread the word elsewhere. Today, Buddhism is fairly marginal in the India of the Brahmans where it originated, but has become the dominant religion in most parts of Asia.

There are two types of Buddhism: *Mahâyâna* (or Great Vehicle) that spread to China, Tibet and Japan, and *Theravâda* (laughingly referred to as the Small Vehicle by disciples of the Great Vehicle) practised in Southeast Asia, including Thailand. Here is not the place to go into the differences between the two, particularly since each form of Buddhism varies according to country, region and ethnic group, and often the traditional beliefs and ancient rituals of the people who practise it.

## THAI BUDDHISM

There are probably more temples in Thailand than churches in Rome – which just goes to show how Buddhism is very much a part of everyday life in Thailand.

Temples are open, convivial places where people go for all sorts of reasons: weddings, funerals, prayer . . . Monks, particularly in the villages, play a part in local affairs and are often called upon for advice – performing a similar role to that of Christian priests, not so long ago. The Thai people have adapted their own form of Buddhism, which includes, as well as the very holy images of the Buddha, an absolute throng of demons and spirits.

To a Westerner, Thai Buddhism is a smiling, tolerant form of religion that plays an inextricable part in people's lives.

Ninety-five per cent of Thais are Buddhist and most men take time out at least once in their lifetime to live as a monk. Some carry out unpaid work building or redecorating the temples, and everyone makes countless offerings of flowers and candles to the statues of the Buddha as well as seeing to the daily needs of the monks.

## MONKS AND NUNS

Monasteries for monks and nuns in Thailand look the same except that the communal buildings for nuns, such as the *sala* and the *bot*, are much smaller. The public is not admitted. Nuns in Thailand are dressed entirely in white, whereas in other Buddhist countries they wear yellow robes like the *bonzes* (monks). But, like the monks, nuns also shave their heads. Cloistered nuns, known as *bikkhunis*, disappeared years ago in Thailand. What's left are novices, or *moechis*, who are destined to remain novices all their lives without ever quite achieving the prestige that goes with being a *bonze*. This is all because the Buddha never wanted to found an order for women, despite their entreaties. When he finally relented, in the face of his aunt's persistence, he set eight very strict rules and made the women totally dependent on the *bonzes*. Since they may not leave the monastery to go out and beg, they share whatever food is given to the monks, which explains why nunneries are always twinned with monasteries.

# THE THAI TEMPLE

The Thai Buddhist temple, or *wat*, is a complex of religious buildings, often of different periods and styles. It is the focus of social and cultural activity for the local community and fulfils a number of needs – as a place of worship and learning, a meeting place and a point of information.

## THE *BOT*

This is the hub of the *wat*, where the monks chant from sacred writings and where they are ordained. The *bot* or *ubosot* is a rectangular room with a single nave and several aisles. It is surrounded by eight boundary stones (*bais simâs*) and these demarcate the area that nobody is allowed to enter during a ceremony. The *bais simâs* are of varying heights and the degree of ornamentation on them depends on the importance of the *wat*. The *bot* is considered sacred and is outside the authority of any lay jurisdiction.

## THE *VIHARA*

This is a large, rectangular room where monks and the faithful gather to listen to sermons. It contains representations of the Buddha as well as sacred temple objects. The sloping, multi-stepped roofs are decorated with *chofas* (birds' heads) and *nâgas* (snakes).

### THE *SALA*

This is one of the first buildings you come across when you visit a monastery. It is a large hall structure where the *bonzes* meet morning and evening to chant the sacred writings, and the faithful come to meditate, attend services or listen to sermons. But you can also eat, speak and even sleep there. An impressive statue of the Buddha sits in state at the back of the room, surrounded by smaller statues offered by the faithful. At the far ends of the room you sometimes find strange decorations, which may differ according to who gave them and what message the superior of the temple is trying to communicate. This explains the collection of objects you see displayed in glass bottles, such as real human skeletons, a foetus or a stillborn child. The Thais have a taste for the macabre and like to remind you that 'nothing lasts' and life is a vale of tears.

### THE OTHER BUILDINGS

– The *bot*, the *vihara* and the *sala*, plus the monks' refectory, are the main communal buildings. The monks live all around them – in little huts called *nutis*, or in buildings when they need more space. That's where they spend most of their time meditating, receiving visitors and resting – they are entirely free to do what they want and answer to nobody.

– The temple also includes a *chedi* or reliquary-tower, which contains relics of the Buddha or the ashes of a saintly man or royal dignitary. The *chedi* is often the reason why the *wat* was built here. It is in the shape of a dome or a bell, with a roof that looks like parasols piled on top of one another.

– There may also be a bell to punctuate the monks' day, a library or libraries (*ho trai*) and a crematorium.

# TRADITION AND CUSTOMS

In Thailand it's a good idea to know 'what goes', so here are the main points to remember:

– You are not allowed to wear shoes inside the temples housing the statue of the Buddha. Don't worry about getting your feet dirty – the place is spotless.

– When you sit down, your feet must not face the Buddha, which is considered to be sacrilege.

– You must dress properly. Leave your Bermuda shorts with the fruit pattern back at the hotel along with your mini shorts and sleeveless T-shirts.

– Women backpackers must not occupy the seats at the back of a bus. These are usually reserved for monks, who are supposed to avoid all physical contact with women. As a general rule, a woman has to use a male go-between if she wishes to give something to a monk.

– All the images and sculptures of the Buddha are sacred, whether large or small, damaged or in ruins.

As far as customs go, there are some you have to respect but it's no big deal.

– People don't usually shake hands in Thailand. The traditional greeting is the *wai*, where you join the hands as if in prayer. This can be tricky if you don't know the rules, as most of the time the *wai* is used to express inequality. It's up to the subordinate person (or the younger person) to make the first move and all he may get in return is a vague smile. Try not to get it wrong. Never *wai* a child, or even a chambermaid (you would only embarrass her). In fact, you're probably better off sticking to a smile, which is easier and as you can see from the Thais, makes you beautiful.

– Expect most people to call you by your first name, which is the custom here, usually preceded by *Khun* (Mr, Mrs or Miss).

– Never touch a person's head. The head is the seat of the soul and your gesture could be interpreted as a sign of contempt.

– Similarly, since the feet are the least noble part of the body, avoid pointing at someone with your feet, as this would be very disrespectful. So, in public, try not to cross your legs at all, if you can, to avoid all possible misunderstandings.

– When eating out, it isn't done to share the bill. Instead, the Thais stick to the simple rule that the person who did the inviting also does the paying. If nobody was invited, then it's up to the superior man to pay (in no area of life is there such a thing as equality in Thailand).

– You eat with a spoon and fork (never a knife). Use the fork to push the food on to the spoon and whatever you do, don't put the fork in your mouth . . .

– If you've got a cold, you must wait for everybody to finish eating before blowing your nose.

– Everyone respects the King and the royal family. If you happen to be standing in the street when the national anthem strikes up (which often happens in towns, at 8am and/or 6pm), or if you're at the cinema and they show the royal portrait before the film starts, you should stand up. It's quite simple really: just do what everybody else does.

– Those of you with an overactive libido should know that holding hands is considered the height of promiscuity in Thailand.

– Thais may appear to have adopted Western standards of behaviour, but the law remains very strict when it comes to sacrilege. There's something called 'Punishment 206' that specifies a fine or up to 3 months in prison if you're caught gesturing or acting in any way that is insulting to their religion.

– Modesty is definitely the best policy in public. The sight of a couple locked in a torrid embrace is deeply embarrassing to the Thais. However difficult, don't forget that what may seem 'normal' back home can prove offensive here. One of the reasons why the Thais aren't quite as welcoming towards Westerners as they used to be is precisely because the tourists don't know how to behave. No one's asking you to be prudish, simply respectful. Remember, even if places like Pattaya seem

**BACKGROUND**

to indicate the opposite, Pattaya isn't the whole of Thailand. Most Thais, even if they are very tolerant, don't hold with prostitution or any other form of sexual excess.

– Looking irritated, losing your cool and raising your voice are other types of behaviour that the Thais frown upon and even consider to reflect badly on you. These are signs of weakness and enough to make even a Thai lose his composure if you draw him into it. There is no greater shame here than loss of face in public, so when a Thai person feels threatened (particularly if there are onlookers) he will try to 'escape' you in any way he can – without even listening to what you have to say.

– There is nothing more versatile than the Thais' legendary smile. They use it every way they can: as a sign of welcome or amusement (and life certainly is *sanouk,* a laugh, in Thailand) but also as an apology or a way of defusing potentially awkward situations. It avoids unnecessary explanations and prevents you from saying or doing things you might later regret.

– You have to watch your step in the streets, where respect for the environment is taken very seriously indeed. Any spitting or littering with paper makes you liable to a large fine. So if you smoke, put the cigarette out between your fingers when you've finished and toss the butt into a dustbin. Bangkok today is astonishingly clean and virtually litter-free. With measures like these, you can see why.

# THE SACRED ELEPHANT

The elephant is the Thai animal par excellence, and it is respected and loved above all others. Visitors are often amazed to learn that these great animals are even entitled to retirement and social security (they have a special hospital and stop work at the age of 60 to live out the end of their days in peace and tranquillity). Although there are fewer elephants nowadays, there still around 4,000 in the country as a whole. However, the mechanization of agricultural work (elephants were used particularly for transporting teak which has now practically disappeared from the country due to over-exploitation) and the exorbitant cost of their upkeep, dealt a harsh blow to the sacred animal. As a result, tourism has become the main livelihood of these great animals.

It is now a rare luxury to actually own an elephant, who then becomes part of the family and is cherished as a sibling or child. In 1997, the prime minister's wife would go nowhere without her elephant, her hand on its trunk (and the elephant dressed in a bridal gown!). In 1998, huge demonstrations brought the Thai people together, calling for the return of the elephants lent to the Indonesians and apparently mistreated: the affair grew to extraordinary proportions and the prime minister and the minister of foreign affairs were obliged to intervene, invoking international law. The elephant was reconfirmed in its status as national symbol, and the consequences would certainly have been dreadful had the five elephants not finally been returned to Phuket where they were greeted by a jubilant, welcoming crowd.

The white elephant, the sacred animal of Buddhism, is venerated still further. A symbol of peace and prosperity throughout Asia, the origin of its legend has been lost: it is sometimes said to have fertilized the mother of Buddha so that she could give birth to the great sage himself. In Thailand, the fate of these exceptional animals has always been associated with the nation. In days gone by they were the emblems of the Siamese flag and the white elephants were traditionally the property of the king, reinforcing his position as a demi-god. The simple fact of trapping such an animal and offering it to the king would lead to popular jubilation  . . . There are currently 12 albino elephants alive and well, albeit retired and very spoiled, in the royal palaces of Bangkok, Phupan and Phuping, near Chiang Mai.

# THE HOUSE OF THE SPIRITS

Alongside most of the buildings – old and new alike – is a small pagoda-like structure on a post. This is the *phra phum*, a miniature shelter for the spirits of the house. No matter what you plan to build in Thailand, your first task is to find the best place in the garden to build a little house where the spirits (*phis*) can come and live. Where to put their house and how to arrange it are for an initiated person to decide, since you can't put a house reserved for the *phis* just anywhere (and particularly not where it might end up overshadowed by the building). In addition, you have to make sure you choose an auspicious day to celebrate the moment when the souls move in.

Their spiritual building consists of one room with a terrace on all sides where people can leave offerings. Every night a bouquet of flowers, a few sticks of incense and numerous candles are left on a small platform as part of a ceremony that draws on animism, Hinduism and Buddhism. It is also customary to leave food before 11am on the morning of the building's birthday, New Year and other important occasions.

If Thai people invite you (a stranger) to their house, you have to ask their permission to enter. Otherwise you're in for a rough night complete with a ghostly visitation when the spirit settles on your chest, which as anybody will tell you gives you nightmares. Likewise in the morning any hope of a good day depends on greeting the spirits first, just as you are required to make offerings if there's something special you want to ask them.

Lastly, any owner who gets rich enough to make improvements to his house but forgets to decorate the spirits' house as well is in for a very nasty surprise.

# RITUALS, SUPERSTITIONS AND BELIEFS

## NÂGAS

According to Buddhist tradition *nâgas* (snakes) protected Buddha from storms during his first long transcendental meditation, by spreading themselves above him with the cobra's head acting as an umbrella (this Buddhist *nâga* is often represented as having seven heads – all the better for keeping the rain off). In this way the snake links the sacred to the profane, the sky to the earth, the spirit to the prophet.

Snakes were significant in ancient Khmer times, when their images were used to decorate the bridges spanning the moats. The Khmer *prasat*, representing the sanctuary tower, was considered the centre of the universe. By linking the sacred *prasat* to the world of man, the snake, which symbolizes water, also links heaven and earth. It allows a constant flow of heavenly blessings to pass through the doors and over the bridges on their way to bring happiness to the world at large.

## THE CULT OF THE DIVINE KING

The cult of the divine king (*deveraja*), a legacy of the Khmers, still survives today. The *prasat* or sanctuary tower, previously used to house the spirits, now serves to house the statues of the kings. An example can be seen in the statue at Wat Phra Keo in Bangkok.

## SETTING BIRDS FREE

One of Buddhism's most fundamental beliefs is respect for all forms of life, but this frequently leads to excess and even abuse. Since it is an act of piety to set captive creatures free, birds and fish are regularly caught in order to be sold to tourists leaving temples and monasteries. It's best not to encourage these practices by buying the creatures' freedom – many of them are born in captivity and could not survive in the wild. What is more, by freeing one you are basically encouraging the practice as another one will be imprisoned in its stead.

## GOOD LUCK CHARMS

Go to any pagoda in town and you'll witness a method of telling fortunes that has nothing very Buddhist about it. Indeed, the Buddha himself would probably dismiss it as pure superstition. Despite this, it has to be the most popular superstition in the whole of the Buddhist canon.

To find out what the future has in store, you consult the 'sticks'. First you pray to the Buddha, then you pick up an open, rounded box containing about 20 sticks and give it a good shake until one of the sticks falls out. On it are various cryptic inscriptions and in exchange for an offering (naturally) the *bonze* will tell you what they mean.

If you donate a coin to an icon representing a god, you will be sprayed with holy water. If you prefer to remain dry, you can buy all sorts of amulets from the *bonzes*, as well as bundles of yellow and blue threads that bring good luck, little wooden bracelets, and images of the Buddha – all aimed at a population with an endless fascination for anything to do with magic.

Finally, in many of the temples, visitors can sound the lovely gongs (use your fist if there is no stick available) and make a wish. It's a delightful tradition and results are guaranteed.

## FLOWER ARRANGING

For a Thai person, any occasion is an excuse for an offering: a walk *en famille*, or welcoming a visitor, for example. The most valued offerings are flowers, which are regarded as little earthly images of the Buddha. The flowers most commonly given are:

– **Malais**: garlands of flowers made of jasmine buds, rosebuds, African marigolds or orchids mainly given for religious reasons and taken as offerings to temples and places of pilgrimage. These fragrant, perishable fetishes are also popular with drivers and chauffeurs, who hang them from car mirrors, *tuk-tuks* and other modes of transport, to bring them good luck and a safe journey.

– **Bais-sris**: pyramidal compositions constructed mainly of expertly folded banana leaves. They are supposed to bring future happiness and success to new-born babies, newly-weds and anyone who has recently been promoted. A *bais-sris* becomes a *bai-sri chan* if the centre is filled with rice, a hard-boiled egg and fruits.

– **Jads pan**: a sort of fat, budding lotus made from lots of coloured flowers, offered at wedding ceremonies. The shape of the budding lotus stands for purity and beauty but also serves as a reminder of the flower's ephemeral nature.

# ART AND ARCHITECTURE

## THE LEADING SCHOOLS

Prehistoric sites discovered in Ban Chiang to the northeast suggest that Thailand was the cradle of a 5,000-year-old civilization. It evolved under the influence of a successive influx of peoples, including the Mons, the Khmers and the Thais, who brought with them their own religious and cultural mores.

– **The Dvâravatî period** (6th–11th centuries). The Mons lived in the southeast of Myanmar, and in the centre and the northeast of Thailand. Not much is known about the political structure of the state they founded, but we do know that their cities were often oval in design and surrounded by moats. Regrettably, all that remains of them today are the brick foundations and a number of fine stone sculptures.

The sculptures were predominantly Buddhist, rarely Hindu, and were influenced by three schools of art: Ceylon (fifth and sixth centuries); Pala (Srîvijaya, 8th to 10th centuries) and lastly Khmer. These three influences resulted in a particular image of the Buddha that departed from the Indian style to become the first original expression of Buddhist art.

The Buddha can be either stone or bronze. He is usually shown standing, and his hands are held in a gesture suggesting argumentation. Or he may be seated in the European manner, his feet resting on a pedestal in the shape of a lotus blossom. He has a wide face, arched eyebrows that meet in the middle, a flat nose and fleshy lips. It's worth going to see the fine collection of Buddhas in the Lamphun Museum.

– **The Srîvjaya** (8th–13th centuries). The history of the Srîvjaya empire is very unclear. It developed between the 8th and 13th centuries in the peninsular part of Thailand and was heavily influenced by the Pala and especially the Javanese civilizations. Chaiya, in the centre-north of the Malaysian peninsula, seems to have been one of the most important administrative and cultural centres. Some of the statues are truly impressive, such as the trunk of Avalokiteçvara in the National Museum of Bangkok. All the statues have generous proportions and are heavily jewelled.

– **The Khmer period or Lopburi school** (11th–13th centuries). The Khmer influence was so significant, right up to the eve of the 19th century, that the northeastern provinces (more than Cambodia) still served as a positive academy of Angkorian artistic and iconographic tradition. The great temples (Prasat Hin Phimai, Phanom Rung, Phanom Wan, Muang Tham) are an expression of both Hindu belief and Mahâyâna Buddhism. The Khmer temples were built in accordance with the symbolic criteria of Hindu cosmology. Their moats and pools represent the ocean, the walls are mountains and the sanctuary tower (*prasat*) is the Meru mountain, axis of the world and land of the gods. The *prasat* was the dwelling place of the principal divinity, first the Hindu god then Buddha in the 12th century. The divinity's wife and the Great Vehicle lived in smaller *prasats* built around the main tower, and cult objects were kept in secondary dwellings beside it. The whole temple was surrounded by a high wall with huge doors. Within it, a second wooden wall surrounded the dwellings of the priests, musicians and dancers. The temple was built in the centre of the town, close to the palace of the king, who was the gods' chosen representative on earth.

The statues of the Buddhas themselves are mainly in stoneware. They have very characteristic features: square-shaped faces, rectilinear eyebrows, wide mouths, a band separating the forehead from the hairline and a growth at the top of the head symbolizing illumination.

– **The kingdom of Lan Na** (11th–17th centuries). The kingdom of Lan Na was principally influenced by the Burmese culture but also developed an artistic style of its own. This is apparent in the temples with multi-stepped roofs and elaborate porches supported by *nâgas* (snakes); the octagonal *chedis*, which are bell-shaped at the top and covered in copper with a fine golden arrow, and the delicate statues.

The period can be divided into two: **Chiang Saen** (11th–13th centuries) followed by what is known as **late Chiang Saen** or **Chiang Mai**. The first is characterized by a sturdy Buddha with a rounded face, the second by a more slender Buddha with an oval face. Most of the statues are made from semi-precious stones, like the Emerald Buddha.

– **The school of U-Thong** (12th–15th centuries). The little kingdom of U-Thong was heavily influenced by the Khmer, Sukhothai and Ceylon styles. Only its sculpture was original, using fine lines to highlight the lips and eyes of the Buddha and to mark the outline of a moustache.

– **The Sukhothai period** (13th–15th centuries). The school of Sukhothai marked the beginning of Thai art proper. It seems that the adoption of Theravâda Buddhism at the end of the Khmer empire (which practised Mahâyâna Buddhism) led to the creation of an original form of art that sought to assert the new kingdom's cultural identity. The Sukhothai Buddha, who first made an appearance in the 13th century, is one of the most characteristic images of Thai art (featuring a perfectly oval-shaped face, long aquiline nose, arched eyebrows, heavily lidded eyes and curly hair). The hands, and all the bodily proportions, have become more stylized and above the head, a tall flame (*usnîsha*) symbolizes the Buddha's spiritual force.

Another very typical image is that of the walking Buddha, moving with a grace and lightness that is personified in the Buddha of the Pâlis writings. The architecture itself brings together various shapes, including Khmer sanctuary towers, tapering Cingalese *stupas*, Chinese concave roofs and Mons cubic structures. It also retains the brick buildings, stucco niches and earthenware figures of the forgotten kingdom of Dvâravatî. The arrow, shaped like an unopened lotus blossom, is regarded by Thais today as the most original legacy of the Sukhothai builders.

**– The Ayutthaya period** (1350–1767). Ayutthaya was founded by a U-Thong prince in 1350 and remained the capital of the kingdom until 1767, when it was destroyed by the Burmese. While art at the time brought together many different influences, the predominant influence was Khmer, which took hold in a big way when the monarchy decided to reinstate the *devaraja* (divine king), and the king became an object of veneration. The Khmer *prasat* (sanctuary tower) became the *prang*, which was shaped like an ear of corn. The kingdom flourished and, as can be seen from the sheer scale and splendour of the temples, the kings were extremely powerful.

The statues of the Buddha became enormous and were covered in flowers.

**– From Ayutthaya to Bangkok**. The Burmese destroyed Ayutthaya in 1767 and Rama I founded the new capital of Bangkok in 1782. The new capital inherited most of its architectural style from the ancient kingdom but lighter materials were used to build the temples and palaces, which were surrounded by Chinese-style gardens (there is a large Chinese community in Bangkok). The temples have elegant, curved roofs arranged in tiers and covered with glazed tiles, again showing a Chinese influence. Inside, the walls are decorated with paintings and lacquered panels.

The Wat Phra Kaeo (in Bangkok), temple of the Emerald Buddha, is a typical example of this kind of architecture. It consists of a rectangular sanctuary with steeply pitched concave roofs lined with brightly coloured tiles, which indicate a Chinese influence. The *bot* (meeting room) may have one or three naves. The statue of the Buddha stands against the wall, facing the entrance. In the northeast is a bell-shaped *chedi* crowned by an arrow made of diminishing concentric rings, derived from the Cingalese *stupa*. In the northwest stands a square *mondop* with tall columns supporting progressively smaller storeys. This too is crowned with an arrow and a profusion of multicoloured decorations. Lastly, in the northeast, is a temple built to house the statues of the kings. This is a Khmer *prasat* surmounted by layered roofs and enclosed by a little *prang*. (*See also* 'Sculpture'.)

BACKGROUND

## FACES OF THE BUDDHA

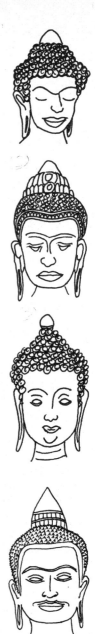

– **Dvâravatî period** (6th–11th centuries). The sculpture of this period is very similar to that of the Gupta dynasty in India from the fourth to the eighth centuries. The Buddha has pronounced features: large square face, flattish nose, thick lips. As he gazes downwards at the person praying at his feet, his expression is absorbed yet kindly. This type of Buddha is found in the centre of Thailand and southern Myanmar and can be seen in museums in Nakhon Pathon, Ratchaburi, Kohn Kaen and Lamphun.

– **Lopburi school** (11th–13th centuries). Found throughout central and northeastern Thailand, this Buddha is identical to the Khmer Buddha: square face, rectilinear eyebrows and wide mouth. A band separates the hairline from the forehead and a conical protuberance at the top of the head symbolizes enlightenment. The seven-headed hood is another feature that dates back to the Khmer cult of the god king (*devaraja*).

– **Period of the kingdom of Lan Na** (11th–17th centuries). Lan Na Buddhas, found in the regions of Chiang Saen and Chiang Mai, are easily recognizable from a number of characteristic features such as their rounded faces, small eyes, small mouths and overall corpulence. Their hair is piled up in curls at the top of the head, crowned with a single lotus blossom. Statues are generally made of crystal or semi-precious stones.

– **U-Thong style** (12th–15th centuries). The pronounced Khmer influence in central Thailand during this period is evident from the very Khmer-like statues of the Buddha. The only original feature was the use of fine lines to highlight the eyes and mouth, which in the latter case looks like a pencil-line moustache.

– **Sukhothai period** (13th–15th centuries). Buddha images during this period are the most characteristic images of Thai art. The Buddha has a slender body, perfectly oval face, long aquiline nose, arched eyebrows, heavy-lidded eyes and hair styled in small curls. Above the head a tall flame (*usnîsha*) symbolizes the Buddha's spiritual strength. The walking Buddha, the first statue of a moving Buddha, was also introduced in this period.

**BACKGROUND**

– **Ayutthaya period** (1350–1767). Buddha imagery from the Ayutthaya period in the centre of Thailand is a combination of previous artistic influences, including the rounded lines of the Sukhothai period and the eyes of the Dvâravatî Buddhas. All the statues are enormous and draped in jewellery like the Khmer gods, reflecting the revival of the cult of the god king.

# SCULPTURE

Almost to the present day, religion, principally Buddhism, has been the greatest source of inspiration in Thai sculpture. The invincible law of the cosmos attributes a place and a role to everything – whether it's the Buddha, real or mythical animals or just plain decoration.

– **Yakshas**. These are the genies of nature – mysterious and sometimes malevolent demons 'rehabilitated' by Buddhism to become the guardians of Buddhist law. You see them at their most terrifying, staring out at you from temple walls, decked out like ancient warriors with gold-encrusted garments inlaid with enamel and glass mosaic decorations.

– **Representations of the Buddha**. A local artform seems to have emerged from different cultural influences (Mon, Khmer, Lanna). In fact, Buddhist art first acquired a structure in the seventh century during the Dvâravatî period. Despite the successive cultural contributions that followed, Buddhist art continued to be guided by traditional principles of originality and continuity, which remain the hallmarks of Thai Buddhist imagery. Any 'innovations' had to conform to a strict iconographic code that originated in southern India.

The appearance of the Buddha is determined by the *lakshanas* (characteristics or signs) that define the 'superior man'. These are qualities you have acquired during your former lives. There are 32 principal characteristics plus 80 that were added later; those you have are obvious from the day you are born. *Lakshanas* are only present in a being called to be king or master of the universe or, if he renounces the world, a Buddha.

Some of the 32 main characteristics relate to psychic qualities that are impossible to translate (the lion's voice, delicacy of taste and so on). But others stem from magical-religious beliefs and are displayed in the Buddha's unique appearance; for example, the growth on the top of the head and his banyan-like plumpness.

– **Gestures and attitudes**. The Buddha is portrayed in four possible positions: standing, sitting, striding and prone (these are the positions in which he appeared to Srâvastî). Statues that show him striding were first seen in the Sukhothai period (13th–15th centuries) and they remain some of the most original expressions of Thai sculpture.

In Thailand, the Buddha's gestures do not have precisely the same meaning as they do in India. There, according to the Mahâyâna conception of Buddhism (Great Vehicle) each *mudrâ* (gesture of the hands and fingers with magical and mystical meaning) is interpreted as a *jina* (conqueror). This makes it possible to differentiate between the figures of the Buddha, which are essentially all the same.

The word *mudrâ* has no place in Theravâda Buddhism or Thai iconography. In fact, the *mudrâs* are not enough to describe the collection of miracles performed by the Enlightened One. But for the sake of simplicity, *mudrâs* is the term used in descriptions.

# GESTURES OF
# THE BUDDHA

– *Bhumisparsa* or '**Calling the earth to witness**'.

The Buddha sits cross-legged; the right hand is held low down, palm uppermost and the left hand rests on the legs. This gesture has come to symbolize the Buddha's enlightenment and features strongly in Thai imagery because it illustrates victory over Mara (death, the demon, the great god of desire). Thwarting Mara's best efforts to disturb His meditation, the Buddha's only response is to touch the earth and ask it to witness His resolve. To the Thais this gesture represents the greatest of all miracles and symbolizes the apogee of the life of the Buddha.

– *Dhyana* or '**Meditative position**'.

The Buddha sits in the lotus position; the right hand rests on the left hand in His lap.

– *Vitarka* or '**Gesture of Argumentation**'.

The Buddha sits or stands, his right arm raised with the hand half open and the thumb and index finger touching to form a circle (the wheel is the symbol of teaching). This gesture is also sometimes made with the left arm raised.

BACKGROUND

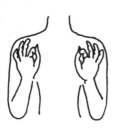

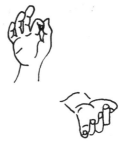

**– *Dharmachakra* (Turning the Great Wheel of Law).**

Both hands are raised, the palms of the hands facing each other and the thumbs and index fingers touching to form a circle. This is the gesture of turning the wheel of Dharma recalling the Buddha's first sermon after enlightenment.

**– *Varada* or 'Gesture of giving'.**

The Buddha sits or stands, arms by his side, hands open. This is the gesture of offering, charity and the giving of favours.

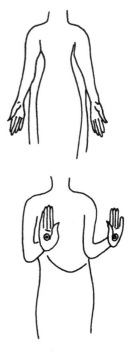

**– *Abhaya* or 'Appeasement of quarrels'.**

The Buddha stands or walks, one or both hands raised, palms facing forward. This is the gesture of fearlessness and appeasement.

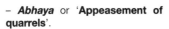

## FURTHER STUDY

If you want to know more, here's a suggested reading list, which is by no means exhaustive. Some of these books are bulky, so dip into them before you go. Note that all publisher details refer to the UK edition.

– *The Sacred Sculpture of Thailand* by J.R. Woodard (Thames & Hudson, 1977)

– *Art and Crafts of Thailand* by Warren Willian (Thames & Hudson, 1995)

– *Art of Thailand* by Van Beek (Thames & Hudson, 1991)

– *The Art of Southeast Asia* by Philip Stanley Rawson (Thames & Hudson, 1967)

# SCUBA-DIVING

## TAKING THE PLUNGE

There can be no better place than Thailand to learn scuba-diving: the sea is warm, calm and welcoming, and the seabed is rich in things to look at. So why not take the plunge? Scuba-diving now ranks as a leisure activity rather than a sport and it's a great thing to do. You find yourself suddenly in another element, where you can fly above nests of clown-fish, have long conversations with curiously attentive wreck fish, dance on an anxious cloud of *anthias* (sea perch) that seem to disappear in a mist around a head of coral; you can glide dreamily over shipwrecks and discover picasso fish.

Nothing in the world glistens like a fish. It's true, you can get a burn from some of the coral, some fish do sting and people do talk (too much) about sharks. But once you get down there you'll find your fears were exaggerated. You must, of course, respect the safety rules, which will be explained to you as you go along. These include being wary of anything that isn't wary of you – such as scorpion-fish, anemones and fire coral.

One golden rule to remember is to respect the delicate environment. Learn to stabilize your depth using your suit rather than by resting on the seabed or leaning against rocks or coral. Do not try to feed the fish, don't leave anything behind and, above all, be careful where you put your flippers.

## YOU NEVER THOUGHT IT WOULD BE THIS EASY

Enter another world where you can swim with multicoloured schools of fish and examine the natural wonders of the seabed or coral reefs. You don't have to be particularly athletic or even a good swimmer to blow your first bubbles. Anyone over eight years old and in good health can have a go. But scuba-diving isn't for anyone on regular medication; if you're pregnant, this is definitely not for you. In your own interests, except if it's for a maiden dive, you will be asked to provide a medical certificate. For children it is especially important to check that the staff are fully qualified and work in a suitable environment (shallow, no current, child-sized equipment).

Diving doesn't hurt your ears – all you have to do is pinch your nose and blow; and no, you don't have to make an effort to inhale through the pressure-reducing valve they put in your mouth. On the contrary, since active exhalation is the basis of all relaxation, you'll find it's surprisingly soothing. Being in the water alters your conscious state, and because the parameters of time and space have changed, you feel 'elsewhere' (which, of course, you are).

## DIVING CENTRES

Depending on where they are based, all the clubs are affiliated to international organizations, the three most important being: the French CMAS (*Confédération mondiale des activités subaquatiques* – Worldwide Confederacy of Underwater Activities), the American PADI (Professional Association of Diving Instructors) and NAUI (National Association of Underwater Instructors). The training and diplomas you receive from each one are valid across the world and in 1996 the CMAS and the PADI signed a convention agreeing to recognize one another's diplomas (but not to consider them as equivalent).

In places influenced by the United States, which includes Thailand, the diving clubs tend to teach the American way and their diving procedures have been standardized so that duration and depth are to a strict rule. Each student has to achieve four separate levels. If the club doesn't recognize your diploma, it will ask you to take a test to check what stage you are at. If a medical certificate is needed, the club will also recommend a local doctor.

A good diving centre obeys all the rules regarding safety but makes sure you enjoy yourself. Be wary of any club that lets you start without first asking you what level you've reached: it's not 'cool' but irresponsible. Check to see whether the centre is properly maintained (look out for rust and general cleanliness), observe whether there is adequate safety equipment on board (look at oxygen, first-aid kit, radio) and be sure that there aren't too many divers to a single instructor (six at most). Check to be sure that you are not carrying too much equipment. Even the carrying of cylinders is a question of culture: in American schools, for example, cylinders are always carried for you no matter how tough you look, while in French schools, people carry their own gear. If in doubt, ask – you are paying after all, so you are entitled to the best. You can choose either the well-oiled 'production line' approach or a smaller, more flexible set-up.

## YOUR FIRST DIVE

The first thing you do is go for a maiden dive, which usually lasts about half an hour during which the instructor looks after you and holds your hand. This session should be just you and the instructor who will take care of everything, so make the most of it. Even if you feel as overdressed as a Christmas tree out of season, you'll forget all about the equipment once you are in the water.

The first time, you're unlikely to go any deeper than 5 metres (16 feet). For maximum comfort, always choose a suit that fits snugly or it can form pockets of water that cool you down. Over the course of the next three to five days you'll gradually progress to the first level, which allows you to dive to a depth of 20 metres (65 feet). To give the depressurization process time to work, make sure you leave a 12- to 24-hour interval before taking the plane or moving to a higher altitude.

Eventually you'll be hooked, totally enraptured by the sea and everything in it. But you can't know until you've tried. Prepare to be amazed – get diving.

## SCUBA-DIVING IN THAILAND

Thailand has some 2,614 kilometres (1,625 miles) of coastline with heavenly beaches and little islands. The appeal is irresistible. Depending on the season, two regions are particularly good for scuba-diving: the Andaman Sea (on the west coast) from November to May and the Gulf of Thailand (on the east coast) from June to October.

Visibility underwater is variable and depends on water temperature (around 28°C/80°F) and plankton which attracts manta rays and whale sharks. You get used to seeing these titans cavorting in tropical waters. A word of warning though: don't touch anything, especially not the white sea-snakes with black stripes. And don't wear a short suit if the waters are teeming with jellyfish; this does happen occasionally but it doesn't stop the diving.

● **Diving clubs**. Whatever your destination, you'll find more than enough diving clubs wherever you go. So you don't always need to book a place in advance (although most clubs now have their own website) particularly since the diving instructors usually approach you when you arrive. What's more, since they are paid on commission, it's in their interest to offer you a good deal to make sure you keep coming back. Your instructor will know the sea like the back of his hand. He will tell you all you need to know about the splendours and pitfalls of the seabed in Thailand and show you all the most interesting sights. Before you get kitted out, listen carefully to what he has to say.

Clubs generally offer you a daily package that includes two diving sessions and a meal. Prices vary from 2,200–3,300 Bts. They rise spectacularly at Chinese New Year.

● **Getting there by boat**. The typical taxiboat (a motorized dugout that holds six people maximum – great if you like the wind in your face) allows you to dive close to your hotel. This is the cheapest option. The classic diving boat holds 15 people and takes you slightly further out. The speedboat holds six people and takes you to the most distant spots – the real sanctuaries of marine life where you might spot the occasional rare species.

● **Diplomas**. Centres provide training which, at each level, gives divers a little more autonomy. You start off with the Open Water Diver certificate, which takes four days and costs 8–12,000 Bts; then you can follow the two-day Advanced Open Water Diver course at a cost of around 7–11,000 Bts before going on to study for the Rescue Diver, costing 8–10,000 Bts and lasting another two days. Finally, the Divemaster diploma is aimed at people wishing to become instructors. As a rule of thumb you should allow 20–30,000 Bts for three weeks' training. Don't be in too much of a hurry to acquire all these certificates – you also need to give yourself time to acquire indispensable experience. Ask your instructor for advice (don't forget, he's been there before). All centres issue a log-book where your experience is recorded, bringing back some lovely memories once your holidays are over. Look after it carefully and don't forget to take this precious 'passport' with you next time you go away.

# THAILAND'S TOP DIVING SPOTS

### In the Andaman Sea

This area is generally reached from the island of Phuket (which has an international airport), where several clubs can take you out to the various diving spots. There are day trips to more distant spots and even four- to five-day 'dive safari' cruises to some particularly lush and wild archipelagos.

Within easy reach of Phuket (ferries go there daily) is the small but heavenly island of Koh Phi Phi. It has first-class accommodation (hotels, guesthouses and bungalows) and lots of diving clubs (particularly along Tonsai Bay). The white, sandy beaches and truly excellent diving conditions are the reason for its great international reputation.

**Koh Phi Phi and the surrounding area**. Less than 50 kilometres (30 miles) to the southeast of Phuket and about the same distance to the south of Krabi (a three-hour crossing), there is a diving-spot *par excellence* in a nature reserve. It's famous for sheer drops, easily accessible underwater caverns and sparkling rocks and corals. The visibility is 8–15 metres (26–50 feet) and the maximum depth is 26 metres (85 feet). Traditional clown fish, angelfish, trumpet fish and shoals of snapper are guaranteed each time you dive. You could even expect to come face to face with a shark in Hin Pae, but just stay calm!

In Koh Phi Phi Lae and Koh Mai Phai you'll find lots of flirtatious lion fish, and in the waters off Hin Klang and Koh Bida you will meet some fairly tame tortoises as well as squid and reef sharks. One of the James Bond films was shot here. Peaceful leopard sharks hang out on the sandy seabed off Mosquito Island. Bamboo Island is a meeting place for stingray, barracuda and sergeant fish. Around Hin Pita and Koh Ku are the most spectacularly beautiful corals in the whole of the archipelago.

**Shark Point**. Some 20 kilometres (12 miles) northwest of Koh Phi Phi, this group of three chalky reefs from 0–22 metres (72 feet) deep is a haven for leopard sharks. These are peaceful creatures as curious as they are harmless. They spend most of their time asleep on the seabed utterly oblivious to the frenzy of activity going on around them (including lion fish, butterfly fish and anemones). It's very colourful and the coral's beautiful.

**Anemone Reef**. Less than 2 kilometres (1.5 miles) northwest of Shark Point is a magnificent isolated reef that goes from 6 to 23 metres (20 to 75 feet) deep, and is completely carpeted with anemones of every kind. Don't be tempted to join the antics of the clown fish as they dart in and out of the anemones' tentacles; only the clown fish can do this in safety, as a result of an understanding they've come to with the anemones – cleaning in exchange for protection. Some barracuda live here too.

**Wreck of the King Cruiser**. You can go aboard an 85-metre long (280-foot) luxury cruise ship that is lying at a depth of between 12 and 33 metres (40 and 110 feet) just off Anemone Reef. It's home to numerous shoals of reef fish and molluscs. Take a torch with you so you can explore the marine life hiding in every nook and cranny. Big holes in the belly of the ship make it easy to find your way back up to the surface, but watch out for unexpected encounters all the same.

**Similan Islands**. This nature reserve consists of nine magnificent islands (white sandy beaches and tropical forests) some 100 kilometres (60 miles) northwest of Phuket and it's reachable by cruise ship (an eight-hour crossing). It's one of the top 10 diving spots in the world, renowned for its reefs, caves, canyons and fabulous coral beds lying in crystalline waters and teeming with fish at a depth of 6–40 metres (20–130 feet). There are frequent sightings of solitary manta rays and black-tip reef sharks on Fantasy Reef, Christmas Point and Elephant Head, all a riot of colour. These waters are a favourite stamping ground for balloon fish, porcupine fish and puffer fish, all of whom like to inflate themselves to impress their enemies (so don't stand in the line of fire).

**Surin Islands**. Just a few hours north of the Similan Islands is another much wilder nature reserve that attracts far fewer tourists. This one is 17–46 metres (56–150 feet) deep. You might see whale sharks around Bon, Koh Tachai and Richelieu. These gentle giants, whose voracious appetite for plankton matches their enormous size, are known to visit these waters. You can amaze the sea tortoises with your flipping skills as you turn 'turtle' in the water. Keep an eye open for the wonderful yellow sea-horses.

**Koh Rajah Yai**. One hour south of Phuket, this little island bordered with heavenly white sandy beaches will appeal to the Robinson Crusoe in you. Dive to a depth of between 9 and 25 metres (30 and 80 feet) to discover the most beautiful bed of coral, with flourishing marine life and some very large fish. Look but don't touch, of course. And watch out for the occasional mean octopus.

**Koh Rajah Noi**. A small desert island surrounded by cliffs just a few kilometres (a mile or so) southwest of Koh Raja Yai. The waters are between 9 and 28 metres (30 and 91 feet) deep, and very clear but the currents are strong, so take care. You'll find lots of crustaceans lurking in the cracks between the coral, and sea bream, barracuda and trumpet fish glide by.

**The Southern Islands**. This small archipelago, some 100 kilometres (62 miles) southeast of Phuket, is reachable by cruise ship (an eight-hour crossing). Diving spots can vary from 6 to 50 metres (20 to 160 feet) in depth. Around the island of Koh Ha you get a chance to visit some enormous underwater caverns before reaching the fascinating reef around Rok Nok. Hin Daeng and Hin Muang are said to be two particularly lush sites, and there's the Koh Tarutao nature reserve near the Malaysian border. It's a feast of really knock-out coral and you get frequent visits from leopard sharks, manta rays and whale sharks.

### In the Gulf of Thailand

This area is best reached from the towns of Chumphon, Surat Thani and Trat (on the opposite coast) where there are plenty of diving clubs to choose from. One idea is to go straight to the island of Koh Tao, a real diver's heaven, with excellent accommodation and a good choice of diving clubs and shops.

**Koh Tao**. About four hours southeast of Chumphon by fast ferry crossing. It's another magnificent island like Koh Phi Phi that is very popular with the tourists. You can take your pick of spots around the island: Hin Bai, Hin Kao and Hin Khiao, plus the little desert island of Nang

BACKGROUND

Yuan (northwest of Koh Tao), which is a real marine-life sanctuary. The waters are clear most of the time, and reveal a rich variety of multi-coloured fish frolicking happily in the finest coral beds in the Gulf of Thailand. It's suitable for divers of all levels.

🐠 **The islands of Koh Samui and Koh Pha Ngan**. South of Koh Tao and some four hours away by boat (the crossing leaves from Surat Thani), these two islands have that same picture-postcard look as their little sister Koh Tao. The diving around Sail Rock and in the Ang Thong nature reserve, which consists of 42 islands, is exquisite. The species of coral you find growing in the sea around Chumphon – black with white, gold and yellow patches – is reminiscent of the 'sea star' gorgonians. You might encounter the occasional whale shark.

🐠 **Koh Chang**. On the coast facing the Gulf of Thailand, near Trat, this is an increasingly popular diving spot, with a rich array of hard corals and some extraordinary undersea life.

# THAI BOXING

For a country where extreme politeness is the norm and violence is distasteful, the national sport of Thai boxing is just about as violent as it gets. The fighting is quite merciless and elbows, knees and feet are used as much as fists. What happens outside the ring is worth watching too.

Try and make time to go and see a boxing match in one of the two stadiums in Bangkok, either in Lumphini stadium – ลุมพินี, on Rama IV Avenue – ถนนพระราม๔, or Ratchadamnoen stadium – ราชดำเนิน, on Ratchadamnoen Nok – ราชดำเนินนอก. There are some good professional fights in Chiang Mai as well. It's an experience you'll never forget. Beer and *mekong* seem to give licence to the kind of behaviour you would never see anywhere else. In fact, an ethnologist would have a field day. But then, Thai boxing is about more than just a sport – it's a betting game and huge amounts are riding on the contestants in the ring.

Before the fight starts, watch the curious gesturing of the two men in the ring. It's a movement halfway between yoga and a more physical expression. In fact it's a personalized ritual, a sort of prayer or incantation that is sometimes performed to popular music. This preliminary delicacy is a sharp contrast to the violence that starts when the contestants actually come to blows. Still, it could be worse. There was a time when boxers used to bind their hands with strips of cloth containing crushed glass.

# TRADITIONAL THAI MASSAGE

Traditional massage came from India and China and has always been linked to Buddhist philosophy, which it expresses through the four states of spiritual divinity taught by the 'Enlightened One' (goodness, compassion, joy of living and serenity). Aside from this spiritual aspect, massage is a very widespread practice in Thailand: mothers teach their daughters who massage their fathers, who massage them in turn, all quite naturally. It is a convivial daily, family routine. There are of course schools (particularly the famous Wat Pho school in Bangkok, and the Moh

Shivagakomarapaj foundation in Chiang Mai), where the three main types of massage are taught: foot massage, traditional full massage (the whole body is given a work-out over two hours) and a massage using herbs.

Some places also offer sexual massages, which often take place in parlours where the masseuses are experts in such matters. However, it should be noted that the limits are not necessarily cut and dried: in many traditional massage places, women may, if they wish, offer this type of massage, without doing so systematically or to order. Having said that, you are under no obligation to experience these 'individual' treatments and the majority of massages offered in guesthouses (normally performed by old Chinese men) or around the southern beaches, are very high quality and completely straight. No visitor to Thailand should leave without having tried a full, traditional massage, where gentle manipulation and pressure in just the right places leave you feeling like a new person.

# GO-GO BARS AND PROSTITUTION

Thailand has a reputation the world over – and so have its famously 'docile' women. Girls in Thailand are generally brought up to be submissive and not to expect pleasure. Why are there so many prostitutes in Thailand? The reason is far from obvious, because while there are many contributing factors, not one of them is in any way conclusive. One major reason is the grinding poverty that afflicts villages in northern Thailand; young girls leave to find work in the towns – sometimes willingly and sometimes less so. Other reasons include the complete lack of any alternative; parents who force their daughters to leave to feed their families and the desire to obtain freedom through money. Many of the girls are in fact sold by their parents – usually poverty-stricken peasants from the northeast – to pimps or brothel owners, who recoup what they paid for them in less than a month. This is modern-day slavery attracting, as it does, punters from all over the world. The sheer scale of prostitution today has created all kinds of problems.

There are said to be at least one million prostitutes in the country, half of them in Bangkok, where the situation has reached epic proportions. These are the girls with the docile smile that you find dancing in G-strings to decadent tunes in the clubs of Patpong. In Thai, the women are called *phouyng ha kin*, which literally means 'women looking for food'. They send most of their earnings back to their villages to feed their families. They usually aim to retire on their earnings by the age of 25–30 when they may return to their village to marry.

The AIDS epidemic, played down by the authorities, has seen new trends emerge in recent years. Today it's no longer young girls who are for sale but children who have barely reached the age of 11 or 12, and there's a growing market for virgins and even 'half virgins' (meaning children who've only had sex once). Clients frightened of AIDS are prepared to pay 10 or 20 times the price of a usual 'trick' to have unprotected sex with someone 'untouched'.

Whether they admit it or not, some of the male tourists who come to

Bangkok on their own come 'for the experience'. For the moment, the Thai government is not taking visible steps to intervene, despite rumblings from various local organizations and growing public awareness. Outside Thailand, the international press and human rights community is also showing signs of activity. The Tourism Authority of Thailand (TAT) condemns the sexual exploitation of children and reminds 'clients' that having sex with a prostitute aged 13–15 years is a crime punishable by a period of imprisonment ranging from 4 to 20 years; exploiting a child under the age of 13 carries a life sentence. To find out how you can help, you can email TAT at: tat@cs.ait.ac.th. Many countries have made child prostitution an extra-territorial offence, so that offenders may be prosecuted even when the offence took place overseas – *see* 'Human Rights' *above*.

## GO-GO BARS IN PATPONG

You will find the biggest concentration of go-go bars in the Patpong area of Bangkok, where they vie for the attention of the never-ending stream of tourists. In case you were wondering, Patpong is named after the old Chinese man, Patpongphanit, who owns the land on which the proliferation of bars are situated. Patpong I and II are two adjoining *sois* between Silom and Surawong Roads. The go-go bars themselves are either a pretty depressing sight or the scene for a great night out, depending on your outlook. On the ground level of the bar, young, practically naked Thai girls dance, offering the male punters expensive drinks and refills every five minutes (they get commission for each drink they sell). Upstairs is where the 'shows', strip-teases and other events take place, all for a price.

Whatever you think about this kind of place, just visiting Patpong I and Patpong II won't cost you anything. In fact, seen by night, you could almost think of it as a cultural stroll through Bangkok. This bedlam of activity, where anything and everything is for sale, makes London's Soho look positively tame by comparison. A word of warning though: the bar touts are merciless and the minute you set foot in a bar, get ready to pay through the nose. People have paid 500 or 1,000 Bts for a soft drink worth 50 Bts. Be careful where you go – they've got conning the tourist down to a fine art in Patpong.

# PRECIOUS STONES

The sheer quantity of 'made in Occident' stones that you will find in markets all over Thailand leaves little room for illusion. It was the French who discovered that synthetic stones, unlike true 'fakes', have the same visual and physical characteristics as real gems.

You can't tell the real thing by its colour and the presence of 'inclusions'. Features like these may mean something to a specialist – but even a specialist will tell you that green garnets, orange opals, green sapphires and yellow tourmalines really are all found in nature and do not necessarily indicate a stone that has been synthesized or treated. Such details therefore, whether natural or artificial, can be misleading. Even a professional jeweller can't be relied on for an opinion, as without any formal training in gemmology, he's bound to make mistakes himself from time to time. But don't worry, because science is there to prevent you from making a big mistake. No fake, however technically perfect, can survive the scrutiny of a scanning electron microscope, a microprobe or other form of spectrophotometer.

But let's face it – you probably won't have a spectrophotometer with you on your travels, and you and every other tourist will probably be tempted to buy stones from what they call the 'place of production', so here are a few hints on what to watch out for while shopping. Citrine or 'smoky topaz' posing as topaz; 'water sapphire' (corderite) and synthetic blue spinel instead of sapphire; serpentine and nephrite instead of jadeite; synthetic rubies and garnets instead of rubies; worthless stony green beryls instead of emeralds; aquamarines that haven't a trace of blue in them (mainly from Brazil and distributed worldwide); and sapphires from Australia (distributed in Thailand) that are more black than blue (and you won't be any the wiser even when you hold them up to the light).

Watch out too for exotic-looking certificates, which are mainly an incentive to buy and are no kind of guarantee or proof that the seller knows what he's talking about. If you are about to part with a lot of money, be firm. Insist on a certificate of analysis from a reputable laboratory that specializes in gemmology.

It almost goes without saying that you have to remember how important it is to be on your guard. The tactics they use on tourists are pretty much to a formula, but it's done extremely skilfully – after all some tourists do fall for the tricks and scams. The routine goes like this: a *tuk-tuk* – ตุ๊กตุ๊ก – conductor or a passer-by strikes up a conversation and starts to chat about this and that. Of course, he's spinning you a line. There's a shop he knows where a massive sale has just started (fancy that!) and you stand to make a real killing. It's so easy to be taken in. They even have statements from other tourists (fakes, obviously) and certificates of authenticity (even faker) to prove what they say. They ply you with tea and attention, which costs them nothing – and suddenly you've fallen for it, although you think you've got a good deal. So tread very carefully because any bargains are strictly in your imagination.

It's also worth remembering that a stone is only worth a sizeable part of your savings provided there is a market for it. Otherwise it will remain buried in some drawer like all the other fine gems that nobody wants because they're the wrong colour, shape, weight or size. Gems are very much a professional's market, so think wisely before purchasing.

In this business, you can never kill two birds with one stone, so remember – a souvenir isn't the same thing as an investment. For more information and suggested reading, contact:

● **The Gemmological Association**: 27 Greville Street, (Saffron Hill entrance), London EC1N 8TN. ☎ (020) 7404 3334.

# ORCHIDS

Thailand is famous for its dazzling array of orchids, half of which are exported to countries all around the world. As well as the cut-flower crops grown on orchid farms and in special nurseries, many varieties flourish in the wild where the humid, tropical conditions are just right.

Orchids remained a mystery in Europe for a long time as they soon perished once removed from their natural environment. Exotic orchids are particularly fragile and should not be planted in a pot. They need airy, mild, humid conditions, as well as shade and a soil that is free from any fertilizer. Although the first orchid hybrid was produced accidentally in 1856, it wasn't until the beginning of the 20th century that the secret of orchid cultivation was finally discovered.

During the 1960s it was found that it was possible to produce identical new orchids by taking tiny cuttings from the vegetative tip of the plant (the meristem). This meant that all that was needed to produce millions of orchids was a few millimetres of plant tissue. Orchids were also the first plants to be successfully crossbred, and today there are 30,000 orchid species in the world (Thailand has over 1,000), with new varieties being added from time to time. The orchid has become a national symbol in Thailand and is often presented to visitors on arrival.

# RECOMMENDED READING

All books listed refer to the British editions.

– *Buddhism, a very short introduction* by Damien Keown (1996, £4.99). Available from the Buddhist Society, 58 Eccleston Square, London SW1V 1PH

– *The Foundations of Buddhism* by Rupert Gethin (OUP, 1998, £8.99)

– *The Elements of Buddhism,* John Snelling (Element Books, 1990, £5.99)

– *The Honourable Schoolboy* thriller by John Le Carré (Hodder & Stoughton, 1977). In Southeast Asia, final battleground of the 'Circus', the British Secret Service is led by George Smiley, trying to rebuild his networks after infiltration by a Soviet spy. John Le Carré displays his talents as a writer in the crowded, multinational setting of Hong Kong and Thailand on the eve of the American withdrawal from Vietnam.

# BANGKOK AND THE SURROUNDING AREA

## BANGKOK (KRUNG THEP) – กรุงเทพ

DIALLING CODE: 02

Bangkok and its suburbs are home to 10 per cent of Thailand's population and 90 per cent of its cars – living proof of the city's ongoing, mushroom-like development. Present-day Bangkok is a chaotic jumble of buildings, most of them hideous, where – and this is what you strikes you more than anything else – the traffic is like bedlam: deafening, demented and exhausting. Leaving that aside, Bangkok is full of good places to live, but don't expect to be staggering under any exotic culture shock or find yourself marvelling at the eternal face of Asia. The years leading up to the economic crisis were a period of runaway growth, when Bangkok developed a seemingly insatiable appetite for more and more buildings, each one taller and more grandiose than the last. What you see today is not very appealing. You'd better get used to it, as it's practically impossible to avoid. And anyway, you might even get to like it – madness can have its attractions.

Bangkok is not without its treasures: superb temples, a magnificent museum, refined cuisine and one helluva nightlife – all of which make up for the heat, the dust and the noise of the place.

**Note**: The Thais most often call Bangkok by the name *Krung Thep,* which means 'City of Angels'. The city's full name is the longest in the world: Krung Thep Maha Nakhorn Amorn Ratanakosin Mahindrayutthaya Mahadilok Phop Noparat Rajdhani Burirom Udom Rajnivet Mahasatan Amorn Pimarn Avatarn Satit, etc. But don't worry about it – Krung Thep will do nicely.

*See Colour Section for maps of Bangkok and the surrounding area*

### TOPOGRAPHY

Bangkok is enormous! Huge distances from A to B and getting anywhere takes ages. There are horrendous traffic jams at peak times and just ordinary jams the rest of the time. The most interesting part of the town is on the banks of the river Chao Phraya. This is where you find the museum, the Grand Palace, the temples and – good news for back-packers – lots of small hotels.

Chinatown is right in the centre of Bangkok. South of Rama IV, Surawong and Silom roads lead out onto Thanon Charoen Krung (New Road), defining an area that's a real hub of activity.

Sukhumvit Road is another major thoroughfare. Many of the hotels, shopping centres and little restaurants at the beginning of the road are having their livelihoods threatened by a flyover under construction at third-floor level aimed at easing traffic congestion. Economic uncertainties, however, may force this nightmarish project to be shelved.

Thonburi, on the western bank of the river, was built well before Bangkok and still has most of its original canals or *khlongs*. On the east bank these have nearly all been filled in. Taking a boat down these *khlongs* is a must. This is Bangkok as it used to be. When you need a break from the frantic goings-on of the city centre, Thonburi is the place to be, because there you're already out in the country. It's compulsory viewing for anyone who wants to understand the way Bangkok has developed.

Addresses in Bangkok usually feature the name of the street followed by the *soi* number. The *soi* is a little road that runs at right angles to the main road. To get your bearings, find the main road first and then the appropriate *soi*. Even and uneven *sois* are on opposite sides of the street.

## ARRIVING AT THE AIRPORT

**● International Airport in Don Muang** – ท่าอากาศยานดอนเมือง (off D1, colour map 1) 25 kilometres (15.5 miles) north of the city.

The tourist information desk is officially open 8am–noon. In practice however it is often closed but if you are lucky enough to find it open, ask for the leaflet called *Getting to the City,* which explains all the different ways of getting to town. Study each option carefully before making up your mind. Left luggage is just to the right of tourist information and is open 24 hours a day, but it's expensive and staff are reluctant to take backpacks. The bureau de change is also open 24 hours a day but exchange rates are poor.

As soon as you can, get yourself a copy of the *Latest Tour Guide to Bangkok and Thailand* – a very detailed map showing bus routes and river stops (for boats). It's a mine of useful information on transport, embassies and things to see and even suggests a limited number of inexpensive guesthouses in Bangkok. Occasionally on sale at the airport although at a premium price, otherwise it's widely available in town, including from hotel bookshops. Also ask for a complimentary *Route Map of Thailand,* which includes a very good map of Bangkok.

**●** The **National Airport** is next door. Transit passengers can cross over to domestic flights using the kilometre (half-mile) long rolling walkway, which is a big help to backpackers.

Alternatively, a free **shuttle-bus** service operates between the two terminals, with buses running every 30 minutes from 6am to 10pm, but it's less convenient than the rolling walkway because you have to leave the airport. Contact Thai Airways International, desk 7 for details.

## GETTING TO TOWN

– **Thai Limousine Service**: air-conditioned cars that take you to the hotel of your choice. They are very expensive (500–650 Bts) so best avoided unless you really are loaded down with bags.

– **Public Taxis**: go to the public taxi counter (just by the exit) and not the airport taxi counter, which is nearly twice as expensive. Public taxis charge a fixed price (250 Bts) regardless of the number of passengers, and you travel in a licensed cab. Watch out for the young people in a suit and tie who greet you in the arrivals hall – they're touts for the more expensive airport taxis. Never use an unlicensed taxi. They'll rob you blind, or worse, so go carefully. Licensed taxis have yellow number-plates. Whenever you can, travel as a group to keep the price down.

– **Taxi-meters**: not many of these, but in theory at least they let the passenger keep an eye on the price. The problem is that the drivers fix the fares among themselves and refuse to use a meter. Instead they quote you a fixed price that is significantly more than you would pay on the meter (around 200 Bts).

– **Buses**: by far the cheapest option – probably 10 times cheaper than everything else. The bus stops just outside the airport. Don't cross the motorway, as cars in Thailand drive on the left and you have to go left to get to Bangkok.

If you're going towards Khao San Road, where there are some cheap hotels, the bus is definitely the best way to get there as it will drop you right where you want to be. Climb aboard a No. A2, which has air-conditioning and luggage space (departs every 15 minutes). Failing that (at night) take a No. 59, which you can identify from its blue number-plate. Get off at Democracy Monument. Khao San Road isn't far (have a map handy). To get to Hua Lamphong Station take the No. 29 bus, which leaves from the same place and which can be either air-conditioned or not. To get to Sukhumvit Road, where there are more and rather classier hotels, take a No. 13, which stops at the Eastern Bus Terminal. Seats are generally available.

The two other air-conditioned buses, the No. 4 and the No. 10, are not so useful for backpackers. The No. 10 goes via the Northern Bus Terminal and Victory Monument; the No. 4 goes towards Silom Road and Charoen Krung Road in south Bangkok. Additionally, chartered minibuses ferry passengers from the airport to guesthouses in Bangkok.

The journey takes about 2 hours depending on traffic conditions and where you want to go – much longer if it's raining. If it's any consolation, even the taxis take at least an hour and they use the toll roads, which are much faster. Lastly, bear in mind that the buses are packed in the mornings until 10am and in the evening until 8pm. Hordes of invading backpackers don't go down too well with the natives and drivers have been known to pull a U-turn when there are no more Thais on board.

At night there's always the shuttle bus to fall back on (details from the limousine counter). It stops in the Khao San Road area and it isn't cheap. Public buses run until about 8pm except for the No. 59 and No. 29 that run throughout the night.

– **Trains**: it's best to take the train only to go to another town or to the area around the station. Otherwise it gets complicated: once at the station, you have to take a bus or a very expensive *tuk-tuk* to get to another part of town. The airport express only leaves every 2 hours 30 minutes on average and it takes about 35 minutes – timetables are available from the tourist office. It's worth taking if there are two of you but for three or more, take a taxi. Remember by the way that the No. 29 bus also goes to the station.

## USEFUL ADDRESSES

### TOURIST INFORMATION

**◨TAT** (Tourism Authority of Thailand, Head Office) – ททท/การท่องเที่ยวแห่งประเทศไทย (off B1, colour map II): 10th Floor, Le Concorde Building, 202 Ratchada-pisek Road, Huai Khwang, Bangkok 10310. ☎ 694-12-22. Fax: 694 12-20-1. Website: www.tourism-thailand.org. Open daily, 8.30am–4.30pm. A rich source of useful leaflets and interesting brochures. Ask for *Where to eat in Bangkok*, a booklet listing over 200 restaurants by type of food served (*see* Thai Cuisine). The TAT can also tell you which buses go to the monuments you want to visit and give you complete lists of bus and train timetables, doctors, hospitals, airlines and so on.

**◨TAT** (Tourism Authority of Thailand) (colour map I, B2): 4 Thanon Ratchadamnoen Nok, Bangkok 10100 (next door to one of the two big boxing stadiums). ☎ 282-97-73(-6). Fax: 282-97-75. Open daily, 8.30am–4.30pm.

**◨ TAC** (Tourist Assistance Centre) – ศูนย์ช่วยเหลือนักท่องเที่ยว: Thanon Ratchadamnoen Nok – ถนนราชดำเนินนอก. ☎ 281-50-51 and 282-81-29. Fax: 281-50-51. Open 8.30am–4.30pm. Can assist with lost documents, help with complaints, etc.

The TAC works in conjunction with the **Tourist Police** – ตำรวจท่องเที่ยว: Unico House Building, 29/1 Soi Lang Suan. ☎ 652-17-21(-6), or dial the 24-hour emergency number direct: ☎ 16-99.

### EMBASSIES

*See* Embassies in 'General Information'.

### SERVICES

✉ **General Post Office (GPO)** – ไปรษณีย์กลาง (colour map I, C4): Charoen Krung Road (or New Road) near the Oriental Hotel. ☎ 233-10-50. Open 8am–8pm weekdays and 9am–1pm weekends and holidays. *Poste restante* facilities. Post office traveller's cheques can be exchanged here. Sells everything you need to send parcels to Europe (cheap boxes, tape). Sending by air is expensive, so send them by sea (very reasonable) and avoid paying excess baggage.

**◨ Telephone**: calls can be made 24 hours a day from the building next to the post office. Otherwise, you can call Europe from any of the telephone kiosks you find in and around the hotels in Bangkok (in the Khao San Road and Sukhumvit areas, for example). Be careful, as there are two kinds of telephone cards. It's cheaper, but less convenient, to call from the post office. Lots of places on the Khao San Road offer very competitive rates.

**◨ Internet, email, fax and call-backs**: Internet Zone, 55 Rambutri Road, in the vicinity of Khao San Road. ☎ 629-41-38. Fax: 629-11-36.

## LEISURE

■ **The Bookseller** – เดอะบุ๊ค เซลเลอร์: 8111 Patpong Road. ☎ 233-17-17. English newspapers and magazines on sale in a major Bangkok hotspot. Open daily until midnight.

■ **D.K. Book Duang Kamol** – ร้านหนังสือดี.เค.ดวงกมล: opposite the Siam Centre, Soi 2, Rama I. ☎ 251-14-67. Books and periodicals in English.

## AIRLINES

■ **British Airways** – 14th Floor, Unit 1402, Abdulrahin Place, 990 Rama IX Road. ☎ 535-22-20. Reservations and fares: ☎ 636-17-83.

■ **Air France** – สายการบินแอร์ ฟรานซ์: Vorawat Building (20th Floor), 849 Silom Road – ถนนสีลม. ☎ 635-11-99. Fax: 635-11-86.

■ **Thai Airways International** – สายการบินไทย: 6 Lanluang Road – ถนนหลานหลวง. Reservations: ☎ 280-01-00. Head Office: 89 Vibhavadi-Rangsit Road. ☎ 513-01-21.

■ **Garuda Airways** – สายการ บินการูด้า: 1168 Rama IV Road – ถนนพระราม4. Lumphini Tower, 27th floor. ☎ 285-64-70.

■ **Philippine Airlines** – สายการ บินฟิลิปปินส์: Chang Kolnee Building, 56 Surawong Road – ถนนสุรวงศ์. ☎ 233-23-50–52.

■ **Bangkok Airways** – สายการ บินบางกอกแอร์เวย์: 140 Pacific Place Building, Sukhumvit Road. ☎ 229-34-34. Three flights a week to Sukhothai and Chiang Mai. Daily connections with Hua Hin, Koh Samui and Phuket.

■ **Air India** – สายการบินอินเดีย: SS Travel Service, SS Building, 10/12–13 Convent Road. ☎ 235-05-57.

## DOCTORS AND HOSPITALS

■ **Dr Philippe Balankura** – หมอฟิลิป: 1 Nares Road – ถนนนเรศ. ☎ 236-14-89 (surgery) or 236-13-89 (home). Speaks English and can see you by appointment. Good but expensive. Also practices at the Nursing Home Hospital (*see below*).

■ **Bangkok Nursing Home Hospital** – โรงพยาบาลบางกอกเนิส ซิ่งโฮม: 9 Convent Road – ถนนคอนแวนต์, Silom. Located in a road at right angles to Silom Road. ☎ 233-26-10. Very good hospital and the staff speak English.

■ **St Louis Hospital** – โรงพยาบาล เซนต์หลุยส์: 215 Sathorn Tai Road – ถนนสาธรใต้, almost opposite the Russian Embassy. ☎ 212-00-33. Good, but very expensive.

## EXCHANGE FACILITIES

There's virtually no black market in Bangkok and you can change money easily at any one of the many banks (generally open 8.30am–3.30pm, Monday to Friday). You'll also find loads of money-changing kiosks in the tourist areas (at least 10 on Khao San Road alone) that stay open until 8 or 10pm. More and more banks let you to draw out money with a Visa card. Passports must be produced at all branches of the Thai Farmers Bank – ธนาคารกสิกรไทย. Thai Farmers Bank kiosks stay open late and many 24-hour cash machines take Visa. Speedy and efficient.

■ **Foreign exchange offices**: you'll find these at the station and in the airport. There are also lots of kiosks on Sukhumvit and Khao San roads. As a last resort, you can change money in the major hotels but the rates are extremely poor.

■ **American Express**: SP Building, 338 Phahon Yothin Road. Ground floor. For lost or stolen traveller's cheques ☎ 273-00-33/44.

■ **Visa** and **MasterCard**: Thai Farmers Bank, Head Office Building, Phahon Yothin. ☎ 270-18-10. For lost or stolen Visa cards ☎ 251-63-33.

## TRAVEL AGENCIES

■ **Siam Exclusive Tours** – สยามเอ็กคลูซีฟทัวร์: 99 Wireless Road – ถนนวิทยุ, Bangkok 10330. 7th floor, Building One. ☎ 256-61-53. Fax: 256-66-65. Asia correspondent in Thailand. Tickets for Myanmar (formerly Burma), Malaysia, Hong Kong. Good quality service at reasonable rates.

■ **Compagnie générale du Siam** – กัมปาญยีเจเนรัลดูสยาม: 645/42– 43 Petchaburi Road – ถนนเพชรบุรี, Bangkok 10400. ☎ 251-02-25 or 252-02-99. Fax: 255-42-22. Unlike the previous agency, only deals in group travel. Organizes personalized, quality packages for groups of four to eight people. Tours leave from Bangkok or Chiang Mai and are accompanied by an English-speaking guide. The Mae Hong Son tour is particularly interesting and includes a river trip in a dugout to Thailand's border with Myanmar. Up-market service that's well worth the price.

■ **J.-P. Travel** – เจ.พี.ทราเวล: 6 Sukhumvit Road – ถนนสุขุมวิท, Soi 4, Bangkok 10110. ☎ and fax: 255-22-33 or 252-96-44. Correspondent for various European agencies (Thailand, Myanmar, Laos, Vietnam). Specializes in difficult trips off the beaten track. Up-market tours at reasonable prices.

■ There's a **Student Travel Agency** in the Royal Hotel.

## GETTING AROUND

When it comes to public transport, Bangkok is a model of Thai efficiency. You will soon realize that the place is immense and it's virtually impossible to go anywhere on foot. But whether you use the taxis, the *tuk-tuks,* the motor-taxis or the bus, make sure you have a copy of the *Latest Tour Guide to Bangkok and Thailand.* This gives details of bus routes and allows you to tell the taxi or *tuk-tuk* driver exactly where you want to go (again and again if necessary).

– ***Tuk-tuks*** (motorized *samlors*): very popular in Bangkok, a *tuk-tuk* is a kind of three-wheeled scooter with a back seat; fiendish contraptions piloted by young bloods whose death-defying skills, however expert, make for a truly buttock-clenching, hair-raising experience. *Tuk-tuks* go anywhere, anytime. The price is negotiable but they are generally not much cheaper than a taxi. Beware of tuk-tuk drivers who quote you an extortionate price for a ready-made tour of the shops (this is where they get commission). Look them in the eye and drop the asking price by at least 30 per cent. Show them where you want to go on the map and get them to repeat the name of the road in Thai (they rarely understand English). One in three *tuk-tuk* drivers will happily drop you anywhere and tell you you've arrived – always with a smile, of course. Notice how lovingly the drivers decorate their machines.

– **Motor-taxis**: great for nipping in and out of the jams (truly horrendous in Bangkok at rush hour) and often cheaper than taxis. You can recognize the drivers from the number they wear. They are probably not for the faint-hearted – wearing a helmet is compulsory but you'd be better off in a suit of armour. Before climbing on, check your insurance.

– **Buses**: usually run until 10pm on a terrific network of routes, long and short distance, all for next to nothing. Lots of tourists panic at the idea of taking the bus but there's really no need. Just watch out for the speciality round here: cutting off your bag with a razor. There are two kinds of bus: with and without air-conditioning. Any map giving the bus routes can show you which bus goes where, but in most cases check with the driver too. If you're staying in Bangkok for 2 or 3 weeks, it's worth taking the bus. If you're only there for a couple of nights, forget it – you waste too much time. Air-conditioned buses are slightly less crowded in the rush-hour than the others but they're more expensive too.

– **Taxis**: there are two kinds of taxi: the **taxi-meter** (definitely favourite) and the **taxi**. Taxi-meters really do have meters and – surprise, surprise – they actually work. No more endless haggling with the driver. If he refuses to go along with it, don't give way – unless of course, you are intimately au fait with the prices and prepared to negotiate the fare. If the fare on the meter seems high when you set off, relax – it rises slowly. Try not to go anywhere in the rush-hour. It can take over an hour to go a short distance at best. Once you have a better grasp of the prices, then you can start to haggle with the other taxi drivers. Bear in mind though, that taxi drivers in Bangkok lead a really terrible life. Some of them even keep a little leakproof bag handy for use in an emergency (car drivers – men and women alike – do the same).

– **Boats**: a very useful, jam-proof way of getting to certain parts of town and there are various alternatives:

• **Chao Phraya River Express**: big, numbered launches that zigzag up and down the Chao Phraya river, stopping on both sides. Fast, convenient and inexpensive, they run every day from 6am to 6pm and are packed in the rush-hour. Details of all stops are shown on the *Latest Tour Guide to Bangkok and Thailand* map. The name of each stop begins with 'Tha' (Tha Oriental, Tha Chang, etc.). Many of them are close to sites such as Wat Arun and the Grand Palace. Tell the conductor where you want to go since boats don't necessarily call at every stop.

• **Ferries**: much the same as the launches but they only take you across the river. Buy your ticket in advance (for a nominal sum) from the ticket office. Don't be conned into crossing in a private boat instead of the official ferry, as you'll pay a lot more. Boats call at the same stops as the river express taxis or just beside. They go back and forth all the time.

• **Long-tail boats** ('long-tails'): so-called because of the extremely long shaft that links the engine to the propeller. These are private taxis with enormous engines; they're difficult to handle but admirably steered by their pilots. Ideal for exploring the network of *khlongs* (little canals) that criss-cross Thonburi.

Don't be taken in by the guys with the impressive photo albums who offer to show you round the *khlongs* (*see* 'What to See'). Deal direct with the boats and don't go through the touts.

## WHERE TO STAY

**A useful tip**: very few *tuk-tuk* drivers are familiar with our alphabet. So before setting foot outside the hotel for the first time, ask for a visiting card with the address written in Thai. Likewise, it's a good idea to have two maps: one for you and one to show the driver where you want to go. Bangkok has done backpackers one small favour – most of the hotels of any interest to you are concentrated in three precise areas: Khao San Road, Soi Ngam Duphli and Sukhumvit Road.

### KHAO SAN ROAD – ถนนข้าวสาร; Banglampoo area – ย่านบางลำพู
(colour map III)

Get off the bus at Democracy Monument – อนุสาวรีย์ประชาธิปไตย (an immense square with a huge and hugely ugly monument in the middle). From here it's a 5 to 10-minute walk to an area that's surprisingly quiet for Bangkok, although the road does get noisier at night when the guesthouses try to drown out each other's sound systems. For years this little road has been a meeting place for all the backpackers who come to Thailand and some of them, it seems, never left. It's a bit of a tourist ghetto but very seductive, with a pleasant atmosphere, lots of local colour and loads of little restaurants. It's also very close to the river and all the main temples. Exasperatingly cool for some but a welcoming refuge all the same in this otherwise tough 'City of the Angels'. You'll find dozens of guesthouses old and new in the street itself and the area around it. Most are cheap (although not as cheap as they were) so don't expect the Ritz. In fact, the best you can hope for in some places is a windowless mousehole built of four sheets of plywood – minus the piece of cheese.

Khao San Road is a good place to stay because there always seems to be room. It's also chock full of travel agencies (reputedly the cheapest in the world) selling everything under the sun: a bus ticket to the southern islands or a world trip with an easy airport transfer. They are not bad as a rule, and are actually very good for inland travel, but ticketing rip-offs have been known, plus overbooking, cancellations and worse. To avoid disappointment, only buy your tickets from agencies that have been in business for several years. Make a few local enquiries and steer well clear of any agencies that aren't well established. The same goes for the small telephone 'centres' from where you can call home, the money-changers and the people selling pirate videos, fake souvenirs, imitation designer T-shirts and lots of other things as well. There is a lively street market at night, which is the reason why everyone comes here.

### BUDGET (100–150 BTS PER PERSON PER NIGHT)

⌂ **Ranee Guesthouse** – ราณีเกสท์เฮาส์ (colour map III, A2, **2**): 77 Trokmayom – ตรอกมะยม. ☎ 282-40-72. Situated in a road at right angles to Khao San Road along with several other guesthouses. A favourite, though the whole area is going downhill. None of the 15 or so small but pleasant bedrooms have en-suite bathrooms or air-conditioning, but they are all cheap. There's a warm welcome, a convivial setting, a lovely shady garden with a cool fountain, and the restaurant serves honest, unpretentious food. Vegetarian food is a speciality.

⚓ **V.S. Guesthouse** – วิ.เอส.เกสท์เฮาส์ (colour map III, A1–B1, **4**): on Khao San Road. Coming from Thanon Tanao, this elegant Chinese wooden house is in the first side street on the right. Tiny bedrooms with fans. Showers on the landing. The place could do with a bit more TLC, but it's particularly worth a visit if you're travelling alone and in search of a cheap place to sleep.

⚓ **Merry V Guesthouse** – เมอรรี่.วิ.เกสท์เฮาส์ (colour map III, A1, **5**): 33–35 Soi Chana Song Khram – ซอยชนะสงคราม, at right angles to Phra Athit Road. ☎ 282-92-67. Once one of the best addresses in our cheap Khao San Road section, this has now come down in the world. Still a favourite with backpackers but definitely looking the worse for wear. Cleaning is only done if guests specifically ask for it. A few coats of paint instead of that dreary wallpaper would work wonders. In short, nothing to write home about but worth a visit if you're broke. Ask for a room on the street side (it's quieter). Some of the rooms have little balconies.

⚓ **Bonny Guesthouse** – บอนนี่เกสท์เฮาส์ (colour map III, A2, **6**): 132 Khao San Road. ☎ 281-98-77. Situated in the alleyway between Khao San Road and Trokmayom Road. Ideal if you're travelling alone and want to meet people as there are few rooms and you practically sleep with your neighbours as none of the partition walls reach the ceiling. There is also a tiny garden where you can have breakfast. Very cosy but pretty basic despite the mosquitonets. Ask to see the room beforehand.

⚓ **Dior Guesthouse** – ดิออร์เกสท์เฮาส์ (colour map III, A2, **7**): 146 Khao San Road. ☎ 282-91-42. Absolutely no relation to the famous fashion designer. The foam mattresses are a bit thin but otherwise OK. Small rooms with fans; shower on each floor. The welcome varies.

⚓ **Joe Guesthouse** – โจเกสท์เฮาส์ (colour map III, A1–2, **10**): Trokmayom – ตรอกมะยม, Chakrapongse Road – ถนนจักรพงษ์. ☎ 281-29-49. Small, teak-and-bamboo guesthouse, tucked away in a very quiet location. Pleasant courtyard has tables and chairs. Accommodation is basic, all wood, but it has decent mattresses and reasonable bathrooms. A bit more expensive than the others but much nicer, it's often full and you can see why. Three prices depending on the size of the room – but none of them are large. If you haven't booked, your best bet is to come early in the morning. A sign on the wall says that, if you just happen to be with a young Thai girl, you won't be allowed to take her to bed with you.

## MODERATE TO EXPENSIVE (200–500 BTS PER PERSON PER NIGHT)

⚓ **Prasuri Guesthouse** – พระสุริย์เกสท์เฮาส์ colour map III, B2, **8**): 85/1 Soi Prasuri. ☎ 280-14-28. Take the No. 59 bus from the airport and get off at Democracy Monument. The guesthouse is a short walk away down Dinsor Road and then first on the right into Soi Prasuri. A little way outside the Khao San Road area and far from the crowds of tourists – so it's pretty quiet. The place gets better every year: pleasant staff, efficient service, clean and relatively spacious rooms with shower, and some with WC and air-conditioning. The more comfortable rooms are double the price and it's best to book in advance. You can make long-distance calls from here, book bus tickets and take advantage of other useful services (left-luggage for example). Good restaurant on the ground floor.

🛌 **Marco Polo Hostel** – มาร์โคโปโลโฮสเทล colour map III, A1, **3**): 108/7–10 Khao San Road. ☎ 281-17-15 or 282-09-39. Situated in a passage between Khao San Road and Rambutri Road. Pretty basic (to say the least) and the windowless rooms are tiny (5.5 square metres/60 square feet) – definitely not for the claustrophobic but undoubtedly the cheapest air-conditioned rooms in the whole area. Very large and lively restaurant on the ground floor serves breakfast. It's not to be confused with the nearby Marco Polo Guesthouse in Trokmayom Road, which has similar prices but is older and not nearly as well kept.

🛌 **New Siam** – นิวสยามเกสท์เฮาส์ (colour map III, A1, **9**): 21 Soi Chana Song Khram – ซอยชนะสงคราม. Small three-storey building in a *soi* at right angles to Phra Athit Road. ☎ 282-45-54. Fax: 281-74-61. The rooms with shower (upstairs) are very pleasant and absolutely spotless. Those with hot water, bathroom facilities and air-conditioning are more expensive, but good value for money on the whole, particularly since there are three standards of comfort on offer. Run by a nice family who like to watch TV but don't get much chance to these days – which is a good sign. One of our own personal favourites and very popular with other readers. Useful to note that even non-residents can use the left-luggage facilities.

🛌 **New Joe Guesthouse** – นิวโจเกสท์เฮาส์ (colour map III, A2, **11**): Trokmayom, Chakrapongse Road. ☎ 281-29-48. Fax: 281-55-47. Near Joe Guesthouse

and on the same side of the street, this small and practically new hotel is deteriorating fast. It seems they pack 'em in but forget about the cleaning. Pretty garden full of flowers and an attractive facade with three-coloured shutters, which are not a common sight round here. Good breakfast. Laundry facilities. The welcome may be non-committal but the service is professional. Still it's pretty good on the whole but a bit pricey.

🛌 **Sawasdee House** – สวัสดีเฮาส์ (colour map III, A1, **13**): 147 Soi Rambutri – ซอยรามบุตรี, Chakrapongse Road. ☎ 281-81-38. This elegant teak house, in a road parallel to Khao San Road, has a terrace overlooking the street. The rooms vary in comfort according to price, which is reasonable overall. Rooms on the street side without bathroom facilities but with balcony are quieter than those at the back of the house, which overlooks a school. None of the rooms has air-conditioning.

🛌 **Orchid House** – ออร์คิดเฮาส์ (colour map III, A1, **14**): 323/2–3 Rambutri Road. ☎ 280-26-91. This pleasant little place is only 2 minutes away from Khao San Road. The smallish rooms are clean and quiet and all have fans or air-conditioning plus bathroom facilities. Small restaurant on the ground floor.

🛌 **Sawasdee Bangkok Inn** – สวัสดีบางกอกอินน์ colour map III, A2, **12**): 126/2 Khao San Road. ☎ 280-12-51. This hotel with a rough-cast pink facade in a side-street off Khao San Road, is part of a hotel group that operates mainly in Pattaya and the south. This one has 100 smallish but clean rooms offering varying degrees of comfort (with or without shower, air-conditioning and so on). It also has a cheap dormitory and there is a traditional massage service on the ground floor.

## SPLASH OUT (1,000–1,700 BTS PER PERSON PER NIGHT)

⌂ **Royal Hotel** – รอยัลโฮเต็ล colour map III, A2, **16**): 2 Ratchadamnoen Klang – ถนนราชดำเนินกลาง. ☎ 222-91-11. Fax: 224-20-83. This well-situated hotel, just 200 metres west of Democracy Monument and near the Wat Phra Kaeo, the Wat Pho and the National Museum, has a charming 1950s facade. Apparently, this was a student rallying point during the May 1992 demonstrations and the scene of the army massacres. Comfortable spacious rooms, some of them recently refurbished. Generous breakfast and buffet. Prices are not by any means cheap, but students can get a 10 per cent reduction on presentation of an International Student Identity Card (ISIC).

## THE THEWET AREA – ย่านเทเวศร์ (colour map I, B1)

This is a quiet area north of the noisy Khao San Road and minutes away from the river and the National Library. Rooms here are cheaper than anywhere else in Bangkok and you can be sure of a warm welcome. You can get here by boat on the Chao Phraya River Express (Tha Thewet stop) or by bus. The No. 53 bus comes here from around Hua Lamphong station (get off at the crossroads with Thanon Samsen Road and Krung Kasem Road); and the No. 10 (air-conditioned) bus comes here from the airport area (get off at the crossroads with Thanon Samsen Road and Ratchawithi Road, north of the library). The Thewet flower market (colour map I, B1, **107**) is moments away and well worth seeing first thing in the morning.

## BUDGET (60–150 BTS PER PERSON PER NIGHT)

⌂ **Back-Packers Lodge** – บ้านพักแบบแพคเกอร์ (colour map I, B1, **44**): 85 Sri Ayutthaya Road, Soi 14. ☎ 282-32-31. The friendliest of all the guesthouses with a terrific welcome.

⌂ **Tavee Guesthouse** – ทวีเกสท์เฮาส์ (colour map I, B1, **44**): 85 Sri Ayutthaya Road, Soi 14. ☎ 280-14-47. Smarter than the Back-Packers Lodge.

⌂ **Sawatdee Guesthouse** – สวัสดีเกสท์เฮาส์ (colour map I, B1, **44**): 71 Sri Ayutthaya Road, Soi 16. ☎ 281-07-57. Right opposite the Shanti Lodge, this is not up to the same standard as the others but it's really cheap.

⌂ **Little-Home Guesthouse** – ลิตเติ้ลโฮมเกสท์เฮาส์ (colour map I, B1, **44**): 23/12 Sri Ayutthaya Road. ☎ 282-15-74. Another very friendly place with very reasonable prices.

## BUDGET TO MODERATE (100–300 BTS PER PERSON PER NIGHT)

⌂ **Bangkok International Youth Hostel** – บ้านพักเยาวชนกรุงเทพฯ (off B1, colour map III, **1**): 25/2 Phitsanulok Road – ถนนพิษณุโลก. ☎ 282-09-50. Fax: 281-68-34. The No. 9, 12 or 19 bus from Democracy Monument takes you practically to the door. You can't miss the building thanks to all the little flags pinned to the front – what you'd expect of a place that caters for young guests from all over the world.There are decent dormitories (eight beds) at reasonable prices; double rooms also very comfortable but cost more. Note that you will have to produce a YHA membership card (you can buy one here, if necessary). There's a friendly, cheap cafeteria on the ground floor. Fairly non-committal welcome.

**Rooms to rent** in one of five virtually adjoining houses owned by some really nice families. What they offer is much the same: clean, quiet rooms with shared WC and shower, as well as dormitories. You can also eat here (this is your chance to go shopping with the cook) and get your washing done too. Additionally, tours organized through local travel agencies leave here every day for the major tourist sites. All the advantages of the Khao San Road in the heart of an authentically working-class area.

**Shanti Lodge** – บ้านพักสันติ (colour map I, B1, **44**): 37 Sri Ayutthaya Road – ถนนศรีอยุธยา, Soi 16. ☎ 281-24-97. This teak house is beautifully decorated in traditional northern style. Each of the 17 rooms has a unique look and atmosphere (try to visit several) and some have air-conditioning. There is also a dormitory on the ground floor. With so many green plants everywhere (including the shower) the house is like an oasis in the middle of Bangkok. Highly recommended, its best to book in advance as people are beating down the door to get in.

## THE SOI NGAM DUPHLI AREA – ย่านซอยงามดูพลี (colour map I, D4)

Before they moved to the Khao San Road, this was where most backpackers used to stay. Situated in a side street off Rama IV Road, it's still quieter and friendlier, and most of the tourists you meet have been here for a very long time. There are several good places to stay, at prices ranging from cheap to average. The atmosphere is friendly, but some places are looking a bit the worse for wear. Definitely a good place to crash if you want to avoid the crowds, and it's well served by buses: Nos. 4, 13, 17, 22, 27, 45, 47, 74, 106 and 116.



### BUDGET TO MODERATE (100–300 BTS PER PERSON PER NIGHT)

Small hard bed cheap try moon House down street

**Salathai** – ศาลาไทยเกสท์เฮาส์ off D4, colour map 1, **21**): 15 Soi Sribumphen – ซอยศรีบำเพ็ญ, Rama IV Road – ถนนพระราม4. ☎ 287-14-36. One of the best hotels and certainly one of the most reliable in terms of quality. It's situated in the *soi* at the end of a cul-de-sac shaped like an elbow. The staff are all new but it's the same owner and she's just as sensitive to the needs of her guests. All the rooms have that personal touch – some of them even have rattan furniture. Others are being refurbished. Clean bathroom facilities and a terrace with a good view (rare in Bangkok) on the second floor. Very good value for money.

**Freddy's Guesthouse** – เฟรดดี้ส์เกสท์เฮาส์ (off D4, colour map 1, **20**): 27/40 Soi Sribumphen. ☎ 286-78-26. Fax: 213-20-97. Coming from Soi Ngam Duphli, the house is practically at the end of the street on the left. Not much to look at from the outside but all the rooms are decent and quiet. Nice shady patio where you can eat. Good value for money.

**Lee 3 Guesthouse** – ลี3เกสท์เฮาส์ (off D4, colour map 1, **22**): 13 Soi Sapankoo. ☎ 679-70-45. Next door to the Salathai, this is much nicer than the very unmemorable Lee 1, 2 and 4 in the same area but not as nice as

Room is a simple box with a hard bed and thin walls, in Bangkok however, its a other places listed here. Decent accommodation and bathrooms and is a useful fall-back if the Salathai is full.

⚑ **T.T.O. Guesthouse** – ที.ที.โอ.เกสท์เฮาส์ (colour map I, D4, **23**): 2/48 Soi Sribumphen. ☎ 286-67-83. Coming from Soi Ngam Duphli, the house is in a small cul-de-sac off to the right and is easily identifiable from its sky-blue facade. Rooms have fans or air-conditioning, shower and WC – all absolutely spotless. Charming, very attentive landlady. More expensive than the houses listed above but still one of the best guesthouses around. Note that they don't serve breakfast.

EXPENSIVE: (600–800 BTS PER PERSON PER NIGHT)

⚑ **Malaysia Hotel** – โรงแรมมาเลเซีย (colour map I, D4, **24**): 54 Soi Ngam Duphli – ซอยงามดูพล. ☎ 286-35-82 or 286-72-63. Fax: 287-14-57. One of the last great backpackers' hotels (it's been going for nearly 80 years now) and a former favourite with the police, not as a place to stay but as a place to raid. Recently refurbished to semi-deluxe standard, it now attracts more tourists with matching luggage than backpacks. Don't be misled by the grand entrance hall: the bedrooms are lacking in charm and some of them could do with a coat of paint. But the service remains excellent, the rooms spotless, the bathroom facilities less so and the (small) swimming pool is

alright. Of the three types of bedrooms, the 'standard' is perfectly adequate. There's a large restaurant on the ground floor.

⚑ **King's Mansion** – คิงส์แมนชั่น (colour map I, D4, **25**): 31 South Sathorn Road – ถนนสาธรใต. ☎ 286-09-40. Fax: 213-14-90. At the end of the avenue, near the intersection with Rama IV Road, this offers spacious, air-conditioned rooms with shower and TV. Well kept but not the sort of place you'd want to stay for any length of time. It's cheaper than the Malaysia Hotel.

⚑ **YWCA** – วาย.ดับเบิ้ลยู.ซี.เอ. (colour map I, D4, **26**): 13 Sathorn Tai Road. ☎ 286-19-36. Fax: 287-30-16. Not what you'd expect of a youth hostel – it's more like a classy hotel. It's quiet, since it doesn't directly face the road, and it attracts lots of young Thai guests as well as tourists. Quite expensive but the price includes breakfast. Single or double rooms have shower and WC, functional furniture and are spotlessly clean, with sheets as white as the driven snow. Male and female guests are welcome and you don't need a YHA card. You even get a copy of the New Testament in English and Thai on the bedside table to help while away those long monsoon evenings.

Prices in the nearby **YMCA** are prohibitive. The restaurant on the other hand, is much more affordable (*see* 'Where to Eat').

**THE AREA AROUND SUKHUMVIT ROAD AND SIAM SQUARE** – ย่านสุขุมวิทและสยามสแควร์ (colour map II)

Sukhumvit Road is the continuation of Rama I Road and a main thoroughfare to the east of Bangkok. It too is packed with hotels that are mainly reserved for the smarter sort of clientele who come here on package holidays – particularly around *sois* 4, 8 and 11.

*sanctuary where you are delighted to return at the end of the day – people were doing it.*

## MODERATE TO EXPENSIVE (400–1,000 BTS PER PERSON PER NIGHT)

⌂ **Dynasty Inn** – ไดนาสตี้อินน์ (colour map II, A3, **27**): 5/4–5 Sukhumvit Road, Soi 4. ☎ 252-45-22. Fax: 255-41-11. This good local hotel in front of the Nana Hotel has everything you'd expect of a grand hotel: large foyer, clocks showing the time in other capital cities, beauty parlour, coffee-shop. The same unostentatious luxury is to be found in the bedrooms, which are all pleasant and well decorated, with air-conditioning, shower/WC and TV.

⌂ **President Inn** – เพรสซิเดนท์อินน์ (colour map II, A3, **45**): 155/14 Sukhumvit Road, Soi 11. ☎ 255-42-30. This hotel comes out tops among the many verging-on-the-up-market hotels in this *soi* (Narry's Inn and Business Inn for example). Very comfortable, fairly charmless rooms (but not unpleasantly so) with or without air-conditioning, and prices vary accordingly. It has modern 1970s-style decor and is ultra-clean and fairly quiet.

⌂ **Stable Lodge** – สเตเบิลลอดจ์ (colour map II, A3, **28**): 39 Sukhumvit, Soi 8. ☎ 253-34-10. Fax: 253-51-25. A semi-luxury hotel with garden and swimming pool. Stylish, luxuriously comfortable rooms with loggia. The more expensive ones have a view over the pool.

⌂ **Nana City Inn** – นานาซิตี้อินน์ (colour map II, A3, **29**): 23/164 Nana City Sukhumvit, Soi 4. ☎ 253-44-68/69. Fax: 255-24-49. Modern and not very big, so more personal than its namesake. Very reasonably priced considering the degree of comfort and the fact that breakfast is included. Small-ish rooms. Discreet, friendly welcome.

⌂ **Reno Hotel** – เรโนโฮเต็ล (colour map I, C2-3, **30**): 40 Soi Kasem-san I – ซอยเกษมสันต์1, Rama I Road – ถนนพระราม1. ☎ 215-00-26/7. Luxury hotel in a small *soi* at right angles to Rama I Road, west of Siam Square and close to Jim Thompson's House. Seventy rooms with air-conditioning, at two-star prices. Not high on charm, but very quiet in this otherwise noisy area. Swimming pool.

⌂ **The Bed & Breakfast** – เดอะเบดแอนด์เบรคฟัสท์เกสท์เฮาส์ (colour map I, C2, **31**): 36/42–43 Soi Kasemsan I. ☎ 215-30-04. This clean, entirely white-tiled guesthouse next to the Reno Hotel has small bedrooms with shower (with or without hot water) and air-conditioning. Minimalist but not objectionable decor. Price includes breakfast.

⌂ **White Lodge** – ไวท์ลอดจ์เกสท์เฮาส์ (colour map I, C2, **32**): 36/8 Soi Kasemsan I, Rama I Road. ☎ 216-88-67. Fax: 216-82-28. Rooms with shower, basin and hot water are decent; you can breakfast in Sorn's Café next door and there's a quiet terrace, making this a nice place to stay.

⌂ **Uncle Rey's Guesthouse** – อังเคิลเรย์เกสท์เฮาส์ (colour map II, A3, **33**): 7/10 Sukhumvit Road, Soi 4. ☎ 252-55-65. Fax: 253-83-07. Friendly little guesthouse at the end of the small Nana Tai Soi, on the left. Don't be put off by the reception area – the rooms are not at all bad and they're clean. Not quite guesthouse prices but reasonable for the area. All the rooms have phone, air-conditioning and spotless bathroom facilities.

⌂ **Nana Guesthouse** – นานาเกสท์เฮาส์ (colour map II, A3, **40**): 4 Sukhumvit Road, Soi 4. ☎ 251-02-91. Coming from Sukhumvit Road, this fairly so-so place is in a cul-de-sac on the left. The welcome is indifferent and some of the rooms are a bit noisy. A useful fall-back all the same, particularly since it's the cheapest place around here.

☗ **Sukhumvit Crown Hotel** – สุขุมวิทคราวน์โฮเต็ล (colour map II, A3, **34**): 7 Sukhumvit Road, Soi 8. ☎ 253-56-72. Fax: 253-56-75. The Crown is a very quiet hotel with old-fashioned rooms, all with air-conditioning and bath. Just so you know: there's a large diamond-shaped mirror hanging over every bed.

## THE AREA AROUND SILOM ROAD AND AS FAR AS HUA LAMPHONG STATION – ย่านถนนสีลมถึงหัวลำโพง (colour map I)

Silom Road is a long avenue running from Charoen Krung Road to the junction with Rama IV Road in front of Lumphini Park, to the south of Bangkok. The hotels of most interest are at the beginning of the avenue, near the Chao Phraya river, in and around the luxury hotels as far as the station, and the rather noisy district on the border with Chinatown. Hotels round there are pretty seedy and are only useful if you're arriving late at night by train or leaving first thing in the morning.

### BUDGET TO MODERATE (100–250 BTS PER PERSON PER NIGHT)

☗ **Sri Hualampong Hotel** – ศรีหัวลำโพงโฮเต็ล (colour map I, C3, **35**): 445 Rong Muang Road – ถนนรองเมือง. ☎ 214-26-10. You'll find this Chinese hotel beside the station, on the left as you exit. Hospitality and hygiene are not its strong points but this is the best of a bad bunch. Strictly a last resort.

☗ **T.T.2 Guesthouse** – ที.ที.2เกสท์ เฮาส์ (colour map I, C3–4, **36**): 516–518 Soi Sawang – ซอยสว่าง, Si Praya Road – ถนนสี่พระยา. ☎ 236-29-46. Fax: 236-30-54. As you come out of the station, take the big Maha Phrutharam Road facing you, then turn left into Soi Kaew Fa as far as the junction with Maha Nakhon Road. The guesthouse is in the little *soi* in front of you. You can't miss it. Take a *tuk-tuk* if you're weighed down with luggage. The house is very friendly, spotless and one of the cheapest places in Bangkok. Single rooms with or without a window are all the same price, so ask to see them first. Cheap dormitory. Laundry facilities available.

### EXPENSIVE TO SPLASH OUT (1,000–1,800 BTS PER PERSON PER NIGHT)

☗ **New Trocadero Hotel** – โรงแรมนิวโทรคาเดโร (colour map I, C4, **39**): 343 Surawong Road. ☎ 234-89-20. A semi-luxury hotel near the river, not far from the corner with Charoen Krung Road. Elegant lobby; pity the rooms are a bit sad, but the cheapest ones are very decent. It's well located and has all mod cons (en suite, TV, etc.). Ask for a room upstairs with a view. Decent-sized swimming pool but surrounded by rather dreary buildings.

### SPLASH OUT (2,600–3,800 BTS PER PERSON PER NIGHT)

☗ **Sri Krung Hotel** – ศรีกรุงโฮเต็ล (colour map I, C3, **38**): 1860 Krung Kasem Road – ถนนกรุงเกษม. ☎ 225-01-32. Fax: 225-47-05. On the right as you leave the station, across the canal. A clean, modern hotel with spacious, air-conditioned rooms with showers. Ask for a room at the back where it's quieter. Note that the hotel is also used by prostitutes. Transfer bus to and from the airport.

🛏 **Tarntawan Place Hotel** – ทาน คะวันเพลสโฮเด็ล (colour map I, C4, **46**): 119/5 Surawong Road – ถนนสุรวงศ์. ☎ 238-26-20. A modern hotel with a warm welcome, just 2 minutes from Patpong Road but shielded from the turmoil of activity there. Bedrooms with all mod cons at negotiable prices (depending on the time of year, the length of stay, your smile, the level of occupancy, and how they feel on the day). No particular charm but you can be sure of quality service plus dozens of added benefits.

## THE CHINESE AND INDIAN QUARTER – ย่านจีนและอินเดีย
(colour map I)

### BUDGET (50–200 BTS PER PERSON PER NIGHT)

🛏 You'll find masses of Indian, Nepalese and Pakistani-run guesthouses, mainly for businessmen from the peninsula, along the Chakraphet Road – ถนนจักรพรรดิ์ – and in the side-streets running parallel to it, up to the junction with Soi Wanit 1 (Sampeng Lane) – ซอยสำเพ็ง. This area is a complete change of scenery – almost like being in Bombay. The accommodation here is generally not up to European standards, and most of the guesthouses are dingy, though some have air-conditioned bedrooms.

### MODERATE TO EXPENSIVE (300–700 BTS PER PERSON PER NIGHT)

🛏 **Chao Phraya Riverside Guest-house** – เจ้าพระยาริเวอร์ไซด์เกสเฮาส์ (colour map I, B3, **41**): 1128 Songwat Road – ถนนทรงวาด. ☎ 222-63-44. Fax: 223-16-96. This small hotel on the banks of the Chao Phraya river, nearly opposite the Chinese School (the only one in Bangkok) is situated in the continuation of Soi Itsaranuphap. It has a few clean, comfortable rooms with fans, but none facing the river. There's a terrific view from the terrace restaurant, particularly at night when the city lights mingle with the rays of the setting sun. Minutes from the Tha Ratchawong jetty, which is very handy if you're travelling.

🛏 **New Empire Hotel** – นิวเอ็ม ไพร์โฮเด็ล (colour map I, B3, **42**): 572 Yaowarat Road – ถนนเยาวราช. ☎ 234-69-90. Fax: 237-69-97. A classical hotel near Wat Traimitr, the Empire is beautifully maintained if a trifle old-fashioned. Some of the rooms are really nice all the same. Ask for one on the upper floors to get a view of the city lights.

🛏 **River View Guesthouse** – ริเวอร์วิวเกสท์เฮาส์ (colour map I, B3, **37**): 768 Soi Panurangsi – ซอยภาณุรังษี, Songwat Road. ☎ 234-54-29. Fax: 237-54-28. One of the very few (not to say only) guesthouses with a view of the river, which is a rare privilege indeed and one you pay for – sometimes through the nose. It's a large, modern complex with no special charm, but the rooms are spacious and well decorated and the welcome friendly. It's the sort of place you'll willingly stay a few days but book in advance because it gets full very quickly. Getting here takes you through some picturesque side-streets full of scrap-merchants and coach-builders.

### EXPENSIVE TO SPLASH OUT (800–1,900 BTS PER PERSON PER NIGHT)

🛏 **The China Town Hotel** – เดอะไชน่าทาวน์โฮเด็ล (colour map

I, B3, **43**): 526 Yaowarat Road. ☎ 225-02-03. Fax: 226-12-95. This is as classical as the New Empire but distinctly smarter and located in a prime position in the heart of Chinatown.

## WHERE TO EAT

Bangkok has all kinds of places to eat, from mobile kitchens that set up shop as the sun goes down, to gourmet and sometimes highly original restaurants. You can eat cheaply just about anywhere, particularly since the economic crisis when many of those who lost their jobs turned to cooking instead. So there's no need to drag yourself across town to find a good Chinese restaurant – you can usually find one right where you are.

Restaurants in general are excellent and highly recommended. But although a few suggestions are given for cheap restaurants in the livelier parts of town, it's impossible to give specific names in the budget category. Just eat where the Thais eat.

Most of the following suggestions are original restaurants serving interesting specialities (to say nothing of the street kiosks that sell fried bamboo worms) but in any case, you are never more than 100 metres from somewhere to eat in Bangkok, any time of day or night.

### ON KHAO SAN ROAD – ถนนข้าวสาร (colour map III)

There's no shortage of restaurants around here: there's one on the ground floor of every guesthouse. The food isn't great but it's cheap. On offer are American music, Chinese soup and an international atmosphere – and it's where most budget travellers eat. It's hard to say whether one restaurant is better than the next. For more authentic cuisine in the same area, explore the little side-streets behind Khao San Road.

✕ **Hello Restaurant** – ร้านอาหารเฮลโล (colour map III, A1, **20**): 63–65 Khao San Road. Apparently as popular as ever with backpackers, this has European or local food, tables on the street, plenty of atmosphere and generous servings. American breakfast. The motto here is 'Good food, good health'. Open until late every night, which is a big plus.

✕ **Small roadside café** at the corner of Thanon Tanao and Soi Damnoen, where they don't speak a word of English and treat 'round eyes' like Martians. Typically Thai and simply delicious. The dishes are displayed on stands, so there's no problem ordering what you want. Very cheap.

✕ **Artsy Fartsy** – ร้านอาหารอาร์ทซี่ฟาร์สที่ (colour map III, A1, **21**): 90/12 Rambutri Road. ☎ 282-23-03. A fairly new and relatively unknown café-restaurant tucked away in a tiny passage linking Khao San Road to Soi Rambutri. They serve a huge selection of traditional Thai dishes and mouth-watering but affordable house cocktails. With stylish, designer decor, it's a great place – pity it's so small.

✕ **Bayon Pub and Restaurant** – ร้านอาหารบาโยน (colour map III, A2, **22**): 249 Khao San Road, on the second floor. ☎ 282-98-00. Very friendly surroundings and good food but worth a visit most of all for the terrace overlooking the Khao San Road.

✕ **La Crêpe** – ร้านอาหารลาแคร์ป (colour map III, A2, **23**): Trokmay-om, Chakrapongse Road. Not so much a restaurant, more a French-type snack bar opposite New Joe Guesthouse; besides pancakes, it serves quiches, milk-bread and sweet or savoury tarts as good as you get in France. Good for eating on the hoof. Open weekdays only, 7am–9pm.

✕ **Buddy Beer and Restaurant** – ร้านอาหารบัดดี้เบียร์ (colour map III, A1, **24**): 153–137/1 Khao San Road. ☎ 282-43-51. This restaurant serving classical cuisine at the back of the Buddy Guesthouse is on your right as you enter the road, coming from Thanon Tanao. It offers predictable food at reasonable prices. Worth seeing for its decorative woodwork and brick floor and walls. It's set back from the street so quieter than the others.

✕ **Khiri** – ร้านอาหารคีรี: 106/4 Rambutri Road. ☎ 629-04-91. Open 9am–midnight. Snack bar with a terrace opposite the Vieng-tai luxury hotel, in the first road parallel to Khao San Road. The Dutch owner has a taste for the *beaux arts* and soft music and it's a great place to escape the rampant commercialism round here. Delicious tea and Laotian coffee – and *the* place to go for a game of chess.

## ON AND AROUND SUKHUMVIT ROAD – ถนนสุขุมวิทและรอบๆ (colour map II)

### BUDGET

✕ **Yong Lee Restaurant** – ร้านอาหารยงลี (colour map II, A3, **51**): 213 Sukhumvit Road. Good Chinese restaurant on the corner of Soi 15. The menu doesn't show the prices, so ask first. Great crab curry, also shrimps, fish and lots of other dishes such as glazed duck; the beef with tomatoes is very good too. There's not much sign of the famous Thai smile but it's an excellent restaurant all the same with a pleasing old-fashioned bar with tables on the street.

### MODERATE TO EXPENSIVE

✕ **Oam Thong Restaurant** – ร้านอาหารออมทอง (colour map II, B3, **52**): 8 Sukhumvit Road, Soi 33. ☎ 258-06-68. Open daily, 11am–11pm. Very good, reasonably priced two-storey restaurant with terrace, opposite the Novotel. Highly imaginative decor: the tables are made of old boats filled with sand and shells, and covered with sheets of glass. It offers simple, well-prepared food – mainly fish in sauces and fried shellfish – in generous helpings, and with friendly service.

✕ **Cabbages and Condoms** – ร้านอาหารแคบเบจแอนด์คอนดอม (colour map II, A3, **53**): Sukhumvit Road, Soi 12, 200 metres on the right as you enter the *soi*. ☎ 249-46-10. Open daily, 11am–10pm. Why the name? You may well ask – the culinary connotations are, after all, not great. The name says something about the mounting concern in certain circles about the ravages caused by AIDS. The owner works for a welfare organization and decided to use his restaurant to make people more aware; this explains the Vasectomy Bar, the poster displaying contraceptive devices and the free condoms. Moving on to the food: they serve classical cuisine, lots of salads and soups, and it's honest cooking at reasonable prices in an agreeable setting. There's an attractive terrace with bamboo tables and chairs surrounded by trees.

✕ **Nan's Place** – น่านเพลส (colour map II, A3, **68**): 20 Sukhumvit, Soi 18. ☎ 258-13-80. Open daily. Restaurant with a lovely, quiet garden, set back from the hubbub of the main street. Sit at the terrace on a Friday or Saturday night at around 7pm and you can watch a display of local dancing. Or you can sit inside, which is much more ordinary but at least it's air-conditioned. It depends whether you want tradition or mod cons. When it comes to the menu, you're spoilt for choice. The red curry scores high marks, but steer well clear of the house wine.

✕ **Juyban Japanese Restaurant** – ร้านอาหารญี่ปุ่นจุยบัน (colour map II, A3, **70**): 1/14 Sukhumvit, Soi 10. ☎ 250-02-99. Open daily from 5pm. One of many generally dis-likeable and expensive Japanese restaurants around here. But this one is alright – it's so small every-one crowds around the bar, and the choice of *sake* is impressive. Stick to one *sake*, and have the noodle soup, to avoid any nasty surprises when the bill comes. There's a good atmosphere and pleasant service.

✕ **Night-time street market** – ตลาดกลางคืน (colour map II, B4, **54**). Every night until midnight you'll find several stands on the corner of Sukhumvit Road and Soi 38 serving fast food perfect for eating on the hoof.

✕ **The Seafood Market and Restaurant** – ภัดคาคารซีฟู้ดมาร์เก็ต (colour map II, B4, **55**): 89 Soi 24, Sukhumvit Road, 200 metres on the left. ☎ 261-20-71. From the outside, it's like watching a non-stop procession of chefs in white hats and red scarves. You can eat on the terrace or in the over-lit restaurant. The very original menu consists of a huge display of pick-your-own ultra-fresh shellfish and fish, with wine and bread also avail-able. Check the price before saying how much fish you want and wait while they weigh it out for you. Then pay at the desk and take the basket of fish to your table where a waiter will come and ask how you want it cooked. All you pay for then is the cooking. Served with a selection of fried baby vegetables.

✕ By the way, if you happen to like mass production try the **Royal Dragon** – รอยัลดรากอน (35/222 Mu 4, Bangna Phrakanong – บางนาพระโขนง, ☎ 398-00-37) about 4 kilometres (2 miles) to the west of town. It's an immense complex with karaoke rooms on the water, built around a six-storey pagoda. Decent food.

✕ **Moghul Room** – ภัดคาคารโมกุลรูม (colour map II, A3, **57**): Soi 11, Sukhumvit Road. ☎ 253-44-65. Undoubtedly one of the best Indian restaurants in town as well as one of the oldest (it's been here for more than 15 years). It's on the left, 100 metres down a little cul-de-sac. Delicious cuisine from the north of India features *tandoori* cooking complete with tikkas, rai-tas and koftas. It's intimate and welcoming and the smokers' area on the first floor is particularly inviting. More expensive than the other two Indian restaurants in the same cul-de-sac but has loads more style. The others are not bad all the same. Visa cards accepted.

## EXPENSIVE

✕ **Lemon Grass** – ร้านอาหารเลมอนกราส (colour map II, B4, **58**): Soi 24, Sukhumvit Road. ☎ 258-86-37. Open 11am–2pm and 6–11pm. A series of little rooms, tastefully de-corated with ornate woodwork, pictures and plants, with soft light-ing and traditional music playing in the background. There are also a few elegantly laid tables in the garden. Refined, varied, melt-in-the-mouth cuisine – great shrimps marinated in coconut milk with lemon – feature in this perfect choice for an exceptional evening out. The prices are very affordable but it gets busy so go early or reserve ahead.

SPLASH OUT

✕ **Le Banyan** – ร้านอาหารเลอบันหยัน (colour map II, A3, **59**): Soi 8, Sukhumvit Road. ☎ 253-55-56. Open evenings only. This is not your ordinary French restaurant nor the sort of food you eat every day but it deserves a mention

because it gives you the chance to sample the joys of gastronomy at non-astronomical prices. There's great art without a doubt, from a kitchen worthy of a two-star Michelin rating: scallop soup, tournedos Rossini, a selection of cheeses and crème brûlée, plus an excellent wine list that you'll regret when you see the bill. All with very professional service in an ultra-chic setting with an exotic, colonial flavour. Save it for the end of your trip if you've got any bahts left. Visa accepted.

**IN AND AROUND SIAM SQUARE AND THE WORLD TRADE CENTER** – ย่านสยามสแควร์, เวิลร์เทรดเซ็นเดอร์และรอบๆ (colour map I, C–D3)

The area around Siam Square consists of a shopping complex and dozens of different restaurants. Prices tend to be high but here are some worth trying if you're in the area.

✕ **Once Upon a Time** (restaurant – in Arcade Jao Khun Ou; colour map I, D2, **81**): 32 Soi 17, Petchburi Road, Pratunam. In the middle of Soi 17, which is opposite the Panthip Plaza. ☎ 252-86-29 and 653-78-57. Open 11am–11pm (or later). This period wooden house, rather like a 1940s-style bungalow, in a tropical garden planted with large mango trees is in the heart of Bangkok but quiet just the same. It serves traditional Thai cuisine at its best: nothing remotely royal or *nouvelle* but a tasteful selection of genuine, provincial home-cooking. You won't be disappointed by such specialities as fried river-fish baked with herbs (pla sawane), crab salad from the northeast (laab pou), yellow curry with crab or shrimps, tamarind soup, seafood soufflé in a coconut shell or chicken with cashew nuts. From the patina on the furniture, the collection of old portraits, dimmed lighting, soft Thai music and waiters' uniforms, you'd think you'd gone back 100 years. An experi-

ence not to be missed, particularly since prices are very reasonable. Major credit cards accepted.

✕ **Maboonkhlong Shopping Centre** – มาบุญครองช็อปปิ้งเซ็นเดอร์ (colour map I, C3, **60**): Thanon Phaya Thai – ถนนพญาไท. Open till 10pm. Just 2 minutes from the Reno Hotel and the National Stadium, this is one of the liveliest places around. Lots of little food stands on the sixth floor serve devilishly good things to eat at angelic prices. Wide selection of Thai dishes.

✕ Yet another **Hard Rock Café** – ฮาร์ดร็อคคาเฟ (colour map I, D3, **61**), right in the heart of Siam Square. Entry is by way of the Thanon Playa Thai, in front of the Maboonkhlong Shopping Centre in the third recess on the right. The usual collection of rock memorabilia – golden records, guitars, posters. Fine for a quick drink but the prices are a real joke. This is where Bangkok's young dudes arrange to meet their permed-hair-babes. The more they spend, the more they love 'em.

✕ **T Restaurant** – ร้านอาหารที (colour map I, D2, **62**): 646/8–10 Soi Talard Nailert Market Pratunam – ซอยตลาดนายเลิศประตูน้ำ, Petchaburi Road, north of Siam Square. ☎ 252-19-84. Open daily, 11.30am–2am. Since the adjacent Pratunam market closed down, the T Restaurant is all that's left round here. It's still popular though, even if it is a bit like eating in a station concourse with lighting that would do justice to a hospital waiting room. The crab curries remain the best in town and the baked prawn and other fish dishes are excellent too. Note that the menu features a photo of each dish but no prices – doubtless omitted out of a sense of propriety. Some dishes are three times as expensive as others, so check before you order.

## IN THE SOI NGAM DUPHLI DISTRICT – ย่านซอยงามดูพลี
(colour map I, D4)

### BUDGET TO MODERATE

✕ **Wong's Place** – ร้านอาหารวงศ์เพลส (colour map I, D4, **64**): Soi Sribumphen. Bar run by a young Chinese fan of 1970s music, as you can see from the decor and the crowds. A popular haunt with long-haul travellers, it offers typical Thai family cooking and is a good place to drink.

✕ **YMCA Coffee Shop** – คอฟฟี่ช็อปไว.เอ็ม.ซี.เอ (colour map I, D4, **65**): Sathorn Tai Road. On the first floor, turn left as you enter. If the price of the rooms is exorbitant, the buffet lunch (every day except Sunday) offers generous helpings at prices that won't break the bank. Choose from a wide selection of Thai starters, main courses and puddings. Sit at a table near the bay window to get a view of the pool.

## TOWARDS SILOM ROAD AND PATPONG – ถนนสีลมและพัฒน์พงษ์
(colour map I, C4–D4)

### BUDGET

– You'll find lots of **Chinese** restaurants along the Silom Road, between Decho Road and Patpong I Road serving *dim sum* (steamed parcels) at lunchtime. They offer great food at low prices, and loads of atmosphere.

– On Silom Road, 50 metres before Patpong Road (on the left-hand pavement coming from Lumphini Park) are lots of terraces serving shellfish and seafood after sunset. Simply point to what you want on the display (a great way of making yourself understood) and 10 minutes later, the food's in front of you. It's like a canteen where the Thais go when they finish work. These are street kitchens, not proper restaurants, so there are no names to mention. An unforgettable experience.

### MODERATE TO EXPENSIVE

✕ **Himali Cha Cha** – ภัตตาคารหิมาลัยชาช่า (colour map I, C4, **67**): 1229/11 New Road – ถนน–เจริญกรุง. ☎ 235-15-69. Open every day for lunch and dinner until 10.30pm. This is another good Indian restaurant at the end of a side-street off New Road, between Silom Road and Surawong, that specializes in cuisine from northern India, including a wide selection of vegetarian dishes. The vegetable koftas curries, kormas and tandoori dishes cost very little and are always a treat. Service is efficient.

✕ **Café de Paris** – ภัตตาคารคาเฟเดอปารีส (colour map I, D4, **69**): Patpong 2 Road. ☎ 237-72-77. Typically French café serving wine and lots of delicious things to eat, to strains of the latest French hits. It's great for homesick French backpackers: almost like being in the Latin Quarter in Paris. But don't get carried away because the prices are extortionate and don't necessarily feature on the menu.

– The buffet-lunches served in all the big hotels are good value too, with good food at low prices and as much as you can eat. To name but one, try the **Sala Rim Nam** – ภัตตาคารศาลาริมน้ำ restaurant in the Oriental Hotel – โรงแรมโอเรียนเต็ล (colour map I, B4, **71**). Open daily, 12–2pm. It's on the other side of the Chao Phraya river. To get there, go through the hotel to the jetty where you'll find a complimentary ferry. Divine cuisine in a magical setting – what more can you ask? It's ultra-luxurious (shorts aren't ideal), and has very varied, super food and lots of it. Booking is essential (☎ 437-62-11 or 437-30-80). The cabaret-dinners in the evening are much more expensive.

✕ **Galaxy** – ภัตตาคารแกแลคซี (colour map I, C4, **75**): 19 Rama IV Road – ถนนพระราม4. This immense nightlife complex includes a restaurant, nightclubs, a café, and massage parlour (included here for information only).

Even more intriguing is the **No-Hand Restaurant** – ภัตตาคารโนแฮนด์, where the hostesses unaccountably spoon-feed the guests – none of whom appear to be armless. You really do find everything in Bangkok, particularly when it comes to service. It's worth noting that dinner (which goes on into the small hours) costs half the wages of a skilled local worker.

SPLASH OUT

✕ **Bussaracum** – ร้านอาหารบุษราคัม (colour map I, C4, **72**): Sethiwan Building, 139 Pan Road. ☎ 266-63-12. This restaurant is in a road that runs at right angles to Silom Road, on the ground floor of a big modern building. A fine old restaurant with a solid-gold reputation (the king of Sweden once ate here . . .), the menu deserves a special mention (no less than 72 dishes, all with photo), as does the complimentary *aperitif*. For the widest selection of dishes, order one of the set menus (minimum of two people) and enjoy a succession of mouth-watering Thai delicacies to strains of the *khim* or the *ranad*. It attracts a stylish, mainly European clientele. Faultless service and priced accordingly. Booking is advised.

✕ **Le Bouchon** – ร้านอาหารเลอบูชง (colour map I, D4, **76**): 37/17 Patpong 2 Road. ☎ 234-91-09. Run by a Frenchman, this restaurant is competition for the nearby Café de Paris. Refined cuisine, jazz or opera playing in the background and, instead of a menu, a large blackboard that they bring to the table (very handy if you're long-sighted). The only snag is the bill – it can be a bit steep.

✕ **Silom Village** – ภัตตาคารสีลมวิลเลจ (colour map I, C4, **73**): 286 Silom Road, near Surawong Road and 10 minutes from Patpong. Open daily for lunch and dinner until 11pm. This elegant complex of rather touristy restaurants and boutiques is a bit too much so, particularly when it comes to the food, which has gone down in standard. Eat outside and sit where you like. It's not exactly cheap, but very pleasant in the evenings despite the rather brash atmosphere (bizarre floor-shows and suchlike). Be careful where you eat and what you eat if you want to keep the price down. Service is slow.

✕ **Ban Chiang** – ร้านอาหารบ้าน เชียง (colour map I, C4, **74**): 14 Srivieng Road – ถนนศรีเวียง. ☎ 236-70-45. A restaurant in a fine, old middle-class house, Ban Chiang is the name of a prehistoric civilization that once occupied Thai Soi I and whose leader collected pottery. Refined decor and perfect cooking with a hint of spice. Traditional specialities.

## THE CHINESE AND INDIAN DISTRICT – ย่านจีนและย่านอินเดีย
(colour map I, B3)

### BUDGET

✕ You'll find lots of cheap and appetizing Chinese restaurants in all the side-streets up and down the Yaowarat Road – ถนนเยาวราช. There's loads of atmosphere at night: twinkling with lights and neon signs, everywhere smoke-filled, and crowds of people. Most places consist of a couple of tables and three chairs, but the food really is the genuine article.

### BUDGET TO MODERATE

✕ **Royal India Restaurant** – ภัตตาคารรอยัลอินเดีย (colour map I, B3, **77**): 392/1 Chakraphat Road. ☎ 221-65-65. Open daily, 10am–10pm. Slightly set back from the Chakraphet Road in a side-street opposite the Chinese pagoda and the ATM department store. Since it opened in the 1970s, this tiny restaurant (just 8 tables and some 30 chairs, so get there early) has become a positive icon of Punjabi cuisine. The exceptional quality of the food – savoury curries plus a wide choice of breads – makes it the perfect place to stop and eat in the Pahurat district. If you like *lassi*, you're in for a treat. Air-conditioned eating area; best to reserve ahead.

✕ **Nangnual Restaurant** – ร้านอา หารนางงวล (colour map I, B3, **78**): ☎ 223-76-86. Open 4pm–midnight. Every Friday the Phra Pokkhlao Bridge – สะพานพระปกเกล้า – facing the Nangnual is the scene of a massive exodus as bumper-to-bumper cars crawl out of Bangkok after a hard working week. Meanwhile, the gilded youth of the business area prefers to hang out on the terrace here, on the banks of the Chao Phraya river. The waiters may be rushed off their feet but the quality of the food is invariably good. It's all very rock 'n' roll, and a good place to stop on your way to your favourite bar.

✕ **Texas Suki Yaki & Noodle** – ภัตตาคารเท็กซัสสุกี้ยากี้ (colour map I, B3, **79**): 17/1 Phadung Dao Road – ถนนผดุงดาว. ☎ 222-06-49. Excellent *sukiyaki* served in traditional Thai chafing dishes (like a fondue dish), delicious cakes and charming waitresses. Where the name 'Texas' came from, nobody knows, but anyone can tell you where to find this wild part of Chinatown.

### SPLASH OUT

✕ **China Town Scala Shark-fins Restaurant** – ภัตตาคารหูฉลามไชน ่าทาวน์สกาล่า (colour map I, B3, **80**): 483–5 Yaowarat Road, Corner Chalermburi. ☎ 221-17-13. For nearly half a century, this restaurant opposite the Chinatown Hotel has attracted affluent Chinese businessmen in search of the celebrated cuisine of the Middle Empire, including braised shark's fin (a house speciality), swallows' nests, abalone, goose thighs and even fish stomachs. Some dishes, famous for their medicinal or aphrodisiac properties, cost as much as a night in a four-star hotel (it takes more than this to deter the Chinese). Other dishes, though, are much more reasonably priced. ' Refined setting and exquisite service.

## WHAT TO SEE

### IN THE WEST

★ **Wat Phra Kaeo and the Grand Palace** – วัดพระแก้วและพระบรมมหาราชวัง (colour map I, A2, **90**): Sanam Chai Road. Lots of buses come here, particularly the No. 12, which crosses Bangkok from east to west. Open all day from 8.30am to 4.30pm. Closed public holidays. The desk closes for lunch (noon–1pm) and permanently at 3.30pm. Guided tours in English at no extra cost at 10am and 2pm. Proper clothing must be worn, but if you haven't got what's needed – something to cover your shoulders, long trousers and shoes (not sandals) – they'll very kindly lend it to you. Try and get there early, partly because of the heat but mainly to avoid the crowds. The admission charge is high but includes a tour of the Vimanmek Mansion (*see* below).

The Grand Palace was built in 1867 in the reign of Rama IV to celebrate the centenary of the Chakri dynasty. Rama V subsequently added his own personal touches. The Grand Palace has a surface area of 219 hectares (541 acres). Inside the precinct are the Grand Palace itself and its outbuildings, and a temple complex that includes the Wat Phra Kaeo. This is the most famous Buddhist temple in Thailand – built as a Holy of Holies to house the Emerald Buddha (it's actually made of jade), the most revered statue in the whole country.

The temple complex surrounding the principal *wat* was built at the end of the 18th century. In architectural terms, this is one of the most homogenous in style, even if it doesn't look it. Beneath an impressive sweep of multi-tiered, multicoloured roofs are numerous *chedis,* sculptures and mythological figures. While most of the temples have been here for more than two centuries, they were regularly restored by a succession of kings, who continuously added new buildings that enriched (or cluttered) what was there before. This explains the mix of styles and the fact that nothing looks really old. You can find magnificent works of art alongside cheap little *chedis.* Apart from the main temples, the place is a jumble of monuments commemorating successive Ramas, plus a main library and annex, a royal pantheon, small lodges and *chedis* galore. But you don't have to see everything – the highlights of the visit are given below. It's principally the temples and particularly the Holy of Holies containing the statuette that everybody comes here to see. For the Thais, its significance is equivalent to that of the Virgin Mary at Lourdes for the French. The Grand Palace itself isn't that interesting.

– **The tour**: buy your ticket before entering the temple precinct; the Coins and Royal Decorations Museum is on your right and you will need a separate ticket for this. If coins and medals aren't your thing, the display of royal regalia – clothes, sceptres, swords, jewels, royal chinaware – is quite simply magnificent. It's astonishing to think of the time it must have taken to create some of these objects and of the quality of craftsmanship involved. Also on display are two of the Emerald Buddha's three sets of robes – the third being the one he's wearing. All these treasures are behind thick metal grilles.

Next, you go through to the temples. Faced with such a kaleidoscope of colour, it's difficult to say whether what you see is magnificent or just plain kitsch: multi-tiered roofs and cluttered facades shimmering with glass mosaics, pieces of multicoloured porcelain and an embellishment of little sculptures. Particularly lovely are the roofs with their multicoloured carpet tiles, the *stupas* glittering with gold and the columns covered in mirrors. This is not the place for a detailed history of each temple, which would be exceedingly dull.

Starting with the Holy of Holies, the Wat Phra Kaeo, temple of the celebrated statuette of the Buddha, which serves as the royal chapel of the Grand Palace, was built by Rama I. The style is reminiscent of chapels of the Sukhothai and Ayutthaya periods. The roof combines the Thai and Cambodian styles (back when the two countries were friends). The temple entrance is to the rear.

The famous legend of the Emerald Buddha dates back to the 15th century, when a stucco statuette of the Buddha was found in a recently destroyed temple in Chiang Rai. Eventually, the stucco peeled away, revealing the very fine jade statue beneath. The statuette remained in Lampang for a while until the king of Chiang Rai decided to retrieve the revered object. A century later it accompanied the conquering princes to Laos and, after still more journeys, it made it back to Thailand thanks to Rama I, who retrieved the statuette when he took the town of Vientiane. The Wat Phra Kaeo, built by Rama I, was completed in 1784 and the statue has remained here ever since. The Buddha is shown cross-legged in the meditation posture. Some believe that the statue originated in the north of the country, whereas other researchers believe that it probably came from southern India or Sri Lanka.

The Buddha sits on a pedestal, protected by a canopy on nine levels, symbol of the universal majesty of the Chakri dynasty. Photography is forbidden. So is pointing to the Buddha with your foot, which is considered an insult. Actually, you can't really see the Buddha anyway, given that it's barely 75 centimetres (2 feet) high and is perched more than 11 metres (30 feet) above your head. Small but perfectly formed, you might say. The Buddha owns three outfits – a blue robe with sequins, and two golden robes that the King himself comes to change each season.

Apart from the Buddha, you can feast your eyes on the gold-encrusted wooden altar beneath the statue and the lacquered door panels inlaid with mother-of-pearl in traditional Ayutthaya style. All around the Emerald Buddha, the life of the Buddha is told in a series of fine mural paintings alluding to the three worlds of desire, form and absence of form. The figures they depict are highly allegorical and often mystifying. One of the murals shows the earth goddess conjuring water out of her hair.

The Wat Phra Kaeo is surrounded by a profusion of other buildings, including the magnificent golden *chedi*, dozens of little temples, statues of monsters, temple guardians and, supporting the structures around some of the *chedis*, monkey-headed demons in ornate costumes studded with multicoloured mosaics.

The walls of the great galleries are covered in an impressive series of paintings that tell the life of the kings from the reign of Rama I. The guides generally give an amusing account of these images, although some of them make it up as they go along. Beside the library is a replica of the Angkor Wat, one of the most beautiful temple complexes ever built. This model was commissioned by King Mongkut, in the days when Thailand had supremacy over Cambodia.

Visitors are also admitted to a number of rooms in the Grand Palace, the former residence of the kings. In fact, it's all a bit of a mess, since each king felt he had to add something of his own. At least take a quick look at the Funeral Hall and the Audience Hall.

Finally, there's a small museum, which looks a bit impoverished on the ground floor but it gets richer upstairs. It contains hundreds of statues of the Buddha of every size, sculpted elephant tusks, panels painted with gold leaf, furniture and so on.

★ **Wat Pho** – วัดโพธิ์ (colour map I, A3, **91**): this is about a 10-minute walk from the Wat Phra Kaeo, going first south along the Saman Chai Road and then turning right into the second road at right angles along it. Open daily, 8am–5pm. Low admission charge. This is another temple complex, where the principal temple contains the celebrated reclining Buddha. The oldest and largest temple in Bangkok, it was built by Rama I in the 18th century. It's undoubtedly the most beautiful temple of all, by virtue of its green and peaceful setting and, unlike the Grand Palace, still very much a working temple. In addition to monks, you'll find a massage school, an ashram for meditation, fortune-tellers and even a little café. This was an important centre for education in the 18th century but actually dates back further than that. Main points of interest:

★ **Temple of the Reclining Buddha**: note the two large stone figures wearing top-hats and holding canes. Fancy finding symbols of European culture in a temple of Thai art! There is barely room inside the little temple for the gigantic reclining Buddha, about 45 metres (150 feet) long and 15 metres (50 feet) high. It was recently entirely regilded. Note also the Buddha's mocking smile, the delicate hair and the feet inlaid with mother-of-pearl designs, representing the qualities of the Buddha. The Buddha is shown reclining and about to enter Nirvana when he is finally freed from the cycle of reincarnation.

● Inside are four large *chedis* decorated with highly ornate pieces of ceramic and all very different in shape and colour. They represent the first kings of the Chakri dynasty and look very fine indeed with their slender, tall spires.

● Beneath two of the galleries, behind a glass wall, a series of anatomical designs depicts the various parts of the body.

● In two galleries around the temple are 394 seated Buddhas.

● At the end of the precinct (on the right as you enter) is a centre for traditional massage. Open 8am–6pm. Run by students who welcome bodies to practise on for sessions lasting from 30 minutes to an hour, with or without herbs. It's so rare to get a real massage in Bangkok, so make the most of it. Arrive early in the morning to avoid the queues. There is also a drinks stand and toilets in the precinct.

★ **Wat Arun** – วัดอรุณ (Temple of the Dawn; colour map I, A3, **92**): on the other side of the Chao Phraya river, in Thonburi – ฝั่งธนบุรี. Take the ferry that crosses the river every 10 minutes, to the Tha Thien stop if you're coming from the Wat Pho, or to the Tha Chang stop if you're coming from the Wat Phra Kaeo. The temple opens early in the morning and, in theory at least, stays open until 5pm. But since it sometimes closes earlier, it's safer to go in the morning. Whatever people tell you, there's no point hiring a boat to cross the river.

The temple is named after Aruna, the Indian dawn goddess. It was built in the 19th century by Rama II and Rama III in this part of town – Thonburi – which was formerly the capital city. This relatively modest temple is quite endearing, and tends to draw fewer crowds than the others. The central *prang* is quite extraordinary: an incredible coloured patchwork of ceramic pieces, 86 metres (259 feet) high and distinctly Khmer in style. There are demons and sculpted gods more or less everywhere. Check before you go, since it has been closed for refurbishment. The smaller *prangs* all around it add the finishing touches. Stairs take you almost to the top of the tower and it's worth the climb for the view of the river and the Royal Palace. Visitors are also admitted inside the *prang* to see the Buddha.

★ **Wat Benjamabopitr** – วัดเบญจมบพิตร (Marble Temple; colour map I, B1, **93**): on the corner of Sri Ayutthaya Road and Rama V Road – มุมถนนศรีอยุธยาและถนนพระราม5. From Democracy Monument, take the No. 12 bus to the crossroads with Sri Ayutthaya Road. From there, the No. 72 bus will drop you close by. Open daily, 8am–5pm. Admission charge. This charming marble temple dates from the late 19th century. All the marble is from Carrara in Italy and the ceramic on the roofs is from China. Two splendidly well-endowed lions flank the sculpted teak door. It is best to visit in the morning to hear the monks chanting in the chapel.

The gold and lacquer decoration inside the main building is remarkable. On the altar, an enormous Buddha watches over the ashes of Rama V, who died in 1910. It features a very fine, gold encrusted ceiling, and in the cloister are 52 bronze Buddhas of different styles and positions, originating from different places. They include seated Buddhas, reclining Buddhas, ascetic, fasting and meditating Buddhas, some original, others simply reproductions, from all over Asia – Thailand, India, Japan, Burma, Cambodia, Pakistan – making this a uniquely varied, iconographic collection of Buddhist art.

★ **Wat Sakhet** – วัดสระเกศ (Temple of the Golden Mount – วัดภูเขาทอง; colour map I, B2, **94**): Chakkaphatdi Road or Boriphat Road – ถนนจักพัฒน์หรือถนนบริพัฒน์. Very near the tourist office, in the woodcrafting district. Take the No. 15 or 47 bus from Democracy Monument. Open daily, 7.30am–5.30pm. A small donation is expected at the top.

Started by Rama III and completed by Rama V, the temple perches at the top of a man-made hill and looks quite unlike any other. High supporting walls on all sides give the mount a fortress-like appearance. The architectural style was copied from a temple in Ayutthaya. It's nothing special in itself but the view you get from the top is unique. A spiral stairway winding round the hill takes you up to the large golden *chedi*, inside which is a relic of the Buddha. At the top of the stairway is a room with open windows hung with charming little bells. From the terrace, you get a magnificent view of almost all of Bangkok. This is the highest point in the city at some 80 metres (240 feet).

★ **Wat Traimitr** – วัดไตรมิตร (Temple of the Golden Buddha; colour map I, B3, **95**): at the junction of Charoen Krung Road and Yaowarat Road – สี่แยกเจริญกรุงเยาวราช, not far from Hua Lamphong station. Bus No 1, 7, 73 and 75 run close by. Open 8.30am–5pm. Of limited in interest itself, the temple is famous for its statue of the Buddha dating from the Sukhothai period. At 3 metres (10 feet) high and weighing more than five tonnes, the statue was originally covered in plaster (possibly to conceal it from the greedy eyes of the Burmese). Its true form remained secret until 1955, when damage in transit revealed the gold beneath. That said, the temple has become a positive tourist trap, swarming with guides and guided tours (they leave every 10 minutes).

★ **Wat Suthat** – วัดสุทัศน์ (Temple of the Giant Swing; colour map I, B2, **96**): enter via Unakan Road – ถนนอุนากาารณ์, or Ti Thong Road. Admission free. Open until 5pm. Built by Rama I and completed by Rama III, in addition to the exceptional wall-paintings, people also come here to see the giant swing just outside the temple on Bamrung Muang Road. Young Brahmans used to swing from it to try to grab in their teeth pouches of money hanging 25 metres (75 feet) above ground. The religious significance of this ceremony isn't clear.

★ If you're still hungry for temples, visit the **Wat Rajabophit** – วัดราชบพิตร (colour map I, B2, **97**) and the **Wat Rajanaddaram** – วัดราชนัดดาราม (colour map I, B2, **98**), surrounded by the amulet market.

★ **The National Museum** – พิพิธภัณฑสถานแห่งชาติพระนคร (colour map I, A2, **99**): Na Phra That Road – ถนนหน้าพระธาตุ. ☎ 224-13-96. Open 9am–6pm. Closed Monday and Tuesday. A map of the museum is available at the entrance. Ask about the guided tours, given on certain days and at set times which are very good and given in English on Wednesday and Thursday. It's a magnificent museum, not to be missed, and is made up of several buildings containing lots of treasures and all the wonders of Thai art, plus some ancient lodges or temples brought here for conservation. It gives a complete resumé of Thai art and provides the perfect introduction to the temples.

These are the most interesting rooms:

**Rooms 1 and 2**: these relate the history of Thailand from prehistoric times (both situated at the entrance).

**Room 3**: in fact a *Buddhaisawan* (chapel) built at the end of the 18th century in the Bangkok style, to house a 15th-century golden bronze Buddha. It looks rather ordinary from the outside, but inside, magnificent painted panels tell the story of the life of the Buddha in allegorical style. The ceiling has ornate beams.

**Room 4**: a huge reception room with a particularly striking ceiling.

**Room 5**: impressive collection of well-guarded treasures, the oldest dating back to the start of the current era, including fine bracelets from the Ayutthaya period and exquisitely designed rings. Some of the jewels are from the royal collection.

**Room 6**: every kind of transport-related object. See in particular the exceptional selection of royal canopies, including one in ivory, and the tall, late 18th-century canopy in sculpted wood.

**Room 7**: collection of Khon masks, theatre figurines, puppet heads and ivory chess sets.

**Room 8B**: magnificent display of sculpted elephant tusks and boxes inlaid with mother-of-pearl.

**Room 10**: arms of every description, some of them very refined, plus full battle-dress for an elephant.

**Room 11:** royal emblems.

**Room 13:** lavishly carved wooden artefacts, including panelled doors and thrones.

**Room 14**: fabrics and traditional military uniforms from across the centuries; Chinese and Cambodian silks, Indian brocades, predominantly from the royal wardrobes.

**Room 15**: collection of musical instruments from all over Asia, plus an audio system so you can hear what they sound like.

**Room 17**: funeral wagons built in the reign of Rama I for royal cremations, including one still in use today: it weighs 20 tonnes and requires several hundred men to pull it.

**Rooms 18**, **19**, **20** and **21**: these are actually lodges used during a variety of ceremonies.

**Room 22**: old teak house, originally the private apartment of a princess. Note the floorboards fastened together with pegs not nails. It's a model of simplicity and refinement and not to be missed.

The rooms in **group N** contain a display of Thai art from different periods: 13th-century artefacts and sculpture from the Lan Na period, when the capital was Chiang Mai; Sukhothai art (lots of Buddhas), Ayutthaya (influenced by Mon and Khmer art) and 19th-century art from Bangkok.

The rooms in **group S** contain a display of art from Lopburi, Dvâravatî and Srivijaya.

★ **Vimanmek Mansion Museum** – พิพิธภัณฑ์วิมานเมม colour map I, B1, **100**): Ratchawithi Road – ถนนราชวิถี in the northwest of Bangkok, near the zoo. Open daily, 9am–4pm (desk closes at 3.15pm). High admission charge, but if you visit the Grand Palace, the price of the ticket includes a visit here. The deal doesn't work both ways so start with the Grand Palace and from there, take the No. 12 or 56 bus for Vimanmek. There are 45-minute guided tours in English, twice an hour. It's particularly important to go properly dressed, so make sure you are. If not, they can lend you a *sarong*. The price of admission includes performances of dance and martial arts staged in the little open-air theatre morning and afternoon.

At the end of a stretch of lawn lies one of the most marvellous houses you will ever see. Considered to be the largest teak residence ever built, this magnificent building was commissioned by Rama V at the end of the 19th century. It was originally built on an island in the Gulf of Siam before being moved to its present position in 1901. The king occupied the third floor of

**BANGKOK**

the house from time to time, leaving the remaining two storeys for the other members of the royal family. Successive kings came here much more infrequently and the house remained closed for nearly 50 years, until major restoration works were undertaken. These are now completed and the house today is a real treat. Inside, it looks exactly the way it did in the days of Rama V.

The tour shows you around 31 rooms, anterooms and verandas arranged on three levels. There are rooms of every description: covered terraces, carved balconies, cosy boudoirs, reception rooms and inviting bed-rooms. A real palace in other words, complete with dozens of portraits of the royal family in ceremonial dress. Showcases in all the rooms contain a display of *objets d'art*, family gifts, personal memorabilia and elegant furniture, which may not have been in place at the time but which adds substance to the visit and helps to turn an architectural treasure into a genuine museum. In case you're interested, one of the bedrooms contains the first bath ever installed in Thailand.

Around Vimanmek Mansion are other smaller, less interesting teak houses, which you can also visit. There is also a long shed-like building containing English harnesses used by Rama kings V, VI, VII, VIII and IX.

★ **The National Theatre** – โรงละครแห่งชาติ (colour map I, A2, **101**): on Na Phra That Road, beside the National Museum. This recent building, half-Thai, half-contemporary, stages magnificent performances of dance in traditional costume and is very reasonably priced. Details are usually advertised in the press but can also be obtained by phoning the theatre on weekdays, 8am–4.30pm (☎ 224-13-42). On the last Friday of every month there are performances of classical Thai dance.

★ **The Royal Barge Museum** – พิพิธภัณฑสถานแห่งชาติเรือพระราชพิธี (ลงจากสะพานพระปิ่นเกล้า) (colour map I, A1–2, **102**): in a boathouse on the Bangkok Noi *khlong*, near Thonburi station. Open 8am–4pm. Admission charge. There are two ways of getting there. Either walk or take the bus to the Phra Pink Lao Bridge. Cross it and look for the sign further up saying 'Royal Barges'. The boathouse lies at the end of a succession of little concrete-and-wood jetties, surrounded by a maze of wooden houses on stilts (now's your chance to see how the locals live). It isn't easy to find. Or you can rent a long-tail boat from Tha Chang or Tha Maharaj and put together a grand tour of the *khlongs* (lasting an hour or two), with a 15-minute stop to see the royal barges (be firm about the price).

The immense boathouse contains a display of eight incredibly ornate barges with decorative carvings, most of them built during the 18th century. Until recently, they served to transport the king during the *Kathin* season, when he presented the *bonzes* with their new robes. The oldest royal barge is some 43 metres (130 feet) long and required a crew of 54. The impressive bows are magnificently carved.

★ **Chinatown** – ย่านเยาวราช colour map I, B3): situated around the Yaowarat and Charoen Krung roads, which run parallel to each other. Take the boat to Tha Ratchawong or Tha Saphan Phut. There's loads of atmosphere, but otherwise it's not an easy place to describe. There are lots of shops as you would expect – jewellery and fabrics mainly – and the area's particularly worth seeing by night, when the neon signs clash with the old Chinese lanterns.

– Yaowarat Road itself is a wide, not very appealing thoroughfare with lots of gold shops and apothecaries, but is criss-crossed by tiny streets that are well worth exploring. The two most colourful are Sampeng Lane (on the map, Soi Wanit I), parallel to Yaowarat Road and particularly Itsaranupha Road, which cuts across it. Here you'll find hundreds of little bric-à-brac shops that occasionally give off the most frightful smell, piles of objects, clothes and assorted antiquities. The atmosphere is pungently Chinese with lots of little restaurants, food stands and old Chinese women setting the tone. Go foraging and your curiosity will be rewarded. There are also imported fruits galore, apples from Korea, pears from Australia, washed and polished grapes from America (they have to be shiny) that cost 10 times as much as local fruit.

– Further east, take a stroll down Phadung Dao Road and the side-streets running off it. On one side there is Soi Texas (a narrow street starting opposite the Chinatown Hotel) packed with hairdressers, where, for just a few bahts, you can get a trim and a pedicure (and much more if they like the look of you). On the other side, there is a tangle of residential streets where the Chinese families you meet become smiling and easy-going. The atmosphere in the many little restaurants (the cheapest in all Bangkok) is positively festive and you may even catch old Chinese guys, whisky or beer in hand, singing along to the latest Cantonese chart-topper. The area bordered by the Charoen Krung, Chakkrawat, Yaowarat and Boriphat roads is the Nakhom Kasem or 'thieves' market, which used to specialize in stolen goods and where you can still go bargain-hunting in the many antiques shops. The Leng Noi Yee temple is worth seeing too, on the corner of Charoen Krung and Mangkon Road. All in all, there's loads of atmosphere.

– Every year on 16 August, Chinatown celebrates the midway point in the Chinese calendar, with street offerings and a general atmosphere of piety.

★ **The Indian district, Pahurat** – ย่านอินเดีย,พาหุรัด (colour map I, B3): at the western tip of Chinatown, all along the Chakraphat Road, the atmosphere becomes more Indian and Pakistani. Visit the fabrics market behind the ATM department store or the enormous Sikh temple, bustling with activity and very typically Indian.

★ **The floating markets** – ตลาดน้ำ: the most famous of these (there are several in Bangkok) was the Wat Sai floating market – ตลาดน้ำวัดสาย, but it floats no more. Today it is a sea of tourist boutiques and is best avoided.

There is another floating market – the **Damnoen Saduak market** – ตลาดน้ำดำเนินสะดวก about 96 kilometres (60 miles) southwest of Bang-kok, in Ratchaburi – จังหวัดราชบุรี. If you're interested, go early to avoid the hordes of tourists (9am is too late) and enjoy the market at its best. The No. 78 bus leaves at 30-minute intervals, from 6am to 8.30pm, departing from the Southern Bus Terminal (allow 90 minutes to 2 hours). There are several markets on each side of the Damnoen Saduak canal and you can hire a taxi-boat to explore the surrounding area. *See* the chapter on Damnoen Saduak *below*.

★ **Boat-trip along the *khlongs*** – นั่งเรือชมคลอง: not be missed and the only way of getting to see a completely different side to Bangkok. The *khlongs* or canals that criss-cross the western part of Bangkok give you a glimpse of some unexpected local colour. Far from the skyscrapers and the traffic jams, covered in mounds of lush vegetation, are hundreds of houses on stilts, rickety old shacks, modest temples, gardens full of flowers and children who spend their days in the water.

Avoid the organized tours – you're better off planning your own. Details on route planning can be obtained from the tourist office (*see* 'Useful Addresses').

Alternatively, why not take one of the many river buses that sail up and down the *khlongs* all day, linking the far reaches of Bangkok with the centre. You can get off where you want and take another boat back. This is public transport and it's really cheap, but beware of touts trying to sell you a trip on a 'long-tail'. Here are a few suggestions:

● **towards Mon Khlong**: leaves from Tha Thien behind the Wat Pho temple, every 30 minutes until 6.30pm.

● **towards Om Khlong**: leaves from Tha Phibul Songkram in Nonthaburi (far north). The last boat leaves at 9pm. To get to Nonthaburi, take the Chao Phraya River Express Taxi north, from any stop.

● **towards Bang Waek Khlong**: leaves from Tha Saphan Phut every 15 minutes until 9.30pm. It's a bit more expensive than the others, but a really great trip.

● **towards Noi Khlong**: frequent departures from the Memorial Bridge beside Thammasat University.

There are lots of other ways of getting from one *khlong* to another.

**Trip up (or down) the Chao Phraya river**: (*see* 'Transportation'). There are lots of jetties (*thas*) where for just a few bahts you can climb on board one of the local river-buses – and of course there's the River Express Taxi, which is great for getting from the Wat Arun to the Wat Pho and the Grand Palace.

Alternatively, why not get together a group of people (10 or more) and agree a price with the driver of a long-tail boat for an hour-long trip on the *khlongs* (or longer, which is even better for seeing the outer suburbs of Bangkok). It's more expensive, but it's up to you where you stop or whether you stop at all. Set a price per person, not per hour, and tell the driver where you want to stop (or not). Be firm about the price and you won't be disappointed. You'll find long-tail boats at Tha Oriental and Tha Chang.

★ **Amulet market** – ตลาดเครื่องรางของขลังสนามหลวง: Mahachai Road – ถนนมหาชัย. This little market, just beside the Wat Rajanaddaram Talat and not far from the main temples, is made up of a handful of shops packed into a space a few metres square, specializing in religious knick-knacks. Choose from a curious collection of wooden rosaries, bronze Buddhas, key-rings, animal amulets, badges of every description, religious pendants and photos of the King.

## IN THE CENTRE

★ **Jim Thompson's House** – ะบ้านจิมทอมป์สัน (colour map I, C2, **103**): Soi 2 Kasemsan – ซอยเกษมสันต์2, Rama I Road – ถนนพระราม1; very near the National Stadium. Take the No. 15 bus from Democracy Monument and get off near a shop called 'Tokyu'. ☎ 215-01-22. Open daily, 9.30am–5pm. Closed Sunday. High admission charge, but you definitely get what you pay for. Concessionary rates now apply for the under-25s. It's definitely worth taking the guided tour in English – you'll be missing something if you don't. Probably the last remaining authentically Thai teak houses in Bangkok, most of which come from the Ayutthaya region, the former capital of Thailand. This is a fine collection of art, elegantly presented in a magnificent setting and very peaceful after the noise and pollution of Bangkok.

Jim Thompson, a reformed ex-CIA agent, set the Thai silk industry back on its feet before disappearing in Malaysia in 1967 in mysterious circumstances. His legacy is a series of rooms and salons decorated in quintessential Thai style and containing a sumptuous collection of *objets d'art*: tableware, sculpture, porcelain, painted panels and, of course, magnificent Buddhas from all over Asia. It's a pity that it's forbidden to take photographs inside the house.

★ **Suan Pakkard Palace** – วังสวนผักกาด (colour map I, D2, **104**): 352 Sri Ayutthaya Road – ถนนศรีอยุธยา, not far from the corner of Thanon Phaya Thai. Open daily, 9am–4pm. Closed on Sunday. High admission charge. This group of five traditional Thai houses set in a beautiful little garden are a real breath of fresh air in an area thick with pretentious architecture. Guided tours are sometimes available – otherwise ask for the information leaflet in English.

These little teak houses joined by walkways were once the property of Princess Chumbhot, a business-woman and one of Thailand's major art collectors.

– **House 1**: collection of Khmer art, mainly fine, stone sculptures, including a magnificent torso of a well-endowed woman dating from the seventh century. Also carved wooden panels.

– **House 2**: fine display of boxes inlaid with mother-of-pearl, and ivory betel boxes.

– **House 3**: collection of musical instruments, bronze Buddhas and elegant if rather bizarre French drawings of Thai costumes dating from the 17th century. Great canopy.

– **House 4**: group of Buddhas on an altar and a collection of painted panels.

– **House 5**: archaeological collection of bronze artefacts, jewellery and pottery, including pieces more than 2,000 years old. There is also a small mineralogical section on the ground floor.

– At the bottom of the garden is a small lodge on stilts that is more than a 100 years old and originally part of a monastery. It was previously situated in the middle of the Chao Phraya river before the princess was granted permission to move it. Inside the lodge, magnificent black-and-gold lacquered wooden panels tell the story of the life of the Buddha and show Hindu gods in everyday scenes, making for a unique and truly astonishing work of art.

The garden is planted on all sides with aromatic plants of differing origins specially selected by the princess. This is a real museum that is sure to delight all aesthetes.

★ **Snake Farm** – สวนงูสภากาชาดไทย (colour map I, D4, **105**): Rama IV Road. ☎ 252-01-61. Open weekdays 8.30am–4.30pm, weekends 8.30am–noon. Fairly high admission charge. This is where the Thai Red Cross and the Pasteur Institute breed snakes to make antivenom serum. Some of the most dangerous snakes in the area (cobras, Russell's vipers, striped kraits) lead a pampered existence, punctuated by daily visits from the vet who, between 11am and 2.30pm every day, goes down into their pit to extract the venom. Brave man. This is your chance to get to know the nicest (and most inoffensive) of them all: the endlessly affable python, 6–8 metres (19–26 feet) long and a real sucker for affection. All the same, it is rather depressing to see so many snakes in cages.

★ **Lumphini Park** – สวนลุมพินี (colour map I, D3–4): Rama IV Road. This is one of the last places in Bangkok to escape the general mayhem and a great place for a walk or a pedalo ride on the lake. Hundreds of Chinese come here at dawn to practise *tai chi* and for young would-be 'Rockies' there's a special body-building area. It's very popular on Sunday and an ideal place to meet people. You'll see lots of kites in the dry season.

★ **Thai boxing matches** – มวยไทย: blockbuster entertainment in Thailand. No blows are barred but biting is forbidden. The fight starts with a ritual dance in slow motion, which is supposed to demonstrate the boxer's expertise and put the spirits on his side. The band plays meanwhile, and keeps playing throughout the fight, turning up the volume when the blows intensify. Spectators bet huge sums and the atmosphere is incredible, with disgruntled spectators throwing bottles at the referee and sounds of *'di!'* ('fight back!') from the crowd every time the contestants hit each other, particularly with their knees.

For details of days and times of matches, contact the Lumphini Boxing Stadium – สนามมวยลุมพินี, Rama IV Road (☎ 251-43-03; usually Monday, Friday, Saturday and Sunday at about 6pm), and the Ratchadamnoen Stadium – สนามมวยราชดำเนิน (☎ 281-42-05; usually Monday and Wednesday at 7pm, Thursday at 5pm and 9pm and Sunday at 2pm and 6pm) on Ratchadamnoen Nok Road, near the tourist office. Seat prices vary but are not cheap, on the whole. Word has it that the best matches are those on Thursday nights in the Ratchadamnoen Stadium.

★ **Khlong Toey Market** – ตลาดคลองเตย (colour map II, A4, **106**): going south towards Rama IV Road. The No. 47 bus goes here direct from Democracy Monument and if you're coming from Sukhumvit Road, the No. 22 (air-conditioned) bus from Asoke Road stops close by. It's well worth a visit at the beginning of the week to appreciate the extraordinary richness of Thai produce: mountains of fruit and vegetables, rice of every description, flowers, cakes and (not for the faint-hearted) meat, fish and frogs. It's a huge maze-like place where you might get the chance to see a display of religious dancing.

★ For tropical plants, flowers and orchids, market-lovers must visit the **Thewet Flower Market** – ตลาดดอกไม้เทเวศน์ (colour map I, B1 **107**) at the other end of town. The **Pak Khlong Market** – ปากคลองตลาด (colour map I, A3, **108**), which specializes in fruits, is a lovely walk too. The River Express goes to both, from Saphan Phut ferry pier or Thewet ferry pier – cheap, fast and very pleasant.

## IN THE NORTH

★ **Chatuchak Park** – สวนจตุจักร (Weekend Market, off colour map I near D1, **122**): Phahon Yothin Road, on the international airport road. Open Saturday and Sunday, 7am–6pm. There aren't too many tourists on Saturday mornings. To get there from the station, take the No. 34 or 29 bus or the No. 44 from Democracy Monument. From the main square around the Wat Phra Kaeo, take the No. 3, 39 or 44 bus. Allow 45 minutes to get there.

Standards seem to be slipping here every year, but rather like Petticoat Lane in London it is still a good source of just about anything: typical Thai clothing, kitchen equipment, food, animals, fabrics, handicrafts, etc. There are also magnificent orchids and bonsai trees at knock-down prices. It's interesting to know that the vendors have to slip a piece of cardboard between the fish bowls on display since the fish attack each other on sight, and you might even witness this astonishing spectacle. There are a few antiques shops, and you can also get something to eat here.

## SHOPPING

There are shopping centres galore in Bangkok, each one more elegant than the last, while many of the older places have had to close down for security reasons pending a face-lift. In other areas, night brings out a swarm of street traders. There is nothing you cannot find in Bangkok – and most of it is fake. When it comes to imitation, this is the place to be: watches, bags, cassettes, shirts, glasses, jewellery – even imitation cars. It seems the Thais now manufacture their own Mercedes bodywork, stick a Japanese engine in it and sell it as the real thing. Fortunately, all of the silks are the genuine article.

– **Silk**: Jim Thompson, who revived the silk industry in Thailand, would be a proud man. Hand-woven Thai silk, with its magnificent designs and flamboyant colours, is now considered among the finest in the world. The Jim Thompson shop (not to be confused with his house) is at ร้านจิมทอมป์สัน: The Thai Silk Company (colour map I, D4, **120**), 9 Surawong Road. ☎ 234-49-00. Open daily, 9am–9pm. Silks of every kind are available, all beautiful, all expensive but still a lot cheaper than in Europe. In addition there are, of course, boutiques specializing in fine silks in all the shopping centres.

– **Tailors**: for men and women, a chance for some bespoke tailoring that doesn't cost the earth. There are hundreds of tailors who can copy the designs from fashion magazines (bring some cuttings with you). The following gave pleasing results: Song Tailor – สองเทลเลอร์ (colour map I, C4, **121**), 8 Trock Chartered Bank Lane (in front of the Oriental Hotel – มิโอเรียลเด็ล). ☎ 235-27-53. Good value for money but watch out all the same because prices can change from one day to the next. There's a limited choice of fabric for women's clothing. If you plan to go to Chiang Mai, you'll find it's a lot cheaper to get your clothes made there.

– **Sukhumvit Road** – ถนนสุขุมวิท (colour map II, A3): at the end of the afternoon the beginning of Sukhumvit Road, between sois 5 and 20, absolutely teems with street traders selling genuine imitations of all the big names – thoroughly reprehensible and not necessarily cheap these days either. Plus, the watches tend to stop almost immediately and the fabrics usually end up as rags, but you'll find lots of souvenirs.

– **Chatuchak Park (weekend market)** – ตลาดนัดสวนจตุจักร (colour map 1, off D1, **122**): formerly one of the biggest open-air markets but now starting to look a bit sorry for itself (*see* 'What to See' in the north).

– **Silom Road and Surawong Road** – ถนนสีลมและถนนสุรวงศ์ (colour map I, C4–D4): antiques shops (you'll be lucky) selling lacquerwork, jewellery and porcelain. Haggling is essential even in the smartest places.

– **Yaowarat Road** – ถนนเยาวราช (colour map I, B3): in the Chinese quarter. There are jewellers from one end of the street to the other, mainly selling gold, plus lots of old shops in the side-streets, specializing in herbs and strange-smelling potions. Further up is the Nakhom Kasem ('thieves' market) and Chinese and Thai porcelain and loads of useless junk. Terrific atmosphere at night – pity not all of the stands stay open late.

– **Patpong Night Bazaar** – พัฒน์พงษ์ในท์บาร์ซาร์ (colour map I, D4): Patpong is not just a major meat market, it's also where hordes of street-traders flock at night to peddle the now-familiar collection of trinkets, cassettes and T-shirts.

– **Khao San Road** – ถนนข้าวสาร (colour map III): has its fair share of nightly street-traders, plus lots of places where you can get photos developed at reasonable prices and on good-quality paper. There's a quick turn-around too and it beats getting it done when you get home.

– **Spectacles**: the price of glasses is lower in Bangkok than anywhere else. A pair of specially made two-tone (light and dark) prescription lenses with frame from a Chinese optician will cost you about £40 (around $60). And they're usually ready within 20 minutes. One address is: Saeng Aroon Optical – ร้านแว่นตาแสงอรุณ, 285 Yaowarat Road. ☎ 223-69-65.

– **Made-to-measure shoes**: Siam Bootery Shoe – สยามบู๊ตเตอรี่ชู, 124–126 Sukhumvit Road, near Nana Post Office. ☎ 253-83-78. Classic designs, cowboy boots, trainers, golfing shoes – you name it, they can make it in about 10 days. There's also the Racha Bootery, Ratchadamri Road, in front of the World Trade Centre. ☎ 252-46-66. It's cheaper and faster, but there's not as much choice.

– Don't forget the many **shopping centres**, which usually stay open until 10pm. You'll find they stock lots of interesting items (lingerie, cosmetics, fabrics, etc.) at prices much lower than you would pay in Europe. Here are just a few: Narayana Bazaar Underground – ชั้นใต้ดินนารายภัณฑ์ (colour map I, D3, **123**), 127 Ratchadamri Road, right in front of the World Trade Center This one is probably the best, and definitely one of the cheapest, in Bangkok, with very competitive prices. Indra Shopping Arcade – อินทราช้อปปิ้งอาร์เคด, in the Pratunam area; Charn Issara Tower – ตึกชาญอิสระ, 942 Rama IV Road. Also, try all the shopping centres in Siam Square.

– And finally, for those who really crave Western food, there is the **Foodland Supermarket** in Sukhumvit Road – ฟู้ดแลนด์ซุปเปอร์มาร์เก็ต, at the entrance to Soi 5, immediately on your left. It has a cafeteria, bakery and bookshop.

## BANGKOK BY NIGHT

This coverage is intended to be fairly brief rather than go on *ad nauseam* about something that tends to sound like more of the same. Basically, after a good meal (remember, most restaurants stop serving at about 10–10.30pm), you can do a bit of shopping and then wind up in some go-go bar for a drink. You can also go to a performance of traditional dance or – much more fun – a Thai boxing match.

– **Shopping at night**: the three liveliest street markets at night are on the Khao San Road (where most of the guesthouses for backpackers are), Sukhumvit Road roughly between sois 5 and 15, and of course on Patpong I and Patpong II. The streets are full of street pedlars hawking nothing but genuine imitations of famous European brands (shirts, glasses, sports-shirts, watches, tapes), which is all very tempting, particularly since some of them are as good as the real thing. Think twice though, because while it may not be illegal to buy them, bringing them back to Europe is strictly forbidden. If found out by customs, the goods will be confiscated and you become liable for a fine amounting to double what you paid for them. So it's definitely not worth the hassle.

– **'Go-go' bars**: before going any further, *see* 'Go-go Bars and Prostitution' earlier in the book. In short, ogling a strip-tease show can be fun – anything more is out of the question. Why? Because what's on offer doesn't conform to Western morals.

– **Patpong I** and **Patpong II** are entirely lined with bars full of go-go girls dancing on stage in bathing costumes. A bit of a giggle that doesn't cost the earth, but make sure you ask the price of a beer before going in. In some places there's also a strip-tease show on the first floor, in which case you pay a fixed admission charge that includes the price of a drink. Drink it slowly otherwise you'll be offered a refill in the next 5 minutes. Likewise be wary of girls who ask for a drink. They only drink cola but nowhere is cola more expensive than here. What's more, once you're upstairs, it isn't easy to slip away and you may be in for a few surprises.

The best thing is to carry only a small amount of money with you and insist that's all you have. As for the 'show', the artistes are the same girls you saw dancing on the ground floor. Their routine includes stunts with bananas, razor-blades, arrow-throwing – definitely not for the faint-hearted.

– Second place for debauchery goes to **Soi Cowboy** –ซอยคาวน์บอย, a little street parallel to Sukhumvit Road, tucked in between Soi 21 and Soi 23. However, the atmosphere here was rather sad.

– **Calypso Cabaret** – คาลิปโซคาบาเร: Sukhumvit Road, Soi 11, beside the Ambassador Hotel. ☎ 261-63-55 (during the day) or 254-04-44 (at night). Nightly performances at 8pm and 10pm lasting just over an hour. High admission charge includes the price of a drink. This is a good place because it seems to take the opposite line to every other place in town. All the artistes are transvestites who perform a dance routine while miming to world-famous tunes. They aren't dressed in Donald Cardwell originals but you'd never guess to look at them. There's nothing in the least debauched about this and the show remains very soft-core and light-hearted throughout, 'with candour rivalling naïvety' as they say in Thai love stories. It's very funny all the same.

– For **performances of traditional dancing** and **Thai boxing**, *see* 'National Theatre' and 'Thai boxing matches' under 'What to See'.

– **Other bars**: dozens of bars have opened in Bangkok in recent years, most of them depressing places popular with foreigners where you'll hear much talk of the 'good old days in Indochina'.

Another fairly lively place until not so long ago, packed with bars of every description, was the **Royal City Avenue** – รอยัลซิตี้อเวนิว (Soi Soonwijai, Rama IX), northwest of the city centre. Sadly though, the RCA (as regulars call it) came a cropper following some administrative hassle involving the police, so its current status is uncertain. It's still worth a visit if you're looking for somewhere off the beaten track, but you never quite know what to expect. It might be great and full of young people or completely deserted. The atmosphere varies from place to place, so take a look around first – by taxi if you plan on making a quick getaway.

## LEAVING BANGKOK

### BY AIR

❶ **Don Muang airport**– ท่าอากาศยานดอนเมือง (off D1, colour map 1) is about 25 kilometres (15 miles) north of town. High airport tax (about 500 Bts in 1999 but likely to increase substantially) on international flights, less high on domestic flights (30 Bts). A shuttle-bus service operates between the two terminals (international and domestic) and takes about 20 minutes. For flight information contact:

❶ **Bangkok International Airport** – ท่าอากาศยานดอนเมืองระหว่างประเทศ (off D1, colour map 1): ☎ 535-12-54 (departures); 535-13-01 (arrivals). Charter flight arrivals: ☎ 535-22-72.

❶ **Domestic Airport Information** – แผนกสอบถามข้อมูลสนามบินภายใน ประเทศ: ☎ 535-12-53 and 535-20-81.

There are lots of daily flights (three times as many in the high season) for Chiang Mai, Chiang Rai, Phuket, Mae Hong Son, Samui, Surat Thani, Trang, Hat Yai.

Be careful when buying international tickets from agencies in the Khao San Road. Watch out for the practice of overbooking, and flights that don't exist. The cheapest tickets aren't necessarily the best. And since the agencies change identity all the time, you have absolutely no come-back. Ask around first and find out where other backpackers go.

**Note**: Be aware of rumours of what can happen at certain airports throughout Asia, notably Thailand and the Philippines. Drugs are said to be planted in the pockets of unsuspecting passengers by crooks who then inform on them in exchange for a pay-off. Just to be on the safe side, be sure to check your pockets before departure.

### GETTING TO THE AIRPORT

#### By Train

All the trains going north stop at the airport, so there are regular departures from the station. They are handy in the rush-hour for avoiding the jams, although there's still the question of how you get to the station.

**By Public Bus**

No. 29 and 59 bus. Take the No. 29 from Hua Lamphong Station, Victory Monument or the Northern Bus Terminal. Take the No. 59 (or the A2, which has air-conditioning and luggage space) from the stop near the Grand Palace, Democracy Monument (near the Khao San Road), Victory Monument or from the Northern Bus Terminal. Take the No. 13 either from the Eastern or Northern Bus Terminals. Allow 2 hours to get there, longer in the rush-hour. It costs next to nothing.

**By Private Bus or Minibus**

Lots of agencies on the Khao San Road or in Soi Ngnam Duphli (both popular stamping grounds with backpackers) can arrange private transport to the airport at prices you can't argue with. The big advantages are frequent departures and being picked up outside your hotel.

**By Taxi**

Much more expensive, of course, but still reasonable particularly since drivers equipped with taxi-meters are more willing to switch them on when going to the airport than when driving away from it. A taxi gets you to the airport about 45 minutes faster than the bus.

**BY TRAIN**

There are two main stations in Bangkok:

🚆 The **Hua Lamphong station** – สถานีรถไฟหัวลำโพง (colour map I, C3) for trains going north and northeast as well as some going south. Left-luggage stays open 4am–10.30pm. For details: ☎ 223-70-10/20. It's best to make reservations as early as possible and tickets can be bought 2 months in advance from the station. Timetables are changeable, so check before you board.

🚆 **Thonburi station** – สถานีรถไฟธนบุรี (colour map I, A2) for other trains going south. So if that's where you're going, find out which of the two stations your train leaves from.

– **For Chiang Mai**: two trains during the day and four at night. Take the night train: it saves wasting a day and makes the 12-hour journey seem shorter. Avoid the Rapid, which is probably the slowest. The best train is the Express Special which has couchettes (remember to reserve yours well in advance since they soon get booked up). Top bunks are cheaper than bottom ones but narrower too. A restaurant service operates in first and second class. A word of warning: try to get a couchette with a fan on the night train. Otherwise, always pack a sweater because it's freezing in the air-conditioned carriages.

Nearly all the trains stop in Ayutthaya and Phitsanulok.

– **Going northeast**: five departures daily for Khon Kaen and Udon Thani, three for Nongkhaï, ten for Surin and seven for Ubon Ratchathani.

– **Going south**: to Surat Thani, Hat Yai and Sungai Kolok (on Thailand's southern border). About ten departures daily for Surat Thani, including two useful night-trains. It takes about 10 hours. Four night-trains go to

Hat Yai and two go all the way to Thailand's border with Malaysia, including one that goes right through to Butterworth (in Malaysia).

– **Going towards Malaysia and Singapore**: it is possible to go to Singapore by train, but you have to change at least twice – once in Butterworth and once in Kuala Lumpur. Seats for these destinations should be booked in advance and, if using a small travel agency, only buy a ticket as far as Butterworth or it could get complicated. Trains often run late, so don't cut your connections too fine. It's worth taking the night-train between Kuala Lumpur and Singapore.

## BY NATIONAL BUS

There are two kinds of bus: with and without air-conditioning. When travelling long-distance, you are strongly advised to take an air-conditioned bus. Fares are cheaper than on private buses but not much. There are three bus terminals depending on your destination.

🚌 **Northern** and **Northeastern Bus Terminal** – สถานีขนส่งสาย เหนือหมอชิด (off D1, colour map 1): behind Chatuchak Park. Take the No. 39 or 59 bus from Democracy Monument. All air-conditioned and non-air-conditioned buses going north and northeast depart from here. The two terminals are just a short distance apart.

Air-conditioned buses leave for Chiang Mai about 20 times a day and for Ayutthaya every 30 minutes from 6am to 6pm.

🚌 **Southern Bus Terminal** – สถานีขนส่งรถปรับอากาศสายใต้ (off A1, colour map 1): Pin Khao Nakhonchaisi Road in Thonburi. ☎ 435-11-99. From Khao San Road, walk to the Phra Pin Khao Bridge (about 5 minutes away). Lots of buses go from there to the terminal. From Silom Road, take the No. 7 or 11 air-conditioned bus. Buses (air-conditioned) go south from the Southern Bus Terminal to Kanchanaburi, Koh Samui, Krabi, Trang, Hua-Hin, Phuket, Phang Nga, Hat Yai, etc.

🚌 **New Southern Bus Terminal** – สถานีขนส่งรถธรรมดาสายใต้ใหม่ (off A1, colour map 1): Pin Khao Nakhonchaisi Road. ☎ 434-55-57/58. Buses for the same destinations as above but not nearly such good value because they're all non-air-conditioned.

🚌 **Eastern Bus Terminal** – สถานีขนส่งสายคะวันออก (off B4, colour map 11): Sukhumvit Road, near Soi 42. ☎ 391-25-04 and 392-92-27 (week-days); 391-00-64 (weekends). Take the No. 2 bus from Democracy Monument. All the buses from here (air-conditioned and non-air-conditioned) go east towards Pattaya, Rayong, Chanthaburi and Trat.

## BY PRIVATE BUS

There are privately operated bus companies all over Bangkok and plenty of agencies that can sell you tickets to wherever you want to go. Many of these are on the Khao San Road, Sukhumvit Road and in the area where you find the big hotels, next to the Indra Hotel (Indra Tour: Rajprarop Road. ☎ 251-61-97. Two departures daily for Chiang Mai). Naturally it's not as cheap as going by national bus but the service is first-class and you get pillows, food and drinks. Booking through an agency costs a few bahts extra but it's worth it for the time you save. Avoid going by minibus: more comfortable in principle but actually there's almost no leg-room.

Private buses are generally pretty luxurious, even very luxurious. If you're travelling long-distance, travel at night. Don't buy your ticket until you've compared the prices in several agencies.

**Note**: everyone's heard of people on the bus being drugged and waking up next morning to find themselves stranded in their underwear by the side of the road with none of their belongings. It's all very well to laugh but it does happen, even if it isn't as common today as it used to be. Never accept sweets from strangers and that goes for fruit, food and drinks too. They could contain a soporific. There's no need for alarm, but watch your back.

Another thing: when buying tickets for Chiang Mai, some agencies offer you a bus ticket at a knock-down price plus a night's free accommodation in a hotel they have an arrangement with. Very nice too, you might think, but actually this is a plot to get you to sign up for a trek organized by the hotel agency. Decline at your peril – people have been thrown out who didn't sign up immediately.

And one more thing: all the private buses leaving from the Khao San Road stop about 10 kilometres (6 miles) from Chiang Mai, usually at a car-park where thousands of touts descend upon you with offers of pick-ups to take you to the centre. Since there's no other way of getting there, you're entirely at their mercy so be warned.

It's as well to be aware, too, that the number of bus accidents is on the increase – perhaps because buses are driven too fast by drivers battling to keep to impossible schedules. When going to Chiang Mai, or travelling any long distance, you're better off on the train, even if it is much more expensive than the prices advertised by the bus companies.

## BANGKOK TO SINGAPORE

If you're in a hurry to go south from Bangkok, it's worth taking the international Express, which does go slightly faster than the local trains. Bangkok to Singapore takes about 48 hours.

Additionally, plenty of agencies on the Khao San Road and next to the Malaysia Hotel have plane tickets from Bangkok to Singapore at 'bucket shop' prices. Do check that the flight exists, just the same.

BANGKOK

## SOUTHEAST OF BANGKOK

# ANCIENT CITY AND CROCODILE FARM – เมืองโบราณและฟาร์มจระเข้

DIALLING CODE: 02

Both of these are about 30 kilometres (19 miles) southeast of Bangkok, on the old Pattaya road. For the Crocodile Farm, take the No. 25 or 102 bus to Samutprakarn Town (going towards Paknam) then the S1 or S55 minibus to the farm, which is 2 kilometres (just over 1 mile) away. For the Ancient City, get off at Paknam, then take the 36 minibus. Allow about 30 minutes to get there. The quickest way is by direct bus: the red, route 38 bus opposite the Eastern Terminal (on Sukhumvit Road). Otherwise, take the No. 11 bus opposite the Mercedes office at the Democracy Monument to the terminal in Paknam, then a minibus to Muang Boran (ancient Thai name for the Ancient City). Do the same in reverse for the return journey, having first crossed the motorway on foot. One final possibility is to club together with others and hire a taxi or, probably cheaper still, go on a tour.

★ **Ancient City** – เมืองโบราณ. Sadly, this is one excursion often over-looked by tourists. Open daily, 8am–5pm ☎ 323-9253.

● Website: www.ancientcity.com

The entire visit takes about 3–4 hours. This is in fact a folly, donated to Thailand by a nostalgic millionaire Mercedes dealer with a taste for culture. In an area covering about 80 hectares (200 acres) he recreated some 80 large monuments (life-size or one-third life-size) from Thailand's past – and used up most of his money doing so. Magnificent though they are, the buildings today are being swallowed up by the jungle for lack of funds. Our bold millionaire it seems, simply can't afford to maintain them and as a result these rather-too-new buildings have acquired a 'patina' of moss and grass and the whole place has a quietly decadent atmosphere that's rather pleasing. During the week there's hardly anyone here, so it's the perfect place to escape for half a day from Bangkok's jams and pollution. This is somewhere 'zen', to be seen ideally at the start of your trip to give you an idea of the local architecture.

– Some outstanding buildings: the Khao Phra Wihan (No. 72 on the complimentary map you receive on the way in) is a magnificent Khmer temple built on a huge artificial hill overgrown with jungle.

– Another masterpiece is the Sanphet Prasat (No. 27 on the map). Demolished by the Burmese, this magnificent palace from Ayutthaya was reconstructed using period documents. The present replica is a third of the building's original size.

– You will also find a replica of the delightful floating market (No. 45 on the map) with its walkways, wooden houses and stalls. Very beautiful, very calm, the whole place is a remarkable open-air museum in the real sense of the word. You can eat lunch here quite cheaply.

★ About 3 kilometres (1.5 miles) from the Ancient City is **Crocodile Farm** – ฟาร์มจระเข้. Open daily, 7am–6pm. To be avoided at weekends when it's packed. The admission charge seems expensive if you haven't got children, considering what there is to see. In the space of a few years, the farm itself has been transformed into a full-blown amusement park complete with zoo, dinosaur museum, go-karts, little train, pedalos, crocodile and elephant displays (alternating every 30 minutes from 9am to 4pm), rifle-shooting, and the inevitable restaurants and souvenir shops galore (specializing in things made out of crocodile skin).

Seeing so many saurians in one place is fairly mind-blowing – there are about 40,000 crocs in all and nine different species. The most impressive are the salt-water crocodiles, which can grow to 5 metres (15 feet) long and live for several months without food. When underwater, special membranes stop the water from entering their ears and throat. Like all reptiles, these are cold-blooded animals that need external warmth to accelerate their bodily functions, which explains why crocs only copulate in broad daylight and in full sun – so much for privacy.

The best time to go is between 4.30pm and 5.30pm, when you get to see the wee beasties being fed.

# PATTAYA – พัทยา                      DIALLING CODE: 038

Some 144 kilometres (90 miles) southeast of Bangkok and about 2 hours 30 minutes away by bus, Pattaya is no longer the delightful fishing village it was just 10 years ago. The sad truth is that Pattaya is now the biggest brothel in the world, with more prostitutes per square metre than anywhere else. Over the past few years, the urban landscape around this pleasant seaside town nestling around a very pretty beach has broken out in a rash of jerry-built hotels with hideous towers, and bars where every other seat is taken by an obliging girl.

To be blunt, Pattaya has gone over the top. This is a place where even the local people are reluctant to say where they live. Plus the beach is polluted, the atmosphere stinks and this is the ideal place to catch whatever disease happens to be all the rage at the moment. Give it a miss.

### PATTAYA THE SEEDY

The booming sex industry attracts the type of tourist that you may well be trying to avoid on your trip to Thailand. Pattaya is a popular destination for package tours and legions of wild-eyed tourists from all over the world come here solely to take advantage of the cheapest rates available in the sex industry in southeast Asia. If witnessing groups of drunken Westerners trawling the streets and bars, eyeing up the talent is not your idea of a fun time, then you are advised to steer well clear. Pattaya earned its reputation as a thriving sex industry in 1959 when American GIs stationed nearby came looking for a good time, and local businessmen figured that selling sex was one way to get rich quick. The place is now unrecognisable from its humble origins as a fishing village, with its flashing neon signs in English and German, tawdry strip-tease shows, cafes serving fish and chips, bratwurst and burgers and the generally tacky atmosphere. The main street is lined with bars that make no attempt to disguise what they are offering. Pattaya is now also renowned for its gay scene, with some bars catering to an exclusively gay clientele. You may also see *katoeys* (transvestites) soliciting in the street, alongside other male and female hookers. Racketeering, prostitution and crime sustain the economy here, and the general atmosphere can be pretty depressing, if you are trying to discover the 'real Thailand'.

The one thing that saves Pattaya from a completely negative reputation is the wide range of watersports on offer in the area, although participating in these can be expensive if you want to try your hand at water-skiing, riding a waterscooter or diving. Windsurfing is probably the only activity that's reasonably priced, so take advantage of the opportunity if you come to Pattaya.

## GETTING THERE FROM BANGKOK

**Eastern Bus Terminal** – สถานีขนส่งสายตะวันออก: Sukhumvit Road, near Soi 42. National bus service, non-stop, very cheap, every 30 minutes from 5.30am to 10.30pm.

Minibuses can be booked through any travel agency. They are much more expensive than public transport but they do pick you up at your hotel.

## USEFUL ADDRESSES

**TAT** (Tourism Authority of Thailand) – ททท: 246/1 Chaichat Road or Pattaya Beach Road. ☎ 428-750 or 427-667. Open daily, 8am–4.30pm. Very helpful staff, well-thought-out street plan.

**Post office** – ไปรษณีย์: on Pattaya 2, Soi Chaiyasit. Open Monday–Friday, 8.30am–4.30pm.

**Telephone exchange** – ศูนย์โทรศัพท์: on South Pattaya Road, near the corner with Pattaya 3 Road. Open Monday–Friday, 8.30am–4.30pm, noon on Saturday.

**Pattaya Memorial Hospital** – โรงพยาบาลพัทยาเม็มโมเรียล: on Central Pattaya Road. ☎ 429-422/ 424.

**Tourist police** – ตำรวจท่องเที่ยว: ☎ 29-371 or 425-937. Emergency number: ☎ 16-99.

## WHERE TO STAY

If you do need a bed for the night, you'll find the cheapest guesthouses are around sois 12 and 13, in a quiet area very near the beach. The price tends to be negotiable off season.

**LEAVING PATTAYA**

– **For Bangkok**: by bus from North Pattaya Road, 200 metres before Sukhumvit Road. Departures every 30 minutes, from 5am to 9pm.

– **For Koh Samet**: the terminal is on Sukhumvit Road, just beyond the junction with Central Pattaya Road. There are no direct buses for Ban Phe. Take a non-air-conditioned bus as far as Rayong, then a *songthaew* (pick-up) to Ban Phe (where the boats leave for Koh Samet). Departures about every 30 minutes, from 7am until late afternoon. It takes 2 hours.

# KOH SAMET (KO SAMET) – เกาะเสม็ด

DIALLING CODE: 038

A lovely little island just a few hours from Bangkok, the delightful Koh Samet escaped the concrete invasion and remains a haven for backpackers. It's probably because the island forms part of a nature reserve that it is protected from ecological disasters elsewhere. The coast is lined with heavenly beaches: white sand, coconut trees, bungalows on the beach, warm waters – this place seems to have it all.

There are one or two drawbacks just the same. First, lots of young Thais come here during the holidays and at weekends, which means it can get quite noisy – great if you like riotous gatherings around the campfire with much guitar playing and imbibing of *Mekong*.

That apart, the island apparently is still a breeding ground for malarial mosquitoes, however much the locals deny it. Watch too for shoals of jellyfish in January and February that can bring you out in hives. If you get stung, there is ointment made of raw banana, which is very effective. Lastly, while this may be a nature reserve, you'll still find piles of rubbish behind every bungalow. However, the refuse collection service is being looked at, so things are set to improve.

What you're left with is a place with sensational beaches as yet untouched by mass tourism (no concrete hotels or surfaced roads, except for a short stretch around the village of Na Dan), where you can spend a few blissful days. It's as well to know that anyone landing on the island has to pay 50 Bts to enter the so-called nature reserve (the ticket is valid for the duration of your stay).

**GETTING THERE**

– **From Bangkok**: from the Eastern Bus Terminal on Sukhumvit Road take the bus to Ban Phe (from where the boats leave for Koh Samet). Air-conditioned buses at 7am, 4pm, 6pm and 8.30pm. Non-air-conditioned buses eight times a day between 6.30am and 5.15pm (they take 4 hours).

– **From Pattaya**: *see* 'Leaving Pattaya'.

**SOUTHEAST OF BANGKOK**

### CROSSING FROM BAN PHE – บ้านเพ

There are three jetties in front of the bus terminal. Frequency of departure depends on the number of passengers (20 on average) and the crossing takes about 45 minutes. Often the boats belong to people who own bungalows on the island, who will inevitably try to rent you a room, but there's no obligation. The last boat leaves at about 4pm. A return ticket costs less but you have to travel on the same boat both ways (which won't always be the first to leave).

There are several jetties on the island: either in the north, in the island's only village of Na Dan, or on the beaches at Cho and Wong Duan, unless you prefer to isolate yourself on the beach at Phrao (the only beach on the west of the island) or Klu Na Nok. The choice is yours, but do find out where each boat goes (since they only go to one place) or you might end up stranded.

### GETTING AROUND THE ISLAND

Only the coastal part of the island is inhabited, where the beaches are. Given how small the island is (7 kilometres long by 3 kilometres wide/3 miles by 1.5 miles at its widest), walking is ideal along the footpaths and beaches unless you're carrying a lot of luggage (in which case take a taxi-van). There are no roads in the south of the island, only footpaths.

### WHERE TO STAY AND WHERE TO EAT

Not bad in terms of bungalows for backpackers: basic and friendly. A word of advice just the same: all the electricity on the island is provided by generators and there is one generator per compound of bungalows. Do check that it isn't next to the bungalow you plan to stay in, otherwise it could get very noisy when night falls. Also, remember to pack a torch if you want to go out at night.

All the addresses below serve food and the best ones are indicated. Nearly all of them have a selection of books in English, French and Swedish (something to while away those long evenings) and many of them also show a video at night, in the dining room.

Here's the lowdown on the different beaches, starting in the north.

### HAT SAI KAEW BEACH (HAT SAI KAEW) – หาดทรายแก้ว

The largest beach on the island, and the prettiest, too, before all these bungalows were built here, one on top of the other. Not the quietest place either, so if you want a decent night's sleep, give it a miss and go down south.

### HIN KHOK BEACH (AO HIN KHOK) – หาดหินโกก

Only separated from the previous one by rocks with a statue of a mermaid sitting on top.

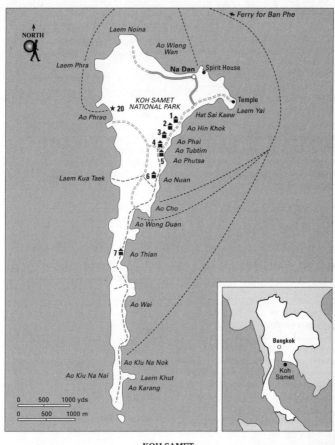

**KOH SAMET**

---

**⌂ Where to Stay and Where to Eat**

1 Naga Bungalows
2 Tok's Little Hut
3 Ao Phai Huts
4 Sea Breeze
5 Silver Sand

6 Nuan Kitchen
7 Lung Dam Beach

★ **What to See**

20 Ao Phrao Beach

---

⌂ ✕ **Naga Bungalows** – นาค
าบังกาโล (map, **1**): ☎ 038-652-
448. On the far left of the beach
as you look out to sea. Unpretentious bamboo bungalows, built on
a little hill. Four walls, mattress on
the floor, strip-lighting, with or
without fan – that's it. Shared

bathroom facilities. It's basic, but the atmosphere is good (young and informal) and so is the food (delicious fried noodles, chicken in peanut sauce, sweet-and-sour pork). Great breakfast too, served on the pleasant overhanging terrace, and a mouth-watering selection of homemade cakes: banana pie, fudge cake (a must), and brownies. The kind of place that appeals to backpackers – let's hope it stays that way when the owner has finished making it bigger. You can borrow books, provided you leave a deposit.

🛏 ✗ **Tok's Little Hut** – โต๊กลิตเดิ้ลฮัท (map, **2**): beside Naga Bungalows. These well-maintained wooden bungalows all have private shower, fan and mosquito net. Best value for money on the island. Prices vary according to the bungalow's position on the beach (some of them are almost at the top of the hill). Food is also available, but eating at Naga Bungalows is recommended.

## PHAI BEACH (AO PHAI) – หาดไผ่

This one is a favourite.

🛏 ✗ **Ao Phai Huts** – กระท่อมอ่าวไผ่ (map, **3**): next to the beach but not directly on it. ☎ 353-2-44. Very well-maintained compound of bungalows old and new, for two or four people. Range of facilities (WC, shower, air-conditioning or fan) at prices that vary accordingly. Visit several, avoiding those nearest the path (four-wheel-drives often pass early in the morning). The restaurant is good, with food served on a terrace that's surrounded by trees and has a view of the sea. There is a safe and a selection of books. Bungalows at the water's edge are more expensive but generally cleaner than the ones away from the beach.

🛏 ✗ **Sea Breeze** – ซีบรีส (map, **4**): good site for cheap bungalows. There are three types in all: the cheapest have no fan and the more expensive ones have a fan, WC and shower. Some are really close to the beach. Avoid those nearest to the restaurant as they show videos at night and it can get a bit rowdy. Laundry service available.

### EXPENSIVE

🛏 **Silver Sand** – ซิลเวอร์แซนด (map, **5**): much prettier little bungalows in a charming corner of the beach. The most luxurious ones offer good value for money, with private shower, attractive furniture and air-conditioning.

## NUAN BEACH (AO NUAN) – หาดนวล

Not easy to get to, this tiny beach nestles in a little inlet surrounded by rocks. To reach it, you have to follow the coastal path up into the forest and from there go back down to the beach. It's easy to miss, so keep your eyes open.

🛏 ✗ **Nuan Kitchen** – นวลคิทเช่น (map, **6**): just eight bungalows arranged around a deliciously fragrant garden. The ideal place for lovers. Delightfully simple traditional straw huts with mosquito nets. No electricity (the owner refuses to install it), but charming tilly-lamps instead. Shared bathroom facilities. Divine food, blissfully quiet – Robinson Crusoe would be in his element. The only snag, as you would expect, is that it's often full. Try to find out from those already there when they are leaving, and make a reservation.

### WONG DUAN BEACH (AO WONG DUAN) – หาดวงเดือน

The biggest beach on the island along with Hat Sai Kaeo. Very beautiful, of course, but not ideal for several reasons – it's where the ferries arrive from Ban Phe; it's where the rich and famous come, since they're the only ones who can afford the bungalows; it's full of boats that make a noise during siesta time. There's no point spending any time here, particularly as other, wilder places beckon.

### THIAN BEACH (AO THIAN) – หาดเทียน

This must be the quietest beach on the island – ideal for those who just want to be alone.

🛏 ✗ **Lung Dam Beach** – ดุงดำบิช (map, **7**): ☎ 01-458-840. Very simple bungalows with mosquito nets, with or without private shower room. A bit more expensive than the others and not up to the same standards (tranquillity has its price). But the food is pretty good (which is just as well since there's nowhere else to eat) and the owner's a nice guy who speaks good English.

## WHAT TO SEE

– **The sunset**: to see this, go to the only beach on the western side of the island: **Ao Phrao** – อ่าวพร้าว (map, **20**). You'll find the turn-off on the main path going north to south, roughly in between Tubtim and Phutsa beaches (*see* map). You can sleep on the beach, but while it's very deserted, it isn't quiet.

– **Other beaches**: south of Thian, there are some lovely walks to other beaches.

## WHAT TO DO

Not a lot and so much the better.

– On the other hand, you could always have a little massage on the beach. You'll generally find some masseuses on **Hin Khok** beach. Each massage lasts an hour and – ladies rest assured – your partner is in safe hands. This is an energetic massage – just what you need to sort your head out (along with everything else . . . ). It would be a shame to miss it.

– **Windsurfing**, **surfing**, **jet-skiing**, **water-skiing**, particularly on the Hat Sai Kaeo and Wong Duan beaches.

– **Boat trips** around the island or to surrounding islands.

## LEAVING KOH SAMET

– Take the boat back to **Ban Phe**: lots of boats leave every day from the village of Na Dang and the Wong Duan beach.

– **For Bangkok**: the bus terminal is on the Nuanthip Pier, to the right of the landing stages in front of a large, covered market. It's somewhere to go while you wait, and sells mainly shellfish and dried fish. Regular air-conditioned bus service, 10 times a day, 4am–6pm; nine non-air-conditioned buses, 5am–5.30pm.

– **For Pattaya**: you can also go by bus. Find one immediately on the right as you come from the port.

– **For Koh Chang**: *see* 'Getting There', or enquire at S.T. Travel, which has a little agency on the first pontoon on the right, as you face the sea. Their minibuses from Bangkok drop people off in Koh Samet on the way to Koh Chang.

# KOH CHANG (KO CHANG) – เกาะช้าง

DIALLING CODE: 039

Mu Koh Chang is an archipelago of about 50 islands that together form a national park. The largest is Koh Chang, a magnificent island with impressive mountains, (the highest, at 744 metres/2,440 feet is Khao Jom Prast), and the second-largest island in Thailand (in terms of size) after Phuket. It remains largely unspoilt. Seen from the boat some 8 kilometres (5 miles) offshore, the island looks fiercely virginal, with vast, beautiful beaches, some totally wild and deserted, others thick with coconut palms. There are lots of coconut palms on the island and they add to the charm of the surroundings. Legend has it that the island was named after an elephant's backside *(chang)*, and one family did try to raise elephants here, without ever quite getting the hang of it.

Hardly anyone lives here, despite the 500 square kilometres (300 square miles) of available space, apart from fishermen, coconut-growers, rubber-farmers, bungalow-owners and tourists. If you're into nature and doing daring things, (diving and walking through the jungle, for example), you could be in for the time of your life, against the backdrop of the white sand and the turquoise sea. Make the most of it while you can, because things always seem to change. Note that there's no cash machine on the island, so come prepared.

**Note**: malaria is reputed to be particularly prevalent here, although locals and resident backpackers deny it. The local advice is not to go walking in the jungle at sundown (so don't say you weren't warned). There's a **Health Centre** in Ban Khlong Prao (a sort of bush hospital, with the word 'Malaria' written on the front . . .).

Find out what's what before leaving Britain, by calling: **Medical Advisory Service for Travellers Abroad (MASTA)**. ☎ (0891) 224100 (UK number). They will send you written information tailored to your journey.

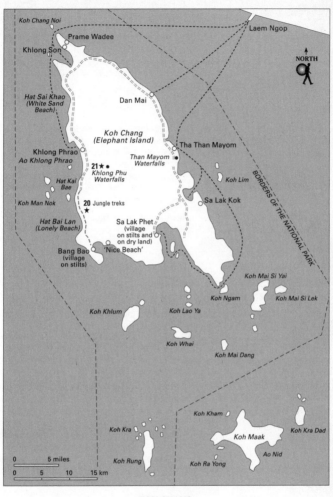

**KOH CHANG**

★ **What to Do and What to See**

**20** Jungle trips

**21** Khlong Phu Waterfalls

## GETTING THERE

– **By boat**: departures for Koh Chang every hour, 9am–6pm, from the little village of Laem Ngop – แหลมงอบ (boats can be late if there aren't enough passengers). There are six boarding points around the island, but the two main ones are north of White Sand Beach (very overcrowded) and in the northeast, which is the coast nearest to Laem Ngop.

## GETTING TO LAEM NGOP

– **From Bangkok**: East Bus Terminal. First you have to get to Trat, a province and large town in the east of Thailand, where any of the *songthaews* near the market on Sukhumvit Road can take you to Laem Ngop (30 minutes). Air-conditioned buses leave for Trat six times a day, 9am–noon (the trip is 370 kilometres/230 miles and takes 5 hours); non-air-conditioned buses leave nine times a day, 3.30am–2.30pm, and there's a 6-hour ride on a night bus, leaving at 11pm.

Lots of agencies in Bangkok offer to take you straight to the island (by minibus and boat). Contact S.T. Travel: 102 Rambutri Road (opposite the Vieng Thai Hotel). ☎ 281-3662 or 282-7312. It's a lot simpler by minibus, but you experience much more of the real thing if you take the bus.

– **From Koh Samet**: going by bus isn't a very practical option. From Ban Phe you have to take a *songthaew* to Rayong, then a bus to Trat, followed by another *songthaew* to Laem Ngop.

It's much simpler to book a boat/minibus trip through S.T. Travel in the Wong Duan Resort. Boats leave at 8.30am and noon, but book ahead.

## GETTING AROUND THE ISLAND

Pending the completion of works currently underway (let's hope progress is slow) there are only two roads (actually, tracks would be more appropriate) on Koh Chang. One goes east, to link up with the village of Sa Lak Pet; the other follows the coast west to Kaï Bae Beach (where you're recommended to go). Wherever you land on the island (landings are basic pontoons surrounded by a few houses on stilts), there will be taxis waiting to take you to the beach of your choice. Once there, you'll find motorbikes and four-wheel-drives for hire, and there's hardly any traffic so they're a great way to enjoy the countryside.

## WHERE TO STAY AND WHERE TO EAT

Most of the bungalows are on the west coast where you also find the best beaches. The island still doesn't have mains electricity, which is mainly provided by generators.

### WHITE SAND BEACH (HAT SAI KHAO) – หาดทรายขาว

The longest beach on the island, and not recommended unless you like noisy video shows and bars that stay open all night serving a mainly young clientele. If you do fancy staying here, there's no problem finding a bungalow – there are loads of them.

## KHLONG PHRAO BEACH (AO KHLONG PHRAO) – หาดคลองพร้าว

Immense white sandy beach with just two bungalows, which you get to from the little village of Khlong Phrao. If you're after peace and quiet, this is for you. Bike or motorbike is a must if you want to get around.

🛏 ✕ **K.P. Bungalows** – เค.พี. บังกาโล: traditional bamboo-and-straw houses. Private/shared bathroom facilities (cold shower with jugs), mosquito nets. Cost more facing the sea. Restaurant facilities, motorbike hire, telephone, laundry service. Simple and cheap.

🛏 ✕ **P.S.S. Bungalows** – พี.เอส.เอส. บังกาโล: right at the end of the beach, near the Khlong Phrao river (opposite a little fishing village on the water). Twenty simple bungalows in an idyllic setting, overgrown with moss and shaded by coconut trees. Shared bathroom facilities. Warm welcome.

## KAÏ BAE BEACH (HAT KAÏ BAE) – หาดไก่แบ้

A great beach – this is where the road ends, so it's the perfect place for exploring deserted beaches or trekking into the jungle. A haven of authentic hospitality, full of simple, cheap bungalows shaded by coconut palms. No sense of overcrowding, loads of charm and many of the bungalows face the sea. Most places serve food and the cooking is usually excellent.

🛏 ✕ **Nang Nuan** – บังกาโลนางนวล: one of the first places you come across, on the right of the entrance to the beach. Nineteen simple straw huts with shared bathroom facilities, fans and mosquito nets, plus two bungalows for six people with private bathroom facilities (price per person). The owner, known to everyone as 'Mama', is warm and welcoming and an excellent Thai cook. Her yellow curry and the tuna steak are highly recommended. Mama can also arrange boat trips to three islands where you can snorkel at very reasonable prices. Friendly atmosphere.

🛏 ✕ **Corol Bungalow Resort** – คอรัลบังกาโลรีสอร์ท: just beyond Nang Nuan. ☎ 012-193-815 (mobile). Traditional bungalows as well as newer ones built of solid materials, with private bathroom facilities (cold water) fan and mosquito nets. Nice decor. Great restaurant

at the end of a little dyke, where the *ho mok* (dried curry seafood) is unbelievably good: selection of fish cooked in coconut milk and served in aluminium foil (don't miss it). Welcome not so great.

🛏 ✕ **Kaï Bae Hut** – กระท่อมหาด ไก่แบ้: on the left at the entrance to the beach. Plain wood-and-bamboo bungalows with or without private bathroom facilities. Visit several before you choose. Nice welcome, good restaurant.

✕ **Comfortable Bar** – บาร์คอม ฟอร์เทเบิลของคุณวิวัฒน์: small bar/restaurant set back from the beach, on the far right as you face the sea. Wood-and-bamboo decor with shells and snakeskins (there are lots of snakes on the surrounding islands). Run by a Thai-boxing instructor called Vivat, the restaurant features a punchball for aspiring boxers. Friendly welcome.

## WHAT TO SEE AND DO

🐟 **Diving** – ดำน้ำ: most of the landlords can arrange to take you snorkelling for the day, in the waters that teem with marine life off the islands surrounding Koh Chang (*see* 'Mama' at the Nang Nuan). For scuba-diving (day trips or maiden dives), the person to contact is Adrien Luedtke – a Swiss guy who's been living here since 1994. You'll find his shop behind the Kaï Bae Hut restaurant (on the right at the entrance to the beach).

★ **Khlong Phu Waterfalls** – น้ำตกคลองภู (map, **21**): these waterfalls are not as high as those on Than Mayom (reachable from the east coast). An opportunity to explore the jungle and take a dip when you get there. The best way to go is by mountain bike (which you can hire in Corol Cove). It takes about 1 hour 15 minutes by bike and 2 hours 30 minutes on foot. From Kaï Bae Beach, take the track going north (5 kilometres/3 miles) then turn right along a little road marked with an arrow. Take the bicycle across the first river and carry on until you reach the car-park, where you can leave the bikes and climb the path leading to the falls (the drop is 30 metres/90 feet). Dive into a natural pool of cool, clear water.

# TRIP TO BANG BAO

★ **Bang Bao** – บางเบ้: is a typical little fishing village consisting of about 40 houses with corrugated iron roofs, built on stilts. There are only about 80 inhabitants. The only way to get there is by long-tail boat or on foot through the jungle. Supplies reach Bang Bao just twice a week. The only water supply here is a communal one. At certain times of day, water is piped to each house in turn, and people fill basins, buckets, bowls and containers of every description. You get from one dwelling to another on makeshift roads made of planks.

## GETTING THERE

– **By long-tail boat**: from Kaï Bae Beach. Perfect if you haven't got the energy but you do have the money. Just keep an eye out for the fishermen who sometimes come to the beach to check people out.

– **On foot**: from Kaï Bae Beach. Only for those who are basically fit and have a sense of direction. Leave early in the morning when it's cool. Takes about 3 hours.

## CROSSING THE JUNGLE

First, follow Kaï Bae Beach south, to the end, past the elegant Sea View bungalow compound (map, **20**) with its well-kept garden, until you reach some bungalows on a hillside. This is where you start the climb up into the jungle, and you'll find a rope there to help you. Follow the winding path through the lush vegetation; it's a good idea to arm yourself with a stick and strike the tree trunks as you go, to announce your presence to the local wildlife. On your right, you can feel the sea is really close. Then, you begin a long descent to Lonely Beach, which lives up to its name (though not for long perhaps . . .) and which you follow almost to the end. Branch off when you reach a little path on the left that leads through the coconut grove to a collection of five traditional straw huts. These are owned by a young German girl called Pamela who has settled here and is gradually signposting the path to Bang Bao. From here, the path penetrates deeper and deeper into the jungle, effectively cutting off the southwestern point of the island (very steep in places, with several stiff climbs and precipitous descents) before descending once again towards a huge coconut grove leading to the village.

● **Getting back**: there are two alternatives – either hitch a lift back to Kaï Bae Beach with a local fisherman (agree the price first) or walk back the way you came (but spend at least a night in Bang Bao).

● **From Bang Bao**: seasoned trekkers only can also walk to the village of Sa Lak Phet – หมู่บ้านสลักเพชร (at least a 6-hour hike through the jungle). Take food, water, a torch and, if possible, a compass, walking-boots and mosquito repellent.


## WHERE TO STAY

♗ The young people of Bang Bao are crazy about snooker and you can't miss the two snooker halls in the little main street. Before the first one (on the right as you come from the land), you'll find a little restaurant that can offer you a bed for the night if you need it (highly recommended). Anyone staying here has access to the lovely beach called 'Nice Beach' just 10 minutes east of the village.


## A FEW WORDS OF ADVICE

– Anyone intending to cross the jungle on foot is advised to wear a pair of sturdy walking boots).

– If in doubt as to which road to take at a junction (there aren't many), always take the one that runs nearest the coast.

– On your way, you'll pass a number of isolated dwellings for people who work in the coconut groves or on the *heveas* (latex plantations). To ask them the way, simply say: 'Paï Bang Bao' – ไปบางเบ้า ('I'm going to Bang Bao') and they'll point you in the right direction.

# WEST OF BANGKOK

# NAKHON PATHOM – นครปฐม

DIALLING CODE: 034

Believed to be the cradle of Buddhist teaching in Thailand, Nakohn Pathom is home to the tallest *chedi* (or *stupa*) in the world – it's 120 metres (350 feet) high and richly decorated with glazed Chinese tiles. Some say that the Buddha rested there, and others that it contains relics belonging to him – but everyone agrees that the building is a very sacred place. Just in case you had any doubts, the arrow on the pagoda was struck by lightning during a thunderstorm in 1995 and the next day the story was in all the papers – proof, if any more proof were needed, of the holiness of the Phra Pathom.

## A BRIEF HISTORY

Once upon a time a long, long time ago – 'three centuries before the present era' – there was a mighty Indian king called Ashoka who converted to Buddhism and immediately sent out missionary monks to the 'Land of Gold' to spread the word throughout Asia. It was then that Nakhon Pathom was founded. Hundreds of years later, from the sixth century onwards, Nakon Pathom became a site of major archaeological discovery, which eventually led the Mon people to build the first Sri Lankan-style *chedi* there in the 10th century.

Built on the site of the present-day pagoda, the Mon *chedi* was destroyed in the 11th century by the new Khmer occupants, who replaced it with a Hindu-inspired *prang*. The city then sank into oblivion once again and did not re-emerge until 1860 when King Mongkut went there on a pilgrimage and ordered the site to be restored. The new *chedi* was subsequently completed by the well-loved king Chulalongkorn.

## GETTING THERE FROM BANGKOK

– **By train**: ten departures a day from Hua Lamphong, three from Thonburi. Takes from 1 hour to 1 hour and 30 minutes. Very convenient.

– **By bus**: departures every 20 minutes between 6am and 10.30pm, from the Southern Bus Terminal on Pin Khao Nakhonchaisai Road. Should take about an hour but can take longer in the rush-hour.

## WHERE TO STAY AND WHERE TO EAT

There's really no good reason to spend the night. The town has very few places, and only one of them is any good.

🛏 **Mitr Paisal Hotel** – โอเด็ลมิตร ไพศาล: 120/30 Phypan Road. ☎ 242-422. In the first side-street on the right as you leave the train station. About 250–350 Bts for a double room with fan or air-conditioning. A bit old-fashioned but clean. Not very welcoming and not cheap either but it's central.

🍴 It's worth eating at the **market**, held daily in the street leading from the station to the *chedi* and the nearby side-streets. Try the *khao lam,* a local speciality based on sticky rice and coconut milk, steamed and served on a split bamboo. Masses of fruit kebabs too. Incredible atmosphere on Sunday when the local blind people put on a concert and the Thais smile more than ever.

🍴 There are three good **restaurants** at the edge of the *khlong,* on the right coming from the *chedi.*

## GUIDED TOUR OF THE FAMOUS *CHEDI*

It's a good idea to start the tour early in the morning or late in the evening. Otherwise, your best chances of avoiding groups of tourists are between the hours of 1 and 2.30pm. There aren't many tours in English and the monks aren't very helpful. Allow 1 hour 30 minutes for a detailed visit.

Following the guide on a tour that leaves from the northern entrance (opposite the station) and proceeds in a clockwise direction (always keep the building on your right):

● A short flight of steps leads to the two circular terraces where you'll find the first chapel or **northern *viharn*** (there are three similar ones on each of the other cardinal points), which is famous for its standing Buddha in the Sukhothai style. This is where you get your first glimpse of the *chedi* bells that are designed to proclaim the Buddha's illumination. You'll see them all around you throughout your visit. Each November at the full moon, pilgrims flock here with offerings of new bells, and some of these are placed at the top of the dome during religious festivals.

● The **museum** on the left (open 9am–noon and 1–4pm) contains pendants of effigies of the Buddha and Dvâravatî statuettes, and also a strange collection of curios that includes some old banknotes under glass.

● Next, on the right, is the **Chinese temple**, followed by the **eastern *viharn*** with its Buddha meditating under the tree of illumination.

● Opposite the museum, and facing south, is the ***bot***, where young monks are ordained. This contains a much-revered Buddha in the Dvâravatî style.

● Shortly before the southern door is a group of **grottoes** (one of which is said to be more than 1,000 years old) containing dozens of statues of the Buddha. Just beside them is the replica of an ancient *chedi* that lies buried beneath the present-day pagoda.

● Another replica, displayed a little further on, beyond the **southern *viharn***, has a statue of the Buddha, seated on a *nâga,* delivering his first sermon to his five disciples. Further on again, on the left and below the terrace, is a group of bungalows for use by pilgrims on meditative retreat.

● There are many sacred trees to be seen on all sides, including the *bo*

**WEST OF BANGKOK**

(banyan) tree. Lastly, the **western *viharn*** features a reclining (but not sleeping) Buddha about to enter Nirvana. Just beyond on the left is a charming little park, where you can sit and meditate on the principles of the famous 'Middle Way' that fascinates so many Europeans today.

To complete your visit, you can go with the young monks to attend a lecture given by a professor of theology (inside the first wall, every weekday 1–4pm).

## WHAT TO SEE IN THE SURROUNDING AREA

★ **The Rose Garden** – สวนสามพราน: on the road to Bangkok – the No. 83 bus can drop you on the way. Afterwards any of the following buses will take you back to the Bangkok bus station: Nos. 12, 72, 76 or 83. Open daily, 8am–6pm. The amusement park is mainly interesting for its reconstruction of a Thai village, and you can watch a variety of craft activities, including weaving, pottery and mask-making. Plus, daily at 2pm and 2.45pm, there are so-called 'cultural' shows, featuring Thai boxing, sword fighting, *takraw,* Northern dancing and working elephants. These are rather artificial and strictly for the tourists, so only worth catching if you're on a flying visit to Thailand. They're expensive too.

## LEAVING NAKHON PATHOM

– **For Kanchanaburi and the River Kwai**: two trains (one in the morning, one in the afternoon) taking 1 hour 30 minutes. You can also travel by bus (No. 81), from the stop near the eastern door of the *chedi*.

– **For Damnoen Saduak**: the No. 78 bus leaves every 30 minutes between 6am and 11.30am. It stops near the police station opposite the southern entrance to the *chedi*.

– **For Bangkok**: thirteen trains a day for Thonburi. Also, the Nos. 997 and 83 buses (both air-conditioned) leave every 20 minutes from the Phayaapun Road, at the edge of the *khlong* (second road on the left before the station).

# DAMNOEN SADUAK (FLOATING MARKET) – ดำเนินสะดวก (ตลาดน้ำ)

DIALLING CODE: 038

This little town, 100 kilometres (62 miles) west of Bangkok, is famous for its floating market.

## GETTING THERE

– **By bus**: take the No. 78 bus from the Southern Bus Terminal in Bangkok, on Charan Sanitwong Road. Departures every 20 minutes from 6am (it takes 2 hours). Same frequency of buses coming back.

– If you want to go south (after your visit) there is no need to go via Bangkok. Lots of buses from Damnoen Saduak go to Ratchaburi, where you can catch a train.

## WHERE TO STAY AND WHERE TO EAT

⌂ **Little Bird Hotel** – ลิตเติ้ลเบิร์ดโฮเต็ล: ☎ 254-382. Very quiet little two-storey motel-style hotel, slightly set back from the main street (almost opposite the bus terminal). Rooms with fan or air-conditioning. The paintwork and bathroom facilities have seen better days but the bedding is clean.

### BUDGET

Cheap food in the many little **restaurants** in the main street – open daily until about 7.30pm.

## WHAT TO SEE

★ Damnoen Saduak is a **floating market** similar to the one – now long-since disappeared – that made Thonburi famous. It's definitely worth a look, even if it is rather touristy. The market is only open 7am–1pm and closes for three days during Chinese New Year. Most of the vendors are women who sell their wares from dugout canoes. Everything changes hands on the water, from one canoe to another, and it's all very picturesque. You might notice that the meat-sellers tend to be men – this is because of a belief held by many ethnic groups that menstruating women pollute meat.

To get there from the bus terminal, keep going straight and cross the bridge over the Damnoen *khlong* (the most interesting floating market is less than 1 kilometre (0.5 miles) away, in a *khlong* at right angles to the canal). From there, you can get to the market in a number of ways. A long-tail boat (boarded under the bridge) will drop you at the entrance to the *khlong* (since they aren't allowed in, it's a quick trip but not a very interesting one). Or you can walk back beside the houses to a boarding point about 500 metres further up on the left of the canal (going back up it). From here, you can hire a canoe that will take you to the heart of the market where all the vendors are. It's relatively inexpensive (try to go as a group and don't hesitate to haggle) and lots of fun bobbing up and down on the waves created by the long-tails.

Alternatively, you can walk the whole distance via the little stairs that lead to the balconies of the houses overlooking the canal. This is your chance to see local people close up, including lots of boatbuilders and repairers. The ideal solution is to go there by canoe and come back on foot, and the laziest solution is to go there by *tuk-tuk*. When you get to the floating market, there are lots of souvenir stands lined up along the sides of the *khlong*.

# KANCHANABURI AND THE
# RIVER KWAI – กาญจนบุรีและแม่น้ำแคว

DIALLING CODE: 034

Kanchanaburi is some 130 kilometres (80 miles) west of Bangkok. It extends about 5 kilometres (3 miles) along the River Kwai, a position that gives it a peculiar and not unattractive atmosphere, particularly since tourists are few and far between, although the famous bridge remains its chief and probably only attraction. For anyone planning to stay here, you'll find the best guesthouses are on the river. Bicycles cost next to nothing to rent and boat hire is pretty cheap too. Then there is the town, near the river, which is very popular with the Thais themselves at weekends.

## USEFUL ADDRESS

**🛈 TAT** – ททท (map B3): on the Saengchuto Road (next to the bus terminal). ☎ 511-200. Open daily, 8.30am–4.30pm. Friendly welcome. They can provide a list of hotels and guesthouses, a map of the town, as well as bus and train timetables.

## GETTING THERE FROM BANGKOK

– **By bus**: departures every 15–20 minutes from the Southern Bus Terminal on Charan Sanitwong Road. Guaranteed service between 4am and 6.30pm, depending on the type of bus (with or without air-conditioning). Takes about 3 hours 30 minutes by ordinary bus, 2 hours by air-conditioned bus.

– **By train**: two departures from Thonburi station at 7.50am and 1.45pm. Takes about 3 hours, but since timetables change all the time and there are few departures in any case, you might do best to take the bus.

---

### ■ Useful Addresses

🛈 TAT
🚂 Train station
🚌 Bus terminal
✉ Post office

### 🛏 Where to Stay

1 Nita Rafthouse
2 River Guesthouse
3 Sugar Cane Guesthouse
4 C&C River Kwai Guesthouse
5 Bamboo House
6 PS Guesthouse
7 River Inn
8 River Kwai Hotel

### ★ Things to See

20 Bridge over the River Kwai
21 JEATH Museum
22 Market

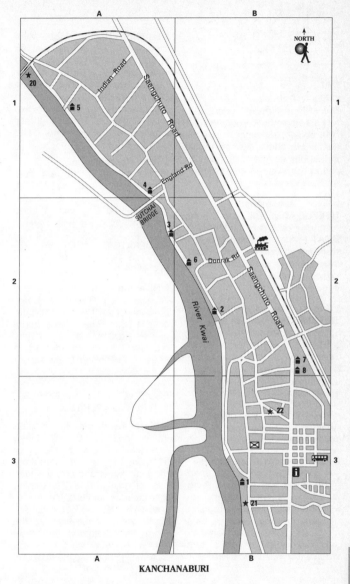

KANCHANABURI

## WHERE TO STAY

### BUDGET (50–200 BTS PER PERSON PER NIGHT)

All the places listed below are on or near the river.

**Nita Rafthouse** – เรือน แพนิต้า(ใกล้พิพิธภัณฑ์) (map, B3, **1**): 27/1 Phakphrak Road. ☎ 514-521. about 100 metres from the JEATH Museum. Bamboo rooms on a boat on the river, with or without shower. Relaxed atmosphere. Delicious food.

**River Guesthouse** – ริเวอร์ เกสท์เฮาส์ (map, B2, **2**): 42 Rong Heeb Oil Road. ☎ 512-491. About 20 local-style bungalows, on stilts (with or without shower). Quiet, well run, very backpackerish atmosphere. You eat sitting cross-legged on a cushion.

**Sugar Cane Guesthouse** – ชูการ์เคนเกสท์เฮาส์ (map, A2, **3**): 22 Soi Pakistan, Maenam Kwai Road. ☎ 624-520. Newly built guesthouse right on the edge of the River Kwai, with small, bamboo bungalows arranged around a well-kept lawn. Private shower, fan and mosquito net. A bit more expensive than the others but loads more charm and quite a seductive atmosphere.

**C&C River Kwai Guesthouse** – ซีแอนด์ซีริเวอร์แควเกสท์เฮาส์ (map, A1, **4**): 265/2 Maenam Kwai Road. ☎ 624-547 or 548. Very simple, bamboo bungalows surrounded by coconut and banana trees. Also, space for less fortunate backpackers to put up a tent. Warm welcome. Bicycle hire.

**Bamboo House** – แบมบูเฮาส์ (map, A1, **5**): 3–5 Soi Vietnam Tha Makha. ☎ 512-532. Some 500 metres before the famous bridge. Quiet house with a lovely garden and six wooden bedrooms. Also two floating huts, each with two very simple bedrooms (mattress on the floor). Bicycle hire. Good food.

**P.S. Guesthouse** – พี.เอส. เกสท์เฮาส์ (map, B2, **6**): 48/4 Chao Khoon Nain Road. ☎ 513-039. Very simple bungalows on the banks of the river with a good restaurant overlooking the water.

### MODERATE TO EXPENSIVE (400–700 BTS PER PERSON PER NIGHT)

**River Inn** – ริเวอร์อินน์ (map, B2, **7**): next to the River Kwai Hotel, on Saengchuto Road. ☎ 511-184 or 511-565. Small, three-storey motel-style hotel. Very ordinary rooms with bathroom (hot water) and air-conditioning. Pretty expensive considering the lack of charm.

### SPLASH OUT (1,000–2,300 BTS PER PERSON PER NIGHT)

**River Kwai Hotel** – ริเวอร์ แควโฮเด็ล (map, B2, **8**): 284/3 Saengchuto Road. ☎ 511-184 or 511-565. Slightly set back from the main street and only included here for those who can't do without their creature comforts. Large, Stalinist-style hotel, and it's clean enough to eat off the floor. All the rooms have bathroom, air-conditioning and hot water. There's also a swimming pool and billiard room.

## WHERE TO STAY IN THE SURROUNDING AREA

SPLASH OUT (1,000–2,300 BTS PER PERSON PER NIGHT)

⌂ **River Kwai Village** – ริเวอร์แควิลเลจ: some 70 kilometres (44 miles) from Kanchanaburi, shortly before Namtok. ☎ 251-75-52. Spacious rooms with air-conditioning, on the banks of the river, plus a few floating bungalows. Swimming pool available. Quiet and very rural. Book from Bangkok.

## WHERE TO EAT

✗ Most of the **guesthouses** serve good Thai food at attractive prices.

✗ You can also eat in any of the **floating restaurants** you find up-river, near the jetty on Song Kusae Road where you board the ferry. Avoid those nearest the bridge.

✗ Lastly, you'll find lots of little **mobile kitchens** all along the Songkwai Road. They serve excellent chicken kebabs.

## WHAT TO SEE

★ **The Bridge over the River Kwai** – สะพานแม่น้ำแคว (map, A1, **20**): 3 kilometres (2 miles) north of town. A place immortalized in the book by Pierre Boulle and the film by David Lean. In 1942, the Imperial Japanese Army were ordered to build a railway line between Siam and Burma. Some 30,000 Allied prisoners-of-war and 100,000 Asian workmen laid 415 kilometres (260 miles) of track in conditions of the most appalling hardship, crucified by a rate of work that intensified when the Japanese decided they needed the railway link to invade India – which they never actually achieved. Thousands died from the effects of forced labour, starvation and rampant malaria. In the final months, the Japanese guards themselves were put to work to keep up the schedule. There is a cemetery commemorating the Allied soldiers who died building the notorious 'death railway' nearby.

The bridge was bombed around 10 times in 1945. Eventually the Thai government decided to restore the line as a tourist attraction and, ironically, had no hesitation in applying to the Japanese banks for finance. The Japanese declined for obvious reasons. Today, visitors can walk across the bridge, close to which are two wartime trains, one of which is a truck converted into a locomotive.

Every year (at the end of November/beginning of December) the bridge is the centre of a major week-long festival that includes a reconstruction of the events of 1942, and a *son et lumière*. Lots of working steam trains are brought in for the occasion.

★ **JEATH Museum** – พิพิธภัณฑ์อักษะเชลยศึกหรือพิพิธภัณฑ์สงคราม (map, B3, **21**): in the centre, near the river. Open daily, 8.30am–4.30pm. The museum features a collection of objects, wartime photographs and engravings that recall the appalling sufferings endured by the prisoners who built the railway. The name, JEATH, is made up of the initials of Japan, England, America/Australia, Thailand and Holland, creating a word that could be used instead of DEATH because that was considered too provocative. The museum is housed in a bamboo cabin that is an exact replica of the prison-camp dormitories. Moving stuff.

★ **The market** – ตลาดในเมือง (map, B3, **22**): in the town centre. Lively and colourful – the kite-shop in particular is not to be missed (out of the rainy season).

★ **Lak Muang Temple** – วัดหลักเมือง: Lak Muang Road, in the centre, opposite the fire station. Women come here to pray for fertility, and it features a gigantic phallus covered in gold-leaf.

★ **The Floating Nun** – แม่ชีลอยน้ำ: in the Wat Tham Mongkon Thong temple – วัดถ้ำมังกรทอง. Every day hundreds of people flock here to see Among, 'the floating nun', who sits waist-deep in a pool of water, performing the different positions adopted by the Buddha. Cross-legged, hands folded on her chest, she sits like the ascetic Buddha; lying on her side, with her head on her right arm, she finishes in the same position adopted by the Buddha before death, about to enter Nirvana. Concentrating and deep in meditation, Among goes through her sequence of positions literally floating on the waves. At the end of the ceremony, the faithful are blessed with holy water from the pool. Among is the temple's second floating nun; thanks to their presence, the temple has become an important place of pilgrimage.

★ **Short trip by slow train to Namtok** – ขึ้นรถไฟไปเที่ยวน้ำตก: pleasant journey lasting about 2 hours. The railway follows the river and passes some pretty impressive overhanging rocks. Sit on the left, facing the same way as the train. The train often stops for no apparent reason and it whistles noisily before crossing a road since there aren't any level crossings. The scenery on one particular section of the route is magnificent.

There are three departures from Kanchanaburi station at 6.10am, 11am and 4.35pm, but the last isn't recommended unless you plan to sleep there. Return trains leave Namtok at 1pm and 3.15pm.

★ **In Namtok** – เที่ยวน้ำตก, take a communal taxi for Pak Saen then rent a canoe. There's a raft hotel here, though sadly the owner is much keener on group bookings than individuals. As well as serving European and Thai food, the hotel also offers hiking excursions, but you may find the prices offputting. All that said, the countryside is sensational; this is Mon country.

★ **Walk to the Erawan Waterfalls** –ไปเที่ยวน้ำตกเอราวัณ: magnificent scenery, and waterfalls on seven levels in a national park 65 kilometres (41 miles) from Kanchanaburi. You can follow a path leading up to each level (it takes 2 hours in all). Wear walking-boots and bring your swimsuit as there are lots of natural swimming pools. There are also bungalows and tents for hire, plus little places where you can eat. To get here, take the No. 8170 bus from Kanchanaburi, which leaves every 50 minutes between 8am and 4.30pm (takes 2 hours). If you don't want to sleep here, the last bus leaves the falls at 4pm and, as you might expect, it's packed.

★ Other waterfalls: **Sai Yok Noi** – น้ำตกไทรโยคน้อย, lovely little place to swim, except in summer when the water-level drops, and **Sai Yok Yai** – น้ำตกไทรโยคใหญ่, which is bigger. You can take a raft from here back to Kanchanaburi along the River Kwai, which takes two days and costs quite a lot. The two falls are 60 kilometres (37 miles) and 66 kilometres (41 miles) from Kanchanaburi respectively. The No. 8203 bus goes to both, leaving the Kanchanaburi terminus every 30 minutes between 6.45am and 6.30pm.

★ **Big rafting trips** – ล่องแพ, One-, two- or four-day trips depending on demand. Most of the guesthouses have their own routes, and the tourist office has some good routes too.

★ There are some fine temples you can see in a day if you rent a bike or motorbike: the **Wat Ban Tum** – วัดบ้านทุ่ม, which is built inside a cave, and a Thai temple right next door to a Chinese pagoda, the **Wat Tham Sua** – วัดถ้ำเสือ and **Wat Tham Kaeo** – วัดถ้ำแก้ว, 20 kilometres (12 miles) from Kanchanaburi.

---

# NORTH OF BANGKOK

# BANGKOK – CHIANG MAI – CHIANG RAI

There are various ways of making this trip:

– **By air**: fast, safe and not as expensive as you'd think (for the address of Thai Airlines *see* 'Air Travel' at the front of the guide or 'Useful Addresses' in the Bangkok chapter).

– **By bus**: cheap and fast.

– **By train**: the best way of getting to Chiang Mai, despite minor hassles like booking and getting to the station. It's much less risky than taking the bus.

For details of buses and trains, *see* 'Leaving Bangkok'.

### A WORD OF WARNING ABOUT CREDIT CARDS

At the risk of being repetitive, here are a few words of warning. Most people have heard of the traffic in tourist credit cards that used to go on (and still does) in northern Thailand, particularly Chiang Mai.

It usually goes something like this: you go on a trek for two or three days and leave your credit card in the guesthouse safe. The landlord, meanwhile, is in league with a gang of international racketeers and, while you're away, he slips your card to a fence who goes to Bangkok to buy hi-fi equipment, gold or jewels from crooked shopkeepers who do this all the time. Having stacked up purchases to the value of £2–3,000, your card is then put back where it was and no one is any the wiser. You return from your trek unaware that your account is drained or in the red. The truth only comes out when you get home but you can't prove a thing. They've taken you to the cleaners and it's up to you to sort it out with the credit card company.

While this kind of fraud is on the way out, always take your credit card and passport with you when you go trekking. Also, make sure you tear up the carbon between the copies of the sales voucher. Otherwise it can be used again or the amount changed.

# BANG PA IN – บางปะอิน

This is a recently restored, late 19th-century summer palace built by the kings of Thailand. There's nothing really to write home about, with the possible exception of the Aisawan Thi Paya, which is a pretty lodge in the middle of the lake and an exact replica of one of the Grand Palace lodges in Bangkok. But it has a magnificent well-manicured garden with avenues of mango trees, wild orchids and topiaried bushes that look like animals. Open 8.30am–3.30pm; admission charge.

Most of the buildings are in the European style, except for a Chinese palace furnished with Chinese antiques. Disaster struck here in 1881 when Queen Sunanda, wife of Rama V, arrived at the palace on the Chao Phraya river and drowned before the very eyes of her hapless servants, who were forbidden by royal protocol to lay a finger on the queen. A tragic twist of fate.

From Ayutthaya you can get here by private boat, which takes 2 hours but is worth it if there are several of you. From Bangkok, you can come here for the day on a River Express Boat (8am–5.30pm). Details and bookings from the Tha Chang Pier at the end of Na Phra Lan Road – ท่าช้าง ถนนหน้าพระลาน. ☎ 221-22-97.

# AYUTTHAYA – อยุธยา

DIALLING CODE: 035

Some 88 kilometres (55 miles) from Bangkok, Ayutthaya is the ancient capital of Thailand and an interesting archaeological site. Obviously, if you haven't got much time, Sukhothai is the place to visit first. Otherwise see Ayutthaya at your leisure. You can even take a day trip there from Bangkok.

### A BRIEF HISTORY

The ancient capital of Siam was founded in 1350 and ruled by 33 kings. In 1662, the kingdom struck up a strange relationship with France when two French missionaries were warmly welcomed by the king of Siam, Phra Narai. So delighted was the French King Louis XIV by this reception that he sent out a new delegation to woo Phra Narai and eventually convert him to Catholicism. François de Chaumont led the mission, accompanied by the Abbot of Choisy, whose *Journal du voyage de Siam* (Diary of a Journey to Siam) ranks as one of the first ever backpacker accounts. The abbot was an eccentric – a man of the cloth who liked nothing better than to dress up as a woman. This bold seafarer could be as coquettish as a little girl. If you read French, you can find out more in Nathalie Reznikoff's *Un Homme de robe à la cour du Roi-Soleil* (published by Ramsay). Back

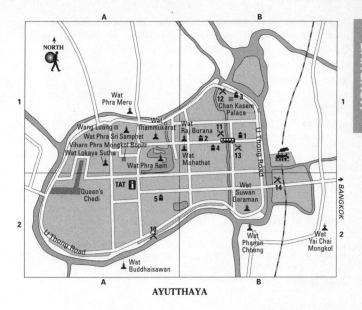

**AYUTTHAYA**

| ■ Useful Addresses | 4 | Thai-Thai Bungalow |
| --- | --- | --- |
| 🛈 TAT | 5 | U Thong Inn |
| 🚆 Train station | | |
| 🚌 Bus station | ✕ **Where to Eat** | |
| | 10 | Ruan Rup Rong Restaurant |
| | 11 | Samanya |
| ⌂ **Where to Stay** | 12 | Hua Raw market |
| | 13 | Moon Café |
| 1 Ayutthaya Guesthouse | 14 | Krung Sri River Hotel |
| 2 B.J. Guesthouse | | Buffet |
| 3 U Thong Hotel | | |

in France, meanwhile, the Siamese ambassadorial mission received by Louis XIV caused such a sensation that the town of Brest decided to commemorate the event by calling its main street 'rue de Siam'.

The success of the mission in Siam was largely due to a francophile Greek opportunist by the name of Phaulkon, who had enormous influence over King Narai. Phaulkon got rid of the English and the Dutch in favour of the French, who set up a garrison in Siam. But the honeymoon came to an end in 1688 when Phaulkon was assassinated by nationalists, the king was deposed and all foreigners were thrown out.

In 1767, Ayutthaya was flattened by the Burmese and Bangkok became the capital. The Siamese then cannibalized the old temples and pagodas in Ayutthaya to build new ones in Bangkok. Anything they didn't use was left to decay until restoration work started some 30 years ago, when, despite these trials and tribulations, the ruins were found to be very significant and quite enough to show us what this great city of more than a million people must have been like.

## GETTING THERE

There are several ways of getting there from Bangkok:

– **By bus**: from the Northern Bus Terminal. Air-conditioned buses every 30 minutes, 6am–7pm; non-air-conditioned buses every 15 minutes, 4.30am–7.15pm. Takes about 1 hour 30 minutes.

– **By train**: from the main station in Hua Lamphong. Daily departures, hourly from 4.20am to 11.30pm. Trains take about 1 hour 30 minutes. The 4.20am train is strongly recommended.

## USEFUL ADDRESSES

🛈 **TAT** – ททท (map, A2): Sri Samphet Road. ☎ 246-076 or 246-077. Fax: 246-078. Open 8.30am–4.30pm.

■ **Thai Farmers Bank** – ธนาคารกสิกรไทย: Naresuan Road. ☎ 24-37-91.

## WHERE TO STAY

Ayutthaya isn't really an ideal place to stay and there isn't much to choose from in terms of quality or alternatives.

BUDGET TO MODERATE (150–400 BTS PER PERSON PER NIGHT)

🛏 **Ayutthaya Guesthouse** – อยุธยาเกสท์เฮาส์ (map, B1, **1**): Chao Phrom Road. ☎ 25-14-68. In a little road that connects with Naresuan Road in the north. Close to the train station and Chaophrom market, and by far the best place in town. Wooden rooms on the ground floor and upstairs, all tastefully decorated. Simple but well kept by a hospitable family, plus good, traditional food prepared by the lady of the house. Friendly place and very cheap. Cycle hire.

🛏 **B.J. Guesthouse** – บี.เจ. เกสท์เฮาส์ (map, B1, **2**): 19/29 Naresuan Road. ☎ 24-60-46. About 300 metres from the monuments and 15 minutes' walk from the station. Spartan but relatively clean, with a decent dormitory. Terrace, furnished with teak furniture, overlooking the street. Good food.

🛏 **U Thong Hotel** – โรงแรมอู่ทอง (map, B1, **3**): U Thong Road. ☎ 25-11-36. Leaving the station, cross the river as you go towards the town centre. The hotel is in the first road on the right coming from the Pa Sak bridge, opposite the post office. It's quite a long walk, which hardly seems worth it when you get there, but at least the place is pretty clean – particularly the rooms on the top floor, which have been redecorated. Some of the rooms with air-conditioning overlook the river but they're also quite noisy. A bit more expensive than the others.

🛏 **Thai-Thai Bungalow** – โรงแรม ไทยไทย (map, B1, **4**): 13/1 Naresuan Road. ☎ 24-47-02. The worst of the lot but possibly the most convenient if you plan to visit the site. The rooms are so-so (ask to see more than one), and some have air-conditioning. The rooms upstairs have wooden floors and have a certain charm.

## SPLASH OUT (FROM 1,500 BTS PER PERSON PER NIGHT)

🛏 **U Thong Inn** – โรงแรมอู่ทองอินน์ (map, A2, **5**): Rotchana Road. ☎ 24-22-36. Despite having air-conditioning and a swimming pool, this hotel is not very central nor is it particularly good value.

## WHERE TO EAT

### BUDGET

🍴 **Ruan Rup Rong Restaurant** – ร้านอาหารเรือนรับรอง (map, A2, **10**): 13/1-2 U Thong Road. A great setting, with the tables arranged across a wide terrace overlooking the river. Very restful. Specialities include fried fish, soups and steamed dishes, all served by an army of waitresses. Undoubtedly the best food in Ayutthaya.

🍴 **Samanya** – ร้านอาหารสมันยา (map, B1, **11**): opposite the mini-bus terminus on Naresuan Road. Large, rather dark room with karaoke. A good place to get break-fast when you arrive.

🍴 You can also eat in the **Hua Raw market** – ตลาดหัวรอ (map, B1, **12**) near the river: lots of **street kitchens**, all clean and inexpensive. Or there's the area near the station and at night, the area at the end of the U Thong Road.

🍴 **Moon Café** – มูนคาเฟ (map, B1, **13**): Chao Phrom Road. Not far

from the Ayutthaya Guesthouse. Beers, cocktails, drinks and a few Thai dishes. More a place to meet for a drink than somewhere to eat. The decor is original and shows a house seen from the outside, with tables arranged across a false roof and stars painted on the ceiling. There are a few tables on the terrace. Great place – makes a change after all the others. You can add to the young landlady's collection of coins from all over the world.

### MODERATE

🍴 **Krung Sri River Hotel Buffet** – บัฟเฟ่ที่กรุงศรีริเวอร์โฮเต็ล (map, B2, **14**): Rotchana Road. Buffet lunches every day in the ground-floor coffee-shop of this big, modern, charmless building. Lots of Thai-style salads, soups, stews, vegetables and puddings served in a large canteen-like space. Good food – shame about the tour groups.

## WHAT TO SEE

What's curious about Ayutthaya is that it's almost like an island with rivers on all sides. The archaeological excavations are extensive and almost too big to cover on foot. The best idea is to rent a rickshaw for a few hours, in which case haggling is not only recommended but a must (the driver always asks for an extortionate amount to begin with). It's cheaper to rent a different rickshaw at every site and it doesn't usually take long to find one. Expect to visit four or five sites at most. It's up to you to do your sums, bearing in mind that all the temples charge an admission fee.

★ **Wat Yai Chai Mongkol** – วัดใหญ่ชัยมงคล (map, B2): one of the most interesting *wat* compounds, beyond the island and about 4 kilometres (2 miles) from the station. Built in 1360, it is now entirely restored and well planted – a remarkable achievement if rather overrun with tourists. The *chedi* was built in 1592 by King Naresuan to celebrate victory over the Burmese (who didn't invade again for another two centuries). It is surrounded by dozens of Buddhas draped in orange robes. Inside the sanctuary there is a corpulent Buddha made of copper. Look out for the reclining Buddha on the path to the big *chedi*.

★ **Wat Phanan Choeng** – วัดพนัญเชิง (map, B2): not far from the previous one, facing the southeastern side of the island. This recently built classical temple is mainly interesting for the enormous Buddha that rises out of the blue incense smoke and for the enthusiasm that it arouses. At about 19 metres (60 feet), this is the tallest seated brick Buddha in Thailand.

★ **Wat Phra Sri Samphet** – วัดพระศรีสรรเพชญ์ (map, A1): in the north-eastern part of the island. Built in the 15th century, this is Ayutthaya's most imposing temple compound. The three big *chedis* symbolize the first three kings who ruled here. If you want to indulge in the peaceful contemplation of elegant architecture in a green and pleasant setting, then try to get here before the crowds.

★ **Viharn Phra Mongkol Bopitr** – วิหารพระมงคลบพิตร (map, A1): not far from the previous *wat*, the recently built *viharn* houses the country's tallest bronze Buddha (nearly 20 metres/65 feet high). It dates from the 15th century and, as you would expect of something that has survived centuries of unrest, it is held to be highly sacred.

★ **Wat Phra Meru** – วัดพระเมรุ (or Wat Na Phramen; map, A1): in the north, outside the ring of water and facing the old palace. Having miraculously survived the Burmese occupation at the end of the 18th century, the *wat* retains a very fine 15th-century ceiling with wooden coffers and gold lacquerwork, plus majestic columns surmounted by lotus blossom decorations. What's most interesting is the Buddha dressed in royal costume.

★ **Wat Phra Ram Uchaya** – วัดพระรามอุชญา: going towards the Wat Mahathat, on the edge of the lake is this now ruined *wat* compound with echoes of the Angkor style.

★ **Wat Raj Burana** – วัดราชบูรณะ (map, B1): next to the Mahathat and built in 1424, this *wat* retains a miraculously intact and magnificent *prang* (Khmer-style tower with a square base).

★ **Wat Mahathat** – วัดมหาธาตุ (map, B1): the compound is now sadly in ruins, although from the foundations and walls that are still standing you can imagine how imposing it must have been. The valuable jewellery and religious objects discovered during the excavations are now on show in the museum.

★ **The National Museum of Chao Sam Phraya** – พิพิธภัณฑ์สถาน แห่งชาติเจ้าสามพระยา: open 9am–noon and 1–4pm. Closed Monday, Tuesday and holidays. Admission charge. Magnificent exhibition of finds made on the site. On the ground floor: superb sculpted doors, temple *toranas*, porcelain and ceramic objects, small bronzes etc. On the first floor: the fabulous Wat Burana treasury. Display of gold-work of religious origin, including golden 'votive trees', statuettes, magnificent jewellery, votive plaques, a prince's tiara and an amazing carved elephant studded with precious stones. The Wat Mahathat Room contains painted chests, votive tablets, a standing Buddha and a model of a 17th-century *viharn.*

★ If you have time, see the elephant **kraal** – เพนียดคล้องช้าง, in the north. The last remaining *kraal* in Thailand, it was built in the 16th century and was used for training elephants right up until 1903.

★ Another lovely trip is to take a boat around the town as far as **Bang Pa In** – no particular character but charming anyway and a nice place to have lunch. Take a 4-hour round trip and go sailing on the water among the lily-pads.

## FESTIVALS

– **Grand annual fair**: one week in January or February, depending on the calendar. Major exhibition of locally produced handicrafts (weaving, wood, bamboo etc.) at very reasonable prices.

## LEAVING AYUTTHAYA

### By bus

– **For Bangkok**: air-conditioned buses depart from the Chao Phrom market every 30 minutes, 6am–7pm; non-air-conditioned buses every 15 minutes. Buses take about 1 hour 30 minutes.

– **For Lopburi**: departures from the Chao Phrom market every 30 minutes. Buses take about 2 hours.

### By train

🚆 The **station** (map, B1) is outside the town centre, to the east on the other side of the canal. ☎ 24-15-21.

– **For Lopburi**: it's quicker by train than by bus and the several trains a day all take about 1 hour 15 minutes. The advantage of catching the first train in the morning is that it gives you enough time to visit Lopburi and catch a late morning train to Phitsanulok. This arrives late afternoon, in time to make it to the bus terminus to catch one of the last buses for Sukhothai. So you won't have to sleep in Phitsanulok (which is pretty dull anyway) but more important still, you'll have the whole of the following day to spend in Sukhothai. You can check these details in the Northern Line timetables.

– **For Bangkok**: every 30 minutes.

# LOPBURI – ลพบุรี          DIALLING CODE: 036

Lopburi is a very ancient, peaceful garrison town some 155 kilometres (97 miles) from Bangkok. In the tenth century it was part of the Khmer empire and there developed what became known as the Lopburi style, which marks a stage in the transition from Khmer style to Thai style. In the 17th century, summers in Lopburi were drier and healthier than in Ayutthaya and King Narai established his summer quarters there.

Lopburi will be of interest if you have the time and inclination to study all the major architectural periods in Thailand along the route from Ayutthaya to Sukhothai. If, on the other hand, time is short, Sukhothai is much more fascinating and you can give Lopburi a miss. It's a large, modern, charmless town that has shamelessly swamped its monuments. Still, they are all in one small part of town, which means you can easily visit them on foot in about 2 hours.

## GETTING THERE FROM BANGKOK

– **By train**: from Hua Lamphong station – several trains a day. Takes about 2 hours 45 minutes.

– **By bus**: from the Northern Terminal – takes about the same time as the train, with departures about every 20 minutes, 5.30am–8.30pm.

## WHERE TO STAY

### BUDGET TO MODERATE (150–600 BTS PER PERSON PER NIGHT)

🛏 **Nett Hotel** – เนตด์โฮเต็ล: Soi Rach Chadamnern 2. ☎ 41-17-38. As you leave the station, take the road along the edge of the Wat Phra Sri Ratana Mahathat then the second on the left (barely a 5-minute walk). Don't be put off by the lobby: the hotel is very well kept. Different coloured rooms on each floor: green on the first, pink on the second and blue on the third. All with fan or air-conditioning and very reasonably priced. Choose a room at the back – they're much quieter. It's very decent, all in all and definitely the best in town.

🛏 **Sri Indtra Hotel** – ศรีอินทราโฮเต็ล: 3–5 Prakarn Road. ☎ 41-12-61. This is the main avenue that starts on the right of the station and goes towards Prang Sam Yod. Clean enough place with very decent, inexpensive rooms with fan. Same price range as the previous hotel. There are more Chinese hotels – the cheapest in town – on the same side of the street, but they're not easy to describe.

🛏 **Rama Plaza Hotel** – รามาพลาซ่าโฮเต็ล: 4 Ban Pom Road. ☎ 41-10-65. In the north of town, a 10-minute walk from the station. Take the road that skirts left around the Prang Sam Yod. The hotel is a bit further on, on the right. Very clean, quiet and modern – cheap too. The rooms without windows smell a bit stale, so ask to see the room first.

🛏 **Asia Hotel** – เอเชียโฮเต็ล: Thanon Sorasak. ☎ 41-15-55. Fax: 41-18-92. Opposite the entrance to the Royal Palace. Charmless, unwelcoming and noisy. Rooms with fan or air-conditioning, not all of them very well kept. Choose only as a last resort. Right next door to a place-with-no-name that serves cheap food.

## WHERE TO EAT

🍴 **White House** – ร้านอาหารไวท์เฮาส์การ์เด้น: as you leave the station, take the second road that skirts right around the site and it's just there. Agreeable setting with tables set outside in a garden full of flowers. Selection of cheap Thai dishes.

✖ **Chanchao Restaurant** – ร้าน อาหารจันทร์เจ้า: 3 Ropwatphatad Road. Take the road on the right opposite the station. Open for dinner only, serving delicious food from a tempting menu. Lovely room but prices are a bit steep for Lopburi.

EXPENSIVE

✖ **Lopburi Inn** – ร้านอาหารลพบุ รีอินน์: Only 3 kilometres (1.5 miles) from the centre on Narai Maharat Road. ☎ 41-23-00. Get there by local bus from the stop near the Kala Temple. Terrific restaurant, reasonably priced. Very lively and often full up. Musical entertainment every night.

## WHAT TO SEE

★ **Wat Phra Sri Ratana Mahathat** – วัดพระศรีรัตนมหาธาตุ: the ruins stretch away from the station. Admission charge. Substantial *prang* and *chedi* remains, plus some very fine sculptures particularly on the central *prang* (remarkable pediment). The most peaceful place in town.

★ **King Narai's Palace** – นารายณ์ราชนิเวศร์: Surasonkram Road. Open 9am–noon and 1–4pm. Closed Monday and Tuesday. Huge doors in the wall open onto immense leafy courtyards and rows of ancient outbuildings, shops and stables. Two palace lodges in the second courtyard at the back have been converted into a museum. Interesting collections of Lopburi style sculptures, furniture etc.

The Dusit Maha Prasad Hall was specially built to receive foreign ambassadors. Notice the dozens of leaf-shaped niches built into the walls. These are where the illuminations are placed during major festivals and ceremonies.

★ **Prang Khaek** – ปรางค์แขก: at the busy crossroads formed by the road containing the Asia Hotel and the one going from the Phaulkon Palace to the Prang Sam Yod is this 10th-century Hindu monument in typical Lopburi style.

★ **Constantine Phaulkon Palace** – บ้านวิชาเยนทร์หรือพอลคอนเฮาส์: admission charge. The palace was built in the reign of King Narai for his adviser and is practically as big as the royal palace itself. The architecture has a certain European flavour to it. While only the facade is still standing, the sheer elegance of what remains is quite enough to let you imagine its former glory.

Phaulkon was a real character. Born on the island of Cephalonia, he was a Greek adventurer who sailed with the English fleet for 10 years before turning merchant in Indochina then gunrunner for King Narai's Minister for Finance. He became increasingly influential at court thanks to a series of major business and diplomatic deals and was appointed a Minister of State then chief adviser to King Narai himself. Phaulkon's influence knew no bounds. He was fluent in Greek, French, English, Portuguese, Malay, Latin and, of course, Thai. He received personal letters from the pope and from Louis XIV. The festivities that he held were fabulous.

He also aroused a great deal of jealousy among Thai dignitaries who, egged on by the Dutch, took advantage of the king's illness to plot Phaulkon's downfall. He was arrested and executed on 5 June 1688. The king died the same year. After this episode, Siam was not to reopen its doors to foreigners for almost 200 years.

★ **Prang Sam Yod** – ปรางค์สามยอด: beautiful temple with three laterite and sandstone *prangs*, built on an esplanade at the end of the Na Kala Road (on the right as you leave the station). Of Hindu origin, the temple was strongly influenced by the Khmer style and is probably the best example of 'Lopburi style'. The stucco decorations are particularly interesting. Today the ruins are home to thieving monkeys.

★ **The Kala Temple** – ศาลพระกาฬ: beside the Prang Sam Yod, this ruined temple is now entirely overgrown and as popular with monkeys as the last one.

★ Take a rickshaw and go to watch the **fishermen** on the river casting their large, square, weighted nets. Or, in the morning, you can visit the **Withayalai Kalasilpa School of Traditional Dance and Music** – วิทยาลัยนาฏศิลปกาฬสินธุ์, which is very close to the palace and well worth knowing about.

★ **Procession with decorative floral floats, music and dancing**: held mid-February, in honour of the memory of the good and mighty Narai.

## LEAVING LOPBURI

### By train

– **For Phitsanulok**: several departures daily, including one that leaves late morning and arrives in Phitsanulok just in time to catch a connecting train for Sukhothai. It's guaranteed to get you there as the sun rises and, as you already know, there's no point staying in Phitsanulok.

– **For Bangkok**: several trains a day. The journey takes about 3 hours 30 minutes.

# THE NORTHWEST

## PHITSANULOK – พิษณุโลก  DIALLING CODE: 055

This modern, commercial town is of little interest and has become even less worthy of attention since it was destroyed by fire 30 years ago. *Wat* addicts, however, might want to visit the 15th-century Wat Phra Sri Ratana Mahathat – วัดพระศรีรัตนมหาธาตุ – the only monument to escape the flames. It's on the right of the bridge over the Nan, as you go in the direction of Sukhothai. Inside is the highly revered Phra Buddha Chinara – พระพุทธชินราช, a Buddha of burnished bronze with a delicately chased golden aureole, who symbolizes Sukhothai's victory over the Khmers. This is the most copied Buddha in Thailand. It took more than 100 craftsmen many months to create the magnificent 18th-century chapel doors inlaid with mother-of-pearl. With its wooden interior, this is a truly splendid *wat*.

**USEFUL ADDRESS**

**▪ TAT** – ททท (Tourist Office, map, A2): 209/7 Surasi Trade Centre, Boromtrailokanat Road, Amphoe Muang. ☎ 25-27-42 and 43. This office is a mine of information: maps, hotels, restaurants plus tours, and detailed bus and train timetables.

**GETTING THERE FROM BANGKOK**

– **By train**: this is the easiest way to get to Phitsanulok, which is 390 kilometres (244 miles) from Bangkok on the northern line, and 360 kilometres (225 miles) from Chiang Mai. For a start, all the regular services to Ayutthaya and Lopburi go by way of Phitsanulok, and there are plenty of departures from 6.40am to 10pm. The fastest, although not necessarily the most convenient, train is the Express, which leaves Bangkok at around 6pm and takes about six hours, arriving in Phitsanulok at midnight. For a really comfortable journey, take the Diesel Railcar Super Express which runs three trains a day (morning, afternoon and night), all taking 5 hours 45 minutes, but check the timetable for details. Booking is essential. It has air-conditioned carriages, and on-board meals and drinks (included in the price of the ticket) are served by charming hostesses. However, you cannot reserve couchettes for Bangkok from Phitsanulok, but only from Chiang Mai.

– **By bus**: two regular buses run from the Northern Bus Terminal. Alternatively, Rose Tour (☎ 234-81-76) and Tong Dee Tour (☎ 233-10-25) can get you there by air-conditioned bus.

THE NORTHWEST

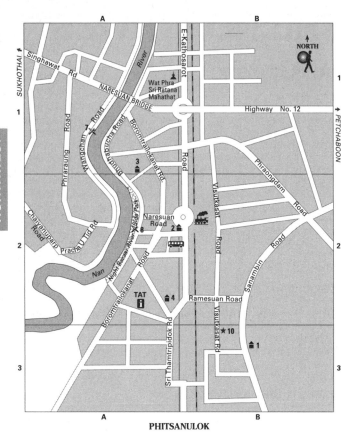

PHITSANULOK

---

- **Useful Addresses**

  - **TAT**
  - **Train station**
  - **Bus station**

- **Where to Stay**

  1 Youth Hostel
  2 Phitsanulok Hotel
  3 Siam Hotel

  4 Thep Nakorn Hotel

- **Where to Eat**

  7 Fahthai Floating Restaurant
  8 Night Bazaar

- **What to See**

  10 Buranathai Buddha Image
     Factory Folk Museum

---

– **By air**: one or two flights from Bangkok. Reasonably priced, so useful if time is short.

## WHERE TO STAY

Phitsanulok is just a place you pass through – definitely not a town that dreams are made of. But, just in case, here are a few addresses.

### BUDGET TO MODERATE (80–300 BTS PER PERSON PER NIGHT)

🛏 **Youth Hostel** – บ้านเยาวชน (map, B3, **1**): 38 Sanambin Road. ☎ 24-20-60. In the southeast of the town, on the way to the airport. From there or from the station, take the No. 1, 8 or 10 bus to the technical college, then the No. 4 bus. Terrific youth hostel in an old house that's been fully converted – without a doubt one of the most charming hostels in northern Thailand. Some work may be still in progress. Very basic five-bed dormitories but clean and very cheap. Lovely double and triple rooms with teak furniture, in a separate wing. Bring your own mosquito net. Air-conditioning and hot water is newly installed. Cleaning service. Two restaurants, including one outside in the garden; a breath of fresh air in this dusty town. YHA card essential: you can buy one here (valid for one year) or stay six nights, in which case you get one anyway. Or you can buy a six-night card. If you don't, the price of rooms goes up and suddenly this isn't such an attractive option.

🛏 **Phitsanulok Hotel** – พิษณุโลกโฮเด็ล (map, A2–B2, **2**): immediately on the left as you leave the station. ☎ 25-84-25. An ugly, rather noisy place but it's clean and better than most of the hotels in this category. Ideal for anyone with a train to catch first thing in the morning or who's arriving at midnight on the Express.

🛏 **Siam Hotel** – สยามโฮเด็ล (map, A1, **3**): 4 Artitwong Road. ☎ 25-88-44. Next to the Paylin Hotel. Decent rooms with shower but the bathrooms aren't too salubrious.

### EXPENSIVE TO SPLASH OUT (700–1,500 BTS PER PERSON PER NIGHT)

🛏 **Thep Nakorn Hotel** – โรงแรมเทพนคร (map A2, **4**): 43/1 Sri Thamtripidok Road. ☎ 25-18-77. As you leave the station, turn left and walk for about 10 minutes, or take a rickshaw if you're loaded down with luggage. Comfortable hotel with rooms at reasonable prices.

## WHERE TO EAT

✗ **Fahthai Floating Restaurant** – ร้านอาหารฟ้าไทยโฟลทดิ่ง (map, A1, **7**): Wangchan Road. Almost opposite the Wat Mahathat, on the other side of the river. Open daily, 11am–11pm. As its name suggests, this is a floating house with tables outside. Come here for the setting more than the food, which is mainly traditional and pretty cheap.

✗ **Night Bazaar** – ตลาดกลางคืน (map, A2, **8**): along the edge of the Nan river, in the south of the town. Open from 7pm until late. Loads of food stands serving all sorts of things to eat on the hoof. The place buzzes.

## WHAT TO SEE

★ **Buranathai Buddha Image Factory Folk Museum** – พิพธภัณฑ์หล่อ พระพุทธรูปบูรณะไทย (map, B3, **10**): 26/43 Visutkasat Road. ☎ 25-87-15. It's best to telephone first since this is first and foremost a Buddha factory and they expect to see your credentials. Learn about how they make Buddhas using the lost-wax method, then visit the shop – you won't have seen anything like it before.

## LEAVING PHITSANULOK

– **By train for Bangkok**: lots of trains every day, plus two night trains. The journey takes about 7 hours. Or there's the Diesel Railcar, which gets you to Bangkok in about 5 hours, and departs three times a day.

– **By train for Chiang Mai**: two night trains that arrive the following morning. But don't go to Phitsanulok specially to catch a train to Chiang Mai, as you can go there directly by bus from Sukhothai.

– **For Khon Kaen** (in the east): a 5-hour bus journey along a lovely road, with several departures daily. Kohn Kaen is the gateway to the East (Phimai, Nakhon Ratchasima, Udon Thani etc.).

– **For Sukhothai**: take one of those little light-blue buses (cheaper than a *tuk-tuk*) from the station to the bus terminal outside town, about 2 kilometres (1 mile) away. The last bus leaves at about 6pm, so anyone arriving at 5.15pm can easily catch it. It's about 60 kilometres (37 miles) from Phitsanulok to Sukhothai – a 90-minute journey.

# SUKHOTHAI – สุโขทัย

DIALLING CODE: 055

Sukhothai, Siam's first capital, nestles in a wide valley flanked by thickly forested, gently sloping hillsides. This is one of the most beautiful archaeological sites in Thailand, rich with man-made treasures and natural delights and now a national park. Not surprisingly, it is also teeming with tourists and everything is highly organized, with car-parks, control posts and barriers.

It's because of this that you are advised to get to Sukhothai the day before and spend a peaceful night there; it's a long way from the bedlam of Bangkok. Then you can get to the first site at dawn and make the most of it before the tour groups arrive. By 10am it's already too late, and it's starting to get hot.

The town of Sukhothai itself is modern and lacks charm – obviously not an ideal place to stay.

## GETTING THERE

– **By bus from Bangkok**: lots of departures from the Northern Bus Terminal, and two night buses. Journey time is about 7 hours 30 minutes.

– **By bus from Ayutthaya**: plenty of direct buses but best to go to Sukhothai on the way back from Chiang Mai (*see* 'Leaving Chiang Mai').

– **By train then bus**: go to Phitsanulok and catch a bus. Bo Ko So national buses depart every 30 minutes from 5.40am to 6pm, and the journey takes an hour.

– **By air**: the airport is about 30 kilometres (19 miles) out of town. There are several connections a day for Bangkok and Chiang Mai.

## A BRIEF HISTORY

It all starts with the Thai Prince Bang Klang Thao who threw the Khmers out of the region at the beginning of the 13th century and founded the dynasty of eight kings who would rule for the next 150 years. The name Sukhothai means 'dawn' or 'birth of happiness' and comes from a Sanskrit or Pali word (the language of *Theravâda* Buddhism). It would be hard to imagine a better place to found a capital, as there is fertile soil, abundant water and all the quarries and forests you could ask for to build temples.

The region even produced a legendary king, Phra Ruang, son of Princess Naga, who is said to have possessed supernatural powers and could turn his enemies to stone, make fruit grow on trees and so on. One day he ordered a fish bone to come to life – hence the name (Phra Ruang) of the strange, transparent fish you see in aquariums in Thailand today. The Sukhothai dynasty did actually produce a mighty king, Rama Khamheng (Rama the Mighty). He ruled from 1275 to 1317 and his life and works are recounted in inscriptions on a stone stele that's thought to be the first known example of Thai writing.

Rama the Mighty was an enlightened monarch with a passion for justice – a wise statesman who opened his country to the outside world. He created the Thai alphabet, established diplomatic relations with China (which he visited twice) and made Buddhism the national religion. He was a firm advocate of free enterprise but it was his sense of justice that had the most profound effect on his reign and the one that is commemorated in the archives: 'When differences arose among the common people, the nobles or the royal princes, the king ordered a fair enquiry and his word was supreme.' Anyone with a complaint to make could ring a bell at the entrance to the palace and the king himself would come and hear the plaintiffs.

On the arts front, Rama Khamheng employed Chinese potters, who founded a flourishing crafts industry that brought fame and wealth to the kingdom. Such a favourable climate naturally led to an extraordinary artistic flowering and a profusion of temples and lavish sculptures. Sukhothai art was born in an atmosphere of creative freedom and openness to the outside world. The style of art it produced easily embraced all the former influences: the artistic traditions of the Khmer oppressors, Chinese techniques, the Burmese contribution with a touch of Singhalese. So it isn't really surprising that this is where you find the famous striding Buddha walking with exaggerated grace towards the 'dawn of happiness'.

The Sukhothai civilization began its decline during the reign of the last kings. As the kingdom of Ayutthaya went from strength to strength, Sukhothai expired with languorous elegance, leaving a wealth of stone treasures and

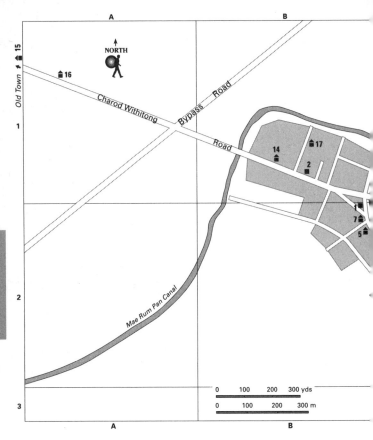

an unparalleled archaeological site that has a dreamlike quality about it, especially when you're all on your own first thing in the morning.

## USEFUL ADDRESSES

✉ **Post office** – ไปรษณีย์ (map I, C2): Nikornkasem Road. You can make long-distance telephone calls here.

🚌 **Bus terminal** – สถานีรถขนส่ง ถนนประเสริฐพงศ์ (map, I, C2): Prasertpong Road. ☎ 61-17-94.

■ **Thai Farmers Bank** – ธนาคารกสิ กรไทย (map, I, B2, **1**): 134 Charod Withitong Road. On the other side of the bridge on the way to the ruins. You can withdraw cash with a Visa card.

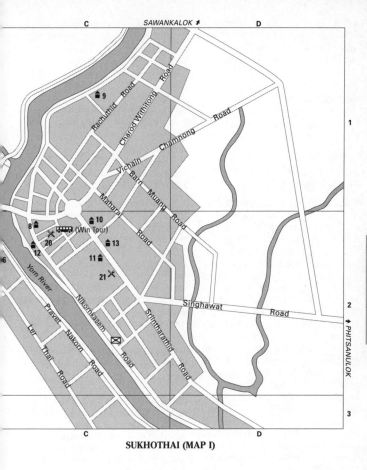

SUKHOTHAI (MAP I)

## ■ Useful Addresses

✉ Post office
🚌 Bus terminal

**1** Thai Farmers Bank
**2** Bus stop for Old Sukhothai

## 🏠 Where to Stay

**5** Somprasong Guesthouse
**6** Banthai Guesthouse
**7** Yupa House
**8** Chinawarat Hotel
**9** Lotus Village

**10** Sukhothai Hotel
**11** Sawaddiphong Hotel
**12** River View Hotel
**13** Northern Palace Hotel
**14** Rajthanee Hotel
**15** Suwan Guesthouse
**16** Thai Village House
**17** No. 4 Guesthouse

## ✕ Where to Eat

**20** Night market
**21** Dream Café

■ Bus stop for Old Sukhothai – สถานีรถสองแถวเพื่อไปอุทยานประ วัติศาสตร์ (map I, B1, **2**): Charod Withitong Road. After the bridge on the right going towards the site. Departures every 10 minutes, 6am–5.30pm.

## WHERE TO STAY

Most of the hotels and guesthouses are comfortable and cheap, and prices are much the same everywhere.

### BUDGET (80–300 BTS PER PERSON PER NIGHT)

🛏 **Somprasong Guesthouse** – สมประสงค์เกสท์เฮาส์ (map I, B2, **5**): 32 Pravet Nakorn Road. ☎ 61-17-09. On the other side of the River Yom, opposite the bus station. Across the bridge is a working-class area of private houses and fragrant gardens, like a delightful little piece of countryside. The rooms in this guesthouse are spotless, light, charming and very cheap. The shared bathroom is alright. Converted terrace at the front of the house on the first floor, overlooking the river. Also more modern rooms in new, solidly constructed, purpose-built bungalows at the end of the garden. These are more expensive but they do all have a terrace and private bathroom facilities and some have air-conditioning. Moped hire by the day, at the usual rates. Also serves a selection of reasonably priced meals. Highly recommended.

🛏 **Banthai Guesthouse** – บ้านไทย เกสท์เฮาส์ (map I, C2, **6**): 38 Pravet Nakorn Road. Just next door to the previous entry. ☎ 61-01-63. Bungalows in a tiny garden full of flowers that's just big enough for a few deckchairs and a washing-line. This place is as simple as it gets and everyone does their own cooking, although the little restaurant serves delicious salads. Decent but very basic rooms plus more rooms in the main building. Honest value for money.

🛏 **Yupa House** – ยุภาเฮาส์ (map I, B2, **7**): 44/10 Pravet Nakorn Road. ☎ 61-25-78. Another very nice place on the other side of the bridge. Large, white villa surrounded by gardens. Not exactly the last word in luxury but very clean. Here too, everyone mucks in and the owners speak a few words of English. Same price as the previous entry. Purified water available.

🛏 **Chinawarat Hotel** – โรงแรมชิน วัฒน์ (map I, C2, **8**): 1/3 Nikornka-sem Road. ☎ 61-13-85. About 500 metres from the bus station, at the entrance to the bridge. The room price depends on degree of comfort. The ones at the back are quieter. The European-style restaurant on the ground floor is not cheap but they do serve a heavenly milkshake. Bus timetables are on display. You can change money here if you need to. Fairly non-committal welcome.

🛏 **No. 4 Guesthouse** – เอ็น4 เกสท์เฮาส์ (map I, B1, **17**): Soi Khlong Maelumpun. ☎ 610-165. Very near to the buses for Old Sukhothai. The owners welcome their guests as warmly as ever and this new location is very pretty. Six rattan bungalows with shower and WC, and others are on the way. Look out for the Thai cookery classes, which are run from time to time.

**⌂ Suwan Guesthouse** – สุวรรณเกสท์เฮาส์ (map I, off A1, **15**): 28/4 Charod Withitong Road. ☎ 61-30-15. Some 100 metres from the entrance to the archaeological site. 'Suwan' in Thai means 'gold' and this place lives up to its name. Rooms in a traditional house at the end of a garden, rustic and clean. Shared bathroom that's hyper-clean. The carved wooden friezes at the tops of the bedroom doors are a nice feature. Also two large rooms in a ground-floor annexe, both new and stylishly decorated, and with air-conditioning. All in all, the place has lots of charm and it's peaceful, which is a particular advantage. The perfect place for early risers who want to see the ruins at first light. Cycle hire available.

## BUDGET TO MODERATE (150–500 BTS PER PERSON PER NIGHT)

**⌂ Lotus Village** – โลดัสวิลเลจ (map I, C1, **9**): 170 Ratchathanee Street. ☎ 62-14-84. Fax: 62-14-63. A charming guesthouse set deep in a lush garden, owned by a French former journalist and his wife, who is from Sukhothai. Three bungalows for two people and three traditional Thai houses with room for six, all built of teak, on stilts and flawlessly furnished. Individual bedrooms as well. Generous Continental breakfast plus French dishes on demand. Lessons in traditional massage at the weekend.

**⌂ Sukhothai Hotel** – สุโขทัยโฮเด็ล (map I, C2, **10**): 15/5 Singhawat Road. ☎ 61-11-33. The rooms here are much more expensive than in the Lotus Village, but double rooms are standard and terrific for the price. Clean and spacious, with or without air-conditioning. The rooms at the rear are quieter. The atmosphere and welcome are nothing special.

**⌂ Thai Village House** ไทยวิลเลจเฮาส์ (map I, A1, **16**): 1 Charod Withitong Road. ☎ 61-10-49. Halfway between the new town and the ruins. Thai-style bungalows groaning under the weight of vegetation. Price depends on degree of comfort. The setting has a certain charm, with streams, lily pads, footbridges, flowerbeds etc. This is a cultural centre that stages dance shows and is as touristy as you would expect. Booking is strongly recommended. Good local cooking. A door at the back of the garden leads to the well-preserved Wat Chang Rom, with its Singhalese *chedi* surrounded by elephants. Admission charge.

## MODERATE TO EXPENSIVE (300–800 BTS PER PERSON PER NIGHT)

**⌂ Sawaddiphong Hotel** – สวัสดิพงษ์โฮเด็ล (map I, C2, **11**): 56/4 Singhawat Road. ☎ 61-15-67. Modern, charmless place in one of the main streets, going towards Phitsanulok. Spacious rooms for four, with fan or air-conditioning. Good value for money and very well kept. The rooms on the street side are very noisy. Warm welcome.

**⌂ River View Hotel** – ริเวอร์วิวโฮเด็ล (map I, C2, **12**): 92/6 Nikornkasem Road. ☎ 61-16-56. Just next door to the bus station. Modern and very clean. Rooms with bathroom, fan or air-conditioning and TV. Very good value for money but the welcome's not too hot. The rooms on the ground floor are very damp, so during the rainy season try to get a room upstairs. There's a restaurant on the ground floor with terrace overlooking the river but it's not as lively as you'd expect. Decent food, and reasonably priced but not much choice.

EXPENSIVE TO SPLASH OUT
(500–1,800 BTS PER PERSON
PER NIGHT)

⌂ **Northern Palace Hotel** –
โรงแรมวังเหนือ (map I, C2, **13**):
43 Singhawat Road. ☎ 61-11-93.
Fax: 61-20-38. Spacious, quiet,
air-conditioned rooms overlooking
the garden, plus family rooms
at reasonable prices for a hotel
in this category. Has a restaurant.

⌂ **Rajthanee Hotel** – โรงแรมราช
ธานี (map I, B1, **14**): 229 Charod
Withitong Road. ☎ 61-10-31. On
the way to the ruins, after the
bridge. Small, new, purpose-built
luxury hotel, with quiet, comfortable rooms. Impersonal welcome
and not always very professional
either.

## WHERE TO EAT AND WHERE TO HAVE A DRINK

✕ **Night market** – ตลาดกลางคืน
(map I, C2, **20**): in front of the River
View Hotel. Lots of **street kitchens** serving good, wholesome
food at low prices. The atmosphere
is much livelier than in the hotel
restaurants.

✕ ♟ **Dream Café** – ดรีมคาเฟ่ (map
I, C2, **21**): only seconds from the
bus terminal. A café for people
who like junk shops, as it's decorated in an original way, with old
furniture and collectables. People
come here mainly to drink – a real
'café' in other words, with a menu
featuring hundreds of coffees,
liqueurs and drinks of every description, plus a few snacks but
nothing very substantial. Great
place.

## GREAT IDEA

Anyone staying in Sukhothai for a few days can give lessons in their own
language to Thai children for 2 hours every night (books are available) in
exchange for their meal. Children hand out leaflets in the area near the
guesthouses and ruins. This is a common practice in towns throughout
northern Thailand.

## WHAT TO SEE IN OLD SUKHOTHAI

The ruins are 12 kilometres (7 miles) outside Sukhothai. It takes about 25
minutes to get there by van, which you catch on the Charod Withitong
Road, beyond the bridge, on the same side as the ruins and on the corner
with Panitsan Road (see map I of Sukhothai, above).The fare is very
cheap with departures every 10 minutes, 6am–5.30pm. You'll also find
bicycles for hire at reasonable rates near the entrance to the site (ask the
man for your free map of the ruin). Going by bike is one of the best ways
to see most of the ruins, but check what condition the bike is in,
particularly the brakes and tyres. You can also hire a *tuk-tuk* for a few
hours and, since there's plenty of competition, it's easy to haggle.
Rumour has it that you can also visit the ruins in an ox-cart driven by a
local farmer – but he won't be allowed inside the walls.

Try to get to the ruins as early as possible (they're open from 7am) and
you'll have the place to yourself for at least 2 hours. The colours in the
dawn light are magnificent and the temperature is pleasantly cool.

SUKHOTHAI

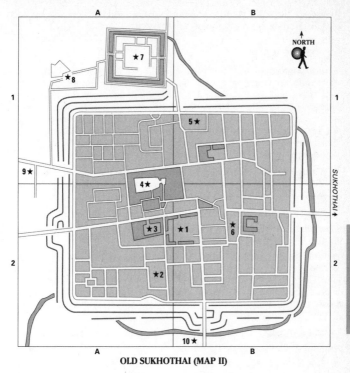

OLD SUKHOTHAI (MAP II)

---

★ **What to See**

1  Wat Mahathat
2  Wat Sri Sawai
3  Wat Trapang Ngoen
4  Wat Sra Si
5  Wat Sorasak

6  National Museum of Rama Kamheng
7  Wat Phra Pai Luang
8  Wat Sri Chum
9  Wat Saphan Hin
10 Wat Chetupon

---

Admission is charged for the main site and some of the temples outside the walls. Some tickets are for several sites. Expect to be there all morning, particularly if you want to linger beneath the big trees and lose yourself in the flowering lotus blossoms.

Originally, the old walled town was 1,800 metres (1 mile) long by 1,500 metres (almost a mile) wide. The main temples inside the city walls were surrounded by moats.

**Tourist Information Centre**: situated outside the walls, in the north-west of the site, near the Wat Phra Pai Luang. The centre issues maps of the site, and there's a model of the ruins to help you find your way around and work out which temples you want to visit.

## INSIDE THE WALLS

★ **Wat Mahathat** – วัดมหาธาตุ (map II, B2, **1**): the most important monument on the entire site, this temple was reserved for the royal family and is surrounded by nearly 1,000 metres of moat. At the front is an imposing esplanade with a series of columns. The base of the central *chedi* is decorated with a frieze showing monks. On either side, two Buddhas are protected by a brick structure. The ruins as a whole, with their lotus-blossom pool, make one of the best photo opportunities of the whole trip.

★ **Wat Sri Sawai** – วัดศรีสวาย (map II, A2, **2**): founded during the period of Khmer domination are these three *prangs* in the Lopburi style for anyone who dreams of seeing Angkor or who isn't going to Phimai.

★ **Wat Trapang Ngoen** – วัดตระพังเงิน (map II, A2, **3**): just next door to the Wat Mahathat, this *chedi* is in the shape of a lotus blossom, and has a magnificent view of the big lake, with its blanket of lotus flowers.

★ **Wat Sra Si** – วัดสระศรี (map II, A1–A2, **4**): one of the loveliest temples on the site, in the middle of a charming little lake on an islet reached by a footbridge. The temple's rounded shape reminds you of Singhalese *stupas.* Look out for the large Buddha with an oddly disproportionate nose. In front are the remains of the *viharn*, with its truncated columns. On the lawn is an extremely graceful, strolling Buddha.

★ **Wat Sorasak** – วัดสรศักดิ์ (map II, B1, **5**): a fine frieze of elephants, with sculptures at the base; perfectly conserved and well worth seeing.

★ **The National Museum of Rama Kamheng** – พิพิธภัณฑสถานแห่งชาติ รามคำแหง (map II, B2, **6**): at the entrance to the site, as you arrive from Sukhothai. Open 9am–4pm. Closed Monday and Tuesday. It houses lots of artefacts unearthed during regional excavations, as well as sculptures, ceramics and mural paintings of outstanding quality. There's a splendid (and extremely rare) striding Buddha and a copy of the stele of Rama Khamheng.

## OUTSIDE THE WALLS

★ **Wat Phra Pai Luang** – วัดพระพายหลวง (map II, A1, **7**): in the northern part of the site is one of the oldest temples in Sukhothai, founded by the Khmers in the 12th century. Vestiges of the series of columns on the *viharn* are still visible and one of the original *prangs* remains practically intact, with magnificent stucco work and sculptures similar to those in Angkor (particularly on the pediment). There is also an astonishing brick statue of a walking Buddha.

★ **Wat Sri Chum** – วัดศรีชุม map II, A1, **8**): in the northwest, not far from the previous temple. Open 8.30am–6pm. This rather unprepossessing blockhouse-type building contains a seated Buddha 15 metres (45 feet) tall. A stairway within the wall leads to the Buddha's head: this may be symbolic of mortal progress towards the Buddha state.

★ **Wat Chang Lom** – วัดช้างล้อม (map II, off B2): at the entrance to the site, next to the Thai Village House. Admission charge. Here there are yet more interesting sculptures, particularly the elephants around the base. It's worth seeing if you're not going to visit the Wat Chang Lom in Sri Satchanalai.

## IN THE SURROUNDING AREA

If you've hired a *tuk-tuk* or a *samlor* (or even a bike) there are some interesting ruins to visit nearby.

★ **Wat Saphan Hin** – วัดสะพานหิน (map II, A1, **9**): about 4 kilometres (2.5 miles) west of the walls. Admission charge. Not an easy site to get to – even dangerous sometimes – but well cleared and worth seeing for the raised pathway of large stone slabs that leads up to it. At the top, you'll find the remains of the *viharn* and a Buddha 12 metres (40 feet) high.

★ **Wat Chang Rop** –วัดช้างรอบ: just beyond the previous temple but not as impressive is a dilapidated *stupa* with elephant sculptures around the base.

★ **Wat Chetupon** – วัดเชตุพน (map II, B2, **10**): in the south, about 2 kilometres (1 mile) away. This is a fine group of remains, including vestiges of the schist walls and moats, and in particular, the principal sanctuary that houses the Four Buddhas. The seated and reclining Buddhas have practically all disappeared, leaving only the standing and walking Buddhas. You can admire the careful carving, subtle curves and delicacy of the Buddha's gait. Other small *wats* all around make the trip out here worthwhile.

## FESTIVAL

– **Loy Krathong**: a major festival, held in the ruins in mid-November, with *son et lumière* and dancing.

## WHAT TO SEE IN THE SURROUNDING AREA

★ **Sri Satchanalai** – ศรีสัชนาลัย: anyone who hasn't overdosed on temples can visit Sri Satchanalai, about 60 kilometres (40 miles) north of Sukhothai (*see* 'Leaving Sukhothai', *below*). There is a bus service from Sukhothai but the ruins themselves are about 20 kilometres (12 miles) from the town itself, on the main road, so don't go into the town centre. Ask the driver to stop where you see the sign pointing to the ruins 500 metres further up on the left. Follow that road over the bridge then take the first road on the right (at the junction, you can hire a bike to visit the ruins). The main entrance to the ruins is about 300 metres further on. Once again, don't go into the town centre or you'll only have to take a taxi to go back to the ruins.

There is something quite extraordinary about the wild, solitary site of Sri Satchanalai, sacred memorial to the Buddha. It was founded in the 13th century for the viceroys of Sukhothai. The ruins today include some interesting remains, particularly the 13th-century Wat Chang Lom that has a *stupa* decorated with 39 elephants. Beside it is the Wat Chedi Chet Thoeo, which has magnificent floral decorations on the walls.

About 2 kilometres (1.5 miles) away, sited in a loop of the River Yom, is the **Wat Phra Mahathat.** Don't miss it. You get to it via the suspension bridge (first entrance coming from Sukhothai). The ruins include a Singhalese-style *chedi* and a magnificent Khmer-style *prang*. Here too, there is another immensely elegant walking Buddha and an interesting Buddha that is watched over by a seven-headed *nâga*.

## LEAVING SUKHOTHAI

– **By train**: you need to go back to Phitsanulok (*see* the relevant chapter).

– **By bus for Chiang Mai**: four Win Tour departures daily (two morning and afternoon). Lots of government transportation buses leave every day: the cost is the same, but they're more comfortable. The journey takes about 5 hours.

**For Chiang Rai**: one Win Tour bus daily, with air-conditioning or fan, leaves mid-morning. Government transportation bus: two departures every morning. Journey lasts about 5 hours.

**For Sri Satchanalai**: lots of buses daily, 6am–6pm. It's a 1-hour journey.

**For Phitsanulok**: Win Tour buses every 30 minutes, 6am–6pm.

**For Bangkok**: nine air-conditioned or non-air-conditioned government buses daily, 7.50am–10.40pm. They will stop in Ayutthaya but ask before setting out. About a 6-hour journey.

**For Khon Kaen** (eastern Thailand): seven buses daily on average. Journey of about 7 hours.

– **By air**: *see* 'Phitsanulok'.

# CHIANG MAI (CHIENG MAI) – เชียงใหม่

DIALLING CODE: 053

Just about every traveller succumbs to the charms of Chiang Mai. This big old provincial town flanked by lush mountainsides is a lovely place, and you can explore it by bicycle (or motorbike) in search of the last remaining traditional wooden houses that still exist here and there. Sadly, the recent period of burgeoning growth has resulted in architectural anarchy – a string of large hotels and gigantic European-style shopping centres lining busier and busier roads. And while it's nothing like Bangkok, traffic jams are now a reality and so is the noise. But despite signs that this 'Rose of the North' may be starting to fade, Chiang Mai retains a certain charm, and life there is sweet indeed.

This is a lively student town, with quite enough life to stop you from being bored, but not so lively that it loses its peaceful atmosphere. Long-term backpackers like to stay here for some time and it's not hard to see why. Pure air, lovely weather, welcoming people, delicious food and lots of terrific little guesthouses buried at the bottom of gardens: Chiang Mai is a pleasure to be in. The town itself, apart from the temples and possibly the museum, if it eventually reopens, does not abound with things to see, but there's plenty to keep you busy in the surrounding area. The town is also the main starting point for mountain treks and you'll find more than 100 agencies battling for your custom.

## A BRIEF HISTORY

Chiang Mai was founded by King Mengrai at the end of the 13th century, and it was then that the canals and ramparts that make up the original, square layout (now in the centre) were excavated and built. The little town became the capital of the kingdom of Lanna at the beginning of the 14th century, when the kingdoms of Sukhothai and Chiang Rai formed an alliance and the two kings agreed to protect each other against acts of aggression. Despite this agreement, the city came under frequent attack, falling first to Ayutthaya and then into the clutches of the Burmese, who maintained control from the mid-16th to the mid-18th century. It remained cut off from the rest of the country for hundreds of years (not a single road went there until the start of the 20th century) leaving the kingdom of Lanna free to develop its own highly original artistic style, inspired by the Burmese and Laotian tradition. You can see examples of it in the museums.

## TOPOGRAPHY

This is not a very big town. The area known as the 'old quarter' (there's no longer anything very old about it) is defined by four canals that form a square around guesthouses, temples and official buildings. The canals make it very easy to get your bearings. The river Mae Nam Ping flows to the east of the square and between the canal and the river lies the new town centre where you'll find plenty of hotels. The main street is the Tha Phae Road and the real heart of Chiang Mai is the Tha Phae Gate, on the corner of Tha Phae Road and the canal. Keep this in mind, and it's difficult to get lost.

## GETTING TO CHIANG MAI

**From the airport**, which is 15 kilometres (9 miles) to the southwest:

● At the **airport** (off A4 on the map) you'll find the tourist office, the post office and the foreign exchange office.

– **Thai Limousine Service**: in theory at least there is a minibus waiting to meet every plane – but only until 6pm. You can be dropped wherever you want in town and it's cheaper than a taxi if you're travelling alone. For two or more people, take a taxi.

– **Airport taxis**: offer an attractive fixed rate that's worth it for two or more people.

**From the station**, which is about 1.5 kilometres (1 mile) from the centre, to the east of the town:

You'll find swarms of guesthouse touts there to meet you, with photos and visiting cards and offers of free transport to the guesthouse they represent. Their pressurized selling tactics are a real pain but you make your choice. Otherwise, you can walk, if you haven't got too much luggage, or take a *samlor*, a *tuk-tuk* or a *songthaew*, one of those vans that serve as buses.

## TRANSPORT IN TOWN

– **By bike**: this is the best way of getting around town, which is fairly flat, but be careful in the rush-hour when there's heavy traffic (early morning and late afternoon). It's easy to find your way around and you'll find people with bikes for hire all over the place, but mainly on the Moon Muang Road. Check the condition of the bike, especially the tyres.

– **By motorbike**: a useful way of getting to places in the surrounding area, and most of the guesthouses have them for hire. Deal directly with the hirer and cut out any middlemen. You'll find lots of bike-hire places on the Moon Muang Road, the Kotchasarn Road and in the main street on the Tha Phae Road. As always, check the brakes, the gears and the tyres, and read the paperwork carefully before you sign. Be aware that insurance isn't compulsory for hired motorbikes but that an increasing number of places will try to sell you a policy that only covers the cost of scrapping the bike – a decision over which you have no control and which could cost you dear if the hirer decides the bike can be repaired. If you are offered insurance, read the small print carefully and get the hirer to confirm all the details. Things usually go swingingly to begin with but the least little accident and you're in no end of trouble. So come prepared: take out a personal insurance policy before leaving home that covers you in the event of an accident. A little Honda 100cc is quite big enough for two people if you plan to keep to the surrounding area. Most hire places will insist on keeping your passport.

Here are two recommended motorbike-hire places, both located oppo-site the Tha Phae Gate, on the left outside the moats: C&P Service, 51 Kotchasarn Road (☎ 273-161) and Deng Bike Hire, 23 Kotchasarn Road (☎ 271-524).

– ***Songthaews***: these are easily recognizable vans: red in town, blue, yellow and other colours in the surrounding regions. Convenient and plentiful, *songthaews* are one-third or two-thirds the price of *tuk-tuks* and operate rather like buses. They are as direct as you would expect of a vehicle in which you are not the only passenger. To stop a *songthaew*, wave to the driver and tell him your destination. If you are his first passenger, the driver will head for your destination and pick up other passengers on the way. In that case, agree a price beforehand and pay when you get there. Fares are more or less fixed according to destination. If the driver refuses to take you it's because the passengers already on board are going a different way.

A tip for those who want to visit the surrounding area but don't want to take public transport: hire a *songthaew* for the day. Agree the price and the number of stops with the driver in advance. It's lots of fun and quite cheap.

– **Local bus services**: there haven't been any buses for some years now.

– ***Tuk-tuks*** (also called motorized *samlors*): local taxi-motorbikes like the ones in Bangkok but more expensive considering the distances they cover. Offer the driver one-third or half the fare he asks for. They're not in such a hurry as in Bangkok – no doubt the mountain air has something to do with it . . .

– **Pedal *samlors***: a convenient and inexpensive way of going short distances, pedal *samlors* have practically disappeared in Chiang Mai. As distances increase on a par with traffic and building development, *samlors* are probably doomed to extinction anyway, unless of course they get their second wind as a result of the economic crisis.

### ■ Useful Addresses

- 🅱 TAT
- ✉ Main post office
- 🚂 Train station
- 🚌 Arcade bus station
- 🚌 Chang Puak bus station
- ✈ Airport
- **1** Thai Airways International
- **3** Immigration office
- **4** Loi Kroa Clinic
- **5** Ram Hospital
- **6** Thai Farmers Bank
- **7** Maharaj Public Hospital

### 🛏 Where to Stay

- **10** C&C Teak House
- **11** Lek House
- **12** Eagle House
- **14** Orchid House
- **15** Pun Pun Guesthouse
- **16** Lamchang House
- **17** Saitum Guesthouse
- **18** Ben Guesthouse
- **19** S.B. House
- **20** Pha-Thai Guesthouse
- **21** Fang Guesthouse
- **22** Rendezvous Guesthouse
- **24** Green Lodge
- **25** Little Home Guesthouse
- **26** Chiang Mai Youth Hostel
- **28** Srisupan Guesthouse
- **29** Paradise Hotel and Guesthouse
- **30** Top North Guesthouse
- **31** Chatree Hotel
- **32** Northlands House Hotel
- **33** YMCA
- **35** Galare Guesthouse
- **36** River Ping Palace Hotel
- **62** Swairaing Chiang Mai Lakeside Town

### ✕ Where to Eat

- **45** Night market in Chaiya Phum Road
- **46** Aroon Rai
- **47** Galare Food Centre
- **49** Grilled Chicken with Honey
- **51** Daret's House and Restaurant
- **53** Kafe Restaurant
- **54** Heun Suntaree
- **55** Fatty
- **56** Tha-Nam Restaurant
- **57** The Gallery Restaurant
- **58** Antique House
- **59** Ta-Krite
- **60** Westin Hotel Buffet Lunch
- **62** Swairaing Chiang Mai Lakeside Town
- **63** Baan Suan
- **65** Old Cultural Centre
- **66** Khum Kaeo Palace
- **67** Lanna Kantoke

### ♈ Entertainment

- **75** The Riverside
- **76** Karaoke Bars
- **77** West-Side
- **79** ID4
- **80** Bar Beer Centre
- **81** Gigi's
- **82** Space Bubble

**CHIANG MAI**

CHIANG MAI

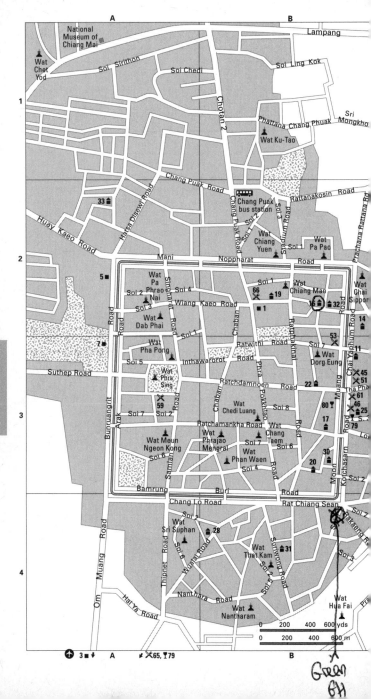

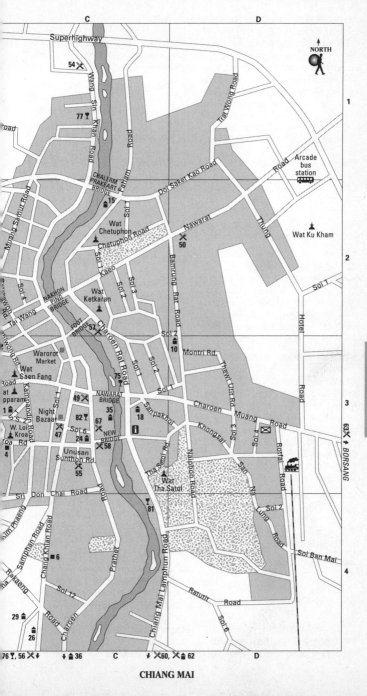

CHIANG MAI

## ADDRESSES AND USEFUL INFORMATION

**🛈 TAT** – ททท (Tourist Office; map, C3): 105/1 Chiang Mai Lamphun Road in the Amphoe Muang district. ☎ 248-604 or 607. Fax: 248-605. Open daily, 8.30am–4.30pm. A bit far from the centre, on the other side of the river opposite the New Bridge (a pedestrian bridge). The building itself is a fine reconstruction of a Thai house. Lots of brochures on Chiang Mai, lists of hotels, bus, train and plane timetables, but don't expect miracles. The tourist police office is on the ground floor. ☎ 248-974 (or 16-99). You can call long-distance from the telephone kiosks outside.

**✉ Main post office** – ไปรษณีย์กลาง (map, D3): Charoen Muang Road. A 10-minute walk from the station. There is another post office in Praisanee Road, 200 metres from the Nawarat Bridge and not far from the big river.

**■ Small private post office** – ไปรษณีย์: 10–12 Ratchadamnoen Road. Immediately on the left of the Shell petrol station. Open daily, 8am–10pm. This is an antiques shop that also offers a range of postal services, including parcel post, long-distance phone calls and fax. Much less crowded than the main post office and so much more convenient.

**🚂 Train station** – สถานีรถไฟ (map, D3): 27 Charoen Muang Road. ☎ 245-363 or 245-364. Trains to and from Bangkok. No trains going north.

**🚌 Arcade bus station** – สถานีรถอาร์เขด (map, D1): Lampang Superhighway. ☎ 242-664. Bus departures for destinations outside the province of Chiang Mai.

**🚌 Chang Puak bus station** – สถานีรถช้างเผือก (map, B2): Chang Puak Road. ☎ 211-586. Buses and *songthaews* covering the province of Chiang Mai.

**■ Tourist police** – ตำรวจท่องเที่ยวถนนลำพูน: same address as the tourist office. ☎ 248-974. Emergency number: ☎ 16-99.

**■ Telephone** – โทรศัพท์: Praisanee Road. Opposite the small post office. Open daily, 8.30am–8pm. Long-distance calls can be made from any of the kiosks and booths you find all over town, particularly on the Moon Muang Road (note that there are two kinds of telephone card). Calls are charged per minute in some places. For reverse-charge (collect) calls, they'll add a commission. These can be made from some booths and guesthouses, which is much more convenient than going to the post office. Still, the best way to make calls is with a telephone card, providing, of course, that you can find a booth that accepts the one you've bought.

**■ Thai Airways International** – สายการบินไทย (map, B2, **1**): 240 Phra Pokkhlao Road. ☎ 210-003 to 005. Same address and telephone number for international and domestic flights. Open daily, 8am–5pm. Airport number: ☎ 270-222–234.

**■ Trans World Travel Co.** – ทรานส์เวิร์ลทราเวล: 259–261 Tha Phae Road. ☎ 272-415 or 273-603. Open 8am–5pm. Travel agency with a reliable reputation.

**■ D.K. Book House** – ร้านขายหนังสือดี.เค.ดวงกมล: 79/1 Kotchasarn Road. Open daily, 9am–9pm. Vast, air-conditioned bookshop selling maps, regional books and guides, and Thai cookery books. Look out for an excellent and amusing map of Chiang Mai, by

Nancy Chandler on sale in lots of bookshops. A bit pricey but well worth it to help you find your way around.

■ **Pichit Stationery** – ร้านพิจิตร สเตชั่นเนอร์: 271 Tha Phae Gate. Some foreign-language newspapers and journals.

■ **Library Service** – ร้านหนังสือ ไลบรารเซอร์วิส: 21/1 Ratchamankha Road, Soi 2. Open daily, 9am–6pm. Buys and sells books in all languages. You'll find the Nancy Chandler map on sale here.

Lots of free magazines *(Welcome in Chiang Mai, Good Morning Chiang Mai, Chiang Mai Guide Line)* sponsored by local advertisers are available from hotels and restaurants. Full of information but proceed with caution.

## DIPLOMATIC REPRESENTATION AND IMMIGRATION

■ **British Consul**: 198 Bamrung Rat Road, Muang, Chiang Mai 5000. ☎ 263-015. Fax: 263-016.

■ **Immigration Office** – สำนักงาน ครวจคนเข้าเมือง (off A4 on the map, **3**): 97 Sanambin Road. Just beside the airport. ☎ 277-510. Usual opening hours: 8.30am–4.30pm. Closed weekends. Applications for visa extensions are made here.

## DOCTORS AND HOSPITALS

■ **Loi Kroa Clinic** – คลีนิคลอย เคราะห์ (map, C3, **4**): 62/2 Loi Kroa Road. Opposite the Wat Loi Kroa. ☎ 271-571. Open weekdays, 7.30am–1pm and 4.30–8.30pm; Saturday 7.30am–1pm, Sunday 4.30–8.30pm. Reliable medical care.

■ **Ram Hospital** – โรงพยาบาลราม (map, A2, **5**): 8 Bunruangrit Road. ☎ 224-861. Ultra-modern and well equipped, but private and therefore expensive.

■ **Chang Puak Hospital** – โรงพยาบาลช้างเผือก: 1/7 Chang Puak Road, Soi 2. ☎ 220-022. It's very clean, with good-quality equipment, and is no more expensive than the others.

■ **Maharaj Public Hospital** – โรงพยาบาลมหาราช (map, A3, **7**): 110 Suthep Road, outside the Suan Dok Gate (western gate). ☎ 221-122. A state hospital, and therefore much cheaper than the Ram Hospital, but also much more crowded so you have to wait. Huge place.

■ **Dentist**: Peerayoot Dental Clinic – พีระยุทธิ์ทันตแพทย์: 141 Somphet Market, Moon Muang Road, Amphur Muang. ☎ 212-653. Patients are seen 9am–8pm every day. Closed on the second and fourth Sunday of the month. Excellent, conscientious dental treatment, but quite expensive. Always find out what it costs before proceeding. Another good place is the Chiang Mai Dental Hospital on Superhighway Road. Lots of dentists and good-quality equipment.

■ **Pharmacy** – ร้านขายยา: 46/3 Charoen Prathet Road. ☎ 274-764. Opposite the Diamond Hotel. Open 7.30am–11pm. Closed on Sunday.

CHIANG MAI

## FOREIGN EXCHANGE

There are lots of banks in Chiang Mai, quite a few with hole-in-the-wall cash dispensers outside. Most are on the Tha Phae Road. Usual opening hour are 8.30am–3.30pm.

■ **Thai Farmers Bank** – ธนาค-ารกสิกรไทย: lets you make cash withdrawals with a Visa card. There are also lots of foreign exchange kiosks that stay open until 7.30pm or 8pm. Two addresses (out of many) are: 169–171 Tha Phae Road (map, C3). The bank is open 8.30am–3.30pm, Monday to Friday, and has a hole-in-the-wall cash dispenser outside, plus a foreign exchange kiosk on the right that opens 8.30am–8pm daily. There is another Thai Farm-ers Bank at 145 Chang Khlan Road (map, C4, **6**), which also has a cash dispenser outside.

■ You can exchange **traveller's cheques or cash** in any of the other banks. Two addresses (out of many) are: The Union Bank of Bangkok, 396 Tha Phae Road, open daily, 8am–9pm; and the Bangkok Bank, 53–59 Tha Phae Road, which offers very competitive rates for exchanging cash.

## LEISURE

■ **Swimming pools** – สระว่ายน้ำ: There are quite a few good ones. One of the best is the Prince Hotel pool: 3 Tai Wang Road, behind the hotel on the left. ☎ 252-025. Open 10am–8pm. Tickets available from hotel reception. Very clean water. There is also the Sara Health Club, 109 Bamrung Rat Road, opposite the British Consulate at the back of a school courtyard. Low admission charge, away from the town centre and therefore quiet. Lovely Olympic pool with deckchairs, chairs and parasols. Very clean water. Great place to spend a lazy afternoon. There's also the Rincome Hotel pool (*see below*).

■ **Tennis** – สนามเทนนิส: in addition to a great pool, the Rincome Hotel – โรงแรมรินค่ำ, 301 Huay Kaeo Road, ☎ 221-044, also has tennis courts, but hiring racquets costs a bomb. The courts for hire opposite the museum are cheaper, but they're not as good.

## A WORD OF WARNING ABOUT DRUGS

It's no secret that Chiang Mai is an important nerve-centre of the drug-running industry. It's also well known that the dealers are the first to grass on you. So a moment's naughtiness can land you in a whole heap of trouble, particularly since the police carry out frequent raids in trekking areas.

## WHERE TO STAY

Chiang Mai deserves praise for the dozens of inexpensive guesthouses that seem to be reserved especially for budget travellers. The nicest of all are teak houses, usually with a lounge area or small garden space.

There are currently more than 300 guesthouses in Chiang Mai. All or nearly all of the landlords organize treks and some of them get sulky if you refuse to go. All they want then is to see you pay up and leave. Likewise, some travel agencies in Bangkok throw in a free night's accommodation on arrival in Chiang Mai in the hope that when you get there you'll sign up for the hotel trek. If you don't, you may be asked to pay for your 'free' night. These commercial tactics are now common practice.

The latest technique to watch out for are *tuks-tuks* or taxis at the bus or train station that refuse to take you to the guesthouse of your choice, saying it's burned down or some such nonsense. Instead, they head for the guesthouse that pays them the most commission and you get taken for a ride in more ways than one.

### BUDGET (80 –150 BTS PER PERSON PER NIGHT)

**Lamchang House** – ลำช้างเฮาส์ (map, B2, **16**): 24 Moon Muang Road, Soi 7. ☎ 210-586. First-class little place in a quiet but central road. Loads of charm, simple and spotlessly kept by a Thai family. Elegant teak house in which everything seems in period, located at the end of a lush garden. Sparingly furnished with woven bamboo furniture of different patterns, creating rooms of positively monastic elegance. The facilities are basic, but there is a hot shower, and the WC outside is very clean. The whole place seems to radiate the softness and languor of the Far East that is sometimes so hard to find in Chiang Mai. And it doesn't organize any treks – what better reference could you ask for? Nice little restaurant, too. Tremendous.

**Lek House** – เล็กเฮาส์ (map, B3, **11**): 22 Chai Yaphum Road. ☎ 252-686. An original brick-and-teak house not far from the Tha Phae Gate by the Chiang Mai Road. Very simple rooms but all with attractive bamboo furniture and private bathroom with cold running water. Very cheap, but not always very well kept. Often fully booked but try to see the room first if you can. This is the kind of place you come to for the setting and the warm welcome. Lovely, peaceful, shady garden even at night in the stark neon lighting.

**Eagle House** – อีเกิ้ลเฮาส์ (map, C3, **12**): 16–18 Chang Moi Kao Road, Soi 3. ☎ 235-387. Fax: 216-368. Nice place, kept by a kind but firm landlady called Annette, an Irishwoman who is most attentive towards her guests. The guesthouse is at the bottom of a shady but prettily lit and beautifully kept terrace garden with wooden tables and chairs. Solidly built rooms with cold shower and WC – cheap too. There is free use of the warm shower outside. Annette manages to give her place a really cool atmosphere, all based on trust. Anyone who wants a drink helps themselves, puts it on the 'slate' and pays later. Not bad eh? There is also a limited menu and all the food is cooked or washed in mineral water. Annette's treks are said to be very good and it appears that she gives priority to trekking customers. Business must be booming, to judge from all the rooms that have recently been redecorated and the new guesthouse she's opened in the old town: Eagle House 2 (Ratwithi Road, Soi 2, ☎ 210-620). Here again, you'll find decent rooms leading off a pleasant garden. A bit more expensive and unfortunately rather noisy.

⌂ **Orchid House** – ออร์คิดเฮาส์ (map, B2, **14**): 11 Chai Yaphum Road, Soi 2. ☎ 874-127. This modern guesthouse in a tiny, quiet sub-*soi* has much to recommend it: spacious, super-clean rooms (ignore the overly-bright floor tiles and the rather dreary lighting), all with WC and cold shower; warm welcome from a young team and very competitive prices. The small adjoining restaurant charges next to nothing and you hear good things about their treks. You can arrange by phone to be picked up from the station. If it's fully booked, you can always go opposite, to the **Chiang Mai Inn** (☎ 251-400): a big, modern building with rooms leading off a patio. A bit more expensive and the furniture and mural paintings have seen better days, but it's decent.

⌂ **Pun Pun Guesthouse** – ปันปัน เกสท์เฮ้าส์ (map, C2, **15**): 321 Charoen Rat Road. ☎ 243-362. Rather a long way from the centre, on the left bank of the river. Little houses on stilts in a garden, all with simple rooms equipped with fans, at low prices. Well-kept bathroom facilities. Airier than places in the centre, so good for those with their own transport. The new landlord is very welcoming. There are other more expensive rooms but most of the guests come here for the cheaper ones. Pity about the new building that's gone up right next door.

⌂ **Saitum Guesthouse** – สายคำเก สท์เฮ้าส์ (map, B3, **17**): 21 Moon Muang Road, Ratchamankha Soi

1. ☎ 278-575. Several small teak houses on stilts in a large walled garden. Lovely mango trees and a well-kept lawn. Very simple, wooden rooms at very reasonable prices. The bathroom facilities are a bit average, but not bad on the whole: pretty and pleasant, if slightly ragged around the edges. Oddly enough they sometimes tell you they're full even when they're not.

⌂ **Chiang Mai Youth Hostel** – บ้านเยาวชนเชียงใหม่ (map, C4, **26**): 21/8 Chang Khlan Road. ☎ 276-737. Coming from the centre, take the side street on the right by the service station. You may even spot the tiny sign. When the YH in the centre was bought up, all that was left was this large, loveless building in the south of town. Simple but very clean rooms with bathroom, at prices you can't argue with. The landlord is pleasant and you hear good things about his treks.

– You'll find lots more guesthouses in the same little street as the **Top North Guesthouse** (*see* 'Moderate to Expensive', *below*). These include places like the **Thailand Guesthouse** and the **Top North Hotel**, all much the same and cheap.

## BUDGET TO MODERATE (100–400 BTS PER PERSON PER NIGHT)

⌂ **C&C Teak House** – ซี.แอนด์ .ซี.ทีคเฮ้าส์ (map, D3, **10**): 39 Bumrung Rat Road. ☎ and fax: 246-966. Coming from the station, turn right at the third set of traffic lights: the guesthouse is within walking distance, 200 metres further up on the right. This is a favourite guesthouse in Chiang Mai – it has it all: a late 19th-century teak house, quiet but in a lively street, friendly atmosphere, simple but carefully prepared food, immaculately clean and very reasonably priced rooms, about 20 in all. Those on the ground floor are dead basic, single or double, with shared bathroom facilities and cold water. The rooms upstairs have fans, mosquito nets and hot water. They cost a bit more but you get (free) use of the bicycles. The room for four people is good value. Next door is a massage parlour in an old colonial-style house. The terrace restaurant serves a tempting assortment of dishes prepared by the Franco-Thai landlords. On the menu are such mouth-watering delicacies as *tom yam* soup with coconut, or fried chicken with coconut, as well as French dishes. Or there is the equally delicious *kantoke* dinner (*see* 'Where to Eat' for a description). Films are shown in the evening. Good organized treks, lasting one or several days. You can also go trekking by motorbike and there are plans for treks by mountain bike too (with Simon the owner). All in all, they get top marks for comfort and hospitality.

🛊 **Ben Guesthouse** – เบญเกสท์เฮ้าส์ (map, C3, **18**): 4/4 Chiang Mai Lamphun Road, Soi 2. ☎ 244-103. At the back of a tiny, quiet *soi*, close to the tourist office, in a very central area that feels far removed from all the hustle and bustle of the town. Solidly built house – nothing special but looks dependable. Very clean rooms with bathroom facilities (cold shower). Courteous, discreet welcome from the owners.

🛊 **S.B. House** – เอส.บี.เฮ้าส์ (map, B2, **19**): 1/1 Soi 13, Phra Pokkhlao Road. ☎ 210-644. Behind the Thai Airways office at the back of a cul-de-sac, next door to a great steak house. Private, solidly-built house run by a friendly family. About 10 comfortable rooms with shower room, hot water, fan or air-conditioning (those with fans are probably cool enough). No particular

charm but very comfortable for the price. You'll find better facilities here than in some of the more expensive guesthouses.

🛊 **Pha-Thai Guesthouse** – ฟ้าไทย เกสท์เฮ้าส์ (map, B3, **20**): 48/1 Ratphakinai Road. ☎ 278-013. Fax: 274-075. Another good place. Recently built house, beautifully kept by a tremendous Thai landlord who is always very helpful. He speaks French, having studied in France for 3 years. Rooms with fan or air-conditioning (some even have both) and all with hot shower. Not the most charming place but surprisingly peaceful. Various levels of comfort.

🛊 **Fang Guesthouse** – แฟงเกสท์เฮ้าส์ (map, C3, **21**): 46–48 Kampandin Road, Soi 1. ☎ 282-940, 272-505 and 272-500. Third road on the left coming from the Pink River on Tha Phae Road, near the Night Bazaar. Recently built house with a large terrace on the third and top floor, offering a fine view of the town. Rather impersonal but the rooms are modern and well kept with telephone, shower, WC, fan or air-conditioning. Single or double rooms – at varying prices. House restaurant.

🛊 **Rendezvous Guesthouse** – รองเดวูเกสท์เฮ้าส์ (map, B3, **22**): 3/1 Soi 5, Ratchdamnoen Road. ☎ 213-763. Fax: 217-229. Small building with complex architecture – half modern, half traditional – in a quiet *soi*. Hospitable bar on the ground floor. Well-equipped rooms, all with telephone, fridge, fan, hot shower and WC. At least one room on the top floor has its own secluded roof-terrace. First-class facilities for the price. From upstairs, there is a view over the quiet part of town.

🛊 There are quite a lot of other places in Soi 5, including **Kavil House** (☎ 224-740), a small, modern, three-storey hotel with decent, slightly cheaper rooms, owned by a *farang*. Not much charm, but it has a good view from the top.

⚐ **Little Home Guesthouse** – ลิตเติ้ลโฮมเกสเฮาส์ (map, B3, **25**): 1 Kotchasarn Road, Soi 3. ☎ 273-662. Charming house with a garden full of flowers, owned by a Thai-Dutch couple. Just 12 simple rooms but all very pleasant and quiet, so it's worth the price despite the somewhat basic facilities (shower, WC, fan), particularly since there's a reduction in price for three nights or more. They talk of opening a restaurant in the lovely lounge area on the terrace but for the time being you don't even get breakfast.

⚐ **Green Lodge** – กรีนลอดจ์ (map, C3, **24**): 60 Charoen Prathet Road. ☎ and fax: 279-188. Large, rather nondescript modern hotel with white walls and red carpets – not quite what you'd expect from the name. New bedding and spacious rooms with fan or air-conditioning. Good value. No restaurant, and no smoking.

⚐ **Northlands House Hotel** – นอร์ธแลนด์เฮาส์โฮเต็ล (map, B2, **32**): 2 Moon Muang Road, Soi 7. ☎ and fax: 218-860. Elegant and modern, but charmless. Spotless rooms with a Thai influence, all with hot shower and WC and choice of fan or air-conditioning. You get what you pay for but the frosted windows let in very little light. Small breakfast area with tables in the covered courtyard.

## MODERATE TO EXPENSIVE (200–700 BTS PER PERSON PER NIGHT)

⚐ **Paradise Hotel and Guest house** – พาราไดซ์โฮเต็ลแอนด์เกสท์เฮ้าส์ (map, C4, **29**): 12 Sri Chandorn Road. ☎ 270-413. Fax: 273-304. To the south of the town and not very central, this place undoubtedly offers the best value for money particularly since price varies with the standard of accommodation and depends on whether you stay in the (budget) guesthouse or the (more expensive) hotel. Both offer all the luxuries of a three-star hotel – or almost – for the price of a night in a European youth hostel. Tastefully decorated rooms, swimming pool, lights in the garden at night – the kind of place anyone would be happy to stay in, although the building's rather lumpen. The hotel restaurant serves good food at low prices, though it's a 5- minute walk away.

⚐ **Top North Guesthouse** – ทอปนอร์ทเกสท์เฮ้าส์ (map, B3, **30**): 15 Moon Muang Road, Soi 2. ☎ 278-900. Fax: 278-485. Three-storey, solidly built hotel with nearly 90 rooms (some family rooms) with hot shower, fan or air-conditioning. Not all the rooms are up to the same standard (visit several and ask for one in the new wing – they're more expensive but more comfortable). The swimming pool, surrounded with greenery and deckchairs, is magnificent. After a busy day spent visiting temples or sightseeing, it's a great place to unwind over a beer. A bit of a shambles in some respects, even surprisingly grubby in places, but good value for money.

⚐ **Srisupan Guesthouse** – ศิริสพรรณเกสท์เฮ้าส์ (map, B4, **28**): 92 Wualai Road, Soi 2. ☎ 270-086. This middle-of-the-range hotel south of the centre has its attractions. It's an immense, elegant private house that is not remotely Thai in style – more like a cross between an ocean-liner and a building by Le Corbusier. It has white-tiled floors throughout and 30 generally spotless rooms, all light and airy with balcony and TV. The price is a bit high but all the rooms have private bathroom facilities and hot water. Hospitable atmosphere and free transport from the station.

🛏 **YMCA** – วาย.เอ็ม.ซี.เอ. (map, A2, **33**): 11 Sermsuk Mengrairasmi Road. ☎ 221-819. Fax: 215-523. Large and rather anonymous but very well-kept five-storey building in the northwest of town, in the mostly residential district of Lanna Villa. Wide range of rooms that start with a shared shower and increase in comfort, with a range of prices to match. Those with fan and mod cons offer the best deal. Very reasonably priced buffet-cafeteria. Booking is essential since the hotel attracts a lot of tour groups.

## SPLASH OUT (OVER 700 BTS PER PERSON PER NIGHT)

🛏 **Swairaing Chiang Mai Lakeside Town** – สไวเรียงเชียงใหม่เลคไซด์วิลล์ (off C4 on the map, **62**): on the road to Lamphun. ☎ 322-061. Fax: 322-062. Two kilometres (1.25 miles) from the crossroads with the superhighway (308 Moo 1 Nong Phung, Soi 8) you'll see a sign (in Thai) telling you to turn right, then more signs (still in Thai) in pink-and-green writing. Follow these signs to what is without a doubt the loveliest place in town. Since you really need some form of transport, car or motorbike to stay here, distance is admittedly a problem. But the hotel compound is superb: traditional Thai houses on stilts, joined by floating pontoons and grouped around a little lake. On one side is a restaurant that serves typically northern cuisine of decent quality – the sort of place where Thais who want to be flashy bring their conquests. On the other side are lots of little bungalows – rustic but comfortable – with a terrace on the water, all very prettily furnished and a model of simple refinement. Loads of charm but rather expensive. Surprising too not to find anyone who spoke anything but Thai and a pity that the noise from the restaurant at night could occasionally be heard in the bedrooms.

🛏 **Galare Guesthouse** – กาแลเกสท์เฮ้าส์ (map, C3, **35**): 7 Charoen Prathet Road, Soi 2. ☎ 818-887. Fax: 279-088. Elegant hotel with masses of charm and rural Thai overtones, located on the river although none of the rooms actually overlooks it. Wooden rooms with rattan furnishings, spotless and with all mod cons but rather pricey. Those at garden level are a treat but of course they're among the most expensive. You'll find others in the newer wing. Lovely shady garden and nice coffee-shop facing the river (remember the mosquito repellent at night).

🛏 **Chatree Hotel** – ชาตรีโฮเต็ล (map, B4, **31**): 11/10 Suriwong Road. ☎ 279-221 or 279-179. Fax: 279-085. Functional, comfortable, predictable place about 300 metres from the Chiang Mai gate to the south of the old town and outside it. Rooms with air-conditioning, bathroom and WC at very reasonable prices in two modern brick buildings. Pleasant swimming pool, although the water is a bit cloudy sometimes. Left-luggage is free and you can eat in the Tamarind Coffee Shop just next door.

🛏 **River Ping Palace Hotel** – โรงแรมริเวอร์ปิงพาเลซ (off C4 on the map, **36**): 385/2 Charoen Prathet Road. ☎ 274-932. Fax: 204-281. Hotel at the edge of the river, going southeast, not far from the Mengrai Bridge and barely 3 kilometres (nearly 2 miles) from the centre. Pretty teak house in the Lan Na style, with 10 rooms furnished with antiques. The price is a bit high considering the facilities – same with the restaurant – but the most expensive room really is magnificent. Pity it's so close to the road.

## WHERE TO EAT

For anyone who likes their food, the restaurants of Chiang Mai have dishes to exercise the taste buds: delicious, refined cuisine packed with mysterious flavours that are unknown in the south. Here are some dishes you'll see on the menus; they're not necessarily typical of northern cooking but you find them here anyway.

– *Phat thai* – ผัดไทย: sautéed noodles served with meat or seafood, raw or cooked soya, ground peanuts, *tofu,* dried shrimps and traditional fish sauce.

– *Sukiyaki* – สุกี้ยากี้: dried pasta with seafood and meat, cooked in a pretty much indescribable sauce.

– *Som tam* – ส้มตำ: salad of green papaya with a sweet crust, in a sauce based on salted, dried shrimps, lemon, tomato, crab, peppers and cucumbers, all finely chopped. Delicious.

– *Tom yam* – ต้มยำ: soup made up of a devilish mixture of tomatoes, mushrooms and fresh lemon grass with chicken, pork or fish.

– *Keng phet* – แกงเผ็ด: seafood or curried meat with coconut milk.

– *Laab* – ลาบ: minced pork with spices, eaten raw *(laab isan)* or cooked *(laab kua)*. Perhaps you should give the former a miss, even if it is delicious. But if raw pork really is what you fancy, then how about the other great northern speciality: soup made from raw pigs' blood and aromatic herbs. The Thais love it, but it's only for those with cast-iron stomachs . . . *Bon appétit,* guys!

## BUDGET

✕ **The Night Market** – ไนท์บาซาร์ ถนนไชยภูมิ (map, B3, **45**): on Chai Yaphum Road; along the canal, about 200–300 metres on the right of the Tha Phae Gate on the outer bank of the canal. Thai and Chinese food for the common man: cheap, tempting and eaten outside. Only open at night but stays open until late. Pleasantly lively.

✕ **Aroon Rai** – ร้านอาหารอรุณไร (map, B3, **46**): 45 Kotchasarn Road, about 100 metres from the Tha Phae Gate, as you face the same way as the cars. ☎ 276-497. Open all day until 10pm, this restaurant is partly outdoors and serves ordinary fare that's simple but good, at very reasonable prices. Range of Chinese dishes and food from the north of Thai-

land – including frogs. The fried noodles and beef-and-tomato sauce are good and so is the *gaeng garee guy* (mildly spicy curried chicken). This is where they shot scenes for *Air America.* The restaurant recently expanded into a large room on the first floor at the back, where there is less noise.

– Almost opposite is the **Café de Paris**, where homesick French backpackers – and others – can re-acquaint themselves with the taste of Ricard and red meat. A bit overpriced and variable in quality.

✕ **Galare Food Centre** – กาแลฟู้ดเซ็นเตอร์หน้าไนท์บาซาร์ (map, C3, **47**): Night Bazaar, Chang Khlan Road. Open daily, 10am–10pm. Large complex with a range of food stands to suit every taste, serving specialities from the north of Thailand, China, India, vegetarian dishes etc. Simply buy your tickets from the desk before going to the stand of your choice, but note that unused tickets are not refunded. There are free shows of traditional music and dancing, 8pm–9pm. Often packed with tourists.

✕ **Grilled Chicken with Honey** – ร้านอาหารไก่ย่างอบน้ำผึ้ง (map, C3, **49**): 40–42 Charoen Prathet Road, very close to the Night Bazaar. Open all day until 9.30pm. ☎ 271-488. Thai equivalent of a fast-food place, specializing, as you'd expect, in grilled chicken with honey. It's rather nondescript but the wooden floor is lovely. The terrace is rather noisy but you couldn't ask for a better welcome, and the chicken is simply delicious. Very popular with the locals.

✕ **Made in France** (map, C3): 23/1 Charoen Prathet Road, not far from the Night Bazaar. ☎ 271-459. French-style patisserie where you can get a real French breakfast, complete with coffee, fresh bread, home-made jam, croissants and *pains au chocolat* (cost about 60 Bts). For big eaters, there's the American version with bacon, eggs etc. (90 Bts). For lunch there's quiche, pâté, stuffed tomatoes, profiteroles etc. (cost about 130 Bts). But the setting isn't up to much and the terrace is rather noisy.

✕ **Daret's House and Restaurant** – ร้านอาหารดาเรศ (map, B3, **51**): 4–5 Chai Yaphum Road. Open 7am–10pm. ☎ 235-440. Large, shady terrace overlooking the street, with lots of tables full of Westerners who come here for the Western cooking (steaks, pizzas etc.). The place is so-so, but prices are very cheap and the cooking is always dependable

even if it's not a gourmet experience. Delicious milkshakes too. Simple, cheap food and lots of it. And, just to be different, they organize treks here.

✕ **Kafe Restaurant** – ร้านอาหารคาเฟ่ (map, B3, **53**): 127–29 Moon Muang Road. Overlooking the canal, on the other side of the road. Open 8am–midnight. ☎ 212-717. This place can do you a Western breakfast or a Thai or Chinese dinner. It's nothing earth-shaking, but they offer a few inexpensive grilled dishes (BBQ) and wine by the glass, all in a lovely teak house with a really nice café atmosphere.

## MODERATE TO EXPENSIVE

✕ **Heun Suntaree** – ร้านอาหารหวนสุนทรีย์ (map, C1, **54**): 46/1 Wang Sin Khan Road. ☎ 252-445. Open nightly 6pm–11pm. Mrs Suntaree's restaurant just beyond the Wild West Café is in a prime position on the river. Lots of terraces sloping down to the water's edge, with tables by the river or on a mezzanine level, where guests sit Thai-fashion on the ground. More tables by the stage where Mrs Suntaree gives her nightly, crystal-clear rendition of traditional songs to a guitar accompaniment. Good local cooking plus northern specialities (the ones that aren't translated at the start of the menu) with a Shans influence. To get an idea of the food try the assorted Muang hors-d'oeuvres or the *laab kua*. Very good food, and this is the genuine article. Stylish too with elegant waitresses. Often fully booked at the weekend.

✕ **Tha-Nam Restaurant** – ร้านอาหารท่าน้ำ (off C4 on the map, **56**): 43/3 Chang Khlan Road. ☎ 275-125. Open 7am–11pm. It's 2 kilometres (1.25 miles) from the centre – so take a *tuk-tuk*. Large, magnificent multi-storey teak house giving onto a lush garden and the river, in a jungle-like setting (despite the housing development on the opposite bank). It also happens to be an antiques shop, so just about everything is for sale: wardrobes, armchairs, porcelain – really memorable. The cooking is classic, refined and substantial. There's music in the evening. Reasonably priced rooms with private bathroom facilities. Has a good reputation.

✕ **The Gallery Restaurant** – ร้าน อาหารเดอะแกเลอรี (map, C2, **57**): 25–29 Charoen Rat Road. ☎ 248-601. Open every day. Cross the Nawarat Bridge and it's 500 metres further up on the left, on the edge of the River Ping. Like the previous entry, this place really belongs under a 'rather stylish restaurant-cum-expo-gallery' heading. At the front is a very fine antiques and crafts shop; at the rear, in the dining room or on the terrace by the water (it's so romantic), is a first-class restaurant serving captivating dishes from the north of Thailand and vegetarian dishes. The fried, minced prawns with plum sauce are divine, and the crab rolls are exquisite. Very generous helpings and they also make excellent coffee. The place itself is charming although a bit overdone, being rather popular with tourists; Mrs Clinton even honoured it with her presence once – but without her husband.

✕ Another similar place is the **Antique House** – ร้านอาหารแอน ทีคเฮาส์ (map, C3, **58**), 71 Charoen Prathet Road. ☎ 276-810. Open 10am–midnight. Lovely teak house, built in 1870 by a rich Burmese businessman. Traditional cooking and *itou* music every night. Pity it's so close to a noisy road.

✕ **Ta-Krite** – ร้านอาหารตะไคร้ (map, A3, **59**): Samlan Road, Soi 1. ☎ 278-298. Open from 10am–11pm. Typical Thai house, close to the Wat Phra Sing and lavishly decorated with big plants and wood. Here you'll find some of the best classical Thai cooking in its price range to be found in Chiang Mai. A good tip is to order lots of side dishes with rice, or go straight for the set menu for two people and share everything out (the set menu works out cheaper, if you're big eaters). Lots of utterly delicious dishes based on lemon grass (tat krite) feature. Intimate atmosphere, though the service is a bit brisk and it's rather difficult to get a smile.

✕ **Westin Hotel Buffet Lunch** – บัฟเฟ่ห์โรงแรมเวสท์อิน (off C4 on the map, **60**): 318/1 Chang Mai–Lamphun Road. ☎ 275-500. It's 3 kilometres (just under 2 miles) from the centre – so take a red minibus (songthaew) or a tuk-tuk. This is a luxurious, international hotel, so you may find it impersonal. The River Terrace restaurant on the right as you step into the hall serves an excellent buffet lunch (11am–2pm) with a range of Thai and international dishes – most people go for the Thai food, as you would expect. The setting is very elegant, with a view of the river, and it's very reasonably priced. Anyway, a bit of luxury never did anyone any harm.

✕ **Swairaing Chiang Mai Lakeside Town** – สไวเรียงเชียงใหม่เลค ไซค์วิลล์ (off C4 on the map, **62**): see 'Where to Stay'.

✕ **Baan Suan** – ร้านอาหารบ้านสวน (off D3 on the map, **63**): 53/1 Chiang Mai–Sankampaeng Road, Moo 1. ☎ 242-116. Open daily, but not always until very late. Slightly to the east of town out towards the craftwork district, about 2 kilometres (just over 1 mile) from the superhighway, in a side-street leading off to the right, not far from the temple. Elegant restaurant in several converted rice-lofts (small buildings on stilts that city people with lots of money often buy as second homes). Good food from the north of Thailand, served in a very pleasant setting with a large lawn and pool. The locals seem to like it and so did we. Classy, rather casual service, and reasonable prices. A good place to go for a gourmet break on a day when you've decided to visit the craft centres. The restaurant has a namesake in the sub-*soi* of the Chiang Inn Plaza shopping centre, next to the Night Bazaar. Same food, or almost, but not nearly such an idyllic setting.

✗ **Fatty** – ร้านอาหารแฟตตี้ตลาด อนุสรณ์ (map, C3, **55**): restaurant with tables on the street in the Anusarn Market that gives on to the Chang Khlan Road, just seconds from the Night Bazaar. No service after 11pm. Easily identifiable from the *Routard* symbol painted on the front. You can get succulent, super-fresh Thai and Chinese cooking, heavy on seafood and fish, some of which are still swimming around in the tank. Try the crab curry (delicious) and the *po teck,* a very spicy fish soup (ask for mild or it will set your mouth on fire) and the banana fritters. Prices have gone up but there is a choice of three portion sizes.

### *KANTOKE* DINNER

A *kantoke* is a wooden tray (teak in the north of the country, bamboo and rattan in the south and the east) on which is laid out a range of regional specialities: Thai curry, spicy dishes, cooked meats from Chiang Mai, all served with sticky rice. In former times, the *kantoke* was brought out on big occasions like weddings and funerals.

A '*kantoke* dinner' is an evening for tourists: a cabaret-dinner with all the trimmings, including full tray, and singing and dancing by mountain tribes and folk groups dressed in marvellous costumes. Organized on a more-or-less regular basis for tour groups, *kantoke* dinners are catching on. New places are opening (and closing) all the time – sometimes quite quickly too. Three are listed here, and in every case it's best to book. But be warned – you might end up with a bus tour group who've had a drink or two, all moaning because they don't like sitting on the floor, because they don't like eating with their fingers or because they don't think much of the spicy food – an independent traveller's nightmare, in other words.

✗ **Old Cultural Centre** – ศูนย์วัฒนธรรมเชียงใหม่ (off A4 on the map, **65**): 183 Wualai Road. ☎ 275-097 or 274-540. Costs about 300 Bts excluding drinks. Nightly performances, 7pm–10pm. The show is one of the best and completely authentic, and you get unlimited quantities of very respectable food – but the drinks are expensive. A tip: get there about 6pm so you can find a table before the busloads of tourists arrive.

✗ **Khum Kaeo Palace** – คุ้มแก้วพาเลซ (map, B2, **66**): 252 Phra Pokkhlao Road (in a small teak palace behind the Vista Hotel). ☎ 210-663. The show starts at 7pm. Some of the best food but the over-hasty welcome is a bit off-putting.

✖ **Lanna Kantoke** – ร้านอาหารขันโตกล้านนา (map, C3, **67**): 33/10 Charoen Prathet Road. ☎ 270-080. Go under the archway of the awful Petch Ngarm Hotel and you'll come across a magnificent wooden house, sadly now surrounded by modern buildings. The show upstairs starts at 7pm. The building's wonderful, and the food and show are not too bad.

## CHIANG MAI BY NIGHT

❣ **The Riverside** – เดอะริเวอร์ไซด์ (map, C3, **75**): 9 Charoen Rat Road. ☎ 243-239. Open until 1am. This is absolutely *the* place to go at night, for backpackers of every nationality. Get there early on Saturday to be sure of a table. Different bands every night, some better than others, but with two stages there are two types of music and two kinds of atmosphere so there's something for everybody. At worst you can always move on to the musical cafés next door *(*Brasserie and Good View*)* – like the Riverside but not nearly as big or as beautiful. Made of wood and bamboo in the Californian style, the Riverside has an open-air terrace overlooking the river. Not a go-go girl in sight, only charming students who come to listen to Western bands and bluegrass music. Serves food and draught beer, and you can even have a dinner-cruise on a boat that takes you on a tour of the river Ping. Leaves at 8pm – lots of fun.

❣ **West-Side** – บาร์เวสท์ไซด์ (map, C1, **77**): 36 Wang Sin Khan Road. ☎ 234-431. Also open until 1am. On the west bank of the river about 2 kilometres (1.25 miles) from the centre. The waterside terrace is a bit like the Riverside but the guests are almost exclusively Thai. So are the rock bands, many of them very good, that perform talent-contest fashion. This is the perfect venue for anyone who's had enough of other tourists. You can also eat here and the food is cheap and good.

❣ **Bar Beer Centre** – บาร์เบียร์เซ็นเดอร์ (map, B3, **80**): on Moon Muang Road, near the Ratchadamnoen Road. Stays open until 3–3.30am. Also known as the BBC. This is in fact not one but a whole complex of bars, arranged around a Thai boxing ring where you can watch matches several times a week (usually at about 11pm). They're rigged, but still entertaining. Women (and occasionally those of indeterminate gender) also get up on stage to sing and dance while miming to a tape. This is where foreigners come, alone or in groups, to down endless beers in a decadent atmosphere pulsating to a discordant cocktail of music from a variety of different bars. This is without mentioning the hostesses, the beggars (some of them pathetically young), the football or billiards on the TV, or the cats and dogs fighting over scraps of food. A strange atmosphere, to be sure – but a real one.

❣ **Gigi's** – จิจิ้ส์ (map, C4, **81**): 62/2 Chiang Mai Lamphun Road. ☎ 302-340. Open every night, this huge space is the nightclub of the moment (well it was, at the time of writing). It's where young people come to have a good time to the rhythm of a Western beat. It puts on concerts every night, usually featuring pretty convincing local bands, and towards midnight everybody dances. The most enthusiastic dancers are captured on video and shown on a big screen – your chance to be discovered perhaps?

CHIANG MAI

**ID4** – ไอดี4 (off A4 on the map, **79**): Rinkean Complex, Voulai Road (south of the centre, not far from the Old Cultural Centre). ☎ 274-565. Open nightly, with live performances of bands on stage. You won't believe this place. To get in, you have to go under a kind of spaceship, next to a piece of rocket. Inside it's like a mega-bad trip: a wicked stage, with dragons and a sensational light show and on the ceiling, a flying saucer and a kind of giant virus. And that's just the decor. As for the atmosphere, there's not a lot to say, as the place can be pretty empty with the army of waiters standing around looking bored. But go there for the setting anyway and see for yourself whether the ID4 makes the grade.

**Space Bubble** – สเปสบับเบิ้ล (map, C3, **82**): 46–48 Charoen Prathet Road. The nightclub at the Pornping Tower Hotel. Real nightclub with all the trimmings: lights, mirrors, designer furnishings – small but nice.

**Karaoke bars**– บาร์คาราโอเกะ (off C4 on the map, **76**): there are lots of karoake bars on Chiang Mai Lane (the side-street at right angles to the Chang Khlan Road) competing for the attention of Thais in good voice and the occasional foreigner who has lost his way. Karaoke has become a very popular leisure activity throughout Southeast Asia, and Thailand is no exception. These bars are where people come to sing a ditty, in the company of young 'hostesses' who offer to keep you company for a price. But they're quite laid-back about it and you can easily refuse. While these bars may not be to everybody's taste, they're fairly innocent. They're ideal places to meet tiddly natives and practise your Thai while joining in with a local refrain – with phonetic translations, if you're lucky.

## WHAT TO SEE AND DO

### TEMPLES AND MUSEUMS

You can visit all the temples in town by bike, all 50 of them – there's one on just about every street corner. So – get on your bike. The ones described below are the most famous but if you're in search of genuine tranquillity, there are others that will open on request. All respectful visitors are welcome, provided they take their shoes off and behave themselves. There are lessons in meditation at certain times of year, particularly in the Wat Ram Poeng. If you're interested, the tourist office has details – and it could do you a lot of good.

★ **Wat Chiang Man** – วัดเชียงมั่น (map, B2): Ratphakinai Road. Open 9am–5pm (usually). This is a temple compound where the two most interesting temples are the large one opposite the entrance and the small one on the right. The large one, founded at the end of the 13th century, is the oldest temple in town. It has an elegant facade and an interior typical of northern Thailand, with a wooden frame and a profusion of wood-carvings. The temple on the right is home to two tiny statues, both protected by thick grilles. The one made of rock crystal is so small that you can barely see it at all. Beside it, also behind a grille, is a marble Buddha that is said to be over 2,000 years old. Behind the principal temple is an elegant *chedi* with a golden dome.

★ **Wat Phra Sing** – วัดพระสิงห์ (map, A3): at the end of Ratchdamnoen Road, on the corner of Singharat Road. Open daily, 8am–5pm. Founded in the 14th century, this is the largest, most important temple compound in town. The main temple features an elegant classical facade, but it is the temple to the left of it, at the back, that is the most interesting. Its facade is decorated with impressive woodcarvings and 16th-century mural paintings. It has elegant, painted pillars, a charming wooden frame and a magnificent lintel over the door. But the climax of the whole visit is an eighth-century Buddha, brought here from Ceylon after a multitude of trials and tribulations.

★ **Wat Chedi Luang** – วัดเจดีย์หลวง (map, B3): Phra Pokkhlao Road. Built in 1391 in the reign of King Saen Muang Ma, this *wat* has a 15th-century *chedi* that stands 85 metres (280 feet) high. It originally housed the Emerald Buddha (the one in Bangkok). It was partially destroyed, first by an earthquake in the 16th century, then by Burmese guns in the 18th century, but the remains are impressive. In front of the *chedi* is the main temple, which isn't very interesting except that, according to legend, the safety of the town depends on the temple being properly maintained . . . One fears for Chiang Mai, although there has been some effort recently to restore the big *chedi* to some of its former glory. The precinct also features some old wooden pavilions.

★ **Wat Suan Dok** – วัดสวนดอก ('Flower Garden Temple', off A3 on the map): west of the central square. This great 14th-century temple isn't that great and the latest restoration works haven't helped. The Buddha inside is not particularly beautiful either. Much more interesting is the range of snow-white *stupas* containing the ashes of the royal family.

★ **Wat Bupparam** – วัดบุพพาราม (map, C3): 234 Tha Phae Gate. Particularly interesting because of its 300-year-old wooden *viharn* covered with stucco floral designs encrusted with coloured mirrors.

★ **Wat Chet Yod** – วัดเจ็ดยอด (map, A1): on the superhighway to Lampang, in the north of town, on the left several hundred metres before the museum. This 15th-century temple is in a lush setting surrounded by smaller temples, *stupas* and monastic cells. It's really peaceful. At last, here's an old temple that hasn't been renovated, and it's much the better for that. Its old *chedi* with seven spires symbolizes the seven weeks that the Buddha spent in India before his enlightenment. All around are the somewhat damaged remains of stucco bas-reliefs that once depicted meditating Buddhas. The temples still attract monks and children and it's a pleasant place to be.

★ **Wat U Mong** – วัดอุโมงค์ (off A3 on the map): out to the west of town. A 14th-century temple, or rather *chedi*, in the middle of a forest. There's not a great deal to see, but it has a strange impact. There are lots of trees covered in English translations of Thai proverbs, which, if you are feeling philosophical, you may like, otherwise you may find them a bit off-putting. The wildlife park is worth seeing, as are the caves and the lakes. This is also a centre for spiritualism.

There are dozens of other temples in town, but you really don't need to see them all.

★ **The National Museum of Chiang Mai** – พิพิธภัณฑ์สถานแห่งชาติ เชียงใหม่ (map, A1): in the north of town, next to the Wat Chet Yod. Open (usually) Wednesday–Sunday, 9am–4pm but often irregularly since it reopened after protracted building works. You'll find a very fine collection of sacred and profane objects reflecting different styles of Thai art. It's an elegant complex of traditionally inspired yet modern buildings, and pride of place goes to Lan Na art, the northern style with a Shans influence. The admission charge is reasonable.

## THE MARKETS

★ **Warorot Market** – ตลาดวโรรส (map, C3): near Foot Bridge, on the corner of Chiang Mai Road and Witchayanon Road. Open daily until nightfall. An enormous, colourful, fragrant market selling just about everything: clothes, fabrics, assorted utensils, fresh vegetables, flowers, huge piles of fish and dried shrimps. The other thing you find here are the collarless, denim shirts that everyone wears in Chiang Mai. This is the place to go before visiting the more touristic – and therefore more expensive – Night Bazaar. Practically the only other people you meet here are Thais doing their shopping. It's a big market that lines both sides of the street, so make sure you leave yourself plenty of time for a good rummage. As you'd expect, the food here is pretty good too.

★ **Night Bazaar** – ไนท์บาซาร์ (night market; map, C3): on the Chang Khlan Road, which runs parallel to Charoen Prathet Road. Actually open 6–11pm and a few stands stay open during the day. This largely overrated and often overpriced market is now mainly for tourists, selling an assortment of souvenirs, T-shirts and designer clothing, hats, bags, stuff made up in the mountains and cheap jewellery. It has lots of imitations too (including fake silk) and poor-quality products. For craftwork see 'Shopping', and for clothes, even if it does seem a bit prosaic, remember the hypermarkets on the outskirts of town. You won't find many bargains in the Night Bazaar.

Some nights there are performances of local singing and dancing on a stage behind the market. Should you be approached by any drug dealers during such an event, treat all offers of narcotics with the contempt they deserve. Dealers make a beeline for anyone who looks like a potential punter and they're much more dangerous than any pickpocket. You have been warned.

## OTHER THINGS TO SEE AND DO

– **Thai boxing**: on Sanpakhoi Khongsai. Take the second turning on the right after the Nawarat Bridge and go left where the road forks. There's usually a match on one night towards the end of the week but it's very variable. Check with the tourist office. Don't forget the rigged but entertaining matches at the Bar Beer Centre (see 'Chiang Mai by Night').

– **The 'Sunday Triple'**: at the racecourse on Chotana Road: past the superhighway, beside the Lanna golf course. The location is slightly outside town going north, on the road that goes to Mae Ring, the elephant training camps and the snake farms. The atmosphere in the tiers is almost one of hysteria as the punters take bets and exchange tips. Quite an experience.

– **The Zoo**: in the northwest of town, not far from the King's summer residence, on the road to Doi Suthep mountain. Open daily, 8am–6pm (last tickets sold at 5pm). The admission charge is reasonable. ☎ 211-179. As zoos go, this one is quite well thought out, and the animals here have more space than they do elsewhere. In fact, the wildlife park is so enormous that you may decide to come here by car, and if so, it will take you at least half a day to see all 6,000 species. Other attractions include little boats, children's games etc.

– **Thai cooking**: it's what every independent, curious tourist wants to do these days. Lessons for beginners in Thai culinary art are all the rage. Try **The Secret of Thai Cooking**, 5 Loi Kroa Road, Soi 1 (a little street behind Kotchasarm). ☎ 271-169. They run one-, two- or three-day courses from 10am to 4pm (booking essential). It's a bit expensive, but the price includes a book and, of course, the food and drink.

– **Meditation**: some temples (especially the Wat U Mong) organize meditation seminars, and these are occasionally open to tourists. If you have time (essential if you plan to meditate) get the details from the tourist office.

– Some guides offer to take you on a **tour of Old Chiang Mai**. Don't bother. It's strictly for tourists and totally devoid of interest or anything remotely resembling charm.

## TRADITIONAL MASSAGE

★ **Thai Massage Conservation Club** – สมาคมนวดแผนโบราณ: 9 Ratdamri Road. ☎ 406-017. Open daily, 8.30am–9pm. This is the most serious of massage centres, and all the masseuses are blind (apparently they're the best) and graduates of the Wat Pho school in Bangkok (first-class credentials).

'Home visits' are possible, for a small extra charge.

★ **Chiang Mai Anatomy Thai Massage**: 1 Changmoi Kao Road (beside the Tha Phae Gate). ☎ 251-407. Another serious place, this time specializing in massage using honey and plants.

## SHOPPING

Chiang Mai is famous as the heart of Thai craft production. Some 90 per cent of all the craftwork you find elsewhere actually originated here, so you're bound to find the greatest choice, although not necessarily at the keenest prices. To make sure the local traders don't lose out, factory prices are kept pretty much in line with retail prices. The big specialities in Chiang Mai are silk, painted umbrellas, Celadon porcelain, lacquerwork, silverware and woodcarvings. One thing you can be sure of is the quality.

Much of the work is carried out in the big workshops and small factories that lie a few kilometres (a couple of miles) to the east of town. Take the road that passes through the villages of Borsang and Sankampaeng (go over the Nawarat Bridge and keep going straight on, once you've passed the station and the superhighway). The first workshops are no more than 3 or 4 kilometres (2.5 miles) from town and the furthest are about 12 kilometres (7 miles) away. There are more than 50 workshops in all, each with its own shop packed with lovely things to buy. But don't expect to find lots of independent craftsmen beavering away at the back of their workshops – they disappeared years ago, thanks to generations of tourists who made their fortunes. You'll find that the shops look more like shopping centres than bamboo shacks.

Still, this is the place to learn about production techniques for silk-making, lacquerwork etc. Most of the workshops are closed on Sunday, but not the shops, where the vendors are, if anything, rather persistent.

Get there under your own steam by bike (but mind the traffic), by motorbike or take a bus (departures every 20 minutes, 8am–6pm, from Chang Puak bus station), a taxi or a *tuk-tuk*. Ask the driver to stop where you want, when you want. Don't leave it up to him or you can be sure he'll take you where he gets the best commission.

The list below is by no means exhaustive but it does include some of the best workshops. As you take the main road out of Chiang Mai, they are on the left-hand side of the road.

🔒 **Lanna Thai Silverware** – ล้านนาไทยเครื่องเงิน: a jewellery workshop on the left. The silverware isn't that fantastic, and nor is the ivory, but you can't expect to like everything. Incidentally, it's forbidden to bring ivory back to Britain.

🔒 **Sudaluck** – สุดาลักษณ์: a huge workshop on the left, where over 1,000 craftsmen work with Burmese rosewood and teak. The shop sells everything from garden furniture to canopied beds. The craftsmen also do designs to order, and will ship goods to any major European city.

🔒 **Borsang** – บ่อสร้าง (small village): an entire district specializing in umbrella production can be found at the corner of a main road on the left. They have been making these umbrellas for at least 200 years, since the day when a monk passed through with a broken umbrella and asked a peasant to repair it. The peasant is said to have fixed the umbrella and then taught the rest of the village how to do it and now that's what everybody does around here. There are no particular preferences as to shops – they're all full of magnificent designs and the prices are tempting. However, umbrella-making does also seem to attract rather too many vendors selling cheap souvenirs. If you're around in January, don't miss the Umbrella Festival (usually the third weekend). *See* 'Festivals', *below*.

🔒 **Siam Celadon** – สยามศิลาดล: a bit further on, and still on the left. Open to visitors daily, 8.30am–5.30pm. Celadon porcelain is green, and is made using production techniques invented in China more than 2,000 years ago, rediscovered not so long ago and now fashionable once again. This shop isn't the largest, but it has the widest choice. Behind the shop is an old kiln.

From here, turn around and head back to Chiang Mai. The places below are now on your left (since you're facing in the opposite direction) but to be consistent, the word 'right' is used here, as if you are still heading *away* from Chiang Mai.

🔒 **Gems Gallery International** – ร้านเพชรเจ็มส์แกเลอรีอินเดอร์เนชั่นแนล: on the right coming from Chiang Mai (so on the left heading back into town). Don't get carried away – this is the biggest jewellery shop in Thailand, which is another way of saying it's as big as an out-of-town superstore and you're bound to be boggled by it. They show foreign-language films, offer a tour of the workshops, and then, of course, you're expected to step right into the shop. From this point, just proceed with extreme caution and, in case you get careless, beware of the baby sharks in the aquariums . . .

🔒 **Laitong Lacquerware** – ร้านเครื่องเงินลายทอง: next door to Gems, this workshop specializes in teak lacquerwork decorated with gold leaf or eggshell. There's an interesting talk that explains about the seven layers of black lacquer, and tells you how to recognize real gold leaf. As for the goods, these things are a matter of individual taste.

🔒 **Bombix** – ร้านผ้าไหมบอมบิก: silk-making workshop a bit further down than Laitong, on the right as you leave Chiang Mai. The fabrics are lovely, although prices here are a bit higher than in the places listed below. Silk clothes made to measure. Guided tours.

🔒 **U Pienkusol and Kinaree Thai Silk** – ยู.เพียรกุศลและกินรีไทยซิลค์: two silk-making workshops a bit

further back towards town, and still on the right as you leave Chiang Mai. You can learn all about the silk-making process, from the spinning of the cocoon to the weaving of the silk. Good guided tour.

🔒 Finally, don't forget that in the town centre there's the **Night Bazaar** and also a tailor where virtually anything can be copied. Pack a favourite item of clothing (or bring a photo) and order several copies but do go for a fitting. For men, there's **Laem Tong** (77 Tha Phae Road), which is reputed to be very good. For women, there's **Patcharin** (340 Tha Phae Road), which is a bit expensive but their work is first class, particularly if you want something made in silk. If you prefer cotton, bring your own. Apart from these two, there are lots of other places where the quality of the work is quite outstanding – provided you know how to make yourself understood and are prepared to go back several times.

## FESTIVALS

– **Umbrella Festival**: held each year on the third weekend in January, in the little village of Borsang (about 8 kilometres/5 miles east of Chiang Mai). Display and sale of hand-made umbrellas plus a 'Miss Umbrella of the Year' contest – a real festival of colour.

– **Carnival of Flowers**: takes place every year in early February, when there is the greatest variety of flowers.

– **Water Festival**: happens in Chiang Mai from 13 to15 April. This is a highly amusing festival when everyone celebrates the Buddhist New Year *(Songkram)* by throwing buckets of water. It's one of the best festivals, particularly in Chiang Mai – and is not to be missed. Incidentally, apart from their own, the Thais also celebrate the Christian and Chinese New Year.

– **Loi Kraton**: a famous festival celebrated at the full moon. There's a procession of floats, and people send thousands of little candles floating down river, to expiate of their sins. Judging from the quantity of candles, they must do a lot of sinning round here.

– **Winter Fair**: a grand fair, held late-December to early-January, when there's wall-to-wall activity that lasts for about 10 days, mainly concentrated around the stadium. There are loads of attractions, including the Miss Chiang Mai contest, which always causes a lot of excitement.

## DAY TRIP AROUND CHIANG MAI

This is a great trip to do in a day (or half a day if you're short of time), either by motorbike or, if there are several of you, by *songthaew* (it's impossible by bicycle and a real hassle by bus). This is a good way of getting out into the countryside and meeting up with some friendly people. The area is very up-and-coming in terms of tourism, with resorts springing up all over the place. If you have time, take a look at the Regent Resort, a mega-luxurious hotel where you get taken to your bungalow in a little electric car.

But despite its touristy side, this is a very pleasant trip that starts off on the road going north before it veers west along a route dotted with orchid farms, snake farms and elephant training centres. Some but not all of these are described below.

Leave Chiang Mai by the Chuang Puak Gate (on the northern road) going towards Fang. You pass the golf course, the racecourse and an immense military base (which is there for Thailand to keep an eye on neighbouring Myanmar).

After about 16 kilometres (10 miles) you come to the village of **Mae Rim**. Stop and eat here, as the restaurants in this area are a lot cheaper than the tourist-traps you'll find once you reach the farms. Try the first place on the right (with a sign in Thai) next to the police station. It has an open-air kitchen, and you can sit on the long, wooden benches and eat delicious noodle soup for next to nothing.

Leaving Mae Rim, take the road on the left, where you see a huge sign to the Mae Sa Butterfly Farm, Mae Sa Waterfalls, Mae Sa Elephant Camp etc.

★ **Mae Sa Butterfly and Orchid Farm** – (Sainamphung Orchids and Butterfly Nursery) – ฟาร์มผีเสื้อแม่สาและสวนกล้วยไม้สายน้ำผึ้ง: it's just over 4 kilometres (2.5 miles) from where the road forks, on the left. Open daily, 8am–5pm; modest admission charge. Orchids are parasitic plants that require no soil in order to grow. They are sold here in bottles and apparently they do quite well back in Europe. You can visit the green-houses, which are full of beautiful orchids of every colour – or marvel at the different phases of the butterflies' magical metamorphosis, in the butterfly house. What you actually see are lots of (rather disappointing) cocoons at various stages of development and not that many butterflies, but there are some beautiful Siamese cats and birds in cages. All in all it's a fairly touristy visit, but quite engaging. The rival farm opposite is smaller, and admission is free.

★ **Mae Sa Snake Farm** – ฟาร์มงูแม่สา: leaving the orchid farm, rejoin the main road and the snake farm is 300 metres further along, on the right. ☎ 860-719. It costs a lot to get in. Try to get there in time for one of the impressive shows that take place at 11.30am, 2, 3 and 3.30pm. You'll see lots of display cases full of snakes that bite, smother or poison anyone who doesn't behave. The main attraction is the 'Cobra

Show' – 20 minutes of realistic, undiluted horror and definitely not for anyone with a snake phobia.

★ **Mae Sa Waterfalls** – น้ำตกแม่สา: about 3 kilometres (2 miles) further on, on the left. You pay a modest charge for entry to the national park. A network of pathways leads to a string of not very thrilling waterfalls, seven in all and each as dull as the last. This is a popular haunt with the Thais, though, so avoid it at weekends unless you want the perfect chance to see the Thais picnicking *en famille* and, for once, not trying to sell you something. Waterfalls apart, this is a great place to stop for lunch, with lots of little restaurants in the car-park selling grilled chicken legs, soups etc.

★ **Mae Sa Elephant Camp** – ปางช้างแม่สา: back on the main road, 4 kilometres (2.5 miles) from the Mae Sa Waterfalls on the left. ☎ 297-060. Admission charge. There are four 40-minute shows in the morning (8am, 8.40, 9.40 and 10.30) and these include demonstrations of elephant trunk prowess and dancing. There are 3,000 elephants in Thailand and about 60 of them live here. You can go for an elephant ride, but since this is one of the smaller camps, it does get very crowded. Lots of vendors have bananas and sugar-cane for sale, to feed their 'big jumbos', who certainly can pack it away. There's a sign telling you not to hold the bananas and your camera in the same hand – very wise.

★ **Pong Yang Elephant Farm** – ปางช้างโป่งยาง: ☎ 215-943. Nearly 6 kilometres (4 miles) further on and very similar to the last place except that it is marginally more expensive and the shows (at 9am and 10.15am) are more homespun and less spectacular. However, it is a good place to take a stroll, as it's much wilder, has a nearby waterfall and, above all, is less crowded.

Having said all that, if you're going to Chiang Dao there's an elephant camp on the way that is preferable to either of these two (*see below*).

– You can carry on along this charming route or turn around and head back to Chiang Mai.

## MORE THINGS TO SEE

### GOING NORTHWEST

★ **Suthep mountain and the Wat Doi Suthep** – ดอยสุเทพและวัดพระ บรมธาตุดอยสุเทพ: Suthep mountain has an altitude of almost 1,000 metres (3,200 feet) and is about 20 kilometres (12 miles) northwest of Chiang Mai, on the road to the zoo. You can get there by *songthaew* for a fixed price, and going up costs more than coming down. Visitors must be properly dressed. Just before you reach the top, you'll see the proud *chedi* of a Buddhist temple that was commissioned by King Guen Na in the 14th century. It has changed a lot since then, of course. Legend has it that the king ordered a white elephant to find the right place to build a temple that would enshrine some of the Buddha's relics, and this is where the elephant stopped.

To reach the temple, there's a fairly strenuous climb up 300 steps, but anyone who finds this a bit daunting can take the escalator. From the top, the view out over the plain is magnificent. In the centre of the temple

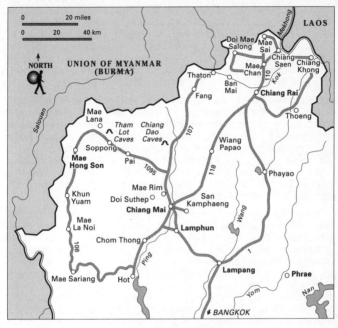

**THAILAND (NORTHERN REGION)**

CHIANG MAI

stands the celebrated and beautiful *chedi* that contains the Buddha's relics. All around it are lovely gilded canopies. Throughout the year, this is one of the temples most revered by pilgrims who come to Chiang Mai. It's also one of the rare temples to be inhabited by nuns, who dress in white. There are food stands and small restaurants to be found at the foot of the temple.

★ **Phuping Palace** – พระตำหนักภูพิงค์ราชนิเวศน์: a few kilometres (a mile or so) from Wat Doi Suthep. This is officially the King's winter residence, although he hardly ever sets foot here. It's worth taking a look at the gardens, but they're only open to visitors at the weekend.

★ **The Meo village of Doi Puy** – หมู่บ้านแม้วดอยปุย: just before the entrance to the Phuping Palace, you'll see a path leading to a thoroughly touristy village – something you might just want to miss.

★ **Doi Puy National Park** – อุทยานแห่งชาติดอยปุย: this whole region is part of a national park conservation area and has lots of places to walk for people who like to go some distance. Details are available at the site.

## GOING NORTH

★ **Elephant Training Centre Chiang Dao** – ศูนย์ฝึกช้างเชียงดาว: about 50 kilometres (30 miles) from Chiang Mai, on the road to Fang and therefore to Chiang Dao, there's an arrow sign to the right. ☎ 298-553.

Admission charge. Shows are at 9am and 10am. This elephant camp is altogether superior to the two described above. The surroundings are much more 'jungly' (there's even a monkey bridge) and the shows focus more on work and less on circus tricks. There's also a very beautiful walk along the river. When you rejoin the road a little further on, you'll see a sign to an information centre on mountain tribes – not the museum you might expect, but an area reserved for mountain people and closed to tourists.

★ **Chiang Dao Caves** – ถ้ำเชียงดาว: about 75 kilometres (46 miles) north of Chiang Mai, on the same road to Fang and about halfway. They are easily accessible by bus, particularly if you're going on to Thaton afterwards, or by motorbike if you're returning to Chiang Mai. If you take the bus, get off where the road forks in the direction of the caves (in the village of Chiang Dao) on the left. The caves are about 5 kilometres (3 miles) from the main road. You'll find motorbike taxis waiting to take you there. There is a modest admission charge and you have to hire the services of a guide equipped with a petrol lamp. Visits daily, 8am–5.30pm.

This impressive group of caves extends for some kilometres (several miles), into the foot of the Doi Chiang Dao mountain (which means 'Town of the Star' in Thai) – the third highest in the country. You can see lots of Buddhas in the first caves, which are illuminated. Then there are chambers branching off in all directions which are packed with stalactites and stalagmites. What with the oppressive atmosphere, the clammy heat and the acrid smell of burning oil from the guide's lamp, there's something quite exciting about exploring the narrow galleries, particularly the tricky bits. Legend has it that the cave was discovered by a king out hunting, who entered in pursuit of a particularly beautiful doe. Neither of them ever re-emerged from the cave, and, so far as we know, no tourist has ever tracked them down . . .

Chiang Dao is also an important place of pilgrimage for the Thais. When archaeological remains were discovered here, the temple was built in front of them. Don't forget to feed the fish in the pool. As far as feeding yourself goes, there are the same good, cheap restaurants that are to be found all over Thailand.

## GOING SOUTH

★ **Lamphun** – ลำพูน: about 25 kilometres (15 miles) south of Chiang Mai, a 45-minute bus journey. Buses leave approximately every 15 minutes, from the northern gate of the ramparts (Chang Puak Gate), or you can take a blue *songthaew* from Nawarat Bridge. Lamphun makes a good half-day excursion. It's the ancient capital of the little Mon kingdom of Hariphuncha and always retained its independence. Take a look at the temples, particularly the 12th-century *Wat Hariphuncha* with its magnificent paintings depicting the various stages in the life of the Buddha. The museum (closed Monday and Tuesday) is nothing special but the gong hanging in one of the open pavilions is one of the biggest in the world. It's struck twice a day at 4pm and 6pm.

You won't find many guesthouses here. The 'Winter Fest' in December is when the town has its annual session of gay follies, best illustrated, perhaps, by the 'Miss Drag Queen' contest.

★ **Lampang** – ลำปาง: about 75 kilometres (47 miles) further on from Lamphun and not an easy journey by bus (take an air-conditioned one –

it's worth spending the extra). It's a pleasant ride by motorbike, though. There's a beautiful 16th-century temple in Lampang, one of the finest in northern Thailand, and it's probably the only town where you can get around by horse-drawn carriage. Lots of fun even if it is for the tourists and a bit expensive.

## GOING SOUTHWEST

★ **Mae Klang Falls** – น้ำตกแม่กลาง: about 60 kilometres (37 miles) southwest of Chiang Mai. These are lovely falls, particularly in the rainy season. You can take the bus from the Chiang Mai Gate, on the corner of Whulai Road, but it's a bit of a hassle. Next to the falls is the little town of Chom Thong – there's a temple at the entrance with a golden *chedi*.

★ If you're travelling by motorbike you can go on to the **Doi Ithanon** – ดอยอินทนนท์ (about 110 kilometres/70 miles from Chiang Mai), the highest peak in the country at 2,590 metres (9,700 feet). There's a good walk, with beautiful scenery, but only if you've got the time. A few kilometres (couple of miles) before you get to the mountain, look out for the two recently built temples – the architecture is interesting. There's an admission charge to get into the national park.

# TREKS IN THE MOUNTAINS

Chiang Mai is the main jumping-off point for all the treks into the surrounding mountains. The main point of the trek ought to be to admire the magnificent villages and scenery. Nowadays however, trekking has become highly organized, with guides talking a lot of nonsense about how these ethnic groups had never seen a tourist before you got there. This is patently untrue, of course – most of these villages are inundated by visits from guides. In Chiang Mai today there are more than 100 agencies organizing treks to meet the rising demand from an ever-increasing number of tourists. But since the number of tribes is the same as it ever was, trekking groups inevitably end up pounding the same tracks and prowling around the same villages. Some regions are less busy than others, but none of them is uncharted territory.

## TREKKING TODAY

For 10 years now, trekking in Thailand has stuck to a fairly rigid formula of two- to four-night outings, and you'll be hard pushed to find an agency in Chiang Mai that offers anything else. How things used to be back in the 1970s is no longer the case now. Gone are the long expeditions lasting more than a week, visiting as many mountain tribes as possible, and the chance to try a variety of mindbending pleasures of dubious legality. If what you seek is adventure with a capital A, be warned that northern Thailand no longer ranks among the world's deepest, darkest regions. But then not many places do these days.

The best time to go trekking is from November to March. Anyone going in July or August could be in for a real soaking. A trek may consist of just a walk, or it can include an elephant ride, a few hours' rafting in a rubber dinghy or shooting the rapids on a bamboo raft. The main physical activity is about 3 to 4 hours' walking a day through moderately difficult terrain, although none of the mountains in northern Thailand is higher than 2,500 metres (7,500 feet). Anyone can do it provided they're reasonably fit, and game for something a bit more demanding than the beaches of the south or the fleshpots of Bangkok.

The other essential aspect of trekking in Thailand is visiting villages inhabited by the ethnic groups – or 'tribes' as they now seem be known – who live in the mountains. These visits, as any travel agent will tell you, are an integral part of any successful trek, except that it's time for a change of register now. The mountain people are not part of the scenery, they are not fairground attractions, and they don't just stand around smiling, waiting for you to drop in on them. Even if the jungle is less dense and inaccessible than it used to be, life isn't always rosy up there.

## THE ETHNIC GROUPS

The minority ethnic groups who live in remote regions in the north and southwest of Thailand still live and dress largely as they have always done.

They have very little in common with the lowland Thais, not even language or religion. Whereas the lowland Thais came here 1,000 years ago, most of the mountain people have only been in Siamese territory for 200 or 300 years. They came in search of a peaceful life and a plot of land to farm at altitude. Northern Thailand had it all, so this is where they settled, protected by dense vegetation on all sides.

Mountain people have been migrating here on a regular basis ever since, although the flow of migration was dealt a serious blow in the mid-20th century, when national borders were drawn up throughout the mountainous massif stretching across the northern regions of Vietnam, Laos, Burma, Thailand and southern China. The reason these mountain people move around so much is because they are itinerant farmers, farming the land using slash-and-burn techniques. The land around the village would be cleared and farmed for a few years until the soil became exhausted, at which point the whole village would move on to another hill site and clear just enough forest to give them the land they needed. This lifestyle was the basis of their social structure and understanding of the world.

But all that came to an end in 1985 when the Thai government forbade the building of any new settlements. What you see today are first-generation 'fixed' mountain people who are struggling to come to grips with methods of commercial farming and are still reeling from the shock of a suddenly stationary way of life that they never expected and cannot get used to. But since the mountain people only account for one per cent of the population, there is little incentive for the government in Bangkok to launch tailor-made development programmes.

These are small, scattered groups of non-industrial people, many of whom made the mistake of siding with the communists during the wars in Indochina. To cap it all, the growing of poppies is now threatened by a

Western campaign, spearheaded by the USA, to convince the growers (these same mountain people), under pressure from the Thai government, to swap their *Papaver somniferum* for *caulis* and the *carota* (cabbage and carrots). The poppy-growers face huge losses in income, not to mention the administrative hassles and too many police and military interventions to keep quiet about. The ultimate objective is a policy of total (and enforced) integration with the culture, language, religion and market economy of Thailand.

But these uncompromising 'Siamization' programmes inevitably call into question the cultural identity of the peoples concerned. The problem is always how to encourage integration through education without at the same time trampling over the only way of life these village people have ever known. As everyone knows (and there are enough examples to prove it) any attempt at forced integration is doomed to failure, destroying the original social fabric and hindering people from adapting to a new way of life.

This is how things stand in Thailand today. Your guide will probably be a Thai and is unlikely to be familiar with the customs of each ethnic group, demonstrating the same lack of cultural interest as the Thai government. And there will be stories with lots of juicy anecdotes and bawdy details. With any luck, you might find your guide is originally from the mountains, although the percentage of local guides who work for the tourist industry is very small indeed.

## ABOUT THE MOUNTAIN TRIBES

In cultural terms, these remote societies, who lived for years completely cut off from the lowlands, have retained some extraordinary traditions, which more than justify your trekking out to see them. In 1998, the ethnic groups living in the mountainous regions of Thailand amounted to some 550,000 people living in 3,500 villages scattered across the northern provinces.

Originally, there were three main linguistic groups: the **Sino-Tibetan** group (with the Tibeto-Karen and Tibeto-Burmese sub-groups), which includes the Karen, Lisu, Lahu and Akha ethnic groups; the **Austro-Thai** group (with the Miao-Yao sub-group), which includes the Hmong and Mien ethnic groups; and the **Austro-Asiatic** group (with the Môn-Khmer sub-group), which includes the Htin, Khamu, Iawa and Mlabri ethnic groups.

That makes 10 main ethnic groups, without the complication of adding other sub-groups to the list. All of these groups are animists by tradition. This means that they worship spirits of every description, including the spirits of things, of the elements and in particular of their ancestors.

Social structure is always based on lineage and the clan and the household may be the sole economic unit. Political structure is largely defined by the extended family. Decisions involving several lineages, or several villages, are taken collectively by the respective males' lineal chiefs.

The settlements are very scattered and each village is completely independent of its neighbour. This entirely random distribution, coupled with a rich variety of cultures, accounts for the confetti-like scattering of multicoloured dots you find on maps, where each dot marks a mountain village according to ethnic group. What that means, in practice, is that you can easily visit several villages and several ethnic groups on the same trek.

### Karens, Lahus, Akhas and Lisus

These four ethnic groups account for 50 per cent, 11 per cent, 6 per cent and 4 per cent respectively of the mountain peoples of Thailand.

– **The Karens** (*Kariang*) were the first to settle in Thai territory nearly 300 years ago. They are originally from the highlands of Burma, where most of them still live today. The majority of Karens live along the border, where there is a certain amount of militant activity in favour of an independent Karen state straddling Thailand and Myanmar (formerly Burma).

Karen is a written and spoken language and there are about 300,000 Karen people living in Thailand, with almost another 2 million in Myanmar. Some of their villages are to the north and east of Chiang Rai.

The Karen ethnic group is divided into four sub-groups: the Saw (or White) Karens; the Pwo Karens (Plongs); the Taungthus (or Black) Karens; and the Kayah (or Red) Karens. They're a colourful people, to say the least.

When they arrived in Thailand, they settled at a relatively low altitude (around 500 metres/1,500 feet), where they were strongly influenced by the culture of neighbouring Thai villages. They are sedentary farmers whose main source of income comes from growing rice. The Karens also keep animals: chickens, pigs, buffaloes and elephants – which they are expert at training. Chickens are often sacrificed on ceremonial occasions. Divorce and adultery are rare, but anyone who has been unfaithful in marriage has to make a sacrifice to pacify the spirits. There are many Christians, too, thanks to the evangelistic zeal of two 19th-century American pastors to whom the Karen Christians owe their profoundly puritanical principle of no alcohol and no drugs. There are also quite a few Buddhists.

Traditional costume is increasingly becoming a thing of the past. So, too, are the traditional bamboo huts that were designed to be dismantled easily. Better-off Karen families now build Thai-style houses, which can make it difficult to distinguish them from their lowland neighbours. A high proportion of families are poverty-stricken and homeless, which is not surprising in a tribe that accounts for 50 per cent of all mountain people. They have never been seriously involved in poppy cultivation.

The Karen ethnic group also includes the tribes where you find the famed 'giraffe' women (*padongs* in Thai). Most of the 8,000 people in these tribes live in the Mae Hong Son region. The women are typical mountain-dwellers to look at, but their shoulder muscles have withered because of all the rings they wear around their necks.

– **The Lahus** (*Musoes*): of Sino-Tibetan origin, there are about 61,000 Lahu people in Thailand, all living along the border with Myanmar, north of Chiang Mai and Chiang Rai. The main sub-groups are the Lahus Nyis

(Red Lahus) and the Lahus Nas (Black Lahus). Lahu people live high up (about 1,000 metres/3,000 feet) in small, scattered villages, isolated from the Thais. Alongside rice and maize they grow opium, which accounts for a large part of their income. They also keep livestock, but their main passion is hunting – they're a dab-hand with a crossbow. They are animists, have witch-doctors, and ancestors play an important role. New Year celebrations are a lively time.

**– The Akhas** (*Ikaws*): of Tibeto-Burmese origin, the Akhas came from Laos and southern China (Yunnan province) and began by settling in Burma at the end of the 19th century before emigrating to the regions around Chiang Rai and Chiang Mai in the 20th century. About 33,000 Akahs live in mountain settlements or on hillsides, and their villages are therefore quite difficult to get to. They famously grow opium, but also cultivate rice, maize, millet and assorted vegetables, and keep livestock – chickens, pigs and buffaloes – which are often used for sacrifice. On festive occasions, a favourite dish is dog soup.

The Akhas are pantheists for whom worshipping their ancestors and making offerings are important events. At the entrance and exit to every village there is a 'door for the spirits', which is the dividing line between the spirit world and the world of men. Anyone entering the village has to pass through this door or gate, in order to purify himself of the evil spirits of the jungle. These highly ornate gates are carved with symbols and signs and should not be touched.

The most important event for the Akhas is the 'swing' ceremony and each village has a giant swing which is the focal point of the annual swinging festival in August. Their traditional costumes are magnificent; their black-and-red designs are hard to beat. Women wear a skirt, decorated leggings and a tall, brightly coloured head-dress made of tin and decorated with dozens of silver coins and other trinkets.

**– The Lisus** (*Lisaos* in Thai): there are currently about 25,000 Lisus living in Thailand, and 400,000 more in Myanmar). Of Sino-Tibetan origin, they migrated here in the same wave as the Akhas. Their villages are concentrated near the Burmese border, north of Chiang Mai, west of Chiang Rai and at quite high altitudes. It seems that the first Lisus only set foot on Thai soil about 60 years ago. They are arable farmers, growing mountain rice, maize and vegetables, who make a bit on the side through opium cultivation. They are strongly influenced by Chinese culture and celebrate the Chinese New Year, when the women wear a brightly coloured head-dress.

### The Hmongs (*Meos*) and Miens (*Yaos*)

These two groups account for 15 per cent and 6 per cent respectively of the total mountain-dwelling population of Thailand. They have close linguistic ties (using the same Chinese characters), and both groups originated in central China, where large numbers of them still live. Others live in Laos and North Vietnam. The total estimated Hmong population in southern China is about 5 million. Both groups share a vision of the world that owes much to Chinese cosmology, and both go in for a particular form of shamanism (if you get the chance, try to see one of their ceremonies – it's an unforgettable experience). Both groups are fairly recent migrants to Thailand (they came here about 100 years ago), which may explain why they built their settlements in the highest mountain ridges, above an altitude of 1,000 metres (3,000 feet). Because they live so high up, both the Hmongs and the Miens build their houses at ground level, which gives a warmer living space than raising them up on stilts as most of the other tribes do.

Living at altitude is also a distinct advantage when the poppy season comes around: the Meos and the Yaos are extremely experienced opium growers.

– **The Meos**: originally from southern China, the first wave of Meo immigrants came to Thailand at the end of the 19th century. The second wave came after the war in Vietnam. Of the total populaton of 5 million, there are currently some 100,000 Meos living in Thailand, mainly along the border with Laos, to the north and west of Chiang Mai.

The Meos are divided into three sub-groups: blue, white and Guas Mbas. The womenfolk of the 'blue' Meos are immediately identifiable by their magnificent and lavishly embroidered indigo pleated skirts, some of them real works of art that display skilful use of batik, embroidery and pleating. The women of the 'white' Meos wear a white skirt on ceremonial occasions and indigo trousers to work in the fields. Their embroidery is outstanding. And there are the Meos 'Guas Mbas', who came here from Laos and most of whom live in refugee camps – the revolution in 1975 didn't help them much. Most of their villages are at relatively high altitude for Thailand, 1,000–1,200 metres (3,000–3,600 feet). They grow rice and maize but most of their income comes from cultivating opium despite numerous attempts by the authorities to force them to change to other cash crops. Opium is mainly smoked by the older people, in accordance with ancient ritual.

Their social structure allows polygamy and their religion is a combination of pantheism and shamanism, although their beliefs reflect a pronounced Chinese influence, as does their language (which is spoken only). The most important festival is New Year (at the end of December), when it is customary for boys and girls who are courting to play ball with each other. The Meo tribes around Chiang Mai have become very much a tourist attraction.

– **The Yaos**: originally migrants from southern China about 150 years ago, the Yaos settled near the border with Laos, around Chiang Rai and Nan. As with some of the other ethnic groups, most of their income comes from opium cultivation, but they grow other important crops as well. The Yao marriage ceremony is steeped in ritual. The future groom chooses his bride from outside the clan, pays her father a hefty bride-price and then takes her to live with his parents. Yao women do beautiful embroidery. Culturally speaking, the Yao way of life has a distinctly Chinese flavour, and the Chinese influence is very much in evidence. Their sacred texts, for example, are written in Chinese characters. Their religion is a cross between pantheism and Taoism. They dress in colourful costumes, particularly the women – touches of red on an indigo background and an amazing scarlet boa worn around the neck. They are renowned for their extremely thrifty nature.

# COLOUR MAPS

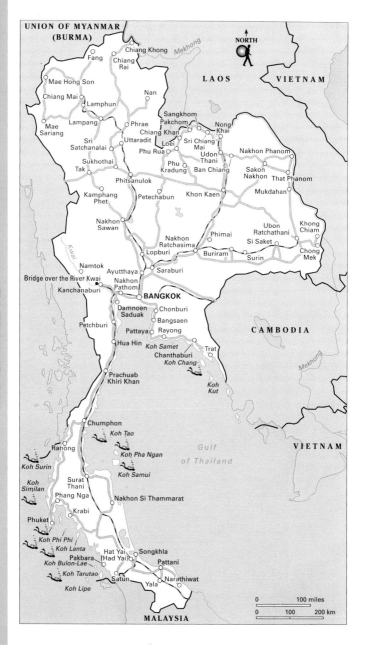

MAP OF THAILAND

THAILAND

# KEY TO BANGKOK MAPS I AND II

■ **Useful Addresses**

🚩 TAT (Map I)
🚃 Railway station (Map I)
🚌 National bus station
   (Maps I and II)
✈ Airport (Map I)
✉ General post office (Map I)

🛏 **Where to Stay**

20 Freddy's Guesthouse (Map I)
21 Salathai (Map I)
22 Lee 3 Guesthouse (Map I)
23 T.T.O. Guesthouse (Map I)
24 Malaysia Hotel (Map I)
25 Kingís Mansion (Map I)
26 YWCA (Map I)
27 Dynasty Inn (Map II)
28 Stable Lodge (Map II)
29 Nana City Inn (Map II)
30 Reno Hotel (Map I)
31 The Bed & Breakfast (Map I)
32 White Lodge (Map I)
33 Uncle Reyís Guesthouse (Map II)
34 Sukhumvit Crown Hotel (Map II)
35 Sri Hualampong Hotel (Map I)
36 TT2 Guesthouse (Map I)
37 River View Guesthouse (Map I)
38 Sri Kung Hotel (Map I)
39 New Trocadero Hotel (Map I)
40 Nana Guesthouse (Map II)
41 Chao Phraya Riverside
   Guesthouse (Map I)
42 New Empire Hotel (Map I)
43 The China Town Hotel (Map I)
44 Shanti Lodge, Back-Packers
   Lodge, Tavee Guesthouse,
   Sawatdee Guesthouse, Little-
   Home Guesthouse (Map I)
45 President Inn (Map II)
46 Tarntawan Place Hotel (Map I)

✗ **Where to Eat**

51 Yong Lee Restaurant (Map II)
52 Oam Thong Restaurant (Map II)
53 Cabbages and Condoms (Map II)
54 Night-time street market (Map I)
55 The Seafood Market and
   Restaurant (Map II)
57 Moghul Room (Map II)
58 Lemon Grass (Map II)
59 Le Banyan (Map II)
60 Maboonkhlong Shopping Centre
   (Map I)

61 Hard Rock Café (Map I)
62 T Restaurant (Map I)
64 Wong's Place (Map I)
65 YMCA Coffee Shop (Map I)
67 Himali Cha Cha (Map I)
68 Nan's Place (Map II)
69 Café de Paris (Map I)
70 Juyban Japanese Restaurant
   (Map II)
71 Sala Rim Nam (Map I)
72 Bussaracum (Map I)
73 Silom Village (Map I)
74 Ban Chiang (Map I)
75 Galaxy (Map I)
76 Le Bouchon (Map I)
77 Royal India Restaurant (Map I)
78 Nangnual Restaurant (Map I)
79 Texas Suki Yaki & Noodle
   (Map I)
80 China Town Scala Shark-fins
   Restaurant (Map I)
81 Once Upon a Time (Map I)

★ **What to See**

90 Wat Phra Kaeo and the Grand
   Palace (Map I)
91 Wat Pho (Map I)
92 Wat Arun (Map I)
93 Wat Benjamabopitr (Map I)
94 Wat Sakhet (Map I)
95 Wat Traimitr (Map I)
96 Wat Suthat (Map I)
97 Wat Rajabophit (Map I)
98 Wat Rajanaddaram (Map I)
99 The National Museum (Map I)
100 Vimanmek Mansion Museum
   (Map I)
101 The National Theatre (Map I)
102 The Royal Barge Museum
   (Map I)
103 Jim Thompson's House (Map I)
104 Suan Pakkard Palace (Map I)
105 Snake Farm (Map I)
106 Khlong Toey Market (Map II)
107 Thewet Flower Market (Map I)
108 Pak Khlong Market (Map I)

🛍 **Shopping**

120 The Thai Silk Company (Map I)
121 Song Tailor (Map I)
122 Chatuchak Park (Weekend
   Market) (Map I)
123 Narayana Bazaar Underground
   (Map I)

**KEY TO BANGKOK MAPS I AND II**

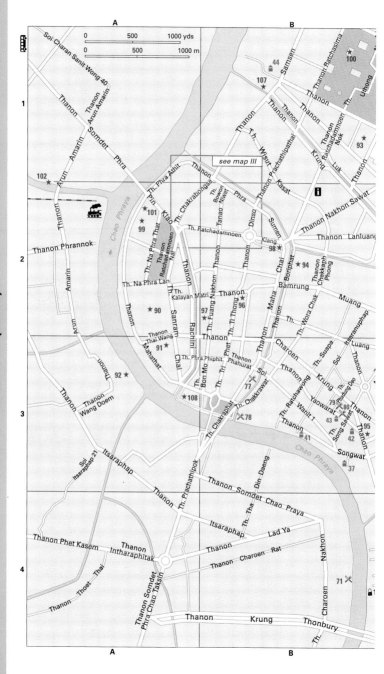

BANGKOK (MAP I)

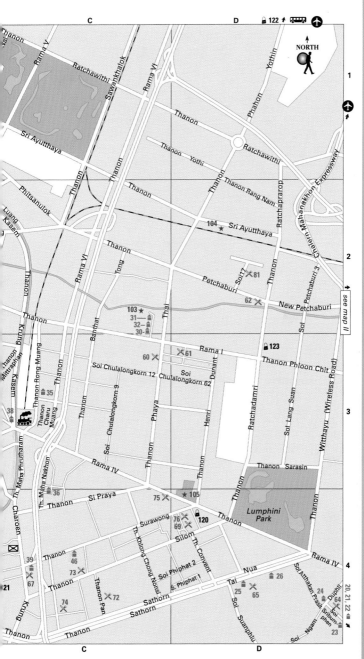

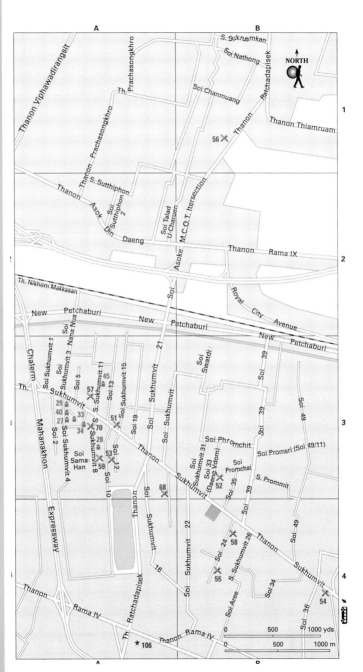

BANGKOK (MAP II)

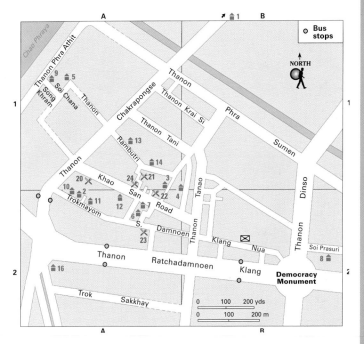

BANGKOK (MAP III)

## KEY TO MAP III

🏠 **Where to Stay**

1 Bangkok International Youth
   Hostel
2 Ranee Guesthouse
3 Marco Polo Hostel
4 V. S. Guesthouse
5 Merry V Guesthouse
6 Bonny Guesthouse
7 Dior Guesthouse
8 Prasuri Guesthouse
9 New Siam
10 Joe Guesthouse

11 New Joe Guesthouse
12 Sawasdee Bangkok Inn
13 Sawasdee House
14 Orchid House
16 Royal Hotel

✕ **Where to Eat**

20 Hello Restaurant
21 Artsy Fartsy
22 Bayon Pub and Restaurant
23 La Crêpe
24 Buddy Beer and Restaurant

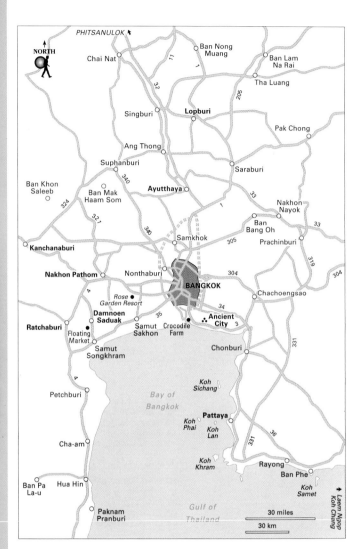

THE AREA AROUND BANGKOK

## The Htins, Khamus, Lawas and Mlabris

The three main ethnic groups of the Mon-Khmer linguistic sub-group collectively account for less than 8 per cent of the mountain-dwelling population of Thailand. In terms of culture, they are considered closer to the Mon and Khmer populations, who founded powerful empires all over the peninsula more than 12 centuries ago. All three groups have been settled for much longer than the other mountain people in the region. They have retained their animistic beliefs, which were the norm throughout the peninsula before Buddhism arrived. You're very unlikely to come across any of these on a trek.

– **The Htins**: migrated from Laos to settle in the provinces of Nan, on the border of Laos, as well as in the regions of Lampang and Kanchanaburi.

– **The Khamus**: live in the same places as the Htins. They are animists.

– **The Lawas**: migrated here in about the seventh century. They number just 8,000 in total, and live mainly to the southwest of Chiang Mai and the southeast of Mae Hong Son. This is the only mountain-dwelling ethnic group that is exclusive to Thailand and most of them are completely integrated with the Thai population.

– **The Mlabris**: also called the Phis Thongs Luangs ('yellow-leaf spirits'), this tiny group of just 150 people lives in the provinces of Nan and Phrae. They are the last surviving mountain nomads and they move camp every three or four days (serious backpackers . . .). They live mainly from hunting, own no land and often work for other people. They live in tiny communities consisting of anything from 3 to 12 members.

## MINDING YOUR MANNERS IN THE MOUNTAIN VILLAGES

It's vital, when visiting the mountain people, to remember that respect and good manners are essential. You are a long way from home and things that might seem obvious to you are actually anything but; and your guide, who isn't at home either, may not understand them any better than you do – there have been many cases of guides behaving deplorably. Simply be guided by good sense.

Mountain people are very welcoming by tradition, so do what you can to keep that tradition alive without taking advantage of their patience. Show respect for their sacred places and their sacred objects. Respect their right to sleep, too, even if you and your friends are on holiday – you don't have to get up at 5am to go to work.

Respect their right to privacy. You wouldn't want to be photographed in your bathroom and they don't want to be either. Ask permission to take photographs, either by using sign language or through the guide as many tribes object strongly to being photographed. If you are in any doubt, don't take any pictures. Tell yourself that it's a privilege to be here and that you're only here out of the goodness of their hearts. In short, be discreet.

## SUGGESTED READING

Those of you who are curious enough to want to return from your trek a little less clueless than when you left should put in some time beforehand doing a bit of ethnological research.

Apart from a small museum, there's also a **Tribal Research Institute**, where you'll find a full range of all available ethnological literature, including books, guides, theses and reference material. Some of these are described below. The institute is in the University of Chiang Mai (about 5 kilometres/3 miles) northwest of town as you go towards the zoo and Doi Suthep mountain; ☎ 221-933; open Monday–Friday, 9am–3pm). Don't hesitate to ask the students questions too.

– *Peoples of the Golden Triangle* by Paul and Elaine Lewis (Thames & Hudson, London, 1998). Expensive but packed with gorgeous photography and good general information.

– *A Trekker's Guide to the Hill Tribes of Northern Thailand* by J.R. Davies and T. Wu. (Footloose Books, Salisbury, Wiltshire, UK, 1990). Good general information, maps and colour photographs.

– *The Hill Tribes of Thailand,* published by the Technical Services Club of the Tribal Research Institute of Chiang Mai, 1986. Simple, straightforward, very cheap and on sale in the bookshops of Chiang Mai.

## WHAT MAKES A SUCCESSFUL TREK

Some of the villages (especially the Akha and Yao villages around Chiang Mai) are visited by an endless stream of minibuses packed with hundreds of tourists for whom the only purpose of the trip is to stop and take photographs before climbing back in the bus again. Clearly the safest solution is to go through an established agency that will put together a standard package with visits to some frequently visited tribes. No surprises (nasty or otherwise) there. Alternatively, you can hire your own guide or use a tiny agency which could be a great success, however, this is more risky than using an established agency.

Broadly speaking, the success of a trek is largely a question of luck. Some trekking tours never keep their promises (maybe the guide doesn't speak English, or the route's been changed, or it's boring, or there isn't enough equipment, or it's all a big swindle and they abandon you en route). Others give complete client satisfaction. Some guides are experts at putting together imaginative routes. Others originally come from the villages where you're heading and are therefore your best chance of getting to know the people who live there. Even your fellow travellers can be difficult. A trek can be tiring, and even quite unpleasant when it rains. This is certainly no Sunday outing and it's no place for people who complain.

To find out how dependable an agency is, ask how long the trek lasts (three days often turn into two); make sure the guide speaks English as well as one or two of the tribal languages; finally, take the precaution of asking to see the route on a map.

Refuse all offers from guides you meet in town. Practically all the guesthouses have an association with an agency. Another good way of checking on an agency is by asking people who've just returned from a trek what they thought of it.

TREKS IN THE MOUNTAINS

## TREKKING EQUIPMENT

There's no point in bringing a lot of stuff out with you from home, since you'll find everything you need in Chiang Mai at half the price, or even less.

**You will need**:

– a pair of good walking shoes;

– a change of underwear and socks (for when you get wet wading through water);

– a sweater to wear at night. From December to February it can get very cold in the mountains and the standard-issue blankets are a bit on the thin side. So if that's when you're coming, bring a thick sleeping bag;

– long trousers (for walking through scrub);

– hat (there's a high risk of sunstroke) and sun cream;

– folding knife;

– mosquito-repellent;

– cagoule, or preferably a waterproof cape;

– iodine-tincture drops for preference, or water purifying tablets;

– water bottle;

– torch;

– medication for stomach upsets;

– do not bring toilet paper – it already litters too many trails;

– do bring your credit card and passport, or leave them locked up at the bank – do not leave them at the guesthouse.

## SOME TREKKING REGIONS

– **Around Chiang Dao** – บริเวณเชียงดาว: rich variety of ethnic settlements about 80 kilometres (50 miles) from Chiang Mai. There are lots of tourists but they're all fairly spread out, thanks to the sheer number of villages. Some agencies take you to less popular regions.

– **Mae Hong Son** – แม่ฮ่องสอน (*see below*): the entire region west of Chiang Mai, where you can go trekking. It was very fashionable at one time when you could cross the border into Burma along the paths used by smugglers and see the 'long-necks' ('giraffe' women or *padongs*). Trekking around Mae Hong takes you through some beautiful countryside. Most of the people you meet are Karens.

– **Golden Triangle** – สามเหลยมทองคำ (north of the Kok river – เหนือแม่น้ำกก): this is the picturesque name for a done-to-death tourist region where you'll find T-shirts, souvenirs and other knick-knacks on sale at every street corner.

There are loads of other possibilities, of course, if you go with an independent guide. But be warned – it's a real jungle out there . . .

## MEETING LOCAL PEOPLE – WITHOUT HELP

If you want to get out and experience some of these cultures under your own steam, starting from the villages of Pai and Soppong west of Chiang Mai on the road to Mae Hong Son it's 1 or 2 hours on foot to various Lisu, Lahu, Karen and Meo settlements. There's no need to go through an agency. All the paths are waymarked and relatively uncrowded, so it's not really what you'd call a trek – more a pleasant stroll.

If you look in Pai and Soppong, you'll find simple, homemade maps (photocopied pages) showing where each tribe lives. Go there during the daytime, and leave yourself plenty of time to get back before nightfall, which comes early in the tropics.

## TREKKING AGENCIES IN CHIANG MAI

Chiang Mai is a mecca for trekkers, with more than 130 agencies responsible for nine out of every ten treks in Thailand. Some of the agencies have been established for years and you may prefer to stick to those we know. Don't forget to do a bit of research in the library of the Tribal Research Institute at the University of Chiang Mai (*see above*, under 'Suggested Reading').

■ **Youth Hostel** – บ้านเยาวชนเชียงใหม่: 21/8 Chang Khlan Road. ☎ 276-737. Offers all sorts of treks, and the organizers try to change their routes regularly. Backpackers usually return contented. Some of the guides speak English.

■ **Mr Wuthi Yunnan, S.T. Tours and Travel** – นายวุฒิยุนนาน,เอส. ที.ทัวร์แอนด์ทราเวล: 143/18 Lanna Villa, Superhighway. ☎ 222-174. Fax: 212-829. Organizes trips of every description, with no complaints so far.

■ **Orchid House** (*see* 'Where to Stay'): lots of trekkers have singled out this guesthouse for the quality of its treks.

## TREKS BY MOTORBIKE

Trekking by motorbike has become increasingly popular in recent years. It's as physically demanding as trekking on foot, and even requires a number of extra skills. Here are a few recommendations and safety hints aimed at making your journey as pleasant as possible.

### Formalities

– Vehicles in Thailand drive on the left.

– You are legally required to have an international driving licence. You are unlikely to be asked to produce it, but bring one just the same.

– Insurance is only just becoming compulsory for motorcycle hire. Find out the score before signing any papers and take out a good personal insurance policy before leaving home.

– You will be asked to leave your passport as a surety, so make doubly sure all parties understand the terms of the hire agreement and above all check that the bike's in reasonable nick.

– There are no speed limit signs, but local people tend to drive rather slowly. So you should do the same, particularly when you're going through villages (watch out for animals and children).

– You are not obliged to wear a helmet (except in Bangkok and Chiang Mai), but since you're used to wearing one at home, wear one anyway – it's in your interests after all. The hire place can supply one (a bit bashed around sometimes, but better than nothing) – all you have to do is ask. Try to get one with a visor, which will keep the dust out of your eyes.

### Equipment

You'll need the same as for trekking on foot (*see above*), plus a few extras:

– Sun cream is essential. You don't always feel the heat on a motorbike, but you're exposed to the sun just the same.

– Long trousers and long-sleeved T-shirts, to protect you from wind, sun, insects, dust and tumbles.

– A pair of gloves and preferably boots, best of all motorcycling boots.

– Large plastic bags, like dustbin liners, are useful to protect your luggage from the dust.

### A few words of advice and technical tips

– Don't follow too close behind the bike in front, in case one of your travelling companions falls off.

– Avoid driving after nightfall – there's less visibility and more traffic.

– Take extra care on very hot days when the rather poor road surface can become greasy and slippery. Bikes often skid going round bends.

– On dirt tracks and going downhill, become an expert at using the front and rear breaks evenly, to avoid locking the wheels and skidding.

A final word of advice: this isn't a motorcycle scramble and you don't have to impress anyone. You're just a hiker – so cool it. And whatever else you do, never go out on your own.

■ **Goodwill Motorcycle Hire** – กู๊ดวิลเช่ารถมอเตอร์ไซค์, 2/6 Chang-moi Kao, Chiang Mai. ☎ and fax: 234-161. In the west of town, on the ramparts and very close to the Suan Dok Gate. Run by an English-man who knows the region like the back of his hand. The top-quality service and well-kept bikes more than justify the price. *See also* Deng Bike Hire under 'Transport' in Chiang Mai.

■ **Safari Moto Adventure** – ซาฟารี โมโต้อาวองตูร์: 39 Bamrung Rat Road, Chiang Mai. ☎ 246-966. Fax: 248-998. The owner of this place is one of the pioneers in this business. He knows every track and trail in the region and can take you on treks lasting one or several days. Only for seasoned backpackers who do a lot of sports. There's also a left-luggage office with 12 lockers.

# WEST OF CHIANG MAI: THE PROVINCE OF MAE HONG SON

The entire region west of Chiang Mai can be explored by bus or motorbike, in which case the grand tour leaving from Chiang Mai takes 4 or 5 days. You can also hire a bike in Mae Hong Son and detour to other villages. Whatever your mode of transport and wherever you started from, you can always make a circuit of the entire region and return to your point of departure without ever having to retrace your steps (this makes more sense when you look at the map). Lots of interesting places and tribes to see on the way, and there's no need to go though an agency, no risk of getting lost and far fewer tourists than in Chiang Mai. The region is populated by 34 per cent ethnic groups, 65 per cent Shans and one per cent 'real' Thais. When you visit the temples, you'll notice a pronounced Shan influence in the Burmese style of the architecture.

The suggested route leaves from the unassuming but appealing capital of the province of Mae Hong Son – which is also called Mae Hong Son. You return to Chiang Mai via Soppong (also called Pang Mapha, the name of the district) and Pai. But there's nothing to stop you leaving from Chiang Mai and visiting Pai, Soppong and lastly Mae Hong Son. The other route is also reversible: going south via Khun Yuam, Mae Sariang and Chom Thong and ending up in Chiang Mai.

Some of the shops and guesthouses in the villages you pass through sell little booklets containing general information and homemade maps of the region. Another useful publication for anyone who wants to go exploring the area is *Maps for Northern Trips*, a series of maps covering the whole of northern Thailand.

## LEAVING CHIANG MAI

### By train for Bangkok

There are lots of night trains that get you into Bangkok the following morning. Most of the guesthouses have up-to-date timetables. Avoid travelling by day – the trains take too long. There are about six departures between 3.30pm and 9pm, and some trains are faster than others. Not all have couchettes so check before booking and reserve well ahead, as the trains are often full.

### By national bus

Buses, with or without air-conditioning, are the cheapest mode of transport. They leave from the Chiang Mai Arcade bus station (map, D1) in the northwest of town, slightly away from the centre. Alternatively, buses to places in the province of Chiang Mai leave from the Chang Puak bus station (map, B2), just beyond the Chang Puak Gate in the northwest of town. If the bus station isn't specified, it means the bus leaves from the Arcade bus station.

– **For Bangkok**: by air-conditioned or non-air-conditioned bus. About 15

MAE HONG SON

departures daily, from early morning until late afternoon for non-air-conditioned buses and until about 9pm for air-conditioned buses. Journey time: 11 hours.

**– For Chiang Rai** (180 kilometres/112 miles): about 12 non-air-conditioned buses daily, 6am to around 5.30pm. At least 10 air-conditioned buses daily, 7am–5pm. Journey time: 3 hours 30 minutes.

**– For Mae Hong Son** (via Mae Sarieng): five non-air-conditioned buses daily, 6.30am–8pm. Two air-conditioned buses daily, one in the morning and one at night.

**– For Mae Hong Son** (via Pai): four non-air-conditioned buses daily.

**– For Fang** (Chang Puak bus station): buses every 30 minutes, 6am–5.30pm. The journey is 150 kilometres (94 miles) and takes 3 hours 30 minutes.

**– For Thaton** (Chang Puak bus station): six buses daily, 6.15am–3.30pm. Journey time: 4 hours. For the river Kok trip, take the one that leaves at 7.20am.

**– For Lamphun** (Chang Puak bus station): the bus service is non-stop from 5am to 9pm.

**– For Sukhothai and Phitsanulok**: several air-conditioned and non-air-conditioned buses daily. They take about 6 hours to get to Sukhothai and 5 hours 30 minutes to get to Phitsanulok.

## By VIP bus

Comfortable, privately operated buses with few passengers and reclining seats, but the price is a bit steep. You'll find most of the agencies in the Anusarn Market, which is also where the buses depart from. Or you can buy your ticket at the guesthouse in exchange for a small commission charge – very handy. Most of the buses go to Bangkok and Chiang Rai.

**– For Bangkok**: five buses daily, from about 7am to 9pm.

**– For Chiang Rai**: it's not that far, so there's no need for a fancy bus, but make sure it doesn't take the old road, which is a much longer journey.

## By air

**– For Bangkok**: at least eight flights daily, 7am–8pm.

**– For Chiang Rai**: two flights daily, morning and afternoon.

**– For Mae Hong Son**: four flights daily, 10am–5pm.

**– For Phuket**: five flights a week, leaving late morning. Flight lasts about 2 hours.

**– For Phitsanulok**: one flight a day. Timetable varies depending on the day.

**– For Sukhothai**: two Bangkok Airways flights a day stop here.

**– Also flights for: Vientiane** (Laos), two flights a week with Lao Aviation; **Singapore**, three flights a week with Silk Air; **Kuala Lumpur** (Malaysia), two flights a week with Malaysia Airlines, which also flies to Europe, the USA and Australia.

MAE HONG SON

# MAE HONG SON – แม่ฮ่องสอน

DIALLING CODE: 053

Mae Hong Son is a large, quiet market town just a short distance from the border with Myanmar and about 250 kilometres (156 miles) from Chiang Mai on the road to Pai and Soppong. It's a peaceful place and absolutely ideal as a base from which to explore the surrounding region. You'll meet a few mountain tribes there, mostly Karens but also black Lahus, Meos and Lisus, who come to market to buy and sell. Mae Hong Son still has the look and feel of a big provincial village that's rather set apart from the rest of the world.

Mae Hong Son is on a small lake at the bottom of a natural basin, nestling in wild and wonderful scenery, flanked by mountains carpeted with teak woods. Being romantic, you might say the lake is a jewel and the town and mountains are the jewellery case. But the view you get of it from the Wat Doi Kong Mu also shows you why Mae Hong Son airport is one of the most dangerous in the world. The town, in any event, is a quiet, friendly place that remains quite unique; like a Swiss spa resort set in exotic mountains fragrant with the aroma of spices. Mae Hong Son also happens to be a nerve-centre of regional opium production, where Burmese growers and Chinese dealers meet to do business.

The town consists essentially of two main roads (Khumlumprapas Road and Singhanat Bamrung Road) that cross each other at right angles. You'll find everything you need, including restaurants and guesthouses, on these two roads, within a short distance of the junction.

## GETTING THERE

– **By air**: about four flights a day leave from Chiang Mai.

– **By bus**: two possible routes, either via Pai (250 kilometres/156 miles) or Mae Sarieng (350 kilometres/218 miles). The first route is better as it's more mountainous. Buses leave from Chiang Mai Arcade bus station and there are five services a day via Pai – an 8-hour journey, or seven a day via Mae Sarieng, which is a slightly longer journey.

## ADDRESSES AND USEFUL INFORMATION

✈ **Airport** – ท่าอากาศยานแม่ฮ่องสอน (map, B2): north of the centre (within walking distance). ☎ 612-221. If you're arriving and leaving by air, confirm your return flight when you arrive. Lots of touts for the guesthouses in town. Currency exchange facilities.

■ **Tourist police** – ตำรวจท่องเที่ยว (map, B2, **1**): Singhanat Bamrung Road, some 50 metres from Thai Airways on the other side of the street. ☎ 611-812. Open daily, 8am–4pm. There's no tourist office in town.

✉ **Post and telegraph office** – ไปรษณีย์กลาง (map, A2): 79 Khumlumprapas Road. Post office open Monday–Friday, 8.30am–6.30pm, weekends 9am–noon. It sells telephone cards and the telephone booths are right outside.

**MAE HONG SON**

## ■ Useful Addresses

| ✉ | Post and telegraph office |
| ✈ | Airport |
| 🚌 | Bus station |
| 1 | Tourist police |
| 2 | Thai Farmers Bank |
| 3 | Bangkok Bank Ltd |
| 4 | Thai Airways |
| 5 | Hospital |
| 6 | T.N. Tours |
| 7 | Motorbike-taxis |
| 8 | Long-distance calls |

## ⌂ Where to Stay

| 10 | Friend House |
| 11 | Prince's House |
| 12 | Johnnie House |
| 14 | Sabannga Guesthouse |
| 15 | Rim Nong Lakeside Guesthouse |
| 16 | Mae Hong Son Guesthouse |
| 17 | Piya Guesthouse |
| 18 | Golden Huts Guesthouse |
| 19 | Yok Guesthouse |
| 20 | Baiyoke Chalet Hotel |
| 21 | Fern Resort |

## ✗ Where to Eat

| 25 | Central market |
| 26 | Kai Mook Restaurant |
| 27 | Thip Restaurant |
| 28 | Fern Restaurant |
| 29 | Vegetarian Restaurant |

## ♈ Where to Have a Drink

| 9 | Sunny Coffee Shop |

■ **Long-distance calls** (map, A2, **8**): Udomchaonitet Road. Big local telecommunications building open 8am–8pm. Same rates as at the post office, so it's cheap. Fax facilities.

■ **Thai Farmers Bank** – ธนาคารกสิกรไทย (map, A2, **2**): in the main street, open Monday–Friday, 8.30am–3.30pm. Hole-in-the-wall cash machine outside, where you can use a Visa card.

■ **Bangkok Bank Limited** – ธนาคารกรุงเทพ (map, A2, **3**): 68 Khumlumprapas Road. Open 8.30am–3.30pm. Hole-in-the-wall cash machine for Visa cards outside. The machine doesn't work 24 hours a day. There's also a currency exchange kiosk outside, open 8.30am–5pm.

■ **Thai Airways** – สายการบินไทย (map, B2, **4**): 71 Singhanat Bamrung Road. ☎ 612-220 and 612-221 (at the airport). Open daily, 8.30am–5.30pm.

■ **Hospital** (map, B2, **5**): east of the centre. ☎ 611-378.

■ **Thai massage** – นวดแผนโบราณ: highly recommended and very clean Institute of Massage, next to the Lakeside Bar, in a road at right angles to the one along the edge of the lake. Look for the yellow sign. Open 11am–11pm-ish. Go there at night and you'll have a massage to the sound of music from the bar next door. Great stuff.

■ **Motorbike hire** – เช่ารถมอเตอร์ไซค์: lots of hire places on the main street, Khumlumprapas Road.

Compare prices before making up your mind.

■ **T.N. Tours** – ที.เอ็น.ทัวร์ (map, B2, **6**): 21 Pradit Chong Kham Road. ☎ 620-059. Fax: 620-060. Most of the guesthouses can take you trekking or walking at reasonable prices in the area around Mae Hong Son. While this agency is overall a bit more expensive, it can put together a tailor-made trip for one or two people, or a small group. Interesting circuits with opportunities for rafting, elephant rides and visits to caves. Reliable professional service – at a price.

■ **Namrin Tour** – น้ำรินทัวร์: 5/2 Khumlumprapas Road. ☎ 611-857. Another place with a good reputation where the owner seems to know what he's doing.

■ **Piya Guesthouse** agency (see 'Where to Stay'). Good things are also said about the treks organized through these people.

■ **Motorbike-taxis** (map, B2, **7**): behind the town market, which is open 8am–6pm. Drivers are easy to spot by the orange or green numbers they wear. Be firm about the price before setting off. You can also hire a regular taxi from here (if you want to visit the surrounding villages) or a tuk-tuk.

■ **Bicycles**: as part of a scheme launched by the town, tourists can now pick up a bicycle free of charge from the airport or the post office (between 8am and 5pm).

■ **Launderettes**: there are quite a few of these near the post office, offering a same-day service at reasonable rates.

## WHERE TO STAY

There are at least 30 guesthouses in town – all modest places offering basic accommodation at reasonable rates. The nicest ones are on the lake.

## BUDGET (50–200 BTS PER PERSON PER NIGHT)

⌂ **Friend House** – เฟรนด์เกสท์เฮ้าส์ (map, B2, **10**): 20 Pradit Chong Kham. ☎ 611-647. Magnificent, newly built teak house with only six bedrooms. The three upstairs rooms have stripped and polished floors, and walls lined with woven bamboo. One of them sleeps four and has a bathroom with hot running water. The spacious terrace-gallery is furnished with cushions and low tables, and overlooks the lake. The three ground-floor rooms have spotless, shared bathroom facilities. Discreet welcome, peaceful setting, friendly atmosphere – an outstanding place in every respect. Breakfast is served after the cock crows – a wake-up call that has proved a bit raucous for some (to judge from comments in the visitors' book), particularly since the cock has been known to crow all night.

⌂ **Prince's House** – พรินส์เฮ้าส์ (map, B2, **11**): 37 Udomchaonitet Road. ☎ 611-137. Elevated building with a very pleasant terrace full of flowers, furnished with low tables and floor cushions, where you get a good view of the temple and the lake. Basic rooms of white plywood, some with a hot shower, but the bathroom facilities are pretty dismal. Not too hot on maintenance but recommended all the same. Limited restaurant service.

⌂ **Johnnie House** – จอนนี่เฮ้าส์ (map, B2, **12**): 5/2 Udomchaonitet Road. ☎ 611-667. On the lake, facing the temples and next to the previous entry. Small and simple but quite charming – wooden rooms with outside shower room, and all very clean. Warm welcome. 'Johnnie', by the way, was the name of the very first tourist who ever slept here.

⌂ **Sabannga Guesthouse** – สบันงาเกสท์เฮ้าส์ (map, A2, **14**):

Udomchaonitet Road. ☎ 612-280. Wooden guesthouse at the end of a garden – not bad overall but looking a bit down-at-heel these days. Long, elevated building with eight bedrooms off a raised passageway, all with linoleum floors, mattresses, floral sheets and blankets. The bathroom facilities are outside. Charming garden with well-kept lawn. Laundry and massage service are so-so.

⌂ **Rim Nong Lakeside Guesthouse** – ริมหนองเลคไซด์เกสท์เฮ้าส์ (map, B2, **15**): 4/1 Chumnansatid Road. Peacefully situated on the edge of the lake, this pocket-sized, higgledy-piggledy guesthouse rents out about a dozen 'cupboards', apparently working on the principle that 'small is beautiful'. The rooms on the first floor are lighter, larger and generally better. There are dormitories on the ground floor and the owners recently added a couple of new, solidly built rooms with bathroom. Useful if you're stuck.

⌂ **Mae Hong Son Guesthouse** – แม่ฮ่องสอนเกสท์เฮ้าส์ ถนนขุมลุมประพาส (map, A1, **16**): set back from the village, in a quiet location about 600 metres north of the centre, which is signposted from the bus station. ☎ 612-510. Choice of accommodation in a fairly dull setting: modest rooms in a long building, or dilapidated huts with mosquito nets and fan, with hot shower outside in each case. Also some brand new and rather expensive bungalows with fake wooden floor tiles. Not bad, but expensive for what it is and in any case a bit too far out for anyone who doesn't have transport.

## MODERATE TO EXPENSIVE (300–600 BTS PER PERSON PER NIGHT)

⌂ **Piya Guesthouse** – ปิยะเกสท์เฮ้าส์ (map, B2, **17**): 1/1 Khumlumprapas, Soi 3. ☎ 611-260. Fax:

612-308. Very near the post office. Delightful, air-conditioned bungalows built by the owners, with wooden floors and bathrooms. More expensive than the two previous places but reduced rates apply for holders of international student cards. There's a large billiard table in the hallway but don't get carried away because it's generally in use as a sideboard. Relaxed, friendly atmosphere and cheap food. Apparently the agency for the guesthouse, Piya Travel (☎ 612-741), has a good reputation.

🛌 **Golden Huts Guesthouse** – โกลเด้นฮัทเกสท์เฮ้าส์ (map, A1, **18**): 253/1 Moo 11, Makasanti Road. ☎ 611-544. It would be hard to imagine anything more original than these bungalows, built on terraces on a mountainside. Prices can triple, from basic straw hut with straw on the floor and cold shower, to luxury pad with private bathroom, hot water, towels and your own terrace. Actually the more expensive ones are rather ugly, not very well kept and the cheaper ones are probably preferable. But this place is as peaceful as it gets with the gentle chirping of birds in cages. The entrance is delightfully kitsch. Serves breakfast.

🛌 **Yok Guesthouse** – หยกเกสท์เฮ้าส์ (map, A1, **19**): 14 Sirimongkol Road; outside the centre, to the northwest of town. ☎ 611-532 or 611-318. Long single-storey building that doesn't look up to much but is lovingly looked after by smiling owners. Nine bedrooms, one with air-conditioning, all with bathroom (hot water); they're nothing special to look at but so clean you could eat off the floor. Very reasonable prices, particularly since you can eat for next

to nothing in the adjoining snack bar.

### EXPENSIVE TO SPLASH OUT (OVER 600 BTS PER PERSON PER NIGHT)

🛌 **Baiyoke Chalet Hotel** – ใบหยกชาเล่ต์โยเด็ต (map, A2, **20**): 90 Khumlumprapas Road. ☎ 611-486. Luxury hotel in the centre of Mae Hong Son. Tastefully decorated rooms, all in wood, Swiss chalet-style. Pity they're so small. The service is what you'd expect of a luxury hotel. Very expensive, of course, but the standard rooms offer good value for money. Avoid those on the ground floor; they're a bit dark and the noise from the hotel pub is a nuisance.

🛌 **Fern Resort** – เฟิร์นรีสอร์ท (off A3 on the map, **21**): not quite 6 kilometres (4 miles) south of town. Follow the signs to the left for another 2 kilometres (1.25 miles) until you come to a remote spot on the river. ☎ 611-374. A group of wooden bungalows with leafy roofs, scattered around a very well-kept garden with little streams and rustling with bamboo. There are three kinds of bungalows, each with its own little terrace and private bathroom. The smaller (cheaper) ones with no air-conditioning are nicer, and there's a lovely wooden floor in place of the absurd fitted carpet you find in the other rooms. Very expensive all the same, but there's a great swimming pool. The owner of this hotel also owns the Fern Restaurant (*see below*) where you'll find a bigger menu and much better food than anything else available here. The setting is divine, but watch out for the mosquitoes (*young* in Thai).

## WHERE TO EAT

### BUDGET

✗ **Central market** – ตลาดกลางถนนขุมลุมประพาส (map, B2, **25**): right in the centre of town, between Singhanat Bamrung Road and Panishawatana Road. A great place to eat at any time of day: lively atmosphere, simple, delicious food, lots of busy market traders and tempting food stands. Eat well for next to nothing from about 7am to 6pm.

✗ **Vegetarian Restaurant** – ร้านอาหารมังสะวิรัด (map, B2, **29**): Singhanat Bamrung Road (next to the tourist police). Open daily, 8am–6pm. A very pleasant, typically Thai miniature restaurant with local TV playing in the background. Very popular with the locals, many of whom don't eat meat. There's no menu, but take a look around the kitchen and lift a few lids to see what's cooking: noodles, rice dishes, fried spring rolls and some (quite spicy) salads too. Exclusively vegetarian cooking full of herbs and spices, at amazing prices. Great.

### MODERATE TO EXPENSIVE

✗ **Kai Mook Restaurant** – ร้านอาหารไข่มุก (map, A2, **26**): 23 Udomchaonitet. ☎ 612-092. Open for lunch (closed 2–5pm) and for dinner until 10pm or 11pm. Lovely dining area, with bamboo pillars ingeniously lit by lamps made of local hats. First-class Chinese and Thai food, including *laab,* a northern dish based on thinly sliced beef with onions and vegetables, and exquisite spring rolls. The house speciality, not to be missed, is roasted duck with basil. All the dishes are available in large or small portions.

– Turn left as you leave the restaurant and go on until you come to a road at right angles. On the pavement opposite is a local restaurant serving uncommonly good banana and papaya fritters.

✗ **Thip Restaurant** – ร้านอาหารทิพย์ (map, A2, **27**): Pradit Chong Kham Road. ☎ 620-553. Open daily, for lunch and dinner. Classical Thai restaurant in a lovely, big teak house with a pretty carved balcony overlooking the lake. Choose from a range of expertly prepared dishes. All the dishes are available in small or large portions but you'll probably find the small portions quite big enough. The crispy spring rolls are particularly good. The subdued lighting in the dining area at night makes the whole place seem quite mysterious.

✗ **Fern Restaurant** – ร้านอาหารเฟิร์น (map, A2, **28**): 87 Khumlumprapas Road. ☎ 611-374. Open daily, 10am–10pm. The best place to eat in Mae Hong Son. It's stylish but relaxed, with a very easy atmosphere. The large and magnificent dining area is tastefully furnished and opens onto the street in front and a courtyard at the back (beware of mosquitoes). Classic cuisine at its best and flawless, charming service. Great choice of spicy dishes all beautifully prepared. Try the *hamok* (seafood cooked with vegetables *en papillote*), or the *chuchi* (shrimps in a sauce served with coconut milk) and above all don't miss the *kai ho bai teoi* – grilled chicken wrapped in a leaf, and one of the best things you can ever eat in Thailand. Prices are very reasonable for a restaurant of this reputation serving such excellent food.

## WHERE TO HAVE A DRINK

☕ **Lakeside Bar** – เลคไซด์บาร์: Pradit Chong Kham Road (not far from Thip Restaurant and run by the same team). This is the favourite watering-hole of the privileged youth from Mae Hong. Lovely terrace with big wooden benches on the water's edge, where you can quietly sip your *singha* to the sounds of the local R 'n' B bands who come on every night at about 8.30pm. Pleasant easy-going place.

☕ If R 'n' B isn't your cup of tea, there's always the **Baiyoke Pub**, on the ground floor of the hotel of the same name (Baiyoke Chalet Hotel; *see* 'Where to Stay'; map A2, **20**). The atmosphere is slightly stale and the music is a bit loud considering the size of the room.

☕ **Karaoke bars** – คาราโอเก้บาร์: there are a few of these in Khumlumprapas Road (up by the junction with Singhanat Bamrung Road), complete with the usual hostesses trying to attract the attention of what passes for a clientele in 'swinging' Mae Hong Son.

☕ The **Sunny Coffee Shop** – ซันนี่คอฟฟี่ช็อป (map A2, **9**) at No. 59, Singhanat Bamrung Road on the first floor of a supermarket, is everybody's idea of a seedy bar, complete with a shady massage parlour. Only really of any interest to sleep-walking ethnographers. The **Josephine Karaoke** opposite, on the other hand, is much more attractive.

## WHAT TO SEE

★ **The market** – คลาดสด (map, A1–A2): in the centre, between Singhanat Bamrung Road and Udomchaonitet. Open 6am–7pm but particularly lively before 10am. Sells mainly fruit and vegetables but also crockery, fabrics etc. Women from the mountain tribes occasionally come to shop here.

★ **Wat Hua Wiang** – วัดหัวเวียง (map, A2): this small Shan temple right next door to the market is uncomfortably close to a chapel of debatable beauty and poor decoration. But do go and see what's left of the magnificent tiling that originally surrounded the 200-year-old Burmese Buddha. The remains are behind a protective grille.

★ **Wat Chong Klang** – วัดจองกลาง (map, B2): south of town, just south of the little lake, this wooden monastery with tiered roofs in the Burmese style is open 6am–6pm. It has a large prayer hall on stilts and old glass panels painted with important scenes from the Buddha's life. The little museum at the back of the temple is very good, with a collection of wooden statues of peasants, animals, old people etc. They are originally from Burma and quite a rarity in Thailand. Many display a kind of mystical pain that is often very moving. There are also lots of scenes depicting the life of the Buddha.

On a lighter note altogether, drop a coin in the collecting box and watch the merry-go-round turn. There's another temple (the **Wat Chong Kham**; map, B2) in the same precinct on the right, with an impressive Buddha, made of painted cement, that is 5.5 metres (17 feet) high. There are lots of lovely gilt *chedis* around the temples.

★ **Wat Doi Kong Mu** – วัดพระธาตุดอยกองมู (map, A2): not quite 3 kilometres (2 miles) from the centre, at the top of a rather steep hill. Perched on a forbidding headland, this temple has been of great importance to the people of Mae Hong Son since the bandits who occupied the site were seen off by their ancestors. Stirring stuff. From the top, you get a magnificent view of the town, the lake, the valley and the airport. There's also a stairway up to the top. The atmosphere in the temple precinct is pleasant, with lots of souvenir-sellers, and strutting chickens.

★ **Wat Phra Non** – วัดพระนอน (map, A2): at the foot of the hill leading to the Doi Kong Mu. The principal, teak-built sanctuary tower houses a reclining Buddha more than 11 metres (36 feet) long. There's also a small museum (which charges admission 'to cover the cost of electricity' – that's what it says above the collecting urn) with a collection of sandal-wood Buddhas and some remarkable Chinese porcelain. It seems that this is where the ashes of the royal family of Mae Hong Son were laid to rest, in a coffin guarded by two fearsome dragons. Not far from here, between the stadium and the prison, is a statue of Phrayasighanat, the first king and founder of Mae Hong Son.

## WHAT TO SEE IN THE SURROUNDING AREA

★ Going north (on the road to Pai), about 19 kilometres (12 miles) on the left, are the sacred fish of the **Tham Pla**. You should pay your respects to these beautiful grey-blue carp that swim in the waters of a subterranean river as it re-emerges above ground, watched over by an eremite Buddha. Just bear in mind that anyone who eats these sacred creatures will die in the most appalling agony. Apart from that, you can take a pleasant stroll in a landscaped park.

## THE MOUNTAIN TRIBES

This mountainous region, densely carpeted with forest on the Thai–Burmese border, is home to the so-called 'giraffe' or 'long-necked' women – members of the Padong tribe, who are related to the Karens. Until recently, the women were kept in settlements on the Thai border by soldiers of the Karen army, who charged admission to anyone who wanted to see them. It's reported that a Thai businessman has now obtained exclusive rights over the Padongs and their families, and they have been moved and brought together in a part of Mae Hong Son called Nai Soi. A Chinese newspaper reported more recently that 46 village women have disappeared and been deported to the Chiang Mai region to be put on show.

Tourists get told a lot of things and you can never be sure what's true and what's false. But generally speaking, tourists are often told that all (or part) of the vast sums of money earned by tourism does go to these long-necked women and their families. In fact, nothing could be further from the truth: it seems that the women end up with just 250 Bts a month to live on – which is what each and every tourist pays to see them. The lion's share meanwhile gets divided up between the tour operators, the army and the town of Mae Hong Son, which attracts large numbers of tourists thanks to the Padongs.

In theory, the Karens and the giraffe women are found only in the Union of Myanmar and, even there, only in limited numbers. The few who live in Thai territory (near Mae Hong Son) are members of refugee groups who fled from the war in Burma between the various armed Karen factions and the Burmese military. As refugees, they do not have the right to cultivate land in Thailand, making their situation quite different from that of the other mountain ethnic groups.

You could argue that it's alright to visit the other unique ethnic groups – the Meo, the Lisu, the Akha and so on – because they have the freedom to come and go. The giraffe women do not have that privilege. They are there to be gawped at whether they like it or not, like animals in a zoo. Everything possible is done to make the visit seem 'natural' and the village entirely 'normal', though this kind of sightseeing is an inhumane business, and you need to decide whether you want to take part.

Lots of guesthouses and small agencies organize treks in the region around Mae Hong, which is much less touristic than the area around Chiang Mai. You'll see mainly Karens but also some Lisus and Lasus. The region of Mae Hong Son is Thailand's major smuggling and opium-trafficking route.

Some travel agencies in Bangkok organize excellent tours of this region, including elephant rides, for small groups of well-heeled people. By the way, if you fancy riding an elephant, it's much more fun doing it here than in an elephant camp. If you don't want to go through an agency but you do have your own transport, you can also hire elephants privately. You'll find family-owned elephants for hire (with their owners) about 8 kilometres (5 miles) south of town, just before the Mae Hong Son Riverside hotel, near the jetty where the boats depart for the villages of the giraffe women. Crossing the river on an elephant is a memorable experience.

## LEAVING MAE HONG SON

– **For Chiang Mai**: about seven buses a day via Mae Sarieng, and about five via Pai. They all stop briefly in Soppong.

# FROM MAE HONG SON TO CHIANG MAI VIA PAI

The northern road is wilder but perhaps more beautiful than the road going via Mae Sarieng. It's described here going one way only, but obviously if you leave from Chiang Mai, you won't go through the towns in the same order.

When you leave Mae Hong Son, the first thing you must see are the Tham Pla caves (*see above*).

Further on, 16 kilometres (10 miles) before Soppong (*see* the end of the section on Soppong), make a detour to visit the Shans, who live in the village of Mae Lana.

To make sure you know exactly where you're going, check all directions on a regional map.

# SOPPONG (PANG MAPHA) – สปพง

DIALLING CODE: 053

This little village is 2 hours from Mae Hong Son (64 kilometres/40 miles) and 1 hour from Pai (45 kilometres/28 miles). The bus from Mae Hong Son to Chiang Mai stops here, despite the smallness of the village and the virtual absence of any tourists. Soppong (or Pang Mapha as the district is called on some maps) is nothing more than a group of houses along a main street, but it's a good jumping-off place for those trekking on their own off the beaten track. The magnificent Tham Lod caves are very close to the village.

If you plan to stay in the area, ask the guesthouse for a map of the region.

## WHERE TO STAY AND WHERE TO EAT

You can always stay in the village of course, but it's much more fun sleeping in the caves.

🛏 ✕ **Jungle Lodge** – จังเกิลลอดจ์: about 1.5 kilometres (1 mile) from the centre, on the road to Mae Hong Son. ☎ 617-099. Little, rustic bamboo huts dotted around a terraced garden, with mattresses on the floor and mosquito nets. Warm shower and outside WC plus some bungalows with their own showers. Spotlessly maintained overall, pleasant and cheap – although you can hear the noise from the road. Lovely wooden terrace where they serve breakfast and foreign or local dishes. The food's not bad.

🛏 **Lemon Hill Guesthouse** – เลมอนฮิลล์เกสเฮาส์: in the centre of the village opposite the bus terminal and the local market, behind the house at the edge of the road (but the only sign is in Thai). These rustic bungalows sloping down towards the river Lang are not as clean as they might be, but they are very well placed. About 10 rooms at reasonable rates. Friendly owner.

## WHERE TO STAY AND WHERE TO EAT IN THE SURROUNDING AREA

🛏 ✕ **Cave Lodge** – เคฟลอดจ์ บ้านถ้ำ: about 9 kilometres (5.5 miles) north of Soppong, 200 metres from the village of Ban Tham and very close to the Tham Lod caves. You can either walk here, hitch a lift with a passing driver (not many of those round here) or hire a motorbike-taxi (☎ 619-024). There's a telephone in the village. The place itself is pretty extraordinary and the setting is unique, with rudimentary bamboo huts on stilts, in a group on the side of a hill overlooking the river. Mattresses on the floor, mosquito nets and a little terrace overlooking the water. Great for would-be Robinson

Crusoes even if some of the cabins, which sleep four, do have their own shower room. Inside the communal house there's a spacious lounge that opens to the outside. It has a fine, wooden floor scattered with cushions, long, low tables and a fire burning in the centre of the room. This place has a good feel, even if the Thai landlady can be a bit tough at times. Her Australian husband is one of the most seasoned explorers of the Tham Lod caves. You'll find plenty of large signs in English telling you what to do if you want to visit the caves, or go trekking in the surrounding area, either alone or with a guide. Plain, cheap food is also available.

🛏 ✕ **Lang River Guesthouse** – ลางริเวอร์เกสเฮาส์: on the river, less than 0.5 kilometres (a few hun-

dred yards) from the caves. ☎ 619-024 (to call a motorbike-taxi, use the telephone in the village). This group of wooden cabins on stilts was recently bought up by Mr Chalong, who smiles a lot and plans to make a better job of it than the previous owners. The bungalows are very simple, with two bedrooms and a shared shower room in between. Each room has a little terrace where you can sit and gaze at the languorous river. There's also a fine dormitory that sleeps about 30, and other classier bungalows under construction. The food is limited but good, prepared by the owner. In short, this place is well located, cheap, friendly and very well kept. It easily rivals the previous entry, which has tended to rest on its laurels.

## WHAT TO SEE IN THE SURROUNDING AREA

★ **The Tham Lod Caves** – ถ้ำลอด: quite close to the two previous entries. Open daily, 9am–5pm. Admission is free but a guide is compulsory. No more than four people to every one guide. The River Lang, which flows underground for 1 kilometre (0.5 miles), crosses the central artery of these huge caves. You'll find pretty good information in English at the entrance to the caves. Be warned, though, that it can be dangerous inside when the river swells. Only the first cave is accessible during the monsoon season.

Follow the guide (who wears flip-flops, although you should wear something sturdier) and discover a fascinating world of stalagmites, huge galleries and narrow tunnels – all very impressive. The guide will probably point out the most famous rocks. Use the wooden ladders (sometimes very rickety) to pull yourself up onto terrace-type ledges that lead to other galleries. The visit lasts a minimum of 2 hours and the price usually includes a tour of at least three lateral caves. The first two can be reached on foot but you have to take (and pay for) a bamboo raft to get to the third, which they close, of course, when the water-level rises. The artefacts found here (including bones, bronze jewellery and ceramics) suggest that these caves were inhabited a long time ago.

Today, they are home to flocks of bats, which congregate mainly in the second cave, which is the warmest chamber (and yes – those things on the ground that the guide is pointing out really are bat droppings). Seeing thousands of bats fly out of the cave at night is a sight not to be missed. It's positively magical. Sometimes they cross with swallows going the other way to spend the night in the caves. There is a path outside leading to a small temple.

★ From Soppong you can get to **Mae Lana,** a village lost in the midd a magnificent site about 16 kilometres (10 miles) from Tham Lod. You get there by car, but hardly anybody does because in scenery as spectacular as this, it's much more fun to walk.

You can also get there on the regular route from Mae Hong Son. About 15 kilometres (9 miles) before you reach Soppong, turn left and follow the road for 1.5 kilometres (1 mile), until you pass through a Lahu village. From there it's about 5 kilometres (3 miles) to Mae Lana. This Shan village, nestling in a natural basin filled with paddy fields, is centred on its beautiful Burmese-style temple. It also has a guesthouse (a bit pricey considering the accommodation). The other thing to say about Mae Lana is how nice it is to escape from the traditional tourist circuit and what a warm atmosphere it has. It's the sort of place where you'd like to linger a while. There are lots of walks in the surrounding area.

★ If you have the time to see them, this entire region abounds with tiny Red or Black **Lahu villages**. The people at Cave Lodge can explain how to get there.

# PAI – ปาย

DIALLING CODE: 054

Pai is a small, sleepy village with a quiet charm of its own, about 112 kilometres (70 miles) from Mae Hong Son. There aren't too many tourists here – yet. The surrounding region is magnificent and great for trekking in search of mountain tribes or long walks. It's perfect for just hanging out too – as others are beginning to discover, if the growing number of guesthouses is anything to go by. Travel agencies have started to sniff around here too. But Pai is well worth a visit and it's a good stopping point halfway to Mae Hong Son.

## GETTING THERE

Pai is on what's called the northern road, between Chiang Mai and Mae Hong Son. Buses going in both directions stop there and there are five buses a day. It takes about 4 hours to get here from Chiang Mai or Mae Hong Son, along a wonderfully rugged mountain road.

## ADDRESSES AND USEFUL INFORMATION

Ask at the guesthouse (Swan & Guy, for example) for the photocopied map of Pai and the surrounding region. It shows all the tribal villages and comes in very handy.

■ There's no tourist office but you'll find the **tourist police** (map, A2, **1**) in the main street.

■ **Thai Adventure** – ไทยแอด เวนเทอร์ (map, A2, **2**): in the main street. ☎ 699-111. Fax: 699-274. This agency is run by an amiable Frenchman (called Guy, otherwise known as 'Khun Ki') who can take you on interesting treks and, in particular, white-water rafting on rubber rafts on the Khong and Pai rivers. The other trek organizers all use traditional rafts. Guy's two-day rafting trips are for four people or more (leaving almost every day, July–February). The boats leave from Ban Khong (where they are kept and where you return to by car) and you spend one night in a bamboo camp. Guy has also launched hydro-speeding in the area.

✉ **Post office** – ไปรษณีย์ (map, A2): in the main street. Open Monday–Friday, 9.30am–5pm; Saturday 8.30–11.45am.

■ **Krung Thai Bank** – ธนาคาร กรุงไทย (map, B1, **4**): open Monday–Friday, 8.30am–3.30pm. It only exchanges cash and traveller's cheques, and the cash withdrawal facilities can be a bit

unreliable. Try to draw out cash somewhere else – but don't miss the incredible bazaar directly opposite.

■ **Motorbike hire** – เช่ารถมอเตอร์ ไซค์: some of the guesthouses have motorbikes for hire. Otherwise there's a large motorbike-hire place opposite the big market.

■ **Traditional massage** – นวดแผนโบราณ: near the river, not far from the bridge. ☎ 699-121. Mr Suttipong massages clients at home Monday–Friday, 4.30–8.30pm, Saturday and Sunday, 9am–8.30pm. Reasonable rates.

## WHERE TO STAY

Choose from an astonishing range of delightfully cheap and comfortable guesthouses. Let's hope the quality will remain the same as tourism increases.

### BUDGET TO MODERATE (50–300 BTS PER PERSON PER NIGHT)

⌂ **Charlie's House** – ชาลีส์เฮ้าส์ (map, B2, **10**): in a road at right angles to the main street. ☎ 699-039. Solidly built, unpretentious, cheap rooms, and some handsome bungalows called 'Sweet House' or 'Romantic House'. These are more expensive but also more comfortable. Also two recently redecorated dormitories. All very clean. A delightful setting in a lovingly kept garden, full of flowers. Often fully booked.

⌂ **Duang Guesthouse** – ดวงเกสท์ เฮ้าส์ (map, B1, **11**): opposite the bus stop. ☎ 699-101. Several rooms of varying levels of comfort in a stylish house surrounded by a small garden. The double rooms with bathroom and hot running water are very cheap but those without bathroom facilities are just as charming. There is also a small family flat with a kitchen

area and terrace for around 400 Bts. Spotlessly clean throughout. The landlady speaks a little English but the doves coo in Thai. Prices to suit every pocket. They also organize good treks here and hire out mountain bikes. Plus there's a board indicating the different points of interest in the area.

⌂ **Shan Guesthouse** – ชาญเกสท์ เฮ้าส์ (map, A2, **12**): south of town on the road to Chiang Mai. ☎ 699-122. An undeniably charming place, thanks to an astonishing reception area on stilts in the middle of a tiny lake. Dotted all around it, on an immense stretch of lawn, are nine bungalows with hot running water and five huts with WC. Each has its own terrace. Very pleasant.

⌂ **Pai River Lodge** – ปายริ เวอร์ลอดจ์ (map, B2, **13**): bamboo and leaf cabins on stilts in a meadow by the river, but close to the

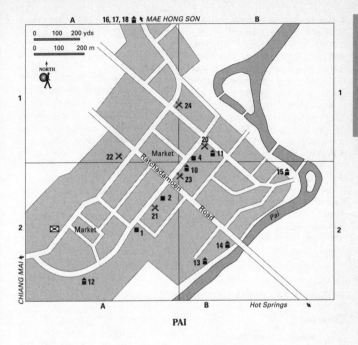

**PAI**

---

- **Useful Addresses**

  🛈 Post office
  **1** Tourist police
  **2** Thai Adventure
  **4** Krung Thai Bank

- **Where to Stay**

  **10** Charlie's House
  **11** Duang Guesthouse
  **12** Shan Guesthouse
  **13** Pai River Lodge

**14** P.S. Riverside & Orchid
       Guesthouse
**15** Rim Pai
**16** Pai Valley
**17** Pai Mountain Lodge
**18** Muang Pai Resort

✕ **Where to Eat**

**20** Duang Restaurant
**21** Swan & Guy
**22** Home Style Kitchen
**23** Market
**24** Prik Waan

---

'pulsating' town centre. Ideal for anyone who finds the pace of life too much in Pai. Basic, very cheap accommodation with mattresses on the floor and mosquito nets. A good place. The architecture of the main house (also bamboo and overlooking the river) is

pretty wild. Rooms on several storeys, mattresses on the floor as before. The whole place would be idyllic if it weren't right next door to a secondary school, which makes it quite noisy during the day. No telephone (but lots of mosquitoes).

⌂ **P.S. Riverside & Orchid Guest-house** – พี.เอส.ริเวอร์ไซด์แอนด์
ออร์คิดเกสท์เฮ้าส์ (map, B2, **14**):
☎ 699-159. A group of huts in the shape of an inverted 'V' in a quiet and welcoming garden, also by the river. Only two of the huts have bathrooms and hot running water. There are a few tables in an arbour at the water's edge. Time stands still in a place like this, and modern-day comforts are something you vaguely remember. The owners have just bought the former Pai Guesthouse (opposite), now the Orchid Guesthouse, which has about 12 slightly plusher rooms but no view of the river – you can't have everything. Decent Thai family cooking.

## EXPENSIVE (FROM 600 BTS PER PERSON PER NIGHT)

⌂ **Rim Pai** – ริมแพ (map, B2, **15**):
☎ 699-133. Fax: 699-234. Group of wooden bungalows not far from the river, arranged around a bar where breakfast is served. All of them have a (hot) shower room but some are more comfortable than others. The cheapest ones are in the long building. The more expensive ones have a view of the river and in the middle are some free-standing bungalows with a little terrace. A very pleasant, clean and quiet place offering excellent value for money.

## WHERE TO STAY IN THE SURROUNDING AREA

### EXPENSIVE

⌂ **Pai Valley** – ปายแวลเลย์ (off A1 on the map, **16**): about 2.5 kilometres (1.5 miles) from Pai, on the road to Mae Hong Son, on the right after the military base. The bus drives right past it and can drop you there or you can hire a mountain bike in Pai. The very nice lady owner, who speaks a few words of English, built her ideal guesthouse in the middle of what's virtually a botanical garden, full of flowers. The smart teak bungalows with sliding shutters and super-trendy pebble-dash bathrooms with hot shower are all pretty good. Less good is the relative closeness of the road and the absence of privacy in the bedrooms, separated only by thin walls. That said, the place is charming and you get to eat home-grown fruits for breakfast.

### SPLASH OUT

⌂ **Pai Mountain Lodge** – ปาย
เมาเทนลอดวช์(ทางไปน้ำโค้ก) (off A1 on the map, **17**): about 10 kilometres (6 miles) from Pai, not far from the falls. ☎ and fax: 699-068. You can cycle here if you're feeling brave, or come by motorbike. Go towards Mae Hong Son for about 7 kilometres (4 miles) then turn left (look out for the sign) and carry on for another 3 or 4 kilometres (2 or 3 miles) until you go through a little village. This extraordinary place is a few hundred metres from the falls on the left. It consists of at least 10 bungalows dotted around a little lake, in a lush, hilly area full of flowers that's wonderfully peaceful. Utterly charming and excellent accommodation for the price: wooden bungalows with brick fireplaces in the mini-lounge at the entrance, wood floor, mattresses on the floor, mosquito nets and hot shower. There are also two large houses that sleep up to 16 people. Large terraced restaurant on several levels. The owners organize one-day walks in the

region. Well worth staying here if you have the time.

⌂ **Muang Pai Resort** – เมืองปาย รีสอร์ท (off A1 on the map, **18**): right next door to the previous place. Book from Chiang Mai. ☎ 270-906. Fax: 272-895. This is another little piece of heaven peeking out from under the greenery: traditional bungalows separated by alleys, each with its own comfortable terrace; light, spacious rooms, all decorated with a personal touch, and tiled bathrooms – the kind of luxury hotel where you'd gladly stay put for a while. The rates here are a bit higher than in the previous place but entirely appropriate, given the wonderful setting with mountains on all sides. Under 14s stay free in their parents' room. Last but not least, the restaurant on the panoramic terrace serves delicious Thai food at prices that won't break the bank.

## WHERE TO EAT AND WHERE TO HAVE A DRINK

✕ **Duang Restaurant** – ร้านอาหารดวง (map, B1, **20**): adjoining the Duang Guesthouse, on the corner of the main street. Open 7am–8pm. Delicious Thai cooking with a touch of Burmese. Generous servings. The *Pad thaï* is first class and you must taste the *khao soï,* a local speciality that originated in Burma. Memorable fruit shakes too. The setting, on the other hand, is nothing special.

✕ **Swan & Guy** – ร้านอาหารสวอนแอนด์กาย (map, A2, **21**): in the main street and therefore very central. ☎ 699-274. Guy, the Frenchman who owns the Thai Adventure travel agency, married a young Thai called Swan, and has opened this agreeable restaurant for anyone nostalgic for a taste of French dishes: *gratin dauphinois*, and *entrecôte marchand de vin* (in a wine sauce), for example. Good food at reasonable prices. Also three rooms to let.

✕ **Home Style Kitchen** – ร้านอาหารโฮมไสตล์คิทเช่น (map, A1, **22**): just seconds from the main crossroads. Very cool-but-friendly teak house owned by a delightfully tripped-out young woman who invites you to carve your initials on the beams when you leave. You eat on the floor *kantoke*-style and despite all the candles and slightly New Age atmosphere, the Thai food is very good even if it is a bit spicy (particularly the curries). Ultra-cool all the same.

✕ In and around the little **market** – ตลาด (map, A2–B2, **23**) you'll find lots of little **food stands** serving local dishes. Some stay open quite late.

✕ **Prik Waan** – ร้านอาหารพริกหวาน (map, A1–B1, **24**): rather stylish restaurant in a recently built but elegant teak house in the centre of Pai. The Thai owners are originally from Bangkok. Beautifully prepared classical cuisine of repute at reasonable prices. On the opposite side of the street is the main 'hotbed' of nightlife in Pai:

♟ **Be Bop** – ร้านอาหารบีบ็อบ: this is where all the young people meet. R 'n' B-style jam-sessions every night unless otherwise specified.

♟ As you leave the bar walk about 200 metres back up the right-hand side of the street to check out the **Mountain Blue** – ร้านอาหารเมาเท่นบลู. Opening times are more variable than in the **Be Bop**.

## WHAT TO SEE AND DO IN THE SURROUNDING AREA

★ **Mo Paeng Falls** – น้ำตกหมอแป๋ง: about 10 kilometres (6 miles) north of Pai, on the road to the hospital. The waterfalls are lovely. Surrounded by forest on every side, they cascade into an inviting pool about 10 metres long by 5 metres wide (32 feet by 16 feet) filled with local children splashing about. It's hard to imagine a more perfect place for a dip. You reach the falls via a tiny Lahu village where mountain pigs frolic in semi-freedom. The shrubs that you see along the road are lychees.

★ About 5 kilometres (3 miles) further on, the **Chinese village of the Kuomintang** (KMT) is worth a visit. The inhabitants are former members of the Chinese Communist army who fought against Mao Zedong. Some of them fled to Burma where they now live off opium-trafficking. Others opted for a quieter life and grow crops in Thailand. Originally they built all their houses of adobe but these days they tend to favour more solid materials.

At the entrance to the village where the road forks, turn right and head towards the falls. Even in a four-wheel-drive this track is almost impassable. A better idea is to head for Pai Mountain Lodge (on the road to Mae Hong Son) and after about 7 kilometres (4 miles) turn left towards the hotel – it's signposted for about 1–2 kilometres (0.5–1 mile) of bad road, so get out and walk. It's not so pretty this way of course, but at least it's possible.

★ **Tha Pai Hot Springs** – น้ำพุร้อน: about 7 kilometres (4 miles) south of Pai. Follow the road to the Mae Yen temple and look out for the wooden sign to the springs. Stay on this path for 1 kilometre (just over 0.5 miles) until you come to a little forest and a warm stream of sulphurous water where you can bathe, water temperature permitting. The springs are at the edge of the stream and they're boiling, so much so that picnickers sometimes hard-boil their eggs in the water. Blissfully quiet, birds singing in the trees and the chance of a warm dip – what could be more agreeable to while away a lazy afternoon? Not many people know about these springs yet so make the most of them while you still can.

Just before the falls there's a family with two elephants who can take you elephant riding.

★ **Trekking**: most of the treks organized by the guesthouses are two- to five-day trips and may or may not include a chance to go rafting. The level of organization varies. On some treks you can shoot the rapids on a bamboo raft. Duang Guesthouse organizes a one-day walk to various Lisu and Lahu villages and some waterfalls, and a three-day trek that includes an elephant ride and rafting. You can always ask Guy Gorias for his advice too (*see* Thai Adventure, under 'Addresses and Useful Information').

A serious word of warning about heroin: it seems that some trek organizers see to it that when you stop for the night someone in the village offers you a cheap fix. Don't be tempted.

If you're travelling by motorbike, there are some great things to see in the area around Pai (always look at a map). Ask when you get there. *See also* the section above on Trekking by Motorbike under 'Treks in the Mountains'.

## LEAVING PAI

– **For Mae Hong Son** or **Chiang Mai**: four buses daily, 8.30am–4pm (about a 4-hour journey).

# FROM MAE HONG SON TO MAE SARIANG

This road – the road going south – is faster and less mountainous than the one via Pai. The selected route starts at Mae Hong Son. If you start from Chiang Mai, you won't go through places in the same order.

Regular buses take this road on average seven times a day in both directions (*see* regional map). It takes just 8 hours to go about 350 kilometres (215 miles).

The region you travel through on leaving Mae Hong Son is full of Karens – White, Red and Black.

About 20 kilometres (12 miles) after the hot springs, where the villagers come to do their washing (roughly 15 kilometres/9 miles away, on the right), there's a road on the left by a small hotel. This road leads to two villages. The first is a remote, tiny Karen village: look for a path on the left, about 3 kilometres (2 miles) from the junction. The second – just under 5 kilometres (3 miles) further on – is home to some eight or ten Hmong families who live as they have always done in traditional single-storey houses with mud floors. Their heavily embroidered black clothes are also traditional.

Despite being easy to get to thanks to a made-up road leading to a television relay on top of the mountain, these two villages are as yet largely untouched by tourism, with all the plus and minus factors that this implies. You are in unfamiliar territory here, so treat the people with respect, keep smiling and everything will be all right. There are lots of similar villages off most of the main roads.

# KHUN YUAM – ขุนยวม          DIALLING CODE: 053

Khun Yuam is a modest market town that stretches out in a long, straight line about 73 kilometres (43 miles) south of Mae Hong Son. It's well away from anywhere, close to the Union of Myanmar (although the border is closed) and is a useful stopping-place on the road going south, for all the usual town services (post office, shops, police etc.). It also has a rather curious museum of the Japanese occupation during World War II. Close by are waterfalls, a church built by a Korean missionary and a pretty temple.

## WHERE TO STAY AND WHERE TO EAT

🛏 ✕ **Ban Farang Guesthouse** – บ้านฝรั่งเกสท์เฮ้าส์: just before the entrance to the town – follow the signs. ☎ 622-086. This guesthouse, previously owned by a now-deceased Frenchman (the *farang* or foreigner in question), is run by his widow. It consists of several solid-looking buildings arranged around a garden, including some very agreeable bungalows with hot running water, though these cost more than the bedrooms. Warm welcome and very good service. The bedrooms are clean and pleasant even if the tiling is grim. There's also a pretty and cheap dormitory above the terraced restaurant on stilts that serves delicious Thai food and a limited range of Western dishes in memory of the former owner.

## WHAT TO SEE

★ **Local Centre Hill-Japanese Tools** – พิพิธภัณฑ์ของเล่นญี่ปุ่น: at the entrance to Khun Yuam. This rather confusing museum with its limited display of rusty artefacts (bodies of old cars, weapons and clothing) recalls the agricultural history of the region and in particular, the period of Japanese occupation. There's not much information in English.

## WHAT TO SEE IN THE SURROUNDING AREA

★ **Wat To Phae** – วัดต่อแพ: Burmese-style temple in a hamlet about 4 kilometres (2.5 miles) from the village. Follow the road opposite the temple, past the Catholic church. The thing to see in this temple, tucked away in a little room on the left, is the beautiful tapestry encrusted with precious stones.

★ **Mae Surin** – น้ำตกแม่สุรินทร์: you can only get here by four-wheel-drive and it takes all day, but if you're prepared to make the effort, these falls, at 240 metres (1,200 feet) high, are the highest in the country. They're about 40 kilometres (25 miles) from Khun Yuam and only accessible by dirt track.

# MAE SARIANG – แม่สะเรียง   DIALLING CODE: 053

Mae Sariang is about 90 kilometres (56 miles) further up, on the River Yuam and slightly set back from the road. On the way you go through the village of Mae La Noi – there's not much to say about it except that it has a good hospital.

The town of Mae Sariang has grown up around a crossroads where three-coloured traffic lights were recently installed. Most of the 4,000 people who live here are Shan and Thai. You'll notice that there are a great many hotels here; Mae Sariang is a busy market town and a compulsory port-of-call for every travelling salesman and trucker in the area. On a more relevant note, this is also where the local mountain people come to do their shopping, and the town itself is very much as it has always been. And there's one hotel here that really deserves a mention.

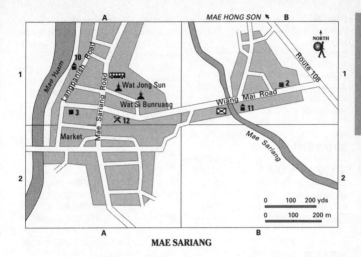

**MAE SARIANG**

---

| ■ Useful Addresses | ≜ Where to Stay |
|---|---|
| ✉ Post office | **10** Riverside Guesthouse |
| **2** Hospital | **11** Mitra Ree Hotel |
| **3** Thai Farmers Bank | |
| 🚆 Train station | ✕ **Where to Eat** |
| | **12** Intira Restaurant |

---

## USEFUL ADDRESSES

■ **Wiang Mai Road** leads into town from the main road, and that's where you'll find the **post office** (map, B1), the **hospital** (map, B1, **2**) and a branch of the **Thai Farmers Bank** (map, A1, **3**) with currency exchange facilities, open 8.30am–3.30pm. There's a Visa cash machine opposite the Intira restaurant.

🚆 **Train station** (map, A1): Mae Sariang Road.

## WHERE TO STAY AND WHERE TO EAT

≜ ✕ **Riverside Guesthouse** – ริเวอร์ไซด์เกสท์เฮาส์ (map, A1, **10**): 85 Langpanish Road. ☎ 681-188. A double room costs about 70–200 Bts. This is a wonderful place. It's a wooden house, set back from the centre and on the water as its name suggests, with delightfully simple, spacious and uncluttered rooms which have a shared shower room. All the rooms face the river, which you get to over a little beach planted with coconut palms. The restaurant serves breakfast and a range of basic dishes, and you can eat while gazing out at the lazy River Yuam. Maybe that's why this place con-

veys such a sense of tropical in-
dolence. Warm welcome.

⌂ **Mitra Ree Hotel** – มิตรอารีย์
โฮเต็ล (map, B1, **11**): Mae Sariang
Road. ☎ 681-109. Fax: 681-280.
Should the previous place happen
to be fully booked, try for a room in
this hotel complex rather than in
the other guesthouses. Prices in
the Mitra Ree start from about
150–400 Bts for a simple room in
the old buildings, or an air-conditioned room in the main building,
which is rather fun with its blue
balustrade, or a luxury bungalow
set back from the others with a
view of the paddy and soya fields.
It has about 100 rooms in all.
There's a little market close by,
with local restaurants.

✕ **Intira Restaurant** – ร้านอา
หารอินทิรา (map, A1, **12**): Wiang
Mai Road. Open daily, 8am–9pm.
There's a choice of dining areas: a
noisy one that opens onto the
street or a closed, air-conditioned
one. There's also a good choice of
excellent, carefully prepared local
dishes including the giant frogs
that local fishermen catch in the
autumn. Bear in mind, though, that
these frogs are a protected species.

✕ The **Renu Restaurant** opposite – ร้านอาหารเรนู – with its rather
kitsch decor specializes in 'wild'
food, including boar and curried
green-and-black woodpecker.
Like the giant frogs, both species
are fairly rare these days.

## WHAT TO SEE

★ The **Wat Si Bunruang** – วัดศรีบุญเรือง and **Wat Jong Sun** – วัดจองสุ่น
(map, A1) are the two most beautiful temples in Mae Sariang. They date
from the 19th century and practically touch each other. While both are in
the Burmese style, there is something quite unique about their recessed
architecture. There are painted *chedis* in front of the more classical Wat
Jong Sun.

★ **The market**: however small the village, the local market is always a
feast of colour, noise and smell. Carry on a bit further and you come to
the bridge over the River Yuam – guarded by two other temples of no
great architectural interest.

# FROM MAE SARIANG TO CHIANG MAI

Route 108 is a well-marked, well-maintained road that drops north from
Mae Hong Son, turns west into Mae Sariang then continues east and
northwards for 190 kilometres (118 miles) to Chiang Mai.

It you're travelling by bus it won't be easy to stop and visit the sites
described below. The distances shown are from Mae Sariang in each
case.

★ 18 kilometres (11 miles): **Thong Bua Ton** (also called **Doi Mae Ho**) is a
mountain you shouldn't miss if you're travelling between October and
December, when the sides are a gorgeous riot of Mexican sunflowers, as
featured on postcards throughout the country.

★ 91 kilometres (56 miles): the **Obluang Gorge**, formed by the Mae

Chaen river, with its impressive little wooden bridge, offers a range of amenities including a picnic area, campsite, swimming and a history trail that takes you past carvings and tombs made by the men who lived here 7–8,000 years ago. Modest admission charge.

★ 105 kilometres (65 miles): the **Hot** village left no lasting impression.

★ 142 kilometres (88 miles): the village of **Chom Thong** is more interesting, with its temple and a magnificent *chedi* housing an important relic of the Buddha. This is the focal point of a big celebration held in the village at the June full moon.

✕ Just behind the temple are several **food stands** serving genuine local food. Point to what you want and don't hesitate to taste things you like the look of. Steer clear of the raw meat and pig's blood soup if you have a weak stomach. Lots of spicy booze.

★ 150 kilometres (93 miles): as you leave **Chom Thong** there's quite a good road on the left leading to **Doi Ithanon**. This is the highest peak in the country (2,590 metres/8,497 feet) and it's in the middle of a national park that is a place of refuge for rare species. The army prevents all access to the top but there's no shortage of other walks. Doi Ithanon is 100 kilometres (62 miles) away and you can get there in a *songthaew* from Chom Thong.

★ 190 kilometres (118 miles): you enter Chiang Mai from the south.

## FROM CHIANG MAI TO CHIANG RAI

There are two ways of getting to Chiang Rai – either take a bus that goes there directly or do what everybody else does and take the bus from Chiang Mai as far as **Thaton** then get out and take a boat down the River Kok to Chiang Rai.

The journey is described here going one way only, but you can also reverse it and go from Chiang Rai to Thaton. If you do that, however, you have no choice but to catch the bus to Chiang Mai, as there's no direct bus from Thaton to Chiang Rai (so you have to take a *songthaew* from Thaton to Fang then a bus from Fang to Chiang Rai). The best way of getting to Chiang Rai from Chiang Mai is by dugout.

# TRIP ON THE RIVER KOK

### GETTING THERE

All the dugouts leave from **Thaton** – ท่าตอน (177 kilometres/110 miles from Chiang Mai). To get there, catch an early-morning bus from the Chang Puak bus station on Chang Puak Road. There are six buses daily, the first one at 6am and the next usually at 7.20am. They take from 3 hours 30 minutes to 4 hours, so you get to Thaton in plenty of time for a leisurely stroll and lunch before the 12.30pm dugout departure. All the official dugouts leave from the jetty, which is 200 metres on the Thaton side of the bridge on the right. These times are liable to change, of course, so check in Chiang Mai before leaving.

If you're travelling in a group of about 8–10 people and don't get to Thaton too late, it's worth hiring a private dugout, in which case you should arrange with the pilot to stop along the way. For reasons that aren't clear, even the private dugouts leave at 12.30pm.

– Doing the trip the other way is highly impractical but directions are as follows. Take an early-morning bus for Chiang Rai where dugouts leave for Thaton at about 10.30am and get you in at about 2.30pm. By that time the last bus back to Chiang Mai has left and since there's no bus from Thaton to Chiang Rai (unless you go by way of Fang which takes longer) you have to spend the night in Thaton.

## THE TRIP DOWNRIVER

The source of the river Mae Kok is high up in the mountains of the Burmese province of Shan. Lots of tribes live all along the river.

You sail downriver in a tapering wooden dugout in which you're uncomfortably squashed at the bottom, with the sides of the boat cutting into your back. It takes about 3 hours to get to Chiang Rai and 4 hours to go the other way (including stops at police checkpoints). Bring water, biscuits in case you get hungry and something to protect your head from the sun as you speed down river.

## IS IT WORTH IT?

Backpackers are fiercely divided as to the relative merits of the trip down the River Kok. Some will tell you it's great – others that it's a rip-off. The truth is that the weather has a lot to do with it. If it rains solidly for 4 hours and you reach Chiang Rai with your teeth chattering and a pain in your back, then you're unlikely to be impressed. But you'll feel quite different after a sunny trip made in good company. Some people also say that the scenery becomes monotonous after a while, and others enjoy the constant flow of subtle variations in landscape and changing colours. Take a good book just in case.

For many it's worth making the trip just for the exotic experience of riding in a dugout. The amount of backwash depends on the time of year. In the dry season when the water level drops too low, passengers often have to get out to make the boat lighter. In the rainy season, the river swells so much that the rapids are hardly noticeable. There's also a brief interval, before and after the rainy season, when the river is level with the rocks and the degree of backwash can be quite significant. At certain times of the year, it's uncrowded and all the better for it or it can be a case of rent-a-mob.

Most people agree on three points: it's a bit expensive, a bit long and a bit touristy. It isn't surprising to find loads of touts waiting to greet you as you arrive in Chiang Rai. Note that the boat drops you about 1.5 kilometres (1 mile) from the centre (you'll find *samlors* and *tuk-tuks* waiting at the landing stage).

## USEFUL INFORMATION

– Before boarding you have to sign the police book in the kiosk by the bridge (open 8.30am–4.30pm).

– There are motorbike-taxis waiting to greet the bus (on the opposite side of the river to the departure point for dugouts).

– Next to the dugout's departure point is a shop where you can buy a very useful brochure called *Welcome to the Hill Tribes*. This includes a map showing the positions of the various tribes. Useful for anyone who wants to get to know the region better.

## ★ THATON

The town is rather attractively situated at the foot of a hill crowned by an imposing Buddha. There has been a considerable increase in the number of tourists who go trekking from here, probably because the surrounding countryside is wilder than around Chiang Mai.

## WHERE TO STAY IN THATON

### BUDGET TO MODERATE (60–250 BTS PER PERSON PER NIGHT)

🛏 **Thip's Travellers' House 1** – ทิปส์ทราเวลเลอร์เฮ้าส์: just before the bridge, on the left. ☎ 459-312. Modest rooms built out of semi-permanent materials, all with fan and cold water – a hot shower and WC cost extra. Small, terrace restaurant overlooking the water. Good breakfast. The landlords organize one- to three-day river treks in floating bamboo cabins, with visits to settlements on the river and usually an elephant ride as well. The guide, who's also the landlady's nephew, speaks English.

🛏 **Chankasem Guesthouse** – จันเกษมเกสท์เฮ้าส์: bungalow with cold shower, fan and WC facing the landing stage but without a view of the river. Decent, but nothing special. More of the same next door.

🛏 **Garden Home** – การ์เด้น โฮมเกสท์เฮ้าส์: go past the bridge and take the path immediately on the left that follows the river. The guesthouse is a few minutes' walk away, on the left, not far from the Mae Kok River Lodge. Great place in a quiet location, with a large garden and a splendid lawn planted with lychee trees. The amiable owner has built some charming bamboo bungalows all with comfortable beds and WC. Free shower outside. You'll even find hens clucking in a corner. Coffee-shop.

### EXPENSIVE (FROM 600 BTS PER PERSON PER NIGHT)

🛏 **Mae Kok River Lodge** – แม่กกริเวอร์ลอดจ์: beyond the bridge, take the path immediately on the left that follows the river. You can book from Chiang Mai (☎ 215-824) or when you get to Thaton (☎ 459-328). Magnificent building of teak and bamboo, run by a huge Irishman who used to be a professional diver. Very stylish and expensive place for people with a taste for adventure who don't like roughing it and who always keep a credit card handy. There's even a little zoo not far from the hotel with a few gibbons. Sadly none of the rooms overlooks the river, unlike the magnificent terrace restaurant. There used to be a little garden with a pretty swimming pool until the authorities closed it down. It seems that the spectacle of people in bathing costumes was considered insulting to the enormous Buddha on top of the mountain. Instead of the pool, there's now an altar for the piously-minded, and for the more practically-minded, a detailed record of all the walks in the area. They also organize treks here.

## WHERE TO EAT IN THATON

✕ **Apple Restaurant** – ร้านอาหาร–รแอปเปิ้ล: opposite the landing stage. ☎ 373-144. Unpretentious bamboo seating and good, plain, cheap Thai food served with a smile. Definitely the best place to eat round here. The restaurant overlooks the landing stage so you can eat here while you wait for the dugout to depart. There are also a few basic but very comfortable rooms to rent.

✕ **Tha Ton River View** – ท่าตอนริเวอร์วิว: luxury hotel on the river, on the other side of the bridge. It's included here mainly because of its restaurant and wonderfully stylish terrace where you can go for a drink or, if you've got the money, a first-class dinner. Run by two sisters who clearly have a good head for business. Incredible setting – the place opens onto a little branch of the river where bamboo rafts are sometimes moored.

## TREKKING IN THE SURROUNDING AREA

Most of the tribes (Lahu, Karen, Lisu and Akha) live within 1 or 2 hours' walk of the river but there are also some Karen and Lahu settlements quite close to the river. This means that you can hire a dugout and guide to explore the area. This isn't cheap, but it's worth it for the sense of adventure.

# CHIANG RAI – เชียงราย   DIALLING CODE: 053

Chiang Rai is the rather dull capital of the province of the same name. It's a small town with nothing much happening, although there's been a recent and unprecedented boom in the property market. The outskirts are now full of big buildings and the town itself has taken on a sad, concrete look – not somewhere to linger for more than a day. However, this is also the jumping-off point for treks into the Golden Triangle, an area that is no longer virgin territory but which remains uniquely beautiful and is a sensational place to explore by motorbike.

Chiang Rai is said to have been founded in 1262 by King Mengrai after the elephant he was hunting on stopped dead in its tracks in this very place. Eventually, the king chose to live in Chiang Mai instead (probably a wise move). The kingdoms of Chiang Rai and Sukhothai were rivals for a long time. The town of Chiang Rai is strategically placed, very close to the borders with Laos and the Union of Myanmar but there are few remaining traces of its past today.

## GETTING THERE

– **By bus**: there are lots of buses from Chiang Mai Arcade bus station that leave more or less every hour from about 6am to 5pm.

– **By air**: two flights a day from Chiang Mai and three or four from Bangkok.

– **By dugout**: down the River Kok from Thaton (*see* 'Trip on the River Kok').

## USEFUL ADDRESSES

### Tourist information and communications

**TAT** – ททท (Tourist Office; map, B2): Singhaklai Road. ☎ 717-433 and 744-674. Open daily, 8.30am–4.30pm. Brochures in English, list of guesthouses, bus timetables, trekking information and more.

■ **Tourist police** – ตำรวจท่องเที่ยว ททท: on the ground floor of the Office of Tourism on Singhaklai

Road. ☎ 717-779. Emergency: ☎ 16-99 day and night.

■ **Chiang Rai Telecommunication** – ศูนย์โทรศัพท์ (map, A2, **1**): Ngam Muang Road. Ultra-modern telecommunications centre, open daily, 7am–10pm (but closed noon–1pm and 6pm–7pm). Inter-

---

■ **Useful Addresses**

- **TAT**
- ✉ Post office and telephone
- ✈ Airport
- 🚌 Bus station
- **1** Chiang Rai Telecommunication
- **2** Thai Airways
- **3** Thai Military Bank
- **4** Overbrooke Hospital
- **5** Pharmacy
- **6** D.K. Book House

▲ **Where to Stay**

- **10** Chian House
- **11** Mae Hong Son Guesthouse of Chiang Rai
- **12** Chat House
- **13** Mae Kok Villa
- **14** White House Guesthouse
- **16** Bowling Guesthouse
- **17** Ben Guesthouse

**19** Boon Bun Dan Guesthouse
**20** Ruang Nakorn Hotel
**21** The Golden Triangle

✕ **Where to Eat**

**21** Golden Triangle Restaurant
**29** Market
**30** Nakhon Pathom
**31** Noi
**32** Mae Oui Kuew
**33** Loy Fa Sea Food
**34** T. Hut
**35** Ton Kao
**36** Wonton Suki
**37** Ga-re Ga-ron

🍷 **Where to Have a Drink**

**40** Station Saloon
**41** Co Coon Pub
**42** Sabun-Nga Pub & Restaurant
**43** Inncome Hotel

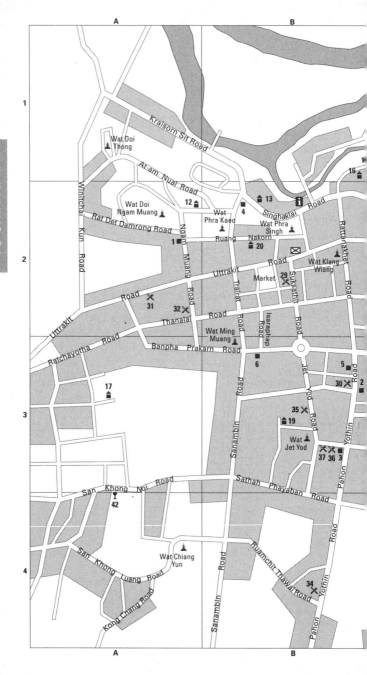

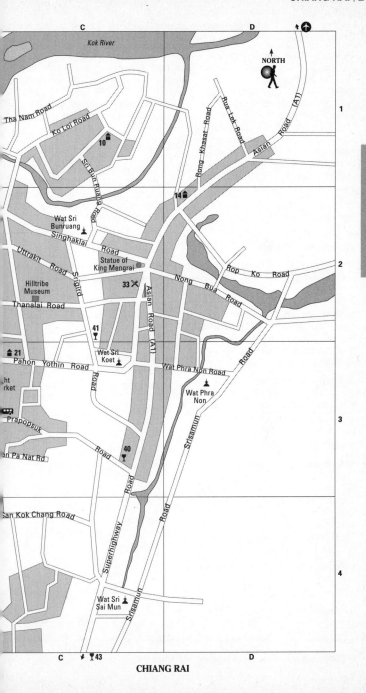

**CHIANG RAI**

national calls, fax and more, at the cheapest rates in town.

**✉ Post office and telephone** – ไปรษณีย์ (map, B2): Uttrakit Road, on the corner with Tha Luang Road. Open Monday–Friday, 8.30am–4.30pm, Saturday 9am–noon. Telephone exchange upstairs, open daily, 7am–10pm. There are some private houses in town (on Thaton Pemavipat) where you can make calls while the owners time you on a stopwatch. Reasonable rates on the whole.

**✈ Airport** – ท่าอากาศยาน (off D1 on the map): ☎ 793-048. 10 kilo-metres (6 miles) north of the town centre. No bus, so take a *tuk-tuk* or taxi.

■ **Thai Airways** – สายการบินไทย (map, B3, **2**): 870 Pahon Yothin Road. ☎ 711-179 or 715-734. Open 8am–5pm; closed at weekends. Their number at the airport: ☎ 793-048.

■ **D.K. Book House** – ร้านขายหนังสือดี.เค.ดวงกมล (map, B3, **6**): 413/1 Banpha Prakarn Road. Specializes in books on Thailand, maps and mini-dictionaries. Not as much choice as in the shop in Chiang Mai.

## Currency Exchange

There are lots of places where you can exchange money or withdraw cash using a credit card. The places below are all close to Thai Airways.

■ **Thai Military Bank** – ธนาคารทหารไทย (map, B3, **3**): 870/12, Pahon Yothin Road. Open daily, 8.30am–8pm. Visa cash withdrawal facilities.

■ **Siam Commercial Bank** – ธนาคารไทยพาณิชย์: 573 Rattanaket Road. Open Monday–Friday, 8.30am–3.30pm. Hole-in-the-wall cash machine outside, in use 7am–11pm.

■ **Thai Farmers Bank** – ธนาคารกสิกรไทย: 537 Banpha Prakarn Road. Open daily, 7am–8pm. Visa cash withdrawal facilities. Another branch at 869/166 Pahon Yothin Road.

## Health

■ **Overbrooke Hospital** – โรงพยาบาลโอเวอร์บรุ๊ค (map, B2, **4**): on the corner of Singhaklai Road and Trairat Road. ☎ 711-366. This is the old Chiang Rai hospital, which is much better than the new one.

■ **Sriburin Hospital** – โรงพยาบาลศรีบุรินทร์: the new hospital, on the superhighway going towards the old airport. ☎ 717-499.

■ **Pharmacy** – ร้านขายยา (map, B3, **5**): 541/1 Pahon Yothin Road, almost opposite the Pizza Napoli. Open daily, 7am–9pm. Some English spoken.

## TRANSPORT

### In town

– **Bicycle *samlors***: good for going short distances.

– **Motorbike hire**: a great way of exploring the area is by motorbike. Lots of places to hire motorbikes in the main street, and you can often hire one through the guesthouse.

– *Songthaews*: in Chiang Rai, these are small blue vans (red in Chiang Mai). They operate like *tuk-tuks* but they also pick people up on the way. Much cheaper than the other forms of transport.

– *Tuk-tuks*: convenient and fast but incredibly expensive, particularly here where the drivers try it on and charge the most outrageous rates. Be firm about the price.

**In the surrounding area**

🚌 **Buses**: all air-conditioned and non-air-conditioned buses leave from the one bus station (map, C3) on Prapopsuk Road, on the corner with Pahon Yothin Road. There's no main telephone number. Private bus operators are also represented at the bus station. Buses depart approximately every 30 minutes for all the villages in the north, including Mae Salong, Mae Sai, Mae Chan, the Golden Triangle and Chiang Saen.

– **Pick-up vans**: at least 50 of these leave early in the morning from the central market on Suksathit Road, almost on the corner of Uttarakit Road. They are the only form of public transport to all the little villages and hamlets in the north where the buses don't go. You can also hire one for the day and make a grand tour of the region – but be sure to fix the price with the driver before setting off.

## WHERE TO STAY

There are lots of good-quality guesthouses and practically all of them organize treks or trips to villages in the north or the Golden Triangle. There are plenty of places to visit without a guide – but remember, too, that it's easy to get lost.

### BUDGET (100–200 BTS PER PERSON PER NIGHT)

🛏 **Chian House** – เชียนเกสท์เฮ้าส์ (map, C1, **10**): 172 Sri Bunruang Road. ☎ 713-388. Take a *tuk-tuk* or *samlor* the first time you go to this guesthouse – it's simpler. Outstanding place for the price, particularly since it has a pool – and not just a glorified paddling pool either, but a real, full-size swimming pool with water in it. Otherwise the layout rather lacks charm with rather dull single rooms at garden level, but they all have warm shower and WC. Also two bungalows and two small detached houses with large family rooms at around 300 Bts. Pleasant atmosphere and good home-cooking. Guesthouses with swimming pools are few and far between.

🛏 **Mae Hong Son Guesthouse of Chiang Rai** – แม่ฮ่องสอนเกสท์ เฮ้าส์เชียงราย (map, B1, **11**): 126 Singhaklai Road. ☎ 715-367. A nice little wooden house not far from the road that follows the river, in the north of town. Go past the tourist office on your left, turn left into a little *soi* and ask for directions. The guesthouse is actually very close by, but you haven't a hope of finding it in this network of *sois*, especially if the building works are still going on. Delightful little garden with rocks, a fountain, bamboo and tables where you can sit and take your time over delicious meals. Nine bedrooms upstairs, some too small but all pretty despite the lino floor. Have a look at more than one. Free use of the warm shower outside; very clean shared WCs. Friendly place with a genuine atmosphere. Motorbikes can be hired here, too, and they also organize treks. You can buy a very detailed map of the region, which even specifies the tribes that live in each village.

⚓ **Chat House** – ชาติเกสท์เฮ้าส์ (map, A2, **12**): 3/2 Soi Sang Kaeo Trirat Road. ☎ 711-481. Maze of little streets in a working-class area that's plainly popular with *samlor* drivers. Warm welcome; pleasantly shambolic atmosphere; lawn and small, shady terrace. Rooms are clean and quiet but rather small; some have fan, and some a shower. There's also a triple room at very reasonable rates and a cheap four-bed dormitory for single people. The treks organized by the landlord's family are said to be quite good. Bike hire and restaurant service.

⚓ **Mae Kok Villa** – แม่กกวิลล่า (Chiang Rai Youth Hostel) – บ้านพักเยาวชนเชียงราย; map, B2, **13**): 445 Singhaklai Road. ☎ 711-786. Very close to the river (although you can't really see it) and about 5 minutes from the tourist office. Neither a hotel nor a guesthouse, but a sort of large, half-brick-half-teak building opposite what was once a green space, sheltered from the road by a large, ordinary-looking house. About 30, stylish and even plush rooms, all spacious and relatively well kept, with private bathroom facilities (cold water only in the case of the cheapest ones). The rooms at the back are much better than those in the annexe. A touch more expensive here than in the last place but still very good quality for the money. There are also large, cheap dormitories in the house in front for hard-up groups. No breakfast.

⚓ **White House Guesthouse** – ไวท์เฮาส์เกสท์เฮาส์ (map, D2, **14**): 789 Pahon Yothin Road. ☎ 744-051. Fax: 713-427. Don't be put off by the road, which happens to be the superhighway (all the rooms are well protected from the noise) nor by the Singha brewery, whose porch you have to pass under to reach the guesthouse. The landlord here is an easy-going, friendly chap from India. Basic, decent rooms with shower room (hot water) at reasonable prices. Good food, lots of it and the treks (particularly going out towards Laos) are supposed to be good.

⚓ **Bowling Guesthouse** – โบว์ลิ่งเกสท์เฮ้าส์ (map, B1, **16**): 399 Singhaklai Road. ☎ 712-704. Small-scale family guesthouse in a well-kept garden close to the River Kok. Very welcoming landlady. Four bedrooms with cold shower only, at very reasonable rates.

All along the river you'll find guest-houses that provide simple, cheap accommodation – all much of a muchness.

## MODERATE (200–500 BTS PER PERSON PER NIGHT)

⚓ **Ben Guesthouse** – เบญเกสท์เฮ้าส์ (map, A3, **17**): 351/10 Ratchayotha Road, Soi 1 or San Khong Luang Road, Soi 4. ☎ 716-775. Magnificent wooden house, built in the very pretty northern Thai style. Rooms with hot shower and WC – some of the rooms opening onto the corridor are noisy. Lots of charming details: carved teak pillars; balcony on the terrace where it's pleasant to sit and have a drink. Not many places offer such good value for money, even if the garden is a bit neglected. By the way, the guesthouse was named 'Ben' after the owners' son, who was born the same year it opened. Run by a very obliging family who usually send a van to meet guests from the boat and to drum up business. They also organize good treks.

**Chai House** – ชัยเฮาส์, 27 San Khong Noi Road, Soi 2, owned by the same family, is where guests are sent when the Ben Guesthouse is full. A bit cheaper, but not such an attractive setting and the rooms are minuscule.

⌂ **Boon Bun Dan Guesthouse** – บุญบันดาลเกสท์เฮ้าส์ (map, B3, **19**): 1005/13 Jet Yod Road. ☎ 717-040 or 041. Fax: 712-914. Two fairly inelegant buildings that face each other in a quiet little street near the Wat Jet Yod. The one on the left is old but clean (ask for a room upstairs – they're lighter and not so damp); the one on the right is newer, built of red brick and the rooms are more expensive. In the middle is a garden surrounded by some little wooden houses with fans, at very reasonable rates. There's something to suit every taste and every pocket. The price includes breakfast. Airport and bus station transfer facilities available (not included in the price). They also organize treks here. A good place to stay.

⌂ **Ruang Nakorn Hotel** – เรืองนคร โฮเต็ล (map, B2, **20**): 25 Ruang Nakorn Road. ☎ 711-566. A central place, included here for those who want more formal accommodation but who are allergic to guesthouses. Concrete hotel of Stalinist charm with warm shower and air-conditioning. Avoid the dark, stuffy rooms on the ground floor. Ask instead for one of the large rooms at rock bottom prices, for four people, with fan, hot shower and WC. Those with air-conditioning are practically double the price. Clean despite the relatively poor state of repair.

## EXPENSIVE (FROM 600 BTS PER PERSON PER NIGHT)

⌂ **The Golden Triangle** – เดอะโกล เด้นไทรเองเกิล (map, C3, **21**): 590 Pahon Yothin Road. Near the bus terminal. ☎ 711-339. Fax: 713-963. Lovely hotel with bags of charm, flawlessly furnished and absolutely spotless. Traditional rooms with all mod cons including bath, and smart, red hexagonal floor tiles. Some of the management speak English. The best place in this town in this category. Treat yourself if the exchange rate is good or if you have the money anyway. Good stylish restaurant, described below.

## WHERE TO EAT

### BUDGET

– Most of the guesthouses serve good home-cooked food but apart from that there are not many decent places to eat.

✗ **In the market** – ตลาด (map, B2, **29**): towards 11am or noon, there are lots of food stands in the central market that serve typical Thai food for next to nothing. It's

the best place to eat – full of steaming cauldrons with intoxicating smells. Behind the market, a Chinese Buddha guards the entrance to a strange-looking temple.

✗ **Nakhon Pathom** – ร้านอา หารนครปฐม (map, B3, **30**): 869/25-26 Pahon Yothin Road. Open daily, 7am–3pm. No sign in English, but it's practically opposite

Thai Airways. Look for the blue plastic seating and you can't miss it. Good working-class meals at reasonable prices. There are food stands on either side of the entrance – rice on the right, noodles on the left.

✕ **Noi** – ร้านอาหารน้อย (map, A2, **31**): Uttrakit Road (opposite the Chiang Rai Condotel). Open daily, 7am–2pm. Tiny cheap place to eat, slightly set back from the centre. The lady owner serves nice little vegetarian dishes for a handful of bahts. There's no sign in English here either but like the previous place, look for the blue plastic.

✕ **Mae Oui Kuew** – ร้านอาหารแม อุ๊ยเขียว (map, A2, **32**): Ngam Muang Road. Agreeable, working-class restaurant with a bamboo roof not far from the flower market. No menu, but a range of mess-tins where you can help yourself. Typically northern cuisine with a Burmese influence – spicy, in other words.

## MODERATE

✕ **Loy Fa Sea Food** – ร้านอา หารลอยฟ้าซีฟู้ด (map, C2, **33**): 897/11 Pahon Yothin Road. Open daily, 6pm–4am. Weird place run by a Chinese guy, opposite one end of the old, rebuilt walls. There's no sign in English, but look for tables on the pavement, fake marble and waiters dressed up as waitresses. Choose from anything that swims, whether fish or shellfish, served boiled, fried or in a sauce. Curious atmosphere, without any doubt, but somewhere to go late at night. The food is good, but it can work out quite expensive ordering fish by weight.

✕ **T. Hut** – ร้านอาหารที.ฮัท (map, B4, **34**): 937/3 Pahon Yothin Road. ☎ 712-162. Open daily, 5pm–11pm. South of the town centre on the right-hand side of the road. Restaurant in a stylishly decorated house (with curtains, tablecloths and real napkins) that serves delicious, traditional food in a Western setting. Lots of *farang* habitués. There is a terraced garden outside (it gets quite cool late in the evening, so bring a sweater) but it's rather too close to the road. The menu's full of delicacies: for example, *kaeng ped ped yang,* a soup made of grilled duck with a curry sauce and coconut milk, or *pad ped pla dook,* an émincé (thin slices) of cat-fish with spices and green pepper. Obliging, smiling, very European service and the prices are very reasonable considering how good the food is.

✕ **Ton Kao** – ร้านอาหารต้นข้าว (map, B3, **35**): 1013/3 Jet Yod Road. ☎ 752-261. A little haven of peace, seconds away from a rather bustling area that's also seething with cheap places to eat (some of them very good). No signs in English. Walk through the long bar to a softly lit garden with swaying lanterns and a gurgling fountain. Big wooden tables where you can eat well-prepared, typically northern Thai food. The perfect place for a romantic dinner, serenaded by a singer who whispers laments most nights. Good place for a drink too.

✕ **Wonton Suki** – ร้านอาหารวัน ทันสุกี้ (map, B3, **36**): 897/18-19 Jet Yod Road. ☎ 711-789. Open 11am–2pm and 5pm–10.30pm. The sort of stripped, germ-free environment you would expect of a Japanese restaurant. You tick what you want, then cook your own meat and vegetables at the table in a big wok containing hot oil. Very convivial all round. Also some excellent barbecues including a delicious roast duck. Attentive service.

## EXPENSIVE

✕ **Ga-re Ga-ron** – ร้านอาหารกะ เร่กะร่อน (map, B3, **37**): 897/2 Jet

Yod Road. ☎ 714-779. Open daily for lunch and dinner. Small, sweet but rather fussy restaurant-boutique that's full of antiques. Decent food – bigger helpings would be nice – that you can eat in a little garden. The place is friendly enough but has a pronounced Western feel and clientele.

✕ **Golden Triangle Restaurant** – ร้านอาหารโรงแรมโกลเด้นไทร แองเกิล (map, C3, **21**); *see* 'Where to Stay'. Open for lunch and dinner until 10pm. Pleasantly traditional but unique setting (tree in a display case) with soft lighting, wall lamps, brick-and-bamboo decor and white tablecloths. Thai cuisine with European overtones. Stylish place for a romantic dinner that won't break the bank. Very classy.

## EXPENSIVE – IN THE SURROUNDING AREA

✕ **Chiang Rai Ruenphae** – เชียงรายเรือนแพ: 59 M7T/Pao Don Chai, Amphur Muang. ☎ 758-678. Open daily, 11am–11pm. Marvellous setting on a lake, consisting of lots of pretty floating pontoons where you eat gazing out at the water. About 5 kilometres (3 miles) west of town but not easy to find. Actually, it's about 5 kilometres (3 miles) miles from the Noi restaurant (*see above*), with signposts in Thai pointing right. So go to the Noi and carry on. A restaurant made for lovers: bags of charm and the most delicious, authentically local food. Very popular with the Thais, particularly at the weekend.

## WHERE TO HAVE A DRINK

The bars in Chiang Rai are not like the bars anywhere else in Thailand. Most of them are around the Pramawipat Road, a little road that joins Jet Yod Road with Pahon Yothin Road. As in Bangkok's notorious Patpong district you will find go-go bars and strip-tease shows. The spectacle is pretty sad to behold, with hostesses in mini skirts offering drinks and more to the stream of tourists.

Fortunately for the young people of Chiang Rai, there are other, distinctly less sordid places in town where they can while away the night.

♪ **Station Saloon** – สเตชั่นซาลูน (map, C3, **40**): Prapopsuk Road (not far from the superhighway). ☎ 740-827. Open every night until at least 2am. Very 'in' rock 'n' roll bar with timber interior and local bands playing American-style music on stage. Not bad on the whole – the Thais are gifted musicians. Fairly young clientele and peaceful atmosphere. Limited range of cheap, exclusively Thai food.

♪ **Co Coon Pub** – โคคูนผับ (map, C2, **41**): 711/2 Srigird Road. Open every night, 6pm–3am. Like the previous place but a bit more stylish and expensive, with tablecloths, comfortable wooden armchairs, candles etc. Live music here too, but the stage seems much too big for the room. Things might have changed, though, as the place hasn't been open long. The food is good, and quite refined.

♪ **Sabun-Nga Pub & Restaurant** – สบังงาผับแอนด์เรสโตรอง (map, A3–A4, **42**): 226/50 San Khong Noi Road. ☎ 712-190. More bands playing live on stage but not so much rock 'n' roll as 'easy listening' – to suit the 40-something clientele no doubt. Every night at 7pm in another room there's a *kantoke* show (cabaret-dinner with local dancing).

**☛ Inncome Hotel** – อินน์คำโฮเด็ล (off C4 on the map, **43**): just over 1 kilometre (0.5 miles) from the centre, in the south of town along the superhighway. The hotel basement houses a leisure complex including a rock 'n' roll bar, nightclub, massage parlour, karaoke bar, snooker room etc. Popular but rather down-market. Fun all the same.

## WHAT TO SEE

★ **Market** – ตลาด (map, B2): lively, picturesque covered market. Fun to look around and it sells just about everything: spices, clothing, basins, tongs – all sorts of stuff. Lots of locals and tribal people come here to do their shopping. Good food stands too (*see* 'Where to Eat').

★ **Night Market** – ตลาดกลางคืน (map, B3–C3): in a little street behind the Thai Airways office, on Pahon Yothin Road. This is where the mountain people come to display an unconvincing collection of hand-made junk (every night, 7pm–11pm). It's an expensive tourist trap.

★ **City walls and statue of King Mengrai** – กำแพงเมืองและอนุสาวรีย์พ่อขุนเม็งรายมหาราช (map, C2): a few metres of rebuilt city walls and a royal statue that's covered in flowers, on the edge of the superhighway. They are useful as landmarks but don't go out of your way to see them.

★ **Hilltribe Museum** – พิพิธภัณฑ์ชาวเขา (map, C2): 620/35 Thanalai Road. ☎ 719-167. Open daily, 10am–8pm. Outpost of the PCDA (Population and Community Development Association), an organization responsible for providing aid, teaching and information to the various mountain tribes. You see them described here in a rather soporific but informative slideshow with English commentary. There are also some artefacts on display, and a shop. On a more interesting note, the PCDA also organizes treks lasting several days (expensive but doubtless more respectful of mountain tribes than any other treks) and even humanitarian missions. A good source of literature, particularly in English.

✗ The restaurant on the ground floor, called **Cabbages and Condoms** like the one in Bangkok, is affiliated to the PCDA. It's a bit expensive considering the small portions, but all in a good cause.

★ **Wat Phra Kaeo** – วัดพระแก้ว (map, B2): opposite the Overbrooke Hospital. A 15th-century temple with a pretty facade, which for a while housed the Emerald Buddha (the one in Bangkok). No one knew it was there until the *stupa* that hid it was struck by lightning, to reveal the Emerald Buddha inside. The jade eminence was promptly moved to Bangkok and the temple in Chiang Rai was named the Wat Phra Kaeo after the one in the capital. There's a beautiful carved door and, inside, interesting wooden pillars with floral designs. In 1991 a new replacement Buddha, also made of jade, was installed in the choir, but unlike the one in Bangkok, this one is at eye level for all to see. It's not as sacred as the 'real' Emerald Buddha of course, nor does it have quite the same pose, but it's lovely, all the same. Behind the main temple is an old 14th-century *chedi*.

★ **Wat Jet Yod** – วัดเจ็ดยอด (map, B3): note the elegant, rather over-elaborate facade.

★ **Wat Doi Ngam Muang** – วัดดอยงามเมือง (map, A2): overlooking the town, on a hill with a stairway leading up to it. The *chedi* contains the ashes of King Mengrai.

★ **Wat Doi Thong** – วัดดอยทอง (map, A1): another *wat* on a hill – this one is at the western entrance to the town.

★ The **Wat Phra Singh** – วัดพระสิงห์ (map, B2): not worth visiting.

## AGENCIES AND GUESTHOUSES THAT ORGANIZE TREKS AND TRIPS

Nearly all the guesthouses in Chiang Rai can take you trekking, whether on foot, by motorbike, in a rubber dinghy, on a wooden raft or on an elephant. Always choose a guesthouse that is approved by the tourist office.

Apart from the guesthouses, there are at least 10 trekking agencies in Pramawipat Road (a narrow road tucked in between Jet Yod Road and Pahon Yothin Road) that can take you shooting the rapids in a bamboo raft, elephant riding or exploring the Golden Triangle in a minibus.

Of course you don't have to go through an agency. Provided you take a few elementary precautions and have no plans to go rafting or elephant riding, it's perfectly possible to explore the Golden Triangle and all the villages along the Burmese border on your own. So don't be conned into thinking it's more complicated than it actually is.

Generally speaking, compare the price of treks in more than one guest-house – some charge twice as much as others. And don't forget that the treks organized by the Hilltribe Museum (*see above*) are less intrusive than the treks organized by the agencies.

■ **Chiang Rai Travel and Tour Co. Ltd** – เชียงรายทราเวลแอนด์ทัวร์: 869/95 Pramawipat Road. ☎ 711-800. Fax: 713-967. This is a one-day, very expensive trip for people who haven't got much time. It includes visits to the Akha, Yao and Lahu tribes, the town of Mae Sai, the Golden Triangle and the Chiang Saen Museum.

■ **Golden Triangle Tour** – โกลเด้นไทรแองเกิลทัวร์: 590/2 Pahon Yothin Road. ☎ 711-339. Well-organized trips with a good reputation.

🏠 **Chat House** – ชาดิเฮาส์: *see* 'Where to Stay' for the address. Good tailor-made treks between Thailand and the Union of Myanmar.

Lots of other people in Chiang Rai organize treks, of course, but you should find out what other backpackers recommend when you get there.

– **Note**: unless you want to wind up in a Laotian gaol (reputedly very damp) turn down all offers of illegal trips to Laos. So long as the borders stay closed, this is not the time to play at being Indiana Jones. The only way to enter Laos is with a visa, preferably obtained in Bangkok, where it's a lot cheaper than on the border.

FROM CHIANG MAI TO CHIANG RAI

You will definitely need a guide if you want to go trekking along the mountain paths.

## TREKKING BY MOTORBIKE

*See* the section on trekking by motorbike under 'Trekking in the Mountains', and make sure you've got a good map of the area – which is easier said than done.

– **Chiang Rai–Mae Chan** – เชียงราย–แม่จัน (about 29 kilometres/18 miles; takes about 30 to 45 minutes). Start by making a detour to see the beautiful Hue Mae Sai – น้ำตกห้วยแม่สาย waterfalls. Set off from the second bridge in town, near the landing-stage, and continue along this road until you reach the village of Ban Tuan (which is only signposted in Thai: บ้านทวน. Once you're in the village, turn left and follow the signs (in English) to the waterfalls. The sign gives the falls as 4 kilometres (2.5 miles) away but actually the trail continues for another 8 kilometres (5 miles) when you reach first a Yao then an Akha village. Take a path that runs alongside a house on stilts before forking right. The falls are a good 15-minute walk away. Lots of other interesting walks lead off in all directions.

Go back to the main bridge over the River Kok on route 110 (the superhighway) and after about 29 kilometres (18 miles), fork left towards Mae Chan – แม่จัน, which is about 150 metres up the road.

Once in Mae Chan, set off from the police station, crossing the motorway, and go straight on for about 5 kilometres (about 3 miles), until you reach a crossroads, where you turn left. Continue up this road for 6 kilometres (nearly 4 miles), until you reach the Yao village of Thummajaric. The Akha village of Cho Pa Kha – ช่อผกา is 500 metres away. Then return to Mae Chan.

🛏 If you want to go on a two-day expedition, you can spend the night in the **Laan Tong Lodge** – ลานทองลอดจ์: ☎ 772-049. At the big junction not quite 3 kilometres (2 miles) from the entrance to Mae Chan, take route 1089 towards Mae Ai, Doi Mae Salong and Thaton. The Lodge is tucked into a valley 11 kilometres (7 miles) away on the left, about 49 kilometres (30 miles) before you reach Thaton. The road is well made-up, so it's easy to get to. The Lodge is quite expensive, but the location is charming, with well-appointed bungalows and your own terrace and garden. It's an ideal place from which to go visiting villages that are only accessible on foot.

– **Mae Chan–Mae Sai** via **Mae Salong** and **Doi Tung** (100 kilometres/67 miles away – allow a day but consult the entries about each place a bit later): from Laan Tong – ลานทอง (about 11 kilometres/7 miles from Mae Chan on route 1089) to Doi Mae Salong – ดอยแม่สลอง. There are two routes to choose from.

● The first route is for skilled bikers only. Start by going left north of Mae Chan and after 7 kilometres (4 miles) turn towards the village of Pang Sa – ป่างสา. You are now on route 1130. The first kilometre (half mile) is very steep and often slippery. Keep going straight along this road until it becomes route 1234, when you turn left towards Mae Salong (44 kilometres/27 miles).

• The second and by far the simpler option is to follow route 1089 for 24 kilometres (15 miles). Then turn right at the crossroads where you see signs to Mae Salong (this is 36 kilometres/22 miles of surfaced road). You will pass through several ethnic settlements on your way over the mountain.

You can go back down from Mae Salong along the road you didn't take to go up. If you do decide to take route 1234, and you're feeling brave, there's no shortage of things to see while you're here, including the village of **Toed Thai** – เทอดไทย, former kingdom of Khun Sa, the opium baron. Since part of the village is blocked off (by the police station), you will have to retrace your steps, turning left just outside the village. There you follow the river, passing the big Chinese temple. The road from here on is easy for about 10 kilometres (6 miles), giving you a chance to enjoy some magnificent scenery.

Once back on route 1234, turn left and keep going straight for about 6 kilometres (4 miles). At the junction, head for Ban Pha Bur – บ้านฟ้าบูรณ์ (going towards route 1149) and carry on for another 8 kilometres (5 miles) until you reach the main road, where you turn left for Doi Tung via Mae Sai. The stretch of land you have just been through is always very lush, even in the dry season. This very new, small road takes you through 24 kilometres (15 miles) of breathtaking scenery, surrounded on all sides by mountains with sheer sides.

When you get to Doi Tung, walk up the little path that starts about 50 metres from the entrance to the temple. You eventually come to a headland, where the views over the Mekong and Chiang Saen Lake are truly awesome. Definitely worth the slog.

From Doi Tung, it's about another 35 kilometres (21 miles) to Mae Sai (takes approximately 1 hour).

The simplest way to get to Mae Sai from Doi Mae Salong is to go back to route 110, and then northwards for a few kilometres (a mile or so) before turning left and joining up directly up with route 1149, which goes up to Doi Tung, and then straight back to Mae Sai.

FROM CHIANG MAI
TO CHIANG RAI

## LEAVING CHIANG RAI

### By bus

🚌 All the buses for Chiang Mai and Bangkok, whether air-conditioned, non-air-conditioned or VIP, leave from the big **bus station** (map, C3) on the corner of Pahon Yothin Road and Prapopsuk Road. There are frequent services throughout the day. To reassure nervous passengers, the authorities (who are not without a sense of humour) have put up a display of black-and-white photographs showing all the bus accidents over the year: crumpled buses, flattened buses, upside-down buses. So reassuring.

– **Bangkok**: journey time 13 hours (845 kilometres/528 miles). There is usually a bus at about 8.30am or the might bus leaves late afternoon. There are frequent services run by several companies.

– **Chiang Mai**: journey time 3 hours, with buses approximately every 30 minutes, 6am–4.45pm.

– **The villages in the north**: buses leave every 15 minutes, 6am–6pm.

– **Mae Salong**: take the bus for Ban Pasang and from there take a *songthaew*. Plenty of buses.

### By air

✚ **Airport** (off D1 on the map): about 10 kilometres (6 miles) north of town. There's no bus, so get there by taxi or *tuk-tuk*.

– Four flights a day leave **for Bangkok,** two **for Chiang Mai.**

# THE GOLDEN TRIANGLE –
## สามเหลี่ยมทองคำ

More than half the illegal opium consumed worldwide comes from the notorious 'Golden Triangle' or 'Region of the Three Frontiers', so called because this is where the borders of Thailand, Laos and the Union of Myanmar (formerly Burma) meet. Broadly speaking, the triangle extends from Kentoung in the Union of Myanmar, to Chiang Rai in Thailand (Mae Hong Son, Mae Sarieng, northeast of Nam) and Ban Houay Sai in Laos. That's the 'Triangle' bit. 'Golden' refers to opium, which was originally worth its weight in gold and was indeed paid for in gold.

The opium is grown by Chinese and Sino-Burmese tribes who live in remote, inaccessible mountains densely covered with jungle.

The area is dominated by a climate of fear created by the warring factions of rival bands and frequent interventions from the more or less official army. The mountains have become a breeding ground for crime and, sadly, no place for a European without a guide. But for a really cheap thrill, you can go along with a busload of tourists to photograph the very spot on the Mekong river where the three countries meet – the actual 'Golden Triangle' – from the safety of your seat. The spot in question couldn't be less interesting. The most beautiful region lies to the northwest of Chiang Rai. The Thai part of this region is full of villages buried deep within dense forests.

The opium caravans come down from the borders of Myanmar, Laos and Thailand between March and June. The biggest caravans can ship as much as 20 tonnes of opium at a time. The organization in charge of this lucrative trade is the Kuomintang, whose troops are former members of the Chinese nationalist army led by Chiang Kaï-Chek who were kicked out of communist China after the victorious People's Revolution in 1949. During the 1950s, the troops of the KMT helped the CIA to seal off the Sino-Burmese border. Today they take part in counter-guerrilla offensives launched in the mountainous regions of the north. It's also worth pointing out that there have been no opium fields on the site of the actual Golden Triangle since 1965, when the authorities pulled up the poppies and replaced them with coffee and tobacco.

For details of how to get there *see* 'Transport' under 'Chiang Rai'.

**Suggested reading**:

*Opium: a History* by Martin Booth (Simon & Schuster). For more information, refer to the section on the history of opium in the chapter on drugs at the start of the book.

## EXPLORING THE REGION WITHOUT A GUIDE

One of the most exciting things about this region is that it presents no end of trekking possibilities and you can travel by whatever means appeals to you.

If you plan to stay in the Golden Triangle region for a few days and simply want to visit the villages of the north, there's absolutely no point going through an agency. Any local bus will take you where you want to go at half the price, and there are vans that go to the more remote parts where the buses don't go. The ideal solution, provided you're careful, is to hire a motorbike (a 125cc will do fine) either in Chiang Rai (the best place to hire one since you have to go back there) or in Mae Sai. Leave your belongings at the guesthouse and take off for two or three days to explore the villages along the border. It's an experience you'll never forget. *See* 'Trekking by Motorbike', *above*, for details of two possible routes around Chiang Rai.

Then there's the minibus option for groups of travellers, and you can go trekking on foot. The suggested routes all include visits to the most famous villages – but there are lots more just waiting to be discovered.

### ★ MAE CHAN – แม่จัน

This is a small town 29 kilometres (18 miles) north of Chiang Rai and 30 kilometres (19 miles) south of Mae Sai, where nothing much happens except for the market. So drive straight through, and after about 2 kilometres (1.25 miles) you will come to a road on the left going towards Mae Salong (36 kilometres/22 miles away). Ten kilometres (6 miles) further up on the right is a Hill Tribe Centre.

After another 5 kilometres (3 miles) you come to the Yao village of Pa-Dua on the left. This is very popular with the tour operators, as you can see from all the junk on sale in the main street. But you might also find some lovely embroidered clothes, coloured dolls, boxes and other things.

There's another little Akha village a few kilometres (a mile or so) further on.

### ★ MAE SALONG – แม่สลอง

The route to Mae Salong (there are two roads, both surfaced – *see above* for our suggested bike routes around Chiang Rai) is very beautiful: lush green hills, deep valleys, little mountain peaks, undulating crop planta-tions, a scenic tour of pastoral serenity. The village, entirely created by and for the Kuomintang (KMT) refugees, is equally astonishing.

The story of the Chinese rebels is a strange one. These were the troops who fled the Chinese revolution in 1949 and settled in Burma where they were allowed to stay until the beginning of the 1960s. When the Burmese government asked them to pack their bags, they settled in Thailand, where they had refugee status. Next came the question of what to do in such inhospitable country and like a shot they turned to drugs. For people who knew the jungle like the back of their hand, what could be easier than opium-smuggling? In short, these new refugees became very trouble-some guests, turning Mae Salong into a major drug-running centre. It seems as though the Thai authorities are now addressing the situation.

Mae Salong is currently the largest KMT village in Thailand with about 4,000 inhabitants. Despite a brand new temple and people of various religious beliefs (Thai and Chinese Buddhists, Muslims, Christians) the town remains distinctly Chinese in origin, with signs in Chinese and houses shaped like pagodas. In recent years, busloads of tourists have done much to dispel the mystique of Mae Salong and put prices up. There are even a few luxury hotels here now.

## WHERE TO STAY

### BUDGET

Just outside the village (on route 1234) this group of three guest-houses offers very similar accomodation at similar prices. Horse riding is available.

☗ **Shin Sane Guesthouse** – ชิน แสนเกสท์เฮ้าส์: ☎ 765-026. Pleasant Chinese house with a range of clean rooms, with or without shower. The simplest ones are very cheap. There's a map on the wall showing all the villages in the region (Akha, Lisu, Lahu etc.).

☗ **Akha Guesthouse** – อักข่าเกสท์ เฮ้าส์: ☎ 765-103. Just next door to Shin Sane: four quite nice rooms with wood floors. Very clean. Friendly welcome.

☗ **Mae Salong Guesthouse** – แม่สลองเกสท์เฮ้าส์: ☎ 765-102.

Slightly further up the village, at the foot of a big radio mast (you can't miss it). Rooms and upkeep all a bit basic – it's nothing special, but they do organize 6-hour riding tours of four villages.

### EXPENSIVE

☗ **Mae Salong Villa** – แม่สล อง วิลล่า: ☎ 765-114. On the left at the entrance to the village, coming from the road to Chiang Rai (route 1234). Bungalows side by side, all with private terraces and magnificent views over the valley. Rooms almost to luxury standard with full bathroom facilities. The price is a bit high, probably because of the view. There's a restaurant where they have cabaret-dinners from time to time, with dancing by Akha and Lahu tribes.

## WHAT TO SEE

★ At the top of the village, there's a street market with stands selling things made of jade and ruby (there are several factories in the area), pots of Chinese herbs, tea and weird concoctions made from bits of animals. The regional speciality is a kind of whisky that's strictly illegal but you can buy it anywhere – very popular with the tour groups. It's not that cheap considering it's undrinkable. There are also a few noodle stands where you can eat lunch.

## WHAT TO SEE IN THE SURROUNDING AREA

★ If you fancy a bit of a challenge, you can follow the dirt tracks to the temple of **Doi Tung**. Otherwise, rejoin the main Mae Chan–Mae Sai road (route 110) and carry on for a few kilometres (a mile or so) until you come to the village of **Huay Krai** – ห้วยไคร้, where a road on the left (route 1149) leads directly to the temple (24 kilometres/15 miles from the junction). If you go to Huay Krai by public transport, get off the bus at the crossroads (where you'll also find some food stands) and take one of the mauve *songthaews* to Doi Tung. Note that the two roads to Doi Tung (the new one and the old one) cross each other several times along the way.

★ **Wat Noi Doi Tung and the Doi Tung mountain** – วัดน้อยดอยตุง: as you ride up to the temple, you pass through magnificent countryside crowded with opium fields even if you can't see them from the road. This entire region is the scene of repeated fighting between the army and the drug-smugglers. People who go off exploring on their own often end up in Burma without knowing how they got there and liking it even less – so on your head be it. The temple, at an altitude of about 1,500 metres (4,500ft), was a gift from the King to his mother, who already owned a magnificent house in the area (*see below*). In fact it's nothing special, but the road leading up to it is lovely and wide and a fine ride on a motorbike.

What strikes you most about this trip is the beauty of the scenery which is steeped in atmosphere. The view from up here is quite extraordinary, and it's well worth stopping to admire the landscape that lies halfway up, often shrouded in mist. The last kilometre (half mile) or so gets a bit tricky, but as you reach the top there's a deliciously fragrant and beautiful pine forest and, just before the temple, a strange garden full of scary sculpture and spirit houses.

Outside the temple are various Akha stands selling trinkets, snacks and drinks. The temple is an important place of worship because of the *chedi*, which is supposed to contain one of the Buddha's collarbones, and the footprint (which you can see) proving that he did set foot in this very place. There are also numerous elephant sculptures, an impressive collection of bells and a monumental stairway, guarded by dragons.

★ **Doi Tung Royal Villa and Garden** – ดอยตุงรอยัลวิลลาแอนด์การ์เด้นท์: this divine pine and teak chalet about 1,000 metres (3,300 feet) up (slightly downhill from the temple), was built in the 1980s by the queen mother, who died in 1995 but who remains adored by her people to this day. The building helped to bring peace to a region that saw repeated fighting over opium and it also created employment for the local mountain people.

There is a guided tour (it's in Thai and there is a charge) every day between 8.30am and 5pm. Be careful not to point your foot at the picture of the Queen when you sit on the teak floor, as this would be a mark of disrespect.

Slightly further down and adjoining the house is a magnificent botanical garden where you can go for a walk (7am–6pm; separate admission charge) through a wonderland of ornamental trees, multi-coloured flowers, strange plants and fountains.

✗ Opposite the entrance to the garden is a self-service cafeteria that sells a range of good canteen food.

– From Doi Tung you can go straight back to Mae Sai along a little-used but excellent mountain road (suitable for motor vehicles) that follows the Burmese border.

## WHAT TO SEE ALONG ROUTE 110

★ Rejoin the main road going towards Mae Sai (route 110). About 5 kilometres (3 miles) north of Huay Krai, just before you get to the village of Ban Thun, there's a sign on the left to the **Saohim Cave and Lake** (keep your eyes open because there's no sign in English).

Follow the path for about a kilometre (half a mile) to a pretty stretch of water at the foot of a mountain. At weekends this becomes the main municipal swimming pool where everyone from Chiang Rai comes for a family dip. Don't be put off by the greenish-looking water – it is clean. And the place itself is great, complete with huts at the water's edge where you can have a drink. Or cross the lake in a pedalo (if you can find one) and go on a candle-lit exploration of a deep cave that's teeming with bats. This is the perfect place to relax. Come here during the week if you want peace and quiet, and at the weekends to meet the locals.

A few hundred metres from the lake, on the right, is another cavern, known as the **Tham Pla Cave**. It's surrounded by a temple and a pool filled with sacred carp. The fish are harmless enough – not so the local colony of monkeys. Funny they may be (you could watch them for hours) but gibbons also bite, steal and can be surprisingly devious. So feed them by all means, but be on your guard.

★ Back on route 110 a bit further up (6–8 kilometres/4–5 miles to be precise) there's another sign, also on the left, to the **Tham Luang Caves**. This group of caves is actually a gallery several kilometres (a mile or so) long which you can visit. A visitor centre has recently been built.

★ A few kilometres (a mile or so) before you get to Mae Sai, the road forks for Chian Saen, and it runs along a mountain that is supposed to look like a woman asleep – hence its name: **The Sleeping Lady**.

## ★ MAE SAI – แม่สาย

Thailand's northernmost village consists of a large main street lined with charmless buildings with a bridge at one end. This is Thailand's border with the Union of Myanmar. Beneath it flows the Mae Sai river, which separates the two countries. On the left, as you come from the bridge, is a path leading to some great guesthouses and the nicest part of town.

All around you are the happy sights and sounds of rural village life; children shrieking and fooling about in the river; people from both countries having a wash and just chatting in the water as if there were no such thing as 'border problems'.

Likewise, nobody seems too bothered about the ferries that go endlessly up and down between the two countries on the other side of the frontier post on the bridge. You might think this is a great way of crossing the border – but take a look at the customs officers keeping watch on either side of the river and you might change your mind. Don't go asking for trouble.

Otherwise, this is a peaceful spot with its endless comings and goings, worth staying in for 24 hours. Be there at the end of the afternoon, when the low, flat sunlight bathes the river and the huts on either side in a magical glow.

The area around the bridge is always alive with activity, full of tribal people from the Union of Myanmar, particularly the Akha and Burmese peasants dressed in the traditional *longyi*, a kind of sarong, who cross the border regularly to buy provisions or look for work. Mae Sai for them is like El Dorado. Rest assured, you too can cross the border, but you'll need a visa (*see below*).

## USEFUL ADDRESSES

■ **Police** – สถานีตำรวจ: in the main street, 200 metres before the bridge.

■ **Immigration Office** – สำนักงาน ตรวจคนเข้าเมือง: either on the main street leading to the bridge, on the left as you come into town, or at the frontier post on the bridge. Bring a photocopy of your passport to leave with Thai customs (who sometimes ask for the original) and US$5 to pay the Burmese (the cost of a visa in 1999). After that, welcome to the Union of Myanmar – or rather to the area a few kilometres (miles) long that was open to tourists at the time of writing and which could well change from one day to another. Note the fake temple-boutique-restaurant complex as you enter the country.

■ **Thai Farmers Bank** – ธนา คารกสิกรไทย: 122/1 Pahon Yothin Road, on the main street a few hundred metres before the bridge on the right. Visa cash withdrawal facilities at the desk or from the hole-in-the-wall cash machine.

■ **Bus terminal**: on the same street at the entrance to town.

■ **Telephone**: there is now a brand new telephone exchange and post office (or at least there should be, given that building works were close to completion at the time of writing) on the left, about 800 metres from the bus terminal and slightly set back from Pahon Yothin Road.

There are lots of guesthouses where you can hire a motorbike.

## WHERE TO STAY

There are lots of guesthouses on the river to the left of the bridge. Some of them have very similar sounding names and landlords are only too happy to make the most of this confusion. So put your glasses on and read the names properly.

### BUDGET

■ **Mae Sai Plaza Guesthouse** – แม่สายพลาซ่าเกสท์เฮ้าส์: on the road that runs along the river, left of the bridge. ☎ 732-230. Costs about 100 Bts for the night.This is a great place despite its rather faded-looking little bungalows that cling to the hillside overlooking the river. Rooms with a range of mod cons at prices to match; some are very decent, with balcony, bath-

room and hot running water; others more rudimentary. Ask to see several if you don't mind the stairs. Village-type guesthouse with bags of charm even if cleanliness isn't the first priority. View over Myanmar. The restaurant on the huge covered terrace serves good working-class food.

■ **Riverside Guesthouse** – ริ เวอร์ไซด์เกสท์เฮ้าส์: on the same road as the previous place, a bit further up on the right. ☎ 732-554. Modest, featureless rooms and bungalows without much character. There are some slightly better ones with little balconies overlooking the river though, so make sure you ask to see several before making a final choice. Hot and cold shower. Nice atmosphere in the terrace restaurant, which also has a view of the river. Classic cuisine and lots of it at reasonable prices.

⚱ **Chad Guesthouse** – ชัชเกสท์ เฮ้าส์: 52/1 Soi Wiengpan. ☎ 732-054. In a quiet residential corner on the left as you come into town, signposted from the Honda dealer. Cheap dormitories and rooms with shared bathroom facilities and hot running water. No view of course – only the old bangers that the landlord likes to tinker with. Restaurant service. They sell an incredibly simple but very useful map of the region here.

## MODERATE

⚱ **Mae Sai Guesthouse** – แม่สาย เกสท์เฮ้าส์ ซอยเวียงพานคำ: the oldest guesthouse in Mae Sai, right at the end of the path. ☎ 732-021. This place has it all: bamboo bungalows with very pretty shower rooms; private terrace overlooking the water where you can watch the kids splashing about; lovely garden on all sides with a well-manicured lawn despite all the dogs. A great place with loads of charm and not too expensive, where you can feel a part of village life. The restaurant, on the other hand, is a bit disappointing. Ask about the trekking.

## EXPENSIVE

You will find quite a few ugly, impersonal and expensive concrete hotels on the main street leading to the bridge. There are even more under construction.

## WHERE TO EAT

You won't find much better than the good, home-cooked food they serve in all the guesthouses.

✕ **Jojo Coffee Shop** – โจโจคอฟฟ ช็อป: in the main street, on the left coming into the village, by the market. Open daily, but only 6am–4pm. Simple food but with a good reputation. The menu, complete with photographs, is in Thai, Burmese, Chinese, Japanese and English – so you can't go far wrong.

✕ **The market** – ตลาด: slightly set back from Pahon Yothin Road, on the left, about 300 metres from the bridge but not visible from the road. It includes stands selling simple country dishes for next to nothing.

✕ **Rimnam Restaurant** – ร้าน อาหารริมน้ำ: at the foot of the bridge, opposite the border with Myanmar. Open 7.30am–8pm. Two long terraces with no particular charm except that they overlook the river, but they do serve some delicious food, particularly the spicy fish soups and fried fish. Try the fried beef with oyster sauce too, and the Chinese specialities. Pity about the dismal service and the complete absence of any prices on the menu.

– There's no point starting a new section just to cover the nightlife in Mae Sai. The sole source of entertainment is a series of bars along the river.

Be warned that some look like perfectly respectable pubs from the outside but you will be harrassed by hostesses once you sit down.

## WHAT TO SEE

★ Jade, as you may already know, originates from Burma and one of the things to visit round here is the little **Thong Tavee Factory** – โรงงานทองทวี jade-cutting factory at 17–17/1 Pahon Yothin Road (the main street). Visits are free: 9am–5pm. After you've seen the video with English commentary, you're shown around the noisy, dusty workshops where the jade is cut and polished and finally of course, you end up in the shop. And don't get carried away by the magnificent-looking rubies at unbeatable prices you find on sale in town – most of them are fakes.

★ The **market** is directly opposite the factory. This is what being in Mae Sai is all about: strolling up and down the little streets (muddy when it rains) and seeing how the local population lives. It isn't everybody's cup of tea and an hour will be more than enough for some. Others will spend several days here, exploring the surrounding area, reading a good thriller, watching time go by.

★ Just before the bridge, off the main street on the left, there's a little road that leads up to the entrance of the **Wat Doi Wao** – วัดดอยว่าว. The temple itself is nothing special, but the location is fantastic: at the top of a hill with a splendid view over Myanmar. It's worth seeing even if it does mean climbing 100 or so stairs. There's a sculpture of a giant scorpion (*doi* in Thai) at the top of the temple.

## LEAVING MAE SAI

– **For Mae Chan**, **Chiang Rai** and **Chiang Mai**: buses leave from the new terminal, which is 1 kilometre (0.5 miles) from the bridge. There are frequent departures in the morning, and not quite as many in the afternoon. Get to Mae Chan by *songthaew* only.

– **For Sop Ruak** and **Chiang Saen**: by *songthaew* only, approximately every hour, 7am to about 1pm. All the *songthaews* leave from Pahon Yothin Road (the main street), by the jade factory, on the right-hand side going towards the bridge.

## ★ THE ROAD FROM MAE SAI TO THE GOLDEN TRIANGLE

The main road forks before Mae Sai to to give a pleasant drive through soft, flat, peaceful countryside along a wide road, recently resurfaced, that doesn't follow the river. You'll see lots of Lahu and Lisu peasants dressed in traditional costume who still use traditional farming equipment and traditional means of transport.

### ★ SOP RUAK – สปรวก

This is it, Sop Ruak, also known as the 'Golden Triangle' – the place where the river Mae Nam Ruak meets the Mekong river and you get to see three countries at once: Thailand, Myanmar (the strip of land between the two rivers; the big building is a casino) and Laos (on the left bank of the Mekong).

There's nothing remotely interesting about this place: it isn't even a proper village – nobody had ever heard of Sop Ruak before it started to attract busloads of tourists. Today it's a nightmare of souvenir stands selling T-shirts, complete with a newly built Golden Triangle Gateway that overlooks the river so the tourists have something to photograph.

The view is lovely, of course, and so are the two ruined temples, one of them dating from the eighth century.

It's not even as though Sop Ruak has ever seen any action – it's much too exposed. The drug-smugglers use the remote, largely inaccessible mountain paths. Whichever way you look at it, the Golden Triangle is strictly for the birds. Stop and and take a picture so you can impress your mates back home but don't waste any time here. Well-heeled tourists sometimes spend a couple of nights in the swanky Meridien hotel that you pass on your way into Sop Ruak.

## THINGS TO DO AND SEE

★ **Boat trip from Sop Ruak to Chiang Saen:** worth it if you're travelling in a group, although it will still make a dent in the budget. A trip lasts about 30 minutes, and it can work out cheaper if you charter a private boat or one of the slower ones. A short trip up the Mekhong is cheaper still.

★ **House of Opium** – พิพิธภัณฑ์ดอกฝิ่น: in the centre. Open daily, 8am–7pm. Admission charge. Despite its ultra-touristy side, this little museum houses an interesting display of opium pipes, knives, scales etc., and there is some explanation in English. There are also some signs pointing out the dangers of drug taking but not a word about the government's role in the rise of the opium industry. The plant (*Paver somniferum*) originated in the Mediterranean and was introduced to the rest of the world by Alexander the Great.

# CHIANG SAEN – เชียงแสน   DIALLING CODE: 053

About 35 kilometres (21 miles) from Mae Sai, Chiang Saen is the most authentically traditional village in the whole region, stranded in the middle of nowhere with hardly another tourist in sight. It was originally the walled capital of a much older kingdom than Chiang Mai and contains a wealth of 10th-century remains. The whole town was subsequently flattened in the 18th century. With its colourful but modest market and friendly people, this is a lovely place to stop along the river and watch the barges arrive with goods from China.

There's a handful of guesthouses that makes it tempting to spend the night here, just to sit and watch 4,200 kilometres (2,600 miles) of Asian history washing by on the Mekhong.

THE GOLDEN TRIANGLE

## USEFUL ADDRESSES

**ℹ** There is a small **tourist office** – ททท (map, A2) opposite the museum. Open 8.30am–4.30pm. Not a vast amount of information but there's a great children's room.

■ **Police** – สถานีตำรวจ (map, B2, **1**): in the main street that comes from the river.

✉ **Post office and telephone** – ไปรษณีย์สื่อสาร: in the same street, by the two old *chedis*.

■ **Motorbike-taxis**: opposite the town hall. Drivers wear red armbands.

You can also hire a **pedal bike** to explore the region – particularly nice since there's very little traffic.

■ There are Visa cash withdrawal facilities at the **Siam Commercial Bank** – ธนาคารไทยพาณิชย์ (in the main street), open Monday–Friday, 8.30am–3.30pm.

## WHERE TO STAY

BUDGET (80–200 BTS PER PERSON PER NIGHT)

⬡ **Gin Guesthouse** – ยินเกสท์เฮ้าส์ (map, B1, **10**): 71 Rimkhong, Mu 8. ☎ 650-847. On the right coming from Sop Ruak, about 1 kilometre (0.5 miles) before you get into Chiang Saen. The setting is great – very lush, with a well-manicured lawn and cart-wheels scattered around, to make it look like a ranch. At the bottom of the garden are some simple, bamboo-and-leaf huts with mattresses on the floor, fan and mosquito nets. The WCs are rustic. There are also three family rooms for four, upstairs in the main house, all tiled throughout and with spacious bathrooms. Nice and quiet. Lovely terrace. You can also hire bikes, motorbikes and cars here and the landlords organize treks. Warm welcome and reasonable rates.

⬡ **Siam Guesthouse** – สยามเกสท์ เฮ้าส์ (map, B1, **11**): beyond the Gin Guesthouse on the right coming from Sop Ruak. Modest guesthouse with single rooms, with or without shower; cold water only. Cheap, but the barrack-like accommodation is a bit off-putting. Terrace restaurant.

⬡ **Chiang Saen Guesthouse** – เชียงแสนเกสท์เฮ้าส์ (map, B1, **12**): next door to the previous place. ☎ 650-196. In a prime position overlooking the Mekhong river and Laos and facing the road but a reasonable distance away from it. Bungalows with shower and WC or single rooms at reasonable prices, very clean but completely lacking in charm. The welcome is off-hand and the atmosphere commercial. Bicycle hire.

EXPENSIVE

⬡ **Chiang Saen River Hill Hotel** – เชียงแสนริเวอร์ฮิลล์โฮเต็ล (map, B2, **13**): 714 Moo 3 Tambol Viang. ☎ 650-826. Signposted from the main street. Probably the best hotel in this price range in town, despite the ugly, charmless building and cold, pink tiling. But the rooms are spacious and air-conditioned with a very pleasant lounge area. Breakfast is included.

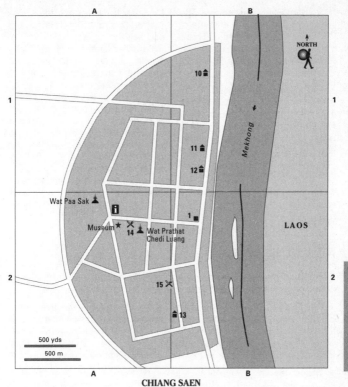

CHIANG SAEN

■ **Useful Addresses**

  **ⓘ** Tourist office
  **1** Police

🏠 **Where to Stay**

  **10** Gin Guesthouse

**11** Siam Guesthouse
**12** Chiang Saen Guesthouse
**13** Chiang Saen River Hill Hotel

✕ **Where to Eat**

**14** Sam Ying
**15** Vegetarian Restaurant

## WHERE TO EAT AND WHERE TO HAVE A DRINK

✕ **Sam Ying** – ร้านอาหารสามหญิง (map, A2, **14**): in the main street next to the Krung Thai Bank. Open daily, 8am–8pm. The name is only written in Thai so look out for the red-and-white awning. The plas- tic-covered menu, on the other hand, is bilingual so ordering shouldn't be too difficult. It doesn't say what things cost but all the dishes are reasonably priced. De- licious food from the north of Thailand, particularly the soups. The landlady used to work in some of the big northern hotels. If you have the stomach for it, try the *kep moo* – like pork scratchings Thai-style and really delicious.

✗ **Vegetarian Restaurant** – ร้าน อาหารมังสะวิรัต (map, A2–B2, **15**): a small vegetarian restaurant not far from the Chiang Saen River Hill Hotel. The kitchen area is open and there are just three tables and four stools. Open 8am–5pm. Local clientele and good, simple food.

❢ The next place is outside the village so it's only for those who have their own transport. Follow the road to Mae Chan for 4 kilometres (2.5 miles), fork left where you see the big sign and carry on for another kilometre or so (nearly 1 mile). Ignore the Chiang Saen Lake, a fish restaurant that has probably gone bust, and carry on until you come to the **Chiang Saen Lake Hill Resort** (☎ 650-599). It's right on the edge of the lake and could be idyllic if it were not for the ugly hotel buildings, lazy service and excessive prices – all of which are a serious turn-off. But there are some large armchairs on the terrace where you can sit back with a drink and watch the birds skimming over the lake.

## WHAT TO SEE AND DO

Throughout the town, there are ruined temples and *stupas* that once belonged to the kingdom of Chiang Saen.

★ **Wat Prathat Chedi Luang** – วัดพระธาตุเจดีย์หลวง: a distinctively 13th-century temple and very charming because of it. All that's left of it today is a brick perimeter with a corrugated iron roof but this is still a very holy place. Beside it stands a big *chedi* about 40 metres (120 feet) high, covered in grass and entirely in ruins but moving nonetheless.

★ **The museum** – พิพิธภัณฑ์: is just next door. Open Wednesday to Sunday, 9am–4pm. The museum contains all the archaeological finds made in the region: statues and heads of Lan Na Buddhas dating from the 14th to the 18th centuries; various examples of the Buddha's hands; a small number of ceramics; fabrics, coins, arms, musical instruments; Thai costumes.

★ There are more **wats** in the area around the village if you fancy a stroll.

★ A **trip on the Mekhong** is always a possibility, but not before you've checked on the state of relations between Myanmar and Thailand.

## LEAVING CHIANG SAEN

– From Chiang Saen you can either head straight back to Chiang Rai via Mae Chan (by bus), or you can detour via Chiang Khong. Since Chiang Khong has little to recommend it and hardly anywhere to stay, it may be better not to bother. Catch the bus in the main street, at right angles to the river. Buses leave at regular intervals throughout the day.

# THE NORTHEAST

While some people may remember Thailand as a mecca for all things exotic, those who visit the northeast will come away with quite a different impression. This whole area, known as I-san (with an 'i' pronounced like the 'i' in little) is completely unpretentious, but what it loses in refinement, it more than makes up for in human warmth and spontaneity. This is your chance to experience a different kind of tourism, focusing on the local people and showing greater respect for their heritage and traditions.

For a region that has attracted few tourists in the past, I-san is not without its attractions. It is richly endowed with national parks (including the Phu Kradung National Park) and nearly 600 kilometres (400 miles) of land along the banks of the Mekhong – as well as a cultural heritage. Thanks in particular to excavations conducted by Ban Chiang, there is now archaeological evidence to show that civilization saw the light of day in I-san long before the birth of the Thai people. The northeast is also home to some of the finest Khmer masterpieces outside Cambodia.

Last but by no means least, I-san boasts an abundance of popular traditions (including music, dancing, silk production, pottery and cooking) that owe much to the intermingling of the local population with their Khmer and Laotian neighbours.

Plan to stay at least a week here – more if you're interested in ethnography, photography or nature, or simply love peace and quiet.

## THE PARKS IN THE PROVINCE OF LOEI

For quiet souls who haven't got much time, this unspoilt conservation area is *the* place to go. It already attracts a growing number of back-packers who seek refuge here from the overcrowded treks in the north. If nothing else, it's worth making the journey just to see the famous Phu Kradung National Park.

# LOEI – เลย

DIALLING CODE: 042

This friendly little town, about 520 kilometres (325 miles) north of Bangkok, is particularly interesting as a starting point for trips to Phu Kradung, Phu Luang and Phu Rua.

### GETTING THERE

**– From Bangkok**: several air-conditioned or non-air-conditioned buses headed for Loei leave from the northern bus station (Mo-Chit) towards early evening.

– **From Chiang Mai and Phitsanulok**: at least six buses a day for Lomsak. Magnificent route from Dan Sai to Loei (route 203), crossing an undulating, lush green landscape.

– **From Khon Kaen**: buses every 30 minutes from 6am.

– **From Nong Khai**: collective taxis every 20 minutes from 5am.

## WHERE TO STAY

### BUDGET (FROM ABOUT 100 BTS PER PERSON PER NIGHT)

⌂ **Muang Loei Guesthouse** – เมืองเลยเกสท์เฮ้าส์: 103/128 Soi A. D. Rouam Chai Road. ☎ 832-839. About 150 metres on the left as you come out of the non-air-conditioned bus terminal. The landlady, Somdy Ming (everybody calls her Noï) lets out four new rooms with shared bathroom at extremely reasonable prices. She also serves breakfast and is an invaluable (and fairly unstoppable) source of tourist information – providing you speak French. So brush up your *français*, and you can find out everything you need to know about bus times, trips in the surrounding area, the weather . . .

⌂ **Sarai Thong Hotel** – สาหร่าย ทองโฮเต็ล: 25/5 Ruanchitra Road. ☎ 811-582. Opposite the Bank of Ayudhia. Clean and quiet, but the rooms are a bit dreary. More expensive than the previous place.

### EXPENSIVE (300–1,000 BTS PER PERSON PER NIGHT)

⌂ **Kinghotel** – คิงโฮเต็ล: 11/9-12 Chumsai Road. ☎ 811-701. The best value for money in this particular category. Rooms with fans or air-conditioning and hot running water.

## WHERE TO EAT AND WHERE TO HAVE A DRINK

✗ **The night market**: on Charoenrat Road about 100 metres before the Phu Luang Hotel. Lots of stands that set up as night falls, selling take-away specialities: grilled meats, meat in sauces, fruits and Chinese sweets. Or there's a wide terrace with tables and chairs where you can have a picnic.

✗ **Sawita Bakery**: 137–139 Charoenrat Road. Treat yourself to a mini-Swiss roll and a banana-split, all served with a smile.

🍷 **Kun-Yai Bar**: 12/13 Kud Pong. Near the lake, opposite the Chinese temple (Sanjao Por Kud Pong). This little bar is where all the young trendies congregate in the evenings. Don't miss it. Very friendly place run by a young team – has ranch-like decor and rock 'n' roll music. Stays open till 2am.

## THINGS TO DO

– There's not a lot to do apart from going for a dip in the **Muang Loei Lan** swimming pool to the north of town. Take a *songthaew* from the bus terminal.

PARKS IN THE PROVINCE OF LOEI

## FESTIVALS

– If you're around in June, find out the exact dates of the **Phi Ta Khon** festival, which is still known as the 'Festival of the Spirits'. Two days of processions in an overheated atmosphere of masks and disguises commemorate the return to his home town of Prince Vessandorn (the Buddha's penultimate incarnation).

# PHU RUA NATIONAL PARK –
## อุทยานแห่งชาติภูเรือ

DIALLING CODE: 042

From the top of Boat Mountain (1,365 metres/4,000 feet) – so-called because the peak resembles a Chinese junk – there is a wonderful view of the mountain ranges and valleys of Laos, and the border is only a few kilometres (couple of miles) away.

## GETTING THERE

– **From Loei (or Phitsanulok)**: frequent buses in both directions from Phitsanulok (or Loei) along route 203. The first bus leaves from Loei at the crack of dawn (5am) followed by two more at 6am and 8am. They stop about 48 kilometres (30 miles) away in the village of Phu Rua. After that, you either walk or hitchhike the rest of the way to the park (it's easy to get a lift at the weekend). It's about 2 kilometres (1.5 miles) to the first checkpoint and another 4 kilometres (3 miles) to the reception desk. There's a perfectly good surfaced road that twists and turns for 10 kilometres (6 miles) from the village to the top of the park, so you might think it's worth hiring a car. Watch out for the engine though – it's a very steep climb (more than 1:5 towards the top).

## WHERE TO STAY

### BUDGET (INSIDE THE PARK)

⛺ **Camping**: there are about 100 tents for hire at the top of the park, about 1,300 metres (4,000 feet) up – and 900 metres (2,700 feet) before you get to the top. Fork left towards the 'Forest Ranger Station' (you can't miss the sign) and carry on walking for about 1.5 kilometres (1 mile) along a flattish, easy trail. Remember to bring warm clothes and a sleeping-bag, even in the dry season (Phu Rua holds the record for being the coldest place in Thailand at -4°C/25°F).

⛺ **Bungalows**: six very rudimentary bungalows (four at reception and two at the ranger station), with five mattresses, bucket shower and no electricity. Cost is about the same as the tents if there's a group of you. Ask when you get to reception.

### EXPENSIVE (OUTSIDE THE PARK)

⛺ **Two bungalow residences** with loads of charm for upper-class Thais on holiday. On the right, along route 203 going towards Loei, surrounded by lush rolling hills and English-style gardens. None of them has air-conditioning but, as in the mountains, the nights are cool here. Coming from Loei, the best thing is to get the driver to drop you off.

⌂ **Phu Rua Chalet** – ภูเรือชาเล่ต์: about 4 kilometres (2.5 miles) from Phu Rua. ☎ 899-012. A really great place. Delicious Thai and European cooking, exceptionally warm, refined welcome (but completely unpretentious) and very reasonable starting prices.

⌂ **Phu Rua Resort** – ภูเรือรีสอร์ท: about 2 kilometres (just over 1 mile) from Phu Rua. ☎ 899-048. Bungalows with discreet terraces, some of which overlook a pretty stream lower down. But there's definitely 'no English spoken here', or written either – the menu is exclusively in Thai.

### THINGS TO DO AND SEE

★ **Trekking in the park**: a rudimentary map is available at reception, but fortunately all the paths are properly waymarked. The park covers a relatively small area – about 120 square kilometres (46 square miles) – so it isn't difficult to plan a fairly complete loop that takes in all the high spots, including the main waterfalls and the walk to the top (1,365 metres/ 4,478 feet).

★ **The Phu Rua Vineyard:** a few kilometres (couple of miles) from the village, on the left going towards Dan Sai, the Château de Loei estate, at an altitude of 650 metres (2,130 feet), is a relative newcomer, yet it produces the finest quality wine in Thailand. Production is currently running at 38,000 bottles a year with only a fifth of the 90-hectare estate (about 220 acres) as yet under cultivation. The stuff is like gold dust in Bangkok where 'vinomania' recently caught on in a big way. If you love wine, this could be your one and only chance to dip your lips into a glass of Chenin Blanc for a long time.

# PHU KRADUNG NATIONAL PARK –
## อุทยานแห่งชาติภูกระดึง

DIALLING CODE: 042

This is without a doubt one of the most beautiful natural parks in Thailand. At the top, at an altitude of 1,200 metres (4,265 feet), stretches 55 square kilometres (21 square miles) of sandstone plateau, with a breathtaking view of the lowlands and surrounding hills. Legend has it that the area was discovered just two centuries ago by a Laotian hunter pursuing a *gaur* (doe). To this day, Phu Kradung remains an important wildlife reserve, with Asian jackals, giant black squirrels and white-handed gibbons, as well as about 20 elephants and some tigers. However, what makes the Bell Mountain unique is the sheer variety of flora that grows here, including tropical, Mediterranean and oceanic species.

### GOING UP

Having paid your dues at reception (open daily, 6.30am– 3pm), you make your way up to the reserve along a path that runs through the forest for 5.5 kilometres (3.5 miles) before it eventually emerges onto the plateau at an altitude of 1,288 metres (4,265 feet). It climbs from about 1,100 metres

(3,300 feet). Expect a very steep climb with a gradient of approximately 1:2. Depending on how fit you are, it can take anything from 2 hours to 3 hours 30 minutes of punishing physical effort (plus another hour to get back to park headquarters). But it's a magnificent walk and there are lots of places that sell drinks along the way.

When you get to the top, you emerge suddenly from dense jungle onto a plateau scattered with pines. It is recommended to hire porters (for just a few bahts), because you will need all your strength for clinging onto creepers and rocks and clambering up bamboo ladders where the cliff face gets too steep to do anything else.

## WHEN TO GO THERE

The park is closed during the monsoon season from mid-June to the end of September. Otherwise, the best time to go depends on what you like to do. From October to December the water that has accumulated during the rainy season flows lazily across the plateau to the edge, where it cascades down the mountainside as waterfalls. The rest of the year it's dry. After that comes the cold season, which lasts until mid-February, when sporty types can trek to their heart's content along more than 50 kilometres (30 miles) of waymarked paths. And do remember to bring warm clothing – temperatures can hover around 0°C/32°F at night.

The best time to come if you want to see nature at its best is from March to April, when the land seems to rejoice in a symphony of colour with the blooms of azaleas, rhododendrons and many other flowers.

Because the Thais like it so much, the reserve gets very crowded at weekends between October and January. Try to come during the week if you can. Later, in March and April when the schools are on holiday, it attracts teenagers dreaming of their first romance as the sun sets on Lomsak Cliff. Expect to be asked to take their photograph and brace yourself for repeated choruses of 'The Last Mekhong' sung around the campfire to the sound of a small guitar.

## GETTING THERE

– **From Bangkok**: catch the Loei bus and ask the driver to drop you near Phu Kradung on the main road 77 kilometres (48 miles) before you get to Loei – where you see the sign. You arrive in the wee small hours. From there, take a collective taxi to the foot of the cliff, 7 kilometres (4 miles) away.

– **From Phitsanulok**: catch an air-conditioned or non-air-conditioned bus for Khon Kaen and get off in Chum Phae, where there are local buses for Loei every 30 minutes, from 6am. Get off near Phu Kradung.

– **From Khon Kaen** (or **Loei**): catch the Loei bus (or the Khon Kaen bus) and ask for the stop nearest to Phu Kradung. Buses leave every 30 minutes, from 6am.

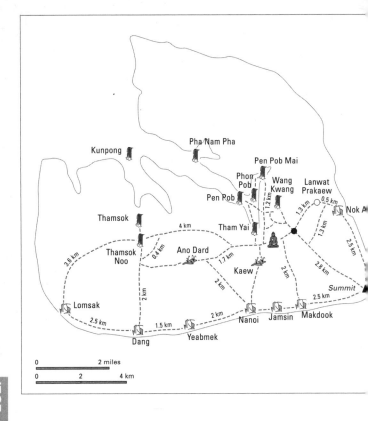

## WHERE TO STAY

It's a good idea to book in advance if you are planning a weekend trip between October and January.

### AT THE FOOT OF THE PLATEAU

#### BUDGET

⛺ There are a few **tents** for hire, at the entrance to the park near the drinks stands.

#### MODERATE TO EXPENSIVE

🏠 **Phu Kradung Resort** – ภูกระ ดึงรีสอร์ท (map, **1**): small bunga- low village on the lake, 3 kilo-

metres (just under 2 miles) from the entrance to the park, on the left. ☎ 871-076. The accommoda- tion is a bit basic but there's a nice shady terrace where they serve good Thai food.

🏠 **Phu Kradung Paradise Resort** – ภูกระดึงพาราไดซ์รีสอร์ท (map, **2**): about 1 kilometre (0.5 miles)

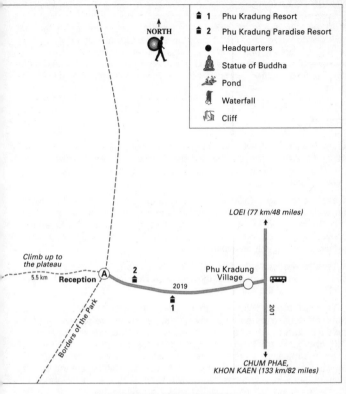

NORTH

| | |
|---|---|
| 🛏 1 | Phu Kradung Resort |
| 🛏 2 | Phu Kradung Paradise Resort |
| ● | Headquarters |
| 🧘 | Statue of Buddha |
| 🐟 | Pond |
| 🎍 | Waterfall |
| 🗻 | Cliff |

*LOEI (77 km/48 miles)*

*Climb up to the plateau*

5.5 km  **Reception**  (A)

**2**
🛏

Phu Kradung Village

2019

**1**
🛏

201

*Borders of the Park*

*CHUM PHAE,*
*KHON KAEN (133 km/82 miles)*

**PHU KRADUNG NATIONAL PARK**

from the entrance to the park, on the right. ☎ 871-146. Very like the previous place, but better – and also twice the price, probably because the bungalows look charming from the outside even though the standard of accommodation inside is fairly rudimentary. Still, at least there's hot running water.

## ON THE HIGH PLATEAU CLOSE TO PARK HEADQUARTERS

🛏 Lots of **tents** for hire and some sleeping-bags too. Check what state they are in as soon as you arrive, since many of the tents have seen better days.

🛏 **Bungalows in the park**: large rudimentary bungalows (mattress on the ground) that sleep eight – only worth it if you're travelling in a group. Singles should book a tent, which you can only do from the National Parks Bureau in Bangkok on Pahon Yothin Road. ☎ 579-5269. It's only 15 kilometres (9 miles) from the centre but it takes at least 2 hours to get there by bus.

## WHERE TO EAT

✕ At the entrance to the park (in the visitors' centre) and also near the park headquarters, you'll find cheap restaurants that stay open all day serving Chinese soups, fried rice, eggs, sweets and drinks (there's no shortage of alcohol round here). Or they can do you a picnic to take on a trek. Torches, batteries and matches are also on sale, and the welcome is great.

## TREKKING

All the treks suggested below start from the park headquarters. You are advised to keep to the paths (which are very clearly marked). The public is not allowed into the northern and northwest areas of the park, which form a wildlife sanctuary.

★ **Trek to the waterfalls**: can take anything from 30 minutes to 2 hours depending on which falls you visit (Wang Kwang, Pen Pob Mai, Phon Pob, Tham Yai or Pen Pob). They are all west of the park headquarters. On your way back, notice how the plateau starts to slope away more gently as the vegetation thickens.

★ **Trek to the azaleas**: about 12 kilometres (7.5 miles) there and back. Head west in the direction of the Thamsok Noo falls, past the statue of the Buddha and the Ano Dard pond.

★ **Tour of the precipices**: about 21 kilometres (13 miles), so the complete tour takes about a day and there's nowhere to buy food on the way. Start as early as you can and set off in the direction of Nok An Cliff, about 2 kilometres on (1.25 miles), and aim to get there in time to watch the majestic sunrise. There are lots of pretty wild flowers around Lanwat Prakaew. Make your way back to Lomsak Cliff (where the view is quite outstanding) by following the cliff from east to west for about 13 kilometres (8 miles). Return via Thamsok Noo. Alternatively, if you have a tent, you can camp on Lomsak Cliff and watch the sun set.

# PHU LUANG WILDLIFE RESERVE

Like so many aspects of Phu Kradung park (including the hills and the vegetation), the wildlife reserve is unique in that it can only be visited by small groups at any one time, under the watchful eye of the forestry guards. As a result, man has had virtually no effect on the wildlife or its natural habitat and everything feels more unfamiliar than ever. At a height of 1,572m (5,157 feet) Phu Luang is also the highest point in the province.

## GETTING THERE

This is no easy matter. From Loei, you have to start by getting back to Wang Saphung, which is about 25 kilometres (15 miles) south along route 201. The reserve is another 35 kilometres (21 miles) west from there, along route 2250 – and there's almost no hope of hitching a lift. Basically, if you haven't got your own transport, all you can do is apply to the tourist office in Wang Saphung (☎ 042-841-141), which, depending on the number of takers, may (or may not) decide to organize a tour. The park is closed from June to October.

# FROM CHIANG KHAN TO NONG KHAI, ALONG THE BANKS OF THE MEKHONG RIVER

The Mekhong river, mother of all rivers, bordered by majestic views, untamed landscapes and visions of 'paradise lost', is the river that bridges the two contrasting worlds of Laos and Thailand – the first steeped in tradition, and the second a part of the modern world. Its banks are home to a small number of French-speakers who can still recall the days of French-Indochina not so very long ago. Within its waters, as anyone will tell you, lives the famous Phrayanak, the Mekhong snake-dragon that sometimes appears just before midnight to shoot clusters of fireballs up at the stars.

On a more prosaic note, collective taxis go endlessly back and forth between Chiang Khan and Nong Khai via Pakchom, Sangkhom, Sri Chiang Mai and Tha Bo. So why not set off in search of adventure and the prospect of a chance encounter? Human warmth guaranteed.

# CHIANG KHAN – เชียงคาน    DIALLING CODE: 042

This large village on the banks of the Mekhong, 48 kilometres (30 miles) north of Loei, is a haven of peace disturbed only by the occasional roar of a speedboat (the only rapid means of transport in the north). It even has a certain charm, with its traditional teak houses on stilts. But like so many other villages along these banks, Chiang Khan is probably doomed to disappear under mountains of concrete as development thrusts ahead.

## GETTING THERE

– **From Bangkok**: four departures daily (two in the morning and two in the late afternoon) from the Northeast Station. The journey takes roughly 10 hours.

– **From Loei**: collective taxis every 20 minutes, 5am–5pm. The journey takes an hour.

– **From Nong Khai**, **Sri Chiang Mai**, **Sangkhom** and **Pakchom along the River Mekhong**: buses and collective taxis every hour, starting at daybreak, from Nong Khai to Pakchom, where there are *songthaews* every 30 minutes.

## WHERE TO STAY

The standard of accommodation is remarkable – in fact, you're spoiled for choice.

### BUDGET (70–200 BTS PER PERSON PER NIGHT)

⚑ **Zen Guesthouse** – เซ็นเกสท์เฮ้าส์: 126/1 Chaikhong Road, Soi 12. ☎ and fax: 821-119. Even if it sounds corny, this place seems the embodiment of freedom and mutual respect, the peaceful traditional house that is run by an American woman called Katie and her husband Dtaw. Three lovely bedrooms with fan and mosquito nets; and an off-beat atmosphere and decor (not like on Khao San Road) – the kind of place you could stay a week or a month without feeling like a character in an agitprop movie. Katie and Dtaw, who have cycled their way across America, Laos and Tibet, also organize mountain-bike treks along the Mekong for four people or more. All the equipment is top-of-the range. Or you can hire mountain bikes by the day. Finally, you can have a steam bath or traditional massage here (see below). An exceptional place in every respect.

⚑ **Nong Sam Guesthouse** – น้องสามเกสท์เฮ้าส์: ☎ 821-457. Two new three-bedroom bungalows outside the village, along the river (less than 1 kilometre/0.5 miles to the east). Slightly set back from the owners' house in a peaceful, lush setting. Charming proprietor, married to an Englishman – nice kids too. Motorbike hire.

⚑ **Ton Khong Guesthouse** – ต้นโขงเกสท์เฮ้าส์: 299/3 Chaikhong Road, Soi 10. ☎ 821-097. Clean, friendly place a few steps from the Rimkhong Pub. Magnificent view of the Mekong from the terrace. Two shared showers on the landing. Good local cooking, delicious breakfasts, all at very reasonable prices. Warm welcome from the owners.

⚑ **Chiang Khan Guesthouse** – เชียงคานเกสท์เฮ้าส์: 282 Chaikhong Road, Soi 19. In the same location as the previous place, with the river lower down. Slightly old-fashioned but the prices more than make up for it (if the last place was cheap then this place is a steal) particularly when you think how nice and cosy it is here (they have hot showers). Motorbike and pedal-bike hire. Attentive landlord.

### MODERATE (200–500 BTS PER PERSON PER NIGHT)

⚑ **OK Guesthouse** – น้ำเกสท์เฮ้าส์: French-colonial-style villa (it's quite close to Laos here) on the river as before, by Soi 5. Four clean and spacious rooms, including two with air-conditioning. Very clean, shared bathroom facilities. The flower-filled terrace is one of the most beautiful in Chiang Khan. Make the most of the first rays of sunlight to watch the landscape come alive to the sound of birdsong. A place with a noticeably intimate atmosphere and a very warm welcome.

### EXPENSIVE (FROM 800 BTS PER PERSON PER NIGHT)

⚑ **Chiang Khan Hill Resort** – เชียงคานฮิลล์รีสอร์ท: ☎ 821-285. Elegant hotel building in a well-kept garden 5 kilometres (3 miles) west of Chiang Khan, opposite the Kaeng Khut Khu rapids. A broad range of prices. The terrace restaurant (which serves a tasty selection of Thai and Chinese specialities) looks down on the restless movement of this great river. Lots of Thais at the weekends.

## WHERE TO EAT AND WHERE TO HAVE A DRINK

✗ Lots of **decent little restaurants** all over the place, but actually nothing fantastic. For a taste of the exotic, choose one of the terrace restaurants on the Mekhong, where the sunsets are simply sublime. If one stands out above the rest, it would be the **OK Guesthouse**, for its wonderful soups and no less delicious pork with basil. Booking is essential.

❢ **Rimkhong Pub** – ริมโขงผับ: 294 Thanon Chaikong, Soi 8, on the Mekhong. ☎ 821-125. Open 8am–midnight, closed Monday. Run by three amiable, energetic guys, two of them Frenchmen. Somewhere to sip a cocktail while you listen to music, or to grab a real French-style breakfast. A great opportunity to pick up a stack of information (maps, routes etc.) based on years of travelling in Thailand by a group of men who can direct you every step of the way. They also organize their own treks. The written account of their adventures – shooting the rapids on the Mekhong on a raft-pedalo – makes absorbing reading. They also let out a few rooms in a teak house.

## THINGS TO DO AND SEE

★ **The market**: between sois 9 and 10. This is one of the most interesting markets in the province, but you have to get up early to see it (things are in full swing between 5am and 7am). There's another market in the evening, near soi 17.

★ **The temples**: there are about 10 of these, scattered all over town.

★ **Weaving**: lots of houses where you can watch women weaving silk and cotton in the traditional way (particularly blankets and *sarongs*).

★ **Steam baths** (1 hour) and **traditional massage** (1 hour 30 minutes): experiences not to be missed in the Zen Guesthouse, at any rate. The first to discover the secrets of the steam bath was Dtaw's great-great-grandfather, a famous healer who settled in Chiang Khan in the mid-19th century. His knowledge of medicinal plants was handed down to subsequent generations and today, no less than 40 plants, including basil, ginger, lime, lemon leaves, tamarind and bamboo as well as honey-based lotions are used to prepare the bath. As for the massages, these are softness itself and performed by a highly renowned elderly masseur from the village.

## THINGS TO DO AND SEE IN THE SURROUNDING AREA

★ **The Kaeng Khut Khu rapids** – แก่งคุดคู้: you can hire a bicycle for next to nothing and pedal all the way to the Kaeng Khut Khu rapids, where the Mekhong narrows and bends sharply, creating a little beach in the dry season. Follow the road going towards Pakchom for about 1 kilometre (0.5 miles), then fork left where you see the sign and carry on for just over another kilometre. Legend has it that a huge rock used to block the river until it was removed by divine intervention, and it was this that brought the lower Mekhong back to life. At the start of the walk you will notice the big rock commemorating the incident. It's impossible to miss – just head for the spot that's swarming with Thais having their picture taken. On Sunday it's a favourite picnic spot and there are lots of stands that sell food, including traditional sweets based on tamarind, coconut and dried bananas. Other stands sell fabrics. However much you fancy a dip, you are strongly recommended to stay out of the water. The current is ferocious and people drown every year. Another way of getting to Kaeng Khut Khu is to hire a little boat from a family in Chiang Khan or from the guesthouse. It takes 2 hours there and back and it's very cheap.

★ **Phu Tok**: a little hill about 8 kilometres (5 miles) from Chiang Khan with a superb view of the Mekhong valley and the wide rice-growing plains to the south. The best time to go there is at sunset. Head for Pakchom as if you were going to the rapids and take the right fork after 4 kilometres (2.5 miles). The top of the hill can be seen, over to the south.

★ **The Paben cave**: magnificent route through cotton fields, paddies, vegetable and fruit plantations where they grow such things as bananas, mangoes, papayas, grenadines, tamarinds, longans, pineapples and mangousteen. From Chiang Khan, follow the road to Pakchom as before until you get to the village of Paben (8 kilometres/5 miles). Once past the bridge, where you see the blue sign, take the track on the right. When you come to a Y-shaped junction, turn right then left, still following the blue signs. Carry straight on until you come to some wide steps on the left: you've arrived.

On the way, you'll find a little lake where you can cool down. The scenery changes with the seasons but the village people are invariably warm and friendly. Allow half a day (or even a day) to get here by bike. The total distance is about 16 kilometres (10 miles) but the cave is worth seeing just for the armies of bats that fly around it (bring a torch).

★ **The river Huang**: what's special about this river is that it forms a border with Laos before merging with the mighty Mekhong about 10 kilometres (6 miles) west of Chiang Khan. One possibility is to take a motorized dugout up the Mekhong as far as the Huang river (4 hours there and back, best to go at dawn or late afternoon). Another possibility is to hire a motorbike (or hitch a lift, which isn't easy) and ride to Pak Huay in the district of Tha Li (about 40 kilometres/25 miles in all, by way of Na Chan, Nam Khaem and Pakkan).

This is undoubtedly one of those great moments in life – travelling through lush countryside, past hills thick with banana and papaya plantations. When you reach your destination, you'll see a sign for Chieng Ton on the right. The road leads to the Huang river. On the opposite side, and barely 50 metres away, is the Lao village of Chieng Ton (also known as Kengton). In the dry season, there's even a ford where you can cross and it's perfectly safe to swim. It's a sobering sight seeing all those children, Thais and Laos, having so much fun. You may be tempted to explore the other bank for a few bahts. It's up to you, of course, but do ask yourself if you really want to be one of hundreds of foreigners (and Thais too for that matter) who've ended up stranded in the middle of nowhere. Perhaps you should just hang loose here in Kengton resort and watch the rapids from your comfortable bamboo hut. The whole place is in party mood at the weekend and you get to hear all the latest tunes. About 300 metres upriver is the O.T.S. Guesthouse – a very friendly place with a guaranteed 'middle of nowhere' atmosphere.

# PAKCHOM – ปากชม

DIALLING CODE: 042

Lovers of nature in the raw will find this one of the most beautiful spots in the region. In the dry season the water levels of the river that some call the 'Mother of Waters' start to drop, revealing vast expanses of white sand. This is when the local fishermen spring into action, each hoping to catch the first *pla buk* of the season. These are migrating catfish that can weigh as much as 250 kilograms (550 pounds) and measure 3 metres (10 feet) long. Catching one brings honour and respect to the whole village.

## WHERE TO STAY AND WHERE TO EAT

### BUDGET (FROM 80 BTS PER PERSON PER NIGHT)

⌂ ✕ **Pakchom Guesthouse** – ปากชมเกสท์เฮาส์: coming from Chiang Khan, take the track on the left (Soi 1) just before the bank. The guesthouse is about a dozen bamboo bungalows (all with mosquito nets) facing the Mekhong, with a beach lower down. The view is amazing, and the welcome is always warm. Delicious Laotian specialities made to order. Traditional massage.

### EXPENSIVE

⌂ **Pakchom Resort** – ปากชมรีสอร์ท: as you leave the village going towards Sangkhom, just beyond the post office. ☎ 881-033. Seven brand-new, very comfortable bungalows (hot water, air-conditioning and even a TV so you can brush up on your Thai). Charming but quite out of character for the area – more like a Swiss chalet. Very warm welcome. No direct access to the river.

## WHAT TO SEE AND DO

★ **The market**: takes place each morning, next to the *songthaew* rank. Masses of fruit, vegetables and fish (including catfish) but also an alarming collection of squirrels, badgers and ant eggs – which they really do eat . . .

Other than that, there isn't a great deal to do, and so much the better. It leaves all the more time to hang out in the sun and take full advantage of the beauty all around you.

# SANGKHOM – สางคม

DIALLING CODE: 042

Like Pakchom, this is another place that time forgot, on the Mekhong in the depths of deepest, darkest Asia. Judge for yourself which of the two is more beautiful or more strange.

## WHERE TO STAY AND WHERE TO EAT

All the places in Sangkhom are sufficiently special to be worth mentioning, so for once the whole list is given here. What they have in common is an uninterrupted view of the Mekhong, which at this point divides into two channels separated by a little mud island. They are all equally cheap (less than 100 Bts a night) and everyone speaks fluent English.

🛏 ✕ **Mama Guesthouse** – มาม่าเกสท์เฮาส์ coming from Pakchom, the first place you come to, on the left. Four bamboo bungalows, and an extremely helpful landlady. Laotian specialities, prepared with garden vegetables (the *som tam* is particularly delicious). This is the genuine article.

🛏 ✕ **Bouy Guesthouse** – บ๊วยเกสท์เฮาส์: more bungalows about 150 metres from the previous guesthouse. ☎ 441-065. Same deal as there, but much more elaborate:

wide choice of dishes, sauna, tai chi, telephone and international fax facilities. But the welcome might seem a bit noncommital, by comparison.

🛏 ✕ **River Huts Guesthouse** – ริเวอร์ฮัทเกสท์เฮาส์: about 300 metres from the Bouy Guesthouse. ☎ 441-012. More bungalows run by Hawaiian and occasional sculptor Yigal, who's made his name serving delicious food. Try to get one of the four bungalows by the river.

## THINGS TO DO AND SEE IN THE SURROUNDING AREA

★ **Than Tip Waterfall** – น้ำตกธารทิพย์: about 18 kilometres (11 miles) before you get to Sangkhom coming from Pakchom, on the right, and 3 kilometres (less than 2 miles) back from route 211. There are narrow waterfalls on three levels – quite impressive in the rainy season but less so the rest of the year when it shrinks to just a trickle of water. The rubbish that tends to collect there on busy days isn't too attractive either.

★ **Than Thong Waterfall** – น้ำตกธารทอง: about 11 kilometres (7 miles) from Sangkhom going towards Nong Khai, on the left. It gets very crowded at the weekend.

★ **Wat Pha Tak Seua**: a little monastery at the top of a steep mountain, with an astonishing view of the Mekong valley. About 5 kilometres (3 miles) out of Sangkhom, you take the road on the right that goes to Nong Khai. For further details, drop in on Yigal at the River Huts Guesthouse (*see above*) – this is his favourite walk.

# SRI CHIANG MAI – ศรีเชียงใหม่

DIALLING CODE: 042

This little place, populated by a significant minority of Laotians and Vietnamese who fled the neighbouring Communist regimes, is now a thriving commercial town (mainly food-processing and trade). Most of the original houses disappeared long ago, much to the dismay of tourists in search of tradition and local colour – but there's plenty of that across the river in Vientiane, which bustles with eastern promise from morning to night. Staying in Sri Chiang Mai is also a good opportunity to visit the celebrated village of Ban Phu.

## WHERE TO STAY AND WHERE TO EAT

🛏 ✕ **Tim Guesthouse** – ทิมเกสท์เฮ้าส์: Rimkhong Road, Soi 16. ☎ and fax: 451-072. Eight clean, quiet bedrooms ranging in price from 60 to 120 Bts depending on size and aspect. The landlord – an amiable French-speaking Swiss called Daniel who married a local girl – is a mine of information on Thai religion and culture. It's a friendly place, serving a selection of Thai and European food: delicious pancakes, milkshakes, real bread and a wide variety of French *saucissons*, which you eat on the terrace at night watching the lights in Vientiane. Daniel also organizes trips on the Mekhong, notably to the Wat Hin Mak Pen (4 hours there and back).

## WHAT TO SEE

★ **Spring rolls**: the streets are full of places run mainly by former refugees, where you can watch spring rolls being made daily, 3am–5pm. The pastry, made with rice flour and salt, is formed into translucent white discs and hung out to dry in the sun on rods of woven bamboo. Spring rolls are eventually exported the world over.

## WHAT TO SEE AND DO IN THE SURROUNDING AREA

★ **Wat Hin Mak Pen** – วัดหินหมากเป็น: about 20 kilometres (12 miles) from Sri Chiang Mai going towards Chiang Khan, on the right of route 211. This revered temple in a serene setting of cliffs and bamboo groves is a regular place of pilgrimage for the royal family. Behave with discretion when you go there so you do not disturb the pilgrims.

★ **Wat Ban Kanoun** – วัดบอนขนุน: also on the road to Chiang Khan, on the left near Lumphini, this small canyon boasts a cave, waterfalls and rock formations.

★ **Tha Bo market** – ตลาดท่าบ่อ: about 15 kilometres (9 miles) from Sri Chiang Mai, Tha Bo is the first big village you come to on the way to Nong Khai. It's famous for the quality of its market (daily, 6am–noon), which sells fish and shellfish, fruits and vegetables. Tomatoes are the local speciality, sometimes crystallized and tinned for export. This is also where the taxis leave for Ban Phu.

# BAN PHU – บ้านภู

This little village, famous for being close to Phu Phra Bat – ภูพระบาท (actually it's about 12 kilometres/7.5 miles from Bantiu), is unavoidable if you want to go trekking in the park. The best way of getting here is by early-morning *songthaew* from Sri Chiang Mai or Nong Khai to Tha Bo, where you hire another *songthaew* all the way to Ban Phu 25 kilometres (15 miles) away.

To get into the park itself, you hire a motorbike-taxi to take you the last few kilometres (couple of miles). It takes 2–3 hours to get to Ban Phu. When you get there, remember to check what time the last *songthaew* leaves for Tha Bo (about 3pm). Another possibility is to hire a motorbike and go the whole way under your own steam.

FROM CHIANG KHAN TO NONG KHAI

## WHAT TO SEE IN THE SURROUNDING AREA

★ **The Historic National Park of Phu Phra Bat** – อุทยานประวัติ
ศาสตร์แห่งชาติภูพระบาท: this park at the top of Phupan hill is famous for
its bizarre (to say the least) rock formations, which, from 1500 to 3000 BC,
were used as shelters by the first human settlers. What remains today is a
series of geometric and figurative paintings in red ochre (mostly of men
and animals). These are thought to reflect the religious and spiritual
beliefs of the time. Sadly, the paintings are now under threat from
repeated exposure to sun and heavy rains, which the visibly diminishing
forest can no longer keep in check.

When Buddhism came to Thailand, the rock shelters were converted into
places of worship for use in religious ceremonies. The high spots of the
visit are:

– **the Ha Nang Ou Sa** (local map, **1**), which is shaped like a mushroom
and features a statue of the Buddha in long robes surrounded by *semas* –
stones characteristic of the Dvaravatî period – marking the eight cardinal
points in space;

– **the Wat Poh Ta** (map, **2**) or temple of the father-in-law;

– **the Tham Phra** (map, **26**), representing the finest example of a prehistoric shelter turned Hindu-Buddhist temple (the Khmers came this
way);

– **the Tham Kon and the Woor** (map, **5**), which depicts seven walking
men and bulls. Begin by visiting the little museum near reception.

The park is meticulously maintained (lots of signs in English, dustbins,
picnic area with bamboo tables under a bower by the Phra Sadej Cliff), and
this makes for a very pleasant tour that lasts at least 2 hours. An English-
speaking guide is on hand every day except Monday and Tuesday.

★ **Wat Praphutabat Buabok** – วัดพระพุทธบาทบัวบก: take the road on the
left, about 1 kilometre (0.5 miles) from the entrance to the park, by the
checkpoint with the barrier. The temple at the top is a modern replica of
the famous *stupa* at That Phanom, and is said to have been founded on
the Buddha's footprints. His relics are believed to be inside the arrow.
Many pilgrims come here to celebrate the Enlightenment and in addition
to all the offerings they leave inside the temple (incense, flowers and gold
leaf) they also drop coins into no fewer than 108 saucers at the entrance.
The whole place has a party atmosphere with popcorn, maize and grilled
chicken, proving that it is a joy to meditate.

# NONG KHAI – หนองคาย  DIALLING CODE: 042

With every backpacker in the northeast making a beeline for Nong Khai,
the place has changed a great deal since the opening of the Friendship
Bridge in 1994 – สะพานมิตรภาพไทยลา – which now provides an easy link
between Thailand and Laos. Much of its charming provincial atmosphere
has been lost in the race to develop tourism and commerce, but here and
there, vestiges of its past have survived. You still see the occasional
traditional house along the river and of course they continue to make their
famous baguettes. But for how much longer?

## ADDRESSES AND USEFUL INFORMATION

**🅑 TAT** – ททท (Tourist Office): next door to the Friendship Bridge. Useful source of information but quite a way from the town centre.

■ **Immigration Head Office** – สำนักงานตรวจคนเข้าเมือง: as you leave town going towards Udon Thani, on the left. This is where to go to renew your Thai visa.

### To get to Laos

– **Departures for Laos**: a ferry service still operates between Nong Khai and Tha Dua but it's only for Thais and Laotians. Foreigners have to use the Friendship Bridge, which is open daily, 8.30am–6pm. The bridge is exclusively for vehicles and no one is allowed across on foot. The bus shuttle service leaves from the minibus station situated at the junction of routes 2 and 212, just before the immigration checkpoint. Your passport is stamped with an exit stamp at the checkpoint and with a visa stamp on the other side of the bridge. From there, it's another 19 kilometres (11 miles) to Vientiane by bus or *tuk-tuk*. There are no rip-offs to warn you about.

– **Visas for Laos**: if you can afford it (roughly US$100 but likely to get cheaper) the best solution is to obtain a visa (valid for two weeks and renewable in Vientiane) on the spot in Nong Khai, through an agency approved by the Central Office of Tourism in Vientiane. It's more-or-less official and remarkably quick – less than 4 hours. The three guesthouses listed below can arrange it for you. Otherwise, 30-day visas are available from the consulates in Khon Kaen (they take three days and cost about US$40) and Bangkok (to be avoided – too many rip-offs).

## WHERE TO STAY AND WHERE TO EAT

### BUDGET (ABOUT 100 BTS PER PERSON PER NIGHT)

🛏 ✕ **Mekong Guesthouse** – แม่โขงเกสท์เฮ้าส์: 519 Rimkhong Road. ☎ 412-119. Lovely teak house with terrace on the river. The rooms are nothing special but they are very cheap. A friendly place that's well situated; also serves food.

🛏 ✕ **Meeting Place** – มีทติ้งเพลช เกสท์เฮ้าส์: 1117 Soi Chuen Jitt. ☎ and fax: 421-223. Friendly, spotless guesthouse-bar-restaurant near Prajak Bungalows. The owner is an old hand at obtaining visas for Laos and can handle the whole shebang – *tuk-tuk,* bus and papers – at no extra charge. The only snag is the restaurant, where the prices are a little high.

### BUDGET TO MODERATE (80–200 BTS PER PERSON PER NIGHT)

🛏 ✕ **Mutmee Guesthouse** – มัดหมี่เกสท์เฮ้าส์: 1111/4 Kaew Worawut Road. Several houses with two, three or four nicely furnished rooms complete with reproduction paintings in every corner. Pleasant garden on the Mekong, where you can eat. This is the place preferred by backpackers the world over, which is hardly surprising considering what's laid on for them: cycle rides, tai chi, yoga, information on trekking in the surrounding area and a very good map of the town. The downside is the rather ghetto feel to the place on some nights and the prices, which you couldn't say were expensive but you couldn't call them cheap either. Still – a nice place, all the same.

## MODERATE TO EXPENSIVE (300–500 BTS PER PERSON PER NIGHT)

🛏 **Prajak Bungalows** – ประจักษ์ บังกาโล: 1178 Prajak Road. ☎ 412-644. Several wooden bungalows with one, two or three rooms with or without air-conditioning. Very comfortable, spotlessly clean, spacious and quiet.

## WHERE TO EAT AND WHERE TO HAVE A DRINK

✘ **Songtawan Restaurant** – ร้าน อาหารสองตะวัน: Rimkhong Road, Soi 4. ☎ 421-209. Not a bad idea to book, because it can get busy in the evenings. This absolute dream of a restaurant is a short distance from the centre, in the east of town, 500 metres beyond the old immigration offices on the path that runs along the Mekhong. Traditional mini-terraces on stilts, where everybody sits around the *kantoke,* a typically Laotian small low table. Lush greenery, tranquil atmosphere and a delicious selection of Thai specialities, particularly the local fish soup (seafood *tom yam).* Warm welcome and almost exclusively local clientele.

🍷 **Le Bistro** – เลอบริสโทร: Rimkhong Road. Facing the river; you can order a draught beer and play billiards while listening to music.

## WHAT TO DO AND SEE

★ **Boat trip on the Mekhong**: every day at 5.30pm a boat leaves the landing stage near the Mutmee Guesthouse for a 1-hour tour of the river. Lovely sunset, bar and restaurant on board. Touristy, but nice all the same.

★ **Village Weaver Handicrafts** – หมู่บ้านทอผ้า: 786 Prajak Road. Visits daily, 8am–5pm. Exhibition and sale of fabrics (particularly Mutmee and Ikat-style indigo cottons) produced by the women members of this non-profit-making organization, founded in 1982 by the Sisters of Berger to help stop the mass exodus of women from the province and save them from almost certain misery and degradation (prostitution in particular).

★ **Friendship Bridge** – สะพานมิตรภาพไทย์ลาว: this bridge, built with Australian funding, is more than 1 kilometre (0.5 miles) long and the only bridge over the Mekhong outside Chinese territory. It completes the Friendship Route, built by the Americans during their time in Vietnam to link Bangkok with Vientiane.

## WHAT TO SEE IN THE SURROUNDING AREA

★ **Wat Kaek** – วัดแขก: very kitsch temple about 5 kilometres (3 miles) out of town on the right going towards Phon Phisai (route 212). It's not easy to find, particularly since the sign is in Thai, but all the *tuk-tuks* in the town centre know how to get there. Open daily, 7am–5.30pm. There are statues galore, including a bizarre procession of dogs in dark glasses following an elephant, and less extravagant images of the principal deities in the Hindu pantheon: Shiva and his wife Uma, Vishnu and his famous avatar Krishna. What you see here is a temple created by a Yogi with a feverish imagination, who wanted to bring together Buddhism and Hinduism – a tall order, to say the least. A new building (in baroque New-Age style) bigger than a station concourse was recently added, to house the pilgrims who visit the temple.

★ **Wat Bang Phuan** – วัดบางผวน: about 18 kilometres (11 miles) west of Nong Khai (on route 211). This group of ruins includes two large statues of the Buddha and a large white tapering *chedi*. There is also an astonishing little museum with a display of wooden statues. This is a quiet, peaceful place in the heart of the country; it is also home to some friendly monks.

## LEAVING NONG KHAI

– **By non-air-conditioned bus**: from the terminus slightly to the east of the town centre on Praserm Road (between Prajak Road and Highway 212). Plenty of buses go south every day (15 to Bangkok, 19 to Udon) and also to the west (13 to Loei, and three, all in the morning, to Sri Chiang Mai).

– **By VIP bus**: there are lots of agencies on Prajak Road.

– **By train**: the station is slightly away from the centre, near the Friendship Bridge. The three trains a day for Bangkok all stop in Udon Thani, Khon Kaen and Ayutthaya (one in the morning, two in the evening).

## FROM UDON THANI TO PHIMAI

# UDON THANI – อุดรธานี    DIALLING CODE: 042

Udon Thani is a large and noisy commercial centre that grew rich on the American presence during the Vietnam War. Practically all the affordable hotels are crummy and there's virtually nothing to see here in any case. If guidebooks mention it at all, it's simply as a place you pass through en route for Ban Chiang. But just in case you do have to spend the night here, you will find two acceptable hotels on Prajak Road near the Clock Tower: Pracha Pakdee Hotel and Sri Sawat Hotel.

## LEAVING TOWN

– **By bus**: there are buses to Bangkok and Nakhon Ratchasima from the bus station on Sai Uthit Road, near the Charoen Sri shopping centre. Buses to Nong Khai leave from the stop near Rungsina market and buses to Loei and Chiang Mai leave from the bus station in the northwest of town.

– **By train**: there are three trains a day for Nong Khai and the towns in the south, from the station on Prajak Road.

– **By air**: three Thai Airways flights daily to Bangkok. Contact their agency on Markkeng Road. ☎ 243-222.

# BAN CHIANG – บ้านเชียง

DIALLING CODE: 042

This once quiet and unassuming little village about 50 kilometres (30 miles) from Udon Thani shot to worldwide fame overnight in 1966 when a young American tourist happened to find some pottery. Like the discovery made in the caves at Lascaux in France 15 years earlier, this was a chance discovery that would change the face of history. The results of archaeological analysis later confirmed that some of the pieces (not only pottery but also bronze and iron artefacts and jewellery) were more than 5,000 years old.

This discovery had the effect of turning received wisdom on its head and revolutionized our knowledge of the history of the Far East. It proved that the region of I-san, like China and Mesopotamia, had been a cradle of civilization. Its bronze culture clearly pre-dated the first Thai settlers, who did not start to arrive from China until about 1000 BC.

## GETTING THERE

**There are two possibilities**:

– The first is to take a bus for Sakhon Nakhon (along route 22) from the southern station in Udon Thani on Sai Uthit Road (near the big Charoen Sri shopping centre). There are buses every 25 minutes. Get off after 50 kilometres (30 miles), where the road forks for Thung Fon (route 2225), and go the last 6.5 kilometres (4 miles) by *tuk-tuk*.

– The second possibility is to go straight from Udon to Ban Chiang by *songthaew*, which you catch opposite the Top World supermarket, at the junction of Phosi Road and Surakarn Road.

## WHERE TO STAY

🛏 **Lakeside Sunrise Guesthouse** – เลคไซด์ซันไรส์เกสท์เฮาส์: ☎ 208-167. A wooden chalet facing the lake overlooked by the archaeological museum. Run by Mrs Tong Lak, who works at the museum, and her Australian husband Alex. An absolute jewel of a place – it's more like staying with a family than renting a room, particularly since you all eat together. Cheap and very clean.

## WHAT TO SEE

★ **Ban Chiang National Museum** – พิพิธภัณฑสถานแห่งชาติบ้านเชียง: open daily, 8.30am–4.30pm. ☎ 223-091. Admission charged. English-speaking guide. Well laid-out museum housing an interesting display of artefacts in two adjoining buildings. The collections include a wealth of ceramics, arranged chronologically to illustrate the development of the craft in terms of shapes, designs and colours over four millennia; plus bronze and iron objects such as axe-heads, spears, arrows, knives, hooks and jewellery including bracelets and necklaces. There is also an exhibition of lifestyles and popular traditions in prehistoric times. Allow about 2 hours for the visit.

★ **Wat Pho Si Nai** – วัดโพธิ์ศรีนาย: opposite the post office. This is the centrepiece of the archaeological excavations that were declared a UNESCO World Heritage Site in 1992. The site has recently been renovated to show off the excavations to better effect, particularly the bones and pots.

### IN THE SURROUNDING AREA

★ **Potters' villages**: **Kham O**, 2 kilometres (1.25 miles) before the road forks for Chiang, on Route 22, and **Ban Pu Lu**, which is 4 kilometres (2.5 miles) before Ban Chiang after the fork in the road. In these two villages the potters have kept alive the skills and traditions of their forefathers who used Greek production techniques and Egyptian designs to produce the distinctive pottery discovered in Ban Chiang. Not surprisingly, some of their pots look exactly like Ancient Greek and Egyptian urns. You'll find many of them on sale in the shops in Ban Chiang facing the museum.

# KHON KAEN – ขอนแก่น     DIALLING CODE: 043

Khon Kaen is the fourth most important town in Thailand, traditionally famous for its agriculture and textiles but now looking to the future. It is home to an ambitious university (the first in I-san) and recently acquired a big luxury hotel, which towers over the whole town, in anticipation of the privileged role that it expects to play when trade opens up with its Laotian neighbours. Nice place to stop, with a magnificent museum and lots of craft shops. It's also the jumping-off point for the village of Chonnabot.

### USEFUL ADDRESSES

**❶ TAT** – ททท (Tourist Office): 15/5 Prachasamosorn Road. ☎ 244-498 and 244-499. Fax: 244-497. The staff are welcoming and speak reasonable English. A particularly clear and useful map of the town is also available.

■ **Laotian Consulate** – สถาน กงศุลลาว: 19/3 Photisarn Road. ☎ 221-961. Fax: 223-849. Open weekdays only, 8.30–11.30am and 1.30–4.30pm. About 2 kilometres (1.25 miles) from the town centre, east of Lake Kaen Nakhon.

A 30-day visa is half the price it would be in Nong Khai and you don't need to go through a local travel agency (just give an address where you'll be staying in Vientiane – a hotel will do). The only snag is the three-day waiting period – there's no getting round that.

■ **Currency exchange**: easily done through the Bangkok Bank in Na Muang Road, next to the Charoen Thani Princess Hotel. This is the most central place and it has a 24-hour cash machine.

■ **Thai Airways** – สายการบินไทย: 183/6 Maliwan Road. ☎ 236-523. As you leave town, going towards the airport. Provided you don't turn up mob-handed and do arrive in time, they might even let you on the next flight with the staff (if you smile sweetly and are prepared to wait).

■ **Municipal swimming pool** – สระว่ายน้ำ: Sri Road, 2–3 kilometres (1.5 miles) from the centre. Take a yellow *songthaew* (with orange doors) from the corner of Klang Muang Road and Sri Chan Road. The pool is on the right. Look for the little sign showing a blue swimmer. This is where the gilded youth of the area hang out.

## WHERE TO STAY

### BUDGET (ABOUT 200 BTS PER PERSON PER NIGHT)

Not many decent hotels in this price range. This is the only one that might do.

⌂ **Sansumran Hotel** – โรงแรม–แสนสำราญ: 55–59 Klang Muang Road. ☎ 239-611. Clean, but pretty basic all the same. Ask for a room on the ground floor because upstairs it's like a steam bath, despite the fan. The owner is a wonderfully genial chap who prides himself on knowing a thing or two about the area – which he can tell you in English.

### EXPENSIVE TO SPLASH OUT (300–1,500 BTS PER PERSON PER NIGHT)

⌂ **Roma Hotel** – โรงแรมโรมา: 50/2 Klang Muang Road. ☎ 236-276. Practically opposite the previous entry. Well-kept but fairly featureless hotel with rooms at a wide range of prices. The rooms with fans are affordable.

⌂ There are lots more hotels of a similar standard, especially the **Kosa Hotel** – โรงแรมโกษา and the **Khon Kaen Hotel** – โรงแรมขอนแก่น.

## WHERE TO EAT

### BUDGET TO MODERATE

✗ There are lots of little restaurants serving Thai or Chinese dishes on the Klang Muang Road and in the night markets.

✗ **First Choice Restaurant** – ร้านอาหารเฟิร์สช้อยส์: 18/8 Phimpasut Road, opposite the Khon Kaen hotel. Good Asian cooking served in an agreeable air-conditioned room. The traditional set lunchtime menu is certainly worth a try, and the service is impeccable.

### MODERATE

✗ **The Parrot Restaurant** – ร้านอาหารเดอะแพรรอท: 175 Sri Chan Road, opposite the Bangkok Bank. Open from 7am (for breakfast) to 11pm. Particularly plush setting that appeals to expats and Thais alike, serving a range of Thai and international dishes (including Italian). Particularly recommended are the steaks (which have to be quarter-pounders otherwise it's not *sanouk* – that means fun, remember), served for some reason with soup and a starter (even more *sanouk*). There's a concert every night and as much locally brewed Singha beer as you can drink. A real winner of a place.

## WHAT TO SEE

★ **The National Museum** – พิพิธภัณฑสถานแห่งชาติขอนแก่น: Lung Soon Rachakarn Road, north of town. Open Monday to Friday, 9am–4pm. Admission charged. The building houses one of the richest collections in Thailand, displayed on two storeys around a delightful patio full of flowers. The exhibition is in three broad sections:

– **Section 1**: from the Mesozoic era (dinosaur skeletons) to the time of *Homo sapiens* with pottery, bronze artefacts etc.

– **Section 2**: Dvâravatî and Khmer history as illustrated by religious works of art: Hindu-Buddhist statues, votive tablets, *semas* etc.

– **Section 3**: the popular traditions of I-san: traditional dwellings, costumes and musical instruments such as the *kaen* (like an American Indian flute) after which the town is named.

★ **The banks of Lake Kaen Nakhon** – ริมบึงแก่นนคร: south of town, this is a nice place to go for a walk at the end of the afternoon to mix with Thai families enjoying barbecued chicken I-san style (it needs a bowl of rice to cool the mouth down) or a papaya salad. While you're there, take a look at the nearby Wat Tat and Wat Klang Muang Kao.

★ **The markets**: bustling with activity all along the Klang Muang Road. It's best to go after dark when there are still lots of people, particularly up by the post office.

## SHOPPING

– **The culinary specialities of I-san**: the Klang Muang Road is lined with an impressive selection of shops mainly specializing in cooked meats and local confectionery. You'll find smoked sausages and chitterlings, biscuits, crystallized fruits – lots of original gift ideas that don't cost a fortune.

– **Silks and cottons from I-san or Laos**: south of town visit the Prathamakant Local Goods Centre at 81 Ruen Rom Road. Definitely worth a look as much for the sheer choice of fabrics as for the way they are displayed. Sophon, who speaks good English, can give you an expert tour of the northeast based on the fabrics produced in each province.

## WHAT TO SEE IN THE SURROUNDING AREA

★ **Chonnabot**: *Mutmee* silk-weaving takes place beneath houses on stilts 57 kilometres (35 miles) south going towards Nakhon Ratchasima (roughly 12 kilometres/7.5 miles from Ban Phai on Route 229). You can admire the skill with which the women tie, dye and weave the silk according to the *mutmee* tie-dyeing technique that enables them to create designs of many different colours. Or you might get to see how they make pillows and decorative cotton cushions (in the *prakit* style). To learn more about silk production from silkworms to the finished article, visit the *Thai Silk Exhibition Hall* on the way out of town. Unfortunately, the staff don't speak any English.

★ **Khok Sanga Na Ngam**: a little village quite unlike any other – to say the least. There's not a guard dog in sight, just a colony of cobras (the most venomous of all the reptiles – one bite can kill sensitive subjects in less than 5 minutes) that live cheek-by-jowl (well, fang actually) with the villagers. For more than a century man and snake have been mesmerizing crowds at fairs and local celebrations. This is a great place to visit if you're feeling suicidal – otherwise feel free to leave it out.

## LOCAL FESTIVAL

– **Silk festival**: takes place from the end of November to early December. Seven days and nights of celebrations with processions, music, traditional dancing and, of course, exhibitions.

## LEAVING KHON KAEN

### By non-air-conditioned bus

Take the bus from the station in Prachasamonsorn Road, a 15-minute walk from Klang Muang Road.

– **To Loei**, **Udon Thani** and **Nong Khai**: buses every 30 minutes until 5.30pm.

– **To Phitsanulok** and **Sukhothai**: five buses a day.

– **To Nakhon Ratchasima**: three buses first thing in the morning.

– **To Bangkok**: three buses first thing and in the evening.

### By air-conditioned bus

From the centre of town, 50 metres back from the Klang Muang Road. Air-conditioned buses go to the same places as non-air-conditioned buses but there are not so many of them.

🚂 The station is slightly away from the centre of town at the end of Ruen Rom Road.

There are three trains daily to Nong Khai, two to Nakhon Ratchasima and five to Bangkok.

### By air

There are four flights daily to Bangkok.

# MUKDAHAN – มุกดาหาร          DIALLING CODE: 042

This large village with a population of 45,000 makes a matched pair with Savannakhet, a boom town in the south of Laos that has become the first trade link between Thailand and Vietnam. Mukhadan itself could soon open out to trade with China and attract the same sort of investment activity as Nong Khai, if the rumoured second bridge over the Mekong actually happens.

## INFORMATION AND USEFUL ADDRESSES

– **Boats to Savannakhet** – เรือไป สุวรรณเขต: five crossings a day on weekdays, three at the weekends. From Savan there are daily links with Vientiane (noon) and Pakse (6am). From June to September, there is also a twice-daily ferry service operating between Savannakhet and Vientiane. Note that no visa is issued at the border, only in London, Khon Kaen or Bangkok (which is best avoided because of all the rip-offs). Specify your port of entry on the visa or you might be sent back to Nong Khai.

■ **Immigration Office** – สำนักงาน ตรวจคนเข้าเมือง: opposite the landing stage. This is the place to go to extend your Thai visa.

## WHERE TO STAY

The choice of accommodation is pretty dire: only one guesthouse (and even that's out of town) and a few second-rate hotels. But there are just a few that might be worth a look.

### BUDGET TO MODERATE (150– 350 BTS PER PERSON PER NIGHT)

🛏 **Pirom's Guesthouse** – ภิรมย์ เกสท์เฮาส์: about 12 kilometres (7.5 miles) north of Mukdahan, in the little village of Wan Yai on the river. Choose from a dormitory or double room – it's a clean place with a family atmosphere. Bicycle hire and boat trips.

🛏 **Bantom Kasame Hotel** – บรร ทมเกษมโฮเด็ล: 25/25-2 Samud Sakdarak Road. ☎ 611-235. Central and very clean, with mosquito screens on the window and hot water. The only decent hotel in this price range.

🛏 **Huanom Hotel** – ฮั่วนำโฮเด็ก: 36 Samud Sakdarak Road. ☎ 611-197. Near the previous place, by a noisy crossroads. The rooms have hot water, and some have air-conditioning. Fairly indifferent welcome but alright otherwise.

### MODERATE TO EXPENSIVE (200– 500 BTS PER PERSON PER NIGHT)

🛏 **Saensuk Bungalows** – แสนสุข บังกาโล: 2 Phitak Santirad Road. ☎ 611-214. About 50 metres from the post office, past the big crossroads. Not much more expensive than the previous place but distinctly smarter and more comfortable and all the rooms have air-conditioning. Nice place.

## WHERE TO EAT

### BUDGET

✕ There are lots of cheap little restaurants all over town.

✕ **Pith Bakery** – พิทย์เบเกอรี: just a few metres beyond the post office, past the Hong Kong Hotel. Absolutely spotless. Delicious brownies, ice-cream and breakfast as good as you could make yourself. Owned by a lovely lady who knows everything there is to know round here and loves nothing better than to be asked for her advice – and it's well worth taking.

MODERATE

✕ **Morris Ship Restaurant** – ร้าน
อาหารมอริสชิป: all aboard for a
short trip down memory lane to
the days of French Indochina. The
year is 1907 and to maintain control, France needs a flat-bottomed
boat capable of getting to all the
main provinces flooded by the
Mekhong whatever the season.
They decide to call the boat 'Morris'. During World War II, this was
the boat that shipped arms to the
Indochinese forces. In the mid-
1980s, it was bought by a Thai
businessman, who converted it
into a floating restaurant. Go there
for lunch, sitting in the shade looking out to Savannakhet, enjoying
good Thai and Chinese food to the
rhythm of the latest disco sounds.

It's a bit expensive and the service
can be a bit clumsy.

BUDGET TO EXPENSIVE

✕ **Riverview Restaurant** – ร้าน
อาหารริเวอร์วิว: slightly away from
the centre, about 600 metres south
of the Immigration Office – just far
enough to give you an appetite.
The setting is very refined – almost
swanky – on a magnificent terrace
on stilts overlooking the Mekhong.
Clearly it's the best restaurant in
town but it serves some surprisingly cheap dishes in addition to a
range of fish specialities (catfish,
*tom yam, som tam*). The perfect
place for a romantic tête-à-tête
whatever the state of your bank
account.

## WHAT TO SEE AND DO

★ **The Indochinese market**: stands all along the river to the right of the
Immigration Office and in the little streets off to the side. This is the place
to go for anything and everything: kitsch items galore, tools and
machines principally imported from China via Vietnam and Laos. Go
there mainly for the atmosphere.

★ **Walk along the Mekhong**: this is a very shady and agreeable stroll
even during the hottest hours of the day. Along the way, near the
Immigration Office, take a look at the Wat Sri Mongkol Thai. It was built
by grateful Vietnamese refugees during the 1950s. Compare this with the
Wat Sri Sumong about 200 metres to the south. Notice the striking
contrast between the brand-new *viharn* of the former and this ancient,
very dilapidated *bot* with its French architectural influence.

## WHAT TO SEE IN THE SURROUNDING AREA

★ **Phu Narom**: this hill about 3 kilometres (1.25 miles) from the town
centre overlooks the town bordered by the Mekhong. It's an easy climb
and the view is wonderful.

★ **The Mukdahan National Park** – อุทยานแห่งชาติมุกดาหาร (Phu Pha
Thoep): about 16 kilometres (10 miles) from Mukdahan going towards
Khemarat on Route 2034. Open daily, 6am–6pm. Collective taxis go there
every 30 minutes starting at 8am, leaving from a point 200 metres south
of the Mukdahan Hotel. You have to walk the last kilometre (half mile) or
so. If you want to camp in the park, take a tent. Drinks are available. It's a
lovely walk to some pretty waterfalls if you go in the rainy season, and you
pass rocks featuring human and animal figures (sharks, sphinxes,

hippopotami, crocodiles and so on). There are also prehistoric rock paintings that have seen better days, and fossilized dinosaur bones. From the top of Camel Cliff (so-called because it's shaped like a dromedary) there's a splendid view of the Mekhong and the Laotian plain. Other curiosities not to be missed include the 'Cave of a Thousand Buddhas' and the Wang Deuan Ha lake further down in the park. If he's still there, you can be sure of an enthusiastic welcome from Thongbiane, an elderly guide with a great sense of humour (speaks English and a little French) who is ready to take you off in search of squirrels, monkeys, foxes and wild cats.

## LEAVING MUKDAHAN

🚌 These days, buses leave from the new bus station about 3 kilometres (1.25 miles) north of town on Route 212 (going towards Nakhon Phanom). It's best to go there by *tuk-tuk*.

There are lots of buses every day to **Bangkok** (in the evening), **Ubon Ratchathani** and **That Phanom**.

# THAT PHANOM – ธาตุพนม    DIALLING CODE: 042

This small provincial village on the Mekhong is the quietest, most peaceful place for miles. Steeped in history, with very few streets and hardly any cars, it's the perfect spiritual retreat for lost souls who need to spend a few days, months or years finding themselves. No kidding – it worked wonders for a Danish woman who emerged from the Buddhist convent reborn and hand in hand with the love of her life. You can't cross to Laos from That Phanom (only locals can) but you can get to Nakhon Phanom about 56 kilometres (35 miles) to the north. When you apply for a visa, it's a good idea to specify that you want to go to Laos via Tha Kaek.

## WHERE TO STAY

### BUDGET (LESS THAN 100 BTS PER PERSON PER NIGHT)

🏠 **Pom's Guesthouse** – ป้อม เกสท์เฮาส์: 110 Soi Anurakjaydee. ☎ 541-450. In the second side-street left of the boarding point for Laos, beyond the Immigration Office. Pom speaks fluent English and a little French and passes for something of an intellectual in hotel circles. He's your man if you want to know more about the vagaries of Thai society. You can sit down with Pom and ask him anything you like – anything goes. As for the accommodation, it consists of some nice little rooms and a dormitory, all clean and very

reasonably priced. Good breakfast, free coffee the day you arrive and unlimited Chinese tea throughout the rainy season. Bicycle hire, boat trips and long-distance telephone facilities also available. A great place.

🏠 **Niyana Guesthouse** – นัยนา เกสท์เฮ้าส์: Rimkhong Road. Also on the left of the boarding point, on the promenade beside the Laotian market. When Niyana 1 closed down, the landlady set off in search of adventure and opened this new place in the middle of a huge sports ground (it's full of football-crazy locals). There's the same 'peace and love' atmosphere as there always was, the same activities (cycling, boating, Thai lessons) and the same kettle on the hob for tea. When it comes to tourism, this lady knows it all – except perhaps that the Khao San Road isn't everybody's cup of tea. The rooms and dormitories are a shade more expensive here than in the last place. Standards of up-keep are fairly rudimentary.

## MODERATE TO EXPENSIVE

â **Sangthong Hotel** – โรงแรม–แสงทอง: Phanom Panarak Road. ☎ 541-397. For information and bookings, enquire at the photo shop on the second road that runs parallel to the Mekhong not far from the big arch. It also lets out a few old-fashioned rooms but most are in the new building on the Mekhong, to the right of the boarding point. All the rooms are new, with fans (impossible to adjust so there's a force 7 or 8 gale blowing all night) or air-conditioning (a bit pricey for what they are) and hot water. The premises are guarded 24 hours a day. Good, but nothing more than that.

## WHERE TO EAT

There's not a great choice and no really nice place that stands out above the rest. For lunch, try one of the stands outside the temple, for barbecued chicken or fish, sticky rice and seasonal fruit. For dinner, you could try one of the restaurants near the bus station, but don't expect a warm welcome.

✗ There's also the **Go All Night** restaurant to the left of the temple opposite the bank. Thai and Chinese food is served late into the night, as its name suggests.

## WHAT TO SEE

★ **Wat Phra That Phanom** – วัดพระธาตุพนม: open 6am–5.30pm. This Lao and Khmer-style *chedi* of imposing dimensions (roughly 53 metres high by 12 kilometres wide/160 feet by 36 feet) is decorated with 110 kilograms (250 pounds) of pure gold at the top and is famous for its holiness. It attracts thousands of pilgrims who go there regularly to offer their prayers to the many resident Buddhas. According to Buddhist legend, one of them is supposed to be 2,535 years old (actually it's more like 1,500 years according to archaeologists but that's quite a long time even so). It has been restored several times: first in 1940, then in 1975 because the arrow had collapsed, and most recently in 1979. For a handful of bahts you can earn yourself some credits releasing birds from their cages – not something you do every day.

★ **The Laotian market**: held twice a week, on Monday and Thursday, 6am–11am. It's about 300 metres from the boarding point along the Mekhong on the left. On market days the border on the Thai side is pushed back a few metres and bamboo barriers are erected, under the watchful eye of customs officials and soldiers. When it comes to trade, they're not going to let a little thing like a border stand in their way. This lively market sells the perfect presents (were it not for the excess baggage charge): Vietnamese black pigs. Less amusing to see were all the wild animal furs still being sold.

## WHAT TO SEE IN THE SURROUNDING AREA

★ **Renu Nakhon** – เรณูนคร: about 15 kilometres (9 miles) inland, this is an excellent place to walk to for three reasons. First, the temple in the village (the Wat Renu Phanom) is a replica of the famous Phra That Phanom and houses, among other things, an image of the Buddha in meditative pose symbolizing Renu. Secondly, the village specializes in embroidered fabrics such as sheets, shirts and sarongs that you won't find anywhere else. Thirdly, and this is quite enough reason in itself, because there's nothing quite as nice as a walk through such luxuriant countryside with lots of traditional houses on the way.

## LEAVING THAT PHANOM

– **For Bangkok**: air-conditioned buses leave from the Chayangkun Road opposite the Lim Charoen hotel.

– **For Renu Nakhon** and **Nakhon Phanom**: catch buses in the same street, on the opposite pavement about 100 metres away going towards the *wat*.

– **Other destinations**: buses leave from the bus station beyond the Go All Night restaurant, in the first street on the left.

# NAKHON RATCHASIMA (EX-KORAT) –
## นครราชสีมา/โคราช
DIALLING CODE: 044

To judge from the buildings and offices on every street corner (to say nothing of the flourishing trade in mobile phones) this place more than any other in the northeast, has gone the way of its big sister Bangkok, which is in any case only 260 kilometres (160 miles) away. An American base during the Vietnam War, Nakhon Ratchasima today is a modern, rather sprawling city of no particular charm on the way to Phimai.

## USEFUL ADDRESS

**🛈 TAT** – ททท (Tourist Office): 2104 Mittraphap Road. ☎ 213-666 or 213-030. Fax: 213-667. About 3 kilometres (just under 2 miles) west of the town centre. Catch the No. 2 or 3 bus from the centre of Nakhon Ratchasima. It's quite a good source of information and they can provide you with an excellent map of the town. Open daily, 8.30am–4.30pm.

## WHERE TO STAY

### BUDGET TO MODERATE (150–500 BTS PER PERSON PER NIGHT)

🛏 **Doctor's House** – ด็อกเตอร์ เกสท์เฮ้าส์ : not far from the tourist office on Suep Siri Road, Soi 4 (just before the railway). ☎ 255-846. The landlady (a retired nurse) speaks good English and actually lived in Chicago for a few years. She's a mine of information on tourist matters: tours, bus and train times, regional information etc. The place itself is clean and quiet and you can eat with the family if you want. An oasis of peace and good manners, but a bit expensive considering that it's on the outskirts of town.

🛏 **Farthai Hotel** – ฟ้าไทยโฮเด็ล: 35–39 Phoklang Road. ☎ 242-533. Just a few steps from the statue of Thao Suranari and conveniently situated right in the centre of town. Despite the rather urban view from the fourth floor, the rooms are clean and comfortable (with fan or air-conditioning) and the owners are very welcoming.

🛏 **Thaï Pokaphan Hotel** – โรงแรม ไทยโภคภัณฑ์: 106–110 Asadang Road. ☎ 242-564. Near the post office opposite the K Star Hotel. Old fashioned but clean and cheap.

### SPLASH OUT (FROM 1,200 BTS PER PERSON PER NIGHT)

🛏 **Chomsurang Hotel** – โรงแรม ชมสุรางค์: 270-1/2 Mahadthai Road. ☎ 257-080. Quite central. The cheapest luxury hotel in town. Spotless, with a terrific restaurant and a swimming pool.

## WHERE TO EAT AND WHERE TO HAVE A DRINK

✕ **The night market** – ตลาด กลางคืน: along Manat Road, between the two side roads called Chumphon Road and Mahadthai Road.

✕ **Doksom Restaurant** – ร้าน อาหารดอกส้ม: 130-142 Chumphon Road. Opposite Thao Suranari's statue. Divine patio surrounded by lush vegetation, where you can sit and enjoy a variety of local specialities as well as delicious milkshakes and ice-creams. Waitresses in traditional I-san costume; young and trendy clientele; rock 'n' roll music; reasonable prices.

The landlord also runs the **Tom Som** – ต้มส้ม, 125 Watcharasit Road (the extension of Chakri Road) very close to the Wan Varn (*see below*). Same deal as the previous place but with a more classical decor.

✕ **Wan Varn Restaurant** – ร้าน อาหารวันวาน: 101–103 Mahadthai Road. By the junction with Chakri Road. Very 'those were the days' (Wan Varn) place where the owner has succeeded in creating a comfortable middle-class interior stuffed full of antiques from all over the world: tables from Vietnam, lampshades from France, clocks from Germany, a piano from America and 78s from India. No such eclecticism where the food is concerned – the dishes are classical, exclusively Thai and absolutely delicious.

🍷 **V.F.W. Café** – วี.เอฟ.ดับเบิ้ลยู .คาเฟ่ (ใกล้ศิริโฮเด็ล): on Phoklang Road to the west of town (slightly away from the centre). Shabby American bar that appeals to former veterans of the Vietnam and Korean wars. As you might expect, they serve lots of steak and chips with unlimited amounts of ketchup and mayon-naise. Seedy atmosphere guaran-teed.

## WHAT TO SEE

★ **The Archaeological Museum** – พิพิธภัณฑ์โบราณคดี: on Thanon Ratchadamnoen Avenue beside the Wat Suthachinda. Open daily, 9am–4pm. This little museum houses a private collection belonging to a prominent I-san monk and is mainly interesting for a few period Dvâravatî and Khmer pieces. Only for enthusiasts.

★ **The Thao Suranari Memorial** – อนุสาวรีย์ท้าวสุรนารี: as you leave the museum, further up on the left on the same avenue (by Chumphon Gate). Thao Suranari is a much-revered local heroine who led the resistance movement against the Laotian invasion in 1826. Every year, towards the end of March/beginning of April, the villagers organize a festival in her honour. For 10 nights Chumphon and Mahadthai Roads are transformed into an immense commercial bazaar where crowds of people inch their way past stands selling clothes, drinks and antiques. Meanwhile, dancers and singers improvise on stage to the beat provided by the sound system.

★ **Wat Sala Loi** – วัดศาลาลอย: in the extreme northeast of town. Catch the No. 2 bus on Mittraparp Road (a kind of ring road to the north of Ratchadamnoen Avenue) and ask the driver to drop you at Sala Loi. If you like pretty temples, here's a delightful little modern number on the water – like a boat. Look for the paintings on the front of the temple illustrating the Buddha's fight against the devils and, on the gable at the back, the magnificent ceramic mosaic inspired by the Buddha's return to the world of men.

## WHAT TO SEE IN THE SURROUNDING AREA

★ **The Prasat Phanom Wan** – วัดปราสาทหินพนมวัน: about 20 kilometres (12 miles) from Korat. Follow Route 2 in the direction of Khon Kaen for 15 kilometres (9 miles) until you come to a little side road on the right leading off into the country – it's signposted. Buses from Korat leave roughly every hour from 7am to 5.30pm from the No. 1 and No. 2 bus stations and from the Pratu Phonsaen gate.

When you've seen the temple you can go on from there to Phimai. The visit and the return journey will take at least a morning. The temple, which is being restored, was originally dedicated to Shiva and dates from the 9th or the 11th century to judge from the classical design of the Khmer sanctuary (with its choir, corridor and ante-room) surrounded by a square wall with four identical doors (gopuras). Sadly, only one of the carved lintels now remains. It shows a god seated on the head of a kala and is over the northern entrance of the sanctuary. The others have all been moved to museums in Phimai and Bangkok.

The sanctuary also houses several stone Buddhas, including one more than 2.5 metres (8 feet) high. From the 13th century onwards, the monastery became a place of worship for Mahayana Buddhists and it remains home to a community of monks, who keep the sanctuary alive with their prayers.

✘ There is a restaurant about 50 metres from the temple.

## LEAVING NAKHON RATCHASIMA

### By bus

🚌 These days, nearly all the buses leave from the No. 2 bus station on the Friendship Highway in the north of town. It's less than 1 kilometre (0.5 miles) from the centre – so take a *tuk-tuk*). The No. 1 bus station (in Burin Lane) is now only used by local buses going short distances (although even buses for Phimai leave from the No. 2 station now).

– **To Phimai**: bus No. 1305 – departures every 30 minutes, 5.30am–10pm.

– **To Nong Khai**: air-conditioned buses every hour, noon–3am.

– **To Ubon Ratchathani**: three air-conditioned and four non-air-conditioned buses daily.

– **To Phitsanulok and Chiang Mai**: five air-conditioned and three non-air-conditioned buses.

– **To Bangkok (via Saraburi)**: departures every hour, with non-air-conditioned buses approximately every 20 minutes, air-conditioned buses every 40 minutes.

### By train

Seven trains a day go to **Saraburi**, **Ayutthaya** and **Bangkok** in one direction and to **Surin** in the other. There are also six trains to **Ubon Ratchathani.**

### By air

Just one flight a day to **Bangkok**, except on Monday and Saturday when there are two.

# PHIMAI – พิมาย                           DIALLING CODE: 044

This peaceful little market town about 60 kilometres (37 miles) from Nakhon Ratchasima on the road to Khon Kaen is famous for its wonderful Khmer temple built between the end of the 11th century and the end of the 12th. If you despair of ever seeing Angkor, this temple will more than make up for it. Phimai itself, built at the confluence of the Moon and Lamjakarat rivers, comes as something of a rest cure after the hustle and bustle of big city life, particularly since there aren't many tourists and the people are friendly and very natural.

## A BIT OF HISTORY

Eight centuries ago, the Khmer kingdom stretched all the way from Sukhothai to the borders with Burma and Malaya. At the time, there was a direct road link between Phimai and Angkor (which is, after all, a mere 250 kilometres/150 miles away). According to the inscriptions, the temple in Phimai actually pre-dates and was the model for the temple that was built in Angkor.

The village was once surrounded by ramparts and a moat, vestiges of which can still be seen, particularly the Victory Gate *(Pratou Chai)*, which used to guard the road to Angkor. No one seems to know why Phimai was abandoned in the 13th century and left to fall into ruin.

## GETTING THERE

– **From Nakhon Ratchasima**: buses every 30 minutes, 5.30am–10pm from the No. 2 bus station (No. 1305 bus).

## USEFUL ADDRESSES

◼ **Tourist information**: available from the Bai-Teiy Restaurant. You can also get a map of the town there, and the times of buses.

◼ **Currency exchange**: is available at the Thai Farmers Bank in the main street.

## WHERE TO STAY AND WHERE TO EAT

⌂ **Phimai Youth Hostel (P.P. House)** – บ้านพักเยาวชนพิมาย(พี.พี. เฮาส์): 552/1 Anantajinda Road. ☎ 471-912. About 1 kilometre (0.5 miles) west of town, in the first road on the left, 150 metres) beyond the only bridge on the River Lamjakarat. This is the latest in a celebrated chain of international youth hostels: brand-new and with rooms ranging from 150 to 400 Bts for the night depending on the level of comfort. Absolutely spotless dormitories and rooms (with or without air-conditioning) – there are even mouldings in the dormitories and carpet on the walls. Lots of facilities: breakfast, cool drinks, cycle hire, tourist information, long-distance telephone calls and even a laundry service – your own mother couldn't do better. A real treat.

Slightly out of the way so not as crowded as its competitors.

⌂ **Old Phimai Guesthouse** – โอลด์พิมายเกสท์เฮ้าส์: 214 Chomsudasapet Road. ☎ 471-918. In a little cul-de-sac leading to the main street, just before the Bai-Teiy Restaurant. It's a clean, quiet, wooden house with dormitories and rooms costing 60–400 Bts a night. Some have air-conditioning, all have mosquito nets, some with roof terrace, some overlooking the shady garden. Masses of tourist information: map of the town, times of buses, things to see in the surrounding area. Also cycle hire. A first-rate place associated with the YHA.

⌂ **S&P Guesthouse** – เอส.แอนด์. พี.เกสท์เฮ้าส์: ☎ 471-992. Directly opposite the last place. Decent rooms at reasonable prices (60–200 Bts). Very pleasant welcome.

⚓ **Phimai Hotel** – พิมายโฮเด็ล: 305 Harutairome Road. ☎ 471-306. In the last street before Pratou Chai, Phimai's southern gate and not very far from the previous two guesthouses (2-minute walk). A hotel without the charm of a guesthouse but probably slightly superior in terms of comfort. It's very well kept, and the prices are reasonable.

✗ **Bai-Teiy Restaurant** – ร้านอาหารใบเคยถนนกลางเมือง: in the main street, on the left-hand pavement going in the direction of the temple. Open 6.30am–midnight. You can eat on the airy terrace or in the air-conditioned dining room, which has two wooden elephants either side of the entrance. There are two menus. Ask for the illustrated one featuring the house specialities – snake-head fish and charcoal grills Thai style. Refined cuisine, proper breakfast.

✗ Alternatively, there are some very nice cheap restaurants near the bus stop for Nakhon Ratchasima and the Phimai Hotel.

## WHAT TO SEE

★ **Prasat Hin Phimai** – ปราสาทหินพิมาย: open 6am–6pm. Admission charge. There are several reasons to get there as early as you can: you have the site all to yourself before the first tour groups arrive at 8am; the light couldn't be better if you want to take photographs; and, of course, it's cool. Plan to spend between 1 hour 30 minutes and 2 hours there.

The temple is a typical *prasat hin,* (which means 'stone castle') built according to the principles of the Hindu *mandala* (cosmic centre of the universe). The water that surrounds Phimai represented the oceans; the city walls were the mountains that protected it; the temple was the magic mountain; the principal sanctuary was the legendary Mount Meru. The latter does not appear to have been a feature of the Hindu faith but of Mahayana Buddhism, to judge from the many statues of the Buddha, and the two lintels either side of the central corridor in the sanctuary, which depict the Buddha under assault from Mara and meditating beneath a serpent (*nâga*).

The temple is square in shape and the doors around it are rigorously symmetrical and aligned with the town gates. Its main distinguishing feature is the terrific sense of perspective created by so many doors in a row. There used to be a hospital by the main entrance and it has been discovered that a number of samples of the mortar once contained medicinal herbs. Next came the lustral basins, then another inner wall. Fascinating architecture of virtually perfect proportions.

The main building of white sandstone has been lovingly restored (even if the mixture of sculptures on the pediment is a bit odd) and is surrounded by two other buildings which appear never to have been completed: the *prang* Hin Daeng, in red sandstone and the *prang* Brahmada, built of laterite. Behind the Hin Daeng is a small Hindu temple, also in laterite. The sculptures on the outside of the temple illustrate a variety of themes but none is so striking as the many allusions to the celebrated Indian epic tale of the *Râmâyana*. The curious western lintel, for instance, shows Rama, the seventh avatar of Vishnu and his brother Lakshmana, gripped by a serpent. The eastern pediment illustrates the death of Ravana.

★ **National Museum of Phimai** – พิพิธภัณฑสถานแห่งชาติ: about 300 metres away going towards the giant banyan tree, on Route 206 shortly before the Moon river. Open daily, 9am–4pm. This two-storey museum has a rich collection of pottery and ceramics from Ban Prasat, Dvâravatî *semas,* and Khmer statues, columns, lintels and pedestals, and it prides itself on being the leading showcase of I-san culture. It is also exceptionally well appointed, is properly laid out, as well as being light and airy, which makes your visit that much more agreeable. Major works include magnificent carved lintels from buildings throughout the region, not only Phimai but also Phanom Rung and Phanom Wan. The jewel in the museum's crown, which comes from the Phimai sanctuary, is the stone statue of Jayavarman VII – the last great Khmer king – who ruled the empire in its heyday from 1181 to 1219. Outside, take a look at the great mural paintings opposite the museum car-park, featuring pottery, spinning-wheels and other stuff.

★ **The giant banyan tree** – ต้นไม้ยักษ์: about 2 kilometres (1.25 miles) northeast of Phimai. Once you have passed the museum, the first turning on the right leads to the bridge over the Moon river. Go on foot or by cycle-rickshaw. The giant banyan tree is a sight not to be missed. It's the largest in Thailand and has stood in the middle of this pretty park for more than 350 summers. The locals, who love the park and love superlatives as well, say it's the biggest banyan tree in the world. It certainly is big – so big in fact that it now needs to be supported. Its branches have rooted all over the place and now extend over 0.4 hectares (more than an acre). While you're there, pay a visit to the fortune-tellers you'll find nesting near the main trunk, next to a little temple.

## LEAVING PHIMAI

– **For Korat**: buses leave every 30 minutes from the bus stop at the junction of Harutairome and Chomsudasapet roads (near the Phimai Hotel).

– **For Bangkok (direct)**: buses leave from the stop north of the temple at the junction of Vonprang Road (which leads to the museum) and Chomsra Road. It's much simpler to go to the No. 2 bus station in Korat where there are buses for Bangkok all the time.

# THE ROUTE TO THE KHMER CITADELS, FROM KORAT TO SURIN

This route off the beaten track is an opportunity for lovers of Far Eastern art to discover some temples that give one of the most moving accounts of the Khmer civilization. Given the distances between the sites and how far most of them are from the main road, this is one occasion when you should definitely consider hiring a motorbike or a car. A bit of a treat perhaps, but actually not that expensive (roughly 150–250 Bts a day for a little single-cylinder motorbike, 500–800 Bts for a second-hand car). That said, provided you have the time and the patience, it's perfectly feasible to do the whole trip by public transport.

## GETTING THERE

– **From Bangkok**, there are various alternatives:

● Catch a bus for Surin and ask to be dropped in Nang Rong, Ta Ko or Prakhon Chai. Make sure before you board that the bus goes along Route 24 and not Route 226 via Buriram.

● Go back to Nakhon Ratchasima and carry on to Surin.

● Go to Buriram by bus (six air-conditioned buses a day, 10 non-air-conditioned from the northeastern station) or by train (seven a day but only three of them get into Buriram in the daytime). From the bus station, which is 3 kilometres (just under 2 miles) from the train station on Thani Road, take a *tuk-tuk*. There are buses for Prakhon Chai every hour.

– **From Nakhon Ratchasima**: buses throughout the day (roughly a 30-minute journey) for Surin via Nang Rong, Ta Ko, Prakhon Chai and Prasat (Route 24). Tell the driver where you want to get off.

– **From Surin**: Route 24 as before, but going the other way.

## WHERE TO STAY AND WHERE TO EAT

The best places to stay in the area are Prakhon Chai – ประโคนชัย and Nang Rong. The advantage of Prakhon Chai is that you can go straight from there to Prasat Phanom Rung by *songthaew* (something you can't do from Nang Rong).

🛏 **Sukpaïboon Hotel** – สุขไพบูลย์ โฮเด็ล: Pakdedomrong Road, Prakhon Chai. ☎ (44) 671-125. Wooden hotel barely a 10-minute walk from the bus station, beside the market place. Rooms with fans or indoor shower room. Very cheap and rich in local colour.

🛏 ✕ **Honey Inn** – ฮันนีอินน์: 8/1 Soi Srikoon, Nang Rong. ☎ (44) 624-057. Coming from Ta Ko, on the right of the main road, slightly beyond the post office (look for the blue sign). A well-kept little guesthouse owned by two charming teachers, one of whom has retired and plans to do this full-time from now on. He has even opened a new annexe in a large but sadly rather charmless building. You're better off in the family home, particularly since you get to taste the landlady's delicious cooking. Mr Phaisan hires out his motorbike and car by the day at very attractive rates.

## GETTING THERE

– **From Nang Rong**: take a *songthaew* to Don Nong Nae (Route 2117) and get out where you see the blue sign for the 'Phanom Rung Resort'. From there, take another *songthaew* or motorbike-taxi to the temple, which is 6 kilometres (just over 3 miles) away on Route 2221.

– **From Ta Ko**: there are *songthaews* for Don Nong Nae roughly every 10 minutes. Do the last part of the journey as above.

**ROUTE TO THE KHMER CITADELS**

– **From Prakhon Chai**: *songthaews* leave from the collective taxi rank roughly every 2 hours from 10am to 5.30pm. They drop you at the foot of the hill and you walk the last kilometre (half mile) or so.

## WHAT TO SEE

★ **The Prasat Phanom Rung** – ปราสาทหินพนมรุ้ง: This temple, like the Prasat Hin Phimai, needs to be seen at dawn, or failing that, just after nightfall. It is beautifully situated on an extinct volcano that overlooks the ancient road to Angkor. It is bordered by fertile plains and, during the rainy season, rice fields that extend as far as the eye can see. It took 300 years (from the 10th to the 12th centuries) to build the colossal Prasat Phanom Rung. The temple is dedicated to Shiva but Vishnu is never far away.

The eastern side of the *prasat* is entered up the first flight of stairs, which leads to a cruciform terrace. On the right is the 'White Elephant' room, whose purpose remains a mystery. Next comes a 160-metre avenue bordered on either side by 67 stones that represent the sacred lotus blossom. At the end is the first bridge, flanked by a balustrade of five-headed snakes (*nâgas)*, symbolizing the transition from the profane to the divine. Next comes the second staircase, the customary lustral basins, a second snake bridge and finally the eastern entrance to the *prasat* precinct, with its embellishment of magnificent sculptures (a goddess seated on a monstrous *kala* gripped by two lions and, higher up, the pediment, representing Shiva surrounded by celestial dancers).

Just beyond, the eastern facade of the sanctuary boasts the most famous lintel in the whole of Thailand (representing Vishnu lying on a serpent in the mythical sea of milk). The lintel was the focus of a public outcry in the late 1980s following the discovery that it had been stolen in 1966 and sold on the streets of Bangkok to a New York art collector who then sold it to the Chicago Art Institute. It remained there for 10 years until the Thai government found out and demanded its return, which finally happened in 1988. Since then all but one of the art thieves have met with accidental deaths – victims of a curse, no doubt.

This is your chance to discover the wealth of remarkable sculptures in this sanctuary. Before you leave, it's worth making a detour to take a quick look around the museum at the entrance to the temple, on the right. There for safe-keeping are some of the finest stones and statues in the Phanom Rung. On the way to the museum, look out for Agni, the Goddess of Fire, mounted on a rhinoceros, and Indra on her elephant. Finally, there is lots of activity around the temple, including restaurants and refreshment stalls.

### ★ MUANG THAM – เมืองต่ำ

About 8 kilometres (5 miles) southeast of the Prasat Phanom Rung. Follow Route 2221 in the direction of Prakhon Chai for 3 kilometres (nearly 2 miles) then turn right where you see the sign in Thai. Get there by taxi or even on foot – it's downhill all the way. This 'low city' at the foot of the hill crowned by the Phanom Rung actually pre-dates the celebrated temple. The shrine is dedicated to Shiva as can be seen from the *lingam* situated in the very heart of the sanctuary and the large lintel on the northeast tower featuring Shiva and Uma astride the bull Nandin. It is curiously similar in layout to the Prasat Kamphaeng Yai – ปราสาทหินกำแพงใหญ่. Two rows of towers are flanked by two traditional libraries, surrounded by two walls with lustral basins in between. The walls are punctuated by four entry doors (*gopuras*) at the four cardinal points. The place is very peaceful, with loads of charm and fewer tourists than at the Prasat Phanom Rung.

### ★ PRASAT PLUANG – ปราสาทหินบ้านพลวง

An 11th-century monument about 2 kilometres (1.25 miles) from Prasat and very easy to get to either by *songthaew* south along Route 214 or on foot. The temple is on your left, set back from the road by about 500 metres. It's officially open 7.30am–6pm but in fact you can visit at any time. It consists of a single sandstone tower (*prang*) that is raised up on a laterite cruciform pedestal (on the east side).

The building appears to have been dedicated to Indra, the king of the gods of the Vedic pantheon. He features on the two lintels to the south and east, sitting in majesty astride his faithful mount Airavata (the white elephant with the four tusks). The sculptures are of remarkable quality and the tops of the lintels display a wealth of carvings (cows, monkeys and squirrels). On the pediment opposite the eastern entrance, the ubiquitous Krishna can be seen picking up a bull by the horns. Meanwhile in the background the traditional house of the spirits promises to protect Indra from hellfire and damnation.

## ★ PRASAT TA MUAN – ปราสาททาเมือน

Not easy to get to, as transport is limited, but few places can be more fascinating than this powerfully evocative group of ruins lost in the jungle on the border with Cambodia. Nowhere else in Thailand is there such a poignant expression of the profoundly tragic aspect of Khmer culture. A few *songthaews* go from Prasat to Ta Miang where a taxi or motorbike-taxi can take you the last 12 kilometres (7.5 miles) along a laterite path (known to everybody in Ta Miang). After about 8 kilometres (5 miles) you get to a police cordon where someone is bound to offer to take you to the ruins (anything to relieve the tedium).

– The **Prasat Ta Muan**, about 3 kilometres (2 miles) further up, is a laterite building dating from the late-12th to early-13th centuries. It was originally used as a chapel by pilgrims and travellers staying in the nearby inn. Besides a lintel and a series of open-work columns on the facade, it is of limited figurative interest.

– The **Prasat Ta Muan Thot** – ปราสาททาเมือนโต๊ด, 200 metres further up, is the former chapel of a hospital built in the reign of the last great king of the Khmer empire, Jayavarman VII. Any trace of the hospital or the inn has long since vanished, probably because neither was built to last. All that remains today are a few solitary scrolls.

– Walk another 500 metres into the forest until you come to a fork in the path. On the left, about 2 kilometres (1.25 miles) further up, is the **Ta Nam Tô** military border camp. Visitors are admitted. Ask to be taken to the fountain, where you get a fantastic view of the Cambodian plain.

– The **Prasat Ta Muan Thom** – ปราสาททาเมือนธม, the jewel of Ta Miang, is on the right another 200 metres further up; it's by far the most impressive of the three buildings. It too dates from the reign of Jayavarman VII and consists of a central sanctuary with two northern towers and two wings at either side. Like Phimai itself, the Ta Muan Thom faces south and was probably a landmark on the road from Phimai to Angkor. The sanctuary is built around a *lingam* carved out of the rock and remains richly decorated with floral scrolls, serpent-*nâgas* and geometric designs. Sadly though, the lintels and carved pediments have completely disappeared, either torn down (or blown up) by the Khmer Rouge, who occupied the site until 1980. The ground around the *prasat* is littered with thousands of stones lining up to get into the mysterious celestial citadel. Nature seems poised to take the place by storm – an awesome prospect. The birds meanwhile are quite unstoppable. You are in no real danger provided you don't venture further into the forest, where there are still some live mines.

## LEAVING THE REGION

– **From Nang Rong** or **Ta Ko**: stops all along the main road.

– **From Prakhon Chai**: the bus terminal is 500 metres north of the junction of the two main roads (Routes 219 and 24).

ROUTE TO THE
KHMER CITADELS

# FROM SURIN TO KHONG CHIAM

# SURIN – สุรินทร์
DIALLING CODE: 044

Every year on the third weekend in November, Surin holds its famous elephant festival, when almost 200 elephants join in processions and shows of strength for the amusement of thousands of spectators. The 'street theatre' is particularly worth seeing: elephants stopping at red lights surrounded by cycle-rickshaws or spraying themselves with water in the middle of traffic jams. On the remaining 363 days of the year, Surin is an excellent base from which to go exploring the fabulous Khmer ruins for which the region is famous.

## WHAT FUTURE FOR THE ELEPHANTS?

Actually, what's happening to the elephants is no laughing matter. Their prospects look bleak, to say the least, as more and more forest is replaced by more and more plantations driving more and more elephants into the towns. With no forest to return to, it seems that elephants are for ever doomed to play the clown or the heavyweight boxer. True to form, man always hurts those he loves. This time it's the elephants' turn.

## GETTING THERE

**– From Bangkok**:

● **By train**: seven trains a day including four in the evening. Avoid those that leave in the afternoon or early evening because they arrive in Surin in the middle of the night.

● **By bus**: six air-conditioned buses a day (one in the morning and five in the evening). Non-air-conditioned buses run all day long.

**– From Korat**: lots of buses every day.

## WHERE TO STAY

It isn't easy finding a place to stay during the festival, particularly since you can't even book because the hotels know they'll be full. Some people get here the week before just to be on the safe side.

⌂ **Pirom Guesthouse** – ภิรมย์ เกสท์เฮ้าส์: 242 Krungsrinai Road, about 150 metres from the market. ☎ 515-140. Simple but clean and really cheap, at 60–150 Bts for the night. A particular favourite with passing backpackers and you can see why. At weekends, the landlady's husband takes groups of up to five people in his Land Rover to visit the Khmer ruins near the Cambodian border, or the elephant village. It's the ideal way of getting a feel for the region, complete with masses of detail and excellent commentary. There was talk of the landlady moving to Tasawang Village about a kilometre (half a mile) west of the train station (via Nong Tom Road, the rail crossing and Buranawit Road), so call to confirm beforehand.

🛏 **Krung Sri Hotel** – กรุงศรีโฮเต็ล: 185 Krungsrinai Road. ☎ 511-037.

About 150–200 Bts for the night. It's well located opposite the market and rooms come with fans or air-conditioning (and hot water). It's a very clean place and the welcome's terrific.

🛏 **Nid Drew Hotel** – นิดครูวีโฮเต็ล: Thanasarn Road. ☎ 512-009. Hotel facing the post office, with rooms at a wide range of prices – from an overheated and tiny room on the roof (where you get a wonderful view of the town) to air-conditioned rooms with all mod cons. Expect to pay about 200–500 Bts for the night. It's a well-kept, friendly place.

## WHERE TO EAT

### BUDGET

✕ **Night market** – ตลาดกลางคืน: Krungsrinai Road. The market is in full swing early in the morning from 5 to 7am but takes on a new face at nightfall. There are lots of appetizing food stands and plenty of local colour.

### MODERATE

✕ **Samrep Thong Criang Restaurant**: Tatmailang Road. About 100 metres from the bus terminal going towards the Tarin luxury hotel. Very cosy decor. It's got antique European clocks, miners' lamps hanging from the ceiling, first-generation telephones and even Phileas Fogg's famous suitcase. Well-presented, flavourful Thai food. Concert every evening from 8pm. A first-rate place.

✕ **Country Roads Café** – ร้านอาหารคันทรีโรดส์: 165/1-2 Sirirat Road. ☎ 515-721. One of the best restaurants in town. It's run by a man who once had a dream that he would indulge his nostalgia for the heights of Nice, cheese and good wine by opening a place called the 'French Riviera'. Luckily, he decided instead to settle in Surin with his charming wife and open a place serving pizzas and American-style burgers, Thai cuisine and beef (which doesn't come cheap). They also make their own French bread, sausages and ham. Open late into the night, with long-distance fax and telephone facilities. They also rent out rooms during the festival but not as much as they used to during the rest of the year.

## ANNUAL ELEPHANT FESTIVAL

All the festivities take place during the third weekend in November. First there is a small welcoming ceremony when enthusiastic crowds gather outside the bus station to cheer and wave to the elephants as they arrive in town after their two-day march. Next comes the spectacle itself (impressive but not as spontaneous) when the elephants perform their tricks in the stadium. This is the highlight of the festival. In between the two events, the beasts lumber around town carrying tourists.

★ **The spectacle**: there is an admission charge as you would expect. The cheapest seats are on the terraces, where you get quite a good view, but the back-light isn't great for photography. The spectacle includes demonstrations of forestry and logging work; a re-enactment of the famous battle of Ayutthaya when the elephants charged the Burmese; and the eagerly anticipated football match.

– **Elephant rides**: very hyped up, considering that all you get is a 5-minute walk around the stadium. The walk around the town is more fun even if it is a bit expensive.

## WHAT TO SEE IN THE SURROUNDING AREA

★ **Ta Klang, the elephant village** – หมู่บ้านช้างท่ากลาง: about 58 kilometres (36 miles) north of Surin. Follow Route 214 for roughly 15 kilometres (9 miles) until you get to Nong Tat where the road forks towards Ta Klang. It's nice to see the gentle giants away from all the hype of the festival – particularly if you go there with Mr Pirom (from the Pirom Guesthouse).

★ **Prasat Sikhoraphum** – ปราสาทศรีขรภูมิ: open 7.30am–6pm. Three trains a day from Surin (two of which leave early in the morning), each taking about 30 minutes. It's an easy journey, particularly since the temple is less than 1 kilometre (0.5 miles) from the station. The *prasat* is surrounded by a U-shaped pond (ancient sacred basin) and consists of five towers arranged in a quincunx, as in Angkor (this sort of arrangement is very rare and was exclusively reserved for state temples at the time).

Building was started by the Khmers in the 12th century and completed by the Laotians in the 16th century. This little temple is a real treasure, with its exceptionally fine stonework (in a warm pink sandstone) and rich carvings.

The magnificent lintel on the central *prang* features the head of a terrifying demon *(kala)* crowned by a Shiva with 10 arms dancing on a pedestal supported by two mythical birds *(hamsas)*. Beside the *kala* are two lions, while on the right stands Ganesh, the elephant of wisdom. Lastly, a few dragons illustrate the impact of the Chinese influence. The columns are richly carved with guardians *(dvarapalas)* and the famous *apsaras* or celestial mistresses, so characteristic of Khmer art, but for some reason virtually unknown outside Cambodia. Each side of the pediment features Garuda, the white eagle with a human head surrounded by *nâgas* (sacred serpent-guardians of treasure). It's a very interesting visit in a lush setting – and there is a restaurant close by.

★ **Prasat Kamphaeng Yai** – ปราสาทกำแพงใหญ่: about 40 kilometres (25 miles) east of Sikhoraphum on Route 226. It makes sense to visit this *prasat* and the previous one on the same day. Take a bus to Si Saket and ask to be dropped in Kamphaeng Yai by the railway, which is roughly 27 kilometres (17 miles) before you get to Si Saket. This 11th-century Khmer temple was built in honour of Shiva and converted to Buddhism at the beginning of the 13th century. It remains home to a community of monks. There are six structures: four central towers that form the sanctuary (were it not for a missing tower on the north side, the *prasat* would be symmetrical); and two libraries (set back on the eastern side). The temple complex is surrounded by a huge gallery punctuated by doors *(gopuras)*. The visit starts from the eastern entrance (against the new temple). The most beautiful sculptures include Indra on his elephant Airavata (look for the inner lintel of the central *prang* on the eastern side), Shiva and Uma (on the inner lintel of the southern library), Vishnu lying down with his two wives, Lakshmi and Bhumidevi, both trying to calm him down (on the lintel of the northern library). There are also some magnificent pediments, including the one on the central tower facing south, which features Shiva and Uma once again, this time sitting astride the bull Nandin. On your way out, there's soup for sale at the entrance (exit) to the *wat*.

# UBON RATCHATHANI – อุบลราชธานี

DIALLING CODE: 045

This town is to the north of the Emerald Triangle (so-called because of its proximity to Laos and Cambodia) and about 560 kilometres (350 miles) from Bangkok – so it is ideally placed to make the most of whatever opportunities open up with its neighbours. In a prime position on the river Moon (the second most important river in Thailand after the Mekhong) Ubon is the last agreeable stopping place before you head back to Khong Chiam.

## USEFUL ADDRESSES

**🛈 TAT** – ททท (Tourist office): 264/1 Khuan Thani Road. ☎ 243-770. Open daily, 8.30am–4.30pm. Centrally located and very welcoming. Ask for the very good map of the town that gives the names of the streets in English.

■ **Post office** and long-distance telecommunications: two blocks from the tourist office, on the same side of the same street.

■ **Thai Airways** – สายการบินไทย: 364 Chaiyangkun Road. ☎ 313-340.

## WHERE TO STAY

### BUDGET TO MODERATE (100–350 BTS PER PERSON PER NIGHT)

**🛏 River Moon Guesthouse** – ริ วอร์มูลเกสท์เฮาส์: 65/3 Si Saket Road. In the south of Ubon, roughly 4 kilometres (2.5 miles) from the centre, near the train station and opposite the fire station. It's also not far from the southern train station, which is handy if you plan to go

on to Khong Chiam. There's no point looking anywhere else – this is the only guesthouse in Ubon. Ideal for people who are broke and great for anyone arriving by train, but otherwise the Warin market is just about all there is to do round here.

**🛏 Tokyo Hotel** – โตเกียวโฮเด็ล: 360 Upparat Road. ☎ 241-739. By far the best place in Ubon. It is set back from the street by about 25 metres, between two side-streets, Pichitrangsan Road and Subpasit Road. A very clean and quiet place with nice reception staff. Rooms with fans and air-conditioning but there's no hot water, which might be a problem if you feel the cold.

**⌂ Sri Issan 2 Hotel** – ศรีอีสาน 2 โฮเด็ล: Ratchabutr Road. ☎ 254-544. On the river facing the River Moon market (downriver from the bridge, on the left bank). Ask for a room on the river side – there's a lovely view from the third floor. Not exactly up to American standards but it's well kept despite being a bit old-fashioned. Some rooms with air-conditioning (with hot water this time). Warm welcome. Not to be confused with the rather grubby Sri Issan 1 Hotel just next door.

## MODERATE TO EXPENSIVE (350–900 BTS PER PERSON PER NIGHT)

**⌂ Racha Hotel** – โรงแรมราชา: 19 Chayangkun Road. ☎ 254-155. In the north of town, one block from the bus station where the buses leave for Bangkok, in a *soi* that is slightly set back from the Chayangkun Road. Absolutely spotless, quiet place in a very lively part of town full of little shops. The rooms with air-conditioning are the only ones with hot running water.

**⌂ Ratchathani Hotel** – โรงแรม ราชธานี: Khuanthani Road. ☎ 244-388. Fairly charmless place but ideally situated opposite the museum and the tourist office, about 50 metres from the night market. The entrance hall and visiting cards are deceptive: this is by no means the Ritz. Some of the rooms are rather sad even if they are very comfortable. The positively icy staff play their part to perfection – the mind boggles to think what an effort it must be. Much more expensive than the previous place.

## WHERE TO EAT

### BUDGET

✕ Lots of **little places to eat** near the bus station in the north of town, plus two good Chinese restaurants next to the Ratchathani Hotel.

✕ **Night market** – ไนท์มาร์เก็ต: on Ratchabutr Road, next to the National Museum. A nightly procession of about 20 mobile restaurants that turns the pavement into one huge terrace. As for the food, you're spoiled for choice: Chinese soup, grilled chicken, kebabs, stuffed pancakes, freshly squeezed fruit juices and much, much more.

✕ **Aree Restaurant** – ร้านอาหารอ ารีย์: Ratchabutr Road. Great canteen serving cheap fast food, not far from the museum, going towards the river. Local dishes, sometimes quite spicy, based on steamed green vegetables. The only drawback (as is so often the case) is the TV going full blast.

### MODERATE

✕ **S.P. Bakery** – เอส.พี.เบเกอรี: Ratchabutr Road, slightly south of the last place on the opposite pavement. Unashamedly kitsch place with salmon-pink armchairs and walls covered in a confetti of little balloons. Serves ice-creams, biscuits, sweets and every kind of sugary thing imaginable. Full of Prince Charmings and flirtatious Cinderellas on Sunday afternoons. Loads of fun.

✕ **The Restaurants of the Ko Hat Wat Tai** – ร้านอาหารโกหาด วัดใต้: three rival restaurants in bamboo huts on stilts on a little islet in the middle of the Moon river. Accessible via a walkway in the dry season only. Come here for a meal or a drink – quite expensive and a bit businesslike but worth it all the same. After a few whiskies, some of the guests like to go for a dip.

## WHAT TO SEE AND DO

★ **National Museum I** – พิพิธภัณฑสถานแห่งชาติอุบลราชธานี: Khuanthani Road, by the junction with Ratchabutr Road. Open daily, 9am–4pm. Interesting museum in a former palace of King Rama VI built around two luminous patios full of flowers. Nine exhibition rooms present a succession of displays on the geography, history and popular traditions of the region. The high points of the visit are the reproductions of the Pha Taem rock paintings and an 8th-century Khmer statue of Ardhanar-isvara (Shiva and Uma's symbolic union). To see the displays in chronological order, start with the rooms on the left and keep going in a clockwise direction.

★ **Wat Supattanaram** – วัดสุปัฏนาราม: at the extreme western end of the Promtap Road, on the river Moon. Interesting temple because of its composite architecture: Khmer-style foundations, stone walls of Germanic influence and strictly traditional Thai roof. In front of the temple is the largest wooden bell in Thailand.

★ **Wat Nongbua** – วัดหนองบัว this replica of the celebrated *Mahabodhi Chedi* (Chedi of the Great Enlightenment) in Bodhgaya, in India, is north of town going towards Mukdahan. Opposite the *chedi* is a new, ultra-modern temple decorated with marble, cut-price gilding and (if you look upwards) paintings illustrating the different stages in the life of the Buddha (strangely reminiscent of the Nepalese *thangkas*).

★ **River Moon market** – ตลาดแม่น้ำมูล: big market on the left bank, downriver from the bridge on the river Moon. Intoxicating smells, lots of people pushing and shoving – it's good to get there early in the morning.

## WHAT TO SEE IN THE SURROUNDING AREA

★ **Wat Pananachat** – วัดป่านานาชาติ: look for the sign in English about 20 kilometres (12 miles) from Ubon on Route 226 going towards Si Saket. Visitors are admitted from 6am to noon, after which silence returns once again. This temple in the middle of the forest is run, for once, by Western monks committed to the preservation of man's natural and cultural heritage. They have even founded a group called Sacred Nature and from time to time hold ecologically proselytizing meetings with neighbouring villagers.

★ **Prasat Khao Phra Viharn** – ปราสาทเขาพระวิหาร: this temple that straddles the Dangkrek mountain range about 160 kilometres (100 miles) south of Ubon is without a doubt one of the most mysterious jewels of Khmer art, similar in structure and style to the Prasat Phanom Rung. Sadly, because the area around the temple on the Cambodian side is still in the hands of rebel Khmer Rouge forces, the temple remains closed to the public. But keen art lovers would do well to check with the tourist office because things may have changed.

## LEAVING UBON RATCHATHANI

– **By bus**: there are frequent buses to Bangkok from the bus station in the north of town on Chayangkun Road near the Racha Hotel. Buses to Udon Thani and Mukdahan leave from a stop 4 kilometres (2.5 miles) further up the same road, going north, beyond the *wat* Nongbua. Buses to Khong Chiam also leave from the southern bus station near the Warin market.

– **By train**: six trains a day (two early in the morning, four in the afternoon) going to Surin, Nakhon Ratchasima, Ayutthaya and Bangkok, from the train station in the south of town. Get there by white bus from the centre (lots of stops on Upparat and Khuanthani roads) or by *tuk-tuk*.

– **By air**: two flights a day to Bangkok (morning and afternoon).

# KHONG CHIAM – โขงเจียม   DIALLING CODE: 045

FROM SURIN TO KHONG CHIAM

This little piece of paradise is where the Moon river joins forces with the 'Asian giant' to start the 800-kilometre (500-mile) trek downriver through Indochina all the way to the South China Sea. See the dark waters of the Mekhong merge with the deep blue flows of its tributary to create a single 'River of Two Colours'. It has a wonderfully restorative effect. Khong Chiam itself is a good jumping-off point to lots of interesting places, the most famous being the Pha Taem rock face with its sensational view and celebrated rock paintings that are unique in Thailand. For some strange reason there are few Western visitors in these parts, which can only add to your sense of adventure.

## GETTING THERE

– **From Ubon Ratchathani** (via Phibun Mangsahan): departures every 30 minutes, 6am–3.30pm from the Warin market, less than 3 kilometres (2 miles) south of town. Leave it to the *tuk-tuk* drivers.

– **From Bangkok**: four buses daily (two ordinary and two VIP buses) from the northeast bus station on Phahon Yothin Road.

## WHERE TO STAY

### BUDGET
⌂ **Apple Guesthouse** – แอปเปิ้ล เกสท์เฮาส์ (map, **1**): Kaewpradit Road. ☎ 351-160. About 300 metres from the bus station is this very clean place run by a really friendly family who speak a bit of English. Around 12 rooms with fans and three with air-conditioning (three times as expensive). Motorbike hire and restaurant service.

⌂ **Khong Chiam Hotel** – โขงเจียม โฮเต็ล (map, **2**): Pukumchai Road.

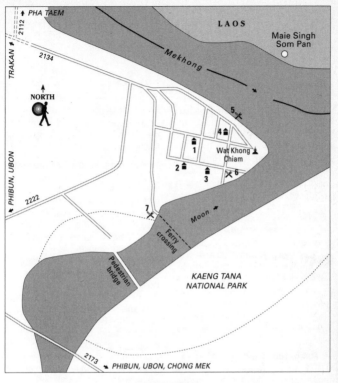

**KHONG CHIAM**

🏠 **Where to Stay**

1 Apple Guesthouse
2 Khong Chiam Hotel
3 Araya Resort
4 Rimkhong Resort

🍴 **Where to Eat**

5 Araya and Nampoon Restaurants
6 Pakmoon Restaurant
7 Hat Mae Moon Restaurant

☎ 351-074. Same price as the previous place but not nearly as good. The rooms are damp and sad and upkeep isn't what it should be.

**EXPENSIVE**

🏠 **Araya Resort** – อารยารีสอร์ท (map, **3**): Pukumchai Road. ☎ 351-191. All the comforts that you'd

get at a holiday village in Europe, with bungalows laid out in a pretty garden full of flowers. No restaurant.

**SPLASH OUT**

🏠 **Rimkhong Resort** – ริมโขงรีสอร์ท (map, **4**): Kaewpradit Road. ☎ 351-101. About 30 metres from the Mekhong, is this group of roomy, very comfortable little chalets (with air-conditioning, bathrooms, and brand-new leather suites) in the middle of an idyllic garden. It has all the trimmings and is absolutely first-rate if you can afford it (twice as expensive as the previous place).

## WHERE TO EAT

✗ **Araya** and **Nampoon Restaurants** – ร้านอาหารอารยาและน้ำพูน (map, **5**): two floating restaurants, one beside the other on the Mekhong, very close to the Rimkhong resort. Both serve Thai and Chinese dishes but the Araya has a better reputation with the Thais, partly because it's been going for 40 years and partly because of the house specialities (turtle, wild boar and venison – which aren't always on the menu – it depends how well the hunting went the day before). On the downside, the Araya tends to be packed at weekends with groups of tourists (exclusively Thai) who turn up for lunch after a quick trip across the border. Very noisy.

✗ **Pakmoon Restaurant** – ร้านอาหารปากมูล (map, **6**): on the banks of the Moon river, beyond the *wat*. The food isn't quite up to the standard of the previous two places but it is the only restaurant with a view of both rivers at the same time. Not to be missed even if you only go there for a drink, particularly since prices are very reasonable. It seems that the Pakmoon undergoes a transformation at a certain hour of the day and becomes the hottest place in town. No comment.

✗ **Hat Mae Moon Restaurant** – ร้านอาหารหาดแม่มูล (map, **7**): on the banks of the Moon river, slightly outside the village. Two dining rooms, one nestling into the side of the hill, the other on a little boat. Blissfully serene atmosphere during the day and a guaranteed rest-cure (the only perceptible movement is the slow toing and froing of a ferryboat downriver). But here too passions stir as night falls and, on another floating restaurant, the **Song Sakorn** near the landing stage, there are sounds of people letting their hair down to the rhythm of karaoke. As for the food, the Hat Mae Moon serves some good freshwater fish specialities, including catfish (together with the inevitable *tom yam*). The only snag is the menu, which is exclusively written in Thai. Check the price before ordering: somehow it always seems higher than you expected when the time comes to pay.

## WHAT TO SEE AND DO

★ **Wat Khong Chiam** – วัดโขงเจียม: there's not a lot to say about the temple. Most people go there for the huge outcrop that overlooks the point where the Mekhong merges with its tributary. There's no view more majestic.

– **Trip on a long-tail boat** – ล่องเรือหางยาว: explore the islets and sandbanks along both rivers. Boats leave from the Araya Restaurant. Once again, you will probably be invited to cross over to Laos to visit Maie Singh Som Pan, the village directly opposite. On your head be it. The Thais may be allowed to spend the day on the other side but it's strictly forbidden for *farangs*. Things can change at any moment of course so, if you're in any doubt, check at the police station, which is located between the Araya and the Apple Guesthouse.

## WHAT TO SEE AND DO IN THE SURROUNDING AREA

★ **Pha Taem** – ผาแต้ม: about 20 kilometres (12.5 miles) north of Khong Chiam. Go back to Huay Pai then turn right towards Nam Thaeng and after 2–3 kilometres (1–2 miles), you'll see a road on the right leading to the cliff. There's no public transport but the road is excellent and well signposted so you could consider hiring a motorbike in Khong Chiam. This impressive sandstone cliff overlooking the Mekong is famous for its ancient rock paintings that date back 2–3,000 years. Remarkably well-preserved images of hunting and fishing stretch out in front of you like scenes from a book: elephants and turtles, the famous *pla buk* or giant catfish, human hands and also a few geometric designs. What you have is a poignant, living account of history, more than 200 metres long. Once you've seen the breathtaking view from the top of the cliff, you can walk around it (about 3 kilometres/2 miles) and head back through the lush forest. All the paths are well waymarked and the terrain is pretty easy going, with refreshment stalls at the end. It's a great walk.

★ **The Kaeng Tana National Park** – อุทยานแห่งชาติแก่งตะนะ: on both sides of the Moon river, upstream from Khong Chiam. You get to the left bank of the park via a turning on the left about 4 kilometres (2.5 miles) up Route 2222. You get to the right bank (where the entrance gate is) either by crossing the suspension bridge over the river in the park or by walking along the dam further upriver. The highlights of the park are: the rapids *(Kaeng Tana)* which are quite a sight in the dry season when the riverbed is partially exposed; the islet *(Don Tana)*, covered in teak forest in the middle of the river; and the waterfalls during the rainy season.

★ **Yasithon beach** – หาดยโสธร: Kok Thiang, on Lake Yasithon, is a nice place to stop on Route 217 going towards Phibun, 12 kilometres (7.5 miles) from the junction with Route 2173 coming from Khong Chiam. It attracts lots of people at weekends.

★ **Chong Mek** – ช่องเม็ก: this little place on Route 217 going towards Pakse, just by the border with Laos, is the one and only dry border between the two countries. The prospect of an increasingly open Laos seems to have sparked off a property boom in the village. The market, which sells all Laotian produce, is a hive of activity selling not only fruit and vegetables but also Chinese medicines, Buddhas of every description, patched jeans of the kind that Westerners seem to like and shipments of teak on their way to Bangkok. The atmosphere is positively feverish and unlike anything you've ever come across before. *Farangs* are allowed to cross provided they have a visa for Pakse, not easy to obtain on an individual basis. Find out what's what when you're there.

★ **The Kaeng Saphue rapids** – แก่งสะพือ: in the town of Phibun Mangsahan, which lies about 30 kilometres (19 miles) from Khong Chiam going towards Ubon Ratchathani. The rapids are 300 metres downstream from the bridge over the Moon river beyond the bus station. During the dry season the rocks that lie on the riverbed are visible above the surface of the water and local youngsters hire lorry-tyre inner-tubes to go bouncing in and out of the boulders. There's a path along the right bank with stands and refreshment stalls, and straw mats are for hire to sit and have a picnic or take a nap.

# THE SOUTH

## FROM BANGKOK TO HAT YAI

For most backpackers, the south is either the end of their journey or the last place they visit before leaving for Malaysia. This part of Thailand on the frontier with the Union of Myanmar and Malaysia is mainly popular not for the ruins (there are either none or very few) but for the white sandy beaches, turquoise sea, sun and thousands of little islands (*koh* in Thai) fanned by coconut palms. The time you spend here, however, could be heaven or hell depending on which island you pick. Steer well clear of sleazy Patong beach (on the island of Phuket) and Chaweng and Lamai beaches (on Koh Samui island). That leaves you with lots of beaches to choose from – some lively, some overcrowded, some practically deserted (although these are harder to find these days).

The south is also rich in national parks, where regulations tend to be a bit lax. The parks include whole strings of islands such as Koh Phi Phi, Koh Lanta and Koh Tarutao. Most of the waterfalls are also in conservation areas, and some of the falls, such as the Hat Yai, are quite magnificent. If you like diving or even just snorkelling, you'll find the seas a haven of wildlife teeming with fish of all colours, harmless sharks and superb coral.

# HUA HIN – หัวหิน
DIALLING CODE: 032

This is the oldest seaside resort in Thailand, about 230 kilometres (150 miles) from Bangkok, and it's still popular with the Thais, although not as much as it used to be. Hua Hin is a very pleasant little town with a large beach where you can swim in safety. It's also where King Prachadipok was staying in 1932 (in his palace) when a *coup d'état* put an end to the absolute monarchy.

Many backpackers don't even know Hua Hin exists but the atmosphere and the surrounding area are definitely worth the detour.

### GETTING THERE FROM BANGKOK

– **By train**: from Hua Lamphong station, 10 trains leave between 1.30 and 10.30pm and the trip takes about 4 hours.

– **By bus**: from the Southern Bus Terminal there are 30 air-conditioned buses leaving every 40 minutes between 4am and 10.30pm. The journey takes about 3 hours 30 minutes.

– **By air**: there's only one flight in the late afternoon and it takes about 30 minutes.

## USEFUL ADDRESSES

🛈 **TAT** – ททท (map, A1): at the junction of Damnoen Kasem Road and Phetkasem Road (the main street). ☎ 511-047. Minutes from the station. Open daily, 8.30am–4.30pm.

✉ **Post office** – ไปรษณีย์ (map, A1): Damnoen Kasem Road. Open weekdays, 8.30am–4.30pm, weekends 9am–noon.

■ **Telephone exchange** – ชุมสายโทรศัพท์ (just next door to the post office): open daily, 9am–noon. Visa cards accepted.

■ **Police** – สถานีตำรวจ: opposite the post office.

■ **Metropolitan Bank of Bangkok** – ธนาคารศรีนคร: on Phetkasem Road (opposite the tourist office). Not many banks exchange traveller's cheques.

■ **Bangkok Bank Limited** – ธนาคารกรุงเทพ and the **Thai Farmers Bank** – ธนาคารกสิกรไทย: these banks face each other on Phetkasem Road beyond the junction with Chomsin Road, as you go north.

## WHERE TO STAY

Just so you know – taxis, *samlors* and *tuk-tuks* get a commission from the hotels for any guests they bring in, which means you wind up paying more for the room. In the interests of economy try to walk to wherever you're staying.

### MODERATE (200–500 BTS PER PERSON PER NIGHT)

The accommodation in this price range is very basic and not very well kept in some cases.

🛌 **All Nations** – ออลเนชั่นเกสท์เฮาส์ (map, A2, **1**): 10/1 Deachanuchit Road. ☎ 512-747. Small, very well-kept guesthouse. Two rooms with shared shower room on the landing. Great backpacking atmosphere.

🛌 **Usaah Guesthouse** – อุษาเกสท์ เฮาส์ (map, A2, **2**): 162/4 Naret-damri Road. ☎ 532-062. Nice cheap rooms in a place owned by a Dutchman, with a bar-restaurant called – you guessed it – 'The Amsterdam'. Relaxed, backpacking atmosphere.

🛌 There are lots of other **guest-houses** in Naretdamri and Dam-noen Kasem roads.

🛌 **Chatchai Hotel** – โรงแรมฉัตรชัย (map, A1, **3**): 59 Phetkasem Road (practically under the walkway). ☎ 511-034. Clean rooms with no particular charm in a rather noisy road. Try to get a room that doesn't overlook it. There's a warm welcome and a few tables downstairs where you can get something to eat.

🛌 **Tananchai Hotel** – โรงแรม ธนัญชัย (map, B1, **4**): 11 Damron-graj Road. ☎ 511-755 or 513-431. Modern, three-storey building in the north of town. Single rooms with fan or air-conditioning, but they're twice as expensive. Quiet but not very central and not well signposted either.

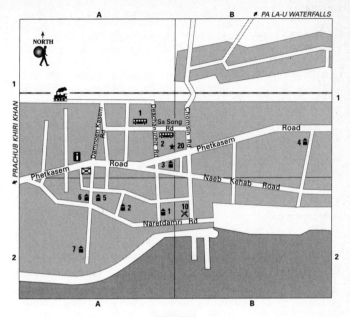

**HUA HIN**

■ **Useful Addresses**

**🛈** TAT

**✉** Post office and telephone

**🚌** **1** Air-conditioned bus terminal.

**🚌** **2** Non-air-conditioned bus terminal

**🚂** Train station

🛏 **Where to Stay**

**1** All Nations
**2** Usaah Guesthouse
**3** Chatchai Hotel

**4** Tananchai Hotel
**5** Ban Boosarin Hotel
**6** Puangpen Villa Hotel and Guesthouse
**7** Sofitel Central Hotel

✕ **Where to Eat**

**10** Sang-Thai King Seafood

★ **What to See**

**20** The night market (Chatchai market)

EXPENSIVE (600–1,000 BTS PER PERSON PER NIGHT)

🛏 **Ban Boosarin Hotel** – โรงแรม บ้านบุษรินทร์ (map, A2, **5**): 8/8 Poon-sook Road. ☎ 512-076 or 089. Offers excellent value for money, with immaculate rooms, some with a pleasant balcony, but full of unne-

cessary gadgets like TVs and fridges – for backpackers in need of a little luxury. Smart decor and guaranteed peace and quiet.

🛏 **Puangpen Villa Hotel and Guesthouse** – พวงเพ็ญวิลล่าโฮเด็ล แอนด์เกสท์เฮาส์ (map, A2, **6**): 11 Damnoen Kasem Road. ☎ 533-

785 or 786. In two parts: the guest-house at the front has nice rooms with TV, fan and hot shower; the little three-storey hotel at the back has cosy, more expensive rooms with balcony and air-conditioning. The complex is very well situated. There's also a swimming pool and deckchairs.

## SPLASH OUT (AROUND 4,000 BTS PR PERSON PER NIGHT)

🏠 **Sofitel Central Hotel** – โรง แรมโซฟิเทลเซ็นทรัล (map, A2, **7**):

Damnoen Kasem Road. ☎ 512-021 or 038. To book from England: ☎ (0208) 283 4570. One of the finest hotels in Thailand was recently bought up by the French chain Sofitel. Built in 1923, it has all the retro elegance of the period, with a first-class restaurant service, swimming pool and big garden that leads directly onto the beach, with magnificent topiary in the shape of animals. Worth a look even if you don't spend the night there.

## WHERE TO EAT

There are places near the landing stage that serve charcoal-grilled fish. You must taste this, but watch out for the sauce, which is red hot.

✕ The **market** at night is another cheap place to eat (see 'What to See').

✕ If you're feeling flush, try the seafood restaurants in the port. There's a particularly handy photographic menu at the **Sang-Thai King Seafood** – ร้านอาหารซีฟู้ดแสงไทยกิง (map, B2, **10**): ☎ 512-144. The restaurant is on a pontoon where the fishing boats come in and serves very good fish, even if the place itself is a bit of a production line.

## WHAT TO SEE IN HUA HIN AND THE SURROUNDING AREA

★ **The night market (Chatchai market)** – ตลาดกลางคืน (map, A1–B1, **20**): lots of stalls at the junction with Phetkasem and Dechanit Roads. For an encounter with authentic Thai cuisine, make sure you come to this market, where you will find excellent dishes at low prices, including a wide range of seafood. Rather this than the European food served at nearby bars and restaurants offering pasta, pizzas, burgers and the like.

★ **The white sandy beach**: 3 kilometres (nearly 2 miles) long, on the right as you look out to sea. It faces east, so it's in the shade after 1pm. Nice walk to the Wat Kao Lad on the water. At night, don't miss seeing the fishing boats come ashore.

★ **The Pa La-u waterfalls**: about 60 kilometres (40 miles) away.

## LEAVING HUA HIN

### For Bangkok

– **By air-conditioned bus**: the bus terminal is at the corner of Sa Song and Dechanuchit roads (map, A1, 🚌 **1**). Buses every 45 minutes from 3am to 9pm and every 30 minutes in the middle of the day. Takes about 3 hours 30 minutes.

– **By non-air-conditioned bus**: the bus terminal (map, A1, 🚌 **2**) is on Sa Song Road (on the opposite corner to the air-conditioned bus terminal) near the night market. Buses leave every 30 minutes from 4.30am to 6pm. Allow about 4 hours.

– **By train**: for the station, *see* map, A1 🚂 . There are 11 trains a day, 1.10am–4.30pm, taking about 4 hours 30 minutes.

#### Going south

– **By air-conditioned bus**: to Surat Thani only. These are private buses coming from Bangkok. Ask at the Western Tour agency on Damnoen Kasem Road.

– **By non-air-conditioned bus**: from the bus terminal on Sa Song Road (behind the night market). Ten buses to Surat Thani, 8am–10.55pm. Takes about 8 hours 30 minutes. Seven buses to Phuket, 1.30am–midnight. Takes about 11 hours.

– **By train**: nine trains to Surat Thani, 1.35am–11.30pm (takes about 7–8 hours). Four trains to Hat Yai, 4.50–7.50pm (takes about 13 hours).

# SURAT THANI – สุราษฎร์ธานี DIALLING CODE: 077

This is a town with absolutely nothing to recommend it except as the place where you board the boat for Koh Samui and Koh Phangan. Avoid spending the night there.

## GETTING THERE

– **By national air-conditioned and non-air-conditioned bus**: from the Southern Bus Terminal in Bangkok. Four air-conditioned buses between 8 and 10pm (it takes 10 hours); two non-air-conditioned buses at 9.20am and 11pm (takes 11 hours). You should aim to get there early.

– **By train**: from Hua Lamphong station in Bangkok: 10 trains, 1.30am–10.30pm (takes 11 hours). Note that the station in Surat Thani is actually in Phun Phin, about 14 kilometres (9 miles) out of town, but if you're trying to make a connecting boat to Koh Samui, there's bound to be a bus going to whichever one of the two landing stages it happens to be.

– **By air**: lots of Thai Airways flights to Surat Thani every day from Bangkok. If your final destination is Koh Samui, it's probably simpler to fly there direct with Bangkok Airways (15 flights a day). Be warned, however, that since the airline holds a monopoly on the Bangkok–Koh Samui route, it costs twice as much to fly there as it does to fly from Bangkok to Surat Thani.

## USEFUL ADDRESS

🛈 **TAT** – ททท: 5 Talat Mai Road, Bandon Amphoe Muang. ☎ 288-818 and 288-819. Fax: 282-828. Open 9am–4.30pm.

## WHERE TO STAY

Try to arrange things so that you don't have to stay in Surat Thani, where the hotels are not only rather grim but also very expensive.

### BUDGET TO MODERATE (LESS THAN 500 BTS PER PERSON PER NIGHT)

🛏 **Phanfa Hotel** – โรงแรมผ่านฟ้า: Na Muang Road (beyond the Grand City Hotel going away from the port). ☎ 272-288. A rather dirty-looking hotel that's on its last legs but at least the sheets are clean. Mentioned here because it's the cheapest place in town.

🛏 **Grand City Hotel** – โรงแรมแกรนด์ซิตี้เมืองทองสุราษฎร์: 428/6-10 Na Muang Road. ☎ 272-560. A bit decrepit but clean, with lots of rooms with bathroom facilities off huge corridors. Noisy, but the rooms on the upper floors are quieter.

🛏 **Thai Hotel** – ไทยโฮเด็ล: 24/4 Chaiya Road (the road that runs parallel to the port). ☎ 272-932. This is the nearest hotel to the landing point for Koh Sui. It's a sleazy place but the rooms are large with bathrooms, and it is not too expensive. You're also sure to be woken up early when the shops open in the street.

### EXPENSIVE (OVER 500 BTS PER PERSON·PER NIGHT)

🛏 **Tapee Hotel** – โรงแรมดาปี: 100 Chonkasen Road. ☎ 272-575. Very central but in a noisy street. This modern-looking hotel is a bit decrepit inside but decent enough. Rooms have fans or air-conditioning and bathroom. Avoid those that overlook the street. The hotel has a lift, car-park and also a restaurant on the ground floor. Prices are reasonable considering the standard of comfort.

🛏 **Seree Hotel** – โรงแรมเสรี: 2/2-5 Seri Tompo Road. ☎ 272-279. Slightly away from the centre and similar in style to the previous place, with rooms that are lacking in charm although they're clean. There's a coffee-shop on the ground floor.

# KOH SAMUI – เกาะสมุย

DIALLING CODE: 077

This is the biggest island in the Gulf of Thailand (about 21 kilometres long by 25 kilometres wide (13 miles by 15 miles) and a place so steeped in fantasy that it seems to be about time somebody painted a more realistic picture. Koh Samui is no longer the marvellous, idyllic island that every backpacker used to dream of. But, despite more and more concrete hotels and a proliferation of girlie bars, the island does have its attractions: beautiful uncrowded beaches, great walks, reasonably priced bungalows on the water, varied and delicious food, ideal climate. Much as one may regret the island's development, the news isn't all bad, but the island is changing at lightning speed.

How much you enjoy your stay on Koh Samui depends on how well you choose your beach. It's all a question of taste and to help you make up your mind, the beaches are reviewed below. There are beaches like **Chaweng Beach** and **Lamai Beach** where new pick-up bars seem to open every day. And there are quieter, more intimate beaches like **Mae Nam Beach** and **Bo Phut Beach.**

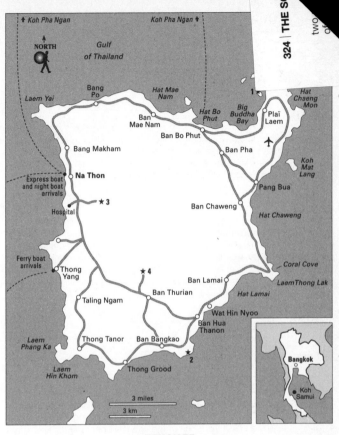

**KOH SAMUI**

| ★ What to See | 2 Butterfly Garden |
|---|---|
| | 3 Hinlat Waterfall |
| 1 Big Buddha | 4 Na Muang Waterfalls 1 and 2 |

## DEVELOPMENT ON THE ISLAND

After Pattaya and Phuket, Koh Samui is without a doubt the island most damaged by the passion for property development that seems set to engulf the whole of southern Thailand. The point of no return was when they built the airport. Today there are no fewer than 15 flights a day from Koh Samui to Bangkok and 2 to Phuket. The best that can be said is that for the time being at least, property development is confined to the

...nain beaches (Chaweng Bay and Lamai Bay). The growing number visitors has also created problems of its own, traffic being one of them (*see* 'Getting Around the Island').

The people of Koh Samui are a welcoming lot who consider themselves first and foremost as Koh Samui islanders complete with all their little idiosyncrasies. So much for the introductions.

## CLIMATE

It generally rains in Koh Samui from November to December but, unlike Phuket, you stand a good chance of fine weather during the (theoretical) rainy season from May to September. In July and August in particular, it rains a lot less here than in the rest of Thailand.

## HEALTH

You should be aware that for some time now there's been dengue fever on Koh Samui and Koh Pha Ngan. The virus is transmitted by mosquitoes and causes a fever that can be anything from mild to severe depending on how strong you are. Anyway, it's nothing to worry about. Just ask a doctor for something to bring down the fever. Incidentally, dengue is nothing to do with malaria, so don't panic.

## GETTING THERE

### By boat

– **From Bangkok**: you have to go to Surat Thani (*see below*) and take the boat. Some agencies sell combined bus and boat tickets.

– **From Surat Thani**: there is a choice of three boarding points: Surat Thani (Ban Don), Ta Tong or Donsak (the slowest crossing). The simplest solution is to buy a ticket from one of the agencies near the port, who will arrange to get you to the port by bus. If you're coming from Krabi or elsewhere, buy a bus and boat ticket from your point of departure. The bus usually gets you there in time for the boat. At Surat Thani station, which is 14 kilometres (9 miles) out of town, there's always a bus waiting to take tourists to the boat. It's all very efficient.

Boats for Koh Samui are as follows: two express boats a day that leave Ta Tong at 8am and 2.30pm (each taking about 2 hours 30 minutes); five ferries from Donsak (practically every 2 hours, 8am–6pm); one night boat that leaves Surat Thani (Ban Don) at 11pm. It does get you into Koh Samui rather early (5am) but at least you don't have to spend the night in Surat Thani; instead, you sleep side by side with the locals on narrow mattresses. Keep an eye on your luggage.

### By air

– **From Phuket**: two Bangkok Airways flights a day (40-minute flight).

– **From Bangkok**: Bangkok Airways flies direct to Koh Samui 15 times a day, between 7.20am and 5.50pm. The flying time is 1 hour 20 minutes.

## GETTING AROUND THE ISLAND

– **Songthaews**: covered vans with seats, which cruise the island from about 6am to 5.30pm. They're fast (a bit too fast sometimes) and very convenient. Their final destination is displayed on the van. To stop one, simply stand on the roadside and wave. When you want to get out, press the switch on the roof. Always have some change handy and never ask the fare before setting off or you'll be overcharged. Find out the price of a typical fare from the locals sitting next to you and work out what yours should be according to the distance covered. At night between 8pm and 9pm, *songthaews* also organize pick-ups from some of the beaches and take the *farangs* boozing in the bars on Chaweng or Lamai beach. The return journey is between 3am and 4am. Prices rocket at these times, as you might expect.

– **Motorbikes**: these are obviously the best way of getting anywhere under your own steam, but read on and you may go off the idea. The roads on Koh Samui are narrow and getting busier all the time. The Thais drive like maniacs and they're not alone: many of the tourists have never ridden a bike in their lives but have hired one here because nobody ever asks to see any papers. First prize for stupidity goes to *farangs* who career around the island in flip-flops and swimming trunks with the throttle flat out. You are advised to wear a helmet and keep an eye on the wing-mirror (that's what it's there for, after all). It's worth knowing that the reason it costs so little to hire a bike is because none of the bikes is insured. What you break you pay for. Otherwise, hiring a bike is great.

## WHERE TO STAY AND WHERE TO EAT

There are always touts waiting to meet the boats, so try to decide in advance which beach you plan to stay on and go there by *songthaew*.

As for which beach to opt for, you're spoiled for choice. There are now bungalows on every beach on the island and you need a really detailed map that shows them all – the best one is V. Hongsombud's *Guide Map of Koh Samui*.

When you get to the bungalow don't hesitate to ask for a reduction if you're staying longer than a week (usually no problem in the off-peak season). Nobody's entirely clear what constitutes the high season these days, but it's generally taken to run from December to February and June to July. On Mae Nam and Bo Phut Beach in particular there are also two-bedroom houses with shower room and kitchen to let by the month – useful if you're planning an extended stay.

The rapid growth in tourism in Koh Samui means that places to stay come and go at an alarming rate. Sadly, mentioning them in a guidebook seems to make things worse because landlords become complacent and let things slide.

This guide does not list many good places to eat either, but you won't generally find much better than the very decent home-cooked food prepared by the *mamma* right where you're staying.

**KOH SAMUI**

## IF YOU PLAN TO DIVE WITHOUT BREATHING APPARATUS

As a general rule, the water is clearer in the east when the wind is from the west and vice versa. There is some magnificent coral around the island but you can only see it properly when the sea is dead calm. The waters in this part of Thailand are relatively shallow and the sand tends to make them cloudy.

## CURRENCY EXCHANGE

There are currency exchange booths on all the beaches. Many of them close at 10pm, but on Na Thon (*see below*) they close at 6pm.

### ★ NA THON – หน้าทอน

This is the main town on the island and the port of arrival and departure for express boats to Surat Thani and Koh Pha Ngan, and ferries land about 10 kilometres (6 miles) away. There's not a lot to see or do here but the place has a nice feel to it. Everything happens on the Taweratphakdee Road where there are lots of craft shops and clothes shops, as well as a partly covered **traditional market** (map, A2,**9**).

## USEFUL ADDRESSES

**🛈 TAT** – ททท (map, B 1): in front of the post office; open daily, 8.30am–4.30pm. Warm welcome.

**✉ Post office** – ไปรษณีย์ (map, B1): on the seafront, about 300 metres to the left as you step off the boat. Open weekdays only, 8.30am–4.30pm. Telephone facilities on the first floor; open daily, 8.30am–10pm.

■ **Doctor**: Dr Surasit Clinic – คลีนิคหมอสุรสิทธิ์: 167 Taweratphakdee Road. ☎ 42-10-11. Very competent doctor who speaks English, in the village centre (on the ground floor of the building). Consultations held Monday–Friday 7am–4pm, Saturday 7am–2pm.

■ **Immigration Office** – สำนักงาน–ตรวจคนเข้าเมือง: behind the post office – the place to go to extend your visa.

■ **Banks** (map, A–B 1–2, **2**): there are lots of banks on the Taweratphakdee Road: Thai Farmers Bank (where you can hire a locker), Krung Thai Bank.

■ **Collective taxis** – รถสองแถว: these leave at frequent intervals from the landing stage and go to all the different beaches on the island. The destination is displayed on the windscreen.

■ **Travel agencies**, **Thai Airways**, **market** on the Taweratphakdee Road.

■ **Boat tickets and sailing times** (map, B1, **1**): from the Songserm offices in the port, in the street between the small landing stage and the big landing stage. Songserm is a legitimate company that owns most of the boats to Koh Pha Ngan, Koh Tao and Surat Thani.

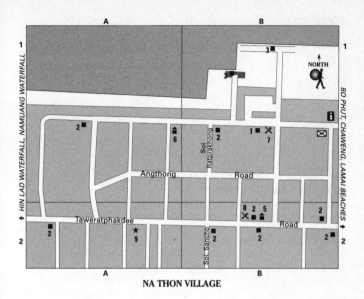

**NA THON VILLAGE**

■ **Useful Addresses**

**ℹ** TAT
**✉** Post office
**1** Boat tickets and sailing times (Songserm)
**2** Banks
**3** Arrival and departure points for boats to Surat Thani, Koh Pha Ngan, Koh Tao

⌂ **Where to Stay**

**5** Sea View Guesthouse
**6** Seaside Palace Hotel

✕ **Where to Eat**

**7** Jelly Roll
**8** Hot Bread Shop

★ **What to See**

**9** Market

## WHERE TO STAY

There's nothing much to be gained from spending the night in Na Thon.

⌂ **Sea View Guesthouse** – ชีวิว เกสท์เฮาส์ (map, B2, **5**): Tawerat-phakdee Road, in the centre of town next to the Thai Military Bank. Roughly 150–300 Bts for the night. Soulless, rather decrepit rooms with shared or private shower room – but the bedding's clean.

⌂ **Seaside Palace Hotel** – โรงแรม ชีไซด์พาเลซ (map, A1, **6**): facing the port, on the right about 300 metres from the landing point. ☎ 421-079 or 420-237. Roughly 600–800 Bts for the night. This is a palace in name only these days, with paint-work that is definitely past its best. But the rooms are clean and well kept and there's a choice of fan or air-conditioning. Plus a warm welcome.

KOH SAMUI

## WHERE TO EAT

✕ **Jelly Roll** – ร้านอาหารเยลลี่โรล (map, B1, **7**): about 40 metres to the left of the landing stage is this large anonymous canteen-style place with a menu written in French (handy if you can speak it) and lots of French specialities. They also do breakfast here and sell good cakes, including chocolate cake, muffins and banana cake. Make sure they're freshly baked.

✕ **Hot Bread Shop** – ฮ็อทเบรด ช็อป (map, B2, **8**): in Taweratphakdee Road. Thai version of a tea-shop serving delicious cakes and good coffee to tourists and Thais who come here for a 'Continental' breakfast.

## LOWDOWN ON THE BEACHES

The beaches are reviewed in clockwise order starting from Na Thon.

### ★ MAE NAM BEACH – หาดแม่น้ำ

Going north from Na Thon, this extremely pretty beach is the first beach you come to. It's wonderfully quiet and the bungalows are among the cheapest on the island. The village of Mae Nam doesn't quite have the charm of nearby Bo Phut (there are no wooden houses) but there are fewer tourists, which makes it feel more like the real thing.

## WHERE TO STAY

### BUDGET TO MODERATE (80–300 BTS PER PERSON PER NIGHT)

Note that the three places listed below are relatively far from the road – which is ideal if you want peace and quiet and are prepared to walk or hire a motorbike. Definitely worth the effort.

⌂ **Mae Nam Villa** – แม่น้ำวิลล่า บังกะโล: not to be confused with Mae Nam Village Bungalows. Coming from the main road, look for the dirt track on the left about 50 metres before the Smile Shop grocery store (almost opposite the exit to Mae Nam coming from Na Thon). The guesthouse is about 800 metres up that track. ☎ 425-501. This is a great place that reminds you of what Koh Samui used to be like a few years ago: lovely little bungalows, solidly built, in the middle of a magnificent garden facing a gorgeous beach. Each bungalow has its own secluded terrace, fan, cold shower and WC. It's run by a nice family and the food is good too. Quiet, far from the madding crowd – it's a particular favourite.

⌂ **Laem Sai Bungalows** – แหลม ทรายบังกะโล: you have to go through Mae Nam Villa to get to this place. ☎ 425-133. Authentic bamboo-and-straw huts dotted among the coconut palms (watch out for falling coconuts). Some of the huts have a mezzanine floor for a second bed. They're fairly basic, but so is the price. Cool place, good food.

⌂ **Rainbow Bungalows** – เรนโบว์ บังกะโล: just before the Mae Nam Villa. ☎ 425-425. Small, solidly built bungalows with cold shower and fan. Basic but clean and reasonably priced. Warm welcome.

⬢ **Mae Nam Village Bungalows** – แม่น้ำวิลเลจบังกะโล: in the middle of the village on the main road, turn left going towards the sea and after about 300 metres, take the path on the right. ☎ 425-151. There are about 15 bungalows plus more rooms in several solidly built houses, all with fan and cold shower (hot shower costs more). Warm welcome. You're not directly on the beach but being so close to the village has its advantages.

## MODERATE TO EXPENSIVE (200–700 BTS PER PERSON PER NIGHT)

⬢ **New Lapaz Villa** – นิวลาปาช วิลล่า: well signposted from the main road. ☎ 425-296. Around 50 well-equipped brick bungalows ranging from basic rooms with fan and cold shower to more luxurious pads with air-conditioning and hot water. Something to suit every purse. Warm welcome, relaxed atmosphere and a very nice restaurant on the beach. A place worth knowing about.

⬢ **Lolita Bungalows** – โลลิต้า บังกะโล well signposted on the left, just before the village of Mae Nam (still coming from Na Thon). ☎ 425-134. Very large, very stylish bungalows with lovely secluded terrace, some on the beach, some in a lush exotic garden, the most luxurious ones with air-conditioning and hot water. Bath towels supplied. There's also an extraordinary circular restaurant with pillars and ornate mosaics that's straight out of the movies. Warm welcome. Good place if you can afford it.

## ★ BO PHUT BEACH – หาดบ่อผุด

Besides being a pretty beach, this is also a charming village that retains many of its traditional wooden houses despite the boom in tourism and the liberal use of concrete. The atmosphere here is quite unique too, bustling with local fishermen and smiling, friendly locals.

As for the beach, it may not be the most beautiful on the island but it's far from the road, relatively secluded and quiet. The beach is at its narrowest near the village where it's not so good for swimming.

## WHERE TO STAY

### MODERATE TO EXPENSIVE (300–500 BTS PER PERSON PER NIGHT)

⬢ **Peace Bungalows** – พีซบังกะโล: ☎ 425-357. Sweet little bungalows old and new, well spaced out in an agreeable setting. The oldest ones have fan, shower and WC. The most recent ones are air-conditioned and stylishly decorated. There's a good restaurant here too. Warm welcome, friendly place giving good value for money all round.

⬢ **Starfish and Coffee**: ☎ 425-085. Fax: 425-191. Near the Sandy Resort (*see below*) and owned by a Franco-Thai couple. About 15 light, well-kept bungalows of different sizes, each tastefully furnished with fan and private bathroom. There's also a restaurant here.

### EXPENSIVE TO SPLASH OUT (500–1,300 BTS PER PERSON PER NIGHT)

⬢ **Sandy Resort** – แซนดี้รีสอร์ท: ☎ 425-353 or 354. Sweet, spotless bungalows with shower room, fan or air-conditioning (towels and sheets changed daily – now there's a luxury). Pleasant decor and rooms at a wide range of prices, the most expensive being by the sea where the deckchairs are. There's also a nice swimming pool overlooking the beach. Very holiday-village atmosphere.

⌂ **World Bungalows** – เวิร์ลด์ บังกะโล: ☎ 425-355 or 358. A selection of bungalows that vary in size and price from a basic room with fan and cold shower to a luxury suite with lounge, TV, air-conditioning etc. All the rooms are spotlessly clean and facing the nicest part of the beach. There's a swimming pool and even an area where you can play *boules*.

## WHERE TO EAT

Bo Phut, despite being very touristy, still has a nice atmosphere which is why it's the only place on the island where we list any restaurants. By the way, lots of Europeans now live in Bo Phut so if you've had enough of Thai food, you can try French, Belgian, German, English or Italian.

### BUDGET

✗ On the main road opposite the go-kart track there's a typical **country restaurant** with tables on a terrace beneath a corrugated iron roof. Excellent traditional food at low prices.

✗ **Tid Restaurant** – ร้านอาหาร– ตินด: in the village. Open 8.30am– 10.30pm for fish caught by the owner himself, including such specialities as crab, prawns, squid and shark. Or if you're broke, the fried noodles are excellent too. Just eight tables, three of them on a little terrace with a magnificent view of the sea, especially when the sun goes down. They also serve breakfast here. Warm welcome and lots of local colour.

### EXPENSIVE

✗ **Le Bateau** – ร้านอาหารเลอ บาโด: as you enter the village, at the beginning of the main road that leads to the landing stage. ☎ 425- 297. Closed on Tuesday and from September to December every other year (the last time was in 1998). Run by an amiable Belgian called Christian, with a Thai wife, who called this restaurant after the first place he opened in 1981. There's no connection between this place and the other place known as The Boat. Nice balance of Thai, Belgian and French food: bread baked in a wood fire, delicious pâté, tasty swordfish with mustard. Not cheap though. Christian also organizes boat trips to Koh Pha Ngan to explore the coral reef, and four-wheel-drive trips into the jungle.

✗ **La Sirène** – ร้านอาหารลาซิแรน: in the village. ☎ 425-301. Another place run by a *farang* who married a Thai girl; this time it's a Frenchman called Gérard. You walk into a pink room with a pleasant terrace and views of Koh Pha Ngan in the background. Lots of different things to eat, all flawlessly prepared – good coffee too (so it should be for the price). Gérard also takes people for boat trips (aboard the restaurant's namesake). Pity about the rather chilly welcome.

✗ **Bird in the Hand** – ร้านอา หารเดอะเบิร์ดอินเดอะแฮนด์: in the village, with four tables on a terrace facing the sea. ☎ 425-248. The owner is an amiable Englishman straight out of *Robinson Crusoe*. Simple, refined European or Thai food; wooden decor with fishing nets hanging on the walls; old nautical atmosphere, and honest prices.

## DIVING SCHOOLS

⤜ **Samui International Diving School** – โรงเรียนดำน้ำสมุย: conscientious but quite expensive diving school in the village opposite the Bird in the Hand restaurant. It runs a well-designed, week-long course for students planning to take the international diving diploma and also organizes day-long maiden dives.

## ★ BIG BUDDHA BEACH – หาดพระใหญ่

This is another pretty beach, facing the setting sun and not too crowded. The only snag is that it's a bit shady and right by the road – not that it's noisy exactly, but you do feel rather exposed. Its principal attraction is how few people go there.

## WHERE TO STAY

### BUDGET

🛏 **Number 1 Bungalow** – นัมเบอร์วันบังกะโล: ☎ 425-446. Rather rustic wooden bungalows in a semicircle facing the beach, some with two bedrooms. Pretty basic, but what you'd expect for the price.

🛏 **Phayorm Park Resort** – พยอมพาร์คริสอร์ท: ☎ 425-137. Row of small wood-and-concrete bungalows, each with private shower room and fan. Nice restaurant on the beach.

### MODERATE

🛏 **Sunset Song** – ซันเซ็ททสองบังกะโล: ☎ 425-155. Very large wooden bungalows each with a nice little terrace, table and tiled bathroom. The cheapest come with fan, the others with air-conditioning and hot water and there's even a bath in some of them. They're a bit crammed together but the landlord sees to it that they're very well kept. Good value for money.

🛏 **Ocean View Resort** – โอเชียนวิวรีสอร์ท: ☎ 425-439. What strikes you about this place is how clean and quiet it is. Fifteen bungalows in an avenue full of flowers that's at right angles to the sea: five straw huts with private shower room and fan (the cheapest option) and ten solidly built bungalows with private shower room, windows and mosquito nets. There's also a restaurant with a covered terrace. Very friendly welcome.

## WHAT TO SEE

★ **Big Buddha** – พระใหญ่ (general map of Koh Samui, **1**): an immense and very kitsch golden Buddha built in 1971 stands on a rocky promontory to the right of the beach of the same name. The monastery close by is home to a community of monks, so no shorts or bare shoulders, please, when you visit the statue.

## ★ CHAENG MON BEACH – หาดเชิงมนต์

This beach in the northeast of the island used to be a heavenly crescent-shaped strip of white sand and coconut palms until the arrival of a hotel complex called the Imperial Boat House. In its wake came hordes of investors who smothered the back of the beach with a string of restaurants. Competition is fierce and waiters come touting for business when things start to look a bit quiet. Not the quietest beach on the island by a long chalk, but great if you like that sort of thing.

## WHERE TO STAY

### MODERATE

⌂ **Chat Kaeo Resort** – ฉัตรแก้ว รีสอร์ท: in the middle of the beach. ☎ 425-109 or 245-178. A complex of simple wooden bungalows with cold shower and fan or not very pretty concrete bungalows with air-conditioning, hot water and private roof terrace. But there's a restaurant facing the sea where they serve good food and the service is flawless.

### SPLASH OUT

⌂ **White House** – ไวท์เฮาส์รีสอร์ท: ☎ 245-315 or 317. Huge detached houses built to look like Buddhist temples scattered around a lush garden. Each one has four huge bedrooms that are arranged as a suite in the more expensive ones. Pleasant decor, air-conditioning, satellite TV and even a mini-bar. There's also a swimming pool, jacuzzi, massage parlour and stylish restaurant. As for the price, this place isn't called the White House for nothing.

## WHAT TO SEE

★ The little pebble beach at **Thong Son Bay** near Chaeng Mon beach is more secluded and relatively uncrowded, and it has a magnificent view. There are also a few bungalows where you can stay.

### ★ CHAWENG BEACH – หาดเฉวง

This is the main beach on the island and the kind of beach every photographer dreams of – wide and beautiful with nearly 3 kilometres (2 miles) of fine white sand rolling gently down to crystal-clear blue water. Except that Chaweng beach today reeks of tourism and has a distinctly Pattaya-like air about it – witness the arrival of the girlie bars. All a bit sordid really. Beautiful it may be, but this beach has sold its soul to the tourist industry and it's the least likeable because of that.

As for 'Where to Stay and Eat': it's all 'Give us yer bahts'-type landlords and expensive restaurants serving indifferent food. What more is there to say?

## WHERE TO STAY

In view of this, there's no rush to suggest places to stay, particularly since they're not difficult to find. Whether you can afford them is another matter. All the same, here are a few places where prices are just about reasonable considering what's on offer.

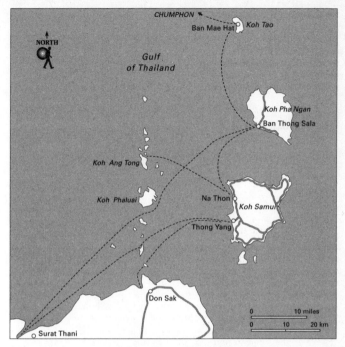

**THE ISLANDS OF KOH SAMUI**

## TOWARDS THE MIDDLE OF THE BEACH

MODERATE TO EXPENSIVE (200–800 BTS PER PERSON PER NIGHT)

🏠 **Long Beach Bungalows** – ลองบีชบังกะโล: ☎ 422-162. One of the few remaining places where there's still a nice atmosphere, although the music next door tends to be a problem. Small wooden bungalows, with cold shower and fan, laid out in two rows either side of a big coconut grove that leads to the beach where you'll also find the restaurant. The Swiss landlord speaks six languages.

SPLASH OUT (OVER 1,500 BTS PER PERSON PER NIGHT)

🏠 **Princess Village** – พรินซ์เซส วิลเลจ: ☎ 422-216 or 245-315. A group of bungalows buried in a lush garden, owned by the man who owns the White House on Chaeng Mon beach. The rooms are nicely decorated, with air-conditioning as you would expect, and hot water. They're bang in the middle of Chaweng Beach but really quiet – and there's a swimming pool too. An ideal place for a honeymoon.

🏠 **Sans-Souci Samui** – ซองซูชีสมุย: opposite the Eden seafood restaurant. ☎ 422-044 or 230-829. Nice, comfortable bungalows dotted around a tropical garden. Restaurant too, and the welcome is warm.

KOH SAMUI

## HEADING SOUTH ALONG THE BEACH

### EXPENSIVE

🛏 **Samui Paradise** – สมุยพาราไดซ์: ☎ 230-294 or 384. Series of pretty wooden huts stylishly arranged on an English lawn shaded by coco- nut palms. High standard of com- fort, with air-conditioning and fan. There's also a restaurant that serves international food. Price in- cludes breakfast.

## WHAT TO SEE IN THE SURROUNDING AREA

★ **Coral Cove** – คอรัลโคฟ: nice little beach between Chaweng and Lamai with not a concrete hotel in sight (truly miraculous). It's a good place to dive and you can even stay there:

🛏 **Coral Cove Resort** – คอรัล โคฟรีสอร์ท: ☎ 422-126. The only place on a little beach surrounded by rocks. Nice wooden bungalows with cold shower and fan or more solidly built ones of a similar stan- dard that cost a bit more. Quite cheap, particularly if you plan to stay a few days. The creek is blissfully quiet and teeming with fish that come and nibble your fingers as they dart in and out of the magnificent coral.

🛏 **Hi Coral Cove Bungalow** – ไฮคอรัลโคฟบังกะโล: in the neigh- bouring creek. ☎ 422-495. Bunga- lows on a hillside, some wooden (the cheapest) – others more so- lidly built, with air-conditioning and mini-bar. No beach, only rocks, so great for snorkelling. Not so good for basking in the sun. There's just about room for a towel if you don't mind the rather coarse sand. Alter- natively, try the Coral Cove Resort next door.

### ★ LAMAI BEACH – หาดละไม

After Chaweng beach, this is the second most popular beach on Koh Samui. It used to be famous for its coconut palms until vast numbers of them were felled to make bungalows. This bit of environmental sabotage was just the beginning. Lamai today is a wasteland of girlie bars, nightclubs and exotic restaurants (Italian, German and French). All totally phoney and no place for a backpacker.

## WHERE TO STAY

There's hardly any need to suggest places to stay here either. But here are one or two, in case you're desperate. Note that the quietest places are at the northern end of the beach.

### GOING NORTH TO SOUTH

### MODERATE

🛏 **Rose Garden Bungalow** – โรสการ์เด้นบังกะโล: one of the first groups of bungalows that you come to. ☎ 424-115. Bungalows of different types and levels of com- fort (fan or air-conditioning) but all beautifully kept. The ones near the road are noisy, so ask for one close to the beach. Good restaurant and a nice welcome too.

KOH SAMUI

⚓ **Marina Bungalow** – มาริน 'าบังกะโล: not to be confused with the more expensive Marina Villa right next door. ☎ 233-116. Old-fashioned bungalows (wood with thatched roof) typical of the *belle époque*, in a pleasant garden shaded by coconut palms. Beautifully kept, and with cold shower and fan. Affable, attentive owner; good food; all-round quality for the price.

⚓ **Bill Resort** – บิลรีสอร์ท: ☎ 424-403 or 424-287. Much further south than the previous place. Bungalows to suit more or less any pocket, from ones with fan to the more luxurious versions with air-conditioning. Well kept overall but rather crammed together. Decent restaurant. Nice welcome.

## EXPENSIVE

⚓ **Marina Villa** – มารีน่าวิลล่า: right beside Marina Bungalow. ☎ 424-426. Solidly built bungalows either side of a shady avenue. Large rooms, with fan or air-conditioning. Each bungalow also has its own terrace and garden area. The restaurant is on the beach.

## WHAT TO SEE

★ On a point to the south of the beach stands a long **cylindrical rock** – หินดาหินยาย of explicit proportions made more explicit still by the presence of the narrow slit in the rocks beside it. It forms a rude natural phenomenon of rare precision: nature rarely gets this realistic. Not to be missed.

★ **Ban Hua Thanon** – บ้านหัวถนน: south of Lamai. An ordinary little village with a difference because it's populated by Muslim fishermen who built it themselves. Their passion is turtle doves and they even organize cooing contests.

★ **Lamai Cultural Hall** – ละไมคัลทูรอลฮอล: north of the village of Lamai, at a right angle in the road, this wooden house in the courtyard of the Wat Lamai is home to a museum of sorts, where the odd collection of objects reminds you more of your granny's attic than a real museum. Culturally sound in intention if not in content.

## ★ BAN LAEM SOR – บ้านแหลมสอ

This is a magnificent beach where there aren't many people because it's not great for swimming. You have to walk out some distance before it gets deep. But it is wonderfully peaceful and there are some great diving spots out towards the coral reef.

## WHERE TO STAY

⚓ **Diamond Villa** – ไดมอนด์วิลล่า: from Na Thon, take Route 4170 and 100 metres past the sign for Ban Laem look for the turning on the right along a sandy track Follow the track for about 700 metres. ☎ 424-442. Down at the end of the beach, by the coral reef, you'll find eight cheap, basic wooden bungalows made of planks, with cold shower, WC (shared or private) and fan. Great welcome from the friendly lady owner, who also serves very good food. Out of season, it's tranquillity itself.

**KOH SAMUI**

## WHAT TO SEE

★ **Butterfly Garden** – สวนผีเสื้อสมุย (general map of Koh Samui, **2**): on Route 4170 between Ban Hua Thanon and Ban Bangkao. Open daily, 9am–7pm. This large tropical garden is draped in an immense net that's supposed to keep in more than 30 different species of butterfly. What you also see are swarms of extremely busy, surprisingly tiny bees, about half the size of European bees. Honey is on sale, of course. There's also a room full of butterflies from all over the world. All a bit of a tourist trap but if you've got nothing better to do . . .

★ **THONG GROOD** – ท้องกรูด

Not so much something to see as somewhere to eat. This small fishing village at the southernmost tip of the island is home to two traditional little restaurants that face the sea. They serve the most delicious fish, prepared any way you like (sautéed, steamed or barbecued) at very reasonable prices. The Ging Pagarang Restaurant is particularly good.

★ **LAEM PHANG KA** – แหลมพังกา

Huge, almost desert-like bay tucked into the southwestern corner of the island on a road off Route 4170, virtually opposite the Snake Farm. This strange, almost desolate place is your chance to escape the tourist bedlam of Koh Samui and enter a world of tranquillity where the sunset is the most beautiful on the island. Don't come here for the swimming though, because the sea is very shallow. At high tide, it only comes up to your knees and at low tide you have to paddle out for a very, very long way.

## WHERE TO STAY

BUDGET (60–200 BTS PER PERSON PER NIGHT)

⌂ **Emerald Cove Bungalows** – เอเมอรอลโคฟบังกะโล: the first group of bungalows you come to on the road. ☎ 423-082. Traditional wooden bungalows with small shower rooms or more solidly built ones with small terraces and tiled bathrooms. Cold water only. Excellent value for money and warm welcome. At night you can sometimes hear the monks chanting in the moonlight.

⌂ **Sea Gull Bungalows** – ซีกัล บังกะโล: the last bungalows along the bay. ☎ 423-091. Very nice, very reasonably priced, some facing the bay, others higher up. Nice terrace restaurant. Wonderfully quiet and the view at night is divine. A great place.

⌂ **Pearl Bay** – เพิร์ลเบย์บังกะโล: just before the Sea Gull Bungalows. ☎ 423-110. Very simple wooden bungalows on the slopes overlooking the bay. Not too hot on upkeep, but cheap.

## WHAT TO SEE INLAND

★ **Buffalo-fights** – ชนควาย: very much part of the Thai way of life and particularly popular in the southern islands. Practically every village has its own 'arena', which may be no more than a space cordoned off by a bamboo screen; there are six on Koh Samui. People bet heavily on these fights, as you'd expect, and the attraction is not so much what's happening inside the ring as what's going on around it. Steer clear of any fights that are laid on especially for the benefit of the tourists (the Thais don't go to these). Find out where the best fights are from your landlords. For your information, a buffalo starts fighting at the age of six or seven and may fight every month thereafter until he turns 25, when he takes a well-deserved retirement (eventually dying in his 40s). As with boxers, contestants must be of equivalent weight and size. According to the Thais, the buffalo's strength is in his neck. The loser is the animal who turns away from his adversary and refuses to go on fighting.

★ **Hinlat Waterfall** – น้ำตกหินลาด (general map of Koh Samui, **3**): 3 kilometres (nearly 2 miles) south of Na Thon, on the left, and about 1 kilometre (0.5 miles) from where you see the sign. Follow the path up into the jungle for about 2 kilometres. Great thing to do on a rainy day. If you're (very) lucky you might get to see a basking monitor lizard – which is harmless, by the way. There's a refreshments stand at the start of the walk.

★ **Na Muang Waterfall 1** – น้ำตกหน้าเมือง (general map of Koh Samui, **4**): about 10 kilometres (just 6 miles) south of Na Thon. This is a nice little waterfall, which you can get to by motorbike and which is only 200 metres from the car-park, so you hardly have to walk at all.

★ **Na Muang Waterfall 2** – น้ำตกหน้าเมือง (general map of Koh Samui, **4**): lovely waterfalls above the Na Muang Waterfall 1, signposted from the car-park. It takes a good 30 minutes to walk there through the coconut groves. The falls are at their most impressive in the rainy season but in the dry season there are lots of natural pools where you can take a dip.

## TRIPS FROM KOH SAMUI

– Why not **explore the area around Koh Pha Ngan by boat** – ท่องเรือเที่ยวเกาะพะงัน, with Christian who runs Le Bateau restaurant on Bo Phut Beach (*see* 'Where to Eat on Bo Phut Beach'). He organizes day trips to spots where you can admire the marine life. Masks and snorkels are provided.

★ **The Ang Tong National Marine Park** – อุทยานแห่งชาติหมู่เกาะอ่างทอง: this is a string of islands west of Koh Samui and about 2 hours 30 minutes away by boat. You leave Na Thon in the morning and return at night. Two companies organize trips there and tickets are available from most of the guesthouses. Always compare prices (which include a meal) because the same trip can cost two completely different prices. Actually this trip is mega-touristy and not that great: the once-clear waters are now cloudy, the fish have had enough of being disturbed and moved on, and 5 hours there and back is a long time to be one of the herd. If you do decide to go, don't forget your mask and snorkel (or you can hire them there).

## LEAVING KOH SAMUI

– **For Surat Thani**: from Na Thon there are two express boats daily (7.15am and 2.30pm) and eight ferries to Donsak, between 7am and 5pm. Whether the boat goes to Surat Thani itself or to the landing stage in

Donsak, which is 60 kilometres (37 miles) away, there are always buses waiting to take passengers to town, to the train station, to the bus station or to the airport. Combined bus and boat tickets are available from any agency in Na Thon. Remember to compare prices. Some of the ferries leave from a point about 10 kilometres (6 miles) from Na Thon but there's a complimentary bus shuttle service.

– **For Koh Pha Ngan**: four boats daily from Na Thon: two express boats at 11.20am and 5.15pm (a 50-minute crossing) and two ferries at 10am and 2pm (a 1-hour crossing). There are also two boats that leave the Big Buddha beach near Sunset One Bungalows bound for Had Rin beach.

– **For Koh Tao**: take the boat to Koh Pha Ngan and carry on to Koh Tao.

– **For Phuket**: two 40-minute Bangkok Airways flights a day.

– **For Bangkok**: 15 Bangkok Airways flights a day, between 7.40am and 7.10pm (a 1 hour 40-minute flight).

# KOH PHA NGAN – เกาะพะงัน DIALLING CODE: 077

This small island a few miles north of Koh Samui is not short of pleasant beaches where you can stay provided you don't mind a long walk each time you fancy a swim.

With the exception of Hat Rin beach, where bungalows seem to have shot up overnight and the hippie-dippie atmosphere gets on your nerves after a while, Koh Pha Ngan is great for backpackers. There are lots of lovely, quite wild spots, particularly on the northwest coasts where the beaches aren't very good for swimming but the landscape, lost in the middle of nowhere, is magnificent in a forlorn sort of way. The people on Koh Pha Ngan are always smiling and welcoming and the bungalows are the cheapest you'll find on any of the islands round here. All of which goes to make it a favourite place.

## GETTING THERE

– **From Koh Samui**: *see* 'Leaving Koh Samui'.

– **From Surat Thani**: one boat a day leaves the Ta Tong Pier at 8am (stops in Koh Samui) and arrives at 11.30am. There's also a night ferry that leaves Ban Don at 11pm, arriving at 6am the following morning.

– **From Chumphon**: one boat a day leaves at 7.30am (stops in Koh Tao) and arrives at 1pm.

## PUBLIC TRANSPORT ON THE ISLAND

Getting around the island isn't easy because there aren't many surfaced roads. It can take a long time to find a *songthaew* or motorbike-taxi, particularly off-season. If you want to explore the island, hire a motorbike in Thong Sala, the main village on the island, but go carefully because there's no insurance and the roads are really quite treacherous.

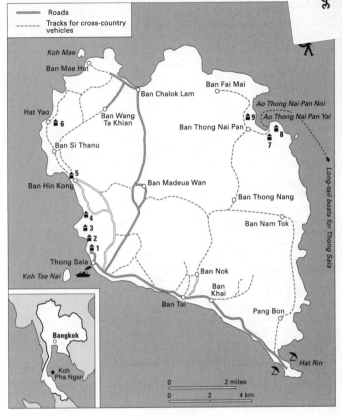

**KOH PHA NGAN**

| ⌂ Where to Stay | | |
|---|---|---|
| | **4** | OK Bungalows |
| **1** Siripun Bungalows, Charn's Bungalows | **5** | Lipstick Cabana |
| | **6** | Blue Coral Beach |
| **2** Cookie Bungalows, Porn Sawan | **7** | Pen's Bungalows |
| | **8** | Central Cottage |
| **3** Darin Bungalows | **9** | Panviman Resort |

– Taxis and boats leave the landing stage in Thong Sala for the beaches in the southeast of the island.

– Hire a boat to take you to the more remote beaches of Thong Nai Pan Noi and Thong Nai Pan Yai.

## ★ THONG SALA – ท้องศาลา

The only disturbance in this otherwise peaceful village is the arrival of the boats from Na Thon (Koh Samui). As you leave the landing stage, Thong Sala is an L-shaped one-way street about 500 metres further up on the right. It's a nice little place with one or two concrete buildings but lots of traditional wooden houses as well. There are also dozens of little restaurants, several guesthouses and even a few craft shops.

## USEFUL ADDRESSES

■ **Siam City Bank** – ธนาคารสยาม ซิตี้: at the end of the main street. Open daily, 8.30am–4.30pm.

⊠ **Post office** – ไปรษณีย์: next door to the bank, slightly set back from the street. Open Monday–Friday, 8.30am–noon and 1pm–4.30pm, Saturday 9am–noon.

■ **Police** – สถานีตำรวจ: about 2 kilometres (1.25 miles) away on the northern road. Open 24 hours a day.

■ **Motorbike hire**: in the street facing the landing stage or in the village itself.

## WHERE TO EAT

✕ **Meeting Point Restaurant** – ร้านอาหารมีทติ้งพ๊อยท์: at the entrance to the village on the right coming from the landing stage. This little restaurant doesn't look like much but it serves delicious Thai food at reasonable prices. Good fish and a nice breezy little terrace.

## ★ ALONG THE COAST GOING NORTH FROM THONG SALA

There are some wild stretches of sand along this coastline where the shallow water makes swimming difficult. This is not a conventional beach by any means, and because of that it is sure to remain the quietest part of the island.

The seascape at low tide reminds you of the beaches in the north with its tarpaulins, boats resting on the sand and greyish waters – undeniably charming in its solitary way.

## WHERE TO STAY

The places below are listed in geographical order, from south to north and not by order of preference. Note that in each case, electricity is provided by a generator – make sure your bungalow isn't right beside it.

🏠 **Siripun Bungalows** – ศิริพรรณ บังกะโล (map, **1**): decent accommodation, well situated within walking distance of the landing stage, at prices that range from 100 to 400Bts. There's a choice of simple wooden bungalows or more solidly built ones, all with bathroom facilities and fan. The landlord is an excellent cook who is happy to give occasional cookery lessons.

♙ **Charn's Bungalows** – ชาญบังกะโล (map, **1**): next door to the previous place and the same sort of thing but not so good and cheaper (about 80–150 Bts for the night).

♙ **Cookie Bungalows** – คุ้กกี้บังกะโล (map, **2**): slightly further out than the last two places, beyond the big hill, in a magnificent setting with the beach on one side and the hill on the other. Basic bungalows with or without bathroom facilities. Lovely place and hard to resist.

♙ **Porn Sawan** – พรสวรรค์บังกะโล (map, **2**): next door to the last place. Very simple bungalows that are hard to miss because they're green. With or without bathroom facilities but each with a secluded terrace and groovy hammock. Good food too, particularly the frit-ters (otherwise known as 'no-name').

♙ **Darin Bungalows** – ดารินบังกะโล (map, **3**): a bit further still. Cheap, unpretentious bungalows in a shady position on a pretty little beach. Small garden area; good restaurant; warm welcome. Cheap too.

♙ **OK Bungalows** – โอ.เค.บังกะโล (map, **4**): along a path which you can walk up or ride up by motor-bike. Basic, reasonably priced huts arranged in tiers on the slope of a hill that runs down to an isolated, wild little creek. The ador-able Chinese landlady called Mrs Ruangtong (Ruan to her friends) organizes a little celebration at Chinese New Year especially for her guests (don't let anyone else in on it). The atmosphere in this place is great – to say nothing of the chocolate cakes.

## SLIGHTLY FURTHER NORTH

♙ **Lipstick Cabana** – ลิฟสติ๊คคาบาน่า (map, **5**): simple straw huts with or without bathroom facilities, set in an isolated little creek. They're really cheap and run by a charming landlord who raises fighting-cocks.

♙ **Blue Coral Beach** – บลูคอรัลบีชบังกะโล (map, **6**): even further north, you find these bungalows nestling into the rocks at one end of a wild but secluded bay (Hat Yao Beach). About as remote as it gets, and only accessible from the sea or along a furrowed path that gets very steep towards the end. Basic comforts at reasonable prices, and every bungalow has its own hammock. Run by a family of fishermen who are happy to take anyone who stays with them out fishing.

♙ If you really want to get it away from it all, there are a few more huts at the extreme northwestern tip of the island.

## ★ GOING EAST FROM THONG SALA

This is not a very attractive stretch of coast, rather rocky and flat with no beach to speak of. Just because there are bungalows there doesn't mean you have to stay in them.

## ★ HAT RIN BEACH – หาดริ้น

This is in fact two beaches back to back at the extreme southeastern tip of the island. The beach that faces northwest is the most beautiful as well as the most popular. The one that faces southwest is certainly much quieter, but you can't really swim there.

If you choose to stay round here, the chances are you'll end up stuck between a noisy bar blaring out what they think is cool music, an electricity generator and a rubbish dump. Every night there's a film show in all the bungalows – how depressing to come all this way to watch a second-rate video. At the full moon, thousands of youngsters descend on the island to indulge in an orgy of dope, drink and repetitive music, otherwise known as Full Moon parties. The police look on apparently unmoved – but they're not of course, as anyone languishing in a Thai jail will tell you.

★ **THONG NAI PAN NOI** AND **THONG NAI PAN YAI BEACHES** (AO THONG NAI PAN NOI AND AO THONG PAN YAI) – หาดท้องนายปาน น้อยและหาดท้องนายปานใหญ่

These are a haven of peace and quiet that are also suitable for swimming, at the extreme northeast tip of the island. Accessible by boat or on foot along a deeply furrowed path that crosses the island from south to north (*see below*). Ferries to Bo Phut leave from these beaches.

## WHERE TO STAY

### BUDGET TO MODERATE (80–300 BTS PER PERSON PER NIGHT)

🏠 **Pen's Bungalows** – เพ็ญบังกะโล (map, **7**): a choice of three categories of bungalow ranging from the most basic to the nearly luxurious that are very well equipped for the price. The owner speaks good English.

🏠 **Central Cottage** – เซ็นทรัลคอท เทจบังกะโล (map, **8**): cheap and cheerful traditional straw huts with or without shower rooms.

### EXPENSIVE TO SPLASH OUT (OVER 800 BTS PER PERSON PER NIGHT)

🏠 **Panviman Resort** – ปานวิมาน รีสอร์ท (map, **9**): there's either a four-wheel-drive or a boat waiting by the landing stage to take you there. Really lovely bungalows with immaculate bathrooms and fans, nestling in magnificent shady grounds full of flowers. The panoramic restaurant up among the rocks gives you a view of both creeks. There are also some hotel bedrooms but the price is ruinous.

## SUGGESTED INLAND TRIP (NOT FOR THE FAINT-HEARTED)

This is a motorbike trip (if there are two of you it's better to hire two bikes) – but be warned, the road is dangerous.

Slightly beyond Ban Tai in the southeast of the island, look for a concealed road that climbs steeply up into the mountains through dense jungle. It isn't an easy climb by any means because of all the potholes and gullies left by the rain. When you get to the top, there's a magnificent view of part of the island and the sea. Go back down the other side of the hill then turn right towards Thong Nai Pan Noi beach.

# KOH TAO – เกาะเต่า

Koh Tao or 'Turtle Island' is a tiny island north of K become famous as a place to dive because of its r and rich sealife (particularly the many species of shark most of them harmless). In just a few years, more than 20 diving schools have opened in Ban Mae Hat, which is the only village on the island and the place where all the boats land.

The people who go there are generally much younger than those who go to Koh Samui and Koh Pha Ngan and they tend to converge on the main beach in the northwestern part of the island. That said, there are other parts of Koh Tao where you feel far from anywhere, including lots of deserted bays or creeks with just a few huts that you can only get to on foot or by boat.

Sadly, like Koh Pha Ngan, Koh Tao is not suitable for swimming because the water stays shallow into the distance.

## GETTING THERE

– **From Koh Pha Ngan** (Thong Sala): there's a slow boat at 11am (a 4-hour crossing), an express boat at 11.30am (a 2 hour 30-minute crossing) and a speedboat at 1pm (a 1 hour 15-minute crossing).

– **From Koh Samui**: there are lots of boats to Koh Pha Ngan from Na Thon (see 'Leaving Koh Samui') plus there's a boat that leaves Mae Nam beach at 9.30am and stops for 10 minutes in Koh Pha Ngan.

– **From Chumphon**: there's an express boat at 7.30am (2 hour 15-minute crossing).

– **From Surat Thani** (Ta Tong Pier): take the express boat to Koh Samui and Kho Pha Ngan that leaves at 8am and arrives at 2pm.

## USEFUL ADDRESSES

✉ **Post office** – ไปรษณีย์: in the middle of the village (Ban Mae Hat) on the right. Open 8am–8pm.

■ **Clinic** – คลีนิค: just before the post office on the right but it tends to move. Also serves as a pharmacy.

■ **Police** – สถานีตำรวจ: follow the road north for about 200 metres and the police station is opposite the school. Opening hours depend on whether the one and only police officer is awake or taking (another) nap.

■ **Krung Thai Bank** – ธนาคาร กรุงไทย: recently opened a bureau de change about 50 metres from the landing stage. Open 11am–3pm.

■ **Motorbike hire:** lots of places in the main street.

## GETTING AROUND THE ISLAND

This is no easy matter. You do see taxis on the main road but mainly when the boats arrive or leave. Otherwise you walk, hire a motorbike (watch out

...otholes) or take a taxi boat to the more remote creeks. Try to get the ...dlords where you're staying to take you where you want to go.

## WHERE TO STAY

There are now lots of bungalows on Laem Cho Pho Ro, the only large beach on the island, to the north of the port. But you're not advised to stay there. The bungalows are one on top of the other, the restaurants show noisy videos and the ultra-hip atmosphere is over the top. This is also where the fishing boats come ashore so there's more rubbish than shells. The creeks are infinitely better.

## ★ CHALOK BAN KAO BEACH (AO CHALOK BAN KAO) – หาดโฉลกบ้านเก่า

A little beach that you get to from the road. It's quiet enough, but places to stay get snapped up in no time in the high season so step on it when you get off the boat. Other places will only rent you a bungalow if you sign up for a diving course first, which can be a rip-off.

## WHERE TO STAY

### BUDGET

🛏 **Porn Resort** – พรรีสอร์ท (map, **1**): in the middle of the beach. ☎ 01-229-5515 (mobile). Simple but very well-kept bungalows that sleep two and four, with private shower room. Run by a charming Thai family who also own the grocery store on the beach.

### EXPENSIVE

🛏 **Ko Tao Cottage Resort** – เกาะเต่าคอทเทจรีสอร์ท (map, **2**): on the far left of the beach as you face the sea. ☎ 377-198. These are the most luxurious bungalows on the island: very well appointed, beautifully decorated, each with its own modern tiled bathroom. Two or three times as expensive as the previous place but you get a magnificent view from the cheapest ones higher up the slope. A pretty cool terrace-restaurant too. Average sort of welcome.

## ★ THIAN OK BEACH (AO THIAN OK) – หาดเทียนออก

The end of the road: nice creek, no good for swimming because of the coral but a snorkeller's paradise (hire your equipment in the village of Ban Mae Hat because you won't find any on the spot). You can almost see the fish from the beach. This place is a natural aquarium, and there are even sharks a bit further out. Tread carefully at low tide though, because the coral is practically above the surface of the water. If you do want to swim, it's an easy walk to Chalok Ban Kao beach (*see above*).

## WHERE TO STAY AND WHERE TO EAT

### BUDGET

🛏 ✕ **Rocky Resort** – ร็อคกี้รีสอร์ท (map, **3**): these pretty white bungalows among the rocks beside a coconut grove are the only ones on this creek. They're laid out like a village and sleep two to six people,

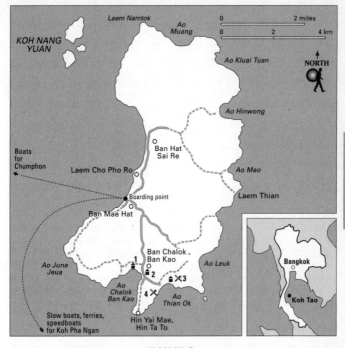

**KOH TAO**

---

## ■ Where to Stay and Where to Eat

1 Porn Resort              3 Rocky Resort
2 Ko Tao Cottage Resort    4 New Heaven

---

with private or shared bathroom, at prices that vary accordingly. A relaxed, peaceful atmosphere, an excellent restaurant and it's great for backpackers. The only problem is that it's often full.

✕ **New Heaven** – ร้านอาหาร นิวเฮเว่น (map, **4**): pleasant rest-aurant on the slopes overlooking Thian Ok, halfway between Chalok Ban Kao and Thian Ok beach. Delicious Thai food that you eat sitting on a mat at a low table. Good fish and a choice of cock-tails. Pleasant atmosphere and reasonable prices.

## WHAT TO DO

There are some **great walks** along the paths that lead from the creeks to the rest of the island. Detailed maps are available from the local travel agencies or in Koh Samui.

There are also lots of diving spots all around the island. Find out where from the diving schools.

## LEAVING KOH TAO

– **For Koh Pha Ngan**: there are four boats a day: a slow boat at 9.30am (a 4-hour crossing), two express boats at 10am and 3pm (taking 2 hours 30 minutes) and a speedboat at 9.30am (1 hour 15 minutes). The same boats also go to Koh Samui and Surat Thani.

– **For Chumphon**: there's a speedboat at 10.30am (a 2-hour crossing) and an express boat at 3pm (2 hours 45 minutes).

# PHUKET – ภูเก็ต
DIALLING CODE: 076

It's time now to talk of this 'Pearl of the Indian Ocean', this sun-kissed island blessed by the gods and rich in the gentle pleasures of life. That was the view a few years ago but not any more. Phuket (pronounced 'pooh-kett'!) has changed. The beaches are still beautiful but the whole place reeks of overdevelopment. The famous Patong Beach is lined with concrete buildings and a depressing number of girlie bars that pull in growing numbers of punters. Every smile has a price and prices go up by the day. As for bungalows suitable for backpackers, they've all been scooped up by a mechanical shovel and replaced by hotels for Westerners with beer bellies.

Some say Phuket is on the way up. For independent travellers it's already going down. It's a shame really, because there are still some pretty places to see, including several beaches untouched by concrete (particularly Kamala and Surin beaches) or one of those charmingly isolated hotels with its own fashionable beach where you can escape the rabble provided you've got the cash.

There's no getting away from it though: Phuket has had enough of backpackers. It may have felt like our territory back in the early 1970s, but the welcome isn't there any more.

## CLIMATE

Few things are more important than the weather. The monsoon season runs from May to October when it rains a lot – particularly in September. Winter is therefore the best time to visit the western coast of Thailand. The dry season starts in December and it's very hot from March to April. In summer you get the fine weather in the Gulf of Thailand (Koh Samui). In other words weather conditions are inverted. The sea is calm from November to April but can be treacherous during the rest of the year because of currents from the Indian Ocean. Check what colour flag is flying before you swim.

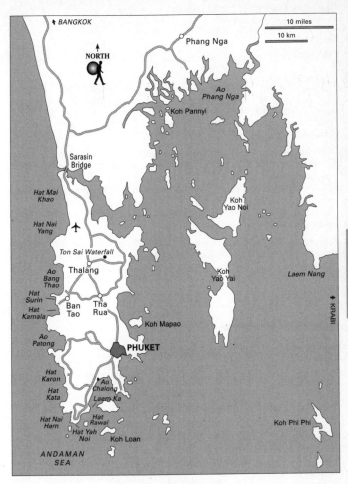

**PHUKET (MAP I)**

## ABOUT THE ISLAND

The main thing about Phuket is how varied it is. The island is about 50 kilometres (30 miles) long from north to south, with hills and valleys in the centre. The most beautiful beaches are on the western coast. The reason Phuket has grown so fast is because it's so close to the mainland, to which it's joined by a bridge. Phuket Town is just a place you pass through on your way to your chosen beach.

The island is home to some of the richest farmers in Thailand – they own the coconut groves and *hevea* plantations that you'll walk through when you explore the island.

## GETTING THERE FROM BANGKOK

### By bus

The 870-kilometre (550-mile) journey from Bangkok takes about 14 hours.

– **National air-conditioned and non-air-conditioned buses**: Southern Bus Terminal. ☎ 435-1199 or 435-1200. From seven to ten non-air-conditioned buses daily, between 7.30am and 10.30pm. Eight air-conditioned buses daily, from 7am–8pm, of which five leave between 5pm and 7pm.

– **Private buses**: faster, more comfortable but more expensive and less like the real thing. Lots of private operators go to Phuket, including Phuket Central Tour (☎ 412-11-99 or 63-34) and Phuket Travel Service (☎ 412-48-47). Both are on Charan Sanit Wong Road. Remember to keep an eye on your luggage at night.

### By air

Depending on the time of year, Thai Airways do between five and ten Bangkok to Phuket flights each day. The flight time is about 1 hour 15 minutes. You can also get to Phuket from Koh Samui (two 40-minute flights a day with Bangkok Airways) Penang, Kuala Lumpur and Singapore.

## TRANSPORT FROM THE AIRPORT

The best way to get to your destination is to take a Thai Limousine minibus either to Phuket Town or the beaches (Kamala Beach, Surin Beach, Patong Beach, Kata Beach or Karon Beach). Tickets are available at the air terminal.

## GETTING AROUND THE ISLAND

– **In Phuket Town**: use the *tuks-tuks*. The price per person is reasonable.

– **To go to the beache**s: *songthaews* leave the market on Ranong Road (map II, A2, ▨ 2) every 30 minutes, 7am–5pm. They're cheap and they go to all the beaches. A list of approved fares is available from the tourist office.

Outside service hours, you can always get to the beach by *tuk-tuk* but the price is usually prohibitive no matter how hard you bargain (about five or ten times the price of *songthaews*).

– **Motorbike hire**: a 50cc bike, which you can hire in town or on any of the beaches, is quite enough to see around all the beaches the day you arrive and get an idea of where you want to stay. It's a risky business, mind you, because none of the bikes is insured – so any damage to the machine or to a third party is your look-out. 'If you break, you pay' – as they say in Thailand.

## ★ PHUKET TOWN

This is the main town on the island, located in the southeast. Setting aside such spectacular events as the Vegetarian Festival in October and the Thai New Year *(Songkram)* there's not a lot happening in Phuket. One or two old houses in the Sino-Portuguese style, a few craft shops, banks and that's about it. Nobody stays in Phuket except the Hong Kong Chinese, who live there.

## USEFUL ADDRESSES

**🛈 TAT** – ททท (Tourist Office, map II, B2): 73–75 Phuket Road, beyond the Imperial Hotel. ☎ 212-213 or 211-036. Fax: 213-582. Open daily, 8.30am–4.30pm. Can supply a complete list of hotels, map of the island (make sure you get one), map of the town, approved *tuk-tuk* fares, list of guesthouses in the peak season and off-peak too. Competent staff.

**✉ Post office and telegrams** – ไปรษณีย์โทรเลข (map II, B2): not easy to find on the first floor of a big building that faces a Novotel in front and looks onto the bus terminal at the back. ☎ 211-020. Open Monday–Friday, 8.30am–4.30pm, Saturday and Sunday, 9am–4pm.

■ **Telecommunications centre** – ศูนย์โทรศัพท์: Phang Nga Road, next to the Pearl Cinema. Open 24 hours. ☎ 216-861. Good for calling overseas, which you can also do from the post office. Plus there are lots of pharmacies and agencies where you can make overseas calls, but it's much more expensive.

■ **Currency exchange**: Phuket Town is not short of banks – there are three in the Phang Nga Road alone. The Thai Farmers Bank (opposite the On On Hotel) offers a good exchange rate and is open daily, 8.30am–6pm. Some currency exchange kiosks stay open till 10pm.

■ **Andaman Hospital** – โรงพยาบาลอันดามัน: Rat-u-Thit Road. ☎ 212-901, ext. 026.

■ **Immigration** – สำนักงานครวจคนเข้าเมือง: Phuket Road. ☎ 212-108. The place to go to extend your visa.

■ **Thai Airways** – สายการบินไทย: Ranong Road. ☎ 211-195. Also at Montri Road. ☎ 211-400.

■ **Bangkok Airways** – สายการบินบางกอกแอร์เวย์: ☎ 212-341.

■ **Bowling** – โบว์ลิ่ง: next to the Pearl Hotel, on Montri Road.

■ **English newspapers**: on sale in several kiosks, including one at 61 Ragada Road, opposite the Thavorn Hotel.

■ **Lee Travel Agent** – ลีทราเวลเอเจนท์ Villa 5, 78/413 Soi 6 – Chawfa Road, Wichit Muang. ☎ 248-517 and 01-60-69-095 (mobile). Owned by Arnaud, a Frenchman, and his Thai wife, who speaks English. A good place to go for general directions, information on the island and even car hire.

## WHERE TO STAY

Only spend a night in the town if you really have to (i.e. because you got in late or are leaving early the next morning). If this is the case then the nicest places can be found near the beach.

### BUDGET TO MODERATE (100–400 BTS PER PERSON PER NIGHT)

⌂ **On On Hotel** – โรงแรมออนออน (map II, A2, **1**): 19 Phang Nga Road. ☎ 211-154 or 225-740. Centrally located near the tourist office, the market, banks and shops. Charming hotel with a nice retro feel, built in 1929 in the old Sino-Portuguese style. Couples should ask for a single (a room with a large single bed). Rooms have fans and padlocked wooden partitions. The more luxurious ones have air-conditioning. Backpacking clientele.

⌂ **Crystal Guesthouse** – คริส ตัลเกสท์เฮาส์ (map II, B2, **2**): 41/16 Montri Road. ☎ 222-774 or 775. Five-storey guesthouse with 40 bedrooms, most with cold shower and fan, some with air-conditioning. Clean and well kept. Warm welcome.

⌂ **Kosawan Hotel** – โรงแรมเกาะ สวรรค์ (map II, A2, **3**): 19/8 Phoonpol Road (at the corner with Soi 9), slightly away from the centre. ☎ 211-867. You'd never guess this was a hotel; in place of reception, you enquire at the grocery store on the ground floor. On the first floor, a huge corridor leads to bedrooms that are tiled from floor to ceiling. The rooms on the street side are noisy. It's a fairly charmless place, but well kept and the rooms have showers. The owners don't speak a word of English so it isn't easy making yourself understood.

⌂ **P.S. Inn Hotel** – พี.เอส.อินน์โฮเด็ล (map II, B3, **4**): 54/1 Ong Sim Phai Road. ☎ 212-216 or 212-893. Beside the covered market (some distance from the centre). Huge, single-storey hotel with 80 indifferent rooms opening off equally huge, starkly lit corridors. Rooms with shower and WC, some with fan, some with air-conditioning. Very much a last-ditch solution.

### EXPENSIVE (FROM 500 BTS PER PERSON PER NIGHT)

⌂ **Thanaporn Guesthouse** – ธนา พรเกสท์เฮาส์ (map II, B2, **5**): 41/7 Montri Road. ☎ 216-504 or 819. This small hotel built in the Sino-Portuguese style ranges from simple rooms with fan and cold shower to more luxurious rooms with air-conditioning and hot water. Price-wise there's not a lot of difference.

⌂ **Sinthavee Hotel** – โรงแรมสินทวี (map II, A2, **6**): 85-91 Phang Nga Road. ☎ 211-186. Large hotel that must have been quite stylish when it was built. The rooms today are past their best but have air-conditioning and (hot) shower, and TV. Quite expensive. Predominantly Asian clientele.

## WHERE TO EAT

✕ **Mae Porn** – ร้านอาหารแม่พร (map II, A2, **10**): Phang Nga Road, on the corner with Soi Pradit. Very central, near the On On Hotel. Traditional and not too expensive. You can eat on the big terrace outside or in the air-conditioned dining room. The huge

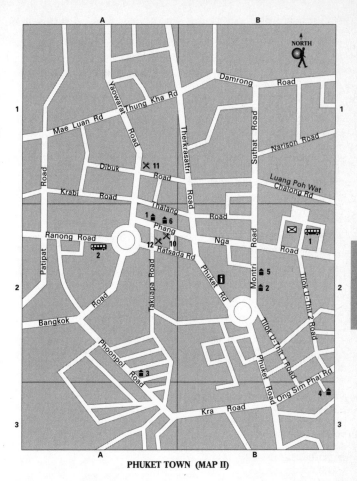

**PHUKET TOWN (MAP II)**

PHUKET

---

- **Useful Addresses**

  - **i** TAT (Tourist office)
  - ✉ Post office and telegrams
  - 🚌 1 Phuket bus terminal
  - 🚌 2 Songthaews to the beaches

- **Where to Stay**

  - **1** On On Hotel

  **2** Crystal Guesthouse
  **3** Kosawan Hotel
  **4** P.S. Inn Hotel
  **5** Thanaporn Guesthouse
  **6** Sinthavee Hotel

- ✕ **Where to Eat**

  **10** Mae Porn
  **11** Kota Restaurant
  **12** Kanda Bakery

menu features Thai cuisine and shellfish. Typical working-class place.

✖ **Kota Restaurant** – ร้านอาหาร โกด้า (map II, A1, **11**): Yaowarat Road (at the corner with Dibuk Road). Open 6am–2pm. Note that the name of the restaurant is written in Thai. Cheap, everyday food served in the small family dining room. Particularly recommended is the Chinese noodle soup, or the chicken served with rice cooked in coconut milk. There are other little places of a similar style on either side of the junction. It's the genuine article and you're sure of a warm welcome.

✖ **Kanda Bakery** – กานดาเบเกอรี (map II, A2, **12**): 33 Ratsada Road. Closes at 9pm. A restaurant-patisserie decked out in lively colours that sells all sorts of croissant-type pastries, cream cakes (including some stunning birthday cakes in glorious technicolour) and a few Thai dishes. Great place to go for breakfast.

## THINGS TO SEE

★ **Phuket Aquarium Marine Centre** – อควาเรียมภูเก็ต: south of town, just beyond Phuket Pier, where the boats leave for Koh Phi Phi. Open 8.30am–4pm. No charge for children under 1.2 metres (4 feet) tall. Lots of fresh- and saltwater aquariums, many of them in need of attention but home to some fine specimens all the same, including stone fish, leopard sharks and impressive moray eels. Strictly for those who've got the time.

★ **Phuket Orchid Garden** – ภูเก็ตออร์คิดการ์เด้น and **Thai Village** – ไทยวิลเลจ: north of Phuket, on the far right-hand side of Yaowarat Road are greenhouses full of orchids of every colour and a so-called traditional Thai village with a range of tourist attractions, including elephant demonstrations, dancing and a floating market. Lots of pricey souvenir shops.

## LOWDOWN ON THE BEACHES

The beaches on the western coast going from north to south are reviewed below.

### ★ SURIN BEACH – หาดสุรินทร์

Divine, almost deserted beach with just a few bungalows on its northern and southern sides. This and Kamala Beach are two favourites, but watch out for the big waves and occasionally treacherous currents in winter. Two kilometres (1.25 miles) away, by a small car-park and bar, a steep path leads down to an exquisite creek called Lampsing Beach. There are no bungalows, just two little restaurants and girls offering a massage. Park before you get to the car-park to avoid paying the fee.

## WHERE TO STAY

MODERATE TO EXPENSIVE (300–500 BTS PER PERSON PER NIGHT)

🛏 **Thangthai Guesthouse** – แดงไทยเกสท์เฮาส์: north of the beach. Has eight bedrooms with private shower and WC, air-conditioning or fan. Lovely view of the beach from the terraces on the third floor. Motorbike hire. Nice atmosphere.

## SPLASH OUT (OVER 4,000 BTS PER PERSON PER NIGHT)

⌂ **The Chedi** – เดอะเจดีย์: ☎ 324-017. Fax: 324-252. This hotel complex entirely on stilts was built by two Frenchmen on its own delightful beach north of Surin Beach.

Little thatched cottages are joined by open-air connecting passages. Bamboo and rattan decor, swimming pool, windsurfing, 18-hole golf course. A real treat if you've got the money. Well-heeled backpackers can find out more from TRI Hotel Marketing, 2 Gerrard Road, London SW13 9RG. ☎ (020) 8563 2100.

## ★ KAMALA BEACH – หาดกมลา

For some reason, this magnificent beach south of Surin Beach seems to have been overlooked by the developers and remains one of the few havens for backpackers left on Phuket. Small groups of bungalows open on to a mini-promenade facing the sea. You see remarkably few people except for one or two guests from the nearby luxury hotel, which doesn't have its own beach (but fortunately does have a swimming pool) and sets up loungers here. Watch out when you swim because the currents here are said to be treacherous.

## WHERE TO STAY

The handful of bungalows (fewer than 10) all facing the sea belong to six different owners but are otherwise identical in terms of standard of accommodation and price. The two below were picked for their warm welcome.

### MODERATE

⌂ **Isi's Bungalows and Restaurant** – อีซีบังกะโลแอนด์เรสโครอง: one of the first places you come to on the northern side of the beach. ☎ 324-432. Nice well-kept, well-spaced bungalows with shower rooms (cold water) and mosquito nets. The charming owner speaks perfect English and serves delicious food.

⌂ **Mayas Bungalows** – มาย าส์บังกะโล: in the middle of the beach. ☎ 324-510. Sweet, solidly built bungalows, small but roomy with mosquito nets. Nicely decorated and beautifully kept. Friendly welcome.

## ★ PATONG BEACH – หาดป่าตอง

Back in the 1970s, Patong Beach was a magnificent bay with a single solitary café. Today it's the most famous beach on the island: a flashy seaside resort where bungalows suitable for backpackers disappeared long ago under mountains of concrete. Wooden huts on the beach have made way for bars, and the only things that aren't for sale are the gentle pleasures of life. This is another place that has fallen victim to prostitution. Everything costs a bomb and backpackers couldn't be more out of place.

– Watch out, because it's dangerous to swim here. Every year too many people get hurt by jet skis that run in too close to the beach.

## WHERE TO STAY

Here are a few places to stay; note that the places referred to as 'cheap' are two or three times as expensive as anywhere else – and tourists on a budget don't go down too well round here.

### BUDGET

⛵ **Sea Dragon Guesthouse** – ซีดราก้อนเกสท์เฮาส์: on Bangla Road. ☎ 342-313 or 314. Decrepit rooms with cold showers – definitely the cheapest round here but also the least clean. The rooms that overlook the string of Pattaya-like bars get pretty noisy at night, so ask for one overlooking the courtyard. When everywhere else is full, you might have some luck here.

### MODERATE

Prices can double depending on what's on offer, so check the price range. Outside the peak season, don't hesitate to haggle because you might get as much as a 50 per cent reduction.

⛵ **Andaman Square** – อันดามัน สแควร์: small square in Kebsap Soi on Thaveewong Road (or Beach Road) where lots of guesthouses let out a handful of rooms with fan or air-conditioning. Prices are reasonable for Patong. Places of a similar standard include the **Cosmos Inn** – คอสมอสอินน์ (☎ 292-074), the **Sea Sun Sand** – ซีซัน แซนด์ (☎ 343-047) and the **B&B Guesthouse** – บีแอนด์บีเกสท์เฮาส์.

⛵ **Bamboo Hut** – แบมบูฮัท: the favourite place in Andaman Square. ☎ 344-012 or 292-043. Just four rooms with hot water, fan or air-conditioning above a small bar-restaurant run by a charming lady. Warm atmosphere guaranteed – if you can get in, that is.

⛵ **Paradise Bungalows** – พาราไดซ์ บังกะโล: 93 Patong Beach. By the sea, next to the Holiday Inn. ☎ 340-172. Small, solidly built houses with balconies scattered around a well-kept garden. Rooms are very simple with fan or air-conditioning.

### EXPENSIVE

⛵ **Tropica Bungalows Hotel** – ทรอปิกาบังกะโลโฮเต็ล: by the sea, not far from the Rat-U-Thit Road. ☎ 340-204/205. About 600–1,800 Bts for the night. Magnificent bungalows buried under dense, tropical vegetation, with 79 rooms in all plus swimming pool. As romantic as it gets, particularly since it's slightly away from the madding crowd. What a shame the rest of Patong isn't like this. Charming place with a warm welcome, where prices remain reasonable for the area.

⛵ **Patong Beach Bungalows** – ปาตองบีชบังกะโล: 96/1 Thawiwong Road. North of the beach (where the road becomes one-way). ☎ 340-117 or 344-240. Costs about 1,500–3,500 Bts for the night, depending on size of room and standard of accommodation. This is one of the only places that gives directly onto the sea without having to cross the road. Choose from bedrooms in a large, long motel-style building or bungalows that aren't too bad except that they're rather too close together. The family bungalows can sleep as many as six people. Restaurant. Swimming pool. More expensive and not as friendly as the previous place.

PHUKET

## WHERE TO EAT

Try as we might, we couldn't find a single nice restaurant in the whole of Patong. This place is rip-off city: overpriced restaurants specializing in poor food at inflated prices. And not just restaurants either. Even the local everyday eateries can spot a tourist a mile off. You're just as likely to be taken to the cleaners in the market or buying food on the street. Not everybody seems to mind though: some people think this is the real face of Thailand. There's one born every minute.

Your only fallback is the buffet lunches served in the luxury hotels to the south of the beach. Prices aren't excessive and the menu changes every day. There are always the pizzerias too (no shortage of those). And if this doesn't suit you, then what are you doing in Patong in any case?

## WHERE TO HAVE A DRINK

If you like a drink, you're spoiled for choice. About a dozen new bars open every year, some of them with room for 50 people or more. The company's great too: lots of willing girls and tribal punters from a long way west of Thailand (like Germany, France, Italy or England). This is the Costa Brava of the East folks – cheers!

## WHERE TO DIVE

**Fantasea Divers** – แฟนตาซีไดเวอร์ส: on Patong Beach. This affiliated PADI diving school runs courses for every level of ability. Three boats daily take a maximum of 20 people out for the day or half-day to explore the seabed that literally teems with creatures of the reef: little coral fish, a rich variety of sharks, rays and coral. The best time to go is from October to May.

## ★ KARON BEACH – หาดกะรน

This beach just under 3 kilometres (2 miles) long has fared rather better than Patong although the developers have had a field day nonetheless. The road runs from one end of the beach to the other, so practically none of the accommodation gives directly onto the beach. A sad sight to be sure, even if it is much quieter and less developed than Patong.

Watch out because strong currents make it dangerous to swim here whatever the season and even when there aren't any waves. Check whicht flag is flying before you swim.

## WHERE TO STAY

BUDGET TO MODERATE (150–300 BTS PER PERSON PER NIGHT)

**Kata Tropicana** – กะคะทรอปิกานา: south of the beach on the other side of the road. ☎ 330-141 or 330-142. Large, single-storey buildings that rise in tiers up a hill. Rows of single rooms with cold shower and WC. Charmless but decent. Cheaper the longer you stay. There's also a restaurant and you can hire a motorbike here.

## EXPENSIVE TO SPLASH OUT (300–1,300 BTS PER PERSON PER NIGHT)

⌂ **Karon Silver Resort** – กะรนซิล เวอร์รีสอร์ท: 127/9 Soi Bangla (first on the right off Luang Por Chuan Road). ☎ 396-187. Small, well-kept hotel in the heart of the resort with rooms of various standards, from those with fan and cold water to more luxurious ones with air-conditioning and hot water. Great place to crash if you want to be near the beach and the centre of activity – particularly since it's hardly ever full.

⌂ **Kata Garden Resort** – กะดะการ์ เด้นรีสอร์ท: 121/1 Kata Beach. ☎ 330-627 or 628. Comfortable brick bungalows buried in lush vegetation between Karon Beach and Kata Beach. Everything is just as it should be, and even the interior decoration is nice. Private shower room (hot or cold water). The price includes American-style buffet breakfast. Laundry service and motorbike hire. Good standard of comfort.

⌂ **Ruamthep Inn** – รวมเทพอินน์: 120/4 Pratak Road. ☎ 330-281 or 282. This motel-style building sandwiched between the road and the beach is the previous place to the south of Karon beach. All the rooms have a view of the sea. Average welcome. One of the very rare places that gives directly onto the beach.

## SPLASH OUT (MORE THAN 1,300 BTS PER PERSON PER NIGHT)

⌂ **Marina Cottage** – มาริน่า คอทเทจ: ☎ 330-625. Luxury bungalows joined by teak walkways, submerged below lush vegetation in a mini jungle reconstruction on the slopes south of the beach. The setting is magnificent, and comes complete with the most extraordinary animal cacophony at certain hours of the day. Some of the bungalows have a wonderful view of the sea. Hot water and air-conditioning. Swimming pool and a restaurant that overlooks the sea and has direct access to the beach. Charming place if you can afford it.

## WHERE TO EAT

✗ **Sunset Restaurant** – ร้านอาหารชันเซ็ท: Luang Por Chuan Road (the main road at right angles to the beach). Very good food, including an excellent selection of seafood at reasonable prices and a choice of menus. Try the muesli, porridge and house yoghurt for breakfast. Attentive, smiling service.

★ **KATA BEACH** – หาดกะดะ

Yet another place that's grown rather too suburban. Here again, a rash of large buildings has pushed all the bungalows suitable for backpackers further and further inland. Kata Beach is in fact two beaches separated by rocks: Kata Yai to the north and Kata Noi to the south.

## THE NORTHERN BEACH (KATA YAI) – กะตะใหญ่

### WHERE TO STAY

MODERATE TO EXPENSIVE (200–700 BTS PER PERSON PER NIGHT)

🛏 **Friendship Bungalows** – เฟรนด์ชิพบังกะโล: about 500 metres from the beach on the slopes above Kata Yai. ☎ 300-499. Brand-new bungalows in a pleasant, shady garden. Very well kept: sheets changed regularly, mosquito nets etc. Fan or air-conditioning. Very friendly staff too, always ready to be of service. Closed in June and July.

🛏 **Cool Breeze Bungalows** – คูลบรีซบังกะโล: ☎ 330-484. On the slopes of the hill about 400 metres from the sea. Double, solidly built and simply decorated bungalows plus a few old-style wooden ones. Air-conditioning is the next thing (by popular request). Private bathrooms. Lovely big shady garden. Welcoming landlady who sees to it that the place is cleaned every day.

🛏 **Over Sea Bungalows** – โอเวอร์ซีบังกะโล: right next door to the previous place, on the slopes above Kata Beach. ☎ 330-116. Bungalows with shower rooms, fans and mini refrigerators. The inside is well kept even if things are a bit slack outside and in the reception area. But the price is reasonable and you're sure of a friendly welcome.

## ★ THE SOUTHERN BEACH (KATA NOI) – กะตะน้อย

There's nothing suitable for backpackers on this beach so there's nothing much to suggest. All the bungalows were flattened when the developers moved in.

Between Kata Noi and Nai Harn Beach is a little beach called **Nui** (pronounced 'nooyer') **Beach** that fortunately isn't that easy to get to. From the View Point, there's a track suitable for motorbikes that you follow for about 20 minutes and then a footpath that leads down to the beach (another 15 minutes). At the bottom is a little restaurant with tables and parasols outside.

## ★ NAI HARN BEACH – หาดในหาน

To think this was a backpacker's favourite spot a few years ago. Today a large part of the beach is littered with loungers and deckchairs, while the rest groans under take-away restaurants and tents full of masseuses. Rather more interesting are the many cheap-and-cheerful places to stay. Note that the beach is also home to the Phuket Yacht Club. Be careful if you swim there in winter when the currents can be dangerous, although no more so than anywhere else. Check when you're there.

### WHERE TO STAY

BUDGET (LESS THAN 300 BTS PER PERSON PER NIGHT)

🛏 **Coconut Bungalows** – โคโคนัทบังกะโล: next door to the Phuket Yacht Club, on the right as you reach the beach. Rather decrepit, fairly basic bungalows with corrugated iron roofs and shared bathroom facilities. The ones on the

**PHUKET**

slopes above the beach are quieter and have a lovely view of the sea. Despite its scruffy appearance, this is the cheapest thing around here. Good restaurant.

🏠 **Ao Sane** – อ่าวเสนบังกะโล: reached via the Phuket Yacht Club (don't worry about the nightwatch-men). ☎ 288-306. Very simple wooden bungalows on the rocks in an isolated little creek. Reason-ably comfortable and far from the madding crowd. The sand could be whiter but the sea is lovely. Shame they don't make more of an effort in the area around the bungalows and in the restaurant – but you can't have everything. Oc-casionally closed off-season.

## MODERATE (AROUND 300 BTS PER PERSON PER NIGHT)

🏠 **Jungle Beach Resort** – จังเกิ้ลปิ๊ชรีสอร์ท: beyond the Ao Sane, going via the road that passes through the Phuket Yacht Club. ☎ 288-264 or 288-341. The sim-plest rooms are excellent value for money.

## EXPENSIVE TO SPLASH OUT (UP TO 4,000 BTS PER PERSON PER NIGHT)

🏠 **Jungle Beach Resort** – จังเกิ้ลปิ๊ชรีสอร์ท: *see above.* Large bungalows with two or more bed-rooms, scattered around some fairly wild (and quite untidy) grounds. Facilities range from private shower rooms (outside in some cases with cold water only) to a luxurious suite of rooms with air-conditioning, balcony and view of the sea. At the end of the grounds is a tiny private beach surrounded by rocks.

## ★ YAH NOI BEACH – หาดหญ้าน้อย

Small, uncrowded beach surrounded by rocks on the coastal road between Nai Harn and Rawai Beaches. The only thing on the beach is a very simple restaurant with tables outside. The clientele is a mixture of Thais and tourists.

## WHERE TO STAY

### BUDGET

🏠 **Ya Noi Bungalows** – หญ้าน้อยบังกะโล: facing the beach on the other side of the road. ☎ 288-982. Small, simple but clean bungalows with shower rooms (cold water), fans and mosquito nets. Relaxed atmosphere and friendly welcome.

## ★ RAWAI BEACH – หาดราไว

This is in fact a narrow stretch of sand fringed with coconut palms about 17 kilometres (10 miles) south of Phuket Town on the east coast. The sea is not very deep on this side of the island and can be sludgy at low tide. At the southern end of the beach is an area with small, low tables on straw mats between the trees. This is where the Thais come for a romantic dinner or with family or friends to share a meal and gaze out to sea. The barbecued fish is delicious and not expensive at all. Not a great beach in terms of looks but it is the genuine article.

## WHERE TO STAY

Since there's no proper beach, not many tourists spend the night here. Nevertheless, there are some good, reasonably priced places to stay where the smile and the welcome aren't necessarily forced (which is good to see).

### BUDGET TO MODERATE (200–400 BTS PER PERSON PER NIGHT)

⌂ **Pormae Bungalows** – พรแม่บังกะโล: 58/1 Wisas Road. ☎ 380-306. Facing the sea at the southern end of the beach. Solidly built bungalows and cheaper but more basic straw huts. Neat and tidy inside, quite new and well equipped. You only have to cross the road to eat on the beach. Nice, friendly welcome. Good value for money.

### MODERATE TO EXPENSIVE (300–700 BTS PER PERSON PER NIGHT)

⌂ **Salaloy Resort** – ศาลาลอยรีสอร์ท: ☎ 381-297. Facing the sea like the previous place but at the northern end of the beach. Pleasant, solidly built bungalows around a large garden full of flowers. The rooms are nicely decorated, with tiled bathroom, fan or air-conditioning and there's an excellent fish restaurant on site. Friendly welcome.

## WHAT TO SEE AND DO

★ **Gypsy Village** – หมู่บ้านยิปซี: at the far northern end of the beach. The village is populated by Moken sea gypsies who were originally from the Andaman Islands. They are a small community of animists with very distinctive looks and traditions. The men are easy to identify from the cloth that most of them wear around their waists instead of trousers. You see the same thing in the Union of Myanmar. They earn their living fishing or diving (some can stay 3 minutes under water).

The village itself is poverty-stricken but that doesn't stop bus-loads of curious tourists (not too many fortunately – most go to Patong) from coming out here to take a look and snap a few pics. Anyway, despite its poverty the village comes alive every afternoon when the fishermen return and set up a fish market in the little street that runs along the sea. What you see then is a fishy display of many different colours, including all sorts of shellfish and lobster and some incredible Mediterranean-type prawns with long blue pincers.

– **Boat trips**: the beach is lined with long-tail boats waiting to take such tourists as there are for a tour of the surrounding islands. You should drive a hard bargain – customers are few and far between.

★ **LAEM KA BEACH** – หาดแหลมกา

This delightful little sandy creek nestling in the shade among the rocks is surrounded by four little islands, Coral Island among them. To get there, leave Rawai Beach (in the north) heading towards Chalong. After the service station, take the little road on the right and carry on for just over 1 kilometre (0.5 miles). The only places to stay are some bungalows that share the beach with a restaurant run by the same landlords. Very popular with the Thais at weekends – not least because of the restaurant.

**PHUKET**

## WHERE TO STAY

EXPENSIVE TO SPLASH OUT (500–1,300 BTS PER PERSON PER NIGHT)

🛏 **The Laem Ka Beach Inn** – เดอแหลมกาบีชอินน์: ☎ 381-305. Pleasant bungalows on a coconut palm-covered hillside that overlooks the sea. Private shower rooms (cold water), fans or air-conditioning. The perfect solitary retreat. Ask for Mo since the rest of the family only speaks Thai. Often full at weekends, so book in advance if you can. Bike or motorbike essential if you want to get around.

### ★ AO CHALONG – อ่าวฉลอง

Large cove where boats and the occasional luxury yacht drop anchor. It's also the point of departure for boats to Koh Phi Phi.

## WHERE TO EAT

If you're not too hard up, there's an original place about 200 metres up from the landing stage on the left (looking out to sea):

✗ **Jimmy's Lighthouse** – ร้านอาหารจิมมี่ไลท์เฮาส์: open 8am–midnight. Everything about this place says 'an American has been here', from the mini lighthouse (after which the restaurant is named) to the plush, spacious, open-air dining area that's heavy on timber and copper pots and pans. The walls are lined with photographs with a military theme and there are some signed dedications by American celebrities. The food is international (American, Italian, French and Thai) and ranges from breakfast to cocktails, so you can end the day there sipping a *Mekhong*.

### ★ IN THE INTERIOR OF THE ISLAND: THE TON SAI WATERFALLS – น้ำตกต้นไทร

The falls are in the northeast of the island in the Khao Phra Theo National Park. To get there take the airport road and at the Thalang crossroads, turn right and carry on for 3 kilometres (2 miles). Open 6am–6pm. The falls themselves are nothing great and they dry up completely in the dry season. But the park is home to an authentically 'virgin' forest (meaning untouched by man) with trees so tall that in places they block out the light entirely. Some of the plants and species you find growing here are now extinct elsewhere. On a grey day or when you've had enough of rubbing shoulders with the other people on the beach, this is a good place to come for a walk.

## LEAVING PHUKET

The tourist office publishes a *Bus Timetable from Phuket* brochure that gives the times of buses to every destination in Thailand.

### By bus

**– To Bangkok**:

🚌 **From the Phuket Bus Terminal** (map II, B2, 🚌 **1**): ☎ 211-480. Six non-air-conditioned buses a day (6am–6.30pm) and five air-conditioned buses (8.25am–5.30pm). The journey takes about 14 hours.

🚌 **Private air-conditioned buses**: several of these in the afternoon run by two private operators, Phuket Travel Service, Ong Sim Phai Road. ☎ 222-107; and Phuket Central Tour, Montri Road. ☎ 213-615.

– **To Hat Yai**: Phuket Bus Terminal. ☎ 211-480. Four non-air-conditioned and air-conditioned buses a day (6.20–10.20am) and six air-conditioned buses (7.30am–12.30pm). Takes 7–8 hours.

– **To Surat Thani**: Phuket Bus Terminal. ☎ 211-480. Eight non-air-conditioned buses a day (4.45am–1.50pm) and two air-conditioned buses at 7.30am and 9am. Takes 5–6 hours.

– **To Phang Nga**: Phuket Bus Terminal. Five non-air-conditioned buses a day (10.10am–4.30pm) plus the bus to Krabi. Takes about 2 hours 30 minutes.

– **To Krabi**: Phuket Bus Terminal. Three non-air-conditioned buses (10.50am–2.30pm) and 17 air-conditioned buses that leave every 30 minutes, 7am–6.30pm. Takes 3–4 hours.

### By air

– **To Bangkok**: five to ten flights a day.

– **To Hat Yai**: three flights a day.

– **To Surat Thani**: one to three flights a day depending on the time of year.

– **To Koh Samui**: two 40-minute Bangkok Airways flights a day.

– **To Penang**: one flight a day.

– **To Kuala Lumpur**: two MAS flights a week.

– **To Singapore**: a few flights a week with either Thai Airways or Trade Winds.

### By boat

– **To Koh Phi Phi**: there are two boarding points to the east and south of Phuket. The best thing is to leave from Phuket Port (in the south) where there are two Songserm boats a day (☎ 222-570 or 574). The immense *King Cruiser* leaves at 8.30am (takes two hours) and the express boat leaves at 1.30pm (which takes 1 hour 30 minutes). Note that out of season there's only one boat in the morning.

# PHANG NGA – พังงา
DIALLING CODE: 076

About 90 kilometres (56 miles) north of Phuket Town, Phang Nga Bay is filled with a profusion of densely overgrown rock pinnacles. The sea has worn away the base of these aquatic totem poles, creating some impressive natural caves. The spectacle is unique but increasingly spoiled by all the tourist hype, with too many travel agencies ferrying too many people out to see it.

### WHEN TO SEE THE CAVES

Just remember that all the tours visit the bay in the morning. The light isn't at its best then and in any case the place isn't quite so magical (to say the least) with all those people milling around. If you've hired a car or motorbike in Phuket, try to get to the bay about 2 or 3 hours before the sun goes down and you'll have the place all to yourselves. It's an experience you'll never forget – in the low, late afternoon light the atmosphere in the bay is quite unique. If coming by bus, try to do the trip in a day so you don't have to spend the night in the village of Phang Nga, which has nothing much to recommend it.

### VISITING THE BAY ON YOUR OWN

The boarding point for boats to the bay is about 7 kilometres (4 miles) from the village of Phang Nga.

There are two ways of getting there:

– **By bus**: from Phuket (*see* 'Leaving Phuket') there is a frequent regular bus service to Phang Nga and Krabi (buses to Krabi go by way of Phang Nga). You can get to the boarding point in several ways: either get off the bus where you see the sign for 'Phang Nga Bay Resort', and hitchhike or walk the last 4 kilometres (2.5 miles) to the boarding point; or get off at the bus terminal in the village of Phang Nga and hire a *songthaew* to take you to the boarding point. Steer clear of the touts unless you want to end up on a boat with 50 other people (and make sure you find out what kind of boat it is). Some of them also offer to take you on a two-day trip to the bay, stopping for the night in the Gypsy Village.

– **By motorbike or hired car**: if you've got the money or there are several of you, the best way to get to the bay is to hire a motorbike or car in Phuket. Not only does that mean you're completely independent, it also gives you the advantage of going to the bay in a long-tail boat rather than in the motorized dugout used by the agencies. Otherwise the trip is exactly the same and lasts from 2 to 3 hours. Agree a price for the boat rather than per person. It's worth it for four people or more (maximum eight people).

### VISITING THE BAY THROUGH AN AGENCY

This is the simplest solution but by no means cheap. It is all right if you don't mind losing the pleasure of seeing the bay because you're packed into a motorized craft with 50 other tourists. Practically all the bungalows and hotels in Phuket can arrange the trip for you.

### WHERE TO STAY IN PHANG NGA VILLAGE

Phang Nga is a charmless sort of place with nowhere but second-rate places to stay. However, if you do end up there for the night, here are a few suggestions:

## BUDGET TO MODERATE (100–250 BTS PER PERSON PER NIGHT)

🛏 **Thawisuk Hotel** – โรงแรมทวีสุข: ☎ 412-100. In the centre, on the right coming from Phuket. The cheapest place in town and easy to spot by its blue facade. Modest but decent rooms with cold shower and fan. This is where all the backpackers stay.

🛏 **Lakmuang Hotel 1** – โรงแรม หลักเมือง: Phetkasem Road. ☎ 411-125. As you leave town going towards Krabi. The reception area and the hall look deceptively comfortable. In fact the rooms are very simple and cheap with cold shower, fan or air-conditioning.

## EXPENSIVE (FROM 400 BTS PER PERSON PER NIGHT)

🛏 **New Lakmuang Hotel** – โรงแรมนิวหลักเมือง: 128 Pechkasem Road. ☎ 411-500 or 412-218. The sister hotel of the previous place, on the left after the service station as you come into town. Clean and modern with air-conditioned rooms. The ones overlooking the street are very noisy. Not very central.

## WHERE TO STAY IN THE BAY ITSELF

🛏 **Phang Nga Bay Resort Hotel** – พังงาเบย์รีสอร์ทโฮเด็ล: about 100 metres from the landing stage. ☎ 412-067. A futuristic building that looks rather uncool given the surroundings. But at least each bedroom has its own terrace with a view of the bay. Swimming pool, air-conditioning and private bathroom (of course). This is the most luxurious hotel round here (which isn't saying much) so very popular with the agencies. There's also a terrace restaurant overlooking the water that serves indifferent and expensive food.

## WHAT TO SEE

★ The motorized dugout begins by chugging alongside a dense **mangrove forest** that used to be infested with gavials (the biggest crocs in the world). Very *Crocodile Dundee* atmosphere. Try as we might, we couldn't persuade the pilot to stop so we could go exploring.

★ As you pull into the bay, look out for the little rock paintings on the walls of a limestone rock formation.

★ Next you enter the fabulous world of **Phang Nga Bay** itself – อ่าวพังงา. As far as the eye can see, huge limestone formations of every shape and size go sheer down to the sea (a bit like Guillin for those of you who are familiar with that corner of China). Further up, the dugout passes under the marine arch of the **Tham Lot Cave** – ถ้ำลอด.

★ Finally you come to the **Island of Koh Pinggan** – เขาพิงกัน, nicknamed 'James Bond Island' since they filmed some location shots here for *The Man with the Golden Gun*. Not that this place is steeped in mystery – steeped in tourists more like. Every boat large and small stops here and you've never seen so many souvenir stands. You probably won't want to stay long.

★ On the return journey there's a compulsory stop at the waterside village of **Koh Pannyi** – เกาะปันหยี or Gypsy Village. The village is entirely of wood and built on stilts. It's inhabited by Muslim people similar to the 'sea gypsies'. This is where the luckless tour groups who visit the bay in the morning spend their lunch break and free time. The number of souvenir shops (including some in private houses) is simply staggering – so are the tourists who barge into the local school to photograph the children at their lessons. Or those who stride up and down the rickety wooden platforms peering curiously at the villagers in their homes. Some even spend the night in the village. Avoid the restaurants by the landing stage – the price is prohibitive.

## LEAVING PHANG NGA

### By bus

All the buses leave from **Phang Nga bus station**, on the right as you come into town.

– **To Krabi**: eight buses, 10.30am–4.30pm.
– **To Phuket**: buses every 30 minutes, 6.30am–5.30pm.

# KOH PHI PHI – เกาะพีพี       DIALLING CODE: 075

These islands lie exactly halfway between Phuket and Krabi. What can we tell you about Koh Phi Phi (pronounced Ko Pee Pee)? It's rather like talking about an unhappy love affair. Every time you try to say something nice, you get this big lump in your throat.

Koh Phi Phi is in fact two islands, Phi Phi Lee and Phi Phi Don, only the second of which is inhabited. Koh Phi Phi is famous for its magnificent turquoise waters, shining sands and fabulous seabed rich with coral. Alas – that reputation has been the island's undoing. Today Phi Phi Don welcomes far more tourists than it has room for. Witness the incessant toing and froing of long-tail boats up and down the island. The noise is horrible.

However, there are still some quiet, pretty little beaches on Koh Phi Phi including, for those who can afford it, private beaches that you can only get to by boat. The good news is that since 1983, when Koh Phi Phi became a national park, all building works have been banned on the island except for those that replaced a former building. The bad news is that as a result, lots of landlords have made improvements to their bungalows and pushed their prices up. Some of them, not many, refused to be steamrollered into installing air-conditioning and continue to charge reasonable prices – but there are people banging at the door to get in.

## A BIT OF HISTORY

For as long as anyone can remember, Koh Phi Phi, Island of the Spirits, was the impregnable fortress of the formidable pirates of the Andaman Sea. Hiding behind the tall cliffs is a labyrinth of caves where ancient drawings of sailing boats and bamboo buildings bear witness to a culture

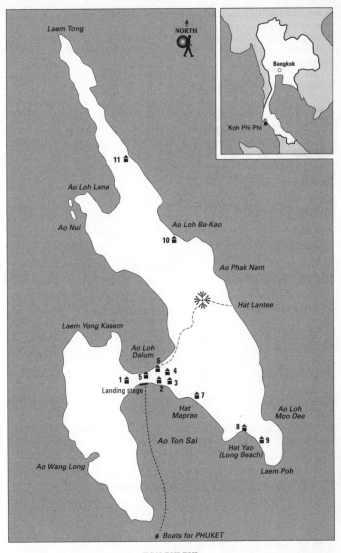

**KOH PHI PHI**

## ☖ Where to Stay

| | | | |
|---|---|---|---|
| **1** | Chong Khao Bungalows | **6** | Pee Pee Charlie Beach Resort |
| **2** | Phi Phi Don Resort | **7** | Maprao Resort |
| **3** | Phi Phi Andaman Resort | **8** | Pee Pee Paradise Resort |
| **4** | Rimna Resort | **9** | Pee Pee Long Beach Bungalows |
| **5** | Pee Pee Princess | **10** | Pee Pee Island Village |
| | | **11** | Phi Phi Palm Beach Resort |

several hundred years old. Like their ancestors before them, the present-day inhabitants of Koh Phi Phi regularly scale the rock face to collect swallows' nests, particularly in Phi Phi Lee. Talking of climbing, Phi Phi Don today is a climber's paradise, as lots of excellent paths have been cleared.

## ★ PHI PHI DON – เกาะพีพีดอน

The island appears roughly H-shaped, the two uprights being the mountains densely covered in virgin forest and the crossbar being the two crescent-shaped beaches of Ton Sai and Loh Dalum that face in opposite directions. Between them lies a strip of land that originally kept them apart but which now brings them together thanks to a friendly little village of wooden houses and corrugated iron roofs that lives only for tourism.

Ton Sai Bay is at its best early in the morning or late in the day, when all the day trippers from Phuket have gone home again. This is where most of the boats land. There's no beach any more, only a stretch of sand packed with long-tail taxi-boats waiting for passengers off the boats. The water is so shallow round here that they're the only means of transport and the racket they make can be heard more than a kilometre (half a mile) away – wherever you are. But since there's only one path on the island from Ton Sai to Lantee Beach, there's no other way of getting around.

In addition to the two main beaches, the island also has a string of golden coves and inlets, many of which, in the northeast, have been snapped up by luxury hotels, whose elegant bungalows now squat respectfully beneath the coconut palms, mindful of their privileged surroundings.

Development in Phi Phi Don hasn't run amok yet but things are deteriorating by the minute. The water supply is often cut off, there are problems to do with the evacuation of soiled water, the litter is becoming an eyesore, the beaches grow steadily dirtier, and so on. Refuse collections are gradually getting under way but so far they haven't made any difference.

The truth is that depending on where you stay, you could be in for a huge treat or a big disappointment. As we've said before, the island itself is magnificent; it's tourism that's made a mess of things.

## AMONG THE MOST BEAUTIFUL WATERS IN THE WORLD

People mainly come to Koh Phi Phi for its fabulous sealife and crystal-clear waters. The cold current that flows to the island from the Indian Ocean makes these azure and turquoise waters a breeding-ground for sea creatures. The island is surrounded by great expanses of fabulous coral. The waters are the most beautiful in the world, so it's like swimming in the Maldives or the Red Sea. The flora and fauna are distinguished by their sheer diversity and the coral is uniquely beautiful.

The star of the animal kingdom is the leopard shark, although the black-tip shark comes a close second. Accidents are almost unheard of and it seems that these gentle fish have never hurt a soul – so don't worry. You might also get to see banks of tuna, amusing dolphins or friendly turtles. Put on your mask and snorkel and away you go!

## GETTING THERE

– **From Phuket**: this is what most people do. The landing stage in Chalong Bay is principally used by tour groups from Phuket. The main boats, including the enormous *King Cruiser* (*see* 'Leaving Phuket'), leave from Phuket Port and take from 1 to 2 hours. The best thing is to buy a ticket at your hotel or from any of the agencies in Phuket. They all charge more or less the same. You'll be picked up from your hotel and taken to the boat. Don't worry about a thing – it's all taken care of with typical Thai efficiency. Do bear in mind though that it costs a lot less to buy a one-way ticket from Phuket and a return in Koh Phi Phi, but don't forget to book it in advance.

– **From Krabi**: the crossing can be rough from Krabi. There are two boats a day, at 9.30am and 2pm (more in the peak season). The journey takes 2–3 hours depending on the boat. Check departure times as they're liable to change.

– **From Ao Nang** (west of Krabi): this crossing can be rough too. There's one boat a day at 9am; it takes 3 hours.

## GETTING AROUND THE ISLAND

No roads, no cars, so it's Shanks's pony, folks. There's only one (steep) path on the island that leads past a sensational view (*see* 'Things to Do and See') to some of the beaches on the east coast. Otherwise you can walk from Ton Sai to Long Beach, but that's it. So the only way of getting to the beaches further north is by long-tail taxi and you'll find plenty of those waiting at the landing stage. They can take you anywhere you want to go but mostly they go from the main beach (Ton Sai) to Long Beach (about 15 minutes away). Price is per person. Find out what it is so you don't get ripped off.

## USEFUL ADDRESSES

A cement slab at the landing stage directs you to a street lined with shops, currency exchange kiosks (with poor exchange rates so use the bank at the end of the street), restaurants, diving boutiques and travel agencies that sell bus tickets, boat tickets etc. (on sale everywhere) and where you can make overseas calls. Bus and boat departures are on display all over the place. There's also a health centre in the village and the one-and-only bank on the island, the Krung Thai Bank, open 8.30am–3.30pm.

## WHERE TO STAY

The boom in tourism has led to dramatic improvements in accommodation and prices have soared accordingly. Virtually the only bungalows suitable for backpackers still left are those where the landlords put client contact before the imperatives of tourism. Be aware that prices can triple and even quadruple depending on the time of year, particularly during the King's Cup (sailing regatta), which usually takes place from 15 November to 15 December.

The best thing is to step into a long-tail taxi the moment you get off the boat and head straight to the beach of your choice because, as we've said before, places are often fully booked and hardly any of them (except for the really classy ones) take bookings over the telephone (considering the level of demand, there's no reason why they should).

## ★ LOH DALUM BEACH – โละดาลัม and **TON SAI** – ต้นไทร

This is not somewhere you'd choose to spend the night. It's too crowded and most of the bungalows are expensive and one on top of the other. Anyway, as we said earlier, there are too many little boats and dugouts on Ton Sai Beach to sunbathe or hang out there. Lots of roads lead from Ton Sai to Loh Dalum Beach.

### BUDGET

⚑ **Chong Khao Bungalows** – ช่องเขาบึงกะโล (map, **1**): left of the landing stage, just about half-way between Ton Sai and Loh Dalum. Simple but clean bunga-lows that don't give directly onto the 'beach'. This is one of the only places round here that hasn't changed and where prices remain reasonable. Run by a very nice family. The restaurant is like the bungalows – simple but cheap and good.

### MODERATE

⚑ **Phi Phi Don Resort** – พีพีดอน รีสอร์ท (map, **2**): on Ton Sai, right of the landing stage. ☎ 017-220-252 (mobile). Three rows of solidly built bungalows at the water's edge that are rather crammed to-gether. Tiled bathrooms and fans. Clean but expensive considering how charmless they are.

⚑ **Phi Phi Andaman Resort** – พีพีอันดามันรีสอร์ท (map, **3**): be-yond the Phi Phi Don Resort further up the coast. ☎ 620-230 or 017-231-073 (mobile). Simple faded green bamboo huts plus more solidly built ones with corru-gated iron roofs. Most of the huts are now past their best although there are some newer ones set back from the sea. The price can double, depending on the level of comfort. About 15 minutes' walk from Long Beach or you can go by taxi-boat.

### MORE EXPENSIVE

⚑ **Rimna Resort** – ริมนารีสอร์ท (map, **4**): this place doesn't give directly onto the sea so it's away from all the hustle and bustle (about halfway between Ton Sai and Loh Dalum). Lovely, solidly built bungalows with all the com-forts of small hotel bedrooms. Try to get one at the back among the palm trees.

### SPLASH OUT

⚑ **Pee Pee Princess** – พีพีพรินซ์เสซ (map, **5**): on the beach in Loh Dalum Bay, directly opposite the landing stage. Bungalows with ter-race and a good range of mod cons, including fan, shower and WC. The price is reasonable for the island.

⚑ **Pee Pee Charlie Beach Resort** – พีพีชาลีบีชรีสอร์ท (map, **6**): on the right of the previous place as you face the sea (they operate as a pair). ☎ 723-0495. Comfortable, nicely decorated bungalows with small terrace, fan or air-condition-ing and cold shower. Massive rest-aurant. Relaxed, slightly holiday-village atmosphere. Quieter than its partner.

## ★ MAPRAO BEACH – หาดมะพร้าว

This tiny creek is reached via a little coastal path that runs along the beach on the right of the landing stage. There's only one group of bungalows and they are a particular favourite of ours: far from the madding crowd, nice easy atmosphere, good food. If you prefer, you can take a long-tail taxi back to the main beach. At low tide it will drop you some way out because of the coral reef, so make sure you take your swimsuit and watch where you put your feet.

**⌂ Maprao Resort** – มะพร้าวรีสอร์ท (map, **7**): this is a favourite place: about 15 basic huts (some with wash basins) surrounded by lush vegetation. Simple but quiet with loads of charm. Shared bathroom facilities (cold shower with a sprinkler only, owing to lack of water). The most expensive huts have an unusual little terrace shaped like the hull of a boat. Run by Marie-Pia and Guy (Mister Guy to his friends), an amiable Belgian couple who settled on the island a few years ago.

Very pleasant bar-restaurant overlooking the water with low wickerwork tables and chairs. Good and reasonably priced Thai and European food and lots of it, including some excellent fish that Mister Guy buys direct from the fishermen. The atmosphere is friendly and unpretentious.

## ★ LONG BEACH – ลองบีช

A long beach, as its name suggests, about 20 minutes' walk from the landing stage (beyond Maprao Beach going east). Pleasant because there aren't too many people. The best way to get there from Ton Sai Bay is by long-tail taxi-boat. The bungalows on the beach are owned by two landlords. A few boats go from Long Beach to Phuket.

## MODERATE TO EXPENSIVE

**⌂ Pee Pee Paradise Resort** – พีพีพาราไดส์รีสอร์ท (map, **8**): on the left as you reach Long Beach. Clean and pleasant bungalows, some bamboo, some more solidly built, with fans, shower rooms and mosquito nets. English landlord. Prices vary considerably depending on the level of comfort and how close the bungalow is to the beach. Try to visit several before deciding. The only drawback is the racket out to sea from the long-tails going endlessly back and forth. Now that there are so many tourists, the welcome can be a bit chilly too. There's also a restaurant.

**⌂ Pee Pee Long Beach Bungalows** – พีพีลองบีชบังกะโล (map, **9**): on the right-hand side of the beach. Expensive, dirty and noisy. Only to be used if you're desperate and the previous place is full.

## BEACHES IN THE NORTHEAST OF THE ISLAND

These beaches are only accessible by long-tail taxi and it costs several hundred bahts to get there (more if you want to take a look around). What that buys you, however, is guaranteed peace and quiet. There's only one luxury place to stay on each beach and you can usually book from Phuket or Bangkok. The boat will drop you on the beach of your choice.

## EXPENSIVE TO SPLASH OUT (900–2,000 BTS PER PERSON PER NIGHT)

🛏 **Pee Pee Island Village** – พีพี ไอส์แลนด์วิลเลจ (map, **10**): 89 Sa-toon Road (for reservations). Muang District, Phuket. ☎ 214-918. Or 34 Suttisarn Road, Huayk-wang, Bangkok. ☎ 766-056 or 770-038. Huge, entirely deserted beach roughly midway up the northeast coast. Watch out at low tide because it's virtually impossi-ble to swim there, because of the coral reef. Very large, charming bungalows dotted among the co-conut palms, luxury well combined with tradition. A little sandy path across the lawn leads up to each one. Tastefully decorated, with fan or air-conditioning. You could never afford a love-nest like this back home.

## SPLASH OUT (APPROXIMATELY 4,000 BTS PER PERSON PER NIGHT)

🛏 **Phi Phi Palm Beach Resort** – พีพีปาล์มบีชรีสอร์ท (map, **11**): 196/1–3 Phuket Road, Phuket (for re-servations). This archetypal luxury spread at the extreme northern end of the island has it all – private beach, tennis courts, snooker room and swimming pool. It's like being in an advertisement or a photograph – or even in a dream. Very expensive, but the setting and the facilities are quite excep-tional. Must be nice being rich.

## WHERE TO EAT

Most of the bungalows serve food but there are also several good restaurants in the village of Ton Sai.

✘ **Le Grand Bleu** – ร้านอาหาร เลอกรองเบลอ: in the main street. Nice restaurant with tables on the street. Good food that's a suc-cessful mixture of Thai and French specialities, but some of the ser-vings are a bit on the small side. Good range of wines, particularly the Australian ones (if you can afford them).

✘ **Chez Mama** – ร้านอาหาร เชมาม่า: in the village centre. Rest-aurant run by a Frenchman (they seem to like it out here) which, sadly, has seen better days. De-cent range of European and Asian food, however, including the house specialities: grilled fish (which you pick yourself from the display), traditional Thai soup and good pancakes.

## WHERE TO GO FOR BREAKFAST

– **Pacharee French Bakery** and **Pee Pee Bakery**: in the main street, a bit further up than Chez Mama, going towards Maprao Beach. Two bakery-cum-tea-shops opposite each other that serve delicious breakfasts. The one calling itself a French bakery goes in for French-type breakfasts (bread, *croissants* and *pains au chocolat* – serve yourself so you get to pick the biggest); the other for American-style breakfasts (doughnuts, cookies etc.).

## WHAT TO DO AND SEE

**Diving**: you can't go all the way to Koh Phi Phi and not take the plunge. A maiden dive in waters as clear as this is not something you forget in a hurry.

– **Snorkelling trips**: the highlight of your stay will be exploring the coral reef around Phi Phi Lee, Phi Phi Don's twin. If there are several of you, it won't cost the earth to hire a little motorboat for the day and it means you're completely independent. Alternatively, all the travel agencies organize boat trips to Phi Phi Lee.

– **View Point**: this is a sight you have to see preferably in the morning when the light is best for photography. Follow the path that starts on the eastern side of Loh Dalum Beach (it's clearly signposted) and after about half an hour's climb you come to a delightful spot full of flowers where there's a tiny bar. The view is sensational and encompasses both coves at once. If you go back down the other side of the hill, through the jungle, you get to Lantee Beach, an isolated beach on the northeast coast where there are a few very simple but cheap bungalows.

## ★ PHI PHI LEE – พีพีเล

This is the smallest island. Nobody lives here but it's famous for its coral and the immense Viking Cave, so-called because of a handful of prehistoric rock paintings, which depict humans and animals, along with more recent paintings of Chinese junks. Anyway, this is where the Thais risk their necks from February to May collecting swallows' nests. These are considered a delicacy by the Chinese, who believe they have aphrodisiac qualities.

The nests are perched precariously at the top of the rock face and the only way up is by means of flimsy ladders and bamboo poles. Accidents happen all the time, of course, witnessed by the shrine in the middle of the cave begging the gods for their protection. Incidentally, the mother swallow builds her nest with saliva. If that nest disappears, she builds a second. If it disappears again she can't build a third because she has no more saliva left, so she has to watch her babies die. Try something else on the menu.

Almost all the agencies in Phuket who organize day trips to Koh Phi Phi stop at the cave. Thousands of multicoloured fish now wait eagerly at the entrance for hordes of tourists to feed them (there's a bread-seller right there). The locals also go there regularly to scoop up sackfuls of bird droppings but even so, it still stinks a bit inside.

## LEAVING KOH PHI PHI

All the agencies in the village (no shortage of those) sell tickets to different destinations. The price is more or less the same wherever you go and mainly depends on the speed of the boat.

– **For Phuket**: lots of boats a day, fast and slow. The journey time varies from 2 to 3 hours, or 45 minutes if you go by catamaran (peak season only).

– **For Krabi**: two boats a day, at 9am and 1pm.

– **For Koh Lanta**: there's one boat that goes there directly in the high season, otherwise you have to go via Krabi.

– **For Ao Phra Nang**: one boat a day in the high season, at 3.30pm.

# KRABI – กระบี่ DIALLING CODE: 075

This is the name of a town and a region. Krabi Town extends gently outwards from the confluence of the Krabi River. Tourists rarely stay here for any length of time. Either they head directly for the beaches or they spend the night waiting to catch a morning boat to Koh Phi Phi, Koh Jum or Koh Lanta. Yet Krabi is a pleasant enough little port with a very provincial atmosphere. There's a market, lots of little restaurants, guest-houses and even some wooden houses that have somehow managed to escape the developers' attentions.

Krabi is also a province, and about 20 kilometres (12 miles) from the town you come to the beaches. To think that in the past you needed a boat to get to all those beaches. That's true of only one now, where an ultra-chic hotel complex has sent prices rocketing in the bungalows around it. Word has it that Richard Gere spent a few days here a while back – all very hush-hush, of course. The other beaches are a lot less charming now that they're easy to get to and have become little more than family seaside resorts. One final word: it's very wet in Krabi during the rainy season, which lasts from May to September, and the entire region is deserted.

## GETTING THERE AND GETTING AROUND

– **From Bangkok**: buses leave from the South Terminal. Five air-conditioned and non-air-conditioned buses. The air-conditioned buses leave every 30 minutes from 6pm to 8pm and the journey takes 12–13 hours. Of the non-air-conditioned buses, one leaves at 7.30am and the rest leave between 6pm and 9.30pm. They take about 14 hours.

– **From Phuket** or **Koh Phi Phi**: *see* 'Leaving Phuket' or 'Leaving Koh Phi Phi'.

– There are taxi-boats at the landing stage waiting to take you to any of the beaches around Krabi Town. They leave several times a day and it's much easier than going by road.

– You can also hire motorbikes in town. Remember to compare prices.

## ★ KRABI TOWN

## USEFUL ADDRESSES

🛈 **TAT** – ททท (Tourist Office; map, A1): at the entrance to the town, coming from the bus terminal in Uttarakit Road. ☎ 612-740. Usually open every day, 8.30am–4.30pm. Watch out for the so-called 'official' agencies that sell you a map of the islands and town.

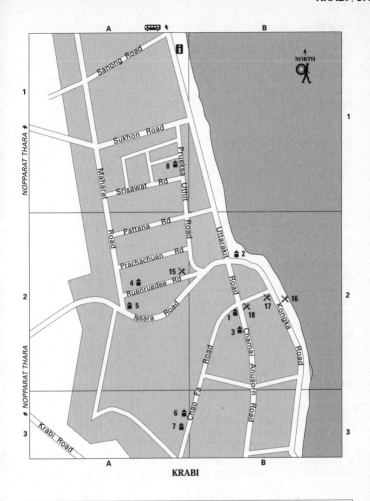

KRABI

■ **Useful Addresses**

🇮 TAT

🚌 Bus terminal

🏠 **Where to Stay**

1 Grand Tower Hotel
2 Thammachart Guesthouse
3 Cha Guesthouse
4 K.L. Guesthouse
5 Seaside Guesthouse

6 Chao Fa Valley Guesthouse
7 KR Mansion Hotel
8 Vieng Thong Hotel

✕ **Where to Eat**

15 May and Mark Restaurant and
   Barn Thai Issara
16 Night market
17 Kotung
18 Good Luck Restaurant

It's available free of charge from the tourist office, which also publishes a little brochure on Krabi, and bus and boat timetables. Friendly welcome.

🚌 **Bus terminal** – สถานีรถประจำทาง (off A1 on the map):

about 5 kilometres (3 miles) from the boarding point for boats to the islands. Lots of *songthaews* can take you from the terminal to the port. You'll find them a the junction down the road, on the right.

## WHERE TO STAY

All the guesthouses sell bus tickets, rent out motorbikes and let you make reservations on neighbouring islands. The price is much the same wherever you go but some places reduce their rates for longer stays.

### BUDGET TO MODERATE (100–300 BTS PER PERSON PER NIGHT)

🛏 **Grand Tower Hotel** – แกรนด์ทาวเวอร์โฮเต็ล (map, B2, **1**): 73/1 at the corner of Uttarakit Road and Chao Fa Road (50 metres up the road from the landing stage). ☎ 621-456. About 100 rooms on six floors, some with private shower room (cold water) and fan. The rest have shared bathroom facilities but no windows. Nice atmosphere and if you're feeling homesick, there are even some foreign-language channels on the TV in the restaurant. Some of the rooms are noisy and not always very clean.

🛏 **Thammachart Guesthouse** – ธรรมชาติเกสท์เฮาส์ (map, B2, **2**): 13 Kongka Road. ☎ 612-536. Small, neat and tidy guesthouse with just four bedrooms. Guests are expected to take their shoes off to go upstairs. Shared bathroom facilities (cold water) on a private terrace overlooking the river. Note that the doors are locked at about 11pm.

🛏 **Cha Guesthouse** – ชาเกสท์เฮาส์ (map, B2, **3**): 45 Uttarakit Road. ☎ 611-141. Very simple bedrooms in three separate buildings that nestle in a tiny garden. Not exactly pristine but the cheapest place in town.

🛏 **K.L. Guesthouse** – เค.แอล.เกสท์เฮาส์ (map, A2, **4**): 24–32 Ruenruedee Road (or Maharat Soi 2). ☎ 612-511 or 512. Cubbyholes more than bedrooms and pretty basic at that, with fan and shared bathroom facilities (cold water).

🛏 **Seaside Guesthouse** – ซีไซด์เกสท์เฮาส์ (map, A2, **5**): 105/55 Maharat Road. ☎ 612-351 or 801. Same landlord as the K.L. Guesthouse and about as comfortable. Single rooms with shared bathroom facilities (cold water).

🛏 **Chao Fa Valley Guesthouse** – เจ้าฟ้าวัลเล่ย์เกสท์เฮาส์ (map, A3, **6**): Chao Fa Road. ☎ 612-499. Two streets up from the port, turn left and the guesthouse is about 10 minutes' walk away on the right. Huge bungalows with fan, shower (cold water) and WC in a garden below the road. All the bungalows are past their best and could do with a face-lift. Visit several before making up your mind. Don't expect to be welcomed with open arms.

🛏 **K.R. Mansion Hotel** – โรงแรมเค.อาร์.แมนชั่น (map, A3, **7**): Chao Fa Road (a bit further than the previous place). ☎ 612-76 or 762. Small four-storey building with about 40 clean, quite well-kept rooms with shared or private bathroom facilities (cold water) and fan. Smiling welcome.

EXPENSIVE TO SPLASH OUT (300–1,200 BTS PER PERSON PER NIGHT)

🛏 **Vieng Thong Hotel** – โรงแรม เวียงทอง (map, A1, **8**): 155 Uttarakit Road. ☎ 611-288 or 620-020.

Modern, rather seedy-looking place with rooms that have private bathroom facilities (hot or cold water), fans or air-conditioning. Quite expensive for what it is – price depends on facilities.

## WHERE TO EAT

✗ **May and Mark Restaurant** – ร้านอาหาร เมย์ แอนด์ มาร์ค (map, A2, **15**): Ruenruedee Road (next to the K.L. Guesthouse). This is the place to come for an English, American or even French breakfast, including hot chocolate, jam, pancakes and homemade yoghurt.

✗ **Barn Thai Issara** – ร้านอาหาร บ้านไทยอิสระ (map, A2, **15**): Ruenruedee Road (next to the previous place). Delightful little tea-shop with lots of exposed timber, knick-knacks and old engravings. Delicious coffee and homemade bread. Get there early to grab a table on the little balcony that's cluttered with green plants. More expensive than the previous place.

✗ **Night market** – ตลาดกลางคืน (map, B2, **16**): opposite the landing stage. Great food and loads of atmosphere. Packed with tempting little food stands that are all as good as each other.

✗ **Kotung** – ร้านอาหารกอตุง (map, B2, **17**): 36 Kongka Road. Facing the Night Market. Clearly the best restaurant in town and as popular with the Thais as with the tourists. Working-class food served in a simple, honest setting. The menu is exhaustive and includes all the fried and sweet-and-sour dishes, soups and beautifully prepared fish. Smiling, friendly welcome.

✗ **Good Luck Restaurant** – ร้าน อาหารโชคดี (map, B2, **18**): 226 Uttarakit Road (facing the Grand Tower Hotel). Run by a Thai landlord and his Belgian wife. Good, traditional food including some particularly delicious fish dishes. Popular with the tourists but relaxing all the same. More expensive than the previous place.

## ★ THE BEACH AREA

Lots of tourists head this way, as you might expect. There are three main beaches: Phra Nang, Nam Mao, and Railay and Sunrise (which you need a boat to get to). Bungalow rates fluctuate enormously depending on the time of year and the landlord's mood – but they're never very welcoming. Always compare prices.

Incidentally, because these beaches owe their development to the boom in the tourist industry, there's not a single Thai in sight – which is a shame.

## ★ PHRA NANG BEACH – หาดพระนาง

This is a long, white, sandy beach where the sea is different shades of green and is generally described as the most beautiful beach. It is surrounded by impressive rock formations, including two large caves created by the waves at the far end of the beach. As you look out to sea from the beach, towering rock monoliths add to its unique atmosphere.

All the bungalows are the wrong side of the wide road that runs along the beach. New buildings blot the landscape every day, turning yet another natural beauty spot into a seaside resort.

## WHERE TO STAY

There are lots of bungalows round here but none that gives directly onto the beach.

### MODERATE

⬢ **Gift's Bungalow** – กิฟท์บังกะโล: ☎ 231-128. Traditional straw huts surrounded by lush vegetation. Basic level of comfort with cold shower, WC and fan. Price is reasonable for the area.

– All the other places along the main road are more expensive.

### EXPENSIVE

⬢ **Phra Nang Inn** – โรงแรมพระ นางอินน์: on the left-hand side of the road that runs at right angles to the one along the beach. ☎ 637-130. Luxury hotel with pleasing architecture surrounded by lush vegetation. Interior garden with a small swimming pool and a jacuzzi. All the rooms are air-conditioned and tastefully decorated with seashells on the walls and stonework bathrooms (hot water). Travel club atmosphere. This is luxury for the price of a two-star hotel back home. Pity the restaurant is so ordinary.

## ★ RAILAY AND SUNRISE BEACHES – หาดไรเลย์และหาดชันไรส์

This beach may well be the loveliest of the three beaches but it's hopelessly overcrowded despite being a boat trip away. Actually it's two beaches back-to-back, but it's easy to cross from one to the other through the rows of bungalows. Boats to the western beach leave from Ao Phra Nang and to the eastern beach from Krabi. The toing and froing of the taxi-boats is a constant noise and there is a growing number of tourists being ferried out here. It can be a job finding anywhere to park your towel in the peak season.

⬢ On Railay Beach in the west, you find the **Railay Village Bungalows** – ไรเลย์วิลเลจบังกะโล (☎ 612-728), **Sand Sea Bungalows** – แชนด์ซีบังกะโล (☎ 012-284-426) and **Railay Bay Bungalows** – ไรเลย์เบย์บังกะโล (☎ 611-944 or 945). These are bungalows and huts, all close together and all much the same standard and price. There's not much to choose between them. Bungalows for backpackers are slowly disappearing, to be replaced by more solidly built buildings with air-conditioning and hot water. The cheapest ones with fans get snapped up right away. The most economical solution is to rent a tent in the middle of a coconut grove.

⬢ On Sunrise Beach in the east, **Sunrise Bungalows** are traditional bungalows with fan, cold shower and WC, and are cheaper than the previous places. The beach on this side is quieter because there are fewer taxi-boats from Krabi.

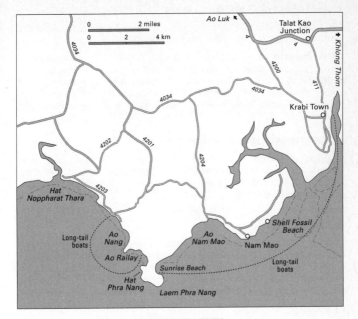

**KRABI'S BEACHES**

– If you like climbing, **Krabi Rock Climbing** mounts assaults on the rocky monoliths in the surrounding area.

## ★ NAM MAO BEACH – หาดน้ำเมา

This narrow, not very sandy beach is the least beautiful of the three beaches and also the least crowded. To get there from Krabi, follow the signs to 'Shell Fossil Beach'. The Dawn of Happiness is just before you get to the beach, on the right (*see below*).

## MODERATE

🏠 **Dawn of Happiness** – ดอว์นออฟแฮปปิเนส: ☎ 612-730. Charming wood-and-bamboo bungalows in a lovely shady setting that's full of flowers. Private bathroom facilities (cold water) and fan; nice decor. Smiling welcome. This is the only place on the beach, so you've got it more or less to yourself.

## ★ THE OTHER BEACHES

The other beaches further north are all reachable by road, so they don't have quite the same magic or mystery.

## ★ SIAM BEACH (AO SIAM) – อ่าวสยาม

This beach remains relatively unspoilt because it's difficult to get to and not signposted. Turn left in the village of Nongthaleh.

🏠 **Pine Bungalows** – ไพน์บังกะโล: ☎ 612-192. The only bungalows on the beach: nice peaceful atmosphere and a choice of two types of bungalow depending on the mod cons; the most comfortable ones give onto the beach. Free transport from Krabi. Ask at the bus terminal or at Pine Tour, 20 Isara Road, near the Thai Hotel. Delicious restaurant – and it's very cheap.

## ★ NOPPHARAT THARA – หาดนพรัตน์ธารา

Very long, pretty beach bordered by the road, and situated in a nature conservation area. There's nowhere to stay on the beach itself, only at the far end of the road on the other side of the river mouth. But this isn't one of the best places to be.

## THINGS TO SEE

★ The entire length of the west coast is punctuated by caves that you can explore by boat. There's a boat-hire place opposite the Phra Nang Inn Hotel (but you can hire one virtually anywhere). The little islands out at sea are surrounded by magnificent coral – Poda Island and Chicken Island are especially beautiful. So give your eyes a treat and spend the morning snorkelling.

★ **The seashell cemetery** – สุสานหอย (Shell Fossil Beach): on one of the points of Krabi Bay, about 19 kilometres (12 miles) from town. This little beach is covered in large patches of seashells that have been slowly transformed over the millennia into great solid slabs that jut out into the sea. Interesting from the geological point of view but aesthetically they look more like large slabs of badly jointed concrete. Not worth going out of your way for.

★ **Wat Tham Seua** – วัดถ้ำเสือ: this highly unusual temple and Buddhist monastery was built right up against a tall rock face at the bottom of a valley inland, in dense tropical forest. Make sure you go properly dressed. From Krabi Town, set off in the direction of Talat Kao, which is about 5 kilometres (3 miles) away, then go towards Trang for about 2 kilometres (1.25 miles). Take the little road on the left by the police station and carry on for 2.5 kilometres (1.5 miles). This is the place.

Carry on up a street bordered by wooden monastic cells. On the left is a stairway that goes up a hill then down again. From there a path leads to some 10 or so natural caves in the cliff that have each been transformed into a temple, some more ornate than others. There's something quite bizarre – even slightly mystical – about these cave-temples in the middle of the forest – particularly if you go there when prayers are being said. Note the narrowness of the monks' cells under the caves. It really is a lovely walk.

## LEAVING KRABI

### By air-conditioned or non-air-conditioned national bus

🚌 All the official buses leave from the bus terminal on Talat Kao, about 5 kilometres (3 miles) north of Krabi. You have to get there by taxi-van.

– **To Bangkok**: two air-conditioned buses at 4.30pm and 5pm and four non-air-conditioned buses between 3.30pm and 5.20pm. It's a distance of 870 kilometres (543 miles) and takes between 12 and 14 hours.

– **To Surat Thani**: three air-conditioned buses at 7am, 11am and 3.30pm (it's about 200 kilometres/125 miles and takes roughly 3 hours and 30 minutes) and two non-air-conditioned buses at 6am and 2.30pm (takes 4–5 hours).

– **To Trang**: buses every 30 minutes.

– **To Hat Yai**: nine air-conditioned buses, between 9.20am and midnight and four non-air-conditioned buses, 10.30am–2.30pm. It's about 310 kilometres (193 miles) and takes 5–6 hours.

– **To Phang Nga and Phuket**: 13 air-conditioned buses, between 9.30am and 5.20pm and 15 non-air-conditioned buses, 6.20am–3.10pm (this is about 185 kilometres/115 miles and takes 4–5 hours).

– **To Koh Lanta**: buses leave from Phattana Road. Check departure times. The bus takes you to Boh Muang Pier where you take a boat to Lanta Pier.

### By private bus

– Lots of guesthouses in Krabi town represent travel agencies and can sell you tickets on very deluxe buses to just about any destination you care to name. You're usually picked up from your guesthouse.

– **To Surat Thani**, **Koh Samui** (a boat connection) **Hat Yai**, **Phuket**, **Bangkok**, **Penang** (Malaysia): two buses a day (in theory) to all these places. You can even buy direct tickets to **Kuala Lumpur**.

### By boat

– **To Koh Phi Phi**: two crossings a day at 9.30am and 2pm (more in the peak season).

– **To Koh Lanta** and **Koh Jum**: two direct crossings a day to Saladan Pier at 10am and 1pm. There's no direct crossing in the rainy season.

# KOH LANTA – เกาะลันตา    DIALLING CODE: 075

Koh Lanta is a string of 15 islands to the south of Krabi. They were declared a national park in 1990, much to the delight of the divers. Several of the islands are uninhabited and the landscape remains wonderfully untamed. The main island of **Lanta Yai** is quiet, rustic and virginal and attracts growing numbers of backpackers fleeing the crowded beaches of Krabi. There is only one road on the island – actually it's more of a red-earth track. It follows the west coast from north to south

FROM BANGKOK TO HAT YAI

and leads to all the bungalows, also on the west coast. **Saladon** is a traditional village of wood-and-bamboo houses on the water. Don't miss the spectacle of the local ferries (like customized long-tails) loading vehicles for the crossing to Lanta Noi on their way back to Trang then Hat Yai. The minibuses leave at 8am.

If you like solitude, arrange for the boat from Krabi to drop you off at Koh Jum, a virtually uninhabited island north of Lanta Yai. There are only two places to stay on this island – both bungalows: the New Village Resort and the New Paradise.

## GETTING AROUND THE ISLAND

There's no taxi service, so getting around the island isn't easy. The only solution is to hire a bicycle or motorbike. If you do, bring some goggles, as the cars create an incredible amount of red dust and it makes visibility rather difficult.

## WHERE TO STAY

Most of the bungalows are on the west coast of the island where you will also find the nicest beaches and the best swimming. Don't worry about all the building work – you'll have no problem finding somewhere to stay. As soon as you arrive in the village of Saladon, you'll be besieged by offers of bungalows. In fact, it's quite a relief when things quieten down. It's best to stay in the north where the beaches are more beautiful and you can walk to Saladon and get a feel for the place. By the way, the bungalows change name at the drop of a hat and grow more modern and more expensive by the minute. Rates fluctuate enormously depending on the time of year.

### BUDGET

☎ **Kaw Kwang Beach Bungalows** – คอกวางบีชบังกะโล: they're signposted from the main road but then it's about a kilometre (half a mile) up a path that isn't marked. Very quiet place at the extreme northwestern end of the island. ☎ 017-220-106 (mobile). Bungalows of different generations, from small, traditional straw huts to large bamboo bungalows with corrugated iron roofs. Cold shower, WC, fan and mosquito nets. Price varies depending on how close the bungalow is to the sea. Nice landlord. Pedal cycle and motorbike hire.

☎ **Khlong Dao Beach Resort** – คลองดาวบีชรีสอร์ท: between Lanta Island and Lanta Villa. Just what you need if you're broke: cheap and cheerful bamboo bungalows, the most basic without windows. The atmosphere is very relaxed.

☎ **Lanta Island Resorts** – ลันตา ไอส์แลนด์รีสอร์ท: next to the Lanta Villa. ☎ 075-621-524 or 012-124-183 (mobile). Bungalows that range from very basic with fan and cold shower to more deluxe with air-conditioning and hot water. A bit crammed together but nicely decorated. Closed out of season.

⚓ **Lanta Palm Beach Bungalows** – ลันดาปาล์มบีชบังกะโล: roughly halfway up the west coast. Tiny concrete bungalows with thatched roofs and shared bathroom facilities (cold water) and other more traditional ones – but you can see daylight between the planks. Warm welcome. Closed May to September.

⚓ **Lanta Coral Beach Bungalows** – ลันดาคอรัลบีชบังกะโล: the most southwesterly bungalows on the list. Attractive, small, solidly built bungalows in a pleasant spot. Nicely decorated with shower rooms (cold water), WC and fans. If you're looking for isolation, look no further. Good value for money. Smiling, friendly welcome. Very good restaurant.

### EXPENSIVE

⚓ **Lanta Villa** – ลันดาวิลลา: on the second beach coming from the northwest. ☎ 75-620-629. Fairly deluxe bungalows on the beach and more basic ones further back, rather too close together but all with private bathroom facilities (cold water). Well-kept garden. There's also a currency exchange bureau at reception.

⚓ **Lanta Sea House** – ลันดาซีเฮ้าส์: about 1 kilometre (0.5 miles) from Saladon going south. ☎ 201-60. Convivial, well-equipped bungalows for two or three people, either side of the restaurant. Pleasant garden full of flowers. Prices can double depending on how close the bungalow is to the beach. Helpful landlords.

⚓ **Golden Bay Cottage** – โกลเด้นเบย์คอทเทจ: one of the best places in the northwest of the island. ☎ 017-230-879 (mobile). Bungalows of different generations ranging from traditional straw huts to more recent solidly built bungalows, all new and very comfortable. Honest prices. Pleasant welcome.

# HAT YAI (HAD YAI) – หาดใหญ่ DIALLING CODE: 074

Practically everyone stops here on their way to or from Malaysia. It's a modern, very lively town that feels distinctly Asian with its streets buzzing with scooters. Incidentally, all the ads refer to Hat Yai as 'the little Paris of Southern Thailand' (which may be a slight exaggeration). Hat Yai is regularly invaded by Malaysian Muslims from the coast who go there to slum it. There are impressive numbers of jewellery shops, hi-fi and video stores, clothes shops and luggage shops. There's hardly any craftwork, so you need to look for that somewhere else. Also restaurants, including some with bizarre specialities (see 'What to See'). Apart from that, there's not a lot to do in Hat Yai itself. Outside town however, don't miss the magnificent Ton Nga Chang ('elephant tusks') waterfalls. West of Hat Yai in Pakbara is where you board the boat to the Tarutao maritime park, a group of five islands where few people go even today (see below).

## WHERE TO GO TO EXTEND YOUR VISA

If your visa is close to expiry you can extend it at the Padang Besar frontier post. Customs officers are quite used to people crossing first one way then the other to extend their visas by 15 days – and it's free of charge. There are lots of buses for Padang Besar from the bus terminal;

or you can catch a collective taxi on the Duang Chan Road that will drop you right in front of the frontier post.

## USEFUL ADDRESSES

**🛈 TAT** – ททท (Tourist office; map, A2): Thanon Soi 2, Niphat Uthit 3 (some way from the centre, next to the police station). ☎ 243-747 and 245-986. Open 8.30am–4.30pm. Loads of information and map in English. Smiling welcome.

**✉ Post office and telephone** – ไปรษณีย์กลาง (map, B1): Ratthakan Road. The main office is on Niphat Songkhrao Road (further away from the centre). Open weekdays 8.30am–4.30pm, weekends 9am–noon.

**■ Thai Airways** – สายการบินไทย: Niphat Uthit 2 Road. ☎ 243-711.

**■ Malaysian Airlines System** – สายการบินมาเลเซีย: Niphat Uthit 2 Road. ☎ 243-729.

## WHERE TO STAY

Most of the cheap hotels are on the Niphat Uthit 2 Road. To get there from the train station walk down the road facing the station, take the third street on the left and then the first street on the right.

### BUDGET (LESS THAN 200 BTS PER PERSON PER NIGHT)

**🛏 Cathay Guesthouse** – คาเธ่ย์ เกสท์เฮาส์ (map, A2, **1**): 93/1 Niphat Uthit 2 Road. ☎ 243-815. Very simple rooms with cold shower and fan, plus a dormitory that sleeps eight that's cheaper still. Friendly welcome and backpacking atmosphere. Price is reasonable even if the rooms are a bit noisy. There's a travel agency on the ground floor.

### MODERATE (200–400 BTS PER PERSON PER NIGHT)

**🛏 Pacific Hotel** – โรงแรมแปซิฟิค (map, A2, **2**): 149/1 Niphat Uthit 2. ☎ 244-062 or 245-202. Clean, well-kept hotel with rooms with fan or air-conditioning, bathroom (hot water) and TV. The rooms that give onto the back of the hotel couldn't be quieter. Nice place that's good value for money.

**🛏 Laem Tong Hotel** – โรงแรม แหลมทอง (map, A2, **3**): 154 Niphat Uthit 2 (at the corner with Thamnoonvitee Road). ☎ 352-301 or 307. The rooms aren't as welcoming as you might expect from the reception area. However, they are clean and well kept, with air-conditioning (and hot water) or fan (and cold water). The street is very noisy, so ask for a room at the back.

**🛏 King's Hotel** – โรงแรมคิงส์ (map, A2, **4**): 126 Niphat Uthit 1 Road. ☎ 234-140. Pleasant rooms with fan or air-conditioning. Once again, the rooms that give onto the street are a bit noisy. Nothing special but all right.

## WHERE TO EAT

You can eat anything you want in Hat Yai, and lots of the Chinese restaurants are first-class.

The restaurants are on Thamnoonvitee Road that leads to the station, and Niphat Uthit 3 Road.

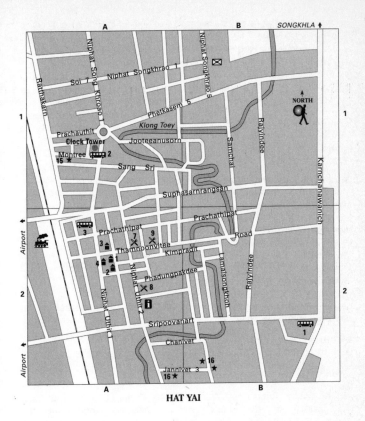

**HAT YAI**

■ **Useful Addresses**

🏢 TAT
✉ Post office and telephone
🚂 Train station
🚌 **1** Terminal for air-conditioned buses
🚌 **2** Terminal for non-air-conditioned buses
🚌 **3** Bus stop for air-conditioned buses

🏠 **Where to Stay**

**1** Cathay Guesthouse

**2** Pacific Hotel
**3** Laem Tong Hotel
**4** King's Hotel

✖ **Where to Eat**

**7** Odean Shopping Mall
**8** Kaneng Restaurant
**9** Sugar Rock

★ **What to See**

**15** Trip by *songthaew* to the Ton Nga Chang waterfalls
**16** Snake House

✕ **Odean Shopping Mall** – ศูนย์ การค้าโอเดียน (map, A2, **7**): 79/ 7 Thamnoonvitee Road. Big department store that specializes in up-market products for Thai and particularly Malaysian customers. Prices aren't that competitive (not even for French and American trainers that are officially manufactured here – perhaps it's done on purpose to discourage imitations). At the top there's a huge room packed with little places that serve delicious **Thai specialities** (this is your chance to try *tom yam* soup) plus ice-creams and fruit juices (avoid the ice-cubes). Good value for money. The floor above is an immense, glazed hangar-type space with merry-go-rounds for kids and a cinema for grown-ups.

✕ **Kaneng Restaurant** – ร้านอา หารแคนง (map, A2, **8**): Niphat Uthit 3 (note that the name on the outside is written in Thai). Another massive hangar-type space, concrete this time with big fans. Packed with locals, who go there for tasty traditional food at reasonable prices. They do an irresistible fried bass in red gravy (chunks of fried fish in a sweet-and-sour sauce) and hot and sour soup Thai-style. This place is the genuine article – and so is all the noise that goes with it.

✕ **Sugar Rock** – ร้านอาหารชูการ์ ร็อค (map, A2, **9**): Thamnoonvitee Road. The place to go for an American breakfast in a half-American-half-French setting (old clock, radio set, bistro tables) with photos of American stars all over the walls.

✕ The **station restaurant** opens at 6am for those arriving early in Hat Yai.

✕ There's a big **market** full of **restaurants** next to the Clock Tower.

## WHAT TO SEE

★ **The Snake House** (map, A2 and B2, **16**): Chanivet (or Jannivet) Soi 3 and Tungso Road (perpendicular roads). There's only one dish on the menu in the Vichai Store, Kieng and Vichai Snake Shop and that's, well, snake, of course. The blood and tripe of vipers, cobras and king cobras are particular favourites with the Chinese, who believe they make them healthy and more virile (what the Thais call 'power'). Naturally, the more dangerous the animal, the greater the demand. Anyway, you can take your pick from bundles of snakes that writhe around in cages. The luckless serpent is then fished out with a long pole and hung in a sort of open-air kitchen area for all to see. Next it's slit open, while still alive. It takes three snakes to obtain half a glassful of snake blood. Mix with alcohol and you've got a snake cocktail.

By the way, snake blood sells for anything from 250 to 2,500 bahts (for a king cobra). The flesh is then made into soup and the skin sold to the local tannery (nothing's wasted, of course). The trade in snake bits keeps snake hunters busy in three neighbouring provinces: Trang, Patthalung and Nakhon Si Thammarat.

★ **Bullfights**: animal fights (fighting fish, bulls, cocks, buffaloes) are part of Thai tradition. For the ancients, they demonstrated the spiritual force of the animal's owner. Before money came into it, the victor was rewarded with jugs of distilled alcohol, which he shared with the loser. Times have changed and betting today is big business. Unlike on Koh Samui or Koh

Pha Ngan where there are buffalo-fights, here it's bullfights – but not the kind of bulls we're used to: Thai bulls have a lump on their backs and look rather like a cross between a bull and a zebu.

The bulls' training programme is impressive: up at dawn, a gambol on the beach, big meal based on fresh grass and eggs and plenty of sleep under a mosquito net. By the time they enter the arena, they're formidable brutes with immense horns. The fighting is fierce and stops when one of them finally collapses. Don't miss the spectacle of the Thais in the stands swearing and shouting at the bulls to make them more aggressive. There are two arenas in Hat Yai and fights take place on the first Saturday and Sunday of every month, between 9am and 4pm. For information and programme contact the tourist office (TAT). ☎ 243-747 or 238-518.

## WHAT TO SEE IN THE SURROUNDING AREA

★ **Ton Nga Chang waterfalls** – น้ำตกโตนงาช้าง: about 20 kilometres (12 miles) from Hat Yai, in a national park. Take a *songthaew* (collective taxi) from Montree 1 Road (near the Clock Tower; map, A1, **15**) but make sure you take the right one. Ask for the 'Nam Tok (waterfall) Ton Nga Chang' and you'll be shown the right vehicle, which will only leave when all the seats are full, so brace yourself for a wait because there aren't that many tourists. The falls are about 45 minutes away and the *songthaew* drops you inside the park.

These extraordinary falls flow as two separate columns of water down through at least seven levels, reminding you of elephant tusks (hence the name *chang*). The first levels are more crowded than the others because the Thais come swimming here, especially at weekends. However, when you enter the jungle by walking along the falls to the right, you find that visitors are few and far between and eventually there's hardly anyone around but you. It takes more than an hour to reach the top but there are waterholes like natural pools on every level so there's no shortage of places to take a dip (you're spoiled for choice). Take a picnic and bathing costume.

The jungle is magnificent and resounds to the most indescribable cacophony of animal calls. In such exuberant vegetation, even the scraps of litter here and there cease to bother you after a while.

Note that the park closes at 6pm, so make sure you come back down in plenty of time. It's a long walk back to Hat Yai.

From Hat Yai, you can get to Krabi, then Koh Phi Phi (*see* 'Leaving Hat Yai').

## LEAVING HAT YAI

### By train

🚆 The **train station** (map, A2) is a busy one:

– **To Bangkok**: it takes 14–17 hours depending on the train. There are five departures daily, between 3.30 and 6.30pm. These stop on the way in Surat Thani, Chumphon, Hua Hin and Nakhon Pathom.

– **To Sungai Kolok** (going towards the Malaysian coast): one express and one fast train a day, at 6am. The journey takes 4 hours.

– **To Butterworth** (on the west coast of Malaysia): one express train at 6.30am. The border crossing is usually fairly straightforward.

## By bus

🚌 Buses go to the same destinations as the trains. Non-air-conditioned buses leave from the **terminal** (map, A1, 🚌 **2**) near the market on Phetkasem Road. AC buses leave from the **bus terminal** (map, B2, 🚌 **1**) or outside the **King's Hotel** and the **President Hotel** (map, A2, 🚌 **3**).

– **To Phuket**: one bus in the morning.

– **To Krabi**: the local bus costs half as much as the express and the journey takes 5 hours.

– **To Malaysia**: private buses only. Check departure times.

– **To Butterworth**: at least three air-conditioned buses.

– **To Singapore**: three direct air-conditioned buses a day, taking 18 hours. Book your ticket at least a day in advance in a travel agency or through the guesthouse. The Modern Tour Service, 14/3 Chee Unit Road, sells tickets at attractive rates. It's located at the first junction on the left coming from the Seiko Hotel. The journey to Singapore can take as much as 23 hours, allowing for rather lengthy border formalities.

– **To Penang and Kuala Lumpur**: buses leave early afternoon. The journey takes 14 hours.

## By air

✚ **Hat Yai Airport**: for information and times of planes: ☎ 244-145 or 246-487.

– Thai Airways has five scheduled flights a day to **Bangkok**, two to **Phuket**, and seven flights a week to **Singapore**.

Don't forget the airport taxes and watch you don't get conned by people telling you that tourists going to Malaysia have to exchange a certain amount of money a day to obtain their visa.

## By collective taxi

– **To Penang**: a bit expensive but fast and comfortable. The driver takes care of all the formalities (in 30 minutes you're through both sets of customs). The journey takes 5 hours. The taxi drops you in Penang, at the hotel of your choice.

# TARUTAO MARITIME PARK –
อุทยานแห่งชาติตะรุเตา

DIALLING CODE: 074

This archipelago of 51 islands, scattered around the Andaman Sea at the frontier with Malaysia, remains largely untouched by tourism (about 70 visitors a day, slightly more in the peak season). Since 1974, when it was declared a UNESCO World Heritage Site, it has successfully resisted attempts to vandalize its natural beauty in the name of development. There are virtually no banks or shops on any of these islands, so bring some cash and provisions out with you.

## GETTING THERE

### By boat

Andrew Tour (☎ 781-509 or 781-159) sail regularly to Tarutao from **Pakbara**, a port about 10 kilometres (6 miles) west of Langu. Sailing times to the various islands within the archipelago are as follows:

– **Pakbara–Koh Tarutao**: a distance of 22 kilometres (14 miles) takes 1 hour 30 minutes. Daily crossings at 10.30am and 3pm returning at 9am (daily) and 2pm (Sunday, Monday, Wednesday and Friday).

– **Pakbara–Koh Lipe** and **Koh Adang**: about 65 kilometres (50 miles) takes 4 hours. A single boat goes to both islands – it leaves at 10.30am Tuesday, Thursday and Saturday and returns at 9am on Wednesday, Friday and Sunday. If requested by passengers, the boat can put in at the islet of Koh Kai, a natural stone arch with a beach of pure white sand that lies about 25 kilometres (15 miles) beyond Tarutao.

– **Koh Tarutao–Koh Lipe** and **Koh Adang**: about 43 kilometres (27 miles) takes 2 hours 30 minutes. The boat leaves at noon on the same days as above (it's the same boat). The return timetable is also the same as above.

There may be more boats in the peak season depending on demand. You can also hire a boat at any time from one of the fisherman in Pakbara. The price is roughly equivalent to eight outward journeys.

### Getting back to Pakbara

– **From Hat Yai**: an air-conditioned minibus to Pakbara leaves from Duang Chan Road near the junction with Niphat Uthit 1 Road, about 300 metres from the train station. As you come out of the station, take the third road on the left then the second on the right (the *tuk-tuks* know the way). The minibus leaves every hour, 7am–4pm and takes 1 hour 30 minutes. What could be simpler? In principle, the boat waits for the arrival of the 9am bus, so calculate your time of arrival in Hat Yai accordingly (night train or bus).

– **From Tran**: buses and *songthaews* go to Langu, from where you take a *songthaew* to Pakbara. There's no direct way of getting back there.

## WHEN TO GO

There are no direct sailings to the islands during the monsoon season from late May to early November, when thunderstorms are common and few fishermen go out to sea. All the restaurants are closed then too. During the rest of the year, provided you avoid public holidays you'll also avoid the crowds (which are nothing like in Phuket or Koh Phi Phi).

## ★ KOH TARUTAO – เกาะตะรุเตา

Sea of deepest blue; white sand as far as the eye can see; coconut palms, virgin forest in the background and not another soul in sight. This may sound too good to be true but actually it's a pretty fair description of Tarutao, a little piece of Paradise Lost where you can leave behind the world and all its ways. To make this dream come true, prepare to forego some of your material comforts for a while and let your sense of adventure do the rest.

## DEVIL'S ISLAND

Despite its many charms, it seems there is a curse on Tarutao. From time immemorial it served as a refuge for Andaman pirates (nightmare creatures from the East), then a prison for Thai criminals, and a penal colony for political dissenters until 1945. Now it's being stalked by Malaysian developers (Koh Langkawi is just 5 kilometres/3 miles away, remember) who just can't wait to turn this much-coveted rock into a second Phuket.

## ADDRESS AND USEFUL INFORMATION

■ **Administration office**: ☎ 729-002 and 781-285. There is a 24-hour radio and telephone link with the mainland – could be handy in an emergency.

■ **Admission charge**: payable on arrival on the island and used to maintain the park.

⚓ **Diving**: there's nowhere to hire equipment on the island. Try around Koh Lipe.

## WHERE TO STAY AND WHERE TO EAT

🛏 The **welcome facilities** managed by the park staff are grouped around Pante Bay in the northwest of the island. The accommodation ranges from hired tents and dormitory-like 'long houses' (rows of attached bamboo huts with palm leaf roofs that each sleep four people) to family bungalows. The price is cheap, certainly, but the facilities are very basic and there are certain rules (bucket shower, no electricity after 10pm). It's best to bring your own tent and bivouac on one of the more isolated beaches on the island (in which case bring supplies from the mainland rather than from Pakbara, where choice is limited).

✕ **Tarutao Restaurant**: open 8am–9pm. This is the only restaurant near the bungalows, so deciding where to eat is quickly done. The welcome is fairly offhand but the food is pretty good (seafood, soups, pasta and so on) and so it should be, for the price.

## THE BEACHES

Starting from the landing stage in the northwest of the island and going along the coast in an anticlockwise direction, the beaches you come to are as follows:

★ **Pante Bay** – อ่าวปันเต (1.5 kilometres/1 mile): stretches southwards from the port, bordered on its eastern side by the village and its coconut palms. This is the most popular beach on the island but nowhere near as crowded as some of the resorts near by. In the peak season you might see the odd towel spread out here and there.

★ **Jack Bay** – อ่าวแจ๊ค (1 kilometre/0.5 miles long): south of Pante Bay from which it is only really cut off at high tide. At low tide you get to Jack Bay by wading 150 metres up to your waist. At high tide you can only swim there or clamber up the limestone and sandstone rocks that separate the two bays. Privacy is virtually guaranteed.

★ **Malae Bay** – อ่าวเมาและ (600 metres long): at the extreme southern end of Jack Bay. Follow the stream that leads off towards the left through the mangrove swamp and cross the stream. After about 200 metres, Malae Bay is visible on the horizon, with its coconut plantations and friendly village that's home to a few fishing families and a community of Buddhist monks. Nice welcoming place where you can have a drink and even pitch your tent if you want.

★ **Sone Bay** – อ่าวสน (3 kilometres/2 miles long): from Malae Bay, carry on along the path past the houses on the left. The path is well waymarked all the way to Sone Bay. It starts by climbing through virgin forest and then descends as it nears the bay. It takes about 2 hours to walk there from your point of departure around 8 kilometres (5 miles) away, including the 4 kilometres (2.5 miles) from Malae Bay. Just before you get to the beach, the path crosses two small streams that flow all year round (feel free to have a drink – the water's perfectly safe) before bending right towards the only bungalow in Sone Bay (Ranger Station) at the extreme northern end of the beach. This is where the forest warden lives with his family.

To the south there is white sand as far as the eye can see and not another soul in sight – a sense of remoteness is guaranteed. This is where the sea turtles come to lay their eggs from December to February. On a more practical note, if you feel like spending the night here (it couldn't be more perfect – the sunset is sublime) try to negotiate with the warden for a dish of home-cooked rice. Passers-by can also use his shower room. There aren't any mattresses however, so bring your camping equipment.

★ **Makham Bay** – อ่าวมะขาม (1 kilometre/0.5 miles) and **Taloh Udang Bay** – อ่าวคะโละอุดัง (2 kilometres/just over 1 mile long): two beaches at the southern end of the island that you can only get to by long-tail boat from the port. Taloh Udang will for ever remain famous as the place that from 1939 to 1945 welcomed large numbers of opponents of Phibun's nationalist regime. You get a magnificent view of Koh Langkawi from the beach.

★ **Taloh Wow Bay** – อ่าวคะโละวาว: this is the only beach (and it's rocky) on the eastern coast of the island, that for a long time served as a jail for highly dangerous Thai prisoners. It's off the only road on the island, so you can walk there, although it's quite hard going with the sun beating down (10 kilometres/6 miles from Pante Bay).

## WHAT TO DO AND SEE

★ **Museum and audiovisual show**: behind the restaurant, on the left, it features a good exhibition of the geography and history of Tarutao, including a large-scale relief map, photographs and all sorts of skeletons. There's an audiovisual show every night, except Sunday, at about 7.30pm. Quite interesting. Some English commentary.

★ **Toh-Boo**: from the park administrative offices, look for the little path off to the east that leads to the top of Toh-Boo, a hill 114 metres (about 350 feet) high where you get a magnificent view of the western coast of the island. Straight ahead, Koh Adang and Koh Lipe (the furthest to the left) are clearly visible in the distance and are roughly 40 kilometres (25 miles) away. The walk to the top takes about 20 minutes.

★ **Crocodile cave**: from the port, look for the natural canal (Malaka Canal) that heads off inland through a dense mangrove swamp, and follow it for just under 1kilometre (about 0.5 miles). Eventually you come to a still partly unexplored cave that used to be notorious for its ferocious crocodiles. These were last sighted in 1974 but have disappeared altogether since then. It's a very interesting expedition – particularly if you remember to take a torch for the cave. Try to go there as a group to share the cost of the journey, which isn't cheap.

## ★ KOH LIPE – เกาะหลีเป๊ะ

This pancake-shaped island surrounded by beautiful, white sandy beaches is principally unique for the fishing community that lives there: some 500 or so Mokens or 'Chaos Lays' (sea gypsies) as they are known in Thai. To this day, very little is known about the origins of these people. With their strong bodies, light-red hair and eyes of intense bronze, it is plain that they are joined to the sea body and soul. Their ritual of 'Loy Rua' symbolizes this relationship. The villagers pack off their sins on a boat that they send out to sea. If the sea rejects the boat and sends it back to shore, the sailors are in for a rough ride. From now on, their lives will be dogged by such misfortunes as bad harvests and accidents at sea.

## USEFUL INFORMATION

– **Getting there**: *see* 'Getting There' *above*. There's no port. Koh Lipe is surrounded by coral reefs and shallow waters. Passengers come ashore in flat-bottomed long-tail boats.

– **Where to stay and where to eat**: unlike Tarutao, Koh Lipe is not exclusively in the hands of the conservation authorities. You can also find bed and board with the families on the island.

## WHAT TO DO AND SEE IN THE SURROUNDING AREA

⚓ **Diving**: the most beautiful coral reefs are around three places: Koh Gra, about 500 metres off the east coast of Koh Lipe and easy to identify from its one solitary palm tree (you can also swim there); Koh Jabang, about 5 kilometres (3 miles) away in the direction of Koh Rawi, and especially Koh Yang, another 3 kilometres (2 miles) on in the direction of Koh Rawi. The best thing to do is get a group of people together and hire a boat for the day or half-day. You can hire masks and snorkels there.

– It's worth making a small detour from Koh Jabang (less than 1 kilometre/0.5 miles), to see the wonderfully polished pebbles that line the beaches of **Koh Hin Ngam** (which means 'island of beautiful stones'). Resist the temptation to take any pebbles away with you as souvenirs. The people round here say it brings bad luck.

★ **KOH ADANG** – เกาะอาดัง

This island is no longer the divers' paradise it used to be. The beautiful coral beds that once surrounded its shores have all sadly deteriorated. At first the damage was attributed to dynamite fishing and the trace elements that this left behind in the water. But it now seems that the wind is also to blame, because of the sand it blows in. The island is not short of attractions, however. The landscape is mountainous (there are dramatic views of neighbouring islands in the archipelago), with dense virgin forests and sensational waterfalls. There are also some of the last remaining Chaos Lays fishing villages here (although most have now decamped to Koh Lipe). This place is only really for determined travellers in search of wild landscapes.

## USEFUL INFORMATION

– **Getting there**: *see* 'Getting There' at the start of the section on the Tarutao Maritime Park. You can also cross at any time from Koh Lipe to Koh Adang (a distance of less than 2 kilometres/1 mile) by long-tail boat. It doesn't cost much and you land on the south side of the island by the administrative centre (Laem Sone).

– **Where to stay and where to eat**: *see above* under Koh Tarutao. The prices are identical.

# KOH BULON-LAE – เกาะบุโหลน

DIALLING CODE: 075

In the heart of the maritime park of Mu Koh Phetra some 15 kilometres (9 miles) north of Tarutao, this little island is a peaceful holiday destination (like Koh Phi Phi 20 years ago, as veteran backpackers will remember) in enchanted surroundings with fine sand, coral and lush undergrowth.

## GETTING THERE

– Andrew Tour (☎ 074-781-509 or 781-159) sails to Koh Bulon-Lae and Tarutao from **Pakbara**. There's one boat daily that leaves at 2pm and returns at 9am, taking between 1 hour 30 minutes and 2 hours.

## WHERE TO STAY AND WHERE TO EAT

🛏 ✕ **Pansand Resort** – พันแชนด์ รีสอร์ท: ☎ 075-218-035 (Andaman Travel in Trang) or ☎ 01-722-0279 (this dials the island directly). A highly efficient bungalow village opposite the landing stage, with bungalows at a wide range of prices, from bamboo huts and traditional bungalows with fan, to family chalets with all mod cons, including air-conditioning, shower and indoor WC. Well-kept garden with direct access to the beach and a magnificent terrace restaurant facing the sea that serves a variety of tasty dishes from 8am to 10pm (Thai, Chinese and European specialities). Smiling welcome, if a touch formal. Overseas telephone facilities. Mask, snorkel and flipper hire. Quality service. Booking essential during public holidays. Ask for the house brochure that includes a map of the island.

🛏 ✕ **Bulon Resort** – บุโหลนรี สอร์ท: much the same as the Pansand Resort, at the extreme northern end of Bulon Beach. Not quite as plush perhaps, but what it loses in comfort it makes up for in authenticity and local colour – the restaurant is much cheaper too. If you want somewhere cool, ask for one of the bungalows in the pine forest.

🛏 **Panka Resort** – ปันการีสอร์ท: further west, beyond the last fishing village, along Panka Yai Bay with its unusual and beautiful beach where you feel miles from anywhere. A handful of bungalows with basic showers and indoor WC, let by the island's indigenous people. The ideal place to join in village life and gain a better understanding of Chao Lays culture. If you're interested in ethnography, look no further.

## BEACHES

★ **Bulon Beach** – หาดบุโหลน: the largest and the most beautiful beach west of Koh Bulon offers clear water, multicoloured fish and coral, creamy yellow sand. Not forgetting the magnificent sunsets.

★ **Mango Bay** – หาดมังโก: in the south of the island, not more than 15 minutes' walk through the fishing villages near Panka Noi Nay. You follow the path on the left to a small sandy beach bordered by a village of very welcoming fishermen. More clear water with coral is only a short distance from the shore. Try to persuade the fishermen to take you out to Bat Cave, slightly to the west of the beach.

★ **Panka Noi Bay** and **Panka Yai Bay** – หาดปันกาน้อยและหาดปันกาใหญ่: in the north of the island. This is the area to visit if you want to see more Chaos Lays villages (don't miss the mid-afternoon smoking break when these big strong men spend long hours drawing on their bamboo pipes), as well as beaches of granite, sandstone and laterite. The only vegetation is a mangrove swamp with its curiously twisted roots. Watch you don't come a cropper when you visit the Nose Cave – the rocks are very sharp and slippery in places.

## WHERE TO DIVE

➤ **Around Koh Bulon**: you can swim to the beds of soft coral that grow along the big beach and in Mango Bay. Equipment can be hired in Pansand Resort.

➤ **White Rock**: if you want to explore the coral reefs, take a boat trip out to White Rock, south of Koh Bulon. You can arrange it through any of the resorts described above but it's simpler, and cheaper, to ask the fishermen direct. There's no fixed price – it largely depends on what the catch is like that morning.

# SONGKHLA – สงขลา          DIALLING CODE: 074

The history of Songkhla goes back a long way. In prehistoric times, the land belonged to a community that lived off fishing and trade. In the 17th century the region became known as Singora and prospered under Malaysian rule. It was renamed Songkhla in 1775 (in the reign of Taskin) after a Chinese man who claimed he was descended from the celebrated Na Songkhla family.

Songkhla is about 30 kilometres (19 miles) from Hat Yai, with which it functions very much as a pair. Built on a peninsula, this is predominantly a seaside resort with its own golf course (where every player has a caddie). Most of the people who visit the town are Asian (Thais, Malaysians and Chinese).

Songkhla is very spread out and you really need a collective taxi to get around. It stretches between the sea in the east (Samila Beach) and an immense lagoon called Songkhla Lake to the west. The guesthouses and hotels are cheaper, incidentally, than in Hat Yai, but are just as good and are quieter and often have more charm.

## GETTING THERE

### By bus

🚌 The No. 1871 bus to Songkhla leaves every 7 minutes, between 6am and 7.30pm, from the **market terminal** in Hat Yai (outside the Clock Tower on Phetkasem Road; map, A1, 🚌 **2**). It takes about 30 minutes, sometimes less.

– Buses back to Hat Yai leave every 20 minutes, between 9am and 6pm, from the Ramwithi Road (opposite Petkiri Road) just under the footbridge. There's also a late bus at 8pm.

– The railway between Hat Yai and Songkhla is no longer in use.

## WHERE TO STAY

**BUDGET (LESS THAN 200 BTS PER PERSON PER NIGHT)**

🏠 **Amsterdam Guesthouse** – อัมสเตอร์ดัมเกสท์เฮาส์: 15/3 Rong Muang. ☎ 314-890. Paula, the charming owner, settled here in 1993. She now lets out seven sweet little rooms with big fans, cold showers and shared WCs. The rest of the house is all green plants, warm tones and loads of retro atmosphere. Price varies according to size of room but none of the rooms is expensive. Paula can tell you what's worth seeing in town.

🛏 **Songkhla Hotel** – โรงแรม สงขลา: 68/70 Vichianchom Road. ☎ 313-505. Very simple, clean rooms with or without bathroom facilities (cold water). Look no further if you're hard up and the previous place is full.

## MODERATE (200–400 BTS PER PERSON PER NIGHT)

🛏 **Sooksomboon 1 Hotel** – โรงแรมสุขสมบูรณ์: 40 Petkiri Road. ☎ 311-049 or 312-428. Small, unpretentious hotel but clean and well kept with charmingly old-fashioned rooms at reasonable prices. Fan or air-conditioning but cold shower only. Young, friendly welcome. It's convivial and good value for money.

🛏 **Sansabai Hotel** – โรงแรม– แสนสบาย: 1 Petkiri Road. ☎ 311-

106 or 441-746. Rather sinister-looking rooms with air-conditioning and shower room (cold water). Total absence of decor. Not worth considering unless the previous place is full.

🛏 **Sooksomboon 2 Hotel** – โรงแรมสุขสมบูรณ์2: 14–18 Saiburi Road. ☎ 323-809 or 810. This hotel is in two parts. The old wing has very simple, cell-like rooms with cold showers and WCs. The new wing has its own entrance and brand-new rooms with air-conditioning and shower rooms with hot running water. Nicely decorated too. Warm welcome. Good value for money in both cases.

🛏 **Queen Hotel** – โรงแรมควีน: 20 Saiburi Road. ☎ 323-273 or 311-138. Next to the Sooksomboon 2 Hotel. Don't be deceived by the luxurious reception area – the rooms aren't as nice as all that, but they do have fan and hot shower (they have hot water next door too, but this place is much more expensive).

## WHERE TO EAT

🍴 There are lots of good **restaurants** and **seafood places** on the road along Samila Beach. Or you can try the little **mobile kitchens** that sell crispy *som tam,* fried balls of unshelled shrimps (they're delicious – and the heads go down a treat!)

## WHAT TO SEE

★ **The night market** – ตลาดกลางคืน: at the far end of Vichianchom Road, it has lots going on and some good little restaurants that specialize in Muslim dishes.

★ **Samila Beach** – หาดสมิหลา: huge beach with a broad, beautiful stretch of sand that gets quite crowded at weekends. Depending on the currents, the sea can be cloudy in places.

★ **Songkhla National Museum** – พิพิธภัณฑสถานแห่งชาติสงขลา: Chana Road. Open Wednesday to Sunday 9am–noon and 1pm–4pm. The museum occupies a strange white house in the Chinese style, with a double stairway, wide balconies and elegant interior gardens. It was built in 1878 and originally served as the Governor's residence. Beautiful stone and bronze sculptures are displayed in various rooms on the ground floor and upstairs, mainly Buddhas, but the style isn't always obvious – Sukhothai, Dvâravatî, Ayutthaya, Lopburi etc. See if you can guess what style they are without reading the labels. Chinese furniture is also displayed.

## IN THE SURROUNDING AREA

★ **Khao Noi** – เขาน้อย: a small hill overlooking the Cape of Songkhla, with a lovely view of the town beneath.

★ **Hat Son Awn** – แหลมสนอ่อน: this is the point that separates the sea from the lagoon in the northwest of town. You can walk there from the beach to admire the beautiful landscape.

★ **Island of Koyor** – ไปชมเกาะยอ: if you're stuck for something to do, there's a boat that leaves at 10am opposite Songkhla post office. It's the local omnibus and very cheap. The crossing takes 2 hours and you arrive on Koyor at noon. Or you can walk there across the bridge. Koyor is a small mountainous island with coconut palms, jungle and an immense orchard. There's a spinning wheel in practically every house. The boat returns to Songkhla at 3pm from the other end of the island.

# INDEX

Page numbers in *italics* refer to maps

Doi Mae Ho *see* Thong Bua Ton